2015/16 FACTS & FIGURES

TABLES FOR THE CALCULATION OF DAMAGES

2015/16
FACTS & FIGURES

TABLES FOR THE CALCULATION OF DAMAGES

Compiled and Edited by:

Members of the Professional Negligence Bar Association

General Editor: Robin de Wilde QC

Editors:

Peter Jennings
Simon Levene
Tejina Mangat
Harry Trusted
and
Maurice Faull FCA MAE
(Forensic Accountant)

SWEET & MAXWELL

THOMSON REUTERS

Published in 2015 by Thomson Reuters (Professional) UK Limited
trading as Sweet & Maxwell, Friars House, 160 Blackfriars Road, London, SE1 8EZ
(Registered in England & Wales, Company No 1679046.
Registered Office and address for service:
2nd floor, Aldgate House, 33 Aldgate High Street, London EC3N 1DL)

Designed and typeset by Wright & Round Ltd, Gloucestershire
Printed and bound in Great Britain by Ashford Colour Press, Gosport, Hants

No natural forests were destroyed to make this product:
only farmed timber was used and re-planted.

ISBN 9780414052758

A CIP catalogue record for this book is available from the British Library.

ACKNOWLEDGMENTS

We are very grateful to the following contributors:

- Adrian Gallop of the Government Actuary's Department for his assistance in preparing *Section A: Ogden Tables & Related Material.*

- Dr Victoria Wass of Cardiff Business School for updating *Section B6: Step-by-step guide to finding the annual estimates for hourly pay in ASHE SOC 2000 6115* and for providing the guide to the ASHE earnings tables at *F7: Average Earning Statistics* and her input into *F4, F5* and *F6.*

- *Rodney Nelson Jones of Field Fisher Waterhouse and Lexis Nexis for allowing us to use and to develop his table for the calculation of special damages interest in C4: Special and General Damages Interest.*

- Maurice Faull's team at Hilton Sharp & Clarke Forensic Accountants, who have helped with the meticulous preparation and updating of annually changing tables at *C2–C5, D1–D3, F1–F3, F8, G1–G5, H1–H3* and *L2*, and for preparing and/or checking the calculations at *A1, A2, A4* and *A5.*

- Michael Perrett and Debra Smith of BWCI Consulting Ltd for their assistance with *E2: Inflation Table*

- *Isabelle Symons and Lynn Bourne of Keith Carter & Associates for the research undertaken for the preparation of the tables F4–F7 in Section F: Earnings.*

- Melissa Chapman and the Family Law Bar Association for their permission to use table *I1 & I2: Social Security Benefits* and *I5: Foster Care Allowances* taken from At A Glance.

- Lynne Bradey and Austin Thornton of Wrigleys for preparing *I3: Personal Injury Trusts.*

- Hugh Jones of Pannone LLP for *J1: Note on the Court of Protection.*

- Adrian Mundell and Tom Cook of Kester Cunningham John, for *J2: The Incidence of Deputyship Costs* over a Claimant's Life and *J3: Deputyship Costs.*

- Alison Somek of Somek & Associates Ltd and James Rowley QC of Byrom Street Chambers, for their work on *K1: Care and Attendance.*

- The RAC Motoring Services in conjunction with Emmerson Hill Associates who compiled the illustrative motorcycle running costs at *L1: Motoring Costs.*

- Nicholas Leviseur for preparing the notes for *L3: Motability Scheme.*

- Margaret McDonald, specialist costs counsel of Kenworthy's Chambers, for permission to reproduce her table of *Senior Court Costs Office Guideline Rates for Summary Assessment* at *M1.*

We are very grateful to the following organisations for kindly granting us permission to use their material:

- The HMSO for their permission to use *Table A3: Life Tables, Table A8: The Ogden Tables, Table C2: Real and Nominal Interest Rates and Price Inflation, Table F5: Average Weekly Earnings Index, Table F6: Average Weekly Earnings, Table F7: Average Earnings Statistics* and the material from the NHS leaflet HC12, NHS charges. Crown Copyright is reproduced with the permission of HMSO.

- HM Revenue & Customs and HMSO for their permission to use the material in *Table L2: Taxation of Car and Fuel Benefits.*

- Sweet & Maxwell for their permission to use the tables from *Kemp & Kemp: The Quantum of Damages* at *C3: Special Investment Account Rates, C8: Judgment Debt Interest Rates, E1: Retail Prices Index* and *E2: Inflation Table.*

- W. Green for their permission to use *Table C9: Judicial Rates of Interest.*

- FTSE Russell for their permission to use the FTSE 100 Index at *Table D1: Share Price Index.*

- Halifax for providing the up-to-date material for *Table E3: House Price Indices* and *Table E4: Average semi-detached house prices by region.*

- Bodily Injury Claims Management Association for their permission to produce the Code of Best Practice on Rehabilitation at *K6: The 2007 Rehabilitation Code* and K7.

- The Automobile Association for their permission to use the AA figures in *Table L1: Motoring Costs.*

- Bauer Media, publishers of Parker's Car Price Guide upon whose figures the calculations in *Table L4: Calculations Involving Cars* are based.

- Collins Debden Australia for their permission to reproduce the perpetual calendar, as featured in the International Management Diary, at *Table M3: Perpetual Calendar.*

FOREWORD TO THE FIRST EDITION

by the Hon. Mr Justice Bell

The assessment of damages for personal injuries and consequential losses has become a matter of increasingly intricate calculation. Detailed schedules of damages and counter-schedules are vital to the proper portrayal of claim and defence to claim but they are arduous and time consuming to compile. Much the same building blocks of information and aids to calculation are required over, and over again. This volume has gathered many of the most frequently used building blocks and aids together in a readily accessible form and those who prepare, argue and settle such cases should be grateful for it. Robin de Wilde and his committee have put a lot of work into what is in fact a manual of very practical assistance and they are to be congratulated on a new venture which should mature year by year with the help of your own suggestions.

May 1996

INTRODUCTION TO THE TWENTIETH EDITION

"He had been eight years upon a project for extracting sunbeams out of cucumbers which were to be put into vials hermetically sealed, and let out to warm the air in raw inclement summers."

Jonathan Swift, *Gulliver's Travels,* "Voyage to Laputa", ch.5

Who we are

It is with a sense of incipient horror that I appreciate that this is now the twentieth edition of this work, conceived in part on the grounds that it might be of some use to the hack personal injury practitioner, which I was and remain. The team of people who are involved are the same as those involved in last year's edition. We have only lost one member and that was due to natural causes, namely retirement from practice. His successor has all the qualities that I suspected he possessed, which includes an obsessive attention to detail! That such an obsession is important became apparent because, last year, a gorilla intervened between typesetting and proofreading and then, even more subtly, between proofreading and printing.

As I have not been besieged with letters, it means that most of our readership neither know nor care. However, as a matter of *"amour propre"*[1] we do care and we have set up a new system, agreed by all. We trust that we have avoided the failings of previous editions. However, like Wavell's book, *Other Men's Flowers,* a delightful collection of English poetry, as Wavell writes in the Foreword: "nothing but the string that binds them is mine own".

It is crucially important in a book of this style, that everyone should know from whence we derive the information contained in it, so that it can be looked up and checked.

The purpose

This continues to be intended as a handy book of reference, which may be carried by the practitioner to some obscure County Court (if there are any left) to be cited to a District or County Court judge, whose experience prior to appointment was entirely based on his or her skill in Rating Cases. As I see from the Reports, it has also been relied upon in the Court of Appeal, where some of the judges have a background ranging from the niceties of tax or the complexities of charter parties. I have a particularly happy experience of one High Court judge, who had been so blessed in that latter speciality, and whose attempts at achieving the correct level of award in a serious brain damage case, was only achieved, in the end, by the Court of Appeal after five days of argument.[2]

Creating the Schedule of Damages

A kind enquiry about the proper use of such information prompted me to reflect upon the basis of my experience when I was learning my trade. As I recall, the Summary used to be referred to as a "Moser

[1] French; but translated into English in this context, it means "self respect".

[2] Actually, I am still sore about one point of the fifteen that we argued, upon which I lost there, only being supported by one judge whose background was that of academia and the Law Commission, which concerned the claim for the actual cost of investment advice from a specialist.

Schedule", named after the splendid, but slightly eccentric, late Mr Justice Michael Davies, and a case of that name over which he presided.

The Schedule itself can either be incorporated in the pleading or attached to the Claim, itself, but in a complex case it is and can become a thing of beauty (I promise) if properly prepared. I do recall spending many happy hours on such a project, when I should have been performing other duties such as being a diligent husband, a proud father or an otherwise public minded citizen. None of the foregoing are, incidentally, mutually exclusive!

Apart from *Kemp & Kemp*, I recall being aided by that excellent book *Munkman on Damages for Personal Injuries and Death*, now in its 12th edition. The late John Munkman, whose prose was always clear and sparkling, has been succeeded by the admirable Gordon Exall, who attempts to make things clear which were once obscure, certainly to me. Some cases in the Law Reports have also covered the subject in detail. William Latimer-Sayer of Cloisters has produced an excellent textbook on the subject, entitled *Personal Injury Schedules*, which is now in the third edition.

What is also clear is, however, that there has to be support from the instructing solicitors, as well as the many experts all of whom are required to work towards providing the supporting evidence, from first witness statements to the detail and analysis of the claim, that the judge can rely upon. It should be apparent how much work is involved when one reads the Section K1, edited by James Rowley QC. He analyses the important developments that occur in each major case. Often major questions of principle arise, as they frequently do in the larger cases, which appears to happen again and again.[3] Like the categories of negligence, heads of damages are never closed and will continue to be developed.

The Lord Chancellor

The cherished and much admired Mr Grayling has departed! It was Mr Grayling who did so much for the ordinary practitioner, whether it was in criminal or civil work and who left, according to the Law Society at least some 600,000 people without the chance of Legal Aid, as a result of his unhappy reign. He, it was, who destroyed the economic viability of the Criminal Bar by reducing their fees, and who also increased court fees by an exorbitant amount.

He was, also, as readers of previous editions of this work will recall, "the Insurer's' friend". The House of Commons Transport Select Committee rightly criticised Mr Grayling for causing it to be suggested that England was the "whiplash capital of the world", a suggestion that the Ministry of Justice, after rigorous questioning by the Select Committee, could produce no evidence of whatsoever. He misrepresented criminal barristers' earnings and denied many people the right to use the Employment Tribunal system by increasing the fees so that the number of claims fell by 80 per cent.

It amused me to see his appearance at various "Magna Carta functions" when he clearly neither knew nor understood the principles or the conception behind Magna Carta. He will always be remembered for his care and understanding of the legal profession, including the judges and court staff, as well as his deep appreciation of what the provision of legal services was for and at whom they have been aimed, namely the poor, the weak, the illiterate and those who would never have any redress against authority without the assistance of lawyers and the courts.

It should be remembered that the Rushcliffe Committee in 1944, which designed the structure of the Civil and Criminal Legal Aid system, later enshrined in legislation, concluded that about 83 per cent of the population would be unable to afford to purchase legal services to protect or enforce their various rights. I doubt that, even today, when enormous sums of money are said to be earned by a few,

[3] As discussed in detail later in this Introduction.

that the actual percentage of those unable to afford legal representation without the support of Legal Aid has changed much, if at all.

So, now we have a new Lord Chancellor, whom, one can only trust, shows a little more sense.

James Badenoch QC's Famous Case

For many years, like many others, he had felt aggrieved at the way the law of negligence had been applied in medical cases. He was brought in to lead in *Montgomery v Lanarkshire Health Board*[4]. The result demonstrated that he was triumphant. The cases of *Bolitho* and *Sidaway* have been overruled, as they no longer reflect modern attitudes to patient centred medicine and failed to respect the ability of patients to understand the treatment options and resulting in unacceptable medical paternalism.

The judgments are a joy to read, even down to Lady Hale's supplementary words—she does not dissent from the judgments of the others but adds her own thoughts on the way people have been treated.

One commentator has suggested that this may be the most important clinical negligence case in the last 30 to 60 years. It causes a profound and fundamental change in the rights of patients and on the grounds upon which litigation can be conducted. Although it is a Scottish case, the principles of law decided apply to the whole of the United Kingdom. It has already been extensively discussed by commentators and I imagine that there will be more thoughts to come. However, one fundamental point is clearly stated and simple: what is to be discussed with a patient is a matter of law and not a matter of professional practice. Thereafter, what is said or not said is not a matter of expert opinion from doctors. It is, now, for the courts and the law to determine and not a question for doctors.[5]

As for James, there are few people so highly regarded practising in this area. He is highly thought of, not only for his professional skill, but also for his natural courtesy and charm towards all with whom he had dealings. A great after-dinner speaker, and someone who is appreciated for being who he is. A friend had been involved in a difficult case, and his professional opponent had lost his personal appeal to my friend. My friend said of his opponent: "Why couldn't he just behave properly, like James Badenoch, for example, and then I could forgive him for his bloody minded behaviour?"

Three substantial Birth Injury cases

Suddenly, there is a flurry of cases on the same cause of action. They are, in order: *Totham v Kings College Hospital NHS Foundation Trust*[6]; Mrs Justice Laing; *Ellison v University Hospitals of Morecombe Bay NHS Foundation Trust*[7]; Mr Justice Warby; and *Robshaw v United Lincolnshire Hospitals NHS Trust*[8]; Mr Justice Foskett.

The claimants are all brain damaged children, who have suffered grievous injuries. Only one of the three judges was a known practitioner in the field. In two of the cases, one can see the fingers of William Latimer-Sayer, who put together the most complex and creative Schedules, based on first class evidence. *Robshaw* is probably the largest award of damages, openly recorded (something in the region of £14.5 million). The facts are interestingly different in each. The latter two are, as I discovered, the subject of "mego" (of which more later). They are all fit to be the subject of lectures for practitioners

[4] [2015] UKSC 11.
[5] I am indebted to Andrew Smith QC, Advocate and Barrister, for his Note, written by him for the benefit of the members of the PNBA, and for his synopsis at the end.
[6] [2015] EWHC 97 (QB).
[7] [2015] EWHC 366 (QB).
[8] [2015] 923 QB.

in this area and set standards to which most will only aspire. I will draw attention to several features that they do have in common, as follows:

(1) Such cases require meticulous preparation by everyone, from the instructing solicitors, junior counsel (who have to be involved at the outset in the planning and the whole preparation process) through to the experts, who have to be not only competent, but also used to this type of litigation. As an example, Warby J was clearly influenced by not only the witness statements, but the "day in a life" video, in addition to the other factual evidence. So was Foskett J in his case, as appears from his judgment.

(2) The hydrotherapy evidence was crucial in Ellison, for there was no other form of treatment that could provide the child with pain relief. The calculations were quite intricate and do not reflect the financial realities in my opinion. The sooner the NHSLA stop arguing that point, the easier life will be. I recall Rose J, as he then was, remarking in the course of argument in *Cassel*, that it is not every purchaser who wants a swimming pool in their garden, plainly having had trouble himself in selling a house with a swimming pool. Friends of mine, who bought a house with a pool when they had small children, ended up fencing the whole pool off and installed a gate, secured with padlock and chain.

(3) *Roberts v Johnstone*[9] was a misguided decision in the Court of Appeal. As I understand it, when it was argued, the point about the discount rate, as it was developed in the course of argument before the court, almost came out of the blue to counsel, who were not properly prepared for either the point or the consequences of the decision. For the most part, neither lawyers, whether counsel or solicitors, nor judges, really understand money and how it actually works. The so-called "rule" in *Roberts v Johnstone* is not only wrong, but does not reflect the real financial consequences. It needs to be re-argued, supported by a report from a forensic accountant and/or an actuary, so that the court fully appreciates the consequences of the decision. Claimants are presently suffering a financial penalty as a result of the original decision. I am not saying that no betterment can occur, but the basic maths do not support the way it is currently applied, as it is described as being the "*Roberts v Johnstone*" discount basis. As the late A.J.P. Taylor said in a different context: "It is not a consequence of men not learning from their mistakes, they do; but they then go on to make different mistakes."

(4) **The Strauss Tables from California (*Robshaw*).** I have never held the view that Professor Strauss fell into the category of "villain", because, having heard him speak, I am satisfied that the views he puts forward are the best that can be provided for on the basic material which he uses. However, as anyone who has been to California will know, the social, economic and cultural structure is so different, that like is not being compared with like. Though his views are interesting, a state that contains 32 million people, whose climate, social conditions and political organisation are so completely different from our own, makes comparisons unreal. Thus, Foskett J's approach in paras 99–101 and then again in paras 135–137 seems to be the correct way of dealing with the Strauss Tables, following Swift J in *Whiten*.

(5) **Deputy Costs and Court of Protection Costs and Expenses.** *Robshaw* is a fine example as to how to deal with these two issues; the case was complicated to the extent that the infant suffered hypoxic ischaemia during delivery, followed by cerebral palsy to all four limbs. It was a bad case, by any standards, needing serious amounts of care and support for his whole life.

(a) **Deputy Past Costs.** This was complicated in that the litigation solicitor had moved firms, her bill had been taxed and reduced on taxation (but not appealed) and an unwarranted attack was

[9] [1989] QB 878.

made on that bill and its reduction on Costs Assessment, without taking into account the 19 files of work which had been done. The case has to be read and studied to see how this problem was managed, with a degree of sensitivity, by Foskett J in a careful passage from para 432 to 442.

(b) **Future management of the Award and Court of Protection Costs.** The judge then dealt with the remaining issues with care from paragraph 447 onwards. I have never seen such detail in a judgment before. However, it shows what has and needs to be done in a case such as this. It is exemplary as the judge moves forward to his conclusions prior to para 480.

There are a host of other points (most of them minor) in these three cases, and the care with which the judiciary have taken is admirable. For Mr Justice Warby, whose background was in defamation, *Ellison* must have been one of the surprises of his life, but he managed to cope with the area both fairly and justly.

Ogden or Periodical Payments

Whilst the Bank of England maintains its base rate, as it presently is, for the next six months, then the question at the head of this paragraph answers itself. For the Ogden Tables, the proper discount rate would still have to be between 0 per cent and -0.5 per cent to be useful in calculating the multipliers. As nothing has changed in the fixing of the discount rate since Lord Chancellor Irvine fixed it at 2.5 per cent on July 27, 2001, the answer has become obvious.

One correspondent has done a survey and calculated that the premium of a Periodical Payments Calculation over an Ogden calculation is 37 per cent. So why, as he asks, is anyone actually using the Ogden Tables in the present climate at all? Don't they understand that a Periodical Payment Award gives a true benefit to the claimant that no Ogden Award ever could in the present financial circumstances? I cannot fathom the answer. Can anyone else?

In a judgment given in the Bermuda Supreme Court by Chief Justice Ian R.C. Kawaley, entitled *Thomson v Thomson* (June 22, 2015) he decided, having heard evidence of fact from an actuary, what the appropriate discount rate for future losses was in England because the claimant now lives in the UK. In making his decision, he was relying on and following the Privy Council decision in *Simon v Helmot*[10]. The appropriate discount rate for the UK should be: (a) -0.5% for heads of damage likely to be affected by price inflation; and (b) -2.5% for heads of damage likely to be affected by real earnings increases (i.e. future loss of earnings).

Bernie Ecclestone

I first came across Bernie Ecclestone some 20 years ago, when I was writing the "First Introduction". I discovered him to be a man who had paid himself some £30 million in one year (1993) which put him out of kilter with the normal bankers, share dealers or other super rich types, such as Directors General of the BBC and others existing in the Blair years. At that stage, Formula One Racing was not a primary interest but slowly it has come to have a grim fascination for me; not for the actual car racing, but rather how it seems to generate great wealth. The king of that world is Mr Bernie Ecclestone.

On January 14, 2014, a court in Munich ruled that Mr Ecclestone would be tried on bribery charges in Germany. On August 5, 2014, the same court ruled that Mr Ecclestone can pay a £60 million settlement, without admitting guilt, to end the trial. That has had consequences for him with the Inland Revenue, namely litigation as to whether the Inland Revenue had been misled by him. That litigation

[10] [2012] UKPC 5.

is continuing. When asked by a journalist about the case, he replied that: "I leave that to the lawyers."

He continues to appear in *The Sunday Times* Rich List (dated April 26, 2015) which suggests that he and his family are worth £2.94 billion, though his fund has been depleted since last year by the sum of £60 million as a result of the Bavarian compromise agreement, by which he escaped any further proceedings. His present wife, Brazilian Fabiana Fosi, was 48 years his junior when he married her in 2012.

"My eyes glaze over" (mego)

I came across this phrase, in the obituary in *The Times* of Ben Bradlee, the Editor of *The Washington Post* at the time of the Watergate affair, who, when reading copy produced by a journalist which he found boring, would say "mego" to indicate that he was less than impressed with that particular part of the copy he had just read. The phrase is cited in one dictionary as synonymous with "This is a smashingly boring affair", which does not do full justice to the literal meaning. It is also cited in *The Dictionary of American Slang*, Fourth Edition by Barbara Ann Kipfer PhD and Robert L. Chapman PhD. I notice that, as I age and decay, I suffer "mego" moments more often, but that may just be my failing faculties. However, there were recent "mego" moments when reading the *Ellison* and *Robshaw* cases, referred to above.

Conclusion

This last year I have received more correspondence than usual amounting to some four letters/emails. That does not include one correspondent, from a previous year, who wishes to replace the Ogden Tables completely with his own scheme, which may turn out to be more practical. However, as he has yet to develop his scheme, as the Chairman of the Ogden Working Party, I am not suffering any nightmares about his idea.

I try and deal with such correspondence as it appears, whether it be a criticism or helpful suggestion. It may be that someone will come up with a new or original idea or an improvement that we can use, such as the proposal to replace the Ogden Tables, referred to above.

As always, I am grateful to everyone involved in assisting the core team and the publishers in any way.

Robin de Wilde, QC

218 Strand Chambers
Third Floor,
218 Strand
London WC2R 1AT

August 1, 2015
rdewilde@clerksroom.com
T: 0845 083 3000
M: 0788 916 1604

INTRODUCTION TO THE FIRST EDITION

Schedules of Damages have become more complex. These tables are intended as an assistance to those who have to check the details which support a Schedule. The Tables themselves come from a variety of primary sources. In one volume they should be easier to use.

The task of compiling this volume has proved more onerous than any of the members of the Committee assigned to the task would have imagined. The discussions as to what should be included or excluded became intense. When dealing with comparative and comparable earnings, should not Mr Bernie Ecclestone of Formula One Promotions and International Sports World receive a mention? He was paid in 1993 the sum of £30,750,109 and became easily the highest paid director by £8,000,000 or so. He is not included in the Table of Comparable Earnings.

We are also conscious that the application of each Table may or may not be easy depending on the contents. We do not intend to triple the size of the volume by setting out worked examples, but would refer the reader to the appropriate text books. It is intended as a source book, easily to hand, so that the practitioner may find what is needed quickly and easily in a single volume.

As this is our first foray into the world of tables, we appreciate that some matters will have been omitted that should be included and some of that which is included should not be present. We rely on our readers to tell us what is wanted and needed, so that the next annual update can be improved. The intention is that each edition is published in late January or early February of each year, incorporating the declarations announced in the Budget in November the previous year.

We have plundered shamelessly from a variety of sources. The final stimulus has been the Family Law Bar Association's "At A Glance" annual publication, but it is designed for practitioners in a different world, facing other demands and needs.

We are also grateful to Mr Justice Bell, who attended the final Advisory Committee Meeting and agreed to write a Foreword to this venture.

We conclude with the thought expressed by the historian Edward Gibbon in *The Decline and Fall of the Roman Empire*, when he states in a footnote about one Emperor that:

> *"Twenty-two acknowledged concubines and a library of sixty-two thousand volumes, attested the variety of his inclinations; and from the productions which he left behind him, it appears that the former as well as the latter were designed for use rather than ostentation."*

These Tables, too, are designed for use rather than ostentation.

199 Strand
London WC2R 1DR
May 1996

Robin de Wilde, QC

CONTENTS

A

Group A

Ogden Tables and Related Materials

A1: 2.5% discount tables "at a glance"

The following tables comprise the 2.5% columns from Ogden Tables 1–26. However, we now include columns for loss of earnings to, and loss of pension from, ages 66, 67, 68 and 69, which have been obtained by interpolation.

The method of interpolation for the multiplier for loss of earnings to pension age is as recommended in paragraph 13 of the Explanatory Notes to the 7th Edition of the Ogden Tables (see table A8).

The Ogden Tables for loss of earnings are not extended below age 16. The appropriate starting figure for loss of earnings where an equivalent age below age 16 is required has been calculated as the difference between the multiplier for life and the multiplier from the equivalent retirement age.

Readers are reminded that the figures for loss of earnings must be adjusted in accordance with Section B of the Explanatory Notes to the Ogden Tables (Contingencies other than mortality) reproduced in Table A8. Multipliers already adjusted for these contingencies are set out in Table A4.

The multiplier for loss of pension commencing at ages 66 to 69 is calculated as the difference between the multiplier for life, as set out in tables 1 and 2 of the Ogden Tables, and the calculated multiplier to pension age.

Multipliers for loss of earnings/loss of pension to and from ages 66 to 69 are shown at the back of Table A1 for a 2.5% discount rate and at the back of Table A2 for a Nil discount rate.

2.5% discount tables "at a glance"—MALE

	Table 1 Pecuniary loss for life	Table 3 Loss of earnings to age 50	Table 5 Loss of earnings to age 55	Table 7 Loss of earnings to age 60	Table 9 Loss of earnings to age 65	Table 11 Loss of earnings to age 70	Table 13 Loss of earnings to age 75	Table 15 Loss of pension from age 50	Table 17 Loss of pension from age 55	Table 19 Loss of pension from age 60	Table 21 Loss of pension from age 65	Table 23 Loss of pension from age 70	Table 25 Loss of pension from age 75
0	35.41							7.00	5.69	4.54	3.54	2.69	1.97
1	35.46							7.20	5.85	4.66	3.64	2.76	2.02
2	35.33							7.37	5.98	4.77	3.72	2.82	2.06
3	35.19							7.54	6.12	4.88	3.80	2.88	2.10
4	35.05							7.72	6.26	4.98	3.88	2.94	2.14
5	34.90							7.89	6.40	5.10	3.97	3.00	2.19
6	34.75							8.08	6.54	5.21	4.05	3.06	2.23
7	34.59							8.26	6.69	5.32	4.14	3.13	2.27
8	34.42							8.45	6.84	5.44	4.23	3.19	2.32
9	34.25							8.65	7.00	5.56	4.32	3.26	2.36
10	34.08							8.84	7.15	5.68	4.41	3.33	2.41
11	33.90							9.05	7.32	5.81	4.51	3.39	2.46
12	33.72							9.26	7.48	5.94	4.60	3.46	2.50
13	33.53							9.47	7.65	6.07	4.70	3.54	2.55
14	33.34							9.69	7.82	6.20	4.80	3.61	2.60
15	33.14							9.91	8.00	6.34	4.91	3.68	2.65
16	32.94	22.80	24.76	26.46	27.92	29.18	30.23	10.14	8.18	6.48	5.01	3.76	2.71
17	32.73	22.36	24.37	26.11	27.61	28.89	29.97	10.37	8.37	6.62	5.12	3.84	2.76
18	32.52	21.91	23.97	25.75	27.29	28.61	29.71	10.61	8.56	6.77	5.23	3.92	2.81
19	32.31	21.45	23.56	25.39	26.97	28.31	29.44	10.86	8.75	6.92	5.34	4.00	2.87
20	32.10	20.99	23.14	25.02	26.64	28.01	29.17	11.11	8.95	7.08	5.46	4.08	2.92
21	31.87	20.50	22.72	24.64	26.30	27.71	28.89	11.37	9.16	7.23	5.58	4.17	2.98
22	31.64	20.01	22.28	24.25	25.95	27.39	28.61	11.63	9.37	7.40	5.70	4.25	3.04
23	31.41	19.51	21.83	23.85	25.59	27.07	28.31	11.90	9.58	7.56	5.82	4.34	3.10
24	31.17	18.99	21.37	23.44	25.22	26.74	28.01	12.18	9.80	7.73	5.95	4.43	3.16
25	30.92	18.46	20.90	23.02	24.85	26.40	27.70	12.46	10.02	7.90	6.08	4.52	3.22
26	30.67	17.92	20.42	22.59	24.47	26.06	27.39	12.76	10.25	8.08	6.21	4.62	3.29
27	30.42	17.36	19.93	22.16	24.07	25.70	27.07	13.06	10.49	8.26	6.34	4.71	3.35
28	30.15	16.79	19.42	21.71	23.67	25.34	26.74	13.36	10.73	8.45	6.48	4.81	3.42
29	29.88	16.21	18.91	21.25	23.26	24.97	26.40	13.67	10.97	8.63	6.62	4.91	3.48
30	29.60	15.61	18.38	20.78	22.84	24.59	26.05	13.99	11.23	8.83	6.76	5.01	3.55
31	29.32	15.00	17.83	20.29	22.41	24.20	25.70	14.33	11.49	9.03	6.91	5.12	3.62
32	29.04	14.37	17.28	19.80	21.97	23.81	25.35	14.67	11.76	9.23	7.07	5.23	3.69
33	28.75	13.73	16.72	19.30	21.53	23.41	24.98	15.02	12.03	9.45	7.22	5.34	3.77
34	28.46	13.08	16.14	18.79	21.07	23.00	24.61	15.38	12.32	9.66	7.38	5.45	3.84
35	28.15	12.41	15.55	18.27	20.60	22.58	24.23	15.75	12.61	9.89	7.55	5.57	3.92
36	27.84	11.72	14.94	17.73	20.13	22.15	23.84	16.13	12.90	10.11	7.72	5.69	4.00
37	27.53	11.01	14.32	17.18	19.64	21.72	23.45	16.51	13.21	10.35	7.89	5.81	4.08
38	27.20	10.29	13.68	16.61	19.13	21.27	23.04	16.91	13.52	10.58	8.07	5.93	4.16
39	26.86	9.54	13.02	16.04	18.62	20.80	22.62	17.32	13.84	10.83	8.24	6.06	4.24
40	26.52	8.78	12.35	15.44	18.09	20.33	22.19	17.74	14.17	11.08	8.43	6.19	4.33
41	26.17	8.00	11.67	14.84	17.55	19.85	21.75	18.17	14.50	11.33	8.62	6.32	4.42
42	25.81	7.20	10.96	14.21	17.00	19.36	21.31	18.61	14.85	11.60	8.81	6.46	4.51
43	25.45	6.38	10.24	13.58	16.44	18.85	20.85	19.07	15.21	11.87	9.01	6.60	4.60
44	25.08	5.54	9.50	12.93	15.86	18.34	20.39	19.54	15.57	12.15	9.21	6.74	4.69
45	24.70	4.68	8.74	12.26	15.27	17.81	19.91	20.02	15.95	12.44	9.43	6.89	4.79
46	24.31	3.79	7.97	11.58	14.67	17.27	19.42	20.52	16.34	12.73	9.64	7.04	4.88
47	23.91	2.88	7.17	10.88	14.05	16.72	18.93	21.03	16.74	13.03	9.86	7.19	4.99
48	23.51	1.95	6.35	10.16	13.42	16.16	18.42	21.56	17.15	13.35	10.09	7.35	5.09
49	23.10	0.99	5.52	9.43	12.77	15.58	17.90	22.11	17.58	13.67	10.33	7.52	5.20
50	22.69		4.66	8.68	12.11	15.00	17.38	22.69	18.03	14.01	10.58	7.69	5.31
51	22.27		3.78	7.91	11.44	14.40	16.85		18.49	14.36	10.83	7.87	5.42
52	21.85		2.87	7.12	10.75	13.80	16.31		18.98	14.72	11.10	8.05	5.54
53	21.42		1.94	6.32	10.05	13.18	15.76		19.48	15.11	11.37	8.24	5.67
54	20.99		0.99	5.49	9.33	12.55	15.20		20.01	15.50	11.66	8.44	5.80

2.5% discount tables "at a glance"—MALE *continued*

	Table 1 Pecuniary loss for life	Table 3 Loss of earnings to age 50	Table 5 Loss of earnings to age 55	Table 7 Loss of earnings to age 60	Table 9 Loss of earnings to age 65	Table 11 Loss of earnings to age 70	Table 13 Loss of earnings to age 75	Table 15 Loss of pension from age 50	Table 17 Loss of pension from age 55	Table 19 Loss of pension from age 60	Table 21 Loss of pension from age 65	Table 23 Loss of pension from age 70	Table 25 Loss of pension from age 75
55	20.56			4.64	8.59	11.90	14.63		20.56	15.92	11.97	8.65	5.93
56	20.12			3.76	7.84	11.25	14.05			16.36	12.29	8.88	6.08
57	19.68			2.86	7.06	10.57	13.46			16.82	12.62	9.11	6.23
58	19.23			1.94	6.26	9.88	12.85			17.29	12.97	9.35	6.38
59	18.77			0.98	5.45	9.18	12.23			17.79	13.32	9.59	6.54
60	18.30				4.60	8.45	11.60			18.30	13.69	9.85	6.70
61	17.81				3.74	7.71	10.95				14.08	10.11	6.87
62	17.33				2.85	6.94	10.28				14.48	10.38	7.04
63	16.84				1.93	6.16	9.61				14.91	10.67	7.23
64	16.35				0.98	5.36	8.93				15.37	10.98	7.42
65	15.86					4.54	8.23				15.86	11.32	7.63
66	15.38					3.70	7.52					11.68	7.86
67	14.90					2.82	6.79					12.07	8.11
68	14.42					1.92	6.04					12.50	8.38
69	13.93					0.98	5.27					12.96	8.67
70	13.44						4.47					13.44	8.97
71	12.94						3.65						9.30
72	12.43						2.79						9.64
73	11.90						1.90						10.00
74	11.36						0.97						10.39
75	10.81												10.81
76	10.25												
77	9.69												
78	9.15												
79	8.61												
80	8.09												
81	7.60												
82	7.13												
83	6.69												
84	6.28												
85	5.88												
86	5.50												
87	5.14												
88	4.78												
89	4.43												
90	4.10												
91	3.79												
92	3.49												
93	3.21												
94	2.96												
95	2.74												
96	2.54												
97	2.37												
98	2.22												
99	2.08												
100	1.95												

2.5% discount tables "at a glance"—FEMALE

	Table 2 Pecuniary loss for life	Table 4 Loss of earnings to age 50	Table 6 Loss of earnings to age 55	Table 8 Loss of earnings to age 60	Table 10 Loss of earnings to age 65	Table 12 Loss of earnings to age 70	Table 14 Loss of earnings to age 75	Table 16 Loss of pension from age 50	Table 18 Loss of pension from age 55	Table 20 Loss of pension from age 60	Table 22 Loss of pension from age 65	Table 24 Loss of pension from age 70	Table 26 Loss of pension from age 75
0	35.94							7.43	6.09	4.92	3.90	3.01	2.25
1	35.97							7.64	6.26	5.06	4.00	3.09	2.31
2	35.86							7.82	6.41	5.17	4.09	3.16	2.36
3	35.73							8.00	6.56	5.29	4.19	3.23	2.41
4	35.60							8.19	6.71	5.41	4.28	3.30	2.46
5	35.47							8.39	6.87	5.54	4.38	3.37	2.51
6	35.34							8.58	7.03	5.66	4.47	3.44	2.56
7	35.19							8.78	7.19	5.79	4.57	3.52	2.61
8	35.05							8.99	7.36	5.92	4.68	3.59	2.67
9	34.90							9.20	7.53	6.06	4.78	3.67	2.72
10	34.75							9.42	7.70	6.20	4.89	3.75	2.78
11	34.59							9.64	7.88	6.34	4.99	3.83	2.84
12	34.42							9.86	8.06	6.48	5.11	3.92	2.90
13	34.26							10.09	8.25	6.63	5.22	4.00	2.96
14	34.09							10.33	8.44	6.78	5.33	4.09	3.02
15	33.91							10.57	8.63	6.93	5.45	4.17	3.08
16	33.73	22.91	24.90	26.64	28.16	29.47	30.59	10.82	8.83	7.09	5.57	4.26	3.14
17	33.55	22.47	24.51	26.29	27.85	29.19	30.34	11.07	9.03	7.25	5.70	4.36	3.21
18	33.36	22.02	24.11	25.94	27.53	28.91	30.08	11.33	9.24	7.42	5.82	4.45	3.27
19	33.16	21.56	23.71	25.58	27.21	28.62	29.82	11.60	9.46	7.58	5.95	4.55	3.34
20	32.97	21.09	23.29	25.21	26.88	28.32	29.56	11.87	9.68	7.76	6.09	4.64	3.41
21	32.76	20.61	22.86	24.83	26.54	28.02	29.28	12.15	9.90	7.93	6.22	4.74	3.48
22	32.56	20.12	22.42	24.44	26.20	27.71	29.00	12.44	10.13	8.12	6.36	4.85	3.55
23	32.34	19.61	21.97	24.04	25.84	27.39	28.71	12.73	10.37	8.30	6.50	4.95	3.63
24	32.12	19.09	21.51	23.63	25.47	27.06	28.42	13.03	10.61	8.49	6.65	5.06	3.70
25	31.89	18.56	21.04	23.21	25.10	26.73	28.12	13.33	10.85	8.68	6.79	5.16	3.78
26	31.66	18.01	20.56	22.78	24.72	26.39	27.81	13.65	11.10	8.88	6.94	5.28	3.85
27	31.42	17.45	20.06	22.34	24.33	26.03	27.49	13.97	11.36	9.08	7.10	5.39	3.93
28	31.18	16.88	19.56	21.89	23.93	25.68	27.17	14.30	11.62	9.29	7.26	5.50	4.01
29	30.93	16.30	19.04	21.43	23.51	25.31	26.84	14.64	11.89	9.50	7.42	5.62	4.10
30	30.68	15.70	18.51	20.96	23.09	24.93	26.50	14.98	12.17	9.71	7.58	5.74	4.18
31	30.41	15.08	17.96	20.48	22.66	24.55	26.15	15.33	12.45	9.94	7.75	5.87	4.27
32	30.15	14.45	17.40	19.98	22.22	24.15	25.79	15.70	12.74	10.16	7.92	6.00	4.35
33	29.87	13.80	16.83	19.48	21.77	23.75	25.43	16.07	13.04	10.40	8.10	6.13	4.44
34	29.59	13.14	16.25	18.96	21.31	23.34	25.06	16.45	13.35	10.64	8.28	6.26	4.54
35	29.31	12.46	15.65	18.43	20.84	22.91	24.68	16.84	13.66	10.88	8.47	6.39	4.63
36	29.01	11.77	15.03	17.88	20.35	22.48	24.29	17.24	13.98	11.13	8.66	6.53	4.73
37	28.71	11.06	14.40	17.32	19.86	22.04	23.89	17.65	14.30	11.38	8.85	6.67	4.82
38	28.40	10.33	13.76	16.75	19.35	21.58	23.48	18.07	14.64	11.65	9.05	6.82	4.92
39	28.09	9.58	13.10	16.17	18.83	21.12	23.06	18.50	14.98	11.92	9.25	6.97	5.02
40	27.76	8.82	12.42	15.57	18.30	20.65	22.63	18.95	15.34	12.19	9.46	7.12	5.13
41	27.43	8.03	11.73	14.96	17.76	20.16	22.20	19.40	15.70	12.47	9.67	7.27	5.23
42	27.09	7.22	11.02	14.33	17.20	19.66	21.75	19.87	16.07	12.76	9.89	7.43	5.34
43	26.75	6.40	10.29	13.69	16.63	19.15	21.29	20.35	16.45	13.06	10.12	7.59	5.45
44	26.39	5.55	9.55	13.03	16.05	18.63	20.82	20.84	16.84	13.36	10.35	7.76	5.57
45	26.03	4.69	8.79	12.36	15.45	18.10	20.35	21.35	17.25	13.68	10.58	7.93	5.69
46	25.67	3.80	8.00	11.67	14.84	17.56	19.86	21.87	17.66	14.00	10.83	8.11	5.81
47	25.29	2.88	7.20	10.96	14.22	17.01	19.36	22.41	18.09	14.33	11.08	8.29	5.93
48	24.91	1.95	6.38	10.24	13.58	16.44	18.86	22.97	18.53	14.67	11.33	8.47	6.06
49	24.53	0.99	5.54	9.50	12.93	15.86	18.34	23.54	18.99	15.03	11.60	8.67	6.19
50	24.14		4.68	8.74	12.26	15.27	17.82	24.14	19.46	15.39	11.88	8.86	6.32
51	23.74		3.79	7.97	11.58	14.67	17.28		19.95	15.77	12.16	9.07	6.46
52	23.33		2.88	7.17	10.88	14.05	16.73		20.45	16.16	12.45	9.28	6.60
53	22.92		1.95	6.36	10.17	13.42	16.17		20.97	16.56	12.75	9.49	6.75
54	22.50		0.99	5.52	9.43	12.78	15.60		21.51	16.98	13.06	9.72	6.90

2.5% discount tables "at a glance"—FEMALE *continued*

	Table 2 Pecuniary loss for life	Table 4 Loss of earnings to age 50	Table 6 Loss of earnings to age 55	Table 8 Loss of earnings to age 60	Table 10 Loss of earnings to age 65	Table 12 Loss of earnings to age 70	Table 14 Loss of earnings to age 75	Table 16 Loss of pension from age 50	Table 18 Loss of pension from age 55	Table 20 Loss of pension from age 60	Table 22 Loss of pension from age 65	Table 24 Loss of pension from age 70	Table 26 Loss of pension from age 75
55	22.07			4.66	8.68	12.12	15.02		22.07	17.41	13.39	9.95	7.06
56	21.64			3.78	7.92	11.45	14.42			17.86	13.73	10.19	7.22
57	21.21			2.87	7.13	10.76	13.81			18.33	14.08	10.44	7.39
58	20.76			1.94	6.32	10.05	13.19			18.81	14.44	10.70	7.56
59	20.30			0.99	5.49	9.33	12.56			19.31	14.81	10.97	7.74
60	19.83				4.64	8.59	11.91			19.83	15.19	11.24	7.92
61	19.35				3.76	7.83	11.24				15.59	11.52	8.11
62	18.86				2.86	7.05	10.56				16.00	11.81	8.30
63	18.37				1.94	6.25	9.86				16.43	12.11	8.50
64	17.87				0.98	5.44	9.16				16.89	12.43	8.71
65	17.38					4.60	8.43				17.38	12.78	8.94
66	16.88					3.74	7.70					13.15	9.19
67	16.39					2.85	6.94					13.54	9.45
68	15.89					1.93	6.17					13.96	9.72
69	15.39					0.98	5.37					14.40	10.02
70	14.87						4.55					14.87	10.33
71	14.35						3.70						10.65
72	13.80						2.82						10.98
73	13.24						1.92						11.32
74	12.66						0.98						11.68
75	12.06												12.06
76	11.45												
77	10.84												
78	10.24												
79	9.64												
80	9.07												
81	8.51												
82	7.99												
83	7.49												
84	7.01												
85	6.55												
86	6.11												
87	5.68												
88	5.26												
89	4.86												
90	4.47												
91	4.11												
92	3.77												
93	3.46												
94	3.18												
95	2.94												
96	2.74												
97	2.56												
98	2.39												
99	2.23												
100	2.08												

A1: 2.5% discount tables for retirement ages 66 to 69 – MALE

	Loss of earnings to age 66	Loss of earnings to age 67	Loss of earnings to age 68	Loss of earnings to age 69		Loss of pension from age 66	Loss of pension from age 67	Loss of pension from age 68	Loss of pension from age 69
16	28.19	28.45	28.70	28.94	**16**	4.75	4.49	4.24	4.00
17	27.88	28.14	28.40	28.65	**17**	4.85	4.59	4.33	4.08
18	27.57	27.84	28.10	28.36	**18**	4.95	4.68	4.42	4.16
19	27.25	27.52	27.79	28.05	**19**	5.06	4.79	4.52	4.26
20	26.92	27.20	27.48	27.75	**20**	5.18	4.90	4.62	4.35
21	26.59	26.88	27.16	27.43	**21**	5.28	4.99	4.71	4.44
22	26.25	26.54	26.83	27.11	**22**	5.39	5.10	4.81	4.53
23	25.90	26.20	26.50	26.79	**23**	5.51	5.21	4.91	4.62
24	25.54	25.85	26.16	26.45	**24**	5.63	5.32	5.01	4.72
25	25.17	25.49	25.80	26.11	**25**	5.75	5.43	5.12	4.81
26	24.80	25.12	25.44	25.75	**26**	5.87	5.55	5.23	4.92
27	24.42	24.75	25.07	25.39	**27**	6.00	5.67	5.35	5.03
28	24.02	24.36	24.69	25.02	**28**	6.13	5.79	5.46	5.13
29	23.62	23.97	24.31	24.64	**29**	6.26	5.91	5.57	5.24
30	23.21	23.57	23.91	24.25	**30**	6.39	6.03	5.69	5.35
31	22.79	23.16	23.51	23.86	**31**	6.53	6.16	5.81	5.46
32	22.36	22.74	23.10	23.46	**32**	6.68	6.30	5.94	5.58
33	21.92	22.31	22.68	23.05	**33**	6.83	6.44	6.07	5.70
34	21.48	21.87	22.25	22.63	**34**	6.98	6.59	6.21	5.83
35	21.02	21.43	21.82	22.20	**35**	7.13	6.72	6.33	5.95
36	20.55	20.96	21.37	21.77	**36**	7.29	6.88	6.47	6.07
37	20.07	20.49	20.91	21.32	**37**	7.46	7.04	6.62	6.21
38	19.58	20.02	20.44	20.85	**38**	7.62	7.18	6.76	6.35
39	19.07	19.53	19.96	20.38	**39**	7.79	7.33	6.90	6.48
40	18.56	19.02	19.47	19.91	**40**	7.96	7.50	7.05	6.61
41	18.03	18.51	18.96	19.42	**41**	8.14	7.66	7.21	6.75
42	17.49	17.98	18.45	18.91	**42**	8.32	7.83	7.36	6.90
43	16.94	17.44	17.92	18.40	**43**	8.51	8.01	7.53	7.05
44	16.38	16.89	17.38	17.87	**44**	8.70	8.19	7.70	7.21
45	15.80	16.33	16.83	17.33	**45**	8.90	8.37	7.87	7.37
46	15.22	15.75	16.27	16.78	**46**	9.09	8.56	8.04	7.53
47	14.62	15.16	15.69	16.22	**47**	9.29	8.75	8.22	7.69
48	14.00	14.56	15.11	15.64	**48**	9.51	8.95	8.40	7.87
49	13.37	13.95	14.51	15.05	**49**	9.73	9.15	8.59	8.05
50	12.73	13.32	13.90	14.45	**50**	9.96	9.37	8.79	8.24
51	12.07	12.68	13.28	13.85	**51**	10.20	9.59	8.99	8.42
52	11.40	12.03	12.64	13.23	**52**	10.45	9.82	9.21	8.62
53	10.71	11.36	11.98	12.59	**53**	10.71	10.06	9.44	8.83
54	10.02	10.68	11.33	11.94	**54**	10.97	10.31	9.66	9.05
55	9.30	9.98	10.64	11.29	**55**	11.26	10.58	9.92	9.27
56	8.56	9.27	9.95	10.61	**56**	11.56	10.85	10.17	9.51
57	7.81	8.53	9.24	9.91	**57**	11.87	11.15	10.44	9.77
58	7.04	7.79	8.51	9.21	**58**	12.19	11.44	10.72	10.02
59	6.24	7.01	7.76	8.48	**59**	12.53	11.76	11.01	10.29
60	5.43	6.22	6.99	7.74	**60**	12.87	12.08	11.31	10.56
61	4.59	5.41	6.20	6.96	**61**	13.22	12.40	11.61	10.85
62	3.73	4.58	5.40	6.18	**62**	13.60	12.75	11.93	11.15
63	2.84	3.72	4.56	5.38	**63**	14.00	13.12	12.28	11.46
64	1.93	2.84	3.72	4.55	**64**	14.42	13.51	12.63	11.80
65	0.98	1.93	2.83	3.71	**65**	14.88	13.93	13.03	12.15
66		0.98	1.92	2.83	**66**	15.38	14.40	13.46	12.55
67			0.98	1.92	**67**		14.90	13.92	12.98
68				0.98	**68**			14.42	13.44
69					**69**				13.93

See notes at the start of section A1 for details of methodology

A1: 2.5% discount tables for retirement ages 66 to 69 – FEMALE

	Loss of earnings to age 66	Loss of earnings to age 67	Loss of earnings to age 68	Loss of earnings to age 69		Loss of pension from age 66	Loss of pension from age 67	Loss of pension from age 68	Loss of pension from age 69
16	28.43	28.70	28.96	29.21	**16**	5.30	5.03	4.77	4.52
17	28.13	28.40	28.68	28.94	**17**	5.42	5.15	4.87	4.61
18	27.82	28.10	28.38	28.65	**18**	5.54	5.26	4.98	4.71
19	27.50	27.79	28.08	28.35	**19**	5.66	5.37	5.08	4.81
20	27.18	27.47	27.77	28.05	**20**	5.79	5.50	5.20	4.92
21	26.85	27.15	27.45	27.74	**21**	5.91	5.61	5.31	5.02
22	26.51	26.82	27.12	27.42	**22**	6.05	5.74	5.44	5.14
23	26.17	26.48	26.79	27.09	**23**	6.17	5.86	5.55	5.25
24	25.81	26.13	26.45	26.76	**24**	6.31	5.99	5.67	5.36
25	25.44	25.78	26.10	26.42	**25**	6.45	6.11	5.79	5.47
26	25.07	25.41	25.74	26.06	**26**	6.59	6.25	5.92	5.60
27	24.69	25.03	25.37	25.71	**27**	6.73	6.39	6.05	5.71
28	24.29	24.65	25.00	25.34	**28**	6.89	6.53	6.18	5.84
29	23.89	24.26	24.62	24.96	**29**	7.04	6.67	6.31	5.97
30	23.48	23.86	24.22	24.58	**30**	7.20	6.82	6.46	6.10
31	23.05	23.44	23.82	24.19	**31**	7.36	6.97	6.59	6.22
32	22.62	23.02	23.41	23.79	**32**	7.53	7.13	6.74	6.36
33	22.18	22.59	22.98	23.37	**33**	7.69	7.28	6.89	6.50
34	21.73	22.15	22.55	22.95	**34**	7.86	7.44	7.04	6.64
35	21.27	21.69	22.11	22.52	**35**	8.04	7.62	7.20	6.79
36	20.80	21.23	21.66	22.08	**36**	8.21	7.78	7.35	6.93
37	20.31	20.76	21.20	21.62	**37**	8.40	7.95	7.51	7.09
38	19.82	20.27	20.73	21.16	**38**	8.58	8.13	7.67	7.24
39	19.31	19.78	20.24	20.69	**39**	8.78	8.31	7.85	7.40
40	18.79	19.27	19.74	20.20	**40**	8.97	8.49	8.02	7.56
41	18.26	18.75	19.23	19.70	**41**	9.17	8.68	8.20	7.73
42	17.72	18.22	18.71	19.19	**42**	9.37	8.87	8.38	7.90
43	17.16	17.68	18.18	18.67	**43**	9.59	9.07	8.57	8.08
44	16.59	17.12	17.64	18.14	**44**	9.80	9.27	8.75	8.25
45	16.01	16.55	17.09	17.60	**45**	10.02	9.48	8.94	8.43
46	15.41	15.97	16.52	17.05	**46**	10.26	9.70	9.15	8.62
47	14.81	15.38	15.94	16.48	**47**	10.48	9.91	9.35	8.81
48	14.19	14.77	15.34	15.90	**48**	10.72	10.14	9.57	9.01
49	13.55	14.15	14.74	15.31	**49**	10.98	10.38	9.79	9.22
50	12.90	13.52	14.12	14.70	**50**	11.24	10.62	10.02	9.44
51	12.23	12.87	13.48	14.08	**51**	11.51	10.87	10.26	9.66
52	11.55	12.20	12.84	13.45	**52**	11.78	11.13	10.49	9.88
53	10.86	11.53	12.18	12.81	**53**	12.06	11.39	10.74	10.11
54	10.15	10.83	11.50	12.15	**54**	12.35	11.67	11.00	10.35
55	9.41	10.12	10.81	11.48	**55**	12.66	11.95	11.26	10.59
56	8.66	9.39	10.10	10.78	**56**	12.98	12.25	11.54	10.86
57	7.90	8.64	9.37	10.07	**57**	13.31	12.57	11.84	11.14
58	7.11	7.88	8.63	9.35	**58**	13.65	12.88	12.13	11.41
59	6.31	7.10	7.87	8.61	**59**	13.99	13.20	12.43	11.69
60	5.48	6.29	7.08	7.85	**60**	14.35	13.54	12.75	11.98
61	4.63	5.47	6.28	7.07	**61**	14.72	13.88	13.07	12.28
62	3.76	4.62	5.46	6.26	**62**	15.10	14.24	13.40	12.60
63	2.86	3.75	4.62	5.45	**63**	15.51	14.62	13.75	12.92
64	1.94	2.86	3.75	4.61	**64**	15.93	15.01	14.12	13.26
65	0.98	1.94	2.85	3.74	**65**	16.40	15.44	14.53	13.64
66		0.98	1.93	2.85	**66**	16.88	15.90	14.95	14.03
67			0.98	1.93	**67**		16.39	15.41	14.46
68				0.98	**68**			15.89	14.91
69					**69**				15.39

See notes at the section A1 for details of methodology

A2: Nil discount tables "at a glance"

MALE

	Table 1 Pecuniary loss for life	Table 3 Loss of earnings to age 50	Table 5 Loss of earnings to age 55	Table 7 Loss of earnings to age 60	Table 9 Loss of earnings to age 65	Table 11 Loss of earnings to age 70	Table 13 Loss of earnings to age 75	Table 15 Loss of pension from age 50	Table 17 Loss of pension from age 55	Table 19 Loss of pension from age 60	Table 21 Loss of pension from age 65	Table 23 Loss of pension from age 70	Table 25 Loss of pension from age 75
0	88.96							39.61	34.80	30.06	25.41	20.90	16.58
1	88.31							39.70	34.87	30.10	25.44	20.91	16.56
2	87.22							39.59	34.76	30.00	25.33	20.81	16.47
3	86.12							39.49	34.65	29.89	25.23	20.70	16.37
4	85.01							39.37	34.54	29.78	25.12	20.60	16.28
5	83.89							39.26	34.43	29.67	25.01	20.50	16.18
6	82.78							39.14	34.32	29.56	24.90	20.39	16.08
7	81.66							39.03	34.20	29.45	24.80	20.29	15.98
8	80.55							38.91	34.09	29.34	24.69	20.19	15.88
9	79.43							38.80	33.97	29.22	24.58	20.08	15.79
10	78.31							38.68	33.86	29.11	24.47	19.97	15.69
11	77.19							38.56	33.74	29.00	24.36	19.87	15.59
12	76.07							38.44	33.63	28.88	24.25	19.76	15.49
13	74.96							38.33	33.51	28.77	24.14	19.66	15.39
14	73.84							38.21	33.40	28.66	24.03	19.56	15.29
15	72.73							38.10	33.29	28.55	23.92	19.45	15.20
16	71.61	33.63	38.44	43.18	47.80	52.26	56.51	37.99	33.17	28.44	23.82	19.35	15.10
17	70.51	32.63	37.44	42.18	46.80	51.26	55.50	37.88	33.06	28.33	23.71	19.25	15.01
18	69.41	31.64	36.45	41.18	45.80	50.25	54.49	37.77	32.96	28.23	23.61	19.15	14.92
19	68.31	30.65	35.46	40.19	44.80	49.26	53.49	37.67	32.85	28.12	23.51	19.06	14.82
20	67.22	29.66	34.47	39.20	43.81	48.26	52.48	37.57	32.75	28.02	23.41	18.96	14.74
21	66.13	28.66	33.48	38.21	42.82	47.26	51.48	37.46	32.65	27.92	23.31	18.87	14.65
22	65.04	27.67	32.49	37.21	41.82	46.27	50.48	37.36	32.55	27.82	23.21	18.77	14.55
23	63.94	26.68	31.49	36.22	40.83	45.27	49.48	37.26	32.45	27.72	23.11	18.67	14.46
24	62.85	25.69	30.50	35.23	39.84	44.27	48.48	37.16	32.34	27.62	23.01	18.58	14.37
25	61.76	24.70	29.52	34.24	38.85	43.28	47.48	37.06	32.24	27.52	22.91	18.48	14.28
26	60.68	23.71	28.53	33.25	37.86	42.29	46.48	36.96	32.15	27.42	22.82	18.39	14.20
27	59.59	22.72	27.54	32.27	36.87	41.29	45.48	36.87	32.06	27.33	22.73	18.30	14.11
28	58.51	21.73	26.55	31.28	35.88	40.30	44.48	36.77	31.96	27.23	22.63	18.21	14.02
29	57.42	20.74	25.56	30.29	34.89	39.31	43.49	36.68	31.86	27.13	22.53	18.11	13.93
30	56.34	19.76	24.57	29.30	33.90	38.32	42.49	36.58	31.76	27.04	22.44	18.02	13.85
31	55.27	18.77	23.59	28.32	32.92	37.33	41.50	36.50	31.68	26.95	22.35	17.93	13.76
32	54.20	17.78	22.61	27.34	31.94	36.35	40.52	36.42	31.60	26.86	22.26	17.85	13.69
33	53.15	16.80	21.63	26.36	30.96	35.37	39.54	36.35	31.52	26.79	22.18	17.77	13.61
34	52.09	15.82	20.65	25.38	29.99	34.40	38.56	36.27	31.44	26.71	22.10	17.69	13.53
35	51.03	14.83	19.67	24.40	29.01	33.42	37.58	36.20	31.36	26.63	22.02	17.61	13.45
36	49.98	13.85	18.69	23.43	28.03	32.45	36.60	36.13	31.29	26.55	21.94	17.53	13.38
37	48.93	12.86	17.71	22.45	27.06	31.47	35.62	36.06	31.22	26.47	21.87	17.45	13.30
38	47.87	11.88	16.73	21.48	26.08	30.50	34.64	35.99	31.14	26.40	21.79	17.37	13.23
39	46.82	10.89	15.75	20.50	25.11	29.52	33.67	35.92	31.07	26.32	21.71	17.30	13.15
40	45.76	9.91	14.76	19.52	24.13	28.55	32.69	35.85	31.00	26.24	21.63	17.22	13.07
41	44.71	8.92	13.78	18.54	23.16	27.57	31.71	35.79	30.93	26.17	21.55	17.14	13.00
42	43.67	7.93	12.80	17.57	22.19	26.60	30.74	35.73	30.86	26.10	21.48	17.07	12.93
43	42.62	6.95	11.82	16.59	21.22	25.63	29.77	35.68	30.80	26.03	21.41	16.99	12.86
44	41.59	5.96	10.84	15.62	20.25	24.66	28.80	35.63	30.74	25.97	21.34	16.92	12.79
45	40.55	4.97	9.86	14.64	19.28	23.70	27.83	35.58	30.69	25.91	21.27	16.85	12.72
46	39.52	3.98	8.88	13.67	18.31	22.73	26.87	35.54	30.64	25.85	21.21	16.79	12.65
47	38.49	2.99	7.90	12.70	17.34	21.77	25.90	35.50	30.59	25.79	21.15	16.72	12.59
48	37.47	1.99	6.92	11.73	16.38	20.81	24.95	35.47	30.55	25.74	21.09	16.66	12.52
49	36.45	1.00	5.93	10.75	15.41	19.85	23.99	35.46	30.52	25.70	21.04	16.60	12.46
50	35.45		4.95	9.78	14.46	18.90	23.04	35.45	30.50	25.66	20.99	16.55	12.41
51	34.45		3.97	8.81	13.50	17.95	22.10		30.49	25.64	20.96	16.51	12.36
52	33.47		2.98	7.84	12.54	17.00	21.16		30.49	25.62	20.93	16.47	12.31
53	32.49		1.99	6.87	11.59	16.06	20.23		30.50	25.62	20.91	16.43	12.27
54	31.53		1.00	5.90	10.63	15.12	19.30		30.53	25.63	20.90	16.41	12.23

Nil discount tables "at a glance"—MALE *continued*

	Table 1 Pecuniary loss for life	Table 3 Loss of earnings to age 50	Table 5 Loss of earnings to age 55	Table 7 Loss of earnings to age 60	Table 9 Loss of earnings to age 65	Table 11 Loss of earnings to age 70	Table 13 Loss of earnings to age 75	Table 15 Loss of pension from age 50	Table 17 Loss of pension from age 55	Table 19 Loss of pension from age 60	Table 21 Loss of pension from age 65	Table 23 Loss of pension from age 70	Table 25 Loss of pension from age 75
55	30.58			4.93	9.68	14.19	18.37		30.58	25.65	20.90	16.39	12.20
56	29.64			3.95	8.73	13.25	17.46			25.69	20.91	16.39	12.18
57	28.71			2.97	7.77	12.32	16.54			25.74	20.94	16.39	12.17
58	27.78			1.99	6.82	11.39	15.63			25.80	20.97	16.40	12.16
59	26.85			1.00	5.85	10.45	14.71			25.86	21.00	16.40	12.15
60	25.92				4.89	9.51	13.79			25.92	21.03	16.41	12.13
61	25.00				3.92	8.58	12.87				21.07	16.42	12.12
62	24.08				2.95	7.64	11.96				21.12	16.44	12.12
63	23.17				1.98	6.70	11.05				21.20	16.47	12.12
64	22.28				0.99	5.77	10.15				21.29	16.52	12.13
65	21.42					4.83	9.25				21.42	16.59	12.16
66	20.57					3.88	8.36					16.69	12.21
67	19.74					2.93	7.46					16.81	12.28
68	18.93					1.97	6.56					16.96	12.37
69	18.12					0.99	5.66					17.13	12.47
70	17.32						4.75					17.32	12.58
71	16.53						3.83						12.70
72	15.72						2.89						12.83
73	14.92						1.95						12.97
74	14.10						0.99						13.12
75	13.29												13.29
76	12.48												
77	11.70												
78	10.93												
79	10.19												
80	9.49												
81	8.83												
82	8.22												
83	7.65												
84	7.13												
85	6.63												
86	6.16												
87	5.71												
88	5.27												
89	4.86												
90	4.47												
91	4.10												
92	3.76												
93	3.44												
94	3.16												
95	2.91												
96	2.69												
97	2.50												
98	2.34												
99	2.18												
100	2.04												

Nil discount tables "at a glance"—FEMALE

	Table 2 Pecuniary loss for life	Table 4 Loss of earnings to age 50	Table 6 Loss of earnings to age 55	Table 8 Loss of earnings to age 60	Table 10 Loss of earnings to age 65	Table 12 Loss of earnings to age 70	Table 14 Loss of earnings to age 75	Table 16 Loss of pension from age 50	Table 18 Loss of pension from age 55	Table 20 Loss of pension from age 60	Table 22 Loss of pension from age 65	Table 24 Loss of pension from age 70	Table 26 Loss of pension from age 75
0	92.57							42.98	38.10	33.26	28.47	23.78	19.22
1	91.86							43.07	38.16	33.30	28.50	23.79	19.21
2	90.77							42.97	38.06	33.20	28.40	23.69	19.12
3	89.68							42.87	37.96	33.10	28.30	23.60	19.02
4	88.58							42.77	37.86	33.00	28.21	23.50	18.93
5	87.49							42.67	37.76	32.90	28.11	23.41	18.84
6	86.38							42.56	37.66	32.80	28.01	23.31	18.75
7	85.28							42.46	37.56	32.70	27.91	23.21	18.65
8	84.18							42.36	37.45	32.60	27.81	23.11	18.56
9	83.07							42.25	37.35	32.49	27.70	23.01	18.46
10	81.97							42.15	37.24	32.39	27.60	22.92	18.37
11	80.86							42.04	37.14	32.29	27.50	22.82	18.28
12	79.76							41.94	37.04	32.18	27.40	22.72	18.18
13	78.65							41.83	36.93	32.08	27.30	22.62	18.09
14	77.55							41.73	36.83	31.98	27.20	22.53	18.00
15	76.44							41.62	36.72	31.88	27.10	22.43	17.91
16	75.34	33.82	38.72	43.57	48.34	53.01	57.53	41.52	36.62	31.78	27.00	22.33	17.81
17	74.24	32.82	37.72	42.57	47.34	52.01	56.52	41.42	36.52	31.67	26.90	22.24	17.72
18	73.14	31.83	36.72	41.57	46.34	51.00	55.51	41.32	36.42	31.58	26.80	22.14	17.63
19	72.05	30.83	35.73	40.57	45.34	50.00	54.51	41.22	36.32	31.48	26.71	22.05	17.54
20	70.96	29.83	34.73	39.57	44.34	49.00	53.50	41.12	36.23	31.38	26.61	21.96	17.45
21	69.86	28.84	33.73	38.58	43.34	48.00	52.50	41.03	36.13	31.29	26.52	21.86	17.36
22	68.77	27.84	32.74	37.58	42.34	47.00	51.49	40.93	36.03	31.19	26.42	21.77	17.27
23	67.67	26.85	31.74	36.58	41.35	46.00	50.49	40.82	35.93	31.09	26.32	21.67	17.18
24	66.57	25.85	30.74	35.58	40.35	44.99	49.48	40.72	35.83	30.99	26.23	21.58	17.09
25	65.48	24.85	29.75	34.59	39.35	43.99	48.48	40.62	35.73	30.89	26.13	21.48	17.00
26	64.38	23.86	28.75	33.59	38.35	42.99	47.47	40.53	35.63	30.79	26.03	21.39	16.91
27	63.29	22.86	27.76	32.59	37.35	41.99	46.47	40.43	35.54	30.70	25.94	21.30	16.82
28	62.20	21.87	26.76	31.60	36.36	40.99	45.46	40.33	35.44	30.60	25.84	21.21	16.74
29	61.11	20.87	25.77	30.60	35.36	39.99	44.46	40.24	35.34	30.51	25.75	21.11	16.65
30	60.02	19.88	24.77	29.61	34.36	39.00	43.46	40.15	35.25	30.41	25.66	21.03	16.56
31	58.94	18.88	23.78	28.62	33.37	38.00	42.46	40.06	35.16	30.32	25.57	20.94	16.48
32	57.86	17.89	22.79	27.62	32.38	37.01	41.46	39.97	35.07	30.23	25.48	20.85	16.39
33	56.77	16.89	21.79	26.63	31.38	36.01	40.46	39.88	34.98	30.14	25.39	20.76	16.31
34	55.69	15.90	20.80	25.64	30.39	35.02	39.47	39.79	34.89	30.05	25.30	20.68	16.23
35	54.61	14.91	19.81	24.65	29.40	34.02	38.47	39.70	34.80	29.96	25.21	20.59	16.14
36	53.53	13.92	18.82	23.66	28.41	33.03	37.47	39.62	34.72	29.88	25.13	20.50	16.06
37	52.46	12.92	17.83	22.67	27.42	32.04	36.48	39.54	34.63	29.79	25.04	20.42	15.98
38	51.38	11.93	16.84	21.68	26.43	31.05	35.49	39.45	34.55	29.71	24.95	20.33	15.90
39	50.31	10.94	15.85	20.69	25.44	30.06	34.49	39.37	34.46	29.62	24.87	20.25	15.82
40	49.24	9.95	14.86	19.70	24.45	29.07	33.50	39.29	34.38	29.54	24.79	20.17	15.73
41	48.17	8.95	13.87	18.71	23.47	28.08	32.51	39.22	34.30	29.46	24.70	20.08	15.66
42	47.10	7.96	12.88	17.73	22.48	27.10	31.53	39.14	34.23	29.38	24.62	20.00	15.58
43	46.04	6.97	11.89	16.74	21.50	26.11	30.54	39.07	34.15	29.30	24.54	19.93	15.50
44	44.98	5.97	10.90	15.75	20.51	25.13	29.55	39.01	34.08	29.23	24.47	19.85	15.43
45	43.93	4.98	9.91	14.77	19.53	24.15	28.57	38.94	34.02	29.16	24.40	19.78	15.35
46	42.87	3.99	8.92	13.79	18.55	23.17	27.59	38.89	33.95	29.09	24.32	19.70	15.28
47	41.83	2.99	7.93	12.80	17.57	22.19	26.62	38.83	33.89	29.02	24.26	19.63	15.21
48	40.79	2.00	6.95	11.82	16.59	21.22	25.64	38.79	33.84	28.97	24.19	19.57	15.14
49	39.76	1.00	5.96	10.84	15.62	20.25	24.67	38.76	33.80	28.92	24.14	19.51	15.08
50	38.73		4.97	9.86	14.65	19.28	23.71	38.73	33.76	28.87	24.08	19.45	15.02
51	37.71		3.98	8.88	13.67	18.31	22.75		33.73	28.83	24.03	19.39	14.96
52	36.69		2.99	7.90	12.70	17.35	21.78		33.70	28.79	23.99	19.34	14.90
53	35.68		1.99	6.92	11.73	16.39	20.83		33.68	28.76	23.95	19.29	14.85
54	34.68		1.00	5.94	10.76	15.43	19.87		33.68	28.74	23.91	19.25	14.80

Nil discount tables "at a glance"—FEMALE *continued*

	Table 2 Pecuniary loss for life	Table 4 Loss of earnings to age 50	Table 6 Loss of earnings to age 55	Table 8 Loss of earnings to age 60	Table 10 Loss of earnings to age 65	Table 12 Loss of earnings to age 70	Table 14 Loss of earnings to age 75	Table 16 Loss of pension from age 50	Table 18 Loss of pension from age 55	Table 20 Loss of pension from age 60	Table 22 Loss of pension from age 65	Table 24 Loss of pension from age 70	Table 26 Loss of pension from age 75
55	33.68			4.95	9.79	14.47	18.92		33.68	28.73	23.89	19.21	14.76
56	32.69			3.97	8.82	13.51	17.97			28.73	23.87	19.19	14.72
57	31.71			2.98	7.85	12.55	17.02			28.73	23.86	19.16	14.69
58	30.74			1.99	6.88	11.59	16.08			28.74	23.86	19.14	14.66
59	29.76			1.00	5.91	10.64	15.13			28.76	23.85	19.12	14.62
60	28.78				4.93	9.68	14.19			28.78	23.85	19.10	14.59
61	27.80				3.95	8.72	13.24				23.85	19.08	14.55
62	26.83				2.97	7.76	12.30				23.86	19.06	14.52
63	25.86				1.99	6.80	11.36				23.88	19.06	14.50
64	24.91				1.00	5.85	10.43				23.92	19.07	14.48
65	23.98					4.89	9.50				23.98	19.10	14.49
66	23.07					3.92	8.57					19.15	14.51
67	22.18					2.95	7.64					19.22	14.54
68	21.29					1.98	6.70					19.32	14.59
69	20.42					0.99	5.77					19.43	14.65
70	19.55						4.83					19.55	14.72
71	18.67						3.88						14.79
72	17.79						2.93						14.86
73	16.89						1.97						14.93
74	15.99						0.99						15.00
75	15.08												15.08
76	14.17												
77	13.28												
78	12.40												
79	11.56												
80	10.77												
81	10.02												
82	9.31												
83	8.65												
84	8.03												
85	7.45												
86	6.89												
87	6.36												
88	5.85												
89	5.36												
90	4.90												
91	4.47												
92	4.08												
93	3.72												
94	3.41												
95	3.14												
96	2.91												
97	2.70												
98	2.52												
99	2.35												
100	2.18												

A2: Nil discount tables for retirement ages 66 to 69 – MALE

	Loss of earnings to age 66	Loss of earnings to age 67	Loss of earnings to age 68	Loss of earnings to age 69		Loss of pension from age 66	Loss of pension from age 67	Loss of pension from age 68	Loss of pension from age 69
16	48.70	49.59	50.48	51.37	**16**	22.91	22.02	21.13	20.24
17	47.69	48.59	49.48	50.36	**17**	22.82	21.92	21.03	20.15
18	46.69	47.58	48.48	49.37	**18**	22.72	21.83	20.93	20.04
19	45.69	46.59	47.48	48.37	**19**	22.62	21.72	20.83	19.94
20	44.69	45.59	46.48	47.37	**20**	22.53	21.63	20.74	19.85
21	43.70	44.59	45.48	46.38	**21**	22.43	21.54	20.65	19.75
22	42.71	43.60	44.48	45.38	**22**	22.33	21.44	20.56	19.66
23	41.71	42.61	43.49	44.38	**23**	22.23	21.33	20.45	19.56
24	40.72	41.61	42.50	43.39	**24**	22.13	21.24	20.35	19.46
25	39.73	40.62	41.50	42.40	**25**	22.03	21.14	20.26	19.36
26	38.74	39.63	40.51	41.40	**26**	21.94	21.05	20.17	19.28
27	37.75	38.64	39.52	40.41	**27**	21.84	20.95	20.07	19.18
28	36.77	37.65	38.53	39.42	**28**	21.74	20.86	19.98	19.09
29	35.78	36.66	37.54	38.43	**29**	21.64	20.76	19.88	18.99
30	34.79	35.68	36.56	37.44	**30**	21.55	20.66	19.78	18.90
31	33.80	34.69	35.57	36.45	**31**	21.47	20.58	19.70	18.82
32	32.83	33.71	34.60	35.47	**32**	21.37	20.49	19.60	18.73
33	31.85	32.73	33.61	34.50	**33**	21.30	20.42	19.54	18.65
34	30.87	31.75	32.64	33.52	**34**	21.22	20.34	19.45	18.57
35	29.90	30.78	31.66	32.54	**35**	21.13	20.25	19.37	18.49
36	28.92	29.80	30.68	31.56	**36**	21.06	20.18	19.30	18.42
37	27.94	28.83	29.71	30.59	**37**	20.99	20.10	19.22	18.34
38	26.97	27.85	28.73	29.61	**38**	20.90	20.02	19.14	18.26
39	25.99	26.88	27.75	28.64	**39**	20.83	19.94	19.07	18.18
40	25.02	25.90	26.78	27.66	**40**	20.74	19.86	18.98	18.10
41	24.04	24.93	25.81	26.69	**41**	20.67	19.78	18.90	18.02
42	23.07	23.96	24.84	25.72	**42**	20.60	19.71	18.83	17.95
43	22.11	22.99	23.87	24.75	**43**	20.51	19.63	18.75	17.87
44	21.14	22.02	22.90	23.79	**44**	20.45	19.57	18.69	17.80
45	20.17	21.06	21.94	22.82	**45**	20.38	19.49	18.61	17.73
46	19.20	20.09	20.97	21.85	**46**	20.32	19.43	18.55	17.67
47	18.24	19.13	20.01	20.89	**47**	20.25	19.36	18.48	17.60
48	17.27	18.17	19.05	19.93	**48**	20.20	19.30	18.42	17.54
49	16.32	17.20	18.09	18.98	**49**	20.13	19.25	18.36	17.47
50	15.35	16.25	17.14	18.02	**50**	20.10	19.20	18.31	17.43
51	14.41	15.29	16.19	17.07	**51**	20.04	19.16	18.26	17.38
52	13.45	14.35	15.24	16.12	**52**	20.02	19.12	18.23	17.35
53	12.50	13.40	14.30	15.18	**53**	19.99	19.09	18.19	17.31
54	11.55	12.45	13.35	14.24	**54**	19.98	19.08	18.18	17.29
55	10.59	11.51	12.41	13.30	**55**	19.99	19.07	18.17	17.28
56	9.65	10.56	11.47	12.36	**56**	19.99	19.08	18.17	17.28
57	8.70	9.61	10.52	11.43	**57**	20.01	19.10	18.19	17.28
58	7.74	8.67	9.58	10.49	**58**	20.04	19.11	18.20	17.29
59	6.80	7.72	8.64	9.54	**59**	20.05	19.13	18.21	17.31
60	5.83	6.77	7.69	8.61	**60**	20.09	19.15	18.23	17.31
61	4.88	5.82	6.75	7.67	**61**	20.12	19.18	18.25	17.33
62	3.91	4.87	5.80	6.72	**62**	20.17	19.21	18.28	17.36
63	2.95	3.90	4.85	5.79	**63**	20.22	19.27	18.32	17.38
64	1.98	2.94	3.90	4.84	**64**	20.30	19.34	18.38	17.44
65	0.99	1.98	2.94	3.89	**65**	20.43	19.44	18.48	17.53
66		0.99	1.97	2.93	**66**	20.57	19.58	18.60	17.64
67			0.99	1.97	**67**		19.74	18.75	17.77
68				0.99	**68**			18.93	17.94
69					**69**				18.12

See notes at the section A1 for details of methodology

A2: Nil discount tables for retirement ages 66 to 69 – FEMALE

	Loss of earnings to age 66	Loss of earnings to age 67	Loss of earnings to age 68	Loss of earnings to age 69		Loss of pension from age 66	Loss of pension from age 67	Loss of pension from age 68	Loss of pension from age 69
16	49.27	50.21	51.14	52.08	**16**	26.07	25.13	24.20	23.26
17	48.27	49.20	50.14	51.07	**17**	25.97	25.04	24.10	23.17
18	47.27	48.20	49.14	50.07	**18**	25.87	24.94	24.00	23.07
19	46.27	47.20	48.14	49.07	**19**	25.78	24.85	23.91	22.98
20	45.27	46.20	47.14	48.07	**20**	25.69	24.76	23.82	22.89
21	44.27	45.20	46.14	47.07	**21**	25.59	24.66	23.72	22.79
22	43.27	44.20	45.13	46.07	**22**	25.50	24.57	23.64	22.70
23	42.27	43.20	44.13	45.06	**23**	25.40	24.47	23.54	22.61
24	41.28	42.20	43.13	44.06	**24**	25.29	24.37	23.44	22.51
25	40.28	41.21	42.13	43.06	**25**	25.20	24.27	23.35	22.42
26	39.28	40.21	41.13	42.06	**26**	25.10	24.17	23.25	22.32
27	38.28	39.21	40.13	41.06	**27**	25.01	24.08	23.16	22.23
28	37.28	38.21	39.14	40.06	**28**	24.92	23.99	23.06	22.14
29	36.29	37.21	38.14	39.07	**29**	24.82	23.90	22.97	22.04
30	35.29	36.22	37.15	38.07	**30**	24.73	23.80	22.87	21.95
31	34.29	35.22	36.15	37.08	**31**	24.65	23.72	22.79	21.86
32	33.30	34.22	35.16	36.08	**32**	24.56	23.64	22.70	21.78
33	32.31	33.23	34.16	35.09	**33**	24.46	23.54	22.61	21.68
34	31.31	32.24	33.17	34.09	**34**	24.38	23.45	22.52	21.60
35	30.32	31.25	32.18	33.10	**35**	24.29	23.36	22.43	21.51
36	29.33	30.26	31.18	32.11	**36**	24.20	23.27	22.35	21.42
37	28.34	29.27	30.19	31.12	**37**	24.12	23.19	22.27	21.34
38	27.36	28.28	29.20	30.13	**38**	24.02	23.10	22.18	21.25
39	26.37	27.29	28.21	29.14	**39**	23.94	23.02	22.10	21.17
40	25.38	26.30	27.23	28.15	**40**	23.86	22.94	22.01	21.09
41	24.39	25.32	26.24	27.16	**41**	23.78	22.85	21.93	21.01
42	23.41	24.33	25.25	26.17	**42**	23.69	22.77	21.85	20.93
43	22.42	23.35	24.27	25.19	**43**	23.62	22.69	21.77	20.85
44	21.44	22.36	23.29	24.21	**44**	23.54	22.62	21.69	20.77
45	20.46	21.39	22.31	23.23	**45**	23.47	22.54	21.62	20.70
46	19.48	20.41	21.33	22.25	**46**	23.39	22.46	21.54	20.62
47	18.50	19.43	20.35	21.28	**47**	23.33	22.40	21.48	20.55
48	17.53	18.45	19.38	20.30	**48**	23.26	22.34	21.41	20.49
49	16.55	17.48	18.41	19.33	**49**	23.21	22.28	21.35	20.43
50	15.58	16.51	17.44	18.36	**50**	23.15	22.22	21.29	20.37
51	14.61	15.54	16.47	17.39	**51**	23.10	22.17	21.24	20.32
52	13.64	14.58	15.51	16.43	**52**	23.05	22.11	21.18	20.26
53	12.67	13.61	14.54	15.47	**53**	23.01	22.07	21.14	20.21
54	11.70	12.64	13.57	14.51	**54**	22.98	22.04	21.11	20.17
55	10.74	11.67	12.61	13.54	**55**	22.94	22.01	21.07	20.14
56	9.77	10.71	11.65	12.58	**56**	22.92	21.98	21.04	20.11
57	8.80	9.75	10.69	11.62	**57**	22.91	21.96	21.02	20.09
58	7.83	8.78	9.72	10.66	**58**	22.91	21.96	21.02	20.08
59	6.86	7.81	8.76	9.70	**59**	22.90	21.95	21.00	20.06
60	5.90	6.85	7.80	8.74	**60**	22.88	21.93	20.98	20.04
61	4.92	5.89	6.83	7.78	**61**	22.88	21.91	20.97	20.02
62	3.94	4.91	5.87	6.82	**62**	22.89	21.92	20.96	20.01
63	2.97	3.94	4.91	5.86	**63**	22.89	21.92	20.95	20.00
64	1.99	2.96	3.93	4.90	**64**	22.92	21.95	20.98	20.01
65	1.00	1.99	2.96	3.93	**65**	22.98	21.99	21.02	20.05
66		1.00	1.98	2.95	**66**	23.07	22.07	21.09	20.12
67			0.99	1.98	**67**		22.18	21.19	20.20
68				0.99	**68**			21.29	20.30
69					**69**				20.42

See notes at the section A1 for details of methodology

A3: Life tables and projected life tables

Interim Life Tables, United Kingdom

Period expectation of life **Office for National Statistics**
Based on data for the years 2011–2013

Age	Males					Females				
x	m_x	q_x	l_x	d_x	e_x	m_x	q_x	l_x	d_x	e_x
0	0.004633	0.004622	100000.0	462.2	78.91	0.003601	0.003595	100000.0	359.5	82.71
1	0.000333	0.000333	99537.8	33.1	78.28	0.000288	0.000288	99640.5	28.7	82.01
2	0.000188	0.000187	99504.6	18.7	77.30	0.000136	0.000136	99611.8	13.6	81.03
3	0.000110	0.000110	99486.0	10.9	76.32	0.000113	0.000113	99598.2	11.2	80.05
4	0.000108	0.000108	99475.1	10.8	75.32	0.000096	0.000096	99587.0	9.6	79.05
5	0.000105	0.000105	99464.3	10.4	74.33	0.000089	0.000089	99577.4	8.9	78.06
6	0.000088	0.000088	99453.9	8.7	73.34	0.000079	0.000079	99568.5	7.9	77.07
7	0.000089	0.000089	99445.2	8.9	72.35	0.000065	0.000065	99560.6	6.4	76.07
8	0.000093	0.000093	99436.3	9.2	71.35	0.000069	0.000069	99554.2	6.8	75.08
9	0.000090	0.000090	99427.0	9.0	70.36	0.000062	0.000062	99547.3	6.2	74.08
10	0.000087	0.000087	99418.1	8.7	69.37	0.000068	0.000068	99541.2	6.7	73.09
11	0.000088	0.000088	99409.4	8.7	68.37	0.000077	0.000077	99534.4	7.7	72.09
12	0.000109	0.000109	99400.7	10.8	67.38	0.000079	0.000079	99526.7	7.9	71.10
13	0.000107	0.000107	99389.8	10.7	66.39	0.000082	0.000082	99518.8	8.2	70.11
14	0.000129	0.000129	99379.2	12.8	65.39	0.000097	0.000097	99510.7	9.7	69.11
15	0.000156	0.000156	99366.4	15.5	64.40	0.000114	0.000114	99501.0	11.4	68.12
16	0.000222	0.000222	99350.9	22.0	63.41	0.000126	0.000126	99489.7	12.5	67.13
17	0.000327	0.000327	99328.9	32.5	62.42	0.000163	0.000163	99477.2	16.2	66.13
18	0.000439	0.000439	99296.3	43.5	61.45	0.000179	0.000179	99461.0	17.8	65.14
19	0.000487	0.000487	99252.8	48.3	60.47	0.000200	0.000200	99443.2	19.9	64.16
20	0.000483	0.000483	99204.5	47.9	59.50	0.000200	0.000200	99423.3	19.9	63.17
21	0.000492	0.000491	99156.6	48.7	58.53	0.000213	0.000213	99403.4	21.2	62.18
22	0.000502	0.000502	99107.8	49.7	57.56	0.000210	0.000210	99382.2	20.9	61.19
23	0.000535	0.000535	99058.1	53.0	56.59	0.000234	0.000234	99361.3	23.2	60.21
24	0.000516	0.000515	99005.1	51.0	55.62	0.000229	0.000229	99338.1	22.8	59.22
25	0.000615	0.000615	98954.1	60.8	54.65	0.000265	0.000265	99315.3	26.3	58.23
26	0.000601	0.000600	98893.3	59.4	53.68	0.000263	0.000263	99289.1	26.1	57.25
27	0.000611	0.000611	98833.9	60.4	52.71	0.000307	0.000307	99262.9	30.5	56.26
28	0.000656	0.000656	98773.5	64.8	51.74	0.000332	0.000332	99232.4	33.0	55.28
29	0.000724	0.000723	98708.7	71.4	50.78	0.000319	0.000319	99199.5	31.7	54.30
30	0.000762	0.000762	98637.3	75.2	49.81	0.000375	0.000375	99167.8	37.2	53.32
31	0.000811	0.000810	98562.1	79.9	48.85	0.000419	0.000419	99130.6	41.5	52.34
32	0.000806	0.000805	98482.3	79.3	47.89	0.000433	0.000433	99089.1	42.9	51.36
33	0.000892	0.000891	98402.9	87.7	46.93	0.000466	0.000466	99046.2	46.2	50.38
34	0.000949	0.000948	98315.2	93.2	45.97	0.000541	0.000541	99000.0	53.5	49.40
35	0.001029	0.001029	98222.0	101.0	45.01	0.000572	0.000572	98946.5	56.6	48.43
36	0.001108	0.001107	98121.0	108.7	44.06	0.000592	0.000592	98889.9	58.5	47.46
37	0.001232	0.001231	98012.3	120.7	43.11	0.000635	0.000635	98831.4	62.7	46.49
38	0.001308	0.001307	97891.6	128.0	42.16	0.000722	0.000722	98768.6	71.3	45.51
39	0.001424	0.001423	97763.7	139.1	41.21	0.000842	0.000842	98697.3	83.1	44.55
40	0.001550	0.001549	97624.5	151.2	40.27	0.000863	0.000863	98614.3	85.1	43.58
41	0.001619	0.001618	97473.3	157.7	39.33	0.000968	0.000968	98529.2	95.3	42.62
42	0.001789	0.001787	97315.6	173.9	38.40	0.001058	0.001057	98433.9	104.0	41.66
43	0.001897	0.001895	97141.7	184.1	37.46	0.001149	0.001149	98329.8	112.9	40.71
44	0.002067	0.002065	96957.6	200.2	36.53	0.001267	0.001266	98216.9	124.4	39.75
45	0.002237	0.002234	96757.4	216.2	35.61	0.001383	0.001382	98092.5	135.6	38.80
46	0.002339	0.002337	96541.2	225.6	34.69	0.001497	0.001496	97956.9	146.6	37.86
47	0.002457	0.002454	96315.6	236.3	33.77	0.001610	0.001609	97810.4	157.3	36.91
48	0.002703	0.002700	96079.3	259.4	32.85	0.001734	0.001732	97653.0	169.2	35.97
49	0.002921	0.002917	95820.0	279.5	31.94	0.001982	0.001980	97483.9	193.1	35.03
50	0.003107	0.003102	95540.5	296.4	31.03	0.002168	0.002166	97290.8	210.7	34.10

Period expectation of life
Based on data for the years 2011–2013

Age	Males					Females				
x	m_x	q_x	l_x	d_x	e_x	m_x	q_x	l_x	d_x	e_x
51	0.003438	0.003433	95244.1	326.9	30.12	0.002398	0.002396	97080.1	232.6	33.17
52	0.003823	0.003815	94917.2	362.1	29.23	0.002604	0.002600	96847.6	251.8	32.25
53	0.004212	0.004204	94555.0	397.5	28.34	0.002875	0.002871	96595.7	277.3	31.33
54	0.004576	0.004565	94157.6	429.9	27.45	0.003086	0.003081	96318.4	296.8	30.42
55	0.005019	0.005007	93727.7	469.3	26.58	0.003433	0.003427	96021.7	329.1	29.52
56	0.005598	0.005582	93258.4	520.6	25.71	0.003757	0.003750	95692.6	358.8	28.62
57	0.006102	0.006083	92737.9	564.1	24.85	0.004102	0.004093	95333.7	390.2	27.72
58	0.006762	0.006739	92173.7	621.2	24.00	0.004388	0.004378	94943.5	415.7	26.83
59	0.007439	0.007411	91552.5	678.5	23.16	0.004942	0.004930	94527.8	466.0	25.95
60	0.008141	0.008108	90874.0	736.8	22.33	0.005312	0.005298	94061.8	498.3	25.07
61	0.008906	0.008866	90137.2	799.2	21.51	0.005863	0.005846	93563.5	547.0	24.21
62	0.009775	0.009728	89338.0	869.1	20.69	0.006338	0.006318	93016.5	587.7	23.34
63	0.010468	0.010414	88468.9	921.3	19.89	0.006864	0.006840	92428.8	632.3	22.49
64	0.011273	0.011210	87547.7	981.4	19.10	0.007329	0.007302	91796.5	670.3	21.64
65	0.012291	0.012216	86566.3	1057.5	18.31	0.008081	0.008049	91126.2	733.5	20.80
66	0.013689	0.013596	85508.8	1162.6	17.53	0.008890	0.008851	90392.8	800.0	19.96
67	0.015200	0.015086	84346.2	1272.4	16.76	0.010153	0.010101	89592.7	905.0	19.14
68	0.016371	0.016238	83073.8	1348.9	16.01	0.010817	0.010759	88687.7	954.2	18.33
69	0.018337	0.018171	81724.9	1485.0	15.27	0.011935	0.011865	87733.5	1040.9	17.52
70	0.020946	0.020729	80239.9	1663.3	14.54	0.013569	0.013478	86692.6	1168.4	16.72
71	0.023123	0.022858	78576.6	1796.1	13.84	0.014720	0.014612	85524.2	1249.7	15.95
72	0.025917	0.025585	76780.4	1964.4	13.15	0.016873	0.016732	84274.5	1410.1	15.17
73	0.027772	0.027392	74816.0	2049.3	12.48	0.018344	0.018178	82864.4	1506.3	14.42
74	0.030948	0.030477	72766.7	2217.7	11.82	0.020666	0.020454	81358.1	1664.1	13.68
75	0.034020	0.033451	70549.0	2359.9	11.17	0.022900	0.022641	79694.0	1804.3	12.96
76	0.037921	0.037215	68189.1	2537.7	10.54	0.025616	0.025292	77889.6	1970.0	12.25
77	0.041670	0.040819	65651.4	2679.8	9.93	0.029041	0.028626	75919.7	2173.3	11.55
78	0.047032	0.045951	62971.6	2893.6	9.33	0.032545	0.032024	73746.4	2361.7	10.88
79	0.051964	0.050648	60077.9	3042.8	8.76	0.036895	0.036227	71384.7	2586.0	10.22
80	0.058676	0.057004	57035.1	3251.2	8.20	0.042123	0.041254	68798.7	2838.2	9.59
81	0.066410	0.064276	53783.9	3457.0	7.66	0.047337	0.046242	65960.5	3050.2	8.98
82	0.075686	0.072927	50326.9	3670.2	7.16	0.053826	0.052415	62910.3	3297.4	8.39
83	0.084527	0.081099	46656.7	3783.8	6.68	0.061583	0.059743	59612.9	3561.5	7.82
84	0.094641	0.090365	42872.9	3874.2	6.23	0.070433	0.068037	56051.4	3813.6	7.29
85	0.106498	0.101114	38998.7	3943.3	5.80	0.079723	0.076667	52237.8	4004.9	6.78
86	0.119260	0.112549	35055.4	3945.4	5.39	0.089840	0.085978	48232.9	4147.0	6.31
87	0.132986	0.124695	31110.0	3879.3	5.01	0.101129	0.096261	44085.9	4243.8	5.85
88	0.148906	0.138587	27230.7	3773.8	4.65	0.114025	0.107875	39842.2	4298.0	5.42
89	0.166694	0.153869	23456.9	3609.3	4.32	0.129846	0.121930	35544.2	4333.9	5.02
90	0.183705	0.168251	19847.6	3339.4	4.02	0.146703	0.136678	31210.3	4265.8	4.64
91	0.208248	0.188609	16508.2	3113.6	3.73	0.167257	0.154349	26944.5	4158.9	4.30
92	0.227223	0.204041	13394.6	2733.1	3.48	0.185711	0.169932	22785.7	3872.0	3.99
93	0.250467	0.222591	10661.5	2373.2	3.24	0.203759	0.184920	18913.7	3497.5	3.71
94	0.259787	0.229922	8288.4	1905.7	3.03	0.221025	0.199030	15416.2	3068.3	3.44
95	0.299963	0.260841	6382.7	1664.9	2.78	0.253868	0.225273	12347.9	2781.6	3.17
96	0.331616	0.284452	4717.8	1342.0	2.59	0.285924	0.250161	9566.2	2393.1	2.95
97	0.368440	0.311125	3375.8	1050.3	2.42	0.305870	0.265297	7173.1	1903.0	2.76
98	0.387597	0.324675	2325.5	755.0	2.28	0.334314	0.286435	5270.1	1509.5	2.58
99	0.421185	0.347916	1570.5	546.4	2.14	0.367172	0.310220	3760.6	1166.6	2.41
100	0.451953	0.368647	1024.1	377.5	2.01	0.392382	0.328026	2594.0	850.9	2.27

Source: Office for National Statistics licensed under the Open Government licence V.I.O.

Expectations of life table

Expectations of life for age attained in 2015 allowing for projected changes in mortality assumed in the 2013-based population projections produced by the Office for National Statistics.

United Kingdom

Age	Males	Females	Age	Males	Females
0	91.0	94.3	**51**	35.1	38.2
1	90.3	93.5	**52**	34.1	37.1
2	89.2	92.4	**53**	33.1	36.1
3	88.0	91.3	**54**	32.0	35.1
4	86.9	90.1	**55**	31.0	34.0
5	85.8	89.0	**56**	30.0	33.0
6	84.6	87.9	**57**	29.0	32.0
7	83.5	86.8	**58**	28.1	31.0
8	82.3	85.6	**59**	27.1	30.0
9	81.2	84.5	**60**	26.2	29.0
10	80.1	83.4	**61**	25.2	28.1
11	78.9	82.2	**62**	24.3	27.1
12	77.8	81.1	**63**	23.4	26.2
13	76.6	80.0	**64**	22.5	25.2
14	75.5	78.9	**65**	21.6	24.3
15	74.4	77.7	**66**	20.8	23.4
16	73.2	76.6	**67**	19.9	22.4
17	72.1	75.5	**68**	19.0	21.5
18	71.0	74.4	**69**	18.2	20.6
19	69.8	73.2	**70**	17.3	19.7
20	68.7	72.1	**71**	16.5	18.8
21	67.6	71.0	**72**	15.7	17.9
22	66.5	69.9	**73**	14.9	17.1
23	65.4	68.8	**74**	14.1	16.2
24	64.3	67.6	**75**	13.3	15.4
25	63.2	66.5	**76**	12.6	14.6
26	62.0	65.4	**77**	11.9	13.8
27	60.9	64.3	**78**	11.2	13.0
28	59.8	63.2	**79**	10.6	12.2
29	58.7	62.1	**80**	9.9	11.5
30	57.6	61.0	**81**	9.2	10.7
31	56.5	59.9	**82**	8.6	10.0
32	55.4	58.8	**83**	8.0	9.2
33	54.3	57.7	**84**	7.4	8.6
34	53.2	56.6	**85**	6.8	7.9
35	52.2	55.5	**86**	6.3	7.3
36	51.1	54.4	**87**	5.8	6.7
37	50.0	53.3	**88**	5.3	6.2
38	48.9	52.2	**89**	4.9	5.7
39	47.8	51.1	**90**	4.6	5.3
40	46.8	50.0	**91**	4.2	4.9
41	45.7	48.9	**92**	3.9	4.5
42	44.6	47.8	**93**	3.6	4.2
43	43.6	46.7	**94**	3.4	3.8
44	42.5	45.7	**95**	3.1	3.5
45	41.5	44.6	**96**	2.9	3.3
46	40.4	43.5	**97**	2.7	3.0
47	39.3	42.4	**98**	2.5	2.8
48	38.3	41.4	**99**	2.3	2.6
49	37.2	40.3	**100**	2.1	2.4
50	36.2	39.2			

Source: Office for National Statistics

Notes:

1. National life tables of various kinds and population projections have been produced for a considerable period, formerly by the Government Actuary's Department and, since February 2006, by the Office for National Statistics. The Decennial Life Tables for England and Wales combined and for Scotland are based on data for the three-year period around a Census. Between Censuses, life tables known as National Life Tables (formerly named Interim Life Tables) are produced which are based on data for the numbers in the population and the deaths by age and sex for the latest three-year period available. These National Life Tables are produced for the United Kingdom as a whole, Great Britain, England and Wales and also for each individual country of the United Kingdom. It is intended to update the life tables in Facts and Figures every year, using the latest data then available.

The historical life tables

2. The latest published Decennial Life Tables are the English Life Tables No.16 and the Scottish Life Tables 2000–2002. These are based on data on the numbers in the population and the numbers of deaths by age and sex for 2000–2002 (the three years around the 2001 Census).

3. Data from the preceding Decennial Life Table, ELT No.15, formed the mortality assumptions underlying the calculations of the multipliers in Tables 1–18 of the 4th edition of the Ogden Tables. Tables of multipliers using mortality from the Decennial Life Tables are no longer reproduced in the Ogden Tables.

4. The tables we produce are the latest available National Life Tables for the United Kingdom (based on data for 2011–2013).

5. The Ogden Tables take account of the possibilities that a claimant will live for different periods, e.g. die soon or live to be very old. The mortality assumptions for the 7th edition relate to the general population of the United Kingdom. Unless there is clear evidence in an individual case to support the view that the individual concerned is atypical and will experience a rather shorter or longer than average life, no further increase or reduction is required for mortality alone. Examples of atypical individuals would be a lifelong heavy smoker, someone suffering from a head injury or epilepsy or an immobile patient.

Projected mortality

6. The life tables referred to above are based on historical data (and expectations of life which are calculated using these data), and effectively assume that the mortality rate for a given age and sex will remain constant in future years. However, there have been large improvements in mortality rates over the last 100 years or so. If improvements in mortality rates carry on into the future, awards of damages calculated on the basis of historical mortality rates are likely to under-compensate claimants, on average.

7. At Appendix A to the Introduction to the 4th edition of the Ogden Tables there is an extract from ELT No.15, which shows graphs indicating rates of mortality expressed in percentages of the 1911 rates of mortality on a logarithmic scale. They demonstrate in stark fashion the improvement in longevity which has taken place since 1911.

8. The sole exception in some recent years has been small increases in the mortality of young males in their 30s due to increases in deaths caused by HIV infection and AIDS; suicide rates and

alcohol-related mortality have also increased for men at young ages in some years. However, even if this slight worsening of mortality were to continue, the effects on the tables of multipliers (in the Ogden Tables) would not be significant.

9. The Office for National Statistics carries out official population projections for the United Kingdom and constituent countries, usually every two years. In particular, these projections include assumptions of improving mortality rates at most ages in the years following the base year of the projections.

10. Tables 1–26 of the 7th edition of the Ogden Tables give multipliers based on the projected mortality rates underlying the 2008-based principal population projections for the United Kingdom. These take as their base the estimated numbers in the population by sex and age in the constituent countries of the United Kingdom in mid-2008. The projections and the underlying assumptions are available on the website of the Office for National Statistics at: *http://www.ons.gov.uk/ons/rel/npp/national-population-projections/index.html.*

11. Multipliers in earlier editions of the Ogden Tables were based on historical or projected mortality rates for the population of England and Wales combined. However, the Ogden Tables are used extensively in Scotland and Northern Ireland. Although it would be possible to produce separate Tables based on projected mortality rates for Scotland and for Northern Ireland, it was agreed for the 6th edition that rather than have three separate sets of tables there should be one set calculated using mortality rates from the population projections of the United Kingdom as a whole and this has been continued in the 7th edition.

12. The 2013-based national population projections were published in September 2014. Table A3, "Expectation of Life Table", shows expectations of life in the year 2015 by age and sex allowing for future improvements based on the mortality assumptions underlying the principal 2013-based population projections for the United Kingdom combined.

13. As mentioned earlier, the mortality rates used are for the population as a whole. In difficult cases, where the sums involved are large and the matter is in doubt, an actuary should be consulted. Expert medical evidence should be obtained in atypical cases.

A4: Loss of earnings multipliers adjusted for education, disability and employment status

The Ogden Tables dealing with loss of earnings (Ogden tables 3–14) are subject to adjustment for contingencies other than mortality (Ogden paras 26–44). The tables which follow incorporate those factors without the need for further calculation.

The contingencies are whether the claimant was in employment or not, whether he was disabled or not, and his educational or skill level. Earlier editions (1st–5th) of the Ogden Tables and of *Facts & Figures*, based on earlier research, made adjustments for the general state of the economy; the nature of the claimant's employment, whether clerical or manual; and for different geographical areas of the country. These are not used in the latest edition as more recent research has shown that when adjustments are made for education, disability and educational attainment the difference made by these other factors is small.

Employment

Employed
Those who at the time of the accident are employed, self-employed or on a government training scheme.

Not employed
All others (including those temporarily out of work, full-time students and unpaid family workers).

Disability

Disabled
A person is classified as being disabled if all three of the following conditions in relation to the ill-health or disability are met:

(i) he or she has either a progressive illness or an illness which has or is expected to last for over a year,

and

(ii) he or she satisfies the Equality Act definition that the impact of the disability substantially limits the person's ability to carry out normal day-to-day activities,

and

(iii) his or her condition affects either the kind **or** the amount of paid work they can do.

Not disabled.
All others.

Paragraph 35 of the Ogden notes (section A8 in this book) gives examples of the ways in which a disability may limit one's day-to-day activities.

Educational attainment means the highest level of education attained by the claimant. It is a shorthand for the level of skill and includes equivalent non-academic qualifications.

Degree or equivalent.

This includes professional qualifications, for example as a nurse.

GCSE grades A–C, O levels, or CSE grade 1, up to A-levels or equivalent.
In the tables which follow this is called "Good GCSE level education or equivalent".

Qualifications below GCSE grade C or CSE grade 1 or equivalent, or no qualifications.
In the tables which follow this is called "Education below good GCSE level".

There are 12 tables each for men and women arranged in the following order.

- Not disabled
  - Employed
    - Degree level education or equivalent
    - Good GCSE level education or equivalent
    - Education below good GCSE level
  - Not employed
    - Degree level education or equivalent
    - Good GCSE level education or equivalent
    - Education below good GCSE level
- Disabled
  - Employed
    - Degree level education or equivalent
    - Good GCSE level education or equivalent
    - Education below good GCSE level
  - Not employed
    - Degree level education or equivalent
    - Good GCSE level education or equivalent
    - Education below good GCSE level

Thus if the claimant is a 32-year-old male solicitor, employed before the accident at a salary of £40,000, not disabled and proposing to retire at 60, the first table on the next page gives the multiplier for loss of earnings to age 60 as 18.22.

By using the tables for disabled claimants it is possible to obtain an estimate of the claimant's residual earning capacity, with an "inbuilt" allowance for employment risks which would otherwise require a separate *Smith v Manchester* award. Thus if the accident has seriously affected the solicitor's ability to work as a solicitor, and he is now employed at a salary of £25,000, the seventh table gives a multiplier of 11.68 for his new earning capacity to age 60. This approach will not always be suitable and there will be cases where a *Smith v Manchester* or *Blamire* award is still needed.

The 6th edition of the Ogden Tables had an adjustment factor for persons aged 16–19 with a degree level education. This caused difficulties. The 7th edition (para.41) recommends that in the case of someone who has not yet reached the age at which it is likely that he would start work, there should be an assessment of the level of education he would have attained, the age he would have started work, and whether he would have been employed or not. The multiplier appropriate to that age and those conditions should then be discounted for early receipt (for the period between the date of trial and the putative date of starting work).

The notes to the Ogden Tables do not provide specific adjustment factors for ages above 54 on the basis that, above that age, the likely course of someone's employment will depend on individual circumstances and the use of statistical averages may be inappropriate.

The adjustment factors as stated in the Ogden Tables are usually constant over a five year age range. This sometimes gives the appearance of anomalies or discontinuities in the figures—for example, in some tables a claimant of 18 or 19 has a smaller multiplier than one in his or her early 20s. The editors have been advised that this is the correct approach.

The tables assume a 2.5 per cent discount rate.

ND E Deg

Loss of earnings: not disabled; employed; degree level education or equivalent

Age	Male to retiring age 50	55	60	65	70	75	Age	Female to retiring age 50	55	60	65	70	75
16	See introductory notes						**16**	See introductory notes					
17							**17**						
18							**18**						
19							**19**						
20	19.31	21.29	23.02	24.51	25.77	26.84	**20**	18.77	20.73	22.44	23.92	25.20	26.31
21	18.86	20.90	22.67	24.20	25.49	26.58	**21**	18.34	20.35	22.10	23.62	24.94	26.06
22	18.41	20.50	22.31	23.87	25.20	26.32	**22**	17.91	19.95	21.75	23.32	24.66	25.81
23	17.95	20.08	21.94	23.54	24.90	26.05	**23**	17.45	19.55	21.40	23.00	24.38	25.55
24	17.47	19.66	21.56	23.20	24.60	25.77	**24**	16.99	19.14	21.03	22.67	24.08	25.29
25	17.17	19.44	21.41	23.11	24.55	25.76	**25**	16.52	18.73	20.66	22.34	23.79	25.03
26	16.67	18.99	21.01	22.76	24.24	25.47	**26**	16.03	18.30	20.27	22.00	23.49	24.75
27	16.14	18.53	20.61	22.39	23.90	25.18	**27**	15.53	17.85	19.88	21.65	23.17	24.47
28	15.61	18.06	20.19	22.01	23.57	24.87	**28**	15.02	17.41	19.48	21.30	22.86	24.18
29	15.08	17.59	19.76	21.63	23.22	24.55	**29**	14.51	16.95	19.07	20.92	22.53	23.89
30	14.36	16.91	19.12	21.01	22.62	23.97	**30**	13.97	16.47	18.65	20.55	22.19	23.59
31	13.80	16.40	18.67	20.62	22.26	23.64	**31**	13.42	15.98	18.23	20.17	21.85	23.27
32	13.22	15.90	18.22	20.21	21.91	23.32	**32**	12.86	15.49	17.78	19.78	21.49	22.95
33	12.63	15.38	17.76	19.81	21.54	22.98	**33**	12.28	14.98	17.34	19.38	21.14	22.63
34	12.03	14.85	17.29	19.38	21.16	22.64	**34**	11.69	14.46	16.87	18.97	20.77	22.30
35	11.17	14.00	16.44	18.54	20.32	21.81	**35**	11.09	13.93	16.40	18.55	20.39	21.97
36	10.55	13.45	15.96	18.12	19.93	21.46	**36**	10.48	13.38	15.91	18.11	20.01	21.62
37	9.91	12.89	15.46	17.68	19.55	21.11	**37**	9.84	12.82	15.41	17.68	19.62	21.26
38	9.26	12.31	14.95	17.22	19.14	20.74	**38**	9.19	12.25	14.91	17.22	19.21	20.90
39	8.59	11.72	14.44	16.76	18.72	20.36	**39**	8.53	11.66	14.39	16.76	18.80	20.52
40	7.73	10.87	13.59	15.92	17.89	19.53	**40**	7.85	11.05	13.86	16.29	18.38	20.14
41	7.04	10.27	13.06	15.44	17.47	19.14	**41**	7.15	10.44	13.31	15.81	17.94	19.76
42	6.34	9.64	12.50	14.96	17.04	18.75	**42**	6.43	9.81	12.75	15.31	17.50	19.36
43	5.61	9.01	11.95	14.47	16.59	18.35	**43**	5.70	9.16	12.18	14.80	17.04	18.95
44	4.88	8.36	11.38	13.96	16.14	17.94	**44**	4.94	8.50	11.60	14.28	16.58	18.53
45	4.02	7.52	10.54	13.13	15.32	17.12	**45**	4.08	7.65	10.75	13.44	15.75	17.70
46	3.26	6.85	9.96	12.62	14.85	16.70	**46**	3.31	6.96	10.15	12.91	15.28	17.28
47	2.48	6.17	9.36	12.08	14.38	16.28	**47**	2.51	6.26	9.54	12.37	14.80	16.84
48	1.68	5.46	8.74	11.54	13.90	15.84	**48**	1.70	5.55	8.91	11.81	14.30	16.41
49	0.85	4.75	8.11	10.98	13.40	15.39	**49**	0.86	4.82	8.27	11.25	13.80	15.96
50		3.87	7.20	10.05	12.45	14.43	**50**		4.02	7.52	10.54	13.13	15.33
51		3.10	6.49	9.38	11.81	13.82	**51**		3.22	6.77	9.84	12.47	14.69
52		2.32	5.77	8.71	11.18	13.21	**52**		2.42	6.02	9.14	11.80	14.05
53		1.55	5.06	8.04	10.54	12.61	**53**		1.62	5.28	8.44	11.14	13.42
54		0.78	4.34	7.37	9.91	12.01	**54**		0.82	4.58	7.83	10.61	12.95

Male: See introductory notes as regards claimants over 54 at date of trial

Female: See introductory notes as regards claimants over 54 at date of trial

ND E GCSE

Loss of earnings: not disabled; employed; good GCSE level education or equivalent

Age	Male to retiring age 50	55	60	65	70	75	Age	Female to retiring age 50	55	60	65	70	75
16	20.52	22.28	23.81	25.13	26.26	27.21	**16**	18.56	20.17	21.58	22.81	23.87	24.78
17	20.12	21.93	23.50	24.85	26.00	26.97	**17**	18.20	19.85	21.29	22.56	23.64	24.58
18	19.72	21.57	23.18	24.56	25.75	26.74	**18**	17.84	19.53	21.01	22.30	23.42	24.36
19	19.31	21.20	22.85	24.27	25.48	26.50	**19**	17.46	19.21	20.72	22.04	23.18	24.15
20	19.31	21.29	23.02	24.51	25.77	26.84	**20**	17.29	19.10	20.67	22.04	23.22	24.24
21	18.86	20.90	22.67	24.20	25.49	26.58	**21**	16.90	18.75	20.36	21.76	22.98	24.01
22	18.41	20.50	22.31	23.87	25.20	26.32	**22**	16.50	18.38	20.04	21.48	22.72	23.78
23	17.95	20.08	21.94	23.54	24.90	26.05	**23**	16.08	18.02	19.71	21.19	22.46	23.54
24	17.47	19.66	21.56	23.20	24.60	25.77	**24**	15.65	17.64	19.38	20.89	22.19	23.30
25	16.98	19.23	21.18	22.86	24.29	25.48	**25**	15.59	17.67	19.50	21.08	22.45	23.62
26	16.49	18.79	20.78	22.51	23.98	25.20	**26**	15.13	17.27	19.14	20.76	22.17	23.36
27	15.97	18.34	20.39	22.14	23.64	24.90	**27**	14.66	16.85	18.77	20.44	21.87	23.09
28	15.45	17.87	19.97	21.78	23.31	24.60	**28**	14.18	16.43	18.39	20.10	21.57	22.82
29	14.91	17.40	19.55	21.40	22.97	24.29	**29**	13.69	15.99	18.00	19.75	21.26	22.55
30	14.21	16.73	18.91	20.78	22.38	23.71	**30**	13.34	15.73	17.82	19.63	21.19	22.52
31	13.65	16.23	18.46	20.39	22.02	23.39	**31**	12.82	15.27	17.41	19.26	20.87	22.23
32	13.08	15.72	18.02	19.99	21.67	23.07	**32**	12.28	14.79	16.98	18.89	20.53	21.92
33	12.49	15.22	17.56	19.59	21.30	22.73	**33**	11.73	14.31	16.56	18.50	20.19	21.62
34	11.90	14.69	17.10	19.17	20.93	22.40	**34**	11.17	13.81	16.12	18.11	19.84	21.30
35	11.17	14.00	16.44	18.54	20.32	21.81	**35**	10.72	13.46	15.85	17.92	19.70	21.22
36	10.55	13.45	15.96	18.12	19.93	21.46	**36**	10.12	12.93	15.38	17.50	19.33	20.89
37	9.91	12.89	15.46	17.68	19.55	21.11	**37**	9.51	12.38	14.90	17.08	18.95	20.55
38	9.26	12.31	14.95	17.22	19.14	20.74	**38**	8.88	11.83	14.40	16.64	18.56	20.19
39	8.59	11.72	14.44	16.76	18.72	20.36	**39**	8.24	11.27	13.91	16.19	18.16	19.83
40	7.73	10.87	13.59	15.92	17.89	19.53	**40**	7.59	10.68	13.39	15.74	17.76	19.46
41	7.04	10.27	13.06	15.44	17.47	19.14	**41**	6.91	10.09	12.87	15.27	17.34	19.09
42	6.34	9.64	12.50	14.96	17.04	18.75	**42**	6.21	9.48	12.32	14.79	16.91	18.70
43	5.61	9.01	11.95	14.47	16.59	18.35	**43**	5.50	8.85	11.77	14.30	16.47	18.31
44	4.88	8.36	11.38	13.96	16.14	17.94	**44**	4.77	8.21	11.21	13.80	16.02	17.91
45	4.02	7.52	10.54	13.13	15.32	17.12	**45**	3.99	7.47	10.51	13.13	15.39	17.30
46	3.26	6.85	9.96	12.62	14.85	16.70	**46**	3.23	6.80	9.92	12.61	14.93	16.88
47	2.48	6.17	9.36	12.08	14.38	16.28	**47**	2.45	6.12	9.32	12.09	14.46	16.46
48	1.68	5.46	8.74	11.54	13.90	15.84	**48**	1.66	5.42	8.70	11.54	13.97	16.03
49	0.85	4.75	8.11	10.98	13.40	15.39	**49**	0.84	4.71	8.07	10.99	13.48	15.59
50		3.87	7.20	10.05	12.45	14.43	**50**		3.93	7.34	10.30	12.83	14.97
51		3.10	6.49	9.38	11.81	13.82	**51**		3.18	6.69	9.73	12.32	14.52
52		2.32	5.77	8.71	11.18	13.21	**52**		2.42	6.02	9.14	11.80	14.05
53		1.55	5.06	8.04	10.54	12.61	**53**		1.62	5.28	8.44	11.14	13.42
54		0.78	4.34	7.37	9.91	12.01	**54**		0.82	4.58	7.83	10.61	12.95

See introductory notes as regards claimants over 54 at date of trial

See introductory notes as regards claimants over 54 at date of trial

ND E <GCSE

Loss of earnings: not disabled; employed; education below good GCSE level

Age	Male to retiring age						Age	Female to retiring age					
	50	55	60	65	70	75		50	55	60	65	70	75
16	19.38	21.05	22.49	23.73	24.80	25.70	**16**	14.66	15.94	17.05	18.02	18.86	19.58
17	19.01	20.71	22.19	23.47	24.56	25.47	**17**	14.38	15.69	16.83	17.82	18.68	19.42
18	18.62	20.37	21.89	23.20	24.32	25.25	**18**	14.09	15.43	16.60	17.62	18.50	19.25
19	18.23	20.03	21.58	22.92	24.06	25.02	**19**	13.80	15.17	16.37	17.41	18.32	19.08
20	18.26	20.13	21.77	23.18	24.37	25.38	**20**	14.34	15.84	17.14	18.28	19.26	20.10
21	17.84	19.77	21.44	22.88	24.11	25.13	**21**	14.01	15.54	16.88	18.05	19.05	19.91
22	17.41	19.38	21.10	22.58	23.83	24.89	**22**	13.68	15.25	16.62	17.82	18.84	19.72
23	16.97	18.99	20.75	22.26	23.55	24.63	**23**	13.33	14.94	16.35	17.57	18.63	19.52
24	16.52	18.59	20.39	21.94	23.26	24.37	**24**	12.98	14.63	16.07	17.32	18.40	19.33
25	16.43	18.60	20.49	22.12	23.50	24.65	**25**	13.36	15.15	16.71	18.07	19.25	20.25
26	15.95	18.17	20.11	21.78	23.19	24.38	**26**	12.97	14.80	16.40	17.80	19.00	20.02
27	15.45	17.74	19.72	21.42	22.87	24.09	**27**	12.56	14.44	16.08	17.52	18.74	19.79
28	14.94	17.28	19.32	21.07	22.55	23.80	**28**	12.15	14.08	15.76	17.23	18.49	19.56
29	14.43	16.83	18.91	20.70	22.22	23.50	**29**	11.74	13.71	15.43	16.93	18.22	19.32
30	13.89	16.36	18.49	20.33	21.89	23.18	**30**	11.77	13.88	15.72	17.32	18.70	19.88
31	13.35	15.87	18.06	19.94	21.54	22.87	**31**	11.31	13.47	15.36	17.00	18.41	19.61
32	12.79	15.38	17.62	19.55	21.19	22.56	**32**	10.84	13.05	14.98	16.66	18.11	19.34
33	12.22	14.88	17.18	19.16	20.83	22.23	**33**	10.35	12.62	14.61	16.33	17.81	19.07
34	11.64	14.36	16.72	18.75	20.47	21.90	**34**	9.86	12.19	14.22	15.98	17.50	18.79
35	11.04	13.84	16.26	18.33	20.10	21.56	**35**	9.72	12.21	14.38	16.26	17.87	19.25
36	10.43	13.30	15.78	17.92	19.71	21.22	**36**	9.18	11.72	13.95	15.87	17.53	18.95
37	9.80	12.74	15.29	17.48	19.33	20.87	**37**	8.63	11.23	13.51	15.49	17.19	18.63
38	9.16	12.18	14.78	17.03	18.93	20.51	**38**	8.06	10.73	13.07	15.09	16.83	18.31
39	8.49	11.59	14.28	16.57	18.51	20.13	**39**	7.47	10.22	12.61	14.69	16.47	17.99
40	7.73	10.87	13.59	15.92	17.89	19.53	**40**	7.06	9.94	12.46	14.64	16.52	18.10
41	7.04	10.27	13.06	15.44	17.47	19.14	**41**	6.42	9.38	11.97	14.21	16.13	17.76
42	6.34	9.64	12.50	14.96	17.04	18.75	**42**	5.78	8.82	11.46	13.76	15.73	17.40
43	5.61	9.01	11.95	14.47	16.59	18.35	**43**	5.12	8.23	10.95	13.30	15.32	17.03
44	4.88	8.36	11.38	13.96	16.14	17.94	**44**	4.44	7.64	10.42	12.84	14.90	16.66
45	4.02	7.52	10.54	13.13	15.32	17.12	**45**	3.80	7.12	10.01	12.51	14.66	16.48
46	3.26	6.85	9.96	12.62	14.85	16.70	**46**	3.08	6.48	9.45	12.02	14.22	16.09
47	2.48	6.17	9.36	12.08	14.38	16.28	**47**	2.33	5.83	8.88	11.52	13.78	15.68
48	1.68	5.46	8.74	11.54	13.90	15.84	**48**	1.58	5.17	8.29	11.00	13.32	15.28
49	0.85	4.75	8.11	10.98	13.40	15.39	**49**	0.80	4.49	7.70	10.47	12.85	14.86
50		3.87	7.20	10.05	12.45	14.43	**50**		3.79	7.08	9.93	12.37	14.43
51		3.10	6.49	9.38	11.81	13.82	**51**		3.07	6.46	9.38	11.88	14.00
52		2.32	5.77	8.71	11.18	13.21	**52**		2.33	5.81	8.81	11.38	13.55
53		1.55	5.06	8.04	10.54	12.61	**53**		1.58	5.15	8.24	10.87	13.10
54		0.78	4.34	7.37	9.91	12.01	**54**		0.81	4.53	7.73	10.48	12.79

See introductory notes as regards claimants over 54 at date of trial

See introductory notes as regards claimants over 54 at date of trial

ND NE Deg

Loss of earnings: not disabled; not employed; degree level education or equivalent

Age	Male to retiring age 50	55	60	65	70	75	Age	Female to retiring age 50	55	60	65	70	75
16	See introductory notes						**16**	See introductory notes					
17							**17**						
18							**18**						
19							**19**						
20	18.68	20.59	22.27	23.71	24.93	25.96	**20**	17.72	19.56	21.18	22.58	23.79	24.83
21	18.25	20.22	21.93	23.41	24.66	25.71	**21**	17.31	19.20	20.86	22.29	23.54	24.60
22	17.81	19.83	21.58	23.10	24.38	25.46	**22**	16.90	18.83	20.53	22.01	23.28	24.36
23	17.36	19.43	21.23	22.78	24.09	25.20	**23**	16.47	18.45	20.19	21.71	23.01	24.12
24	16.90	19.02	20.86	22.45	23.80	24.93	**24**	16.04	18.07	19.85	21.39	22.73	23.87
25	16.43	18.60	20.49	22.12	23.50	24.65	**25**	15.40	17.46	19.26	20.83	22.19	23.34
26	15.95	18.17	20.11	21.78	23.19	24.38	**26**	14.95	17.06	18.91	20.52	21.90	23.08
27	15.45	17.74	19.72	21.42	22.87	24.09	**27**	14.48	16.65	18.54	20.19	21.60	22.82
28	14.94	17.28	19.32	21.07	22.55	23.80	**28**	14.01	16.23	18.17	19.86	21.31	22.55
29	14.43	16.83	18.91	20.70	22.22	23.50	**29**	13.53	15.80	17.79	19.51	21.01	22.28
30	13.58	15.99	18.08	19.87	21.39	22.66	**30**	12.72	14.99	16.98	18.70	20.19	21.47
31	13.05	15.51	17.65	19.50	21.05	22.36	**31**	12.21	14.55	16.59	18.35	19.89	21.18
32	12.50	15.03	17.23	19.11	20.71	22.05	**32**	11.70	14.09	16.18	18.00	19.56	20.89
33	11.95	14.55	16.79	18.73	20.37	21.73	**33**	11.18	13.63	15.78	17.63	19.24	20.60
34	11.38	14.04	16.35	18.33	20.01	21.41	**34**	10.64	13.16	15.36	17.26	18.91	20.30
35	10.55	13.22	15.53	17.51	19.19	20.60	**35**	9.97	12.52	14.74	16.67	18.33	19.74
36	9.96	12.70	15.07	17.11	18.83	20.26	**36**	9.42	12.02	14.30	16.28	17.98	19.43
37	9.36	12.17	14.60	16.69	18.46	19.93	**37**	8.85	11.52	13.86	15.89	17.63	19.11
38	8.75	11.63	14.12	16.26	18.08	19.58	**38**	8.26	11.01	13.40	15.48	17.26	18.78
39	8.11	11.07	13.63	15.83	17.68	19.23	**39**	7.66	10.48	12.94	15.06	16.90	18.45
40	7.20	10.13	12.66	14.83	16.67	18.20	**40**	6.88	9.69	12.14	14.27	16.11	17.65
41	6.56	9.57	12.17	14.39	16.28	17.83	**41**	6.26	9.15	11.67	13.85	15.72	17.32
42	5.90	8.99	11.65	13.94	15.88	17.47	**42**	5.63	8.60	11.18	13.42	15.33	16.97
43	5.23	8.40	11.14	13.48	15.46	17.10	**43**	4.99	8.03	10.68	12.97	14.94	16.61
44	4.54	7.79	10.60	13.01	15.04	16.72	**44**	4.33	7.45	10.16	12.52	14.53	16.24
45	3.60	6.73	9.44	11.76	13.71	15.33	**45**	3.38	6.33	8.90	11.12	13.03	14.65
46	2.92	6.14	8.92	11.30	13.30	14.95	**46**	2.74	5.76	8.40	10.68	12.64	14.30
47	2.22	5.52	8.38	10.82	12.87	14.58	**47**	2.07	5.18	7.89	10.24	12.25	13.94
48	1.50	4.89	7.82	10.33	12.44	14.18	**48**	1.40	4.59	7.37	9.78	11.84	13.58
49	0.76	4.25	7.26	9.83	12.00	13.78	**49**	0.71	3.99	6.84	9.31	11.42	13.20
50		3.36	6.25	8.72	10.80	12.51	**50**		3.00	5.59	7.85	9.77	11.40
51		2.65	5.54	8.01	10.08	11.79	**51**		2.27	4.78	6.95	8.80	10.37
52		1.92	4.77	7.20	9.25	10.93	**52**		1.61	4.02	6.09	7.87	9.37
53		1.22	3.98	6.33	8.30	9.93	**53**		0.98	3.18	5.09	6.71	8.09
54		0.58	3.24	5.50	7.40	8.97	**54**		0.44	2.43	4.15	5.62	6.86

See introductory notes as regards claimants over 54 at date of trial (male)

See introductory notes as regards claimants over 54 at date of trial (female)

ND NE GCSE

Loss of earnings: not disabled; not employed; good GCSE level education or equivalent

Age	Male to retiring age 50	55	60	65	70	75	Age	Female to retiring age 50	55	60	65	70	75
16	19.38	21.05	22.49	23.73	24.80	25.70	**16**	17.64	19.17	20.51	21.68	22.69	23.55
17	19.01	20.71	22.19	23.47	24.56	25.47	**17**	17.30	18.87	20.24	21.44	22.48	23.36
18	18.62	20.37	21.89	23.20	24.32	25.25	**18**	16.96	18.56	19.97	21.20	22.26	23.16
19	18.23	20.03	21.58	22.92	24.06	25.02	**19**	16.60	18.26	19.70	20.95	22.04	22.96
20	18.47	20.36	22.02	23.44	24.65	25.67	**20**	16.03	17.70	19.16	20.43	21.52	22.47
21	18.04	19.99	21.68	23.14	24.38	25.42	**21**	15.66	17.37	18.87	20.17	21.30	22.25
22	17.61	19.61	21.34	22.84	24.10	25.18	**22**	15.29	17.04	18.57	19.91	21.06	22.04
23	17.17	19.21	20.99	22.52	23.82	24.91	**23**	14.90	16.70	18.27	19.64	20.82	21.82
24	16.71	18.81	20.63	22.19	23.53	24.65	**24**	14.51	16.35	17.96	19.36	20.57	21.60
25	16.24	18.39	20.26	21.87	23.23	24.38	**25**	13.92	15.78	17.41	18.83	20.05	21.09
26	15.77	17.97	19.88	21.53	22.93	24.10	**26**	13.51	15.42	17.09	18.54	19.79	20.86
27	15.28	17.54	19.50	21.18	22.62	23.82	**27**	13.09	15.04	16.75	18.25	19.52	20.62
28	14.78	17.09	19.10	20.83	22.30	23.53	**28**	12.66	14.67	16.42	17.95	19.26	20.38
29	14.26	16.64	18.70	20.47	21.97	23.23	**29**	12.23	14.28	16.07	17.63	18.98	20.13
30	13.42	15.81	17.87	19.64	21.15	22.40	**30**	11.77	13.88	15.72	17.32	18.70	19.88
31	12.90	15.33	17.45	19.27	20.81	22.10	**31**	11.31	13.47	15.36	17.00	18.41	19.61
32	12.36	14.86	17.03	18.89	20.48	21.80	**32**	10.84	13.05	14.98	16.66	18.11	19.34
33	11.81	14.38	16.60	18.52	20.13	21.48	**33**	10.35	12.62	14.61	16.33	17.81	19.07
34	11.25	13.88	16.16	18.12	19.78	21.16	**34**	9.86	12.19	14.22	15.98	17.50	18.79
35	10.42	13.06	15.35	17.30	18.97	20.35	**35**	9.22	11.58	13.64	15.42	16.95	18.26
36	9.84	12.55	14.89	16.91	18.61	20.03	**36**	8.71	11.12	13.23	15.06	16.64	17.97
37	9.25	12.03	14.43	16.50	18.24	19.70	**37**	8.18	10.66	12.82	14.70	16.31	17.68
38	8.64	11.49	13.95	16.07	17.87	19.35	**38**	7.64	10.18	12.39	14.32	15.97	17.38
39	8.01	10.94	13.47	15.64	17.47	19.00	**39**	7.09	9.69	11.97	13.93	15.63	17.06
40	7.11	10.00	12.51	14.65	16.47	17.97	**40**	6.35	8.94	11.21	13.18	14.87	16.29
41	6.48	9.45	12.02	14.22	16.08	17.62	**41**	5.78	8.45	10.77	12.79	14.52	15.98
42	5.83	8.88	11.51	13.77	15.68	17.26	**42**	5.20	7.93	10.32	12.38	14.16	15.66
43	5.17	8.29	11.00	13.32	15.27	16.89	**43**	4.61	7.41	9.86	11.97	13.79	15.33
44	4.49	7.70	10.47	12.85	14.86	16.52	**44**	4.00	6.88	9.38	11.56	13.41	14.99
45	3.60	6.73	9.44	11.76	13.71	15.33	**45**	3.00	5.63	7.91	9.89	11.58	13.02
46	2.92	6.14	8.92	11.30	13.30	14.95	**46**	2.43	5.12	7.47	9.50	11.24	12.71
47	2.22	5.52	8.38	10.82	12.87	14.58	**47**	1.84	4.61	7.01	9.10	10.89	12.39
48	1.50	4.89	7.82	10.33	12.44	14.18	**48**	1.25	4.08	6.55	8.69	10.52	12.07
49	0.76	4.25	7.26	9.83	12.00	13.78	**49**	0.63	3.55	6.08	8.28	10.15	11.74
50		3.36	6.25	8.72	10.80	12.51	**50**		2.57	4.81	6.74	8.40	9.80
51		2.65	5.54	8.01	10.08	11.79	**51**		1.93	4.06	5.91	7.48	8.81
52		1.92	4.77	7.20	9.25	10.93	**52**		1.32	3.30	5.00	6.46	7.70
53		1.22	3.98	6.33	8.30	9.93	**53**		0.80	2.61	4.17	5.50	6.63
54		0.58	3.24	5.50	7.40	8.97	**54**		0.35	1.93	3.30	4.47	5.46

See introductory notes as regards claimants over 54 at date of trial

See introductory notes as regards claimants over 54 at date of trial

ND NE <GCSE

Loss of earnings: not disabled; not employed; education below good GCSE level

Age	Male to retiring age 50	55	60	65	70	75
16	18.70	20.30	21.70	22.89	23.93	24.79
17	18.34	19.98	21.41	22.64	23.69	24.58
18	17.97	19.66	21.11	22.38	23.46	24.36
19	17.59	19.32	20.82	22.12	23.21	24.14
20	17.42	19.21	20.77	22.11	23.25	24.21
21	17.02	18.86	20.45	21.83	23.00	23.98
22	16.61	18.49	20.13	21.54	22.73	23.75
23	16.19	18.12	19.80	21.24	22.47	23.50
24	15.76	17.74	19.46	20.93	22.19	23.25
25	15.14	17.14	18.88	20.38	21.65	22.71
26	14.69	16.74	18.52	20.07	21.37	22.46
27	14.24	16.34	18.17	19.74	21.07	22.20
28	13.77	15.92	17.80	19.41	20.78	21.93
29	13.29	15.51	17.43	19.07	20.48	21.65
30	12.64	14.89	16.83	18.50	19.92	21.10
31	12.15	14.44	16.43	18.15	19.60	20.82
32	11.64	14.00	16.04	17.80	19.29	20.53
33	11.12	13.54	15.63	17.44	18.96	20.23
34	10.59	13.07	15.22	17.07	18.63	19.93
35	9.93	12.44	14.62	16.48	18.06	19.38
36	9.38	11.95	14.18	16.10	17.72	19.07
37	8.81	11.46	13.74	15.71	17.38	18.76
38	8.23	10.94	13.29	15.30	17.02	18.43
39	7.63	10.42	12.83	14.90	16.64	18.10
40	6.85	9.63	12.04	14.11	15.86	17.31
41	6.24	9.10	11.58	13.69	15.48	16.97
42	5.62	8.55	11.08	13.26	15.10	16.62
43	4.98	7.99	10.59	12.82	14.70	16.26
44	4.32	7.41	10.09	12.37	14.31	15.90
45	3.46	6.47	9.07	11.30	13.18	14.73
46	2.80	5.90	8.57	10.86	12.78	14.37
47	2.13	5.31	8.05	10.40	12.37	14.01
48	1.44	4.70	7.52	9.93	11.96	13.63
49	0.73	4.08	6.98	9.45	11.53	13.25
50		3.26	6.08	8.48	10.50	12.17
51		2.57	5.38	7.78	9.79	11.46
52		1.89	4.70	7.10	9.11	10.76
53		1.22	3.98	6.33	8.30	9.93
54		0.58	3.24	5.50	7.40	8.97

See introductory notes as regards claimants over 54 at date of trial

Age	Female to retiring age 50	55	60	65	70	75
16	13.52	14.69	15.72	16.61	17.39	18.05
17	13.26	14.46	15.51	16.43	17.22	17.90
18	12.99	14.22	15.30	16.24	17.06	17.75
19	12.72	13.99	15.09	16.05	16.89	17.59
20	12.65	13.97	15.13	16.13	16.99	17.74
21	12.37	13.72	14.90	15.92	16.81	17.57
22	12.07	13.45	14.66	15.72	16.63	17.40
23	11.77	13.18	14.42	15.50	16.43	17.23
24	11.45	12.91	14.18	15.28	16.24	17.05
25	11.32	12.83	14.16	15.31	16.31	17.15
26	10.99	12.54	13.90	15.08	16.10	16.96
27	10.64	12.24	13.63	14.84	15.88	16.77
28	10.30	11.93	13.35	14.60	15.66	16.57
29	9.94	11.61	13.07	14.34	15.44	16.37
30	9.89	11.66	13.20	14.55	15.71	16.70
31	9.50	11.31	12.90	14.28	15.47	16.47
32	9.10	10.96	12.59	14.00	15.21	16.25
33	8.69	10.60	12.27	13.72	14.96	16.02
34	8.28	10.24	11.94	13.43	14.70	15.79
35	7.85	9.86	11.61	13.13	14.43	15.55
36	7.42	9.47	11.26	12.82	14.16	15.30
37	6.97	9.07	10.91	12.51	13.89	15.05
38	6.51	8.67	10.55	12.19	13.60	14.79
39	6.04	8.25	10.19	11.86	13.31	14.53
40	5.29	7.45	9.34	10.98	12.39	13.58
41	4.82	7.04	8.98	10.66	12.10	13.32
42	4.33	6.61	8.60	10.32	11.80	13.05
43	3.84	6.17	8.21	9.98	11.49	12.77
44	3.33	5.73	7.82	9.63	11.18	12.49
45	2.44	4.57	6.43	8.03	9.41	10.58
46	1.98	4.16	6.07	7.72	9.13	10.33
47	1.50	3.74	5.70	7.39	8.85	10.07
48	1.01	3.32	5.32	7.06	8.55	9.81
49	0.51	2.88	4.94	6.72	8.25	9.54
50		2.01	3.76	5.27	6.57	7.66
51		1.52	3.19	4.63	5.87	6.91
52		1.04	2.58	3.92	5.06	6.02
53		0.62	2.04	3.25	4.29	5.17
54		0.27	1.49	2.55	3.45	4.21

See introductory notes as regards claimants over 54 at date of trial

D E Deg

Loss of earnings: disabled; employed; degree level education or equivalent

Age	Male to retiring age 50	55	60	65	70	75
16	See introductory notes					
17						
18						
19						
20	12.80	14.12	15.26	16.25	17.09	17.79
21	12.50	13.86	15.03	16.04	16.90	17.62
22	12.21	13.59	14.79	15.83	16.71	17.45
23	11.90	13.32	14.55	15.61	16.51	17.27
24	11.58	13.04	14.30	15.38	16.31	17.09
25	11.08	12.54	13.81	14.91	15.84	16.62
26	10.75	12.25	13.55	14.68	15.64	16.43
27	10.42	11.96	13.30	14.44	15.42	16.24
28	10.07	11.65	13.03	14.20	15.20	16.04
29	9.73	11.35	12.75	13.96	14.98	15.84
30	9.21	10.84	12.26	13.48	14.51	15.37
31	8.85	10.52	11.97	13.22	14.28	15.16
32	8.48	10.20	11.68	12.96	14.05	14.96
33	8.10	9.86	11.39	12.70	13.81	14.74
34	7.72	9.52	11.09	12.43	13.57	14.52
35	7.20	9.02	10.60	11.95	13.10	14.05
36	6.80	8.67	10.28	11.68	12.85	13.83
37	6.39	8.31	9.96	11.39	12.60	13.60
38	5.97	7.93	9.63	11.10	12.34	13.36
39	5.53	7.55	9.30	10.80	12.06	13.12
40	5.00	7.04	8.80	10.31	11.59	12.65
41	4.56	6.65	8.46	10.00	11.31	12.40
42	4.10	6.25	8.10	9.69	11.04	12.15
43	3.64	5.84	7.74	9.37	10.74	11.88
44	3.16	5.41	7.37	9.04	10.45	11.62
45	2.57	4.81	6.74	8.40	9.80	10.95
46	2.08	4.38	6.37	8.07	9.50	10.68
47	1.58	3.94	5.98	7.73	9.20	10.41
48	1.07	3.49	5.59	7.38	8.89	10.13
49	0.54	3.04	5.19	7.02	8.57	9.85
50		2.47	4.60	6.42	7.95	9.21
51		2.00	4.19	6.06	7.63	8.93
52		1.55	3.84	5.81	7.45	8.81
53		1.05	3.41	5.43	7.12	8.51
54		0.53	2.96	5.04	6.78	8.21

See introductory notes as regards claimants over 54 at date of trial

Age	Female to retiring age 50	55	60	65	70	75
16	See introductory notes					
17						
18						
19						
20	13.50	14.91	16.13	17.20	18.12	18.92
21	13.19	14.63	15.89	16.99	17.93	18.74
22	12.88	14.35	15.64	16.77	17.73	18.56
23	12.55	14.06	15.39	16.54	17.53	18.37
24	12.22	13.77	15.12	16.30	17.32	18.19
25	11.69	13.26	14.62	15.81	16.84	17.72
26	11.35	12.95	14.35	15.57	16.63	17.52
27	10.99	12.64	14.07	15.33	16.40	17.32
28	10.63	12.32	13.79	15.08	16.18	17.12
29	10.27	12.00	13.50	14.81	15.95	16.91
30	9.73	11.48	13.00	14.32	15.46	16.43
31	9.35	11.14	12.70	14.05	15.22	16.21
32	8.96	10.79	12.39	13.78	14.97	15.99
33	8.56	10.43	12.08	13.50	14.72	15.77
34	8.15	10.07	11.76	13.21	14.47	15.54
35	7.60	9.55	11.24	12.71	13.98	15.05
36	7.18	9.17	10.91	12.41	13.71	14.82
37	6.75	8.78	10.57	12.11	13.44	14.57
38	6.30	8.39	10.22	11.80	13.16	14.32
39	5.84	7.99	9.86	11.49	12.88	14.07
40	5.29	7.45	9.34	10.98	12.39	13.58
41	4.82	7.04	8.98	10.66	12.10	13.32
42	4.33	6.61	8.60	10.32	11.80	13.05
43	3.84	6.17	8.21	9.98	11.49	12.77
44	3.33	5.73	7.82	9.63	11.18	12.49
45	2.81	5.27	7.42	9.27	10.86	12.21
46	2.28	4.80	7.00	8.90	10.54	11.92
47	1.73	4.32	6.58	8.53	10.21	11.62
48	1.17	3.83	6.14	8.15	9.86	11.32
49	0.59	3.32	5.70	7.76	9.52	11.00
50		2.81	5.24	7.36	9.16	10.69
51		2.31	4.86	7.06	8.95	10.54
52		1.76	4.37	6.64	8.57	10.21
53		1.21	3.94	6.31	8.32	10.03
54		0.62	3.48	5.94	8.05	9.83

See introductory notes as regards claimants over 54 at date of trial

D E GCSE

Loss of earnings: disabled; employed; good GCSE level education or equivalent

Age	Male to retiring age 50	55	60	65	70	75	Age	Female to retiring age 50	55	60	65	70	75
16	12.54	13.62	14.55	15.36	16.05	16.63	**16**	9.85	10.71	11.46	12.11	12.67	13.15
17	12.30	13.40	14.36	15.19	15.89	16.48	**17**	9.66	10.54	11.30	11.98	12.55	13.05
18	12.05	13.18	14.16	15.01	15.74	16.34	**18**	9.47	10.37	11.15	11.84	12.43	12.93
19	11.80	12.96	13.96	14.83	15.57	16.19	**19**	9.27	10.20	11.00	11.70	12.31	12.82
20	11.54	12.73	13.76	14.65	15.41	16.04	**20**	9.28	10.25	11.09	11.83	12.46	13.01
21	11.28	12.50	13.55	14.47	15.24	15.89	**21**	9.07	10.06	10.93	11.68	12.33	12.88
22	11.01	12.25	13.34	14.27	15.06	15.74	**22**	8.85	9.86	10.75	11.53	12.19	12.76
23	10.73	12.01	13.12	14.07	14.89	15.57	**23**	8.63	9.67	10.58	11.37	12.05	12.63
24	10.44	11.75	12.89	13.87	14.71	15.41	**24**	8.40	9.46	10.40	11.21	11.91	12.50
25	9.97	11.29	12.43	13.42	14.26	14.96	**25**	8.35	9.47	10.44	11.30	12.03	12.65
26	9.68	11.03	12.20	13.21	14.07	14.79	**26**	8.10	9.25	10.25	11.12	11.88	12.51
27	9.37	10.76	11.97	13.00	13.88	14.62	**27**	7.85	9.03	10.05	10.95	11.71	12.37
28	9.07	10.49	11.72	12.78	13.68	14.44	**28**	7.60	8.80	9.85	10.77	11.56	12.23
29	8.75	10.21	11.48	12.56	13.48	14.26	**29**	7.34	8.57	9.64	10.58	11.39	12.08
30	8.12	9.56	10.81	11.88	12.79	13.55	**30**	7.22	8.51	9.64	10.62	11.47	12.19
31	7.80	9.27	10.55	11.65	12.58	13.36	**31**	6.94	8.26	9.42	10.42	11.29	12.03
32	7.47	8.99	10.30	11.42	12.38	13.18	**32**	6.65	8.00	9.19	10.22	11.11	11.86
33	7.14	8.69	10.04	11.20	12.17	12.99	**33**	6.35	7.74	8.96	10.01	10.93	11.70
34	6.80	8.39	9.77	10.96	11.96	12.80	**34**	6.04	7.48	8.72	9.80	10.74	11.53
35	5.96	7.46	8.77	9.89	10.84	11.63	**35**	5.98	7.51	8.85	10.00	11.00	11.85
36	5.63	7.17	8.51	9.66	10.63	11.44	**36**	5.65	7.21	8.58	9.77	10.79	11.66
37	5.28	6.87	8.25	9.43	10.43	11.26	**37**	5.31	6.91	8.31	9.53	10.58	11.47
38	4.94	6.57	7.97	9.18	10.21	11.06	**38**	4.96	6.60	8.04	9.29	10.36	11.27
39	4.58	6.25	7.70	8.94	9.98	10.86	**39**	4.60	6.29	7.76	9.04	10.14	11.07
40	4.21	5.93	7.41	8.68	9.76	10.65	**40**	4.50	6.33	7.94	9.33	10.53	11.54
41	3.84	5.60	7.12	8.42	9.53	10.44	**41**	4.10	5.98	7.63	9.06	10.28	11.32
42	3.46	5.26	6.82	8.16	9.29	10.23	**42**	3.68	5.62	7.31	8.77	10.03	11.09
43	3.06	4.92	6.52	7.89	9.05	10.01	**43**	3.26	5.25	6.98	8.48	9.77	10.86
44	2.66	4.56	6.21	7.61	8.80	9.79	**44**	2.83	4.87	6.65	8.19	9.50	10.62
45	2.25	4.20	5.88	7.33	8.55	9.56	**45**	2.53	4.75	6.67	8.34	9.77	10.99
46	1.82	3.83	5.56	7.04	8.29	9.32	**46**	2.05	4.32	6.30	8.01	9.48	10.72
47	1.38	3.44	5.22	6.74	8.03	9.09	**47**	1.56	3.89	5.92	7.68	9.19	10.45
48	0.94	3.05	4.88	6.44	7.76	8.84	**48**	1.05	3.45	5.53	7.33	8.88	10.18
49	0.48	2.65	4.53	6.13	7.48	8.59	**49**	0.53	2.99	5.13	6.98	8.56	9.90
50		2.28	4.25	5.93	7.35	8.52	**50**		2.62	4.89	6.87	8.55	9.98
51		1.85	3.88	5.61	7.06	8.26	**51**		2.20	4.62	6.72	8.51	10.02
52		1.41	3.49	5.27	6.76	7.99	**52**		1.73	4.30	6.53	8.43	10.04
53		0.95	3.10	4.92	6.46	7.72	**53**		1.21	3.94	6.31	8.32	10.03
54		0.50	2.75	4.67	6.28	7.60	**54**		0.65	3.64	6.22	8.43	10.30

See introductory notes as regards claimants over 54 at date of trial (male)

See introductory notes as regards claimants over 54 at date of trial (female)

D E <GCSE

Loss of earnings: disabled; employed; education below good GCSE level

Age	Male to retiring age 50	55	60	65	70	75
16	7.30	7.92	8.47	8.93	9.34	9.67
17	7.16	7.80	8.36	8.84	9.24	9.59
18	7.01	7.67	8.24	8.73	9.16	9.51
19	6.86	7.54	8.12	8.63	9.06	9.42
20	7.98	8.79	9.51	10.12	10.64	11.08
21	7.79	8.63	9.36	9.99	10.53	10.98
22	7.60	8.47	9.21	9.86	10.41	10.87
23	7.41	8.30	9.06	9.72	10.29	10.76
24	7.22	8.12	8.91	9.58	10.16	10.64
25	7.75	8.78	9.67	10.44	11.09	11.63
26	7.53	8.58	9.49	10.28	10.95	11.50
27	7.29	8.37	9.31	10.11	10.79	11.37
28	7.05	8.16	9.12	9.94	10.64	11.23
29	6.81	7.94	8.92	9.77	10.49	11.09
30	6.24	7.35	8.31	9.14	9.84	10.42
31	6.00	7.13	8.12	8.96	9.68	10.28
32	5.75	6.91	7.92	8.79	9.52	10.14
33	5.49	6.69	7.72	8.61	9.36	9.99
34	5.23	6.46	7.52	8.43	9.20	9.84
35	4.84	6.06	7.13	8.03	8.81	9.45
36	4.57	5.83	6.91	7.85	8.64	9.30
37	4.29	5.58	6.70	7.66	8.47	9.15
38	4.01	5.34	6.48	7.46	8.30	8.99
39	3.72	5.08	6.26	7.26	8.11	8.82
40	3.42	4.82	6.02	7.06	7.93	8.65
41	3.12	4.55	5.79	6.84	7.74	8.48
42	2.81	4.27	5.54	6.63	7.55	8.31
43	2.49	3.99	5.30	6.41	7.35	8.13
44	2.16	3.71	5.04	6.19	7.15	7.95
45	1.83	3.41	4.78	5.96	6.95	7.76
46	1.48	3.11	4.52	5.72	6.74	7.57
47	1.12	2.80	4.24	5.48	6.52	7.38
48	0.76	2.48	3.96	5.23	6.30	7.18
49	0.39	2.15	3.68	4.98	6.08	6.98
50		1.86	3.47	4.84	6.00	6.95
51		1.55	3.24	4.69	5.90	6.91
52		1.18	2.92	4.41	5.66	6.69
53		0.81	2.65	4.22	5.54	6.62
54		0.43	2.36	4.01	5.40	6.54

See introductory notes as regards claimants over 54 at date of trial

Age	Female to retiring age 50	55	60	65	70	75
16	5.73	6.22	6.66	7.04	7.37	7.65
17	5.62	6.13	6.57	6.96	7.30	7.59
18	5.51	6.03	6.49	6.88	7.23	7.52
19	5.39	5.93	6.39	6.80	7.16	7.46
20	5.27	5.82	6.30	6.72	7.08	7.39
21	5.15	5.72	6.21	6.64	7.01	7.32
22	5.03	5.61	6.11	6.55	6.93	7.25
23	4.90	5.49	6.01	6.46	6.85	7.18
24	4.77	5.38	5.91	6.37	6.77	7.11
25	4.64	5.26	5.80	6.28	6.68	7.03
26	4.50	5.14	5.70	6.18	6.60	6.95
27	4.36	5.02	5.59	6.08	6.51	6.87
28	4.22	4.89	5.47	5.98	6.42	6.79
29	4.08	4.76	5.36	5.88	6.33	6.71
30	4.71	5.55	6.29	6.93	7.48	7.95
31	4.52	5.39	6.14	6.80	7.37	7.84
32	4.34	5.22	5.99	6.67	7.24	7.74
33	4.14	5.05	5.84	6.53	7.13	7.63
34	3.94	4.88	5.69	6.39	7.00	7.52
35	4.24	5.32	6.27	7.09	7.79	8.39
36	4.00	5.11	6.08	6.92	7.64	8.26
37	3.76	4.90	5.89	6.75	7.49	8.12
38	3.51	4.68	5.70	6.58	7.34	7.98
39	3.26	4.45	5.50	6.40	7.18	7.84
40	3.35	4.72	5.92	6.95	7.85	8.60
41	3.05	4.46	5.68	6.75	7.66	8.44
42	2.74	4.19	5.45	6.54	7.47	8.27
43	2.43	3.91	5.20	6.32	7.28	8.09
44	2.11	3.63	4.95	6.10	7.08	7.91
45	1.97	3.69	5.19	6.49	7.60	8.55
46	1.60	3.36	4.90	6.23	7.38	8.34
47	1.21	3.02	4.60	5.97	7.14	8.13
48	0.82	2.68	4.30	5.70	6.90	7.92
49	0.42	2.33	3.99	5.43	6.66	7.70
50		2.20	4.11	5.76	7.18	8.38
51		1.86	3.91	5.67	7.19	8.47
52		1.47	3.66	5.55	7.17	8.53
53		1.05	3.43	5.49	7.25	8.73
54		0.56	3.15	5.38	7.28	8.89

See introductory notes as regards claimants over 54 at date of trial

D NE Deg

Loss of earnings: disabled; not employed; degree level education or equivalent

Age	Male to retiring age 50	55	60	65	70	75
16	See introductory notes					
17						
18						
19						
20	11.12	12.26	13.26	14.12	14.85	15.46
21	10.87	12.04	13.06	13.94	14.69	15.31
22	10.61	11.81	12.85	13.75	14.52	15.16
23	10.34	11.57	12.64	13.56	14.35	15.00
24	10.06	11.33	12.42	13.37	14.17	14.85
25	8.86	10.03	11.05	11.93	12.67	13.30
26	8.60	9.80	10.84	11.75	12.51	13.15
27	8.33	9.57	10.64	11.55	12.34	12.99
28	8.06	9.32	10.42	11.36	12.16	12.84
29	7.78	9.08	10.20	11.16	11.99	12.67
30	6.71	7.90	8.94	9.82	10.57	11.20
31	6.45	7.67	8.72	9.64	10.41	11.05
32	6.18	7.43	8.51	9.45	10.24	10.90
33	5.90	7.19	8.30	9.26	10.07	10.74
34	5.62	6.94	8.08	9.06	9.89	10.58
35	4.72	5.91	6.94	7.83	8.58	9.21
36	4.45	5.68	6.74	7.65	8.42	9.06
37	4.18	5.44	6.53	7.46	8.25	8.91
38	3.91	5.20	6.31	7.27	8.08	8.76
39	3.63	4.95	6.10	7.08	7.90	8.60
40	2.90	4.08	5.10	5.97	6.71	7.32
41	2.64	3.85	4.90	5.79	6.55	7.18
42	2.38	3.62	4.69	5.61	6.39	7.03
43	2.11	3.38	4.48	5.43	6.22	6.88
44	1.83	3.14	4.27	5.23	6.05	6.73
45	1.22	2.27	3.19	3.97	4.63	5.18
46	0.99	2.07	3.01	3.81	4.49	5.05
47	0.75	1.86	2.83	3.65	4.35	4.92
48	0.51	1.65	2.64	3.49	4.20	4.79
49	0.26	1.44	2.45	3.32	4.05	4.65
50		1.12	2.08	2.91	3.60	4.17
51		0.87	1.82	2.63	3.31	3.88
52		0.63	1.57	2.37	3.04	3.59
53		0.41	1.33	2.11	2.77	3.31
54		0.20	1.10	1.87	2.51	3.04

See introductory notes as regards claimants over 54 at date of trial

Age	Female to retiring age 50	55	60	65	70	75
16	See introductory notes					
17						
18						
19						
20	12.23	13.51	14.62	15.59	16.43	17.14
21	11.95	13.26	14.40	15.39	16.25	16.98
22	11.67	13.00	14.18	15.20	16.07	16.82
23	11.37	12.74	13.94	14.99	15.89	16.65
24	11.07	12.48	13.71	14.77	15.69	16.48
25	9.28	10.52	11.61	12.55	13.37	14.06
26	9.01	10.28	11.39	12.36	13.20	13.90
27	8.72	10.03	11.17	12.16	13.02	13.74
28	8.44	9.78	10.95	11.96	12.84	13.59
29	8.15	9.52	10.71	11.76	12.65	13.42
30	6.91	8.14	9.22	10.16	10.97	11.66
31	6.64	7.90	9.01	9.97	10.80	11.51
32	6.36	7.66	8.79	9.78	10.63	11.35
33	6.07	7.41	8.57	9.58	10.45	11.19
34	5.78	7.15	8.34	9.38	10.27	11.03
35	5.23	6.57	7.74	8.75	9.62	10.37
36	4.94	6.31	7.51	8.55	9.44	10.20
37	4.65	6.05	7.27	8.34	9.26	10.03
38	4.34	5.78	7.04	8.13	9.06	9.86
39	4.02	5.50	6.79	7.91	8.87	9.69
40	3.35	4.72	5.92	6.95	7.85	8.60
41	3.05	4.46	5.68	6.75	7.66	8.44
42	2.74	4.19	5.45	6.54	7.47	8.27
43	2.43	3.91	5.20	6.32	7.28	8.09
44	2.11	3.63	4.95	6.10	7.08	7.91
45	1.31	2.46	3.46	4.33	5.07	5.70
46	1.06	2.24	3.27	4.16	4.92	5.56
47	0.81	2.02	3.07	3.98	4.76	5.42
48	0.55	1.79	2.87	3.80	4.60	5.28
49	0.28	1.55	2.66	3.62	4.44	5.14
50		1.08	2.01	2.82	3.51	4.10
51		0.80	1.67	2.43	3.08	3.63
52		0.58	1.43	2.18	2.81	3.35
53		0.35	1.14	1.83	2.42	2.91
54		0.16	0.88	1.51	2.04	2.50

See introductory notes as regards claimants over 54 at date of trial

D NE GCSE

Loss of earnings: disabled; not employed; good GCSE level education or equivalent

Age	Male to retiring age 50	55	60	65	70	75
16	11.17	12.13	12.97	13.68	14.30	14.81
17	10.96	11.94	12.79	13.53	14.16	14.69
18	10.74	11.75	12.62	13.37	14.02	14.56
19	10.51	11.54	12.44	13.22	13.87	14.43
20	9.66	10.64	11.51	12.25	12.88	13.42
21	9.43	10.45	11.33	12.10	12.75	13.29
22	9.20	10.25	11.16	11.94	12.60	13.16
23	8.97	10.04	10.97	11.77	12.45	13.02
24	8.74	9.83	10.78	11.60	12.30	12.88
25	7.57	8.57	9.44	10.19	10.82	11.36
26	7.35	8.37	9.26	10.03	10.68	11.23
27	7.12	8.17	9.09	9.87	10.54	11.10
28	6.88	7.96	8.90	9.70	10.39	10.96
29	6.65	7.75	8.71	9.54	10.24	10.82
30	5.31	6.25	7.07	7.77	8.36	8.86
31	5.10	6.06	6.90	7.62	8.23	8.74
32	4.89	5.88	6.73	7.47	8.10	8.62
33	4.67	5.68	6.56	7.32	7.96	8.49
34	4.45	5.49	6.39	7.16	7.82	8.37
35	3.47	4.35	5.12	5.77	6.32	6.78
36	3.28	4.18	4.96	5.64	6.20	6.68
37	3.08	4.01	4.81	5.50	6.08	6.57
38	2.88	3.83	4.65	5.36	5.96	6.45
39	2.67	3.65	4.49	5.21	5.82	6.33
40	2.02	2.84	3.55	4.16	4.68	5.10
41	1.84	2.68	3.41	4.04	4.57	5.00
42	1.66	2.52	3.27	3.91	4.45	4.90
43	1.47	2.36	3.12	3.78	4.34	4.80
44	1.27	2.19	2.97	3.65	4.22	4.69
45	0.94	1.75	2.45	3.05	3.56	3.98
46	0.76	1.59	2.32	2.93	3.45	3.88
47	0.58	1.43	2.18	2.81	3.34	3.79
48	0.39	1.27	2.03	2.68	3.23	3.68
49	0.20	1.10	1.89	2.55	3.12	3.58
50		0.84	1.56	2.18	2.70	3.13
51		0.64	1.34	1.94	2.45	2.86
52		0.46	1.14	1.72	2.21	2.61
53		0.29	0.95	1.51	1.98	2.36
54		0.14	0.77	1.31	1.76	2.13

See introductory notes as regards claimants over 54 at date of trial

Age	Female to retiring age 50	55	60	65	70	75
16	8.02	8.71	9.32	9.86	10.31	10.71
17	7.86	8.58	9.20	9.75	10.22	10.62
18	7.71	8.44	9.08	9.64	10.12	10.53
19	7.55	8.30	8.95	9.52	10.02	10.44
20	6.96	7.69	8.32	8.87	9.35	9.75
21	6.80	7.54	8.19	8.76	9.25	9.66
22	6.64	7.40	8.07	8.65	9.14	9.57
23	6.47	7.25	7.93	8.53	9.04	9.47
24	6.30	7.10	7.80	8.41	8.93	9.38
25	5.94	6.73	7.43	8.03	8.55	9.00
26	5.76	6.58	7.29	7.91	8.44	8.90
27	5.58	6.42	7.15	7.79	8.33	8.80
28	5.40	6.26	7.00	7.66	8.22	8.69
29	5.22	6.09	6.86	7.52	8.10	8.59
30	4.87	5.74	6.50	7.16	7.73	8.21
31	4.67	5.57	6.35	7.02	7.61	8.11
32	4.48	5.39	6.19	6.89	7.49	7.99
33	4.28	5.22	6.04	6.75	7.36	7.88
34	4.07	5.04	5.88	6.61	7.24	7.77
35	3.49	4.38	5.16	5.84	6.41	6.91
36	3.30	4.21	5.01	5.70	6.29	6.80
37	3.10	4.03	4.85	5.56	6.17	6.69
38	2.89	3.85	4.69	5.42	6.04	6.57
39	2.68	3.67	4.53	5.27	5.91	6.46
40	2.03	2.86	3.58	4.21	4.75	5.20
41	1.85	2.70	3.44	4.08	4.64	5.11
42	1.66	2.53	3.30	3.96	4.52	5.00
43	1.47	2.37	3.15	3.82	4.40	4.90
44	1.28	2.20	3.00	3.69	4.28	4.79
45	0.84	1.58	2.22	2.78	3.26	3.66
46	0.68	1.44	2.10	2.67	3.16	3.57
47	0.52	1.30	1.97	2.56	3.06	3.48
48	0.35	1.15	1.84	2.44	2.96	3.39
49	0.18	1.00	1.71	2.33	2.85	3.30
50		0.70	1.31	1.84	2.29	2.67
51		0.53	1.12	1.62	2.05	2.42
52		0.37	0.93	1.41	1.83	2.17
53		0.21	0.70	1.12	1.48	1.78
54		0.09	0.50	0.85	1.15	1.40

See introductory notes as regards claimants over 54 at date of trial

D NE <GCSE

Loss of earnings: disabled; not employed; education below good GCSE level

Age	Male to retiring age						Age	Female to retiring age					
	50	55	60	65	70	75		50	55	60	65	70	75
16	5.70	6.19	6.62	6.98	7.30	7.56	**16**	4.35	4.73	5.06	5.35	5.60	5.81
17	5.59	6.09	6.53	6.90	7.22	7.49	**17**	4.27	4.66	5.00	5.29	5.55	5.76
18	5.48	5.99	6.44	6.82	7.15	7.43	**18**	4.18	4.58	4.93	5.23	5.49	5.72
19	5.36	5.89	6.35	6.74	7.08	7.36	**19**	4.10	4.50	4.86	5.17	5.44	5.67
20	5.04	5.55	6.00	6.39	6.72	7.00	**20**	3.59	3.96	4.29	4.57	4.81	5.03
21	4.92	5.45	5.91	6.31	6.65	6.93	**21**	3.50	3.89	4.22	4.51	4.76	4.98
22	4.80	5.35	5.82	6.23	6.57	6.87	**22**	3.42	3.81	4.15	4.45	4.71	4.93
23	4.68	5.24	5.72	6.14	6.50	6.79	**23**	3.33	3.73	4.09	4.39	4.66	4.88
24	4.56	5.13	5.63	6.05	6.42	6.72	**24**	3.25	3.66	4.02	4.33	4.60	4.83
25	4.43	5.02	5.52	5.96	6.34	6.65	**25**	2.97	3.37	3.71	4.02	4.28	4.50
26	4.30	4.90	5.42	5.87	6.25	6.57	**26**	2.88	3.29	3.64	3.96	4.22	4.45
27	4.17	4.78	5.32	5.78	6.17	6.50	**27**	2.79	3.21	3.57	3.89	4.16	4.40
28	4.03	4.66	5.21	5.68	6.08	6.42	**28**	2.70	3.13	3.50	3.83	4.11	4.35
29	3.89	4.54	5.10	5.58	5.99	6.34	**29**	2.61	3.05	3.43	3.76	4.05	4.29
30	3.59	4.23	4.78	5.25	5.66	5.99	**30**	2.36	2.78	3.14	3.46	3.74	3.97
31	3.45	4.10	4.67	5.15	5.57	5.91	**31**	2.26	2.69	3.07	3.40	3.68	3.92
32	3.31	3.97	4.55	5.05	5.48	5.83	**32**	2.17	2.61	3.00	3.33	3.62	3.87
33	3.16	3.85	4.44	4.95	5.38	5.75	**33**	2.07	2.52	2.92	3.27	3.56	3.81
34	3.01	3.71	4.32	4.85	5.29	5.66	**34**	1.97	2.44	2.84	3.20	3.50	3.76
35	2.48	3.11	3.65	4.12	4.52	4.85	**35**	1.74	2.19	2.58	2.92	3.21	3.46
36	2.34	2.99	3.55	4.03	4.43	4.77	**36**	1.65	2.10	2.50	2.85	3.15	3.40
37	2.20	2.86	3.44	3.93	4.34	4.69	**37**	1.55	2.02	2.42	2.78	3.09	3.34
38	2.06	2.74	3.32	3.83	4.25	4.61	**38**	1.45	1.93	2.35	2.71	3.02	3.29
39	1.91	2.60	3.21	3.72	4.16	4.52	**39**	1.34	1.83	2.26	2.64	2.96	3.23
40	1.32	1.85	2.32	2.71	3.05	3.33	**40**	1.15	1.61	2.02	2.38	2.68	2.94
41	1.20	1.75	2.23	2.63	2.98	3.26	**41**	1.04	1.52	1.94	2.31	2.62	2.89
42	1.08	1.64	2.13	2.55	2.90	3.20	**42**	0.94	1.43	1.86	2.24	2.56	2.83
43	0.96	1.54	2.04	2.47	2.83	3.13	**43**	0.83	1.34	1.78	2.16	2.49	2.77
44	0.83	1.43	1.94	2.38	2.75	3.06	**44**	0.72	1.24	1.69	2.09	2.42	2.71
45	0.51	0.96	1.35	1.68	1.96	2.19	**45**	0.52	0.97	1.36	1.70	1.99	2.24
46	0.42	0.88	1.27	1.61	1.90	2.14	**46**	0.42	0.88	1.28	1.63	1.93	2.18
47	0.32	0.79	1.20	1.55	1.84	2.08	**47**	0.32	0.79	1.21	1.56	1.87	2.13
48	0.21	0.70	1.12	1.48	1.78	2.03	**48**	0.21	0.70	1.13	1.49	1.81	2.07
49	0.11	0.61	1.04	1.40	1.71	1.97	**49**	0.11	0.61	1.04	1.42	1.74	2.02
50		0.47	0.87	1.21	1.50	1.74	**50**		0.47	0.87	1.23	1.53	1.78
51		0.34	0.71	1.03	1.30	1.52	**51**		0.34	0.72	1.04	1.32	1.56
52		0.23	0.57	0.86	1.10	1.30	**52**		0.23	0.57	0.87	1.12	1.34
53		0.14	0.44	0.70	0.92	1.10	**53**		0.14	0.45	0.71	0.94	1.13
54		0.06	0.33	0.56	0.75	0.91	**54**		0.06	0.33	0.57	0.77	0.94

See introductory notes as regards claimants over 54 at date of trial

See introductory notes as regards claimants over 54 at date of trial

A5: Multipliers for fixed periods and at intervals

Introductory notes

1. The purpose of the table is to provide a means of calculating an appropriate multiplier which will produce the present day equivalent of a cost recurring, either continuously or at fixed intervals, over a given number of years. It does not allow for mortality or contingencies.

2. The table is based on a discount rate of 2.5% per annum. The Lord Chancellor fixed the discount rate under the Damages Act 1996 (June 25, 2001) at 2.5%, leaving open the possibility of a different rate in exceptional cases such as the effect of tax on large sums. In recent editions of this book, the range of discount rates was extended as a result of the decision in Helmot v Simon.[1] Readers requiring tables at -1.5% or 1% per annum should refer to the 2013/14 edition.

3. It is assumed that yearly loss is incurred at the *end* of each year in which the loss arises. (Continuous loss obviously accrues from day to day throughout the period. Weekly and monthly losses can in practice be treated as continuous.) For example:

   For expenditure assumed to recur every seven years the expenditure is shown as arising at the end of years seven, 14, and so on.

4. The table contains a number of columns: the number of years; the multiplier for a single payment in *n* years' time; that for a continuous loss over that period of *n* years; that for annual payments in the sense of a series of payments at intervals of one year; and those for payments at intervals of two, three, four and so on years.

5. The multiplier for a single payment in *n* years' time (second column) is the same as the discount factor for deferment for the next *n* years.

6. The table shows a multiplier appropriate to each year in which expenditure is to be incurred, and also cumulative multipliers for expenditure up to the end of that year. For example, at 2.5% discount:

   The multiplier for expenditure at the end of year 10 is 0.781. Thus the current lump sum required to provide £100 in 10 years' time is £78.10.

   And similarly:

   - £100 a year continuously over the next 10 years has a present value of £886;
   - £100 at the end of each of the next 10 years a present value of £875;
   - £100 at the end of two, four, six, eight and 10 years a present value of £432 (row 10, two-yearly column); and
   - £100 at the end of three, six and nine years a present value of £259 (row 9, three-yearly column).

   The cumulative multipliers do not include an immediate payment: where one is needed in addition to the recurring payments add 1.00 to the multiplier.

7. The calculations have been rounded to two places of decimals.

[1] [2010] GCA 31.

Multipliers where there is evidence of life expectancy

8. In some cases there is medical evidence of the particular claimant's life expectancy. As more distant losses have lower present value, the possibility of dying earlier than expected has more effect on the multiplier than that of dying later than expected. The multiplier for life of someone whose life expectancy is *n* years will therefore be lower than the multiplier for a fixed period of *n* years. The difference varies with sex and age. It is not large but at a discount rate of 2.5% it is not negligible.

9. If the conditions set out in the cases of *Sarwar v Ali*[2] and *Burton v Kingsbury*[3] for the estimation of life expectancy are met, then it is appropriate to adopt term certain tables with no further reduction for mortality. In all other cases a reduction to the fixed term multipliers should be adopted for mortality.

Reduction of fixed term multipliers for mortality

10. For the reasons discussed above in relation to cases where there is evidence of life expectancy, in all cases where the period of loss is dependent on someone's life the multiplier for a fixed period will be slightly higher than the true multiplier. In appropriate cases the fixed term multipliers can be reduced by the method discussed in paras 20–23 of the Ogden notes (Table A8 of this book), which calculates an equivalent age based on reduced life expectation.

11. For example:

    The claimant is aged 53 and seven months. His life expectancy is 30 years. For the first 12 years he will need care at £10,000 a year and incur expenditure on equipment of £5,000 at the end of every four years (i.e. after four, eight and 12 years). For the remaining 18 years he will need care at £20,000 a year and expenditure on equipment of £6,000 at the end of every three years (i.e. after 15, 18, 21, 24, 27 and 30 years).

    For a continuous loss of 30 years (eg required to value the future care expenditure) the multipliers—from Table A5 at 2.5%—are:

	First 12 years:	Remaining 18 years[4]	30 years
Care:	10.39	10.80	21.19

The equivalent age to be adopted is calculated from interpolation of the 0% column in the life multipliers shown at Table 1 of the Ogden Tables, as follows:

55 year old multiplier for life at 0%	30.58
56 year old multiplier for life at 0%	29.64

$$\left(\frac{30.58 - 30.00}{30.58 - 29.64}\right) \times 56 + \left(\frac{30.00 - 29.64}{30.58 - 29.64}\right) \times 55 = 55.62$$

The life multiplier at a discount rate of 2.5% for a male aged 55.62 is shown at Table 1 of the Ogden Tables to be 20.29. It is not 21.19 (the multiplier for a continuous loss), because the possibility of dying earlier than expected affects the multiplier more than the possibility of dying

[2] [2007] EWHC 2091 (QB).
[3] [2007] EWHC 2091 (QB).
[4] Calculated by subtraction—see point 13 below.

later. The fixed term multipliers for care are therefore too high and need to be reduced by a factor of 20.29/21.19 = 95.75%.

Multipliers for care adjusted for mortality (that is multiplied by 95.75%):

	First 12 years:	Remaining 18 years	30 years
Care:	9.95	10.34	20.29

For expenditure at fixed intervals (i.e. non-continuous) over a period of 30 years (i.e. required to value the future equipment expenditure) the multipliers—from Table A5 at 2.5%—are:

	First 12 years:	Remaining 18 years[5]	30 years
Equipment:	2.47	3.47	20.93

It was shown above that the equivalent age multiplier is 20.29. Any future multiplier based on fixed interval tables must be reduced by 96.94% (i.e. 20.29/20.93).

Multipliers for equipment adjusted for mortality (that is multiplied by 96.94%):

	First 12 years:	Remaining 18 years	30 years
Equipment:	2.39	3.36	20.29

Modifications

12. Multipliers for continuous loss for periods other than entire years can be obtained by interpolation:

For continuous payments for 10 and 11 years the multipliers are 8.86 and 9.63. So, for weekly or monthly payments for 10 years 3 months (i.e. 10.25 years) the multiplier is:

$$8.86 + \frac{9.63 - 8.86}{10 + \left(\frac{3}{12}\right) - 10} = 9.05$$

Or

$$8.86 + \frac{9.63 - 8.86}{10.25 - 10} = 9.05$$

13. Multipliers for payments beginning after a deferred period can be derived by subtraction or by multiplying by a factor from the single payment column:

Multipliers for five-yearly payments for 15 and for 50 years are 2.36 and 5.40;

So the multiplier for five-yearly payments from years 20 to 50 inclusive is 5.40 – 2.36 = 3.14;

Multiplier for one payment after 18 years is 0.641;

So that for five-yearly payments from years 23–68 inclusive is 5.40 × 0.641 = 3.46.

14. Multipliers for irregular payments can be found by adding individual figures from the single payment column.

[5] Calculated by subtraction: 30 year multiplier for 3-yearly replacements 6.81 (Table A5) less 12 year multiplier for 3-yearly replacements 3.34 (Table A5)—see point 13 below.

Multipliers at 2.5% discount

	Single payment	Continuous loss	Frequency of payments in years											
n			**1**	**2**	**3**	**4**	**5**	**6**	**7**	**8**	**10**	**12**	**15**	**20**
1	0.976	0.99	0.98											
2	0.952	1.95	1.93	0.95										
3	0.929	2.89	2.86		0.93									
4	0.906	3.81	3.76	1.86		0.91								
5	0.884	4.70	4.65				0.88							
6	0.862	5.58	5.51	2.72	1.79			0.86						
7	0.841	6.43	6.35						0.84					
8	0.821	7.26	7.17	3.54		1.73				0.82				
9	0.801	8.07	7.97		2.59									
10	0.781	8.86	8.75	4.32			1.67				0.78			
11	0.762	9.63	9.51											
12	0.744	10.39	10.26	5.07	3.34	2.47		1.61				0.74		
13	0.725	11.12	10.98											
14	0.708	11.84	11.69	5.77					1.55					
15	0.690	12.54	12.38		4.03		2.36						0.69	
16	0.674	13.22	13.06	6.45		3.14				1.49				
17	0.657	13.88	13.71											
18	0.641	14.53	14.35	7.09	4.67			2.25						
19	0.626	15.17	14.98											
20	0.610	15.78	15.59	7.70		3.75	2.97				1.39			0.61
21	0.595	16.39	16.18		5.26				2.14					
22	0.581	16.97	16.77	8.28										
23	0.567	17.55	17.33											
24	0.553	18.11	17.88	8.83	5.82	4.31		2.80		2.05		1.30		
25	0.539	18.65	18.42				3.51							
26	0.526	19.19	18.95	9.36										
27	0.513	19.71	19.46		6.33									
28	0.501	20.21	19.96	9.86		4.81			2.65					
29	0.489	20.71	20.45											
30	0.477	21.19	20.93	10.34	6.81		3.98	3.28			1.87		1.17	
31	0.465	21.66	21.40											
32	0.454	22.12	21.85	10.79		5.26				2.50				
33	0.443	22.57	22.29		7.25									
34	0.432	23.01	22.72	11.22										
35	0.421	23.43	23.15				4.40		3.07					
36	0.411	23.85	23.56	11.63	7.66	5.67		3.69				1.71		
37	0.401	24.26	23.96											
38	0.391	24.65	24.35	12.02										
39	0.382	25.04	24.73		8.04									
40	0.372	25.42	25.10	12.40		6.05	4.78			2.87	2.24			0.98
41	0.363	25.78	25.47											
42	0.354	26.14	25.82	12.75	8.40			4.04	3.42					
43	0.346	26.49	26.17											
44	0.337	26.84	26.50	13.09		6.38								
45	0.329	27.17	26.83		8.72		5.10						1.50	
46	0.321	27.49	27.15	13.41										
47	0.313	27.81	27.47											
48	0.306	28.12	27.77	13.72	9.03	6.69		4.35		3.18		2.01		
49	0.298	28.42	28.07						3.72					
50	0.291	28.72	28.36	14.01			5.40				2.53			
51	0.284	29.00	28.65		9.31									
52	0.277	29.28	28.92	14.28		6.97								
53	0.270	29.56	29.19											
54	0.264	29.83	29.46	14.55	9.58			4.61						
55	0.257	30.09	29.71				5.65							
56	0.251	30.34	29.96	14.80		7.22			3.97	3.43				
57	0.245	30.59	30.21		9.82									
58	0.239	30.83	30.45	15.04										
59	0.233	31.06	30.68											
60	0.227	31.30	30.91	15.26	10.05	7.44	5.88	4.84			2.76	2.24	1.72	1.21

Multipliers at 2.5% discount

n	Single payment	Continuous loss	Frequency of payments in years: 1	2	3	4	5	6	7	8	10	12	15	20
61	0.222	31.52	31.13											
62	0.216	31.74	31.35	15.48										
63	0.211	31.95	31.56		10.26				4.18					
64	0.206	32.16	31.76	15.69		7.65				3.64				
65	0.201	32.36	31.96				6.08							
66	0.196	32.56	32.16	15.88	10.46			5.04						
67	0.191	32.76	32.35											
68	0.187	32.95	32.54	16.07		7.84								
69	0.182	33.13	32.72		10.64									
70	0.178	33.31	32.90	16.25			6.26		4.36		2.94			
71	0.173	33.48	33.07											
72	0.169	33.66	33.24	16.41	10.81	8.00		5.20		3.80		2.41		
73	0.165	33.82	33.40											
74	0.161	33.99	33.57	16.58										
75	0.157	34.14	33.72		10.96		6.42						1.88	
76	0.153	34.30	33.88	16.73		8.16								
77	0.149	34.45	34.03						4.51					
78	0.146	34.60	34.17	16.87	11.11			5.35						
79	0.142	34.74	34.31											
80	0.139	34.88	34.45	17.01		8.30	6.55			3.94	3.08			1.35
81	0.135	35.02	34.59		11.25									
82	0.132	35.15	34.72	17.15										
83	0.129	35.28	34.85											
84	0.126	35.41	34.97	17.27	11.37	8.42		5.48	4.63			2.54		
85	0.123	35.53	35.10				6.68							
86	0.120	35.66	35.22	17.39										
87	0.117	35.77	35.33		11.49									
88	0.114	35.89	35.45	17.50		8.54				4.06				
89	0.111	36.00	35.56											
90	0.108	36.11	35.67	17.61	11.60		6.79	5.58			3.18		1.99	
91	0.106	36.22	35.77						4.74					
92	0.103	36.32	35.87	17.72		8.64								
93	0.101	36.42	35.98		11.70									
94	0.098	36.52	36.07	17.81										
95	0.096	36.62	36.17				6.88							
96	0.093	36.72	36.26	17.91	11.79	8.73		5.68		4.15		2.63		
97	0.091	36.81	36.35											
98	0.089	36.90	36.44	18.00					4.83					
99	0.087	36.99	36.53		11.88									
100	0.085	37.07	36.61	18.08		8.82	6.97				3.27			1.43

1. The single payment column is the appropriate multiplier for one payment in *n* years' time.
2. The continuous loss column is for loss accruing from day to day: in practice it is appropriate for weekly and monthly losses as well.
3. The column headed "1" is for a series of payments at yearly intervals *at the end of each year* for *n* years. If you want an immediate payment as well, add 1.
4. The remaining columns similarly show the multiplier for a series of payments at intervals of two, three, four and so on years.
5. Thus at 2.5% discount £100 paid after 10 years has a present value of £78.10;
   - £100 a year continuously over the next 10 years has a present value of £886;
   - £100 at the end of each of the next 10 years has a present value of £875;
   - £100 at the end of two, four, six, eight and 10 years has a present value of £432 (row 10, two-yearly column);
   - £100 at the end of three, six and nine years has a present value of £259 (row 9, three-yearly column); and
   - £100 now and after two, four, six and eight years (but not the 10th year) has a present value of £454 (row 8, two-yearly column, plus one).

A6: Combination tables

Introductory notes

1. The following table is intended for use when a claimant will suffer a loss over a known number of years, but that loss will not start to run immediately. It has been derived from first principles, but tables at discount rates between 0% and 5% could be obtained by combining Ogden Tables 27 and 28.

2. For example:

   a. The claimant is now 30 years old. He has a reduced life expectation, to the age of 60. For the last 10 years of his life, he will need nursing care at a cost of £7,500 a year. His nursing needs will therefore start in 20 years.

   b. At 2.5% discount, the multiplier for a period of 10 years is 8.86 [Ogden Table 28].

   c. At 2.5% discount, a loss that will not occur for a further 20 years must be discounted by multiplying it by 0.6103 [Ogden Table 27].

   d. The appropriate multiplier is therefore [8.86 × 0.6103] = 5.41 (to two decimal places).

   But see paras 20–33 of the Ogden notes.

3. The following points should also be remembered:

   a. When applying the multipliers to claims for loss of earnings, Ogden Tables 3–14 only take the ordinary risks of mortality into account. They do *not* take into account any other factors such as educational attainment or disability. A further discount must be made for these risks: see Section B of the Introduction to the Ogden Tables (Contingencies other than Mortality).

   b. Ogden Table 27 (Discounting Factors for Term Certain) gives the discount factor for a period of *complete* years. So in the example above, where the date of trial is August 23, 2012, the need for nursing care will start on August 23, 2032.

   c. Ogden Table 28 (Multipliers for Pecuniary Loss for Term Certain) assumes that the loss will occur regularly throughout the year, e.g. a monthly nursing bill.

Combination grid (Discount rate 2.5%)

Years of loss	Years before loss starts to run 1	2	3	4	5	6	7	8	9	10	12.5	15	20	25	30	35	40	Years of loss
1	0.96	0.94	0.92	0.89	0.87	0.85	0.83	0.81	0.79	0.77	0.73	0.68	0.60	0.53	0.47	0.42	0.37	**1**
2	1.90	1.86	1.81	1.77	1.72	1.68	1.64	1.60	1.56	1.52	1.43	1.35	1.19	1.05	0.93	0.82	0.73	**2**
3	2.82	2.75	2.69	2.62	2.56	2.49	2.43	2.37	2.32	2.26	2.12	2.00	1.76	1.56	1.38	1.22	1.08	**3**
4	3.72	3.63	3.54	3.45	3.37	3.28	3.20	3.13	3.05	2.98	2.80	2.63	2.32	2.05	1.82	1.61	1.42	**4**
5	4.59	4.48	4.37	4.26	4.16	4.06	3.96	3.86	3.77	3.67	3.45	3.25	2.87	2.54	2.24	1.98	1.75	**5**
6	5.44	5.31	5.18	5.05	4.93	4.81	4.69	4.58	4.47	4.36	4.10	3.85	3.40	3.01	2.66	2.35	2.08	**6**
7	6.27	6.12	5.97	5.82	5.68	5.54	5.41	5.28	5.15	5.02	4.72	4.44	3.92	3.47	3.06	2.71	2.39	**7**
8	7.08	6.91	6.74	6.58	6.42	6.26	6.11	5.96	5.81	5.67	5.33	5.01	4.43	3.92	3.46	3.06	2.70	**8**
9	7.87	7.68	7.49	7.31	7.13	6.96	6.79	6.62	6.46	6.30	5.93	5.57	4.93	4.35	3.85	3.40	3.01	**9**
10	8.65	8.43	8.23	8.03	7.83	7.64	7.45	7.27	7.10	6.92	6.51	6.12	5.41	4.78	4.22	3.73	3.30	**10**
11	9.40	9.17	8.95	8.73	8.51	8.31	8.10	7.91	7.71	7.53	7.07	6.65	5.88	5.20	4.59	4.06	3.59	**11**
12	10.13	9.89	9.64	9.41	9.18	8.96	8.74	8.52	8.32	8.11	7.63	7.17	6.34	5.60	4.95	4.38	3.87	**12**
13	10.85	10.58	10.33	10.07	9.83	9.59	9.36	9.13	8.90	8.69	8.17	7.68	6.79	6.00	5.30	4.69	4.14	**13**
14	11.55	11.27	10.99	10.72	10.46	10.21	9.96	9.72	9.48	9.25	8.69	8.17	7.22	6.38	5.64	4.99	4.41	**14**
15	12.23	11.93	11.64	11.36	11.08	10.81	10.55	10.29	10.04	9.79	9.21	8.66	7.65	6.76	5.98	5.28	4.67	**15**
16	12.90	12.58	12.27	11.98	11.68	11.40	11.12	10.85	10.58	10.33	9.71	9.13	8.07	7.13	6.30	5.57	4.92	**16**
17	13.54	13.21	12.89	12.58	12.27	11.97	11.68	11.39	11.12	10.85	10.20	9.59	8.47	7.49	6.62	5.85	5.17	**17**
18	14.18	13.83	13.50	13.17	12.84	12.53	12.23	11.93	11.64	11.35	10.67	10.03	8.87	7.84	6.93	6.12	5.41	**18**
19	14.80	14.44	14.08	13.74	13.40	13.08	12.76	12.45	12.14	11.85	11.14	10.47	9.26	8.18	7.23	6.39	5.65	**19**
20	15.40	15.02	14.66	14.30	13.95	13.61	13.28	12.95	12.64	12.33	11.59	10.90	9.63	8.51	7.52	6.65	5.88	**20**
21	15.99	15.60	15.22	14.85	14.48	14.13	13.79	13.45	13.12	12.80	12.04	11.31	10.00	8.84	7.81	6.90	6.10	**21**
22	16.56	16.16	15.76	15.38	15.00	14.64	14.28	13.93	13.59	13.26	12.47	11.72	10.36	9.16	8.09	7.15	6.32	**22**
23	17.12	16.70	16.30	15.90	15.51	15.13	14.76	14.40	14.05	13.71	12.89	12.12	10.71	9.47	8.37	7.39	6.54	**23**
24	17.67	17.24	16.82	16.41	16.01	15.61	15.23	14.86	14.50	14.15	13.30	12.50	11.05	9.77	8.63	7.63	6.74	**24**
25	18.20	17.76	17.32	16.90	16.49	16.09	15.69	15.31	14.94	14.57	13.70	12.88	11.38	10.06	8.89	7.86	6.95	**25**
26	18.72	18.26	17.82	17.38	16.96	16.55	16.14	15.75	15.36	14.99	14.09	13.25	11.71	10.35	9.15	8.09	7.15	**26**
27	19.23	18.76	18.30	17.85	17.42	16.99	16.58	16.17	15.78	15.40	14.47	13.61	12.03	10.63	9.40	8.30	7.34	**27**
28	19.72	19.24	18.77	18.31	17.87	17.43	17.01	16.59	16.19	15.79	14.85	13.96	12.34	10.90	9.64	8.52	7.53	**28**
29	20.20	19.71	19.23	18.76	18.30	17.86	17.42	17.00	16.58	16.18	15.21	14.30	12.64	11.17	9.87	8.73	7.71	**29**
30	20.68	20.17	19.68	19.20	18.73	18.27	17.83	17.39	16.97	16.56	15.56	14.63	12.93	11.43	10.10	8.93	7.89	**30**
31	21.13	20.62	20.12	19.63	19.15	18.68	18.22	17.78	17.35	16.92	15.91	14.96	13.22	11.68	10.33	9.13	8.07	**31**
32	21.58	21.06	20.54	20.04	19.55	19.08	18.61	18.16	17.71	17.28	16.25	15.27	13.50	11.93	10.55	9.32	8.24	**32**
33	22.02	21.48	20.96	20.45	19.95	19.46	18.99	18.52	18.07	17.63	16.58	15.58	13.77	12.17	10.76	9.51	8.41	**33**
34	22.45	21.90	21.37	20.84	20.34	19.84	19.36	18.88	18.42	17.97	16.90	15.89	14.04	12.41	10.97	9.69	8.57	**34**
35	22.86	22.31	21.76	21.23	20.71	20.21	19.71	19.23	18.76	18.31	17.21	16.18	14.30	12.64	11.17	9.87	8.73	**35**
36	23.27	22.70	22.15	21.61	21.08	20.57	20.06	19.58	19.10	18.63	17.52	16.47	14.56	12.86	11.37	10.05	8.88	**36**
37	23.67	23.09	22.52	21.98	21.44	20.92	20.41	19.91	19.42	18.95	17.81	16.75	14.80	13.08	11.56	10.22	9.03	**37**
38	24.05	23.47	22.89	22.33	21.79	21.26	20.74	20.23	19.74	19.26	18.11	17.02	15.04	13.30	11.75	10.39	9.18	**38**
39	24.43	23.83	23.25	22.68	22.13	21.59	21.06	20.55	20.05	19.56	18.39	17.29	15.28	13.51	11.94	10.55	9.33	**39**
40	24.80	24.19	23.60	23.03	22.46	21.92	21.38	20.86	20.35	19.86	18.67	17.55	15.51	13.71	12.12	10.71	9.47	**40**
41	25.16	24.54	23.94	23.36	22.79	22.23	21.69	21.16	20.65	20.14	18.94	17.80	15.74	13.91	12.29	10.86	9.60	**41**
42	25.51	24.88	24.28	23.68	23.11	22.54	21.99	21.46	20.93	20.42	19.20	18.05	15.95	14.10	12.46	11.02	9.74	**42**
43	25.85	25.22	24.60	24.00	23.42	22.85	22.29	21.74	21.21	20.70	19.46	18.29	16.17	14.29	12.63	11.16	9.87	**43**
44	26.18	25.54	24.92	24.31	23.72	23.14	22.58	22.02	21.49	20.96	19.71	18.53	16.38	14.47	12.79	11.31	9.99	**44**
45	26.51	25.86	25.23	24.61	24.01	23.43	22.86	22.30	21.75	21.22	19.95	18.76	16.58	14.65	12.95	11.45	10.12	**45**
Years of loss	**1**	**2**	**3**	**4**	**5**	**6**	**7**	**8**	**9**	**10**	**12.5**	**15**	**20**	**25**	**30**	**35**	**40**	**Years of loss**

A7: Table of adjustments to multiplier for Fatal Accidents Acts dependency

These tables deal with factors to be applied in fatal accident cases to allow for the possibility that the deceased would not have survived until trial. These tables are derived from the Explanatory Notes of the Ogden Tables, para.64 onwards. They are set out here on one page for convenience. (The user will need to consider the current state of authority on the acceptability of this approach.)

PRE-TRIAL damages (factor to be applied to damages from date of accident to trial)

Age of deceased at date of accident	Period from accident to trial (or cessation of dependency if earlier) Male 3	6	9	Female 3	6	9
10	1.00	1.00	1.00	1.00	1.00	1.00
20	1.00	1.00	1.00	1.00	1.00	1.00
30	1.00	1.00	0.99	1.00	1.00	1.00
40	1.00	0.99	0.99	1.00	1.00	0.99
50	0.99	0.99	0.98	1.00	0.99	0.99
60	0.99	0.97	0.94	0.99	0.98	0.97
65	0.98	0.95	0.91	0.99	0.97	0.95
70	0.97	0.92	0.86	0.98	0.95	0.91
75	0.94	0.87	0.78	0.96	0.91	0.84
80	0.90	0.79	0.67	0.93	0.84	0.75

POST-TRIAL damages (factor to be applied to damages from date of trial to retirement age)

Age of deceased at date of accident	Period from accident to trial Male 3	6	9	Female 3	6	9
10	1.00	1.00	1.00	1.00	1.00	1.00
20	1.00	1.00	0.99	1.00	1.00	1.00
30	1.00	0.99	0.99	1.00	1.00	0.99
40	0.99	0.99	0.98	1.00	0.99	0.99
50	0.99	0.97	0.95	0.99	0.98	0.97
60	0.97	0.93	0.88	0.98	0.96	0.92
65	0.96	0.90	0.82	0.97	0.93	0.88
70	0.93	0.84	0.71	0.96	0.89	0.80
75	0.88	0.73	0.55	0.92	0.81	0.66
80	0.83	0.59	0.37	0.86	0.68	0.48

POST-RETIREMENT damages (for the period of dependency after retirement age)

1. First obtain the multiplier for the whole of life dependency by the following steps:
   (a) determine, from 0% tables, the expectation of life which the deceased would have had at the date of trial (or the shorter period for which the deceased would have provided the dependency);
   (b) determine the expected period for which the dependant would have been able to receive the dependency (for a widow, normally her life expectancy from 0% tables; for a child, normally the period until it reaches adulthood);
   (c) take the lesser of the two periods; and
   (d) treat the resulting period as a term certain and look up the multiplier for that period (Table A5, continuous loss column).
2. Obtain the multiplier for dependency from date of trial to retirement age. Do not adjust it for contingencies other than mortality. Do not apply the factors in the Post-Trial table above.
3. Subtract the multiplier for dependency to retirement age (2) from the whole life multiplier (1). Multiply by the factor in the Post-Trial table above.

   Post-retirement multiplier = [Stage 1 figure *minus* Stage 2 figure] × Post-Trial factor.

A8: The Ogden Tables

Actuarial tables with explanatory notes for use in personal injury and fatal accident cases.

Prepared by an Inter-Professional Working Party of Actuaries, Lawyers, Accountants and other interested parties.

7th edition prepared by the Government Actuary's Department.

Table of Contents *Page*

Introduction to the 7th edition

"When it comes to the explanatory notes we must make sure that they are readily comprehensible. We must assume the most stupid circuit judge in the country and before him are the two most stupid advocates. All three of them must be able to understand what we are saying"

Sir Michael Ogden QC, on his explanatory notes to the 1st edition of the Ogden Tables.[1]

1. The Working Party has been eager to see a new set of these tables published, as there have been changes in the official projections of future mortality rates for the UK since the previous, 6th edition was published which produce significant changes in the values of some of the multipliers. The Working Party is grateful that the Ministry of Justice has agreed to fund the production of this edition of the Ogden Tables.

Purpose of the tables

2. These tables are designed to assist those concerned with calculating lump sum damages for future losses in personal injury and fatal accident cases in the UK.

3. The methodology is long-established whereby multipliers are applied to the present day value of a future annual loss (net of tax in the case of a loss of earnings and pension) with the aim of producing a lump sum equivalent to the capitalised value of the future losses. In essence, the multiplier is the figure by which an annual loss is multiplied in order to calculate a capitalised sum, taking into account accelerated receipt, mortality risks and, in relation to claims for loss of earnings and pension, discounts for contingencies other than mortality.

4. This methodology was endorsed by the House of Lords in the famous case of ***Wells v Wells***.[2] In that case the court determined that the discount rate should be based on the yields on Index Linked Government Stock. The discount rate is now fixed by the Lord Chancellor of the day pursuant to his powers under the Damages Act 1996. The above method was further endorsed by Lord Chancellor Irvine in his decision of July 2001, when he fixed the Discount Rate as being 2.5 per cent. He also gave his reasons for his decision, which reasons appear now to be less than happy in the light of the financial turmoil which has since occurred. I will deal with this below. In my view, this present rate is long out of date and does not reflect the substantial reduction in yields on Index Linked Government Stocks since 2001. The present Lord Chancellor Clarke has agreed to review it although his decision may not be available for several months.

First decision of the Working Party

5. It was decided that, with funding now obtained, a new set of tables, based on the most recent mortality rates produced by the Office for National Statistics (ONS), with as few other revisions as possible, should be issued as quickly as was realistically achievable.

Second decision of the Working Party

6. It was decided that, due to the passage of time and the changed circumstances since the tables were first produced, the text of the Explanatory Notes will require a substantial re-write in order to bolster

[1] Memoirs of Sir Michael Ogden QC, *Variety is the Spice of Legal Life*, p.182 (Lewes: The Book Guild, 2002).
[2] [1999] 1 A.C. 345.

its usefulness to practitioners. Not only is there a need to change the language, but the effect of other decided cases has made this a task of importance. The intention of the Working party is to accomplish this re-writing in the next (eighth) edition, which will rely on the further updated mortality projections due to be produced by the ONS later in 2011. It is hoped that the 8th edition will be available in autumn 2012.

Third decision of the Working Party

7. Developments in Guernsey and the review of the discount rate currently being carried out by the Lord Chancellor (see further, below, in respect of both matters) caused the Working Party to decide to include in this edition tables with discount rate columns which range between minus 2 per cent and plus 3 per cent.

8. It is not, we believe, the purpose of these tables or the role of the Working Party to advocate a discount rate, but merely to provide the tools so that, whatever the rate should be, personal injury and fatal accident claims may be quantified.

9. The revised spread of discount rates will assist comparison between lump sums and periodical payments, a process required by the Damages Act 1996, to be more accurately appreciated. The present value of periodical payments is substantially higher than lump sums calculated using the current discount rate of 2.5 per cent. Brooke L.J. remarked in para.34 of the ***Flora v Wakom***[3] judgment: "The fact that these two quite different mechanisms now sit side by side in the same Act of Parliament does not in my judgment mean that the problems that infected the operation of the one should be allowed to infect the operation of the other." This imbalance is a factor which any Lord Chancellor ought to take into account.

Fourth decision of the Working Party

10. The Working Party decided not to increase further the number of tables to reflect different possible retirement ages. The multipliers for retirement ages which do not conform strictly with the five-yearly intervals between 50 and 75 can be calculated with reasonable accuracy by interpolation. We would be interested to learn of other views on this decision which might cause us to think again.

Helmot v Simon

11. The judgment in ***Helmot v Simon***[4] in the Court of Appeal of the Island of Guernsey (September 14, 2010), presided over by Sumption J.A., could be truly described as a decision which has had after-effects. The results have rippled the waters within the English legal establishment, even though the decision creates no precedent in England.

12. The first point to make about the case is that the Damages Act 1996 (as amended) does not apply in Guernsey. Consequentially, neither the 2.5 per cent discount rate prescribed under the power provided by s.1 applies nor is there any power to make an award by way of a periodical payment.

13. The original lump sum award made at first instance on January 14, 2010 was for damages in the sum of £9.3 million plus interest. The court used a single discount rate of 1 per cent for all future losses. The claimant had argued for differential rates of 0.5 per cent for non-earnings-related losses and of

[3] [2006] EWCA Civ 1103; [2007] 1 W.L.R. 282.
[4] [2009–10] G.L.R. 465.

minus 1.5 per cent for earnings-related losses. Some eight months later these arguments succeeded on appeal and the final amount of the award was increased to more than £14 million. Permission has been granted to appeal the decision to the Privy Council.

14. The consequences in England and Wales have been profound. The Lord Chancellor has indicated his intention to reconsider the discount rate and at the time of writing is in the process of doing so. It has also emphasised the disparity between lump sum awards and the provision of periodical payments, to the detriment of lump sum awards, when the discount rate is inappropriate, it not having been revised for a period of 10 years.

Mortality data

15. Projections of future mortality rates are usually produced on a two-yearly basis by the ONS as part of the production of national population projections for the United Kingdom and its constituent countries. Multipliers published in the 6th edition of the Ogden Tables were calculated using mortality rates from the 2004-based projections; this new edition provides multipliers based on mortality rates from the most recent, 2008-based, projections. The 2006-based projections showed rather higher projected life expectancies at many ages than those in the 2004-based projections. The 2008-based projections suggest slightly higher projected life expectancies than those in the 2006-based projections, but which are of relatively little significance in terms of the values of the multipliers at most ages.

16. There is much debate among demographers about whether the factors that have led to the significant improvements in mortality in recent years can continue unabated, thus adding some uncertainty to any projections of future mortality. While the Working Party has continued to use the official projections made by the ONS of future mortality rates in the UK, we propose to monitor developments as new evidence becomes available.

Contingencies other than mortality

17. We have persuaded Dr Victoria Wass to join the Working Party. She has suggested changes to the definition of "disabled" and also clarified some of the language in the Explanatory Notes. We anticipate some further suggestions for amendment in the 8th edition.

18. The Working Party notes that there have been a number of cases in which judges have made significant adjustments to the suggested discount factors. In particular the approach of the trial judges to the calculation of future loss of earnings in ***Conner v Bradman***[5] and ***Clarke v Maltby***[6] has generated some debate. These issues will be discussed in detail when drafting the 8th edition and consideration will be given to whether or not the Explanatory Notes need amendment, especially as regards the circumstances in which it might be appropriate to depart from the suggested non-mortality reduction factors and the size of any adjustments that are made. In the meantime, practitioners performing such calculations are referred to the helpful article by Dr Wass, *"Discretion in the Application of the New Ogden Six Multipliers: The Case of Conner v Bradman and Company"*,[7] which highlights some of the relevant issues.

[5] [2007] EWHC 2789 (QB).
[6] [2010] EWHC 1201 (QB).
[7] [2008] J.P.I.L. 2, 154–163.

Fatal Accidents Act calculations and the "Actuarially Recommended Approach"

19. This is dealt with in detail in Section D of the Explanatory Notes. To those comments I would add one qualification which is that the Court of Appeal in ***Fletcher v A Train & Sons Ltd***[8] was sufficiently concerned with the consequence of following the reasoning of the House of Lords in ***Cookson v Knowles***[9] that it unanimously gave the unsuccessful appellant permission to appeal to the House of Lords on the point; the appeal was subsequently compromised.

20. The Scottish Parliament has since enacted the Damages (Scotland) Act 2011 dealing with the same point and in so doing has demonstrated that it agrees with the point that our predecessors had made on this topic.

21. Section 7(1)(d) of the Damages (Scotland) Act 2011 provides for the multiplier to be calculated at the date of the proof (trial) and the losses over the period between the fatal accident and the proof to be calculated separately, subject to a factor for possible early death, with interest added. Multipliers are determined from the tables based on the age of the deceased had he/she survived to the date of proof. This is the same as our actuarially recommended approach.

Concluding remarks

22. The changes to the Explanatory Notes in this edition are minor; it is the figures that have been updated.

23. As I have previously stated, the figures for the tables themselves are produced by the Government Actuary's Department according to long-established principles.

24. The other matters discussed are the subject of careful and detailed analysis by the members of the Working Party. Its discussions are never less than uninhibited and I am grateful to those members of the Working Party (listed inside the front cover) who give their time and energy to attend the meetings and ensure that all is done which ought to be done.

25. I begin to believe that the journey made by Jason and the Argonauts in search of the Golden Fleece is as nothing in comparison with the desire of those involved in these tables to make the assessment of future losses as simple and accurate as they possibly can be, whilst remaining as clear as we can be in explaining the actual process of calculating the figures. I am conscious that we may not always succeed in that ambition.

Robin de Wilde QC — August 1, 2012

[8] [2008] EWCA Civ 413; [2008] 4 All E.R. 699.
[9] [1979] A.C. 566.

Explanatory Notes

Section A: General

Purpose of tables

1. The tables have been prepared by the Government Actuary's Department. They provide an aid for those assessing the lump sum appropriate as compensation for a continuing future pecuniary loss or consequential expense or cost of care in personal injury and fatal accident cases.

Application of tables

2. The tables set out multipliers. These multipliers enable the user to assess the present capital value of future annual loss (net of tax) or annual expense calculated on the basis of various assumptions which are explained below. Accordingly, to find the present capital value of a given annual loss or expense, it is necessary to select the appropriate table, find the appropriate multiplier and then multiply the amount of the annual loss or expense by that figure.

3. Tables 1–26 deal with annual loss or annual expense extending over three different periods of time. In each case there are separate tables for men and women.

- In Tables 1 and 2 the loss or expense is assumed to begin immediately and to continue for the whole of the rest of the claimant's life.
- In Tables 3–14 the loss or expense is assumed to begin immediately but to continue only until the claimant's retirement or earlier death.
- In Tables 15–26 it is assumed that the annual loss or annual expense will not begin until the claimant reaches retirement but will then continue for the whole of the rest of his or her life. These tables all make due allowance for the chance that the claimant may not live to reach the age of retirement.

Mortality assumptions

4. The tables are based on a reasonable estimate of the future mortality likely to be experienced by average members of the population alive today and are based on projected mortality rates for the United Kingdom as a whole. The Office for National Statistics publishes population projections on a regular basis which include estimates of the extent of future improvements in mortality. Tables 1–26 in this edition show the multipliers which result from the application of these projected mortality rates which were derived from the principal 2008-based population projections for the United Kingdom, which were published in October 2009. (Further details of these projections can be found on the ONS website at: *http://www.ons.gov.uk/ons/rel/npp/national-population-projections/2008-based-projections/index/html.)*

5. The tables do not assume that the claimant dies after a period equating to the expectation of life, but take account of the possibilities that the claimant will live for different periods, e.g. die soon or live to be very old. The mortality assumptions relate to the general population of the United Kingdom. However, unless there is clear evidence in an individual case to support the view that the individual is atypical and will enjoy longer or shorter expectation of life, no further increase or reduction is required for mortality alone.

Use of tables

6. To find the appropriate figure for the present value of a particular loss or expense, the user must first choose that table which relates to the period of loss or expense for which the individual claimant is to be compensated and to the gender of the claimant, or, where appropriate, the claimant's dependants.

7. If, for some reason, the facts in a particular case do not correspond with the assumptions on which one of the tables is based (e.g. it is known that the claimant will have a different retiring age from that assumed in the tables), then the tables can only be used if an appropriate allowance is made for this difference; for this purpose the assistance of an actuary should be sought, except for situations where specific guidance is given in these explanatory notes.

Rate of return

8. The basis of the multipliers set out in the tables is that the lump sum will be invested and yield income (but that over the period in question the claimant will gradually reduce the capital sum, so that at the end of the period it is exhausted). Accordingly, an essential factor in arriving at the right figure is the choice of the appropriate rate of return.

9. The annual rate of return currently to be applied is 2.5 per cent (net of tax), as fixed by the Lord Chancellor on June 25, 2001, and reassessed on July 27, 2001, under the provisions of the Damages Act 1996 s.1. An annual rate of return of 2.5 per cent was also set for Scotland by the Scottish Ministers on February 8, 2002. The Lord Chancellor may make a fresh determination of this rate, after receiving advice from the Government Actuary and the Treasury (and, in Scotland, the Scottish Ministers after consultation with the Government Actuary). In order to allow the tables to continue to be used should a new discount rate be specified, the tables are accordingly shown for a range of possible annual rates of return ranging from –2 per cent to 3 per cent, in steps of 0.5 per cent, rather than the range 0.0 per cent to 5.0 per cent as in the 6th edition. This change has been made because multipliers at negative rates are useful for the financial evaluation of periodical payments in the exercise which is required by the Damages Act in all cases for comparison with lump sums. In addition, it is recognised that multipliers based on discount rates of more than 3 per cent are currently not generally required, and a recent case heard in the Channel Islands (***Helmot v Simon***[10]) has made an award based on negative discount rates.

10. The figures in the 0% column show the multiplier without any discount for interest and provide the expectations of life (Tables 1 and 2) or the expected period over which a person would have provided a dependency (up to retirement age Tables 3–14 or from pension age Tables 15–26). These are supplied to assist in the calculation of multipliers in Fatal Accidents Act cases (see Section D).

11. Section 1(2) of the Damages Act 1996 makes provision for the courts to make variations to the discount rate if any party to the proceedings shows that it is more appropriate in the case in question. Variations to the discount rate under this provision have, however, been rejected by the Court of Appeal in the cases of ***Warriner v Warriner***[11] and ***Cooke & Others v United Bristol Health Care & Others.***[12]

12. Previous editions of these tables explained how the current yields on index-linked government bonds could be used as an indicator of the appropriate real rate of return for valuing future income

[10] [2009–10] G.L.R. 465.
[11] [2002] EWCA Civ 81; [2002] 1 W.L.R. 1703.
[12] [2003] EWCA Civ 1370; [2004] 1 W.L.R. 251.

streams. Such considerations were endorsed by the House of Lords in ***Wells v Wells*** and the same argumentation was adopted by the Lord Chancellor when he set the rate on commencement of s.1 of the Damages Act 1996. In cases outwith the scope of these tables, the advice of an actuary should be sought.

Different retirement ages

13. In para.7 above, reference was made to the problem that will arise when the claimant's retiring age is different from that assumed in the tables. Such a problem may arise in valuing a loss or expense beginning immediately but ending at retirement; or in valuing a loss or expense which will not begin until the claimant reaches retirement but will then continue until death. Tables are provided for retirement ages of 50, 55, 60, 65, 70 and 75. Where the claimant's actual retiring age would have been between two of the retirement ages for which tables are provided, the correct multiplier can be obtained by consideration of the tables for retirement age immediately above and below the actual retirement age, keeping the period to retirement age the same. Thus a woman of 42 who would have retired at 58 can be considered as being in between the cases of a woman of 39 with a retirement age of 55 and a woman of 44 with a retirement age of 60. The steps to take are as follows:

(1) Determine between which retirement ages, for which tables are provided, the claimant's actual retirement age R lies. Let the lower of these ages be A and the higher be B.

(2) Determine how many years must be subtracted from the claimant's actual retirement age to get to A and subtract that period from the claimant's age. If the claimant's age is x, the result of this calculation is $(x + A - R)$.

(3) Look up this new reduced age in the table corresponding to retirement age A at the appropriate rate of return. Let the resulting multiplier be M.

(4) Determine how many years must be added to the claimant's actual retirement age to get to B and add that period to the claimant's age. The result of this calculation is $(x + B - R)$.

(5) Look up this new increased age in the table corresponding to retirement age B at the appropriate rate of return. Let the resulting multiplier be N.

(6) Interpolate between M and N. In other words, calculate:

$$(B - R) \times M + (R - A) \times N$$

and divide the result by $[(B - R) + (R - A)]$, (or equivalently $[B - A]$).

14. In the example given in para.13, the steps would be as follows:

(1) R is 58, A is 55 and B is 60.

(2) Subtracting three years from the claimant's age gives 39.

(3) Looking up age 39 in Table 6 (for retirement age 55) gives 13.10 at a rate of return of 2.5 per cent.

(4) Adding two years to the claimant's age gives 44.

(5) Looking up age 44 in Table 8 (for retirement age 60) gives 13.03 at a rate of return of 2.5 per cent.

(6) Calculating 2 × 13.10 + 3 × 13.03 and dividing by (60 – 58) + (58 – 55) [equals 5] gives 13.06 as the multiplier.

15. When the loss or expense to be valued is that from the date of retirement to death, and the claimant's date of retirement differs from that assumed in the tables, a different approach is necessary, involving the following three steps.

(1) Assume that there is a present loss which will continue for the rest of the claimant's life and from Table 1 or 2 establish the value of that loss or expense over the whole period from the date of assessment until the claimant's death.

(2) Establish the value of such loss or expense over the period from the date of assessment until the claimant's expected date of retirement following the procedure explained in paras 13 and 14, above.

(3) Subtract the second figure from the first. The balance remaining represents the present value of the claimant's loss or expense between retirement and death.

16. If the claimant's actual retirement age would have been earlier than 50, or later than 75, the advice of an actuary should be sought.

Younger ages

17. Tables 1 and 2, which concern pecuniary loss for life, and Tables 15–26, which concern loss of pension from retirement age, have been extended down to age 0. In some circumstances the multiplier at age 0 is slightly lower than that at age 1; this arises because of the relatively high incidence of deaths immediately after birth.

18. Tables for multipliers for loss of earnings (Tables 3–14) have not been extended below age 16. In order to determine the multiplier for loss of earnings for someone who has not yet started work, it is first necessary to determine an assumed age at which the claimant would have commenced work and to find the appropriate multiplier for that age from Tables 3–14, according to the assumed retirement age. This multiplier should then be multiplied by the deferment factor from Table 27 which corresponds to the appropriate rate of return and the period from the date of the trial to the date on which it is assumed that the claimant would have started work. A similar approach can be used for determining a multiplier for pecuniary loss for life where the loss is assumed to commence a fixed period of years from the date of the trial. For simplicity the factors in Table 27 relate purely to the impact of compound interest and ignore mortality. At ages below 30 this is a reasonable approximation but at higher ages it would normally be appropriate to allow explicitly for mortality and the advice of an actuary should be sought.

Contingencies

19. Tables 1–26 make reasonable provision for the levels of mortality which members of the population of the United Kingdom alive today may expect to experience in future. The tables do not take account of the other risks and vicissitudes of life, such as the possibility that the claimant would for periods have ceased to earn due to ill-health or loss of employment. Nor do they take account of the fact that many people cease work for substantial periods to care for children or other dependants. Section B suggests ways in which allowance may be made to the multipliers for loss of earnings, to allow for certain risks other than mortality.

Impaired lives

20. In some cases, medical evidence may be available which asserts that a claimant's health impairments are equivalent to adding a certain number of years to their current age, or to treating the

individual as having a specific age different from their actual age. In such cases, Tables 1 and 2 can be used with respect to the deemed higher age. For the other tables the adjustment is not so straightforward, as adjusting the age will also affect the assumed retirement age, but the procedures described in paras 13–15 may be followed, or the advice of an actuary should be sought. In other cases, the medical evidence may state that the claimant is likely to live for a stated number of years. This is often then treated as requiring payment to be made for a fixed period equal to the stated life expectancy and using Table 28 to ascertain the value of the multiplier. In general, this is likely to give a multiplier which is too high since this approach does not allow for the distribution of deaths around the expected length of life. For a group of similarly impaired lives of the same age, some will die before the average life expectancy and some after; allowing for this spread of deaths results in a lower multiplier than assuming payment for a term certain equal to the life expectancy. In such cases, it is preferable to look up the age in the 0 per cent column in Tables 1 or 2 for which the value of the multiplier at 0 per cent is equal to the stated life expectancy. The relevant multipliers are then obtained from the relevant tables using this age. Take, for example, an impaired male life which is stated to have a life expectancy of 20 years. By interpolation, the age for which the multiplier in the 0 per cent column in Table 1 is 20 is:

$$(20 - 19.74)/(20.57 - 19.74) \times 66 + (20.57 - 20)/(20.57 - 19.74) \times 67$$

which equals 66.7 years.

The value of the whole of life multiplier is then obtained from the 2.5 per cent column of Table 1 for age 66.7 years:

$$(67 - 66.7) \times 15.38 + (66.7 - 66) \times 14.90$$

which equals 15.04 (compared to 15.78 for the value for a term certain of 20 years using the 2.5 per cent column of Table 28).

Fixed period

21. In cases where pecuniary loss is to be valued for a fixed period, the multipliers in Table 28 may be used. These make no allowance for mortality or any other contingency but assume that regular frequent payments (e.g. weekly or monthly) will continue throughout the period. These figures should in principle be adjusted if the periodicity of payment is less frequent, especially if the payments in question are annually in advance or in arrears.

Variable future losses or expenses

22. The tables do not provide an immediate answer when the annual future loss or expense is likely to change at given points in time in the future. The most common examples will be where:

(a) the claimant's lost earnings would have increased on a sliding scale or changed due to promotion; or

(b) the claimant's care needs are likely to change in the future, perhaps because it is anticipated that a family carer will not be able to continue to provide help.

In such situations it is usually necessary to split the overall multiplier, whether for working life or whole of life, into segments, and then to apply those smaller segmented multipliers to the multiplicand appropriate for each period.

There are a variety of methods which could be used for splitting a multiplier, especially where the age at which a payment is increased or decreased, or stops or begins, is one which is tabulated in Tables 1–26. The following examples serve to illustrate how multipliers might be split using the "apportionment method". This method can be extended for use in cases where none of the ages at which payments change are tabulated.

Example 1—Variable future earnings

23. The claimant is female, a graduate with a degree, aged 25 at date of settlement/trial. Her probable career progression, in the absence of injury, would have provided her with salary increases at ages 30, 35 and 40; thereafter she would have continued at the same level to age 60, when she would have stepped down from full-time work to work part-time until 70. Post-accident she is now incapable of working.

The multiplicands for lost future earnings are:

Age 25–30:	£16,000 a year
Age 30–35:	£25,000 a year
Age 35–40:	£35,000 a year
Age 40–60:	£40,000 a year
Age 60–70:	£20,000 a year

The multipliers for each stage of her career are calculated as follows:

(1) The working-life will be 45 years and the Multiplier from Table 12 for that period taking into account mortality risks but without any discounts for any other contingencies will be 26.73.

(2) The multiplier for a term certain of 45 years (ignoring mortality risks) from Table 28 is 27.17.

(3) The multiplier from Table 28 should be split so that each individual segment of the whole working life period (45 years) is represented by a figure. So, the first five years is represented by a multiplier for a term certain of five years, namely 4.70; the next five years is represented by a multiplier of 4.16 (being the difference between the figure for a term certain of 10 years, namely 8.86 and the figure for a term certain of five years, namely 4.70); the next five years by 3.68 (i.e. the 15-year figure of 12.54 less the 10 year figure of 8.86); the next 20 years by 10.89 (i.e. the difference between the 35-year figure which is 23.43 and the 15-year figure of 12.54); then, the final 10 years by the balance of 3.74 (the residual figure being 27.17 less 23.43).

(4) Each of those smaller segmented multipliers can be shown as a percentage or fraction of the whole: so, for the first five years the segmented multiplier of 4.70 is 17.30 per cent of the whole figure of 27.17, and so on for each segment of the 45-year period.

(5) The working life multiplier from Table 12 can now be split up in identical proportions to the way in which the Table 28 multiplier has been treated above: thus the first five-year period is now represented by a multiplier of 4.62, which is calculated by taking 17.30 per cent of 26.73. Each segmented multiplier is calculated in the same way.

(6) Having now obtained multipliers for each segment of working life, taking into account mortality risks, it is then necessary to discount those figures for "contingencies other than mortality". The

discount factor from Table C (using the column for a female, not disabled, with degree level education) is 0.89. So, the figure of 4.62 for the first five-year period now becomes 4.11 (i.e. 4.62 × 0.89). Again, treat each segmented multiplier in the same way.

(7) The multiplicand for each segment of working life is now multiplied by the appropriate segmented multiplier to calculate the loss for that period. The sum total of those losses represents the full sum for loss of future earnings (ignoring any mitigation).

(8) The figures are set out in tabular form below and give a total lump sum award of £716,260:

Ages	Period (years)	Table 28	% Split	Table 12	Discounted Multipliers (Table C) (× 0.89)	Net Annual Earnings £	£ Loss
25–30	5	4.70	17.30	4.62	4.11	16,000	65,760
30–35	5	4.16	15.31	4.09	3.64	25,000	91,000
35–40	5	3.68	13.54	3.62	3.22	35,000	112,700
40–60	20	10.89	40.08	10.71	9.53	40,000	381,200
60–70	10	3.74	13.77	3.68	3.28	20,000	65,600
Totals:	45 years	27.17	100.00	26.73	23.79		**716, 260**

N.B. the figures in the above table have been rounded at each step of the calculation so the totals shown are not necessarily the sum of the individual multipliers in the columns

Example 2—Variable future care costs

24. A male aged 20 years at the date of settlement/trial requires personal care support for life. He has a normal life expectation for his age. Significant changes in his care regime are anticipated at age 30 and again at age 50.

The multiplicands for care costs are:

Age 20–30: £30,000 a year

Age 30–50: £60,000 a year

Age 50 for rest of life: £80,000 a year

The multipliers for each stage of the care regime are calculated as follows:

(1) The life expectation will be 67.22 years (from the 0 per cent column of Table 1) and the multiplier for that period taking into account mortality risks (from Table 1) will be 32.10.

(2) The multiplier for a term certain of 67.22 years (ignoring mortality risks) from Table 28 lies between 32.75 (for 67 years) and 32.94 (for 68 years) and is calculated thus:

$$(68 - 67.22) \times 32.75 + (67.22 - 67) \times 32.94 = 32.79.$$

(3) The multiplier from Table 28 should be split so that each individual segment of the whole period of life expectation is represented by a figure. So, the first 10 years (20–30) are represented by a multiplier of 8.86; the next 20 years (30–50) are represented by a multiplier of 12.33 (being the difference between the 30-year figure of 21.19 and the 10-year figure of 8.86); then, the final

years (50 to death) are represented by the balance of 11.60 (being the difference between the term certain multiplier of 32.79 and the 30-year figure of 21.19).

(4) Each of those smaller segmented multipliers can be shown as a percentage or fraction of the whole: so, for the first 10 years the segmented multiplier of 8.86 is 27.02 per cent of the whole figure of 32.79, and so on for each segment of the life period.

(5) The life multiplier from Table 1 can now be split up in the way in which the Table 28 multiplier was treated above and in identical proportions: thus the first 10-year period is now represented by a multiplier of 8.67 which is calculated by taking 27.02 per cent of 32.10.

(6) The figures are set out in tabular form below and give a total lump sum award of £1,893,100:

Age (years)	Table 28 (67.22 years) Split multipliers	% Split (of Table 28) figure	Table 1 (multiplier allowing for mortality)	Care costs £ a year	Total £
20–30	8.86	27.02%	8.67	30,000	260,100
30–50	12.33	37.60%	12.07	60,000	724,200
50 till death	11.60	35.38%	11.36	80,000	908,800
Totals	32.79 (no mortality discount)	100.00%	32.10 life multiplier		**1,893,100**

N.B. the figures in the above table have been rounded at each step of the calculation.

Spouse's pensions

25. If doubt exists whether the tables are appropriate to a particular case which appears to present significant difficulties of substance, it would be prudent to take actuarial advice. This might be appropriate in relation to the level of spouse's benefits, if these are to be assessed, since these are not readily valued using Tables 1–26. As a rough rule of thumb, if spouse's benefits are to be included when valuing pension loss from normal pension age, the multipliers in Tables 15–26 should be increased by 5 per cent for a female claimant (i.e. benefits to the male spouse) and by 14 per cent for a male claimant if the spouse's pension would be half of the pension that the member was receiving at death. If the spouse's pension would be payable at a rate of two-thirds the member's pension at death the multipliers should be increased by 7 per cent for a female claimant and by 18 per cent for a male claimant.

Section B: Contingencies other than mortality

26. As stated in para.19, the tables for loss of earnings (Tables 3–14) take no account of risks other than mortality. This section shows how the multipliers in these tables may be reduced to take account of these risks.

27. Tables of factors to be applied to the existing multipliers were first introduced in the 2nd edition of the Ogden Tables. These factors were based on work commissioned by the Institute of Actuaries and carried out by Professor S. Haberman and Mrs D. S. F. Bloomfield.[13] Although there was some debate within the actuarial profession about the details of the work, and in particular about the scope for developing it further, the findings were broadly accepted and were adopted by the Government

[13] "Work time lost to sickness, unemployment and stoppages: measurement and application" (1990) 117 *Journal of the Institute of Actuaries*, 533–595.

Actuary and the other actuaries who were members of the Working Party when the 2nd edition of the Tables was published and remained unchanged until the 6th edition.

28. Some related work was published in 2002 by Lewis, McNabb and Wass.[14] For the publication of the 6th edition of the Ogden Tables, the Ogden Working Party was involved in further research into the impact of contingencies other than mortality carried out by Professor Richard Verrall, Professor Steven Haberman and Mr Zoltan Butt of City University, London and, in a separate exercise, by Dr Victoria Wass of Cardiff University. Their findings were combined to produce the tables of factors given in section B of the 6th edition and repeated here.

29. The Haberman and Bloomfield paper relied on data from the Labour Force Surveys for 1973, 1977, 1981 and 1985 and English Life Tables No. 14 (1980–82). The Labour Force Survey (LFS) was originally designed to produce a periodic cross-sectional snapshot of the working age population and collects information on an extensive range of socio-economic and labour force characteristics. Since the winter of 1992/3, the LFS has been carried out on a quarterly basis, with respondents being included in the survey over five successive quarters. The research of Professor Verrall *et al.* and Dr Wass used data from the Labour Force Surveys conducted from 1998–2003 to estimate the probabilities of movement of males and females between different states of economic activity, dependent on age, sex, employment activity and level of disability. These probabilities permit the calculation of the expected periods in employment until retirement age, dependent on the initial starting state of economic activity, disability and educational attainment. These can then be discounted at the same discount rate that is used for obtaining the relevant multiplier from Tables 3–14, in order to give a multiplier which takes into account only those periods the claimant would be expected, on average, to be in work. These discounted working life expectancy multipliers can be compared to those obtained assuming the person remained in work throughout, to obtain reduction factors which give the expected proportion of time to retirement age which will be spent in employment.

30. The factors described in subsequent paragraphs are for use in calculating loss of earnings up to retirement age. The research work did not investigate the impact of contingencies other than mortality on the value of future pension rights. Some reduction to the multiplier for loss of pension would often be appropriate when a reduction is being applied for loss of earnings. This may be a smaller reduction than in the case of loss of earnings because the ill-health contingency (as opposed to the unemployment contingency) may give rise to significant ill-health retirement pension rights. A bigger reduction may be necessary in cases where there is significant doubt whether pension rights would have continued to accrue (to the extent not already allowed for in the post-retirement multiplier) or in cases where there may be doubt over the ability of the pension fund to pay promised benefits. In the case of a defined contribution pension scheme, loss of pension rights may be allowed for, simply by increasing the future earnings loss (adjusted for contingencies other than mortality) by the percentage of earnings which the employer contributes to the scheme represent.

31. The methodology proposed in paras 33–42 describes one method for dealing with contingencies other than mortality. If this methodology is followed, in many cases it will be appropriate to increase or reduce the discount in the tables to take account of the nature of a particular claimant's disabilities. It should be noted that the methodology does not take into account the pre-accident employment history. The methodology also provides for the possibility of valuing more appropriately the possible mitigation of loss of earnings in cases where the claimant is employed after the accident or is considered capable of being employed. This will in many cases enable a more accurate assessment to be made of the mitigation of loss. However, there may be some cases when the *Smith v Manchester Corporation* or *Blamire* approach remains applicable or otherwise where a precise mathematical approach is inapplicable.

[14] "Methods of calculating damages for loss of future earnings" (2002) 2 *Journal of Personal Injury Law*, 151–165.

32. The suggestions which follow are intended as a "ready reckoner" which provides an initial adjustment to the multipliers according to the employment status, disability status and educational attainment of the claimant when calculating awards for loss of earnings and for any mitigation of this loss in respect of potential future post-injury earnings. Such a ready reckoner cannot take into account all circumstances and it may be appropriate to argue for higher or lower adjustments in particular cases. In particular, it can be difficult to place a value on the possible mitigating income when considering the potential range of disabilities and their effect on post-work capability, even within the interpretation of disability set out in para.35. However, the methodology does offer a framework for consideration of a range of possible figures with the maximum being effectively provided by the post-injury multiplier assuming the claimant was not disabled and the minimum being the case where there is no realistic prospect of post-injury employment.

The deduction for contingencies other than mortality

33. Under this method, multipliers for loss of earnings obtained from Tables 3–14 are multiplied by factors to allow for the risk of periods of non-employment and absence from the workforce because of sickness.

34. The research by Professor Verrall et al. and Dr Wass referred to in paras 28 and 29 demonstrated that the key issues affecting a person's future working life are employment status, disability status and educational attainment.

35. The definitions of employed/not employed, disabled/not disabled and educational attainment used in this analysis and which should be used for determining which factors to apply to the multipliers to allow for contingencies other than mortality are as follows:

Employed	Those who at the time of the accident are employed, self-employed or on a government training scheme.
Not employed	All others (including those temporarily out of work, full-time students and unpaid family workers).
Disabled	A person is classified as being disabled if all three of the following conditions in relation to the ill-health or disability are met: (i) the person has an illness or a disability which has lasted or is expected to last for over a year or is a progressive illness, (ii) the person satisfies the Equality Act 2010 definition that the impact of the disability substantially limits the person's ability to carry out normal day to day activities, and (iii) their condition affects either the kind **or** the amount of paid work they can do.
Not disabled	All others.

Normal day to day activities are those which are carried out by most people on a daily basis, and we are interested in disabilities/health problems which have a substantial adverse effect on respondent's ability to carry out these activities.

There are several ways in which a disability or health problem may affect the respondent's day to day activities:

Mobility—for example, unable to travel short journeys as a passenger in a car, unable to walk other than at a slow pace or with jerky movements, difficulty in negotiating stairs, unable to use one or more forms of public transport, unable to go out of doors unaccompanied.

Manual dexterity—for example, loss of functioning in one or both hands, inability to use a knife and fork at the same time, or difficulty in pressing buttons on a keyboard.

Physical co-ordination—for example, the inability to feed or dress oneself; or to pour liquid from one vessel to another except with unusual slowness or concentration.

Problems with bowel/bladder control—for example, frequent or regular loss of control of the bladder or bowel. Occasional bedwetting is not considered a disability.

Ability to lift, carry or otherwise move everyday objects (for example, books, kettles, light furniture)—for example, inability to pick up a weight with one hand but not the other, or to carry a tray steadily.

Speech—for example, unable to communicate (clearly) orally with others, taking significantly longer to say things. A minor stutter, difficulty in speaking in front of an audience, or inability to speak a foreign language would not be considered impairments.

Hearing—for example, not being able to hear without the use of a hearing aid, the inability to understand speech under normal conditions or over the telephone.

Eyesight—for example, while wearing spectacles or contact lenses—being unable to pass the standard driving eyesight test, total inability to distinguish colours (excluding ordinary red/green colour blindness), or inability to read newsprint.

Memory or ability to concentrate, learn or understand—for example, intermittent loss of consciousness or confused behaviour, inability to remember names of family or friends, unable to write a cheque without assistance, or an inability to follow a recipe.

Perception of risk of physical danger—for example, reckless behaviour putting oneself or others at risk, mobility to cross the road safely. This excludes (significant) fear of heights or underestimating risk of dangerous hobbies.

Three levels of educational attainment are defined for the purposes of the tables as follows:

D Degree or equivalent or higher.

GE–A GCSE grades A–C up to A levels or equivalents.

O Below GCSE C or CSE 1 or equivalent or no qualifications.

The following table gives a more detailed breakdown of the allocation of various types of educational qualification to each of the three categories above and is based on the allocations used in the research by Professor Verrall, et al. and Dr Wass.

Categories of highest educational attainment

D Degree or equivalent or higher	GE–A GCSE grades A–C up to A levels or equivalent	O Below GCSE grade C or CSE grade 1 or equivalent or no qualifications
Any degree (first or higher) Other higher education qualification below degree level Diploma in higher education	A or AS level or equivalent O level, GCSE grade A–C or equivalent	CSE below grade 1 GCSE below grade C
NVQ level 4 or 5	NVQ level 2 or 3	NVQ level 1 or equivalent
HNC/HND, BTEC higher, etc	BTEC/SCOTVEC first or general diploma OND/ONC, BTEC/SCOTVEC national	BTEC first or general certificate SCOTVEC modules or equivalent
RSA higher diploma	RSA diploma, advanced diploma or certificate	RSA other
Teaching, Nursing, etc	GNVQ intermediate or advanced	GNVQ/GVSQ foundation level
	City and Guilds craft or advanced craft	City and Guilds other
	SCE higher or equivalent Trade apprenticeship Scottish 6th year certificate (CSYS)	YT/ YTP certificate Other qualifications No qualification Don't know

Note: "educational attainment" is used here as a proxy for skill level, so that those in professional occupations such as law, accountancy, nursing, etc. who do not have a degree ought to be treated as if they do have one.

36. The research also considered the extent to which a person's future working life expectancy is affected by individual circumstances such as occupation and industrial sector, geographical region and education. The researchers concluded that the most significant consideration was the highest level of education achieved by the claimant and that, if this was allowed for, the effect of the other factors was relatively small. As a result, the Working Party decided to propose adjustment factors which allow for employment status, disability status and educational attainment only. This is a change from earlier editions of the Ogden Tables where adjustments were made for types of occupation and for geographical region.

37. A separate assessment is made for: (a) the value of earnings the claimant would have received if the injury had not been suffered, and (b) the value of the claimant's earnings (if any) taking account of the injuries sustained. The risk of non-employment is significantly higher post-injury due to the impairment. The loss is arrived at by deducting (b) from (a).

38. In order to calculate the value of the earnings the claimant would have received, if the injury had not been suffered, the claimant's employment status and the disability status need to be determined as at the date of the accident (or the onset of the medical condition) giving rise to the claim, so that the correct table can be applied. For the calculation of future loss of earnings (based on actual pre-accident earnings and also future employment prospects), Tables A and C should be used for claimants who were not disabled at the time of the accident, and Tables B and D should be used for those with a pre-existing disability. In all of these tables the three left hand columns are for those who were employed at the time of the accident and the three right hand columns are for those who were not.

39. In order to calculate the value of the actual earnings that a claimant is likely to receive in the future (i.e. after settlement or trial), the employment status and the disability status need to be determined as at the date of settlement or trial. For claimants with a work-affecting disability at that point in time, Tables B and D should be used. The three left hand columns will apply in respect of claimants actually in employment at date of settlement or trial and the three right hand columns will apply in respect of those who remain non-employed at that point in time.

40. The factors in Tables A–D allow for the interruption of employment for bringing up children and caring for other dependants.

41. In the case of those who at the date of the accident have not yet reached the age at which it is likely they would have started work, the relevant factor will be chosen based on a number of assessments of the claimant's likely employment had the injury not occurred. The relevant factor from the tables would be chosen on the basis of the level of education the claimant would have been expected to have attained, the age at which it is likely the claimant would have started work, together with an assessment as to whether the claimant would have become employed or not. The work multiplier will also have to be discounted for early receipt using the appropriate factor from Table 27 for the number of years between the claimant's age at the date of trial and the age at which it is likely that he/she would have started work.

42. Tables A–D include factors up to age 54 only. For older ages the reduction factors increase towards 1 at retirement age for those who are employed and fall towards 0 for those who are not employed. However, where the claimant is older than 54, it is anticipated that the likely future course of employment status will be particularly dependent on individual circumstances, so that the use of factors based on averages would not be appropriate. Hence reduction factors are not provided for these older ages.

Table A

Loss of earnings to pension age 65 (males—not disabled)

Age at date of trial	Employed D	Employed GE–A	Employed O	Not employed D	Not employed GE–A	Not employed O
16–19		0.90	0.85		0.85	0.82
20–24	0.92	0.92	0.87	0.89	0.88	0.83
25–29	0.93	0.92	0.89	0.89	0.88	0.82
30–34	0.92	0.91	0.89	0.87	0.86	0.81
35–39	0.90	0.90	0.89	0.85	0.84	0.80
40–44	0.88	0.88	0.88	0.82	0.81	0.78
45–49	0.86	0.86	0.86	0.77	0.77	0.74
50	0.83	0.83	0.83	0.72	0.72	0.70
51	0.82	0.82	0.82	0.70	0.70	0.68
52	0.81	0.81	0.81	0.67	0.67	0.66
53	0.80	0.80	0.80	0.63	0.63	0.63
54	0.79	0.79	0.79	0.59	0.59	0.59

Table B

Loss of earnings to pension age 65 (males—disabled)

Age at date of trial	Employed D	Employed GE–A	Employed O	Not employed D	Not employed GE–A	Not employed O
16–19		0.55	0.32		0.49	0.25
20–24	0.61	0.55	0.38	0.53	0.46	0.24
25–29	0.60	0.54	0.42	0.48	0.41	0.24
30–34	0.59	0.52	0.40	0.43	0.34	0.23
35–39	0.58	0.48	0.39	0.38	0.28	0.20
40–44	0.57	0.48	0.39	0.33	0.23	0.15
45–49	0.55	0.48	0.39	0.26	0.20	0.11
50	0.53	0.49	0.40	0.24	0.18	0.10
51	0.53	0.49	0.41	0.23	0.17	0.09
52	0.54	0.49	0.41	0.22	0.16	0.08
53	0.54	0.49	0.42	0.21	0.15	0.07
54	0.54	0.50	0.43	0.20	0.14	0.06

Table C

Loss of earnings to pension age 60 (females—not disabled)

Age at date of trial	Employed D	Employed GE–A	Employed O	Not employed D	Not employed GE–A	Not employed O
16–19		0.81	0.64		0.77	0.59
20–24	0.89	0.82	0.68	0.84	0.76	0.60
25–29	0.89	0.84	0.72	0.83	0.75	0.61
30–34	0.89	0.85	0.75	0.81	0.75	0.63
35–39	0.89	0.86	0.78	0.80	0.74	0.63
40–44	0.89	0.86	0.80	0.78	0.72	0.60
45–49	0.87	0.85	0.81	0.72	0.64	0.52
50	0.86	0.84	0.81	0.64	0.55	0.43
51	0.85	0.84	0.81	0.60	0.51	0.40
52	0.84	0.84	0.81	0.56	0.46	0.36
53	0.83	0.83	0.81	0.50	0.41	0.32
54	0.83	0.83	0.82	0.44	0.35	0.27

Table D
Loss of earnings to pension age 60 (females—disabled)

Age at date of trial	Employed D	Employed GE–A	Employed O	Not employed D	Not employed GE–A	Not employed O
16–19		0.43	0.25		0.35	0.19
20–24	0.64	0.44	0.25	0.58	0.33	0.17
25–29	0.63	0.45	0.25	0.50	0.32	0.16
30–34	0.62	0.46	0.30	0.44	0.31	0.15
35–39	0.61	0.48	0.34	0.42	0.28	0.14
40–44	0.60	0.51	0.38	0.38	0.23	0.13
45–49	0.60	0.54	0.42	0.28	0.18	0.11
50	0.60	0.56	0.47	0.23	0.15	0.10
51	0.61	0.58	0.49	0.21	0.14	0.09
52	0.61	0.60	0.51	0.20	0.13	0.08
53	0.62	0.62	0.54	0.18	0.11	0.07
54	0.63	0.66	0.57	0.16	0.09	0.06

The factors in Tables A–D will need to be reviewed if the discount rate changes.

Different pension ages

43. The factors in the preceding tables assume retirement at age 65 for males and age 60 for females. It is not possible to calculate expected working life times assuming alternative retirement ages from the LFS data, since the employment data in the LFS are collected only for the working population, assumed to be aged between 16 and 64 for males and between 16 and 59 for females. Where the retirement age is different from age 65 for males or age 60 for females, it is suggested that this should be ignored and the reduction factor and the adjustments thereto be taken from the above tables for the age of the claimant as at the date of trial with no adjustment, i.e. assume that the retirement age is age 65 for males and age 60 for females. However, if the retirement age is close to the age at the date of trial, then it may be more appropriate to take into account the circumstances of the individual case.

44. It should be noted that the reduction factors in Tables A, B, C and D are based on data for the period 1998–2003. Whilst the reduction factors and adjustments allow for the age-specific probabilities of moving into, or out of, employment over future working life time, based on data for the period 1998–2003, the methodology assumes that these probabilities remain constant over time; there is no allowance for changes in these age-specific probabilities beyond this period. It is also assumed that there will be no change in disability status or educational achievement after the date of the accident. Future changes in the probabilities of moving into, and out of, employment are especially difficult to predict with any certainty. It is the intention that the factors should be reassessed from time to time as new data becomes available.

Section C: Summary of personal injury applications

45. To use the tables the guidance below should be followed:

(1) Choose the table relating to the appropriate sex of the claimant and period of loss or expense (e.g. loss for life, or loss of earnings to a set retirement age). Where loss of earnings is concerned, and none of the tables is relevant because the claimant's expected age of retirement differs from that assumed in the tables, the procedure in paras 13–16 of the explanatory notes should be followed.

(2) Choose the appropriate discount column (currently 2.5 per cent).

(3) In that column find the appropriate figure for the claimant's age at trial ("the basic multiplier").

Loss of earnings

(4) When calculating **loss of earnings**, the tables should be used when a multiplier/multiplicand approach is appropriate. If it is, the basic multiplier should be adjusted to take account of contingencies other than mortality. These contingencies include the claimant's employment and disability status and educational qualifications. The basic multiplier should be multiplied by the appropriate figure taken from Tables A–D. It may be necessary at this stage to modify the resulting figure further to allow for circumstances specific to the claimant.

This process gives "the adjusted table multiplier".

(5) Multiply the net annual loss (the multiplicand) by the adjusted table multiplier to arrive at a figure which represents the capitalised value of the future loss of earnings.

(6) If the claimant has a residual earning capacity, allowance should be made for any post-accident vulnerability on the labour market: the following paragraphs show one way of doing this, although there may still be cases where a conventional ***Smith v City of Manchester*** award is appropriate.

Where it is appropriate to do so, repeat steps 1–5 above, replacing the pre-accident employment and disability status with the post-accident employment and disability status in step 4 and replacing the net annual loss by the assumed new level of net earnings at step 5. It will only be necessary to reconsider the claimant's educational attainments if these have changed between the accident and the date of trial or settlement.

The result will represent the capitalised value of the claimant's likely post-accident earnings. It is important to note that, when carrying out this exercise, the *degree* of residual disability may have a different effect on residual earnings depending on its relevance to the claimant's likely field of work. For example, the loss of a leg may have less effect on a sedentary worker's earnings than on a manual worker's.

(7) Deduct the sum yielded by step 6 from that yielded by step 5 to obtain the net amount of loss of earnings allowing for residual earning capacity. Where the above methodology is used there will usually be no need for a separate ***Smith v City of Manchester*** award.

Lifetime losses

(8) Where a **loss** will continue **for life**, follow steps 1–3, above, to find the appropriate multiplier in the table.

Where the normal life expectancy given by the table is inapplicable the approach set out in para.20, using the lifetime tables rather than Table 28, is the correct approach.

(9) This figure may need adjustment to allow for the particular circumstances of the claimant.

(10) Multiply the annual loss or expense by the multiplier as adjusted.

Variable annual losses

(11) In cases where there will be different losses at different periods it may be necessary to split the multiplier. The approach set out at paras 22–24 should be followed.

Fixed period and deferred losses

(12) Where a loss will continue over a fixed period, the appropriate multiplier can be found in Table 28.

(13) Where a loss will not commence until some future date, multiply the appropriate multiplier by a discount figure taken from Table 27 (the use of which is explained in para.18). This paragraph does not apply to loss of pensions, which have their own tables.

Examples

46. The following are examples of the use of the tables in illustrative personal injury cases with simplified assumptions.

Example 3

47. The claimant is female, aged 35 at the date of the trial. She has three A levels, but not a degree, and was in employment at the date of the accident at a salary of £25,000 a year net of tax. She was not disabled before the accident. As a result of her injuries, she is now disabled and has lost her job but has found part-time employment at a salary of £5,000 a year net of tax. Her loss of earnings to retirement age of 60 is assessed as follows:

(1) Look up Table 8 for loss of earnings to pension age 60 for females.

(2) The appropriate rate of return is determined to be 2.5 per cent (the rate currently set under s.1 of the Damages Act 1996).

(3) Table 8 shows that, on the basis of a 2.5 per cent rate of return, the multiplier for a female aged 35 is 18.43.

(4) Now take account of risks other than mortality. Allowing for the claimant being employed, not disabled and having achieved A levels at the date of trial, Table C would require 18.43 to be multiplied by 0.86, resulting in a revised multiplier of 15.85.

(5) The damages for loss of earnings are assessed as £396,250 (15.85 × £25,000).

(6) Allow for mitigation of loss of earnings in respect of post-injury earnings. As before, Table 8 shows that, on the basis of a 2.5 per cent rate of return, the multiplier for a female aged 35 is 18.43.

(7) Now take account of risks other than mortality. Allowing for the claimant being employed, disabled and having achieved A levels at the date of trial, Table D would require 18.43 to be multiplied by 0.48, resulting in a revised multiplier of 8.85.

(8) The amount of mitigation for post-injury earnings is assessed as £44,150 (8.85 × £5,000).

(9) Hence award for loss of earnings after allowing for mitigation is £396,250 − £44,250 = £352,00.

Example 4

48. The claimant is male, aged 48 at the date of the trial. He has no educational qualifications. His retirement age was 65, he was employed at the time of the accident and his pre-retirement multiplicand has been determined as £20,000 a year net of tax. He was not disabled before the accident.

As a result of his injuries, he is now disabled and has lost his job. The multiplicand for costs of care is deemed to be £50,000 a year. He is unemployed at the date of trial but has been assessed as capable of finding work with possible future earnings of £5,000 a year net of tax. His loss of earnings to retirement age of 65 is assessed as follows:

(1) Look up Table 9 for loss of earnings to pension age 65 for males.

(2) The appropriate rate of return is determined to be 2.5 per cent (the rate currently set under s.1 of the Damages Act 1996).

(3) Table 9 shows that, on the basis of a 2.5 per cent rate of return, the multiplier for a male aged 48 is 13.42.

(4) Now take account of risks other than mortality. Allowing for the claimant being employed, not disabled and having no educational qualifications at the date of trial, Table A would require 13.42 to be multiplied by 0.86, resulting in a revised multiplier of 11.54.

(5) The damages for loss of earnings are assessed as £230,800 (11.54 × £20,000).

(6) Allow for mitigation of loss of earnings in respect of post-injury earnings. As before, Table 9 shows that, on the basis of a 2.5 per cent rate of return, the multiplier for a male aged 48 is 13.42.

(7) Now take account of risks other than mortality. Allowing for the claimant being unemployed and disabled with no educational qualifications at the date of trial, Table B would require 13.42 to be multiplied by 0.11, resulting in a revised multiplier of 1.48.

(8) The amount of mitigation for post-injury earnings is assessed as £7,400 (1.48 × £5,000).

(9) Hence award for loss of earnings after allowing for mitigation is £230,800 − £7,400 = £223,400.

49. The damages for cost of care are assessed as follows:

(1) Look up Table 1 for the multiplier at age 48.

(2) The appropriate rate of return is 2.5 per cent.

(3) Table 1 shows that, on the basis of a 2.5 per cent rate of return, the multiplier at age 48 is 23.51.

(4) No adjustment is made for risks other than mortality.

(5) The damages for cost of care are assessed at £1,175,500 (23.51 × £50,000).

Example 5

50. The claimant is female, aged 14 at the date of the trial. She is expected to achieve a degree and to be in employment thereafter on a salary, in current terms, of £30,000 a year net of tax. She was not disabled before the accident. As a result of her injuries, she is now disabled—she is still expected to achieve a degree and to be in employment, but with an average salary in current terms of £20,000 net of tax. She will be aged 21 when she completes her degree. Her loss of earnings to retirement age of 60 is assessed as follows:

(1) Look up Table 8 for loss of earnings to pension age 60 for females.

(2) The appropriate rate of return is determined to be 2.5 per cent (the rate currently set under s.1 of the Damages Act 1996).

(3) Table 8 shows that, on the basis of a 2.5 per cent rate of return, the multiplier for a female graduate aged 21 is 24.83. This needs to be discounted back to age 14. The factor at 2.5 per cent for a period for deferment for seven years is 0.8413 from Table 27, giving a total multiplier of 24.83 × 0.8413 = 20.89.

(4) Now take account of risks other than mortality. Allowing for the claimant at age 21 assessed as achieving a degree, being employed and not disabled, Table C would require 20.89 to be multiplied by 0.89, resulting in a revised multiplier of 18.59.

(5) The damages for loss of earnings are assessed as £557,700 (18.59 × £30,000).

(6) Allow for mitigation of loss of earnings in respect of post-injury earnings. As before, Table 8 shows that, on the basis of a 2.5 per cent rate of return, the multiplier for a female graduate aged 21 is 24.83. As before, after discounting for seven years to age 14 the multiplier is reduced to 24.83 × 0.8413 = 20.89.

(7) Now take account of risks other than mortality. Allowing for the claimant at age 21 assessed as achieving a degree, being employed and disabled, Table D would require 20.89 to be multiplied by 0.64, resulting in a revised multiplier of 13.37.

(8) The amount of mitigation for post-injury earnings is assessed as £267,400 (13.37 × £20,000).

(9) Hence award for loss of earnings after allowing for mitigation is £557,700 – £267,400 = £290,300.

Example 6

51. The claimant is male, aged 40 at the date of the trial. He has achieved O levels. He was unemployed at the time of the accident. His potential pre-retirement multiplicand has been determined as £15,000 a year net of tax. He was disabled before the accident. As a result of his injuries, he has been assessed as having no future prospect of employment. His loss of earnings to retirement age of 65 is assessed as follows:

(1) Look up Table 9 for loss of earnings to pension age 65 for males.

(2) The appropriate rate of return is determined to be 2.5 per cent (the rate currently set under s.1 of the Damages Act 1996).

(3) Table 9 shows that, on the basis of a 2.5 per cent rate of return, the multiplier for a male aged 40 is 18.09.

(4) Now take account of risks other than mortality. Allowing for the claimant being unemployed, disabled and having achieved O levels at the date of trial, Table A would require 18.09 to be multiplied by 0.23, resulting in a revised multiplier of 4.16.

(5) The damages for loss of earnings are assessed as £62,400 (4.16 × £15,000).

(6) As the claimant has been assessed as having no future prospect of employment following the accident, there is no mitigation of loss of earnings in respect of post-injury earnings.

(7) Hence award for loss of earnings after allowing for mitigation is £62,400.

Section D: Application of tables to fatal accident cases

52. The current approach of the courts, except in Scotland, is to assess the multiplier as at the date of death (***Cookson v Knowles***[15]).

53. That approach was criticised by the Law Commission in their Report 263 (*Claims for Wrongful Death*). The Law Commission recommended that multipliers should be assessed as at the date of trial and that the multipliers derived from the Ogden Tables should only take effect from the date of trial. The Law Commission stressed that the current approach incorporates an actuarial flaw in that it incorporates a discount for early receipt in the period prior to trial or assessment.

54. The Working Party, then under the Chairmanship of the late Sir Michael Ogden QC, considered that the Law Commission's criticism was valid. In the Fourth Edition of the Tables published in August 2000, the Working Party set out guidance in Section D of the Explanatory Notes on how damages should be calculated in such cases. We refer to that guidance below as the actuarially recommended approach. We note that the actuarially recommended approach has been adopted in the Damages (Scotland) Act 2011. For further details see paras 20–21 in the Introduction.

55. However, the courts have considered themselves bound by ***Cookson v Knowles*** and hence have not followed the actuarially recommended approach (***White v Esab,***[16] ***H v S***[17] and ***Fletcher v A Train & Sons Ltd***[18]).

The basic law in England and Wales

56. Under the Fatal Accidents Act the loss is that of the dependants, i.e. those who relied upon the deceased for support. They may claim that part of the deceased's income (whether earnings, pension, unearned income or state benefits) that the deceased would have spent on them. They may also claim the loss of the services such as DIY, domestic/household or childcare which the deceased would have undertaken and from which they would have benefited. The position of each dependant must be considered separately.

57. Each head of dependency must be considered separately. For each head of claim for each dependant the court calculates a multiplicand. This is calculated on the basis of what is known at the date of trial. For pre-trial losses, the actual loss to date of trial is calculated. Interest is added. For post-trial losses the multiplicand is calculated as at the date of trial.

58. A multiplier for the period of dependency is applied to the multiplicand to arrive at an overall lump sum for each head of dependency.

59. The remainder of section D deals with how to approach the calculations in fatal accident claims. Three approaches are put forward. Paragraphs 60–63 set out the current approach. The actuarially

[15] [1979] A.C. 556.
[16] [2002] P.I.Q.R. Q6.
[17] [2002] EWCA Civ. 792, [2003] Q.B. 965.
[18] [2008] EWCA Civ. 413, [2008] 4 All E.R. 699.

recommended approach is then set out at paras 64–81. Example 7 illustrates the application of both these approaches whilst Examples 8 and 9 show the actuarially recommended approach applied to more complex situations—these examples make up paras 82–87. The final paragraphs of section D, 88–90, offer an alternative approach using multipliers selected from the date of death.

The current approach

60. Under the approach currently followed by the courts, the multiplier is calculated as at the date of death. However, when making that calculation the court is entitled to take into account matters that have arisen between death and trial. For example, ***Williamson v Thorneycroft***[19] in which the deceased's widow died after her husband but before trial, her dependency terminated at her death. See also, ***Corbett v Barking, Havering & Brentwood HA***.[20]

61. There are two periods to be determined:

(i) the expected period from date of death in which the deceased would have been capable of providing the dependency; and

(ii) the expected period from the date of the death in which the dependant would have been able to receive the dependency.

The shorter of those two periods provides the basis for the multiplier.

62. In respect of each of those periods consideration must be given as to what discount should be made for contingencies other than mortality. The most obvious contingencies other than mortality fall into the following three categories:

(i) Factors relating to the deceased. For example, the deceased's health may have been such as to seriously affect his ability to provide services or work until retirement age. In relation to earnings the starting point for the adjustment factor should be the figures contained in Tables A–D.

(ii) Factors relating to the dependant. For example, at trial it may be proved that a dependant has a significantly reduced life expectancy.

(iii) Factors relating to the relationship of the deceased and the dependant. For example, an unmarried couple who were on the point of separation before the deceased died. See also s.3 (4) of the Act and ***Drew v Abassi***.[21]

63. The assessment of the multiplier involves the following steps:

(1) Determine the expected period from the date of death for which the deceased would have been capable of providing the dependency.

(2) Discount that period for early receipt using the appropriate table as at the date of death and a discount rate of 2.5 per cent.

(3) Apply any adjustment to the above figure to reflect contingencies other than mortality.

[19] [1940] 2 K.B. 658.
[20] [1991] 2 Q.B. 408.
[21] Court of Appeal, May 24, 1995.

(4) Determine the expected period from date of death for which the dependant would have been able to receive the dependency.

(5) Discount that period for early receipt using the appropriate table as at the date of death at a discount rate of 2.5 per cent.

(6) Apply any adjustment to the figure in (5) to reflect contingencies other than mortality.

(7) Take the lower of the figures in (3) and (6) above. That is the overall multiplier from date of death.

(8) Subtract the period elapsed from date of death to date of trial. Losses in this period will be treated as in effect special damages and will attract an award of interest.

(9) The balance of the multiplier will be the multiplier for the post-trial multiplicand.

The actuarially recommended approach

64. Whereas in personal injury cases the problem to be solved is that of setting a value on an income stream during the potential life of one person (the claimant), the situation is generally more complicated in fatal accident cases. Here the compensation is intended to reflect the value of an income stream during the lifetime of one or more dependants of the deceased (or the expected period for which the dependants would have expected to receive the dependency, if shorter) but limited according to the expectation of how long the deceased would have been able to provide the financial support, had he or she not been involved in the fatal accident.

65. In principle, therefore, the compensation for post-trial dependency should be based on the present value at the date of the trial of the dependency during the expected future joint lifetime of the deceased and the dependant or claimant (had the deceased survived naturally to the date of the trial), subject to any limitations on the period of dependency and any expected future changes in the level of dependency, for example, on attaining retirement age. In addition there should be compensation for the period between the date of accident and the date of trial.

66. A set of actuarial tables to make such calculations accurately would require tables similar to Tables 1–26 but for each combination of ages as at the date of the trial of the deceased and the dependant to whom compensation is to be paid. The Working Party concluded that this would not meet the criterion of simplicity of application which was a central objective of these tables and recommends that, in complex cases, or cases where the accuracy of the multiplier is thought by the parties to be of critical importance and material to the resulting amount of compensation (for example, in cases potentially involving very large claims where the level of the multiplicand is unambiguously established), the advice of a professionally qualified actuary should be sought. However, for the majority of cases, a certain amount of approximation will be appropriate, bearing in mind the need for a simple and streamlined process, and taking into consideration the other uncertainties in the determination of an appropriate level of compensation. The following paragraphs describe a methodology using Tables 1–26 which can be expected to yield satisfactory answers.

(i) Damages for the period from the fatal accident to the date of trial

67. The period of pre-trial dependency will normally be equal to the period between the date of the fatal accident and the date of the trial, substituting where appropriate the lower figure of the expected period for which the deceased would have provided the dependency, had he or she not been killed in

the accident, or if the period of dependency would have been limited in some way, for example, if the dependant is a child.

68. A deduction may be made for the risk that the deceased might have died anyway, in the period between the date of the fatal accident and the date at which the trial takes place. In many cases this deduction will be small and could usually be regarded as de minimis. The need for a deduction becomes more necessary the longer the period from the date of accident to the date of trial and the older the deceased at the date of death. As an illustration of the order of magnitude of the deduction, Table E shows some examples of factors by which the multiplier should be multiplied for different ages of the deceased and for different periods from the date of accident to the date of the trial.

Table E
Factor by which pre-trial damages should be multiplied to allow for the likelihood that the deceased would not in any case have survived to provide the dependency for the full period to the date of trial

Age of deceased at date of accident	Period from date of accident to date of trial or date of cessation of dependency, if earlier (years)					
	Male deceased			Female deceased		
	3	6	9	3	6	9
10	1.00	1.00	1.00	1.00	1.00	1.00
20	1.00	1.00	1.00	1.00	1.00	1.00
30	1.00	1.00	0.99	1.00	1.00	1.00
40	1.00	0.99	0.99	1.00	1.00	0.99
50	0.99	0.99	0.98	1.00	0.99	0.99
60	0.99	0.97	0.94	0.99	0.98	0.97
65	0.98	0.95	0.91	0.99	0.97	0.95
70	0.97	0.92	0.86	0.98	0.95	0.91
75	0.94	0.87	0.78	0.96	0.91	0.84
80	0.90	0.79	0.67	0.93	0.84	0.75

N.B. The factor for a period of zero years is clearly 1.00. Factors for other ages and periods not shown in the table may be obtained approximately by interpolation.

69. The resultant multiplier, after application of any discount for the possibility of early death of the deceased before the date of trial, even had the accident not taken place, is to be applied to the multiplicand, which is determined in the usual way. Interest will then be added up to the date of trial on the basis of special damages.

(ii) Damages from the date of trial to retirement age

70. The assessment of the multiplier involves the following steps:

(1) Determine the expected period from the date of the trial for which the deceased would have been able to provide the dependency (see para.71).

(2) Determine the expected period for which the dependant would have been able to receive the dependency (see paras 71 and 72).

(3) Take the lesser of the two periods.

(4) Treat the resulting period as a term certain for which the multiplier is to be determined and look up the figure in Table 28 for this period at the appropriate rate of interest.

(5) Apply any adjustment for contingencies other than mortality in accordance with section B.

(6) If necessary, make an allowance for the risk that the deceased might have died anyway before the date of the trial (see para.73).

71. The expected periods at (1) and (2) of para.70 may be obtained from the 0% column of the appropriate table at the back of this booklet. For (1), Tables 3–14 will be relevant, according to the sex of the deceased and the expected age of retirement. The age at which the table should be entered is the age which the deceased would have been at the date of the trial. For (2), Tables 1 and 2 can be used, according to the sex of the dependant and looking up the table at the age of the dependant at the date of the trial.

72. If the period for which the dependency would have continued is a short fixed period, as in the case of a child, the figure at (2) would be the outstanding period at the date of the trial.

73. A deduction may be made for the risk that the deceased might have died anyway before the date of trial. The need for such a deduction becomes more necessary the longer the period from the date of accident to the date of trial and the older the deceased at the date of death. As an illustration of the order of magnitude of the deduction, Table F shows some examples of the factor by which the multiplier, determined as above, should be multiplied for different ages of the deceased and for different periods from the date of accident to the date of the trial.

Table F
Factor by which post-trial damages should be multiplied to allow for the likelihood that the deceased would not in any case have survived to the date of trial in order to provide any post-trial dependency

Age of deceased at date of accident	Period from date of accident to date of trial (years)					
	Male deceased			Female deceased		
	3	6	9	3	6	9
10	1.00	1.00	1.00	1.00	1.00	1.00
20	1.00	1.00	0.99	1.00	1.00	1.00
30	1.00	0.99	0.99	1.00	1.00	0.99
40	0.99	0.99	0.98	1.00	0.99	0.99
50	0.99	0.97	0.95	0.99	0.98	0.97
60	0.97	0.93	0.88	0.98	0.96	0.92
65	0.96	0.90	0.82	0.97	0.93	0.88
70	0.93	0.84	0.71	0.96	0.89	0.80
75	0.88	0.73	0.55	0.92	0.81	0.66
80	0.83	0.59	0.37	0.86	0.68	0.48

N.B. The factor for a period of zero years is clearly 1.00. Factors for other ages and periods not shown in the table may be obtained approximately by interpolation.

74. The resulting multiplier, after application of any discount for the possibility of early death of the deceased before the date of trial, even had the accident not taken place, is to be applied to the appropriate multiplicand, determined in relation to dependency as assessed for the period up to retirement age.

75. If there are several dependants, to whom damages are to be paid in respect of their own particular lifetime (or for a fixed period of dependency), separate multipliers should be determined for each and multiplied by the appropriate multiplicand using the procedure in paras 70–74. The total amount of damages is then obtained by adding the separate components. If a single multiplicand is determined, but the damages are to be shared among two or more dependants so long as they are each alive, or during a period of common dependency, then the multiplier will be calculated using the procedure in paras 70–74. However, at step (2) of para.70 the expected period will be the longest of the expected periods for which the dependency might last.

(iii) Damages for the period of dependency after retirement age

76. The method described in paras 70–75 for pre-retirement age dependency cannot satisfactorily be applied directly to post-retirement age dependency with a sufficient degree of accuracy. We therefore propose a method which involves determining the multiplier by looking at dependency for the rest of life from the date of trial and then subtracting the multiplier for dependency up to retirement age.

77. The assessment of the multiplier for whole of life dependency involves the following steps:

(1) Determine the expectation of life which the deceased would have had as at the date of trial, or such lesser period for which the deceased would have been able to provide the dependency (see para.78).

(2) Determine the expected period for which the dependant would have been able to receive the dependency (see para.78).

(3) Take the lesser of the two periods.

(4) Treat the resulting period as a term certain for which the multiplier is to be determined and look up the figure in Table 28 for this period at the appropriate rate of interest.

78. The expected periods at (1) and (2) of para.77 may be obtained from the 0% column of the appropriate table at the back of this booklet. For (1), Tables 1 or 2 will be relevant, according to the sex of the deceased. The age at which the table should be entered is the age which the deceased would have attained at the date of the trial. For (2), Tables 1 and 2 can be used, according to the sex of the dependant and looking up the table at the age of the dependant at the date of the trial.

79. Deduct the corresponding multiplier for post-trial pre-retirement dependency, as determined in paras 70–75, but without any adjustment for contingencies other than mortality, or that the deceased may have died anyway before the date of trial. The result is the multiplier for post-retirement dependency, which must then be applied to the appropriate multiplicand, assessed in relation to dependency after retirement age. The adjustment for contingencies other than mortality in respect of the damages for the period of dependency after retirement age will often be less than that required for pre-retirement age damages (see para.30).

80. A deduction may finally be made for the risk that the deceased might have died anyway before the date of trial. The need for such a deduction becomes more necessary the longer the period from the date of accident to the date of trial and the older the deceased at the date of death. As an illustration of the order of magnitude of the deduction, Table F shows some examples of the factor by which the multiplier, determined as above, should be multiplied for different ages of the deceased and for different periods from the date of accident to the date of the trial. The factors for this purpose are exactly the same deductions as used in the calculation at paras 70–75.

81. The layout of paras 70–80 is based on the assumption that the dependency provided by the deceased would have changed at retirement age. This may not be appropriate in some cases, particularly in the important case of the deceased wife and mother whose contribution has been solely in the home or in the case of an adult child caring for an elderly parent or parents. In cases like this, where the deceased might have provided the dependency throughout their lifetime, paras 76–80 should be ignored and paras 70–75 used, with the difference that the expected period required at step (1) of para.70 should be a whole of life expectancy, taken from Tables 1 and 2. This is also the approach to use when the deceased was already a pensioner.

Examples

82. Paragraphs 83 and 84 give calculations of damages awards for Example 7, calculated using first the current approach and then the actuarially recommended approach.

Example 7

83. The dependant is female, aged 38 at the date of the trial, which is taking place three years after the date of the fatal accident which killed her husband, at that time aged 37, on whom she was financially dependent. The deceased had A levels, was in employment and in good health with no disability at the time of the fatal accident. The dependant was, at the date of death, and is at the date of trial, in good health. Their relationship was stable. The court has determined a multiplicand of £30,000 up to the deceased's normal retirement age of 65 with no financial dependency post-age 65, nor any services dependency. The damages are to be calculated as follows:

The current approach

(1) The deceased would have been capable of providing the financial dependency to the dependant for the period of 28 years from the date of his death aged 37 to his 65th birthday.

(2) The appropriate Table is 9. Using the 2.5 per cent column the multiplier = 19.64.

(3) Adjustment factor for contingencies other than mortality (in accordance with section B) for an employed male aged 37 with A levels and who is not disabled = 0.9 to give a multiplier of 19.64 × 0.9 = 17.68.

(4) The expected period for which the dependant would have been able to receive the dependency was between the ages of 35 and 63.

(5) The appropriate Tables are 8 and 10, and using the 2.5 per cent column the multiplier = 19.91.

(6) The parties were married so section 3(4) does not apply. The relationship was stable. The dependant was and is in good health. The court is unlikely to make much of an adjustment to the figure in (5) above to reflect contingencies other than mortality.

(7) The lower of the two figures is that in (3) above, namely 17.68.

(8) The period that has elapsed between date of death and date of trial is three years. The pre-trial loss is therefore £30,000 × 3 = £90,000.

(9) Interest at half rate from date of death to date of trial: three years at 3 per cent a year = 9 per cent.
£90,000 × 9% = £8,100.

(10) The post-trial multiplier is 14.68 (17.68 – 3).

(11) The post trial loss is therefore 14.68 × £30,000 = £440,400.

(12) Total financial dependency is therefore £90,000 + £8,100 + £440,400 = £538,500.

The actuarially recommended approach

84. Applying this approach to Example 7 set out above:

Pre-trial damages:

(1) Period between fatal accident and trial: three years.

(2) Factor for possible early death (Table E for male aged 37 and three years) = 1.00.

(3) Pre-trial damages = 3 × 1.00 × £30,000 = £90,000 (plus interest as special damages).

(4) Interest at half rate from date of death to date of trial: three years at 3 per cent a year = 9 per cent.
£90,000 × 9% = £8,100.

Post-trial damages:

(1) Expected period for which the deceased would have provided the dependency (Table 9 at 0 per cent for male aged 40, the age as at the date of trial): 24.13.

(2) Expected period for which the dependant would have been able to receive the dependency (Table 2 at 0 per cent for female aged 38): 51.38.

(3) Lesser of two periods at (1) and (2) = 24.13.

(4) Multiplier for term certain of 24.13 years at 2.5 per cent rate of return = 18.18.

(5) Adjustment factor for contingencies other than mortality (in accordance with section B) for an employed male aged 40 with A levels and who was not disabled = 0.88 to give a multiplier of 18.18 × 0.88 = 16.00.

(6) Adjustment factor for the risk that the deceased might have died anyway before the date of trial (Table F for male aged 37 and three years): 0.99 to give a multiplier of 16.00 × 0.99 = 15.84.

(7) Post-trial damages = 15.84 × £30,000 = £475,200.

(8) Total financial dependency is therefore £90,000 + £8,100 + £475,200 = £573,300.

85. Examples 8 and 9 in the following paragraphs set out two further examples to show the application of the actuarially recommended approach to more complex examples.

Example 8

86. The dependant is female, aged 50 at the date of the trial, which is taking place four years after the date of the fatal accident which killed the man, at that time aged 47, on whom she was financially dependent. The deceased was in employment at the time of the fatal accident, was not disabled and had achieved A levels. The court has determined a multiplicand, up to the deceased's normal retirement age of 60, of £50,000 and has decided that post-retirement damages should be payable based on a multiplicand of £30,000. The damages are to be calculated as follows:

Pre-trial damages:

(1) Period between fatal accident and trial: four years.

(2) Factor for possible early death (Table E for male aged 47 and four years): 0.99.

(3) Pre-trial damages = 4 × 0.99 × £50,000 = £198,000 (plus interest as special damages).

Post-trial pre-retirement damages:

(1) Expected period for which the deceased would have provided the dependency (Table 7 at 0% for male aged 51, the age as at the date of trial): 8.81.

(2) Expected period for which the dependant would have been able to receive the dependency (Table 2 at 0 per cent for female aged 50): 38.73.

(3) Lesser of two periods at (1) and (2) = 8.81.

(4) Multiplier for term certain of 8.81 years at 2.5 per cent rate of return (interpolating between the values for 8 and 9 in Table 28) = (9 – 8.81) × 7.26 + (8.81 – 8) × 8.07 = 7.92.

(5) Adjustment factor for contingencies other than mortality (in accordance with section B) for an employed male aged 51 with A levels and who was not disabled = 0.82 to give a multiplier of 7.92 × 0.82 = 6.49.

(6) Adjustment factor for the risk that the deceased might have died anyway before the date of trial (Table F for male aged 47 and four years): 0.99 to give a multiplier of 6.49 × 0.99 = 6.43.

(7) Post-trial pre-retirement damages = 6.43 × £50,000 = £321,500.

Post-retirement damages:

(1) Expectation of life of deceased at date of trial (Table 1 at 0 per cent for male aged 51): 34.45.

(2) Expected period for which the dependant would have been able to receive the dependency (Table 2 at 0 per cent for female aged 50): 38.73.

(3) Lesser of two periods at (1) and (2) = 34.45.

(4) Multiplier for term certain of 34.45 years at 2.5 per cent rate of return (interpolating between the values for 34 and 35 in Table 28) = (35 – 34.45) × 23.01 + (34.45 – 34) × 23.43 = 23.20.

(5) Deduct multiplier for post-trial pre-retirement damages before application of adjustment factors for contingencies other than mortality and for the risk that the deceased might have died anyway before the date of trial: 23.20 – 7.92 = 15.28.

(6) Adjustment factor for the risk that the deceased might have died anyway before the date of trial (Table F for male aged 47 and four years): 0.99 to give a multiplier of 15.28 × 0.99 = 15.13.

(7) Post-retirement damages = 15.13 × £30,000 = £453,900.

Example 9

87. There are two dependants, respectively a child aged 10 and a male aged 41 at the date of the trial, which is taking place three years after the date of the fatal accident which killed the woman, at that

time aged 35, on whom both were financially dependent. She had a degree and worked in London for a computer company. The court has determined a multiplicand, up to the deceased's normal retirement age of 62, of £50,000 for the male dependant and £10,000 for the child, up to the age of 21, and has decided that post-retirement damages should be payable based on a multiplicand of £20,000. The damages are to be calculated as follows:

Pre-trial damages:

(1) Period between fatal accident and trial: three years.

(2) Factor for possible early death (Table E for female aged 35 and three years): 1.00.

(3) Pre-trial damages = 3 × 1.00 × (£50,000 + £10,000) = £180,000 (plus interest as special damages).

Post-trial pre-retirement damages:

(1) Expected period for which the deceased would have provided the dependency should be based on female aged 38 at the date of trial with retirement age of 62. First calculate as though deceased were aged 36 and had retirement age of 60 (Table 8 at 0% for female aged 36): 23.66.

Then calculate as though deceased were aged 41 and had retirement age of 65 (Table 10 at 0 per cent for female aged 41): 23.47.

Interpolate for age 38 with retirement age of 62 = (3 × 23.66 + 2 × 23.47)/5 = 23.58.

(2) Expected period for which the male dependant would have been able to receive the dependency (Table 1 at 0 per cent for male aged 41): 44.71.

Expected period for which child would have been able to receive the dependency = 11.00.

(3) Lesser of two periods at (1) and (2) = 11.00 (in case of child)

= 23.58 (in case of man).

(4) Multiplier for term certain of 11 years at 2.5 per cent (Table 28): 9.63.

Multiplier for term certain of 23.58 years at 2.5 per cent rate of return (interpolating between the values for 23 and 24 in Table 28)

= (24 – 23.58) × 17.55 + (23.58 – 23) × 18.11= 17.87.

(5) Adjustment factor for contingencies other than mortality (in accordance with section B) for an employed female aged 38 with a degree and who was not disabled = 0.89 (does not apply to child) to give a multiplier of 17.87 × 0.89 = 15.90.

(6) Adjustment factor for the risk that the deceased might have died anyway before the date of trial (Table F for female aged 35 and three years): 1.00, so multipliers are 9.63 and 15.90 respectively.

(7) Pre-retirement damages = 9.63 × £10,000 + 15.90 × £50,000

= £96,300 + £795,000 = £891,300.

Post-retirement damages:

(1) Expectation of life of deceased at date of trial (Table 2 at 0 per cent for female aged 38): 51.38.

(2) Expected period for which the dependant would have been able to receive the dependency (Table 1 at 0 per cent for male aged 41): 44.71 (no post retirement dependency for child).

(3) Lesser of two periods at (1) and (2) = 44.71.

(4) Multiplier for term certain of 44.71 years at 2.5 per cent rate of return (interpolating between the values for 42 and 43 in Table 28)

$= (45 - 44.71) \times 26.83 + (44.71 - 44) \times 27.17 = 27.07.$

(5) Deduct multiplier for post-trial pre-retirement damages before application of adjustment factors for contingencies other than mortality and for the risk that the deceased might have died anyway before the date of trial: 27.07 – 17.87 = 9.20.

(6) Adjustment factor for the risk that the deceased might have died anyway before the date of trial (Table F for female aged 35 and three years) = 1.00, so multiplier is 9.20 × 1.00 = 9.20.

(7) Post-retirement damages = 9.20 × £20,000 = £184,000.

An Alternative approach

88. If the court wishes to select multipliers from the date of death, it is essential to ensure that the period before the trial does not include a discount for early receipt. This could be achieved by selecting multipliers from the 0% columns of the appropriate tables and then applying the discount for early receipt to the period after the trial (using the discount rate set under s.1 of the Damages Act 1996). The calculation of the multiplier involves the following steps:

(1) Determine the expected period for which the deceased would have provided the dependency at the date of death.

(2) Deduct the period between accidental death and date of trial to give post-trial period.

(3) Determine the expected post-trial period for which the dependant would have been able to receive the dependency.

(4) Take the lesser of two periods at (2) and (3).

(5) Take the multiplier for term certain for the period calculated at (4) at 2.5 per cent rate of return (from Table 28).

(6) Apply any adjustment factor to the figure in (5) to reflect contingencies other than mortality (in accordance with section B). This will give the multiplier for the post-trial multiplicand.

89. Applying this approach to Example 7 set out above:

(1) Expected period for which the deceased would have provided the dependency (Table 9 at 0 per cent for male aged 37, the age as at the date of death): 27.06.

(2) Deduct period between accidental death and date of trial of three years to give post-trial period: 24.06.

(3) Expected post-trial period for which the dependant would have been able to receive the dependency (Table 2 at 0 per cent for female aged 38): 51.38.

(4) Lesser of two periods at (2) and (3) = 24.06.

(5) Multiplier for term certain of 24.06 years at 2.5 per cent rate of return (Table 28) = 18.14.

(6) Adjustment factor for contingencies other than mortality (in accordance with section B) for an employed male aged 37 with A levels and who was not disabled = 0.90 to give a multiplier of 18.14 × 0.90 = 16.33.

(7) Pre-trial damages = 3 × £30,000 = £90,000 (plus interest as special damages of £8,100).

(8) Post-trial damages = 16.33 × £30,000 = £489,900.

(9) Total financial dependency therefore £90,000 + £8,100 + £489,900 = £588,000.

90. As can be seen, the three methodologies (the current approach, the actuarially recommended approach and this alternative approach) give three different amounts of damages in relation to Example 7, namely £538,500 for the current approach used by the courts, £573,300 using the actuarially recommended approach, and £588,000 using this alternative approach. The size of the disparities between the three methods depends on the length of the period between the date of death and the date of trial; if the example had assumed a period of six years then the differences would have been greater.

Section E: Concluding remarks

91. These tables are designed to assist the courts to arrive at suitable multipliers in a range of possible situations. However, they do not cover all possibilities and in more complex situations, such as where there are significant pension rights, advice should be sought from a Fellow of the Institute and Faculty of Actuaries.

GEORGE RUSSELL FIA
Deputy Government Actuary
London
August 2012

Table 1: Multipliers for pecuniary loss for life (males)

Age at date of trial	Multiplier calculated with allowance for projected mortality from the 2008–based population projections and rate of return of											Age at date of trial
	–2.0%	***–1.5%***	***–1.0%***	***–0.5%***	***0.0%***	***0.5%***	***1.0%***	***1.5%***	***2.0%***	***2.5%***	***3.0%***	
0	264.76	195.32	147.14	113.22	88.96	71.35	58.34	48.60	41.17	35.41	30.89	0
1	259.11	191.95	145.15	112.06	88.31	71.00	58.18	48.54	41.18	35.46	30.96	1
2	252.28	187.68	142.46	110.35	87.22	70.30	57.73	48.24	40.98	35.33	30.87	2
3	245.58	183.46	139.78	108.64	86.12	69.58	57.26	47.94	40.78	35.19	30.78	3
4	239.02	179.29	137.12	106.93	85.01	68.86	56.78	47.62	40.56	35.05	30.68	4
5	232.59	175.19	134.48	105.22	83.89	68.12	56.30	47.29	40.34	34.90	30.58	5
6	226.29	171.15	131.87	103.52	82.78	67.39	55.80	46.96	40.12	34.75	30.47	6
7	220.14	167.18	129.29	101.83	81.66	66.65	55.31	46.63	39.89	34.59	30.36	7
8	214.13	163.28	126.74	100.15	80.55	65.90	54.80	46.28	39.65	34.42	30.24	8
9	208.23	159.43	124.21	98.48	79.43	65.15	54.29	45.93	39.41	34.25	30.13	9
10	202.47	155.64	121.71	96.81	78.31	64.39	53.78	45.58	39.16	34.08	30.00	10
11	196.83	151.92	119.23	95.15	77.19	63.63	53.25	45.22	38.91	33.90	29.87	11
12	191.33	148.26	116.79	93.50	76.07	62.86	52.72	44.85	38.65	33.72	29.74	12
13	185.95	144.67	114.37	91.87	74.96	62.09	52.19	44.47	38.39	33.53	29.61	13
14	180.69	141.14	111.98	90.24	73.84	61.32	51.65	44.10	38.12	33.34	29.47	14
15	175.56	137.67	109.62	88.63	72.73	60.55	51.11	43.71	37.84	33.14	29.32	15
16	170.55	134.27	107.30	87.02	71.61	59.77	50.56	43.32	37.57	32.94	29.17	16
17	165.66	130.93	105.00	85.44	70.51	58.99	50.01	42.93	37.28	32.73	29.02	17
18	160.89	127.66	102.74	83.86	69.41	58.22	49.46	42.53	37.00	32.52	28.87	18
19	156.25	124.45	100.52	82.31	68.31	57.44	48.91	42.14	36.71	32.31	28.71	19
20	151.72	121.31	98.32	80.76	67.22	56.66	48.35	41.73	36.41	32.10	28.55	20
21	147.28	118.22	96.15	79.23	66.13	55.88	47.78	41.32	36.11	31.87	28.39	21
22	142.94	115.17	94.00	77.70	65.04	55.09	47.21	40.90	35.81	31.64	28.22	22
23	138.69	112.17	91.87	76.18	63.94	54.30	46.63	40.48	35.49	31.41	28.04	23
24	134.54	109.22	89.77	74.67	62.85	53.51	46.05	40.05	35.17	31.17	27.86	24
25	130.49	106.33	87.69	73.17	61.76	52.71	45.46	39.61	34.85	30.92	27.67	25
26	126.54	103.50	85.65	71.69	60.68	51.91	44.87	39.17	34.51	30.67	27.48	26
27	122.69	100.72	83.63	70.22	59.59	51.11	44.28	38.73	34.18	30.42	27.28	27
28	118.90	97.98	81.63	68.74	58.51	50.30	43.67	38.27	33.83	30.15	27.08	28
29	115.20	95.28	79.64	67.28	57.42	49.49	43.06	37.81	33.48	29.88	26.87	29
30	111.59	92.63	77.69	65.83	56.34	48.68	42.45	37.34	33.12	29.60	26.65	30
31	108.09	90.04	75.78	64.40	55.27	47.87	41.83	36.87	32.76	29.32	26.44	31
32	104.68	87.52	73.89	62.99	54.20	47.06	41.22	36.40	32.39	29.04	26.21	32
33	101.36	85.04	72.04	61.60	53.15	46.26	40.60	35.92	32.02	28.75	25.99	33
34	98.10	82.61	70.21	60.21	52.09	45.45	39.98	35.44	31.65	28.46	25.75	34
35	94.92	80.21	68.39	58.83	51.03	44.63	39.35	34.95	31.26	28.15	25.51	35
36	91.82	77.86	66.60	57.46	49.98	43.82	38.71	34.45	30.87	27.84	25.27	36
37	88.78	75.55	64.83	56.10	48.93	43.00	38.07	33.95	30.47	27.53	25.01	37
38	85.81	73.27	63.08	54.74	47.87	42.18	37.42	33.44	30.06	27.20	24.75	38
39	82.89	71.03	61.35	53.39	46.82	41.35	36.77	32.91	29.65	26.86	24.48	39
40	80.05	68.83	59.63	52.05	45.76	40.51	36.11	32.39	29.22	26.52	24.20	40
41	77.27	66.67	57.94	50.72	44.71	39.68	35.44	31.85	28.79	26.17	23.91	41
42	74.56	64.55	56.28	49.41	43.67	38.84	34.77	31.31	28.35	25.81	23.62	42
43	71.92	62.47	54.63	48.10	42.62	38.01	34.10	30.76	27.91	25.45	23.32	43
44	69.34	60.43	53.01	46.81	41.59	37.17	33.42	30.21	27.45	25.08	23.01	44
45	66.82	58.43	51.41	45.52	40.55	36.33	32.73	29.65	26.99	24.70	22.69	45
46	64.36	56.46	49.83	44.25	39.52	35.49	32.05	29.08	26.53	24.31	22.37	46
47	61.96	54.53	48.28	42.99	38.49	34.65	31.35	28.51	26.05	23.91	22.04	47
48	59.63	52.64	46.74	41.74	37.47	33.81	30.66	27.94	25.57	23.51	21.70	48
49	57.35	50.79	45.24	40.50	36.45	32.97	29.97	27.36	25.09	23.10	21.36	49
50	55.14	48.99	43.76	39.29	35.45	32.14	29.27	26.78	24.60	22.69	21.01	50
51	52.99	47.23	42.31	38.09	34.45	31.31	28.58	26.19	24.11	22.27	20.65	51
52	50.90	45.51	40.89	36.91	33.47	30.48	27.88	25.61	23.61	21.85	20.29	52
53	48.87	43.83	39.49	35.74	32.49	29.67	27.19	25.02	23.11	21.42	19.92	53
54	46.90	42.19	38.12	34.60	31.53	28.85	26.50	24.43	22.61	20.99	19.55	54

Table 1: Multipliers for pecuniary loss for life (males) *continued*

Age at date of trial	Multiplier calculated with allowance for projected mortality from the 2008–based population projections and rate of return of											Age at date of trial
	–2.0%	***–1.5%***	***–1.0%***	***–0.5%***	***0.0%***	***0.5%***	***1.0%***	***1.5%***	***2.0%***	***2.5%***	***3.0%***	
55	44.99	40.60	36.79	33.47	30.58	28.04	25.81	23.85	22.11	20.56	19.18	55
56	43.15	39.04	35.48	32.37	29.64	27.25	25.13	23.26	21.60	20.12	18.80	56
57	41.35	37.53	34.19	31.28	28.71	26.45	24.45	22.67	21.09	19.68	18.42	57
58	39.59	36.04	32.93	30.19	27.78	25.65	23.76	22.08	20.58	19.23	18.02	58
59	37.87	34.57	31.67	29.11	26.85	24.85	23.07	21.47	20.05	18.77	17.62	59
60	36.17	33.12	30.42	28.04	25.92	24.04	22.36	20.86	19.51	18.30	17.20	60
61	34.52	31.69	29.19	26.97	25.00	23.23	21.65	20.24	18.96	17.81	16.77	61
62	32.91	30.30	27.98	25.92	24.08	22.43	20.95	19.62	18.41	17.33	16.34	62
63	31.36	28.95	26.80	24.89	23.17	21.63	20.25	19.00	17.86	16.84	15.90	63
64	29.85	27.63	25.65	23.88	22.28	20.85	19.55	18.38	17.31	16.35	15.47	64
65	28.40	26.37	24.54	22.90	21.42	20.08	18.87	17.77	16.77	15.86	15.03	65
66	27.02	25.14	23.46	21.94	20.57	19.33	18.20	17.17	16.24	15.38	14.60	66
67	25.68	23.96	22.41	21.01	19.74	18.59	17.54	16.58	15.70	14.90	14.16	67
68	24.38	22.81	21.39	20.10	18.93	17.86	16.88	15.99	15.17	14.42	13.73	68
69	23.13	21.69	20.39	19.21	18.12	17.14	16.23	15.40	14.64	13.93	13.29	69
70	21.91	20.60	19.41	18.32	17.32	16.41	15.58	14.81	14.10	13.44	12.84	70
71	20.70	19.52	18.43	17.44	16.53	15.69	14.92	14.21	13.55	12.94	12.38	71
72	19.52	18.44	17.46	16.56	15.72	14.96	14.25	13.60	12.99	12.43	11.91	72
73	18.34	17.38	16.49	15.67	14.92	14.22	13.57	12.97	12.42	11.90	11.42	73
74	17.18	16.32	15.52	14.79	14.10	13.47	12.89	12.34	11.83	11.36	10.92	74
75	16.04	15.27	14.56	13.90	13.29	12.72	12.19	11.70	11.24	10.81	10.40	75
76	14.93	14.25	13.62	13.03	12.48	11.97	11.50	11.05	10.64	10.25	9.88	76
77	13.86	13.26	12.70	12.18	11.70	11.24	10.82	10.42	10.05	9.69	9.36	77
78	12.83	12.31	11.82	11.36	10.93	10.53	10.15	9.79	9.46	9.15	8.85	78
79	11.86	11.40	10.97	10.57	10.19	9.84	9.50	9.19	8.89	8.61	8.34	79
80	10.94	10.55	10.17	9.82	9.49	9.18	8.88	8.60	8.34	8.09	7.85	80
81	10.10	9.75	9.43	9.12	8.83	8.56	8.30	8.05	7.82	7.60	7.38	81
82	9.33	9.03	8.74	8.47	8.22	7.98	7.75	7.53	7.33	7.13	6.94	82
83	8.62	8.36	8.11	7.88	7.65	7.44	7.24	7.05	6.87	6.69	6.53	83
84	7.97	7.74	7.53	7.32	7.13	6.94	6.76	6.59	6.43	6.28	6.13	84
85	7.36	7.16	6.98	6.80	6.63	6.47	6.31	6.16	6.02	5.88	5.75	85
86	6.79	6.62	6.46	6.31	6.16	6.02	5.88	5.75	5.62	5.50	5.39	86
87	6.25	6.11	5.97	5.83	5.71	5.58	5.46	5.35	5.24	5.14	5.04	87
88	5.74	5.62	5.50	5.38	5.27	5.16	5.06	4.96	4.87	4.78	4.69	88
89	5.26	5.15	5.05	4.95	4.86	4.76	4.68	4.59	4.51	4.43	4.35	89
90	4.81	4.72	4.64	4.55	4.47	4.39	4.31	4.24	4.17	4.10	4.03	90
91	4.40	4.32	4.25	4.17	4.10	4.04	3.97	3.91	3.85	3.79	3.73	91
92	4.01	3.94	3.88	3.82	3.76	3.70	3.65	3.59	3.54	3.49	3.44	92
93	3.65	3.59	3.54	3.49	3.44	3.39	3.34	3.30	3.25	3.21	3.17	93
94	3.33	3.29	3.24	3.20	3.16	3.11	3.07	3.03	2.99	2.96	2.92	94
95	3.06	3.02	2.98	2.94	2.91	2.87	2.84	2.80	2.77	2.74	2.71	95
96	2.83	2.79	2.76	2.72	2.69	2.66	2.63	2.60	2.57	2.54	2.52	96
97	2.62	2.59	2.56	2.53	2.50	2.48	2.45	2.42	2.40	2.37	2.35	97
98	2.44	2.41	2.38	2.36	2.34	2.31	2.29	2.27	2.24	2.22	2.20	98
99	2.27	2.25	2.22	2.20	2.18	2.16	2.14	2.12	2.10	2.08	2.06	99
100	2.11	2.09	2.07	2.06	2.04	2.02	2.00	1.98	1.97	1.95	1.93	100

Table 2: Multipliers for pecuniary loss for life (females)

Age at date of trial	Multiplier calculated with allowance for projected mortality from the 2008–based population projections and rate of return of											Age at date of trial
	–2.0%	***–1.5%***	***–1.0%***	***–0.5%***	***0.0%***	***0.5%***	***1.0%***	***1.5%***	***2.0%***	***2.5%***	***3.0%***	
0	285.20	208.39	155.57	118.70	92.57	73.74	59.95	49.69	41.92	35.94	31.26	0
1	279.01	204.72	153.41	117.45	91.86	73.36	59.76	49.62	41.91	35.97	31.32	1
2	271.81	200.28	150.65	115.73	90.77	72.67	59.33	49.34	41.73	35.86	31.24	2
3	264.75	195.89	147.91	114.00	89.68	71.97	58.88	49.05	41.55	35.73	31.16	3
4	257.83	191.56	145.19	112.28	88.58	71.27	58.43	48.75	41.35	35.60	31.08	4
5	251.06	187.30	142.49	110.56	87.49	70.56	57.97	48.45	41.15	35.47	30.99	5
6	244.43	183.11	139.83	108.85	86.38	69.85	57.50	48.14	40.95	35.34	30.89	6
7	237.94	178.98	137.18	107.15	85.28	69.13	57.03	47.83	40.74	35.19	30.80	7
8	231.59	174.92	134.57	105.46	84.18	68.40	56.55	47.51	40.52	35.05	30.70	8
9	225.38	170.93	131.98	103.77	83.07	67.67	56.06	47.18	40.30	34.90	30.60	9
10	219.31	167.00	129.43	102.10	81.97	66.94	55.57	46.85	40.08	34.75	30.49	10
11	213.37	163.14	126.90	100.43	80.86	66.20	55.07	46.52	39.85	34.59	30.38	11
12	207.57	159.34	124.40	98.78	79.76	65.46	54.57	46.18	39.62	34.42	30.27	12
13	201.89	155.60	121.92	97.13	78.65	64.71	54.07	45.83	39.38	34.26	30.15	13
14	196.33	151.93	119.48	95.49	77.55	63.96	53.55	45.47	39.13	34.09	30.03	14
15	190.91	148.32	117.06	93.86	76.44	63.21	53.03	45.12	38.88	33.91	29.90	15
16	185.61	144.77	114.67	92.25	75.34	62.45	52.51	44.75	38.62	33.73	29.77	16
17	180.42	141.28	112.31	90.64	74.24	61.70	51.99	44.38	38.37	33.55	29.64	17
18	175.36	137.86	109.98	89.05	73.14	60.94	51.46	44.01	38.10	33.36	29.51	18
19	170.42	134.50	107.68	87.46	72.05	60.17	50.92	43.63	37.83	33.16	29.37	19
20	165.60	131.20	105.42	85.89	70.96	59.41	50.38	43.25	37.56	32.97	29.22	20
21	160.88	127.95	103.17	84.33	69.86	58.64	49.84	42.86	37.28	32.76	29.08	21
22	156.26	124.76	100.95	82.78	68.77	57.86	49.28	42.47	36.99	32.56	28.92	22
23	151.72	121.60	98.74	81.22	67.67	57.08	48.72	42.06	36.70	32.34	28.76	23
24	147.29	118.50	96.56	79.68	66.57	56.29	48.16	41.65	36.40	32.12	28.60	24
25	142.97	115.46	94.41	78.15	65.48	55.50	47.58	41.23	36.09	31.89	28.43	25
26	138.74	112.47	92.28	76.63	64.38	54.71	47.01	40.81	35.78	31.66	28.26	26
27	134.61	109.53	90.18	75.12	63.29	53.92	46.43	40.38	35.46	31.42	28.08	27
28	130.57	106.65	88.11	73.62	62.20	53.12	45.84	39.95	35.14	31.18	27.90	28
29	126.63	103.81	86.05	72.13	61.11	52.32	45.25	39.51	34.81	30.93	27.71	29
30	122.78	101.02	84.03	70.65	60.02	51.52	44.65	39.06	34.47	30.68	27.51	30
31	119.02	98.29	82.03	69.18	58.94	50.71	44.05	38.61	34.13	30.41	27.31	31
32	115.34	95.60	80.06	67.72	57.86	49.90	43.44	38.15	33.78	30.15	27.11	32
33	111.75	92.97	78.11	66.27	56.77	49.09	42.83	37.68	33.42	29.87	26.89	33
34	108.24	90.37	76.18	64.83	55.69	48.27	42.21	37.21	33.06	29.59	26.67	34
35	104.80	87.81	74.27	63.40	54.61	47.45	41.58	36.73	32.69	29.31	26.45	35
36	101.45	85.31	72.39	61.98	53.53	46.63	40.95	36.24	32.31	29.01	26.22	36
37	98.17	82.84	70.53	60.57	52.46	45.81	40.31	35.75	31.93	28.71	25.98	37
38	94.97	80.42	68.69	59.17	51.38	44.98	39.67	35.25	31.54	28.40	25.74	38
39	91.83	78.04	66.88	57.78	50.31	44.15	39.03	34.74	31.14	28.09	25.48	39
40	88.77	75.71	65.08	56.39	49.24	43.31	38.37	34.23	30.73	27.76	25.23	40
41	85.78	73.41	63.31	55.02	48.17	42.48	37.71	33.71	30.32	27.43	24.96	41
42	82.86	71.16	61.56	53.66	47.10	41.64	37.05	33.18	29.90	27.09	24.69	42
43	80.01	68.94	59.84	52.31	46.04	40.80	36.38	32.65	29.47	26.75	24.41	43
44	77.23	66.77	58.14	50.97	44.98	39.95	35.71	32.11	29.03	26.39	24.12	44
45	74.52	64.65	56.46	49.64	43.93	39.11	35.03	31.56	28.59	26.03	23.82	45
46	71.87	62.56	54.81	48.32	42.87	38.27	34.35	31.01	28.14	25.67	23.52	46
47	69.28	60.51	53.17	47.02	41.83	37.42	33.67	30.45	27.69	25.29	23.21	47
48	66.77	58.50	51.57	45.73	40.79	36.58	32.98	29.89	27.23	24.91	22.90	48
49	64.32	56.54	50.00	44.46	39.76	35.74	32.30	29.33	26.76	24.53	22.58	49
50	61.93	54.62	48.44	43.20	38.73	34.90	31.61	28.76	26.29	24.14	22.25	50
51	59.60	52.73	46.91	41.95	37.71	34.06	30.91	28.19	25.81	23.74	21.92	51
52	57.33	50.88	45.40	40.71	36.69	33.22	30.22	27.61	25.33	23.33	21.57	52
53	55.11	49.07	43.92	39.49	35.68	32.38	29.52	27.02	24.84	22.92	21.22	53
54	52.96	47.30	42.46	38.28	34.68	31.55	28.82	26.44	24.34	22.50	20.87	54

Table 2: Multipliers for pecuniary loss for life (females) *continued*

Age at date of trial	Multiplier calculated with allowance for projected mortality from the 2008–based population projections and rate of return of											Age at date of trial
	-2.0%	**-1.5%**	**-1.0%**	**-0.5%**	**0.0%**	**0.5%**	**1.0%**	**1.5%**	**2.0%**	**2.5%**	**3.0%**	
55	50.86	45.57	41.02	37.09	33.68	30.71	28.12	25.84	23.84	22.07	20.51	55
56	48.83	43.88	39.61	35.91	32.69	29.88	27.42	25.25	23.34	21.64	20.14	56
57	46.84	42.22	38.23	34.75	31.71	29.05	26.72	24.65	22.83	21.21	19.76	57
58	44.89	40.60	36.86	33.59	30.74	28.22	26.01	24.05	22.31	20.76	19.37	58
59	42.99	38.99	35.50	32.44	29.76	27.39	25.29	23.43	21.78	20.30	18.98	59
60	41.12	37.41	34.16	31.30	28.78	26.55	24.57	22.81	21.24	19.83	18.57	60
61	39.30	35.86	32.83	30.16	27.80	25.70	23.84	22.18	20.69	19.35	18.15	61
62	37.52	34.33	31.52	29.03	26.83	24.86	23.11	21.54	20.13	18.86	17.72	62
63	35.79	32.84	30.24	27.92	25.86	24.02	22.38	20.90	19.57	18.37	17.28	63
64	34.11	31.39	28.98	26.83	24.91	23.19	21.65	20.26	19.01	17.87	16.84	64
65	32.50	29.99	27.76	25.77	23.98	22.38	20.93	19.63	18.45	17.38	16.40	65
66	30.94	28.64	26.58	24.73	23.07	21.58	20.23	19.00	17.89	16.88	15.96	66
67	29.44	27.32	25.43	23.72	22.18	20.78	19.52	18.38	17.34	16.39	15.52	67
68	27.99	26.05	24.30	22.72	21.29	20.00	18.83	17.76	16.78	15.89	15.07	68
69	26.57	24.80	23.19	21.74	20.42	19.22	18.13	17.13	16.22	15.39	14.62	69
70	25.19	23.57	22.10	20.76	19.55	18.44	17.43	16.50	15.65	14.87	14.15	70
71	23.83	22.35	21.01	19.79	18.67	17.65	16.72	15.86	15.07	14.35	13.68	71
72	22.47	21.14	19.92	18.81	17.79	16.85	16.00	15.20	14.48	13.80	13.18	72
73	21.13	19.93	18.83	17.82	16.89	16.04	15.25	14.53	13.86	13.24	12.66	73
74	19.80	18.72	17.73	16.82	15.99	15.21	14.50	13.84	13.23	12.66	12.13	74
75	18.48	17.53	16.64	15.83	15.08	14.38	13.74	13.14	12.58	12.06	11.58	75
76	17.20	16.35	15.57	14.84	14.17	13.55	12.97	12.43	11.92	11.45	11.01	76
77	15.95	15.21	14.51	13.87	13.28	12.72	12.20	11.72	11.27	10.84	10.45	77
78	14.75	14.10	13.50	12.93	12.40	11.91	11.45	11.02	10.62	10.24	9.88	78
79	13.62	13.05	12.52	12.03	11.56	11.13	10.72	10.34	9.98	9.64	9.32	79
80	12.56	12.07	11.61	11.17	10.77	10.38	10.02	9.69	9.37	9.07	8.78	80
81	11.58	11.15	10.75	10.37	10.02	9.68	9.36	9.06	8.78	8.51	8.26	81
82	10.67	10.30	9.95	9.62	9.31	9.02	8.74	8.48	8.23	7.99	7.76	82
83	9.83	9.51	9.21	8.92	8.65	8.39	8.15	7.92	7.70	7.49	7.29	83
84	9.06	8.78	8.52	8.27	8.03	7.81	7.59	7.39	7.19	7.01	6.83	84
85	8.34	8.10	7.87	7.65	7.45	7.25	7.06	6.88	6.71	6.55	6.40	85
86	7.66	7.45	7.25	7.07	6.89	6.72	6.56	6.40	6.25	6.11	5.97	86
87	7.01	6.84	6.67	6.51	6.36	6.21	6.07	5.93	5.80	5.68	5.56	87
88	6.41	6.26	6.11	5.98	5.85	5.72	5.60	5.48	5.37	5.26	5.16	88
89	5.84	5.71	5.59	5.47	5.36	5.25	5.15	5.05	4.95	4.86	4.77	89
90	5.31	5.20	5.10	5.00	4.90	4.81	4.72	4.64	4.55	4.47	4.40	90
91	4.82	4.73	4.64	4.55	4.47	4.40	4.32	4.25	4.18	4.11	4.04	91
92	4.37	4.29	4.22	4.15	4.08	4.01	3.95	3.89	3.83	3.77	3.71	92
93	3.97	3.90	3.84	3.78	3.72	3.67	3.61	3.56	3.51	3.46	3.41	93
94	3.62	3.56	3.51	3.46	3.41	3.36	3.31	3.27	3.22	3.18	3.14	94
95	3.32	3.27	3.23	3.18	3.14	3.10	3.06	3.02	2.98	2.94	2.91	95
96	3.06	3.02	2.98	2.94	2.91	2.87	2.84	2.80	2.77	2.74	2.71	96
97	2.84	2.80	2.77	2.74	2.70	2.67	2.64	2.61	2.58	2.56	2.53	97
98	2.64	2.61	2.58	2.55	2.52	2.49	2.47	2.44	2.42	2.39	2.37	98
99	2.45	2.42	2.40	2.37	2.35	2.32	2.30	2.28	2.26	2.23	2.21	99
100	2.27	2.25	2.22	2.20	2.18	2.16	2.14	2.12	2.10	2.08	2.06	100

Table 3: Multipliers for loss of earnings to pension age 50 (males)

Age at date of trial	Multiplier calculated with allowance for projected mortality from the 2008–based population projections and rate of return of											Age at date of trial
	–2.0%	***–1.5%***	***–1.0%***	***–0.5%***	***0.0%***	***0.5%***	***1.0%***	***1.5%***	***2.0%***	***2.5%***	***3.0%***	
16	48.26	43.90	40.05	36.65	33.63	30.94	28.55	26.42	24.51	22.80	21.26	16
17	46.31	42.26	38.66	35.47	32.63	30.10	27.84	25.81	24.00	22.36	20.89	17
18	44.40	40.64	37.29	34.30	31.64	29.25	27.12	25.20	23.47	21.91	20.51	18
19	42.54	39.04	35.93	33.14	30.65	28.41	26.39	24.57	22.94	21.45	20.11	19
20	40.71	37.48	34.58	31.99	29.66	27.55	25.66	23.94	22.39	20.99	19.71	20
21	38.91	35.93	33.25	30.84	28.66	26.70	24.92	23.30	21.84	20.50	19.29	21
22	37.16	34.41	31.94	29.70	27.67	25.84	24.17	22.65	21.27	20.01	18.86	22
23	35.44	32.92	30.63	28.56	26.68	24.97	23.41	21.99	20.69	19.51	18.42	23
24	33.75	31.44	29.34	27.43	25.69	24.10	22.65	21.32	20.11	18.99	17.96	24
25	32.10	29.99	28.06	26.31	24.70	23.23	21.88	20.65	19.51	18.46	17.49	25
26	30.48	28.56	26.80	25.19	23.71	22.36	21.11	19.96	18.90	17.92	17.01	26
27	28.89	27.15	25.55	24.08	22.72	21.47	20.32	19.26	18.27	17.36	16.52	27
28	27.34	25.76	24.31	22.97	21.73	20.59	19.53	18.55	17.64	16.79	16.00	28
29	25.81	24.40	23.08	21.87	20.74	19.70	18.73	17.83	16.99	16.21	15.48	29
30	24.32	23.05	21.87	20.78	19.76	18.81	17.92	17.10	16.33	15.61	14.94	30
31	22.86	21.73	20.67	19.69	18.77	17.91	17.11	16.36	15.66	15.00	14.38	31
32	21.43	20.43	19.49	18.61	17.78	17.01	16.29	15.61	14.97	14.37	13.81	32
33	20.03	19.15	18.31	17.53	16.80	16.11	15.46	14.85	14.28	13.73	13.22	33
34	18.66	17.88	17.15	16.47	15.82	15.20	14.63	14.08	13.57	13.08	12.62	34
35	17.31	16.64	16.00	15.40	14.83	14.29	13.78	13.30	12.84	12.41	11.99	35
36	16.00	15.42	14.87	14.34	13.85	13.38	12.93	12.51	12.10	11.72	11.35	36
37	14.70	14.21	13.74	13.29	12.86	12.46	12.07	11.70	11.35	11.01	10.69	37
38	13.44	13.02	12.62	12.24	11.88	11.53	11.20	10.88	10.58	10.29	10.01	38
39	12.19	11.85	11.52	11.20	10.89	10.60	10.32	10.05	9.79	9.54	9.31	39
40	10.98	10.69	10.42	10.16	9.91	9.67	9.43	9.21	8.99	8.78	8.58	40
41	9.78	9.55	9.34	9.13	8.92	8.72	8.53	8.35	8.17	8.00	7.84	41
42	8.61	8.43	8.26	8.10	7.93	7.78	7.63	7.48	7.34	7.20	7.07	42
43	7.46	7.33	7.20	7.07	6.95	6.83	6.71	6.60	6.49	6.38	6.28	43
44	6.33	6.24	6.14	6.05	5.96	5.87	5.78	5.70	5.62	5.54	5.46	44
45	5.23	5.16	5.10	5.03	4.97	4.91	4.85	4.79	4.73	4.68	4.62	45
46	4.14	4.10	4.06	4.02	3.98	3.94	3.90	3.86	3.83	3.79	3.75	46
47	3.08	3.06	3.03	3.01	2.99	2.97	2.94	2.92	2.90	2.88	2.86	47
48	2.03	2.02	2.01	2.00	1.99	1.98	1.97	1.96	1.96	1.95	1.94	48
49	1.01	1.01	1.00	1.00	1.00	1.00	0.99	0.99	0.99	0.99	0.98	49

Table 4: Multipliers for loss of earnings to pension age 50 (females)

Age at date of trial	Multiplier calculated with allowance for projected mortality from the 2008–based population projections and rate of return of											Age at date of trial
	–2.0%	***–1.5%***	***–1.0%***	***–0.5%***	***0.0%***	***0.5%***	***1.0%***	***1.5%***	***2.0%***	***2.5%***	***3.0%***	
16	48.58	44.19	40.30	36.87	33.82	31.12	28.71	26.56	24.63	22.91	21.36	16
17	46.62	42.53	38.91	35.69	32.82	30.27	27.99	25.95	24.12	22.47	20.99	17
18	44.71	40.91	37.53	34.52	31.83	29.42	27.27	25.33	23.59	22.02	20.60	18
19	42.83	39.30	36.16	33.35	30.83	28.57	26.54	24.71	23.06	21.56	20.21	19
20	40.98	37.73	34.81	32.19	29.83	27.72	25.80	24.08	22.51	21.09	19.80	20
21	39.18	36.17	33.47	31.03	28.84	26.85	25.06	23.43	21.96	20.61	19.39	21
22	37.41	34.64	32.14	29.89	27.84	25.99	24.31	22.78	21.39	20.12	18.96	22
23	35.68	33.13	30.83	28.74	26.85	25.12	23.55	22.12	20.81	19.61	18.51	23
24	33.98	31.65	29.53	27.60	25.85	24.25	22.78	21.44	20.22	19.09	18.06	24
25	32.31	30.18	28.24	26.47	24.85	23.37	22.01	20.76	19.61	18.56	17.59	25
26	30.68	28.74	26.97	25.35	23.86	22.49	21.23	20.07	19.00	18.01	17.10	26
27	29.08	27.33	25.71	24.23	22.86	21.60	20.44	19.37	18.37	17.45	16.60	27
28	27.52	25.93	24.46	23.11	21.87	20.71	19.64	18.65	17.74	16.88	16.09	28
29	25.98	24.55	23.23	22.01	20.87	19.82	18.84	17.93	17.08	16.30	15.56	29
30	24.48	23.20	22.01	20.90	19.88	18.92	18.03	17.20	16.42	15.70	15.02	30
31	23.01	21.86	20.80	19.81	18.88	18.02	17.21	16.45	15.74	15.08	14.46	31
32	21.56	20.55	19.60	18.72	17.89	17.11	16.38	15.70	15.05	14.45	13.88	32
33	20.15	19.26	18.42	17.63	16.89	16.20	15.55	14.93	14.35	13.80	13.29	33
34	18.76	17.98	17.25	16.55	15.90	15.28	14.70	14.15	13.63	13.14	12.68	34
35	17.41	16.73	16.09	15.48	14.91	14.37	13.85	13.36	12.90	12.46	12.05	35
36	16.08	15.49	14.94	14.41	13.92	13.44	12.99	12.56	12.16	11.77	11.40	36
37	14.77	14.28	13.80	13.35	12.92	12.51	12.12	11.75	11.40	11.06	10.73	37
38	13.50	13.08	12.68	12.30	11.93	11.58	11.25	10.93	10.62	10.33	10.05	38
39	12.25	11.90	11.56	11.24	10.94	10.64	10.36	10.09	9.83	9.58	9.34	39
40	11.02	10.73	10.46	10.20	9.95	9.70	9.47	9.24	9.02	8.82	8.61	40
41	9.82	9.59	9.37	9.16	8.95	8.76	8.56	8.38	8.20	8.03	7.86	41
42	8.64	8.46	8.29	8.12	7.96	7.80	7.65	7.51	7.36	7.22	7.09	42
43	7.48	7.35	7.22	7.09	6.97	6.85	6.73	6.62	6.51	6.40	6.29	43
44	6.35	6.25	6.16	6.06	5.97	5.89	5.80	5.72	5.63	5.55	5.48	44
45	5.24	5.17	5.11	5.04	4.98	4.92	4.86	4.80	4.74	4.69	4.63	45
46	4.15	4.11	4.07	4.03	3.99	3.95	3.91	3.87	3.83	3.80	3.76	46
47	3.08	3.06	3.04	3.01	2.99	2.97	2.95	2.93	2.90	2.88	2.86	47
48	2.04	2.03	2.02	2.01	2.00	1.99	1.98	1.97	1.96	1.95	1.94	48
49	1.01	1.01	1.00	1.00	1.00	1.00	0.99	0.99	0.99	0.99	0.98	49

Table 5: Multipliers for loss of earnings to pension age 55 (males)

Age at date of trial	Multiplier calculated with allowance for projected mortality from the 2008–based population projections and rate of return of											Age at date of trial
	–2.0%	***–1.5%***	***–1.0%***	***–0.5%***	***0.0%***	***0.5%***	***1.0%***	***1.5%***	***2.0%***	***2.5%***	***3.0%***	
16	58.33	52.26	47.00	42.43	38.44	34.96	31.90	29.22	26.85	24.76	22.90	16
17	56.17	50.49	45.54	41.22	37.44	34.13	31.22	28.65	26.38	24.37	22.58	17
18	54.07	48.74	44.09	40.02	36.45	33.30	30.53	28.08	25.90	23.97	22.24	18
19	52.00	47.03	42.67	38.83	35.46	32.48	29.84	27.50	25.42	23.56	21.90	19
20	49.99	45.34	41.26	37.65	34.47	31.65	29.14	26.91	24.92	23.14	21.55	20
21	48.01	43.68	39.86	36.48	33.48	30.81	28.44	26.31	24.42	22.72	21.19	21
22	46.07	42.04	38.47	35.31	32.49	29.97	27.72	25.71	23.90	22.28	20.82	22
23	44.17	40.43	37.11	34.14	31.49	29.13	27.00	25.10	23.38	21.83	20.43	23
24	42.31	38.84	35.75	32.98	30.50	28.28	26.28	24.47	22.85	21.37	20.04	24
25	40.49	37.28	34.41	31.83	29.52	27.43	25.54	23.84	22.30	20.90	19.63	25
26	38.70	35.74	33.08	30.69	28.53	26.57	24.81	23.20	21.75	20.42	19.21	26
27	36.95	34.23	31.77	29.55	27.54	25.71	24.06	22.55	21.18	19.93	18.78	27
28	35.24	32.74	30.47	28.42	26.55	24.85	23.30	21.89	20.60	19.42	18.34	28
29	33.56	31.27	29.18	27.29	25.56	23.98	22.54	21.22	20.01	18.91	17.89	29
30	31.91	29.82	27.91	26.17	24.57	23.11	21.78	20.55	19.42	18.38	17.42	30
31	30.30	28.40	26.66	25.06	23.59	22.24	21.00	19.86	18.81	17.83	16.94	31
32	28.73	27.00	25.41	23.95	22.61	21.37	20.22	19.17	18.19	17.28	16.44	32
33	27.19	25.63	24.19	22.86	21.63	20.49	19.44	18.46	17.56	16.72	15.94	33
34	25.68	24.27	22.97	21.76	20.65	19.61	18.65	17.75	16.92	16.14	15.41	34
35	24.20	22.94	21.77	20.68	19.67	18.72	17.85	17.03	16.26	15.55	14.88	35
36	22.75	21.63	20.58	19.60	18.69	17.83	17.04	16.29	15.59	14.94	14.32	36
37	21.33	20.33	19.40	18.52	17.71	16.94	16.22	15.55	14.91	14.32	13.76	37
38	19.94	19.06	18.23	17.46	16.73	16.04	15.40	14.79	14.22	13.68	13.17	38
39	18.57	17.80	17.07	16.39	15.75	15.14	14.56	14.02	13.51	13.02	12.56	39
40	17.23	16.56	15.93	15.33	14.76	14.23	13.72	13.24	12.79	12.35	11.94	40
41	15.92	15.34	14.79	14.28	13.78	13.32	12.87	12.45	12.05	11.67	11.30	41
42	14.63	14.14	13.67	13.23	12.80	12.40	12.01	11.65	11.30	10.96	10.64	42
43	13.37	12.96	12.56	12.18	11.82	11.48	11.15	10.83	10.53	10.24	9.96	43
44	12.13	11.79	11.46	11.14	10.84	10.55	10.27	10.01	9.75	9.50	9.26	44
45	10.92	10.64	10.37	10.11	9.86	9.62	9.39	9.17	8.95	8.74	8.54	45
46	9.73	9.51	9.29	9.08	8.88	8.68	8.50	8.31	8.14	7.97	7.80	46
47	8.57	8.39	8.22	8.06	7.90	7.74	7.59	7.45	7.31	7.17	7.04	47
48	7.43	7.29	7.17	7.04	6.92	6.80	6.68	6.57	6.46	6.35	6.25	48
49	6.31	6.21	6.12	6.02	5.93	5.85	5.76	5.68	5.60	5.52	5.44	49
50	5.21	5.14	5.08	5.01	4.95	4.89	4.83	4.77	4.72	4.66	4.60	50
51	4.13	4.09	4.05	4.01	3.97	3.93	3.89	3.85	3.81	3.78	3.74	51
52	3.07	3.05	3.03	3.00	2.98	2.96	2.94	2.91	2.89	2.87	2.85	52
53	2.03	2.02	2.01	2.00	1.99	1.98	1.97	1.96	1.95	1.94	1.93	53
54	1.01	1.01	1.00	1.00	1.00	1.00	0.99	0.99	0.99	0.99	0.98	54

Table 6: Multipliers for loss of earnings to pension age 55 (females)

Age at date of trial	Multiplier calculated with allowance for projected mortality from the 2008–based population projections and rate of return of										Age at date of trial
	–2.0%	*–1.5%*	*–1.0%*	*–0.5%*	*0.0%*	*0.5%*	*1.0%*	*1.5%*	*2.0%*	*2.5%*	*3.0%*	
16	58.83	52.69	47.37	42.75	38.72	35.20	32.11	29.40	27.01	24.90	23.03	16
17	56.66	50.91	45.90	41.54	37.72	34.37	31.43	28.84	26.54	24.51	22.70	17
18	54.54	49.15	44.45	40.34	36.72	33.55	30.74	28.26	26.07	24.11	22.37	18
19	52.46	47.43	43.02	39.14	35.73	32.71	30.05	27.68	25.58	23.71	22.03	19
20	50.43	45.73	41.60	37.95	34.73	31.88	29.35	27.09	25.09	23.29	21.68	20
21	48.43	44.05	40.19	36.77	33.73	31.04	28.64	26.50	24.58	22.86	21.32	21
22	46.48	42.41	38.80	35.59	32.74	30.20	27.92	25.89	24.06	22.42	20.95	22
23	44.56	40.78	37.42	34.42	31.74	29.35	27.20	25.27	23.54	21.97	20.56	23
24	42.69	39.18	36.05	33.25	30.74	28.49	26.47	24.65	23.00	21.51	20.17	24
25	40.85	37.60	34.70	32.09	29.75	27.64	25.73	24.01	22.46	21.04	19.76	25
26	39.04	36.05	33.36	30.94	28.75	26.78	24.99	23.37	21.90	20.56	19.34	26
27	37.28	34.52	32.04	29.79	27.76	25.91	24.24	22.72	21.33	20.06	18.91	27
28	35.55	33.02	30.73	28.65	26.76	25.04	23.48	22.05	20.75	19.56	18.46	28
29	33.86	31.54	29.43	27.51	25.77	24.17	22.72	21.38	20.16	19.04	18.01	29
30	32.20	30.08	28.15	26.38	24.77	23.30	21.94	20.70	19.56	18.51	17.54	30
31	30.57	28.64	26.88	25.26	23.78	22.42	21.16	20.01	18.94	17.96	17.05	31
32	28.98	27.23	25.62	24.15	22.79	21.53	20.38	19.31	18.32	17.40	16.56	32
33	27.42	25.84	24.38	23.03	21.79	20.64	19.58	18.60	17.68	16.83	16.04	33
34	25.89	24.46	23.15	21.93	20.80	19.75	18.78	17.87	17.03	16.25	15.52	34
35	24.39	23.11	21.93	20.83	19.81	18.86	17.97	17.14	16.37	15.65	14.97	35
36	22.92	21.78	20.73	19.74	18.82	17.96	17.15	16.40	15.69	15.03	14.41	36
37	21.48	20.48	19.53	18.65	17.83	17.05	16.33	15.65	15.01	14.40	13.84	37
38	20.07	19.19	18.35	17.57	16.84	16.14	15.49	14.88	14.30	13.76	13.25	38
39	18.69	17.92	17.19	16.50	15.85	15.23	14.65	14.11	13.59	13.10	12.64	39
40	17.34	16.67	16.03	15.43	14.86	14.32	13.80	13.32	12.86	12.42	12.01	40
41	16.02	15.44	14.89	14.36	13.87	13.40	12.95	12.52	12.12	11.73	11.36	41
42	14.72	14.22	13.75	13.30	12.88	12.47	12.08	11.71	11.36	11.02	10.70	42
43	13.45	13.03	12.63	12.25	11.89	11.54	11.21	10.89	10.59	10.29	10.01	43
44	12.20	11.85	11.52	11.20	10.90	10.61	10.33	10.06	9.80	9.55	9.31	44
45	10.98	10.70	10.42	10.16	9.91	9.67	9.43	9.21	8.99	8.79	8.58	45
46	9.78	9.56	9.34	9.13	8.92	8.73	8.54	8.35	8.17	8.00	7.84	46
47	8.61	8.43	8.26	8.09	7.93	7.78	7.63	7.48	7.34	7.20	7.07	47
48	7.46	7.33	7.20	7.07	6.95	6.83	6.71	6.60	6.49	6.38	6.28	48
49	6.33	6.24	6.14	6.05	5.96	5.87	5.78	5.70	5.62	5.54	5.46	49
50	5.23	5.16	5.10	5.03	4.97	4.91	4.85	4.79	4.73	4.68	4.62	50
51	4.14	4.10	4.06	4.02	3.98	3.94	3.90	3.86	3.83	3.79	3.75	51
52	3.08	3.06	3.03	3.01	2.99	2.97	2.94	2.92	2.90	2.88	2.86	52
53	2.03	2.02	2.01	2.00	1.99	1.98	1.97	1.96	1.96	1.95	1.94	53
54	1.01	1.01	1.00	1.00	1.00	1.00	0.99	0.99	0.99	0.99	0.98	54

Table 7: Multipliers for loss of earnings to pension age 60 (males)

Age at date of trial	Multiplier calculated with allowance for projected mortality from the 2008–based population projections and rate of return of											Age at date of trial
	–2.0%	***–1.5%***	***–1.0%***	***–0.5%***	***0.0%***	***0.5%***	***1.0%***	***1.5%***	***2.0%***	***2.5%***	***3.0%***	
16	69.28	61.13	54.18	48.26	43.18	38.81	35.03	31.77	28.93	26.46	24.29	16
17	66.90	59.22	52.65	47.02	42.18	38.00	34.38	31.24	28.50	26.11	24.01	17
18	64.58	57.34	51.13	45.79	41.18	37.19	33.73	30.71	28.07	25.75	23.72	18
19	62.30	55.49	49.63	44.57	40.19	36.38	33.06	30.17	27.62	25.39	23.42	19
20	60.08	53.68	48.15	43.36	39.20	35.57	32.40	29.62	27.17	25.02	23.11	20
21	57.90	51.89	46.68	42.15	38.21	34.75	31.72	29.06	26.71	24.64	22.80	21
22	55.76	50.13	45.23	40.95	37.21	33.93	31.04	28.50	26.25	24.25	22.47	22
23	53.66	48.40	43.79	39.76	36.22	33.11	30.36	27.93	25.77	23.85	22.14	23
24	51.61	46.69	42.37	38.57	35.23	32.28	29.66	27.35	25.28	23.44	21.80	24
25	49.60	45.01	40.96	37.40	34.24	31.45	28.97	26.76	24.79	23.02	21.44	25
26	47.64	43.35	39.57	36.22	33.25	30.61	28.26	26.16	24.28	22.59	21.08	26
27	45.71	41.72	38.19	35.06	32.27	29.77	27.55	25.56	23.77	22.16	20.71	27
28	43.82	40.12	36.83	33.90	31.28	28.93	26.83	24.94	23.24	21.71	20.32	28
29	41.97	38.54	35.48	32.74	30.29	28.09	26.10	24.32	22.70	21.25	19.92	29
30	40.15	36.99	34.14	31.59	29.30	27.24	25.37	23.69	22.16	20.78	19.52	30
31	38.38	35.46	32.83	30.46	28.32	26.39	24.64	23.05	21.61	20.29	19.10	31
32	36.65	33.96	31.53	29.33	27.34	25.53	23.89	22.40	21.04	19.80	18.67	32
33	34.96	32.48	30.24	28.21	26.36	24.68	23.15	21.75	20.47	19.30	18.23	33
34	33.30	31.03	28.97	27.09	25.38	23.82	22.39	21.09	19.89	18.79	17.78	34
35	31.67	29.60	27.71	25.98	24.40	22.96	21.63	20.42	19.30	18.27	17.32	35
36	30.07	28.19	26.46	24.88	23.43	22.09	20.87	19.74	18.69	17.73	16.84	36
37	28.51	26.80	25.23	23.78	22.45	21.22	20.09	19.04	18.08	17.18	16.35	37
38	26.98	25.43	24.01	22.69	21.48	20.35	19.31	18.34	17.45	16.61	15.84	38
39	25.48	24.08	22.80	21.60	20.50	19.47	18.52	17.63	16.81	16.04	15.32	39
40	24.00	22.76	21.60	20.52	19.52	18.59	17.72	16.91	16.15	15.44	14.78	40
41	22.56	21.45	20.41	19.45	18.54	17.70	16.91	16.17	15.48	14.84	14.23	41
42	21.15	20.16	19.24	18.38	17.57	16.81	16.10	15.43	14.80	14.21	13.66	42
43	19.76	18.90	18.08	17.31	16.59	15.92	15.28	14.68	14.11	13.58	13.07	43
44	18.41	17.65	16.93	16.26	15.62	15.02	14.45	13.91	13.41	12.93	12.47	44
45	17.08	16.42	15.79	15.20	14.64	14.12	13.61	13.14	12.69	12.26	11.85	45
46	15.78	15.21	14.67	14.16	13.67	13.21	12.77	12.35	11.95	11.58	11.22	46
47	14.50	14.02	13.56	13.12	12.70	12.30	11.92	11.55	11.21	10.88	10.56	47
48	13.26	12.85	12.46	12.08	11.73	11.38	11.06	10.75	10.45	10.16	9.89	48
49	12.03	11.69	11.37	11.05	10.75	10.47	10.19	9.93	9.67	9.43	9.19	49
50	10.83	10.56	10.29	10.03	9.78	9.55	9.32	9.10	8.88	8.68	8.48	50
51	9.66	9.44	9.22	9.01	8.81	8.62	8.43	8.25	8.08	7.91	7.75	51
52	8.51	8.34	8.17	8.00	7.84	7.69	7.54	7.40	7.26	7.12	6.99	52
53	7.38	7.25	7.12	7.00	6.87	6.76	6.64	6.53	6.42	6.32	6.21	53
54	6.27	6.18	6.08	5.99	5.90	5.82	5.73	5.65	5.57	5.49	5.41	54
55	5.18	5.12	5.05	4.99	4.93	4.87	4.81	4.75	4.69	4.64	4.58	55
56	4.12	4.07	4.03	3.99	3.95	3.91	3.87	3.84	3.80	3.76	3.73	56
57	3.06	3.04	3.02	2.99	2.97	2.95	2.93	2.91	2.89	2.86	2.84	57
58	2.03	2.02	2.01	2.00	1.99	1.98	1.97	1.96	1.95	1.94	1.93	58
59	1.01	1.00	1.00	1.00	1.00	0.99	0.99	0.99	0.99	0.98	0.98	59

Table 8: Multipliers for loss of earnings to pension age 60 (females)

Age at date of trial	Multiplier calculated with allowance for projected mortality from the 2008–based population projections and rate of return of											Age at date of trial
	-2.0%	*-1.5%*	*-1.0%*	*-0.5%*	*0.0%*	*0.5%*	*1.0%*	*1.5%*	*2.0%*	*2.5%*	*3.0%*	
16	70.04	61.77	54.73	48.72	43.57	39.14	35.32	32.02	29.14	26.64	24.45	16
17	67.65	59.85	53.18	47.48	42.57	38.33	34.67	31.49	28.72	26.29	24.17	17
18	65.30	57.96	51.66	46.24	41.57	37.52	34.01	30.96	28.28	25.94	23.88	18
19	63.01	56.10	50.15	45.02	40.57	36.71	33.35	30.41	27.84	25.58	23.59	19
20	60.76	54.27	48.66	43.80	39.57	35.90	32.68	29.87	27.39	25.21	23.28	20
21	58.56	52.46	47.18	42.58	38.58	35.08	32.01	29.31	26.93	24.83	22.97	21
22	56.40	50.69	45.71	41.37	37.58	34.25	31.32	28.74	26.46	24.44	22.64	22
23	54.29	48.94	44.26	40.17	36.58	33.42	30.64	28.17	25.98	24.04	22.31	23
24	52.21	47.21	42.83	38.98	35.58	32.59	29.94	27.59	25.50	23.63	21.97	24
25	50.18	45.51	41.41	37.79	34.59	31.75	29.24	27.00	25.00	23.21	21.61	25
26	48.19	43.84	40.00	36.60	33.59	30.91	28.53	26.40	24.49	22.78	21.25	26
27	46.24	42.20	38.61	35.43	32.59	30.07	27.81	25.79	23.98	22.34	20.87	27
28	44.33	40.58	37.24	34.26	31.60	29.22	27.09	25.17	23.45	21.89	20.49	28
29	42.46	38.98	35.87	33.09	30.60	28.37	26.36	24.55	22.91	21.43	20.09	29
30	40.63	37.41	34.53	31.94	29.61	27.51	25.62	23.91	22.37	20.96	19.69	30
31	38.83	35.86	33.19	30.79	28.62	26.65	24.88	23.27	21.81	20.48	19.27	31
32	37.08	34.34	31.87	29.64	27.62	25.79	24.13	22.62	21.24	19.98	18.83	32
33	35.35	32.84	30.57	28.50	26.63	24.93	23.37	21.96	20.66	19.48	18.39	33
34	33.67	31.37	29.28	27.37	25.64	24.06	22.61	21.29	20.07	18.96	17.93	34
35	32.01	29.91	28.00	26.25	24.65	23.18	21.84	20.60	19.47	18.43	17.46	35
36	30.40	28.48	26.73	25.13	23.66	22.30	21.06	19.91	18.86	17.88	16.98	36
37	28.81	27.08	25.48	24.02	22.67	21.42	20.28	19.21	18.23	17.32	16.48	37
38	27.26	25.69	24.24	22.91	21.68	20.54	19.48	18.50	17.60	16.75	15.97	38
39	25.73	24.32	23.02	21.81	20.69	19.65	18.68	17.78	16.95	16.17	15.44	39
40	24.24	22.98	21.81	20.72	19.70	18.76	17.88	17.05	16.29	15.57	14.90	40
41	22.78	21.66	20.61	19.63	18.71	17.86	17.06	16.31	15.61	14.96	14.34	41
42	21.35	20.35	19.42	18.55	17.73	16.96	16.24	15.56	14.93	14.33	13.77	42
43	19.95	19.07	18.24	17.47	16.74	16.05	15.41	14.80	14.23	13.69	13.18	43
44	18.58	17.81	17.08	16.40	15.75	15.15	14.57	14.03	13.52	13.03	12.57	44
45	17.24	16.57	15.93	15.33	14.77	14.23	13.73	13.25	12.79	12.36	11.95	45
46	15.92	15.34	14.80	14.28	13.79	13.32	12.87	12.45	12.05	11.67	11.30	46
47	14.63	14.14	13.67	13.23	12.80	12.40	12.01	11.65	11.30	10.96	10.64	47
48	13.37	12.95	12.56	12.18	11.82	11.48	11.15	10.83	10.53	10.24	9.96	48
49	12.13	11.79	11.46	11.14	10.84	10.55	10.27	10.00	9.75	9.50	9.26	49
50	10.92	10.64	10.37	10.11	9.86	9.62	9.39	9.17	8.95	8.74	8.54	50
51	9.73	9.51	9.29	9.08	8.88	8.69	8.50	8.31	8.14	7.97	7.80	51
52	8.57	8.39	8.22	8.06	7.90	7.75	7.60	7.45	7.31	7.17	7.04	52
53	7.43	7.30	7.17	7.04	6.92	6.80	6.68	6.57	6.46	6.36	6.25	53
54	6.31	6.21	6.12	6.03	5.94	5.85	5.76	5.68	5.60	5.52	5.44	54
55	5.21	5.14	5.08	5.02	4.95	4.89	4.83	4.77	4.72	4.66	4.61	55
56	4.13	4.09	4.05	4.01	3.97	3.93	3.89	3.85	3.82	3.78	3.74	56
57	3.07	3.05	3.03	3.00	2.98	2.96	2.94	2.92	2.89	2.87	2.85	57
58	2.03	2.02	2.01	2.00	1.99	1.98	1.97	1.96	1.95	1.94	1.93	58
59	1.01	1.01	1.00	1.00	1.00	1.00	0.99	0.99	0.99	0.99	0.98	59

Table 9: Multipliers for loss of earnings to pension age 65 (males)

Age at date of trial	Multiplier calculated with allowance for projected mortality from the 2008–based population projections and rate of return of											Age at date of trial
	–2.0%	*–1.5%*	*–1.0%*	*–0.5%*	*0.0%*	*0.5%*	*1.0%*	*1.5%*	*2.0%*	*2.5%*	*3.0%*	
16	81.11	70.46	61.56	54.09	47.80	42.47	37.95	34.08	30.77	27.92	25.46	16
17	78.49	68.41	59.95	52.82	46.80	41.68	37.32	33.59	30.38	27.61	25.21	17
18	75.93	66.39	58.35	51.56	45.80	40.89	36.69	33.09	29.98	27.29	24.96	18
19	73.42	64.40	56.78	50.31	44.80	40.10	36.06	32.58	29.58	26.97	24.70	19
20	70.97	62.45	55.22	49.07	43.81	39.30	35.42	32.07	29.16	26.64	24.43	20
21	68.57	60.53	53.68	47.83	42.82	38.50	34.78	31.55	28.74	26.30	24.15	21
22	66.21	58.63	52.16	46.60	41.82	37.70	34.13	31.02	28.31	25.95	23.87	22
23	63.90	56.77	50.65	45.38	40.83	36.89	33.47	30.49	27.88	25.59	23.57	23
24	61.64	54.93	49.15	44.16	39.84	36.08	32.81	29.94	27.43	25.22	23.27	24
25	59.43	53.12	47.68	42.95	38.85	35.27	32.14	29.39	26.98	24.85	22.96	25
26	57.26	51.35	46.22	41.75	37.86	34.45	31.46	28.84	26.52	24.47	22.65	26
27	55.14	49.60	44.77	40.56	36.87	33.63	30.78	28.27	26.05	24.07	22.32	27
28	53.06	47.87	43.34	39.37	35.88	32.81	30.10	27.70	25.57	23.67	21.98	28
29	51.02	46.17	41.92	38.18	34.89	31.98	29.40	27.11	25.08	23.26	21.63	29
30	49.03	44.50	40.52	37.01	33.90	31.15	28.70	26.52	24.58	22.84	21.28	30
31	47.08	42.86	39.14	35.84	32.92	30.32	28.00	25.93	24.07	22.41	20.91	31
32	45.17	41.25	37.78	34.69	31.94	29.49	27.29	25.33	23.56	21.97	20.54	32
33	43.31	39.67	36.43	33.54	30.96	28.65	26.58	24.72	23.04	21.53	20.16	33
34	41.48	38.11	35.10	32.40	29.99	27.81	25.86	24.10	22.51	21.07	19.77	34
35	39.69	36.57	33.78	31.27	29.01	26.97	25.14	23.48	21.97	20.60	19.36	35
36	37.94	35.06	32.47	30.14	28.03	26.13	24.41	22.84	21.42	20.13	18.95	36
37	36.22	33.57	31.18	29.02	27.06	25.28	23.67	22.20	20.86	19.64	18.52	37
38	34.54	32.11	29.90	27.90	26.08	24.43	22.92	21.55	20.29	19.13	18.08	38
39	32.89	30.66	28.64	26.79	25.11	23.57	22.17	20.88	19.70	18.62	17.62	39
40	31.27	29.24	27.38	25.69	24.13	22.71	21.41	20.21	19.11	18.09	17.16	40
41	29.69	27.84	26.14	24.59	23.16	21.85	20.64	19.53	18.50	17.55	16.68	41
42	28.14	26.46	24.92	23.50	22.19	20.98	19.87	18.84	17.88	17.00	16.18	42
43	26.62	25.10	23.70	22.41	21.22	20.11	19.09	18.14	17.26	16.44	15.68	43
44	25.13	23.77	22.50	21.33	20.25	19.24	18.30	17.43	16.62	15.86	15.16	44
45	23.68	22.45	21.32	20.26	19.28	18.36	17.51	16.71	15.97	15.27	14.62	45
46	22.25	21.16	20.14	19.19	18.31	17.48	16.71	15.98	15.30	14.67	14.07	46
47	20.86	19.89	18.98	18.14	17.34	16.60	15.90	15.24	14.63	14.05	13.50	47
48	19.49	18.64	17.84	17.08	16.38	15.71	15.09	14.50	13.94	13.42	12.92	48
49	18.15	17.41	16.70	16.04	15.41	14.82	14.27	13.74	13.24	12.77	12.33	49
50	16.85	16.20	15.58	15.00	14.46	13.94	13.44	12.98	12.53	12.11	11.71	50
51	15.57	15.01	14.48	13.98	13.50	13.04	12.61	12.20	11.81	11.44	11.09	51
52	14.32	13.84	13.39	12.95	12.54	12.15	11.77	11.42	11.08	10.75	10.44	52
53	13.09	12.69	12.30	11.94	11.59	11.25	10.93	10.62	10.33	10.05	9.78	53
54	11.89	11.56	11.24	10.93	10.63	10.35	10.08	9.82	9.57	9.33	9.10	54
55	10.71	10.44	10.18	9.92	9.68	9.45	9.22	9.00	8.79	8.59	8.40	55
56	9.56	9.34	9.13	8.93	8.73	8.54	8.35	8.17	8.00	7.84	7.67	56
57	8.43	8.26	8.09	7.93	7.77	7.62	7.47	7.33	7.19	7.06	6.93	57
58	7.32	7.19	7.06	6.94	6.82	6.70	6.59	6.48	6.37	6.26	6.16	58
59	6.22	6.13	6.03	5.94	5.85	5.77	5.68	5.60	5.52	5.45	5.37	59
60	5.14	5.08	5.01	4.95	4.89	4.83	4.77	4.71	4.66	4.60	4.55	60
61	4.09	4.04	4.00	3.96	3.92	3.89	3.85	3.81	3.77	3.74	3.70	61
62	3.04	3.02	3.00	2.98	2.95	2.93	2.91	2.89	2.87	2.85	2.83	62
63	2.02	2.01	2.00	1.99	1.98	1.97	1.96	1.95	1.94	1.93	1.92	63
64	1.00	1.00	1.00	1.00	0.99	0.99	0.99	0.99	0.98	0.98	0.98	64

Table 10: Multipliers for loss of earnings to pension age 65 (females)

Age at date of trial	Multiplier calculated with allowance for projected mortality from the 2008–based population projections and rate of return of											Age at date of trial
	−2.0%	*−1.5%*	*−1.0%*	*−0.5%*	*0.0%*	*0.5%*	*1.0%*	*1.5%*	*2.0%*	*2.5%*	*3.0%*	
16	82.26	71.41	62.34	54.74	48.34	42.93	38.33	34.41	31.05	28.16	25.66	16
17	79.62	69.34	60.72	53.47	47.34	42.14	37.71	33.91	30.66	27.85	25.41	17
18	77.03	67.31	59.12	52.20	46.34	41.35	37.08	33.42	30.26	27.53	25.16	18
19	74.50	65.30	57.53	50.95	45.34	40.55	36.45	32.91	29.86	27.21	24.91	19
20	72.02	63.33	55.96	49.70	44.34	39.75	35.81	32.40	29.45	26.88	24.64	20
21	69.59	61.39	54.41	48.45	43.34	38.95	35.16	31.88	29.03	26.54	24.37	21
22	67.20	59.48	52.87	47.21	42.34	38.15	34.51	31.35	28.60	26.20	24.08	22
23	64.87	57.59	51.35	45.98	41.35	37.33	33.85	30.82	28.16	25.84	23.79	23
24	62.58	55.73	49.84	44.75	40.35	36.52	33.19	30.27	27.72	25.47	23.49	24
25	60.34	53.91	48.35	43.53	39.35	35.70	32.51	29.72	27.27	25.10	23.19	25
26	58.14	52.11	46.87	42.32	38.35	34.88	31.84	29.16	26.80	24.72	22.87	26
27	55.99	50.33	45.41	41.11	37.35	34.05	31.15	28.60	26.33	24.33	22.54	27
28	53.88	48.59	43.96	39.91	36.36	33.23	30.46	28.02	25.85	23.93	22.21	28
29	51.82	46.87	42.53	38.72	35.36	32.39	29.77	27.44	25.36	23.51	21.86	29
30	49.80	45.18	41.12	37.53	34.36	31.56	29.06	26.84	24.87	23.09	21.51	30
31	47.82	43.52	39.72	36.35	33.37	30.72	28.35	26.25	24.36	22.66	21.14	31
32	45.88	41.88	38.33	35.18	32.38	29.87	27.64	25.64	23.84	22.22	20.77	32
33	43.98	40.27	36.96	34.01	31.38	29.03	26.92	25.02	23.31	21.77	20.38	33
34	42.12	38.68	35.60	32.85	30.39	28.18	26.19	24.39	22.78	21.31	19.98	34
35	40.30	37.11	34.26	31.70	29.40	27.32	25.45	23.76	22.23	20.84	19.57	35
36	38.51	35.58	32.93	30.56	28.41	26.47	24.71	23.12	21.67	20.35	19.15	36
37	36.76	34.06	31.62	29.42	27.42	25.61	23.96	22.47	21.10	19.86	18.72	37
38	35.05	32.57	30.32	28.28	26.43	24.74	23.21	21.81	20.52	19.35	18.28	38
39	33.38	31.10	29.04	27.16	25.44	23.88	22.44	21.14	19.93	18.83	17.82	39
40	31.73	29.66	27.76	26.04	24.45	23.00	21.68	20.46	19.33	18.30	17.35	40
41	30.12	28.24	26.51	24.92	23.47	22.13	20.90	19.77	18.72	17.76	16.86	41
42	28.55	26.84	25.26	23.81	22.48	21.25	20.12	19.07	18.10	17.20	16.37	42
43	27.01	25.46	24.03	22.71	21.50	20.37	19.33	18.36	17.46	16.63	15.85	43
44	25.49	24.10	22.81	21.62	20.51	19.48	18.53	17.64	16.82	16.05	15.33	44
45	24.02	22.77	21.61	20.53	19.53	18.60	17.73	16.92	16.16	15.45	14.79	45
46	22.57	21.46	20.42	19.45	18.55	17.71	16.92	16.18	15.49	14.84	14.23	46
47	21.15	20.17	19.24	18.38	17.57	16.81	16.10	15.43	14.81	14.22	13.66	47
48	19.77	18.90	18.08	17.31	16.59	15.92	15.28	14.68	14.11	13.58	13.08	48
49	18.41	17.65	16.93	16.26	15.62	15.02	14.45	13.91	13.41	12.93	12.47	49
50	17.08	16.42	15.80	15.21	14.65	14.12	13.62	13.14	12.69	12.26	11.85	50
51	15.78	15.21	14.67	14.16	13.67	13.21	12.77	12.35	11.96	11.58	11.22	51
52	14.51	14.02	13.56	13.12	12.70	12.30	11.92	11.56	11.21	10.88	10.56	52
53	13.26	12.85	12.46	12.09	11.73	11.39	11.06	10.75	10.45	10.17	9.89	53
54	12.04	11.70	11.37	11.06	10.76	10.47	10.20	9.93	9.68	9.43	9.20	54
55	10.84	10.56	10.30	10.04	9.79	9.55	9.32	9.10	8.89	8.68	8.49	55
56	9.67	9.44	9.23	9.02	8.82	8.63	8.44	8.26	8.09	7.92	7.75	56
57	8.52	8.34	8.17	8.01	7.85	7.70	7.55	7.40	7.26	7.13	7.00	57
58	7.39	7.25	7.13	7.00	6.88	6.76	6.65	6.53	6.43	6.32	6.22	58
59	6.28	6.18	6.09	5.99	5.91	5.82	5.73	5.65	5.57	5.49	5.41	59
60	5.19	5.12	5.05	4.99	4.93	4.87	4.81	4.75	4.69	4.64	4.58	60
61	4.11	4.07	4.03	3.99	3.95	3.91	3.87	3.84	3.80	3.76	3.73	61
62	3.06	3.04	3.02	2.99	2.97	2.95	2.93	2.91	2.88	2.86	2.84	62
63	2.03	2.02	2.01	2.00	1.99	1.98	1.97	1.96	1.95	1.94	1.93	63
64	1.01	1.00	1.00	1.00	1.00	0.99	0.99	0.99	0.99	0.98	0.98	64

Table 11: Multipliers for loss of earnings to pension age 70 (males)

Age at date of trial	Multiplier calculated with allowance for projected mortality from the 2008–based population projections and rate of return of											Age at date of trial
	-2.0%	*-1.5%*	*-1.0%*	*-0.5%*	*0.0%*	*0.5%*	*1.0%*	*1.5%*	*2.0%*	*2.5%*	*3.0%*	
16	93.75	80.18	69.05	59.87	52.26	45.93	40.62	36.16	32.38	29.18	26.44	16
17	90.86	77.97	67.35	58.57	51.26	45.15	40.02	35.69	32.02	28.89	26.22	17
18	88.04	75.80	65.68	57.27	50.25	44.37	39.41	35.22	31.65	28.61	25.99	18
19	85.28	73.67	64.03	55.99	49.26	43.59	38.81	34.74	31.28	28.31	25.76	19
20	82.58	71.57	62.39	54.71	48.26	42.81	38.19	34.26	30.90	28.01	25.52	20
21	79.94	69.50	60.78	53.44	47.26	42.03	37.58	33.78	30.52	27.71	25.28	21
22	77.35	67.47	59.17	52.18	46.27	41.24	36.95	33.28	30.12	27.39	25.03	22
23	74.81	65.46	57.59	50.93	45.27	40.45	36.32	32.78	29.72	27.07	24.77	23
24	72.32	63.49	56.02	49.68	44.27	39.65	35.68	32.26	29.31	26.74	24.50	24
25	69.89	61.55	54.47	48.44	43.28	38.85	35.04	31.75	28.89	26.40	24.23	25
26	67.50	59.64	52.93	47.20	42.29	38.05	34.39	31.22	28.47	26.06	23.95	26
27	65.17	57.76	51.42	45.98	41.29	37.25	33.74	30.69	28.03	25.70	23.66	27
28	62.88	55.91	49.92	44.76	40.30	36.44	33.08	30.15	27.59	25.34	23.36	28
29	60.64	54.08	48.43	43.54	39.31	35.63	32.41	29.61	27.14	24.97	23.05	29
30	58.45	52.29	46.96	42.34	38.32	34.81	31.74	29.05	26.68	24.59	22.74	30
31	56.31	50.53	45.51	41.14	37.33	34.00	31.07	28.49	26.22	24.20	22.42	31
32	54.21	48.80	44.08	39.96	36.35	33.18	30.39	27.93	25.75	23.81	22.09	32
33	52.17	47.10	42.67	38.79	35.37	32.37	29.71	27.36	25.27	23.41	21.75	33
34	50.16	45.43	41.28	37.62	34.40	31.55	29.02	26.78	24.79	23.00	21.41	34
35	48.20	43.78	39.89	36.46	33.42	30.73	28.33	26.20	24.29	22.58	21.05	35
36	46.28	42.16	38.53	35.31	32.45	29.90	27.63	25.60	23.79	22.15	20.69	36
37	44.39	40.57	37.18	34.16	31.47	29.07	26.93	25.00	23.27	21.72	20.31	37
38	42.55	39.00	35.84	33.02	30.50	28.24	26.21	24.39	22.75	21.27	19.93	38
39	40.74	37.45	34.51	31.88	29.52	27.40	25.49	23.77	22.21	20.80	19.53	39
40	38.96	35.92	33.20	30.75	28.55	26.56	24.76	23.14	21.67	20.33	19.12	40
41	37.23	34.42	31.90	29.63	27.57	25.71	24.03	22.50	21.11	19.85	18.70	41
42	35.53	32.95	30.62	28.51	26.60	24.87	23.29	21.86	20.55	19.36	18.26	42
43	33.86	31.50	29.35	27.40	25.63	24.02	22.55	21.20	19.98	18.85	17.82	43
44	32.23	30.07	28.10	26.30	24.66	23.17	21.80	20.54	19.39	18.34	17.36	44
45	30.64	28.66	26.86	25.21	23.70	22.31	21.04	19.87	18.80	17.81	16.90	45
46	29.08	27.28	25.63	24.12	22.73	21.45	20.28	19.19	18.19	17.27	16.41	46
47	27.55	25.92	24.42	23.04	21.77	20.59	19.51	18.51	17.58	16.72	15.92	47
48	26.06	24.58	23.22	21.97	20.81	19.73	18.74	17.81	16.95	16.16	15.41	48
49	24.60	23.27	22.04	20.91	19.85	18.87	17.96	17.11	16.32	15.58	14.90	49
50	23.17	21.98	20.88	19.85	18.90	18.01	17.18	16.40	15.68	15.00	14.37	50
51	21.78	20.72	19.73	18.81	17.95	17.14	16.39	15.69	15.02	14.40	13.82	51
52	20.42	19.48	18.60	17.78	17.00	16.28	15.60	14.96	14.36	13.80	13.27	52
53	19.09	18.26	17.48	16.75	16.06	15.41	14.81	14.23	13.69	13.18	12.70	53
54	17.79	17.06	16.38	15.73	15.12	14.55	14.01	13.49	13.01	12.55	12.11	54
55	16.51	15.88	15.29	14.72	14.19	13.68	13.20	12.75	12.31	11.90	11.52	55
56	15.27	14.73	14.21	13.72	13.25	12.81	12.39	11.99	11.61	11.25	10.90	56
57	14.05	13.59	13.14	12.72	12.32	11.94	11.57	11.22	10.89	10.57	10.27	57
58	12.85	12.46	12.09	11.73	11.39	11.06	10.75	10.45	10.16	9.88	9.62	58
59	11.68	11.35	11.04	10.74	10.45	10.17	9.91	9.66	9.41	9.18	8.95	59
60	10.52	10.26	10.00	9.75	9.51	9.28	9.06	8.85	8.65	8.45	8.26	60
61	9.39	9.18	8.97	8.77	8.58	8.39	8.21	8.04	7.87	7.71	7.55	61
62	8.28	8.11	7.95	7.79	7.64	7.49	7.35	7.21	7.07	6.94	6.82	62
63	7.19	7.06	6.94	6.82	6.70	6.59	6.48	6.37	6.27	6.16	6.06	63
64	6.12	6.03	5.94	5.85	5.77	5.68	5.60	5.52	5.44	5.36	5.29	64
65	5.07	5.01	4.95	4.89	4.83	4.77	4.71	4.65	4.60	4.54	4.49	65
66	4.04	4.00	3.96	3.92	3.88	3.84	3.81	3.77	3.73	3.70	3.66	66
67	3.02	3.00	2.97	2.95	2.93	2.91	2.89	2.86	2.84	2.82	2.80	67
68	2.01	2.00	1.99	1.98	1.97	1.96	1.95	1.94	1.93	1.92	1.91	68
69	1.00	1.00	1.00	0.99	0.99	0.99	0.99	0.98	0.98	0.98	0.98	69

Table 12: Multipliers for loss of earnings to pension age 70 (females)

Age at date of trial	Multiplier calculated with allowance for projected mortality from the 2008–based population projections and rate of return of											Age at date of trial
	–2.0%	*–1.5%*	*–1.0%*	*–0.5%*	*0.0%*	*0.5%*	*1.0%*	*1.5%*	*2.0%*	*2.5%*	*3.0%*	
16	95.47	81.58	70.18	60.79	53.01	46.54	41.12	36.57	32.73	29.47	26.68	16
17	92.56	79.35	68.47	59.48	52.01	45.76	40.53	36.11	32.37	29.19	26.46	17
18	89.71	77.16	66.79	58.18	51.00	44.99	39.93	35.65	32.01	28.91	26.24	18
19	86.92	75.00	65.12	56.89	50.00	44.21	39.32	35.18	31.64	28.62	26.02	19
20	84.18	72.88	63.47	55.61	49.00	43.43	38.71	34.70	31.27	28.32	25.79	20
21	81.50	70.79	61.84	54.33	48.00	42.64	38.09	34.21	30.88	28.02	25.55	21
22	78.87	68.73	60.22	53.06	47.00	41.85	37.47	33.72	30.49	27.71	25.30	22
23	76.30	66.70	58.62	51.79	46.00	41.06	36.84	33.22	30.09	27.39	25.04	23
24	73.77	64.70	57.04	50.53	44.99	40.26	36.20	32.71	29.68	27.06	24.78	24
25	71.30	62.73	55.47	49.28	43.99	39.46	35.56	32.19	29.27	26.73	24.51	25
26	68.88	60.80	53.91	48.03	42.99	38.65	34.91	31.67	28.85	26.39	24.23	26
27	66.51	58.89	52.38	46.80	41.99	37.85	34.26	31.13	28.41	26.03	23.95	27
28	64.19	57.01	50.86	45.56	40.99	37.03	33.59	30.60	27.98	25.68	23.65	28
29	61.91	55.17	49.36	44.34	39.99	36.22	32.93	30.05	27.53	25.31	23.35	29
30	59.68	53.35	47.87	43.12	39.00	35.40	32.25	29.50	27.07	24.93	23.04	30
31	57.50	51.56	46.40	41.91	38.00	34.58	31.58	28.94	26.61	24.55	22.72	31
32	55.37	49.79	44.94	40.71	37.01	33.75	30.89	28.37	26.13	24.15	22.39	32
33	53.27	48.06	43.51	39.52	36.01	32.92	30.20	27.79	25.65	23.75	22.05	33
34	51.22	46.35	42.08	38.33	35.02	32.09	29.50	27.21	25.16	23.34	21.70	34
35	49.22	44.67	40.67	37.14	34.02	31.26	28.80	26.61	24.66	22.91	21.35	35
36	47.25	43.02	39.28	35.97	33.03	30.42	28.09	26.01	24.15	22.48	20.98	36
37	45.32	41.39	37.90	34.80	32.04	29.58	27.37	25.40	23.63	22.04	20.60	37
38	43.44	39.79	36.54	33.64	31.05	28.73	26.65	24.78	23.10	21.58	20.21	38
39	41.59	38.21	35.19	32.48	30.06	27.88	25.92	24.16	22.56	21.12	19.81	39
40	39.78	36.66	33.85	31.34	29.07	27.03	25.19	23.52	22.01	20.65	19.40	40
41	38.01	35.13	32.53	30.20	28.08	26.18	24.45	22.88	21.46	20.16	18.98	41
42	36.28	33.62	31.23	29.06	27.10	25.32	23.70	22.23	20.89	19.66	18.54	42
43	34.58	32.14	29.94	27.93	26.11	24.46	22.95	21.57	20.31	19.15	18.10	43
44	32.92	30.69	28.66	26.81	25.13	23.59	22.19	20.90	19.72	18.63	17.64	44
45	31.29	29.26	27.40	25.70	24.15	22.73	21.42	20.22	19.12	18.10	17.17	45
46	29.70	27.85	26.15	24.60	23.17	21.86	20.65	19.54	18.51	17.56	16.68	46
47	28.15	26.47	24.92	23.50	22.19	20.99	19.87	18.84	17.89	17.01	16.19	47
48	26.63	25.11	23.71	22.41	21.22	20.11	19.09	18.14	17.26	16.44	15.68	48
49	25.14	23.77	22.51	21.34	20.25	19.24	18.30	17.43	16.62	15.86	15.16	49
50	23.68	22.46	21.32	20.27	19.28	18.36	17.51	16.71	15.97	15.27	14.62	50
51	22.26	21.17	20.15	19.20	18.31	17.49	16.71	15.99	15.31	14.67	14.07	51
52	20.87	19.90	18.99	18.14	17.35	16.60	15.91	15.25	14.63	14.05	13.51	52
53	19.50	18.65	17.85	17.09	16.39	15.72	15.09	14.50	13.95	13.42	12.93	53
54	18.17	17.42	16.72	16.05	15.43	14.83	14.28	13.75	13.25	12.78	12.33	54
55	16.86	16.21	15.60	15.02	14.47	13.95	13.45	12.99	12.54	12.12	11.72	55
56	15.58	15.02	14.49	13.99	13.51	13.05	12.62	12.21	11.82	11.45	11.09	56
57	14.33	13.85	13.40	12.96	12.55	12.16	11.78	11.43	11.09	10.76	10.45	57
58	13.10	12.70	12.31	11.95	11.59	11.26	10.94	10.63	10.34	10.05	9.78	58
59	11.89	11.56	11.24	10.93	10.64	10.35	10.08	9.82	9.57	9.33	9.10	59
60	10.71	10.44	10.18	9.92	9.68	9.44	9.22	9.00	8.79	8.59	8.39	60
61	9.55	9.33	9.12	8.92	8.72	8.53	8.35	8.17	8.00	7.83	7.67	61
62	8.42	8.25	8.08	7.92	7.76	7.61	7.46	7.32	7.18	7.05	6.92	62
63	7.30	7.17	7.05	6.92	6.80	6.69	6.57	6.47	6.36	6.25	6.15	63
64	6.21	6.12	6.02	5.93	5.85	5.76	5.68	5.59	5.51	5.44	5.36	64
65	5.14	5.07	5.01	4.95	4.89	4.83	4.77	4.71	4.65	4.60	4.54	65
66	4.08	4.04	4.00	3.96	3.92	3.88	3.85	3.81	3.77	3.74	3.70	66
67	3.04	3.02	3.00	2.98	2.95	2.93	2.91	2.89	2.87	2.85	2.83	67
68	2.02	2.01	2.00	1.99	1.98	1.97	1.96	1.95	1.94	1.93	1.92	68
69	1.00	1.00	1.00	1.00	0.99	0.99	0.99	0.99	0.98	0.98	0.98	69

Table 13: Multipliers for loss of earnings to pension age 75 (males)

Age at date of trial	Multiplier calculated with allowance for projected mortality from the 2008–based population projections and rate of return of											Age at date of trial
	–2.0%	***–1.5%***	***–1.0%***	***–0.5%***	***0.0%***	***0.5%***	***1.0%***	***1.5%***	***2.0%***	***2.5%***	***3.0%***	
16	107.05	90.16	76.55	65.51	56.51	49.13	43.04	37.99	33.77	30.23	27.24	16
17	103.88	87.79	74.76	64.17	55.50	48.37	42.46	37.55	33.44	29.97	27.04	17
18	100.78	85.45	73.01	62.84	54.49	47.60	41.88	37.10	33.10	29.71	26.84	18
19	97.75	83.16	71.27	61.52	53.49	46.83	41.29	36.65	32.75	29.44	26.63	19
20	94.79	80.91	69.55	60.21	52.48	46.06	40.70	36.20	32.40	29.17	26.42	20
21	91.89	78.69	67.86	58.91	51.48	45.29	40.11	35.74	32.04	28.89	26.20	21
22	89.04	76.51	66.17	57.61	50.48	44.52	39.50	35.27	31.67	28.61	25.98	22
23	86.25	74.36	64.51	56.32	49.48	43.74	38.89	34.79	31.30	28.31	25.74	23
24	83.52	72.24	62.86	55.04	48.48	42.95	38.28	34.31	30.92	28.01	25.51	24
25	80.85	70.15	61.23	53.76	47.48	42.17	37.66	33.82	30.53	27.70	25.26	25
26	78.23	68.10	59.63	52.50	46.48	41.38	37.04	33.32	30.14	27.39	25.01	26
27	75.67	66.09	58.03	51.24	45.48	40.59	36.41	32.82	29.74	27.07	24.75	27
28	73.16	64.10	56.46	49.99	44.48	39.79	35.77	32.31	29.32	26.74	24.48	28
29	70.70	62.14	54.90	48.74	43.49	38.99	35.13	31.79	28.91	26.40	24.21	29
30	68.29	60.22	53.35	47.50	42.49	38.19	34.48	31.27	28.48	26.05	23.93	30
31	65.95	58.33	51.84	46.28	41.50	37.39	33.83	30.74	28.05	25.70	23.64	31
32	63.65	56.48	50.34	45.06	40.52	36.59	33.18	30.21	27.62	25.35	23.35	32
33	61.41	54.66	48.86	43.86	39.54	35.79	32.52	29.67	27.18	24.98	23.05	33
34	59.22	52.87	47.40	42.66	38.56	34.98	31.86	29.13	26.73	24.61	22.74	34
35	57.06	51.11	45.95	41.47	37.58	34.17	31.19	28.58	26.27	24.23	22.43	35
36	54.96	49.37	44.52	40.29	36.60	33.36	30.52	28.02	25.80	23.84	22.10	36
37	52.90	47.67	43.11	39.12	35.62	32.55	29.84	27.45	25.33	23.45	21.77	37
38	50.87	45.98	41.70	37.95	34.64	31.73	29.16	26.87	24.85	23.04	21.42	38
39	48.89	44.33	40.31	36.78	33.67	30.91	28.46	26.29	24.35	22.62	21.07	39
40	46.95	42.69	38.94	35.62	32.69	30.08	27.76	25.70	23.85	22.19	20.70	40
41	45.05	41.09	37.58	34.47	31.71	29.25	27.06	25.10	23.34	21.75	20.33	41
42	43.19	39.51	36.24	33.33	30.74	28.42	26.35	24.49	22.81	21.31	19.95	42
43	41.37	37.96	34.91	32.20	29.77	27.59	25.63	23.87	22.29	20.85	19.55	43
44	39.59	36.43	33.60	31.07	28.80	26.76	24.91	23.25	21.75	20.39	19.15	44
45	37.85	34.93	32.31	29.95	27.83	25.92	24.19	22.62	21.20	19.91	18.73	45
46	36.14	33.45	31.03	28.84	26.87	25.08	23.46	21.98	20.64	19.42	18.31	46
47	34.47	32.00	29.76	27.74	25.90	24.24	22.72	21.34	20.08	18.93	17.87	47
48	32.84	30.58	28.52	26.65	24.95	23.39	21.98	20.69	19.50	18.42	17.42	48
49	31.25	29.18	27.29	25.56	23.99	22.55	21.24	20.03	18.92	17.90	16.97	49
50	29.70	27.81	26.07	24.49	23.04	21.71	20.49	19.37	18.33	17.38	16.50	50
51	28.18	26.46	24.88	23.43	22.10	20.87	19.74	18.70	17.74	16.85	16.03	51
52	26.70	25.14	23.70	22.38	21.16	20.03	18.99	18.03	17.13	16.31	15.54	52
53	25.26	23.85	22.54	21.34	20.23	19.19	18.24	17.35	16.52	15.76	15.04	53
54	23.85	22.58	21.40	20.31	19.30	18.35	17.48	16.66	15.90	15.20	14.53	54
55	22.48	21.34	20.28	19.29	18.37	17.52	16.72	15.98	15.28	14.63	14.02	55
56	21.13	20.12	19.17	18.28	17.46	16.68	15.96	15.28	14.64	14.05	13.49	56
57	19.82	18.92	18.07	17.28	16.54	15.85	15.19	14.58	14.00	13.46	12.95	57
58	18.53	17.74	16.99	16.29	15.63	15.00	14.42	13.86	13.34	12.85	12.39	58
59	17.27	16.57	15.91	15.29	14.71	14.16	13.63	13.14	12.67	12.23	11.81	59
60	16.03	15.42	14.85	14.30	13.79	13.30	12.84	12.40	11.99	11.60	11.22	60
61	14.81	14.29	13.79	13.32	12.87	12.45	12.04	11.66	11.29	10.95	10.61	61
62	13.62	13.18	12.75	12.35	11.96	11.59	11.24	10.91	10.59	10.28	9.99	62
63	12.46	12.09	11.73	11.38	11.05	10.74	10.44	10.15	9.88	9.61	9.36	63
64	11.33	11.02	10.72	10.43	10.15	9.89	9.63	9.39	9.15	8.93	8.71	64
65	10.22	9.97	9.72	9.48	9.25	9.03	8.82	8.61	8.42	8.23	8.04	65
66	9.14	8.93	8.73	8.54	8.36	8.18	8.00	7.83	7.67	7.52	7.36	66
67	8.08	7.92	7.76	7.61	7.46	7.32	7.18	7.04	6.91	6.79	6.66	67
68	7.04	6.91	6.79	6.67	6.56	6.45	6.34	6.24	6.14	6.04	5.94	68
69	6.01	5.92	5.83	5.74	5.66	5.58	5.50	5.42	5.34	5.27	5.19	69
70	4.99	4.93	4.87	4.81	4.75	4.69	4.63	4.58	4.52	4.47	4.42	70
71	3.98	3.94	3.90	3.86	3.83	3.79	3.75	3.72	3.68	3.65	3.61	71
72	2.98	2.96	2.94	2.92	2.89	2.87	2.85	2.83	2.81	2.79	2.77	72
73	1.99	1.98	1.97	1.96	1.95	1.94	1.93	1.92	1.91	1.90	1.89	73
74	1.00	0.99	0.99	0.99	0.99	0.98	0.98	0.98	0.98	0.97	0.97	74

Table 14: Multipliers for loss of earnings to pension age 75 (females)

Age at date of trial	Multiplier calculated with allowance for projected mortality from the 2008–based population projections and rate of return of											Age at date of trial
	−2.0%	*−1.5%*	*−1.0%*	*−0.5%*	*0.0%*	*0.5%*	*1.0%*	*1.5%*	*2.0%*	*2.5%*	*3.0%*	
16	109.63	92.19	78.15	66.79	57.53	49.95	43.70	38.52	34.21	30.59	27.53	16
17	106.42	89.80	76.36	65.44	56.52	49.19	43.13	38.09	33.88	30.34	27.34	17
18	103.28	87.44	74.59	64.11	55.51	48.43	42.55	37.65	33.55	30.08	27.15	18
19	100.20	85.12	72.84	62.78	54.51	47.66	41.97	37.21	33.21	29.82	26.95	19
20	97.19	82.84	71.11	61.47	53.50	46.90	41.38	36.76	32.86	29.56	26.74	20
21	94.24	80.59	69.39	60.15	52.50	46.13	40.79	36.30	32.51	29.28	26.53	21
22	91.35	78.38	67.69	58.85	51.49	45.35	40.19	35.84	32.15	29.00	26.31	22
23	88.51	76.19	66.01	57.55	50.49	44.57	39.58	35.37	31.78	28.71	26.08	23
24	85.73	74.04	64.34	56.25	49.48	43.79	38.97	34.89	31.40	28.42	25.85	24
25	83.01	71.93	62.69	54.97	48.48	43.00	38.35	34.40	31.02	28.12	25.61	25
26	80.34	69.84	61.06	53.69	47.47	42.21	37.73	33.91	30.63	27.81	25.37	26
27	77.73	67.79	59.45	52.42	46.47	41.41	37.10	33.41	30.23	27.49	25.11	27
28	75.17	65.77	57.85	51.15	45.46	40.62	36.47	32.90	29.83	27.17	24.85	28
29	72.67	63.79	56.27	49.90	44.46	39.82	35.83	32.39	29.42	26.84	24.59	29
30	70.22	61.83	54.71	48.65	43.46	39.01	35.18	31.87	29.00	26.50	24.31	30
31	67.82	59.91	53.17	47.40	42.46	38.20	34.53	31.34	28.57	26.15	24.03	31
32	65.47	58.01	51.64	46.17	41.46	37.40	33.87	30.81	28.13	25.79	23.74	32
33	63.16	56.15	50.13	44.94	40.46	36.58	33.21	30.26	27.69	25.43	23.44	33
34	60.91	54.31	48.63	43.72	39.47	35.77	32.54	29.72	27.24	25.06	23.13	34
35	58.70	52.51	47.15	42.51	38.47	34.95	31.86	29.16	26.78	24.68	22.82	35
36	56.54	50.73	45.69	41.30	37.47	34.12	31.18	28.59	26.31	24.29	22.49	36
37	54.42	48.98	44.24	40.10	36.48	33.30	30.49	28.02	25.83	23.89	22.16	37
38	52.35	47.26	42.81	38.91	35.49	32.47	29.80	27.44	25.34	23.48	21.81	38
39	50.32	45.57	41.40	37.73	34.49	31.64	29.10	26.85	24.85	23.06	21.46	39
40	48.33	43.90	40.00	36.55	33.50	30.80	28.40	26.26	24.35	22.63	21.10	40
41	46.38	42.26	38.61	35.38	32.51	29.96	27.69	25.65	23.83	22.20	20.73	41
42	44.48	40.64	37.24	34.22	31.53	29.12	26.97	25.04	23.31	21.75	20.34	42
43	42.61	39.06	35.89	33.06	30.54	28.28	26.25	24.42	22.78	21.29	19.95	43
44	40.79	37.49	34.55	31.92	29.55	27.43	25.52	23.79	22.24	20.82	19.55	44
45	39.00	35.96	33.23	30.78	28.57	26.58	24.79	23.16	21.69	20.35	19.13	45
46	37.26	34.45	31.93	29.65	27.59	25.73	24.05	22.52	21.13	19.86	18.71	46
47	35.55	32.97	30.64	28.53	26.62	24.88	23.30	21.87	20.56	19.36	18.27	47
48	33.88	31.51	29.37	27.42	25.64	24.03	22.56	21.21	19.98	18.86	17.83	48
49	32.25	30.08	28.11	26.31	24.67	23.18	21.81	20.55	19.40	18.34	17.37	49
50	30.66	28.68	26.87	25.22	23.71	22.32	21.05	19.88	18.81	17.82	16.90	50
51	29.10	27.30	25.65	24.14	22.75	21.47	20.29	19.20	18.20	17.28	16.42	51
52	27.58	25.94	24.44	23.06	21.78	20.61	19.52	18.52	17.59	16.73	15.93	52
53	26.08	24.61	23.25	21.99	20.83	19.75	18.75	17.83	16.97	16.17	15.43	53
54	24.63	23.30	22.07	20.93	19.87	18.89	17.98	17.13	16.34	15.60	14.91	54
55	23.20	22.01	20.91	19.88	18.92	18.03	17.20	16.42	15.69	15.02	14.38	55
56	21.81	20.75	19.76	18.83	17.97	17.16	16.41	15.70	15.04	14.42	13.84	56
57	20.45	19.50	18.62	17.80	17.02	16.30	15.62	14.98	14.38	13.81	13.28	57
58	19.11	18.28	17.50	16.77	16.08	15.43	14.82	14.25	13.70	13.19	12.71	58
59	17.80	17.07	16.39	15.74	15.13	14.56	14.02	13.50	13.02	12.56	12.12	59
60	16.52	15.88	15.29	14.72	14.19	13.68	13.20	12.75	12.32	11.91	11.52	60
61	15.26	14.71	14.20	13.71	13.24	12.80	12.38	11.98	11.60	11.24	10.89	61
62	14.03	13.56	13.12	12.70	12.30	11.92	11.56	11.21	10.88	10.56	10.26	62
63	12.83	12.43	12.06	11.70	11.36	11.04	10.72	10.42	10.14	9.86	9.60	63
64	11.65	11.33	11.01	10.71	10.43	10.15	9.89	9.63	9.39	9.16	8.93	64
65	10.50	10.24	9.98	9.73	9.50	9.27	9.05	8.84	8.63	8.43	8.24	65
66	9.38	9.16	8.96	8.76	8.57	8.38	8.20	8.03	7.86	7.70	7.54	66
67	8.28	8.11	7.95	7.79	7.64	7.49	7.35	7.21	7.07	6.94	6.81	67
68	7.19	7.07	6.94	6.82	6.70	6.59	6.48	6.37	6.27	6.17	6.07	68
69	6.13	6.04	5.95	5.86	5.77	5.69	5.60	5.52	5.44	5.37	5.29	69
70	5.08	5.01	4.95	4.89	4.83	4.77	4.71	4.66	4.60	4.55	4.49	70
71	4.04	4.00	3.96	3.92	3.88	3.85	3.81	3.77	3.73	3.70	3.66	71
72	3.02	3.00	2.97	2.95	2.93	2.91	2.89	2.86	2.84	2.82	2.80	72
73	2.01	2.00	1.99	1.98	1.97	1.96	1.95	1.94	1.93	1.92	1.91	73
74	1.00	1.00	1.00	0.99	0.99	0.99	0.99	0.98	0.98	0.98	0.98	74

Table 15: Multipliers for loss of pension commencing age 50 (males)

Age at date of trial	Multiplier calculated with allowance for projected mortality from the 2008–based population projections and rate of return of											Age at date of trial
	-2.0%	*-1.5%*	*-1.0%*	*-0.5%*	*0.0%*	*0.5%*	*1.0%*	*1.5%*	*2.0%*	*2.5%*	*3.0%*	
0	179.64	121.70	83.09	57.16	39.61	27.64	19.42	13.74	9.78	7.00	5.04	0
1	176.24	120.05	82.40	56.99	39.70	27.85	19.67	13.99	10.01	7.20	5.21	1
2	172.05	117.83	81.32	56.54	39.59	27.92	19.83	14.17	10.19	7.37	5.36	2
3	167.93	115.64	80.24	56.09	39.49	27.99	19.98	14.35	10.37	7.54	5.51	3
4	163.90	113.48	79.16	55.63	39.37	28.06	20.13	14.53	10.56	7.72	5.67	4
5	159.97	111.36	78.10	55.18	39.26	28.12	20.28	14.72	10.75	7.89	5.83	5
6	156.12	109.27	77.05	54.73	39.14	28.19	20.43	14.91	10.94	8.08	5.99	6
7	152.36	107.22	76.01	54.28	39.03	28.25	20.59	15.10	11.14	8.26	6.16	7
8	148.69	105.21	74.99	53.83	38.91	28.32	20.74	15.29	11.33	8.45	6.34	8
9	145.10	103.23	73.98	53.39	38.80	28.38	20.90	15.48	11.54	8.65	6.52	9
10	141.59	101.28	72.97	52.95	38.68	28.44	21.05	15.68	11.74	8.84	6.70	10
11	138.17	99.37	71.98	52.51	38.56	28.51	21.21	15.87	11.95	9.05	6.89	11
12	134.83	97.50	71.01	52.07	38.44	28.57	21.36	16.07	12.16	9.26	7.08	12
13	131.57	95.66	70.04	51.64	38.33	28.63	21.52	16.28	12.38	9.47	7.28	13
14	128.40	93.86	69.10	51.21	38.21	28.70	21.68	16.48	12.60	9.69	7.48	14
15	125.31	92.10	68.16	50.79	38.10	28.76	21.85	16.69	12.82	9.91	7.69	15
16	122.29	90.37	67.24	50.38	37.99	28.83	22.01	16.90	13.05	10.14	7.91	16
17	119.35	88.68	66.34	49.96	37.88	28.89	22.17	17.12	13.29	10.37	8.13	17
18	116.49	87.02	65.46	49.56	37.77	28.96	22.34	17.34	13.53	10.61	8.36	18
19	113.71	85.41	64.59	49.16	37.67	29.03	22.52	17.56	13.77	10.86	8.60	19
20	111.01	83.83	63.74	48.78	37.57	29.11	22.69	17.79	14.02	11.11	8.85	20
21	108.37	82.28	62.90	48.39	37.46	29.18	22.87	18.02	14.28	11.37	9.10	21
22	105.78	80.76	62.06	48.00	37.36	29.26	23.04	18.25	14.53	11.63	9.36	22
23	103.25	79.25	61.24	47.62	37.26	29.33	23.22	18.49	14.80	11.90	9.62	23
24	100.79	77.78	60.42	47.24	37.16	29.40	23.40	18.73	15.06	12.18	9.90	24
25	98.39	76.35	59.63	46.86	37.06	29.48	23.58	18.97	15.34	12.46	10.18	25
26	96.06	74.95	58.85	46.50	36.96	29.56	23.77	19.22	15.62	12.76	10.47	26
27	93.80	73.57	58.08	46.14	36.87	29.64	23.96	19.47	15.90	13.06	10.77	27
28	91.57	72.22	57.32	45.77	36.77	29.71	24.14	19.72	16.19	13.36	11.08	28
29	89.39	70.88	56.56	45.41	36.68	29.79	24.33	19.98	16.49	13.67	11.39	29
30	87.27	69.58	55.82	45.06	36.58	29.87	24.52	20.24	16.79	13.99	11.72	30
31	85.23	68.32	55.10	44.71	36.50	29.96	24.72	20.51	17.10	14.33	12.05	31
32	83.24	67.09	54.41	44.38	36.42	30.05	24.93	20.79	17.42	14.67	12.40	32
33	81.32	65.90	53.73	44.06	36.35	30.15	25.14	21.07	17.75	15.02	12.77	33
34	79.44	64.72	53.05	43.74	36.27	30.24	25.35	21.36	18.08	15.38	13.14	34
35	77.60	63.57	52.39	43.42	36.20	30.34	25.56	21.65	18.42	15.75	13.52	35
36	75.82	62.44	51.74	43.11	36.13	30.44	25.78	21.95	18.77	16.13	13.92	36
37	74.08	61.34	51.09	42.81	36.06	30.54	26.00	22.25	19.12	16.51	14.32	37
38	72.37	60.25	50.46	42.50	35.99	30.64	26.22	22.55	19.49	16.91	14.74	38
39	70.70	59.18	49.83	42.19	35.92	30.74	26.45	22.86	19.85	17.32	15.17	39
40	69.07	58.13	49.21	41.89	35.85	30.85	26.67	23.18	20.23	17.74	15.62	40
41	67.49	57.11	48.61	41.60	35.79	30.96	26.91	23.50	20.62	18.17	16.08	41
42	65.95	56.11	48.01	41.31	35.73	31.07	27.14	23.83	21.01	18.61	16.55	42
43	64.46	55.14	47.44	41.03	35.68	31.18	27.39	24.16	21.42	19.07	17.04	43
44	63.01	54.19	46.87	40.76	35.63	31.30	27.63	24.51	21.84	19.54	17.55	44
45	61.60	53.26	46.32	40.49	35.58	31.42	27.89	24.86	22.26	20.02	18.07	45
46	60.22	52.36	45.77	40.23	35.54	31.55	28.14	25.22	22.70	20.52	18.62	46
47	58.88	51.47	45.24	39.98	35.50	31.68	28.41	25.59	23.15	21.03	19.18	47
48	57.59	50.62	44.73	39.73	35.47	31.83	28.69	25.97	23.62	21.56	19.76	48
49	56.34	49.79	44.23	39.50	35.46	31.98	28.97	26.37	24.10	22.11	20.37	49
50	55.14	48.99	43.76	39.29	35.45	32.14	29.27	26.78	24.60	22.69	21.01	50

Table 16: Multipliers for loss of pension commencing age 50 (females)

Age at date of trial	Multiplier calculated with allowance for projected mortality from the 2008–based population projections and rate of return of											Age at date of trial
	–2.0%	*–1.5%*	*–1.0%*	*–0.5%*	*0.0%*	*0.5%*	*1.0%*	*1.5%*	*2.0%*	*2.5%*	*3.0%*	
0	199.59	134.37	91.19	62.37	42.98	29.85	20.87	14.70	10.42	7.43	5.33	0
1	195.74	132.49	90.40	62.16	43.07	30.06	21.13	14.95	10.65	7.64	5.51	1
2	191.18	130.11	89.25	61.69	42.97	30.15	21.30	15.16	10.85	7.82	5.67	2
3	186.71	127.75	88.10	61.23	42.87	30.24	21.48	15.36	11.05	8.00	5.83	3
4	182.34	125.44	86.97	60.76	42.77	30.32	21.65	15.56	11.26	8.19	6.00	4
5	178.06	123.16	85.85	60.30	42.67	30.41	21.82	15.77	11.46	8.39	6.17	5
6	173.88	120.92	84.74	59.84	42.56	30.49	22.00	15.97	11.67	8.58	6.35	6
7	169.79	118.72	83.65	59.38	42.46	30.58	22.17	16.18	11.89	8.78	6.53	7
8	165.80	116.55	82.56	58.92	42.36	30.66	22.35	16.40	12.10	8.99	6.72	8
9	161.89	114.43	81.49	58.47	42.25	30.75	22.53	16.61	12.33	9.20	6.91	9
10	158.08	112.34	80.43	58.02	42.15	30.83	22.70	16.83	12.55	9.42	7.11	10
11	154.36	110.29	79.39	57.57	42.04	30.92	22.89	17.05	12.78	9.64	7.31	11
12	150.73	108.28	78.36	57.12	41.94	31.00	23.07	17.27	13.01	9.86	7.52	12
13	147.17	106.30	77.34	56.68	41.83	31.08	23.25	17.50	13.25	10.09	7.73	13
14	143.71	104.36	76.34	56.24	41.73	31.17	23.43	17.73	13.49	10.33	7.95	14
15	140.33	102.45	75.35	55.81	41.62	31.25	23.62	17.96	13.74	10.57	8.18	15
16	137.02	100.58	74.37	55.38	41.52	31.34	23.81	18.20	13.99	10.82	8.41	16
17	133.80	98.75	73.41	54.95	41.42	31.42	24.00	18.44	14.25	11.07	8.65	17
18	130.66	96.95	72.46	54.53	41.32	31.51	24.19	18.68	14.51	11.33	8.90	18
19	127.60	95.19	71.52	54.11	41.22	31.60	24.38	18.92	14.78	11.60	9.16	19
20	124.61	93.47	70.61	53.70	41.12	31.69	24.58	19.18	15.05	11.87	9.42	20
21	121.70	91.78	69.70	53.30	41.03	31.78	24.78	19.43	15.32	12.15	9.69	21
22	118.85	90.11	68.80	52.89	40.93	31.87	24.97	19.69	15.61	12.44	9.97	22
23	116.05	88.47	67.91	52.48	40.82	31.96	25.17	19.94	15.89	12.73	10.25	23
24	113.32	86.85	67.03	52.08	40.72	32.05	25.37	20.21	16.18	13.03	10.54	24
25	110.66	85.27	66.16	51.68	40.62	32.14	25.57	20.47	16.48	13.33	10.85	25
26	108.06	83.73	65.31	51.28	40.53	32.23	25.78	20.74	16.78	13.65	11.16	26
27	105.53	82.21	64.47	50.89	40.43	32.32	25.99	21.02	17.09	13.97	11.48	27
28	103.06	80.72	63.64	50.50	40.33	32.41	26.19	21.29	17.40	14.30	11.81	28
29	100.65	79.26	62.82	50.12	40.24	32.50	26.41	21.58	17.72	14.64	12.14	29
30	98.30	77.82	62.02	49.74	40.15	32.60	26.62	21.86	18.05	14.98	12.49	30
31	96.01	76.42	61.23	49.37	40.06	32.69	26.84	22.15	18.38	15.33	12.85	31
32	93.78	75.05	60.46	49.00	39.97	32.79	27.06	22.45	18.73	15.70	13.22	32
33	91.61	73.71	59.69	48.64	39.88	32.89	27.28	22.75	19.07	16.07	13.61	33
34	89.48	72.38	58.93	48.28	39.79	32.99	27.50	23.05	19.43	16.45	14.00	34
35	87.39	71.08	58.18	47.92	39.70	33.09	27.73	23.36	19.79	16.84	14.40	35
36	85.37	69.81	57.45	47.57	39.62	33.19	27.96	23.68	20.16	17.24	14.82	36
37	83.40	68.57	56.73	47.22	39.54	33.29	28.19	24.00	20.53	17.65	15.25	37
38	81.47	67.35	56.02	46.87	39.45	33.40	28.43	24.32	20.92	18.07	15.69	38
39	79.59	66.15	55.31	46.53	39.37	33.50	28.66	24.65	21.31	18.50	16.14	39
40	77.75	64.97	54.62	46.19	39.29	33.61	28.90	24.99	21.71	18.95	16.61	40
41	75.96	63.82	53.94	45.86	39.22	33.72	29.15	25.33	22.11	19.40	17.10	41
42	74.22	62.69	53.27	45.54	39.14	33.83	29.40	25.67	22.53	19.87	17.60	42
43	72.53	61.59	52.62	45.22	39.07	33.95	29.65	26.03	22.96	20.35	18.11	43
44	70.88	60.52	51.98	44.90	39.01	34.07	29.91	26.39	23.40	20.84	18.64	44
45	69.28	59.47	51.35	44.60	38.94	34.19	30.17	26.76	23.85	21.35	19.19	45
46	67.72	58.45	50.74	44.30	38.89	34.32	30.44	27.14	24.31	21.87	19.76	46
47	66.20	57.45	50.14	44.01	38.83	34.45	30.72	27.53	24.78	22.41	20.35	47
48	64.73	56.48	49.56	43.73	38.79	34.59	31.01	27.93	25.27	22.97	20.96	48
49	63.31	55.54	48.99	43.46	38.76	34.74	31.30	28.34	25.77	23.54	21.59	49
50	61.93	54.62	48.44	43.20	38.73	34.90	31.61	28.76	26.29	24.14	22.25	50

Table 17: Multipliers for loss of pension commencing age 55 (males)

Age at date of trial	Multiplier calculated with allowance for projected mortality from the 2008–based population projections and rate of return of											Age at date of trial
	–2.0%	*–1.5%*	*–1.0%*	*–0.5%*	*0.0%*	*0.5%*	*1.0%*	*1.5%*	*2.0%*	*2.5%*	*3.0%*	
0	165.74	111.07	74.94	50.90	34.80	23.94	16.57	11.54	8.08	5.69	4.02	0
1	162.56	109.52	74.30	50.73	34.87	24.11	16.78	11.74	8.26	5.85	4.16	1
2	158.64	107.46	73.29	50.31	34.76	24.17	16.90	11.89	8.41	5.98	4.27	2
3	154.79	105.43	72.29	49.89	34.65	24.22	17.02	12.04	8.56	6.12	4.39	3
4	151.03	103.43	71.30	49.47	34.54	24.27	17.15	12.19	8.71	6.26	4.52	4
5	147.35	101.46	70.32	49.05	34.43	24.31	17.27	12.34	8.86	6.40	4.64	5
6	143.76	99.52	69.35	48.63	34.32	24.36	17.39	12.49	9.02	6.54	4.77	6
7	140.25	97.62	68.39	48.22	34.20	24.41	17.52	12.64	9.17	6.69	4.90	7
8	136.83	95.76	67.44	47.80	34.09	24.45	17.64	12.80	9.33	6.84	5.04	8
9	133.48	93.92	66.51	47.39	33.97	24.50	17.77	12.96	9.50	7.00	5.18	9
10	130.21	92.11	65.58	46.98	33.86	24.54	17.89	13.11	9.66	7.15	5.32	10
11	127.02	90.34	64.67	46.57	33.74	24.59	18.02	13.27	9.83	7.32	5.47	11
12	123.91	88.61	63.77	46.17	33.63	24.63	18.14	13.44	10.00	7.48	5.62	12
13	120.87	86.91	62.88	45.77	33.51	24.68	18.27	13.60	10.18	7.65	5.78	13
14	117.91	85.24	62.00	45.37	33.40	24.72	18.40	13.77	10.35	7.82	5.94	14
15	115.03	83.61	61.14	44.98	33.29	24.77	18.53	13.94	10.53	8.00	6.10	15
16	112.22	82.01	60.30	44.60	33.17	24.81	18.66	14.11	10.72	8.18	6.27	16
17	109.49	80.45	59.47	44.22	33.06	24.86	18.79	14.28	10.90	8.37	6.45	17
18	106.83	78.92	58.65	43.84	32.96	24.91	18.93	14.46	11.10	8.56	6.63	18
19	104.24	77.42	57.85	43.47	32.85	24.96	19.07	14.64	11.29	8.75	6.81	19
20	101.73	75.97	57.07	43.11	32.75	25.02	19.21	14.82	11.49	8.95	7.00	20
21	99.28	74.54	56.29	42.76	32.65	25.07	19.35	15.01	11.70	9.16	7.20	21
22	96.87	73.13	55.52	42.40	32.55	25.12	19.49	15.19	11.90	9.37	7.40	22
23	94.52	71.74	54.76	42.04	32.45	25.17	19.63	15.38	12.11	9.58	7.61	23
24	92.23	70.38	54.02	41.69	32.34	25.23	19.77	15.58	12.33	9.80	7.82	24
25	90.00	69.05	53.28	41.34	32.24	25.28	19.92	15.77	12.54	10.02	8.04	25
26	87.84	67.76	52.56	41.00	32.15	25.34	20.07	15.97	12.77	10.25	8.27	26
27	85.73	66.49	51.86	40.67	32.06	25.40	20.22	16.17	13.00	10.49	8.50	27
28	83.67	65.24	51.16	40.33	31.96	25.45	20.37	16.38	13.23	10.73	8.74	28
29	81.64	64.01	50.46	39.99	31.86	25.51	20.52	16.58	13.46	10.97	8.98	29
30	79.68	62.81	49.78	39.66	31.76	25.56	20.67	16.79	13.70	11.23	9.24	30
31	77.78	61.65	49.12	39.35	31.68	25.63	20.83	17.01	13.95	11.49	9.50	31
32	75.95	60.52	48.48	39.04	31.60	25.69	20.99	17.23	14.20	11.76	9.77	32
33	74.17	59.42	47.86	38.74	31.52	25.77	21.16	17.46	14.46	12.03	10.05	33
34	72.42	58.34	47.24	38.44	31.44	25.84	21.33	17.69	14.73	12.32	10.34	34
35	70.72	57.27	46.62	38.15	31.36	25.91	21.50	17.92	15.00	12.61	10.64	35
36	69.07	56.24	46.03	37.86	31.29	25.98	21.68	18.16	15.28	12.90	10.94	36
37	67.45	55.22	45.44	37.57	31.22	26.06	21.85	18.40	15.56	13.21	11.26	37
38	65.87	54.22	44.85	37.29	31.14	26.13	22.03	18.65	15.85	13.52	11.58	38
39	64.33	53.23	44.27	37.00	31.07	26.21	22.21	18.89	16.14	13.84	11.91	39
40	62.82	52.27	43.70	36.72	31.00	26.28	22.38	19.14	16.44	14.17	12.26	40
41	61.36	51.33	43.15	36.45	30.93	26.36	22.57	19.40	16.74	14.50	12.61	41
42	59.93	50.41	42.60	36.18	30.86	26.45	22.76	19.66	17.06	14.85	12.98	42
43	58.55	49.51	42.07	35.92	30.80	26.53	22.95	19.93	17.38	15.21	13.36	43
44	57.21	48.64	41.55	35.66	30.74	26.62	23.15	20.21	17.71	15.57	13.75	44
45	55.90	47.78	41.04	35.41	30.69	26.71	23.35	20.49	18.04	15.95	14.15	45
46	54.63	46.95	40.54	35.16	30.64	26.81	23.55	20.77	18.39	16.34	14.57	46
47	53.39	46.14	40.05	34.93	30.59	26.91	23.76	21.06	18.74	16.74	15.00	47
48	52.20	45.35	39.58	34.70	30.55	27.01	23.98	21.37	19.11	17.15	15.45	48
49	51.04	44.58	39.12	34.48	30.52	27.12	24.20	21.68	19.49	17.58	15.92	49
50	49.93	43.85	38.68	34.27	30.50	27.25	24.44	22.00	19.88	18.03	16.40	50
51	48.86	43.14	38.26	34.08	30.49	27.38	24.69	22.34	20.29	18.49	16.91	51
52	47.83	42.46	37.86	33.91	30.49	27.53	24.95	22.69	20.72	18.98	17.44	52
53	46.84	41.81	37.48	33.74	30.50	27.68	25.22	23.06	21.16	19.48	17.99	53
54	45.90	41.19	37.12	33.60	30.53	27.86	25.51	23.44	21.62	20.01	18.57	54
55	44.99	40.60	36.79	33.47	30.58	28.04	25.81	23.85	22.11	20.56	19.18	55

Table 18: Multipliers for loss of pension commencing age 55 (females)

Age at date of trial	Multiplier calculated with allowance for projected mortality from the 2008–based population projections and rate of return of											Age at date of trial
	–2.0%	***–1.5%***	***–1.0%***	***–0.5%***	***0.0%***	***0.5%***	***1.0%***	***1.5%***	***2.0%***	***2.5%***	***3.0%***	
0	185.47	123.56	82.90	56.01	38.10	26.08	17.97	12.46	8.69	6.09	4.30	0
1	181.85	121.80	82.16	55.81	38.16	26.26	18.19	12.68	8.88	6.26	4.44	1
2	177.57	119.58	81.09	55.37	38.06	26.33	18.33	12.84	9.05	6.41	4.57	2
3	173.37	117.38	80.03	54.94	37.96	26.40	18.48	13.01	9.21	6.56	4.69	3
4	169.26	115.23	78.98	54.51	37.86	26.47	18.62	13.18	9.38	6.71	4.83	4
5	165.25	113.10	77.94	54.08	37.76	26.54	18.76	13.35	9.55	6.87	4.97	5
6	161.33	111.01	76.92	53.65	37.66	26.60	18.91	13.52	9.72	7.03	5.11	6
7	157.49	108.96	75.90	53.22	37.56	26.67	19.05	13.69	9.89	7.19	5.25	7
8	153.74	106.95	74.89	52.79	37.45	26.73	19.20	13.87	10.07	7.36	5.40	8
9	150.08	104.96	73.90	52.37	37.35	26.80	19.35	14.04	10.25	7.53	5.55	9
10	146.51	103.02	72.92	51.95	37.24	26.86	19.49	14.22	10.44	7.70	5.71	10
11	143.02	101.11	71.95	51.53	37.14	26.93	19.64	14.41	10.63	7.88	5.87	11
12	139.61	99.24	71.00	51.12	37.04	26.99	19.79	14.59	10.82	8.06	6.04	12
13	136.29	97.39	70.05	50.71	36.93	27.06	19.94	14.78	11.01	8.25	6.21	13
14	133.04	95.59	69.12	50.30	36.83	27.12	20.09	14.97	11.21	8.44	6.38	14
15	129.87	93.82	68.21	49.90	36.72	27.19	20.25	15.16	11.41	8.63	6.56	15
16	126.78	92.08	67.30	49.50	36.62	27.26	20.40	15.35	11.61	8.83	6.75	16
17	123.76	90.37	66.41	49.10	36.52	27.32	20.55	15.55	11.82	9.03	6.94	17
18	120.82	88.70	65.53	48.71	36.42	27.39	20.71	15.75	12.03	9.24	7.13	18
19	117.96	87.07	64.67	48.32	36.32	27.46	20.87	15.95	12.25	9.46	7.34	19
20	115.17	85.47	63.82	47.94	36.23	27.53	21.03	16.16	12.47	9.68	7.54	20
21	112.45	83.90	62.98	47.56	36.13	27.60	21.20	16.37	12.70	9.90	7.76	21
22	109.78	82.35	62.15	47.19	36.03	27.67	21.36	16.58	12.93	10.13	7.98	22
23	107.16	80.82	61.33	46.81	35.93	27.73	21.52	16.79	13.16	10.37	8.20	23
24	104.61	79.32	60.51	46.43	35.83	27.80	21.68	17.00	13.40	10.61	8.43	24
25	102.12	77.86	59.71	46.06	35.73	27.87	21.85	17.22	13.64	10.85	8.67	25
26	99.70	76.42	58.92	45.69	35.63	27.94	22.02	17.44	13.88	11.10	8.92	26
27	97.34	75.01	58.15	45.33	35.54	28.01	22.19	17.67	14.13	11.36	9.17	27
28	95.02	73.63	57.38	44.97	35.44	28.08	22.36	17.89	14.39	11.62	9.43	28
29	92.77	72.27	56.62	44.61	35.34	28.15	22.53	18.12	14.65	11.89	9.70	29
30	90.58	70.94	55.88	44.26	35.25	28.22	22.71	18.36	14.91	12.17	9.97	30
31	88.45	69.65	55.15	43.92	35.16	28.29	22.88	18.60	15.18	12.45	10.26	31
32	86.37	68.38	54.44	43.58	35.07	28.37	23.06	18.84	15.46	12.74	10.55	32
33	84.34	67.13	53.73	43.24	34.98	28.45	23.24	19.09	15.74	13.04	10.85	33
34	82.35	65.90	53.03	42.90	34.89	28.52	23.43	19.33	16.03	13.35	11.16	34
35	80.41	64.70	52.34	42.57	34.80	28.60	23.61	19.59	16.32	13.66	11.48	35
36	78.53	63.52	51.66	42.24	34.72	28.67	23.80	19.84	16.62	13.98	11.80	36
37	76.69	62.37	51.00	41.92	34.63	28.75	23.99	20.10	16.92	14.30	12.14	37
38	74.89	61.24	50.34	41.60	34.55	28.83	24.18	20.37	17.23	14.64	12.49	38
39	73.14	60.13	49.69	41.28	34.46	28.91	24.37	20.64	17.55	14.98	12.85	39
40	71.43	59.04	49.05	40.97	34.38	29.00	24.57	20.91	17.87	15.34	13.22	40
41	69.76	57.97	48.43	40.66	34.30	29.08	24.77	21.19	18.20	15.70	13.60	41
42	68.14	56.93	47.81	40.35	34.23	29.17	24.97	21.47	18.54	16.07	13.99	42
43	66.56	55.91	47.21	40.05	34.15	29.25	25.17	21.76	18.88	16.45	14.39	43
44	65.03	54.92	46.62	39.76	34.08	29.35	25.38	22.05	19.23	16.84	14.81	44
45	63.54	53.95	46.04	39.48	34.02	29.44	25.60	22.35	19.60	17.25	15.24	45
46	62.09	53.00	45.47	39.20	33.95	29.54	25.82	22.66	19.97	17.66	15.68	46
47	60.68	52.07	44.91	38.93	33.89	29.64	26.04	22.97	20.35	18.09	16.14	47
48	59.31	51.18	44.38	38.66	33.84	29.75	26.27	23.30	20.74	18.53	16.62	48
49	57.99	50.31	43.85	38.41	33.80	29.87	26.51	23.63	21.14	18.99	17.12	49
50	56.70	49.46	43.35	38.17	33.76	29.99	26.76	23.97	21.56	19.46	17.63	50
51	55.46	48.63	42.85	37.93	33.73	30.12	27.01	24.32	21.99	19.95	18.16	51
52	54.25	47.83	42.37	37.70	33.70	30.25	27.27	24.68	22.43	20.45	18.71	52
53	53.08	47.05	41.90	37.49	33.68	30.40	27.54	25.06	22.88	20.97	19.29	53
54	51.95	46.30	41.45	37.28	33.68	30.55	27.83	25.44	23.35	21.51	19.88	54
55	50.86	45.57	41.02	37.09	33.68	30.71	28.12	25.84	23.84	22.07	20.51	55

Table 19: Multipliers for loss of pension commencing age 60 (males)

Age at date of trial	Multiplier calculated with allowance for projected mortality from the 2008–based population projections and rate of return of											Age at date of trial
	–2.0%	*–1.5%*	*–1.0%*	*–0.5%*	*0.0%*	*0.5%*	*1.0%*	*1.5%*	*2.0%*	*2.5%*	*3.0%*	
0	150.59	99.76	66.49	44.58	30.06	20.38	13.89	9.52	6.56	4.54	3.16	0
1	147.63	98.33	65.89	44.41	30.10	20.52	14.06	9.69	6.70	4.66	3.26	1
2	144.02	96.44	64.97	44.02	30.00	20.55	14.16	9.80	6.82	4.77	3.35	2
3	140.47	94.58	64.06	43.63	29.89	20.59	14.26	9.92	6.94	4.88	3.44	3
4	137.00	92.74	63.15	43.25	29.78	20.62	14.35	10.04	7.06	4.98	3.54	4
5	133.61	90.93	62.25	42.86	29.67	20.65	14.45	10.16	7.18	5.10	3.63	5
6	130.29	89.16	61.36	42.47	29.56	20.68	14.54	10.28	7.30	5.21	3.73	6
7	127.06	87.42	60.49	42.09	29.45	20.71	14.64	10.40	7.42	5.32	3.83	7
8	123.91	85.71	59.63	41.71	29.34	20.74	14.74	10.52	7.55	5.44	3.94	8
9	120.82	84.03	58.77	41.33	29.22	20.77	14.84	10.65	7.68	5.56	4.05	9
10	117.81	82.38	57.93	40.95	29.11	20.80	14.93	10.77	7.81	5.68	4.16	10
11	114.87	80.76	57.09	40.58	29.00	20.82	15.03	10.90	7.94	5.81	4.27	11
12	112.01	79.17	56.27	40.21	28.88	20.85	15.13	11.03	8.07	5.94	4.39	12
13	109.22	77.62	55.46	39.84	28.77	20.88	15.23	11.16	8.21	6.07	4.50	13
14	106.50	76.10	54.67	39.48	28.66	20.91	15.33	11.29	8.35	6.20	4.63	14
15	103.85	74.61	53.88	39.12	28.55	20.94	15.43	11.42	8.49	6.34	4.75	15
16	101.27	73.15	53.11	38.77	28.44	20.96	15.53	11.55	8.63	6.48	4.88	16
17	98.76	71.72	52.36	38.42	28.33	20.99	15.63	11.69	8.78	6.62	5.02	17
18	96.32	70.32	51.61	38.07	28.23	21.03	15.74	11.83	8.93	6.77	5.15	18
19	93.94	68.96	50.88	37.74	28.12	21.06	15.84	11.97	9.08	6.92	5.30	19
20	91.64	67.63	50.17	37.41	28.02	21.09	15.95	12.11	9.24	7.08	5.44	20
21	89.39	66.33	49.47	37.08	27.92	21.13	16.06	12.26	9.40	7.23	5.59	21
22	87.18	65.04	48.77	36.75	27.82	21.16	16.17	12.41	9.56	7.40	5.74	22
23	85.02	63.77	48.08	36.42	27.72	21.19	16.28	12.55	9.72	7.56	5.90	23
24	82.92	62.54	47.40	36.09	27.62	21.23	16.39	12.70	9.89	7.73	6.06	24
25	80.88	61.33	46.73	35.78	27.52	21.26	16.50	12.86	10.06	7.90	6.23	25
26	78.91	60.15	46.08	35.46	27.42	21.30	16.61	13.01	10.23	8.08	6.40	26
27	76.98	59.00	45.44	35.16	27.33	21.34	16.73	13.17	10.41	8.26	6.58	27
28	75.09	57.86	44.80	34.85	27.23	21.37	16.84	13.33	10.59	8.45	6.76	28
29	73.23	56.74	44.17	34.54	27.13	21.41	16.96	13.49	10.77	8.63	6.95	29
30	71.44	55.65	43.55	34.24	27.04	21.44	17.08	13.65	10.96	8.83	7.14	30
31	69.70	54.59	42.95	33.95	26.95	21.48	17.20	13.82	11.15	9.03	7.34	31
32	68.02	53.56	42.37	33.66	26.86	21.53	17.32	13.99	11.35	9.23	7.54	32
33	66.40	52.56	41.80	33.39	26.79	21.58	17.45	14.17	11.55	9.45	7.75	33
34	64.81	51.58	41.24	33.12	26.71	21.63	17.58	14.35	11.76	9.66	7.97	34
35	63.25	50.61	40.68	32.84	26.63	21.67	17.71	14.53	11.96	9.89	8.20	35
36	61.74	49.67	40.14	32.58	26.55	21.72	17.85	14.72	12.18	10.11	8.43	36
37	60.27	48.75	39.60	32.31	26.47	21.78	17.98	14.90	12.40	10.35	8.66	37
38	58.83	47.84	39.07	32.05	26.40	21.83	18.12	15.09	12.62	10.58	8.91	38
39	57.42	46.95	38.55	31.79	26.32	21.88	18.25	15.28	12.84	10.83	9.16	39
40	56.04	46.07	38.03	31.53	26.24	21.93	18.39	15.48	13.07	11.08	9.42	40
41	54.71	45.22	37.53	31.28	26.17	21.98	18.53	15.68	13.31	11.33	9.68	41
42	53.42	44.38	37.04	31.03	26.10	22.03	18.67	15.88	13.55	11.60	9.96	42
43	52.16	43.57	36.55	30.79	26.03	22.09	18.82	16.09	13.80	11.87	10.24	43
44	50.93	42.78	36.08	30.55	25.97	22.15	18.97	16.30	14.05	12.15	10.54	44
45	49.74	42.01	35.62	30.32	25.91	22.22	19.12	16.51	14.31	12.44	10.84	45
46	48.58	41.25	35.16	30.09	25.85	22.28	19.28	16.73	14.57	12.73	11.15	46
47	47.46	40.51	34.72	29.87	25.79	22.35	19.44	16.96	14.84	13.03	11.48	47
48	46.37	39.80	34.29	29.65	25.74	22.42	19.60	17.19	15.12	13.35	11.81	48
49	45.32	39.10	33.87	29.45	25.70	22.50	19.77	17.43	15.41	13.67	12.16	49
50	44.30	38.43	33.47	29.26	25.66	22.59	19.95	17.68	15.71	14.01	12.52	50
51	43.33	37.79	33.09	29.07	25.64	22.69	20.14	17.94	16.03	14.36	12.90	51
52	42.39	37.17	32.72	28.91	25.62	22.79	20.34	18.21	16.35	14.72	13.30	52
53	41.49	36.58	32.37	28.75	25.62	22.91	20.55	18.49	16.69	15.11	13.71	53
54	40.63	36.01	32.04	28.61	25.63	23.04	20.77	18.79	17.04	15.50	14.14	54

Table 19: Multipliers for loss of pension commencing age 60 (males) *continued*

Age at date of trial	Multiplier calculated with allowance for projected mortality from the 2008–based population projections and rate of return of											Age at date of trial
	–2.0%	***–1.5%***	***–1.0%***	***–0.5%***	***0.0%***	***0.5%***	***1.0%***	***1.5%***	***2.0%***	***2.5%***	***3.0%***	
55	39.81	35.48	31.73	28.48	25.65	23.18	21.01	19.10	17.41	15.92	14.60	55
56	39.03	34.97	31.45	28.37	25.69	23.33	21.26	19.43	17.80	16.36	15.07	56
57	38.29	34.49	31.18	28.28	25.74	23.50	21.52	19.77	18.21	16.82	15.57	57
58	37.56	34.02	30.92	28.20	25.80	23.68	21.79	20.12	18.63	17.29	16.09	58
59	36.86	33.56	30.67	28.12	25.86	23.86	22.07	20.49	19.06	17.79	16.64	59
60	36.17	33.12	30.42	28.04	25.92	24.04	22.36	20.86	19.51	18.30	17.20	60

Table 20: Multipliers for loss of pension commencing age 60 (females)

Age at date of trial	Multiplier calculated with allowance for projected mortality from the 2008–based population projections and rate of return of											Age at date of trial
	–2.0%	*–1.5%*	*–1.0%*	*–0.5%*	*0.0%*	*0.5%*	*1.0%*	*1.5%*	*2.0%*	*2.5%*	*3.0%*	
0	169.99	112.01	74.27	49.55	33.26	22.45	15.24	10.40	7.14	4.92	3.41	0
1	166.62	110.38	73.58	49.35	33.30	22.59	15.42	10.58	7.30	5.06	3.52	1
2	162.64	108.33	72.60	48.95	33.20	22.65	15.53	10.71	7.43	5.17	3.62	2
3	158.74	106.30	71.62	48.55	33.10	22.70	15.65	10.85	7.56	5.29	3.72	3
4	154.93	104.31	70.66	48.15	33.00	22.75	15.77	10.98	7.69	5.41	3.83	4
5	151.21	102.36	69.71	47.75	32.90	22.80	15.88	11.12	7.83	5.54	3.93	5
6	147.57	100.43	68.76	47.36	32.80	22.85	16.00	11.26	7.97	5.66	4.04	6
7	144.01	98.54	67.83	46.96	32.70	22.89	16.11	11.40	8.11	5.79	4.16	7
8	140.54	96.68	66.91	46.57	32.60	22.94	16.23	11.54	8.25	5.92	4.27	8
9	137.14	94.85	65.99	46.18	32.49	22.99	16.35	11.69	8.39	6.06	4.39	9
10	133.83	93.06	65.09	45.79	32.39	23.03	16.47	11.83	8.54	6.20	4.51	10
11	130.60	91.31	64.21	45.41	32.29	23.08	16.59	11.98	8.69	6.34	4.64	11
12	127.45	89.58	63.33	45.02	32.18	23.13	16.71	12.13	8.84	6.48	4.77	12
13	124.36	87.89	62.47	44.65	32.08	23.17	16.83	12.28	9.00	6.63	4.90	13
14	121.36	86.23	61.62	44.27	31.98	23.22	16.95	12.43	9.16	6.78	5.04	14
15	118.43	84.60	60.77	43.90	31.88	23.27	17.07	12.58	9.32	6.93	5.18	15
16	115.57	83.00	59.95	43.53	31.78	23.31	17.19	12.74	9.48	7.09	5.32	16
17	112.78	81.44	59.13	43.16	31.67	23.36	17.32	12.90	9.65	7.25	5.47	17
18	110.06	79.90	58.33	42.80	31.58	23.41	17.44	13.06	9.82	7.42	5.62	18
19	107.41	78.40	57.53	42.45	31.48	23.46	17.57	13.22	9.99	7.58	5.78	19
20	104.83	76.93	56.76	42.10	31.38	23.51	17.70	13.38	10.17	7.76	5.94	20
21	102.32	75.49	55.99	41.75	31.29	23.56	17.83	13.55	10.35	7.93	6.11	21
22	99.85	74.07	55.23	41.40	31.19	23.61	17.96	13.72	10.53	8.12	6.28	22
23	97.44	72.67	54.48	41.05	31.09	23.66	18.09	13.89	10.71	8.30	6.45	23
24	95.08	71.29	53.73	40.70	30.99	23.70	18.22	14.06	10.90	8.49	6.63	24
25	92.79	69.95	53.00	40.36	30.89	23.75	18.35	14.24	11.09	8.68	6.82	25
26	90.55	68.63	52.28	40.03	30.79	23.80	18.48	14.41	11.29	8.88	7.01	26
27	88.37	67.34	51.57	39.69	30.70	23.85	18.62	14.59	11.49	9.08	7.20	27
28	86.24	66.07	50.87	39.36	30.60	23.90	18.75	14.77	11.69	9.29	7.41	28
29	84.17	64.83	50.18	39.03	30.51	23.95	18.89	14.96	11.90	9.50	7.61	29
30	82.15	63.61	49.50	38.71	30.41	24.00	19.03	15.15	12.11	9.71	7.83	30
31	80.18	62.43	48.84	38.39	30.32	24.05	19.17	15.34	12.32	9.94	8.04	31
32	78.27	61.26	48.19	38.08	30.23	24.11	19.31	15.53	12.54	10.16	8.27	32
33	76.40	60.12	47.54	37.77	30.14	24.16	19.45	15.72	12.76	10.40	8.50	33
34	74.57	59.00	46.90	37.46	30.05	24.22	19.60	15.92	12.99	10.64	8.74	34
35	72.79	57.90	46.27	37.15	29.96	24.27	19.74	16.12	13.22	10.88	8.99	35
36	71.05	56.82	45.66	36.85	29.88	24.33	19.89	16.33	13.45	11.13	9.24	36
37	69.36	55.77	45.05	36.55	29.79	24.38	20.04	16.53	13.69	11.38	9.50	37
38	67.71	54.73	44.45	36.26	29.71	24.44	20.19	16.74	13.94	11.65	9.77	38
39	66.10	53.72	43.86	35.97	29.62	24.50	20.34	16.96	14.19	11.92	10.04	39
40	64.53	52.73	43.28	35.68	29.54	24.56	20.50	17.17	14.44	12.19	10.32	40
41	63.00	51.75	42.70	35.39	29.46	24.62	20.65	17.39	14.70	12.47	10.62	41
42	61.51	50.80	42.14	35.11	29.38	24.68	20.81	17.62	14.97	12.76	10.92	42
43	60.06	49.87	41.59	34.84	29.30	24.74	20.97	17.85	15.24	13.06	11.23	43
44	58.65	48.97	41.06	34.57	29.23	24.81	21.14	18.08	15.52	13.36	11.55	44
45	57.28	48.08	40.53	34.31	29.16	24.88	21.31	18.32	15.80	13.68	11.88	45
46	55.95	47.21	40.01	34.05	29.09	24.95	21.48	18.56	16.09	14.00	12.22	46
47	54.65	46.37	39.50	33.79	29.02	25.02	21.65	18.81	16.39	14.33	12.57	47
48	53.40	45.55	39.01	33.55	28.97	25.10	21.84	19.06	16.70	14.67	12.94	48
49	52.19	44.75	38.54	33.32	28.92	25.19	22.03	19.33	17.01	15.03	13.32	49
50	51.01	43.98	38.07	33.09	28.87	25.28	22.22	19.60	17.34	15.39	13.71	50
51	49.86	43.22	37.62	32.87	28.83	25.38	22.42	19.87	17.67	15.77	14.11	51
52	48.76	42.49	37.17	32.65	28.79	25.47	22.62	20.16	18.02	16.16	14.53	52
53	47.68	41.78	36.75	32.45	28.76	25.58	22.83	20.45	18.38	16.56	14.97	53
54	46.65	41.09	36.34	32.26	28.74	25.70	23.06	20.76	18.74	16.98	15.43	54

Table 20: Multipliers for loss of pension commencing age 60 (females) *continued*

Age at date of trial	Multiplier calculated with allowance for projected mortality from the 2008–based population projections and rate of return of											Age at date of trial
	–2.0%	***–1.5%***	***–1.0%***	***–0.5%***	***0.0%***	***0.5%***	***1.0%***	***1.5%***	***2.0%***	***2.5%***	***3.0%***	
55	45.65	40.43	35.94	32.08	28.73	25.82	23.29	21.07	19.13	17.41	15.90	55
56	44.69	39.79	35.57	31.91	28.73	25.95	23.53	21.40	19.52	17.86	16.39	56
57	43.76	39.18	35.20	31.75	28.73	26.09	23.78	21.74	19.93	18.33	16.91	57
58	42.86	38.57	34.85	31.59	28.74	26.24	24.04	22.09	20.35	18.81	17.44	58
59	41.98	37.99	34.50	31.44	28.76	26.39	24.30	22.44	20.79	19.31	17.99	59
60	41.12	37.41	34.16	31.30	28.78	26.55	24.57	22.81	21.24	19.83	18.57	60

Table 21: Multipliers for loss of pension commencing age 65 (males)

Age at date of trial	Multiplier calculated with allowance for projected mortality from the 2008–based population projections and rate of return of											Age at date of trial
	−2.0%	*−1.5%*	*−1.0%*	*−0.5%*	*0.0%*	*0.5%*	*1.0%*	*1.5%*	*2.0%*	*2.5%*	*3.0%*	
0	134.16	87.81	57.78	38.22	25.41	16.98	11.40	7.69	5.21	3.54	2.42	0
1	131.46	86.50	57.23	38.06	25.44	17.08	11.53	7.82	5.32	3.64	2.50	1
2	128.17	84.80	56.40	37.70	25.33	17.10	11.60	7.91	5.41	3.72	2.57	2
3	124.95	83.11	55.57	37.35	25.23	17.12	11.67	8.00	5.50	3.80	2.64	3
4	121.80	81.45	54.76	37.00	25.12	17.14	11.75	8.09	5.59	3.88	2.71	4
5	118.72	79.82	53.95	36.64	25.01	17.15	11.82	8.18	5.68	3.97	2.78	5
6	115.71	78.22	53.15	36.29	24.90	17.17	11.89	8.27	5.78	4.05	2.85	6
7	112.78	76.65	52.36	35.95	24.80	17.18	11.96	8.36	5.87	4.14	2.93	7
8	109.92	75.11	51.59	35.60	24.69	17.20	12.03	8.46	5.97	4.23	3.01	8
9	107.13	73.60	50.82	35.26	24.58	17.21	12.11	8.55	6.07	4.32	3.09	9
10	104.40	72.11	50.06	34.91	24.47	17.22	12.18	8.65	6.17	4.41	3.17	10
11	101.74	70.65	49.31	34.57	24.36	17.23	12.25	8.74	6.27	4.51	3.26	11
12	99.15	69.23	48.57	34.24	24.25	17.25	12.32	8.84	6.37	4.60	3.34	12
13	96.62	67.83	47.84	33.91	24.14	17.26	12.39	8.94	6.47	4.70	3.43	13
14	94.16	66.46	47.13	33.58	24.03	17.27	12.47	9.04	6.58	4.80	3.52	14
15	91.77	65.12	46.43	33.25	23.92	17.28	12.54	9.14	6.68	4.91	3.62	15
16	89.44	63.81	45.74	32.93	23.82	17.30	12.62	9.24	6.79	5.01	3.71	16
17	87.17	62.53	45.06	32.61	23.71	17.31	12.69	9.34	6.90	5.12	3.81	17
18	84.97	61.27	44.39	32.30	23.61	17.33	12.77	9.45	7.02	5.23	3.91	18
19	82.83	60.05	43.74	32.00	23.51	17.34	12.85	9.55	7.13	5.34	4.02	19
20	80.75	58.86	43.10	31.70	23.41	17.36	12.93	9.66	7.25	5.46	4.13	20
21	78.72	57.69	42.47	31.40	23.31	17.38	13.01	9.77	7.37	5.58	4.24	21
22	76.73	56.54	41.84	31.10	23.21	17.39	13.09	9.88	7.49	5.70	4.35	22
23	74.79	55.40	41.22	30.80	23.11	17.41	13.17	9.99	7.61	5.82	4.47	23
24	72.90	54.29	40.61	30.51	23.01	17.42	13.25	10.11	7.74	5.95	4.59	24
25	71.06	53.21	40.01	30.22	22.91	17.44	13.33	10.22	7.87	6.08	4.71	25
26	69.28	52.16	39.43	29.94	22.82	17.46	13.41	10.34	8.00	6.21	4.83	26
27	67.55	51.13	38.86	29.66	22.73	17.48	13.50	10.46	8.13	6.34	4.97	27
28	65.85	50.11	38.29	29.38	22.63	17.50	13.58	10.58	8.26	6.48	5.10	28
29	64.18	49.10	37.72	29.10	22.53	17.51	13.66	10.69	8.40	6.62	5.23	29
30	62.57	48.13	37.17	28.82	22.44	17.53	13.75	10.82	8.54	6.76	5.38	30
31	61.01	47.18	36.64	28.56	22.35	17.55	13.83	10.94	8.68	6.91	5.52	31
32	59.50	46.27	36.12	28.30	22.26	17.58	13.93	11.07	8.83	7.07	5.67	32
33	58.05	45.38	35.61	28.06	22.18	17.61	14.02	11.20	8.98	7.22	5.83	33
34	56.62	44.50	35.11	27.81	22.10	17.63	14.12	11.34	9.14	7.38	5.99	34
35	55.23	43.64	34.61	27.56	22.02	17.66	14.21	11.47	9.29	7.55	6.15	35
36	53.87	42.80	34.13	27.32	21.94	17.69	14.31	11.61	9.45	7.72	6.32	36
37	52.56	41.97	33.65	27.08	21.87	17.72	14.41	11.75	9.61	7.89	6.49	37
38	51.26	41.16	33.18	26.84	21.79	17.75	14.50	11.89	9.78	8.07	6.67	38
39	50.00	40.37	32.71	26.60	21.71	17.77	14.60	12.03	9.95	8.24	6.85	39
40	48.77	39.59	32.25	26.36	21.63	17.80	14.70	12.18	10.12	8.43	7.04	40
41	47.58	38.83	31.80	26.13	21.55	17.83	14.80	12.32	10.29	8.62	7.24	41
42	46.42	38.09	31.36	25.91	21.48	17.86	14.90	12.47	10.47	8.81	7.44	42
43	45.30	37.36	30.93	25.69	21.41	17.90	15.01	12.63	10.65	9.01	7.64	43
44	44.21	36.66	30.51	25.47	21.34	17.93	15.12	12.78	10.84	9.21	7.86	44
45	43.15	35.97	30.09	25.26	21.27	17.97	15.23	12.94	11.03	9.43	8.08	45
46	42.11	35.30	29.69	25.05	21.21	18.01	15.34	13.10	11.22	9.64	8.30	46
47	41.11	34.64	29.29	24.85	21.15	18.05	15.46	13.27	11.42	9.86	8.54	47
48	40.14	34.01	28.91	24.65	21.09	18.10	15.57	13.44	11.63	10.09	8.78	48
49	39.20	33.39	28.53	24.46	21.04	18.15	15.70	13.62	11.84	10.33	9.03	49
50	38.29	32.79	28.18	24.28	20.99	18.20	15.83	13.80	12.07	10.58	9.29	50
51	37.42	32.22	27.83	24.11	20.96	18.27	15.97	13.99	12.29	10.83	9.56	51
52	36.58	31.67	27.50	23.96	20.93	18.34	16.11	14.19	12.53	11.10	9.85	52
53	35.78	31.14	27.19	23.81	20.91	18.41	16.26	14.40	12.78	11.37	10.15	53
54	35.01	30.64	26.89	23.67	20.90	18.50	16.42	14.62	13.04	11.66	10.46	54

Table 21: Multipliers for loss of pension commencing age 65 (males) *continued*

Age at date of trial	Multiplier calculated with allowance for projected mortality from the 2008–based population projections and rate of return of											Age at date of trial
	–2.0%	***–1.5%***	***–1.0%***	***–0.5%***	***0.0%***	***0.5%***	***1.0%***	***1.5%***	***2.0%***	***2.5%***	***3.0%***	
55	34.28	30.15	26.61	23.55	20.90	18.60	16.59	14.85	13.31	11.97	10.78	55
56	33.59	29.70	26.35	23.44	20.91	18.71	16.78	15.09	13.60	12.29	11.13	56
57	32.92	29.27	26.10	23.35	20.94	18.83	16.97	15.34	13.90	12.62	11.49	57
58	32.28	28.85	25.87	23.26	20.97	18.95	17.18	15.60	14.21	12.97	11.86	58
59	31.65	28.44	25.64	23.17	21.00	19.08	17.38	15.87	14.53	13.32	12.25	59
60	31.03	28.04	25.41	23.09	21.03	19.21	17.59	16.14	14.85	13.69	12.65	60
61	30.43	27.65	25.19	23.01	21.07	19.35	17.81	16.43	15.19	14.08	13.07	61
62	29.87	27.28	24.99	22.94	21.12	19.50	18.04	16.73	15.55	14.48	13.51	62
63	29.34	26.94	24.81	22.90	21.20	19.67	18.29	17.05	15.93	14.91	13.98	63
64	28.85	26.63	24.65	22.88	21.29	19.86	18.56	17.39	16.33	15.37	14.49	64
65	28.40	26.37	24.54	22.90	21.42	20.08	18.87	17.77	16.77	15.86	15.03	65

Table 22: Multipliers for loss of pension commencing age 65 (females)

Age at date of trial	Multiplier calculated with allowance for projected mortality from the 2008-based population projections and rate of return of											Age at date of trial
	-2.0%	*-1.5%*	*-1.0%*	*-0.5%*	*0.0%*	*0.5%*	*1.0%*	*1.5%*	*2.0%*	*2.5%*	*3.0%*	
0	153.09	99.71	65.31	43.01	28.47	18.95	12.67	8.52	5.75	3.90	2.66	0
1	149.98	98.22	64.68	42.82	28.50	19.06	12.81	8.66	5.87	4.00	2.74	1
2	146.34	96.35	63.78	42.45	28.40	19.10	12.90	8.76	5.98	4.09	2.82	2
3	142.77	94.51	62.90	42.08	28.30	19.13	12.99	8.87	6.08	4.19	2.90	3
4	139.29	92.70	62.02	41.72	28.21	19.16	13.08	8.98	6.18	4.28	2.98	4
5	135.88	90.92	61.16	41.36	28.11	19.20	13.17	9.08	6.29	4.38	3.06	5
6	132.55	89.17	60.30	40.99	28.01	19.23	13.26	9.19	6.40	4.47	3.14	6
7	129.30	87.45	59.46	40.63	27.91	19.26	13.35	9.30	6.51	4.57	3.23	7
8	126.13	85.76	58.62	40.27	27.81	19.29	13.45	9.41	6.62	4.68	3.32	8
9	123.03	84.10	57.80	39.92	27.70	19.32	13.54	9.53	6.73	4.78	3.41	9
10	120.00	82.48	56.98	39.56	27.60	19.35	13.63	9.64	6.85	4.89	3.50	10
11	117.06	80.89	56.18	39.21	27.50	19.38	13.72	9.75	6.97	4.99	3.60	11
12	114.18	79.32	55.39	38.87	27.40	19.41	13.81	9.87	7.08	5.11	3.69	12
13	111.37	77.79	54.61	38.52	27.30	19.44	13.90	9.99	7.20	5.22	3.79	13
14	108.63	76.28	53.84	38.18	27.20	19.47	14.00	10.11	7.33	5.33	3.90	14
15	105.96	74.81	53.08	37.84	27.10	19.50	14.09	10.23	7.45	5.45	4.00	15
16	103.35	73.36	52.33	37.50	27.00	19.53	14.19	10.35	7.58	5.57	4.11	16
17	100.81	71.94	51.59	37.17	26.90	19.56	14.28	10.47	7.71	5.70	4.23	17
18	98.33	70.55	50.86	36.84	26.80	19.59	14.38	10.60	7.84	5.82	4.34	18
19	95.92	69.19	50.15	36.52	26.71	19.62	14.47	10.72	7.97	5.95	4.46	19
20	93.58	67.87	49.45	36.20	26.61	19.65	14.57	10.85	8.11	6.09	4.58	20
21	91.29	66.56	48.76	35.88	26.52	19.69	14.67	10.98	8.25	6.22	4.71	21
22	89.05	65.28	48.07	35.56	26.42	19.72	14.77	11.11	8.39	6.36	4.84	22
23	86.86	64.01	47.39	35.24	26.32	19.74	14.87	11.24	8.53	6.50	4.97	23
24	84.71	62.77	46.72	34.93	26.23	19.77	14.97	11.38	8.68	6.65	5.11	24
25	82.63	61.55	46.06	34.62	26.13	19.80	15.07	11.51	8.83	6.79	5.25	25
26	80.60	60.37	45.41	34.31	26.03	19.83	15.17	11.65	8.98	6.94	5.39	26
27	78.62	59.20	44.77	34.01	25.94	19.86	15.27	11.79	9.13	7.10	5.54	27
28	76.69	58.06	44.14	33.71	25.84	19.89	15.38	11.93	9.29	7.26	5.69	28
29	74.81	56.94	43.52	33.41	25.75	19.93	15.48	12.07	9.44	7.42	5.84	29
30	72.98	55.84	42.91	33.12	25.66	19.96	15.58	12.21	9.61	7.58	6.00	30
31	71.20	54.77	42.32	32.83	25.57	19.99	15.69	12.36	9.77	7.75	6.17	31
32	69.46	53.73	41.73	32.54	25.48	20.03	15.80	12.51	9.94	7.92	6.34	32
33	67.77	52.70	41.15	32.26	25.39	20.06	15.91	12.66	10.11	8.10	6.51	33
34	66.12	51.69	40.58	31.98	25.30	20.09	16.02	12.81	10.28	8.28	6.69	34
35	64.50	50.70	40.01	31.70	25.21	20.13	16.13	12.97	10.46	8.47	6.88	35
36	62.93	49.73	39.45	31.43	25.13	20.16	16.24	13.12	10.64	8.66	7.06	36
37	61.41	48.78	38.91	31.15	25.04	20.20	16.35	13.28	10.83	8.85	7.26	37
38	59.91	47.85	38.37	30.89	24.95	20.23	16.47	13.44	11.01	9.05	7.46	38
39	58.46	46.94	37.84	30.62	24.87	20.27	16.58	13.61	11.20	9.25	7.67	39
40	57.04	46.05	37.32	30.36	24.79	20.31	16.70	13.77	11.40	9.46	7.88	40
41	55.66	45.17	36.80	30.10	24.70	20.35	16.81	13.94	11.60	9.67	8.10	41
42	54.31	44.32	36.30	29.84	24.62	20.38	16.93	14.11	11.80	9.89	8.32	42
43	53.01	43.48	35.81	29.59	24.54	20.43	17.05	14.29	12.00	10.12	8.55	43
44	51.74	42.67	35.33	29.35	24.47	20.47	17.18	14.46	12.22	10.35	8.79	44
45	50.50	41.88	34.85	29.11	24.40	20.51	17.31	14.65	12.43	10.58	9.04	45
46	49.30	41.10	34.39	28.87	24.32	20.56	17.44	14.83	12.65	10.83	9.29	46
47	48.13	40.34	33.93	28.64	24.26	20.61	17.57	15.02	12.88	11.08	9.55	47
48	47.00	39.61	33.49	28.42	24.19	20.66	17.70	15.22	13.11	11.33	9.82	48
49	45.91	38.89	33.06	28.20	24.14	20.72	17.85	15.42	13.35	11.60	10.10	49
50	44.85	38.20	32.64	27.99	24.08	20.78	17.99	15.62	13.60	11.88	10.40	50
51	43.82	37.52	32.23	27.79	24.03	20.85	18.14	15.83	13.85	12.16	10.70	51
52	42.82	36.86	31.84	27.59	23.99	20.92	18.29	16.05	14.12	12.45	11.01	52
53	41.85	36.22	31.45	27.40	23.95	20.99	18.45	16.27	14.38	12.75	11.33	53
54	40.92	35.60	31.08	27.22	23.91	21.07	18.62	16.50	14.66	13.06	11.67	54

Table 22: Multipliers for loss of pension commencing age 65 (females) *continued*

Age at date of trial	Multiplier calculated with allowance for projected mortality from the 2008–based population projections and rate of return of											Age at date of trial
	–2.0%	***–1.5%***	***–1.0%***	***–0.5%***	***0.0%***	***0.5%***	***1.0%***	***1.5%***	***2.0%***	***2.5%***	***3.0%***	
55	40.02	35.01	30.73	27.05	23.89	21.16	18.80	16.74	14.95	13.39	12.02	55
56	39.16	34.44	30.38	26.89	23.87	21.26	18.98	16.99	15.25	13.73	12.38	56
57	38.32	33.88	30.05	26.74	23.86	21.36	19.17	17.25	15.56	14.08	12.76	57
58	37.51	33.34	29.73	26.59	23.86	21.46	19.36	17.51	15.88	14.44	13.16	58
59	36.72	32.81	29.42	26.45	23.85	21.57	19.56	17.78	16.21	14.81	13.56	59
60	35.94	32.29	29.10	26.31	23.85	21.68	19.76	18.06	16.54	15.19	13.98	60
61	35.18	31.78	28.80	26.17	23.85	21.79	19.97	18.34	16.89	15.59	14.42	61
62	34.46	31.29	28.51	26.04	23.86	21.91	20.18	18.63	17.25	16.00	14.87	62
63	33.76	30.83	28.23	25.93	23.88	22.05	20.41	18.94	17.62	16.43	15.35	63
64	33.10	30.39	27.98	25.83	23.92	22.20	20.66	19.27	18.02	16.89	15.86	64
65	32.50	29.99	27.76	25.77	23.98	22.38	20.93	19.63	18.45	17.38	16.40	65

Table 23: Multipliers for loss of pension commencing age 70 (males)

Age at date of trial	Multiplier calculated with allowance for projected mortality from the 2008–based population projections and rate of return of											Age at date of trial
	–2.0%	*–1.5%*	*–1.0%*	*–0.5%*	*0.0%*	*0.5%*	*1.0%*	*1.5%*	*2.0%*	*2.5%*	*3.0%*	
0	116.52	75.30	48.89	31.89	20.90	13.76	9.09	6.04	4.02	2.69	1.81	0
1	114.10	74.13	48.39	31.74	20.91	13.83	9.19	6.13	4.11	2.76	1.87	1
2	111.17	72.62	47.66	31.42	20.81	13.84	9.24	6.20	4.17	2.82	1.91	2
3	108.30	71.12	46.93	31.10	20.70	13.84	9.29	6.27	4.24	2.88	1.96	3
4	105.50	69.65	46.20	30.78	20.60	13.85	9.34	6.33	4.31	2.94	2.02	4
5	102.76	68.21	45.49	30.47	20.50	13.85	9.39	6.40	4.37	3.00	2.07	5
6	100.08	66.80	44.78	30.16	20.39	13.85	9.44	6.46	4.44	3.06	2.12	6
7	97.48	65.41	44.09	29.84	20.29	13.85	9.49	6.53	4.51	3.13	2.18	7
8	94.95	64.05	43.40	29.54	20.19	13.85	9.54	6.60	4.58	3.19	2.23	8
9	92.47	62.71	42.72	29.23	20.08	13.85	9.59	6.67	4.65	3.26	2.29	9
10	90.04	61.40	42.05	28.92	19.97	13.85	9.64	6.74	4.73	3.33	2.35	10
11	87.69	60.11	41.39	28.62	19.87	13.85	9.69	6.81	4.80	3.39	2.41	11
12	85.39	58.86	40.74	28.32	19.76	13.85	9.74	6.88	4.87	3.46	2.47	12
13	83.16	57.63	40.10	28.02	19.66	13.85	9.79	6.95	4.95	3.54	2.54	13
14	80.98	56.42	39.47	27.73	19.56	13.85	9.84	7.02	5.02	3.61	2.60	14
15	78.87	55.24	38.85	27.44	19.45	13.85	9.89	7.09	5.10	3.68	2.67	15
16	76.81	54.09	38.25	27.15	19.35	13.85	9.94	7.16	5.18	3.76	2.74	16
17	74.80	52.96	37.65	26.87	19.25	13.85	9.99	7.24	5.26	3.84	2.81	17
18	72.86	51.86	37.06	26.59	19.15	13.85	10.05	7.31	5.34	3.92	2.88	18
19	70.97	50.79	36.49	26.32	19.06	13.85	10.10	7.39	5.43	4.00	2.95	19
20	69.13	49.74	35.93	26.05	18.96	13.85	10.15	7.47	5.51	4.08	3.03	20
21	67.34	48.71	35.38	25.79	18.87	13.85	10.21	7.55	5.60	4.17	3.11	21
22	65.59	47.70	34.82	25.52	18.77	13.85	10.26	7.63	5.69	4.25	3.19	22
23	63.88	46.71	34.28	25.25	18.67	13.85	10.31	7.70	5.77	4.34	3.27	23
24	62.22	45.74	33.75	24.99	18.58	13.85	10.37	7.78	5.86	4.43	3.36	24
25	60.60	44.79	33.22	24.74	18.48	13.86	10.42	7.87	5.96	4.52	3.44	25
26	59.04	43.87	32.71	24.48	18.39	13.86	10.48	7.95	6.05	4.62	3.53	26
27	57.52	42.97	32.21	24.24	18.30	13.86	10.54	8.03	6.14	4.71	3.63	27
28	56.02	42.07	31.71	23.99	18.21	13.86	10.59	8.12	6.24	4.81	3.72	28
29	54.56	41.20	31.22	23.74	18.11	13.86	10.65	8.20	6.34	4.91	3.82	29
30	53.15	40.34	30.73	23.49	18.02	13.87	10.70	8.29	6.44	5.01	3.92	30
31	51.78	39.52	30.27	23.26	17.93	13.87	10.76	8.38	6.54	5.12	4.02	31
32	50.46	38.72	29.81	23.03	17.85	13.88	10.82	8.47	6.64	5.23	4.12	32
33	49.19	37.94	29.37	22.81	17.77	13.89	10.89	8.56	6.75	5.34	4.23	33
34	47.94	37.18	28.93	22.59	17.69	13.90	10.95	8.66	6.86	5.45	4.35	34
35	46.72	36.43	28.50	22.37	17.61	13.91	11.02	8.75	6.97	5.57	4.46	35
36	45.54	35.70	28.08	22.15	17.53	13.92	11.08	8.85	7.08	5.69	4.58	36
37	44.39	34.98	27.66	21.94	17.45	13.93	11.15	8.95	7.20	5.81	4.70	37
38	43.26	34.27	27.24	21.72	17.37	13.94	11.21	9.04	7.32	5.93	4.82	38
39	42.16	33.58	26.84	21.51	17.30	13.95	11.28	9.14	7.43	6.06	4.95	39
40	41.09	32.90	26.43	21.30	17.22	13.95	11.34	9.24	7.55	6.19	5.08	40
41	40.05	32.24	26.04	21.10	17.14	13.97	11.41	9.35	7.68	6.32	5.22	41
42	39.04	31.60	25.66	20.90	17.07	13.98	11.48	9.45	7.80	6.46	5.36	42
43	38.06	30.97	25.28	20.70	16.99	13.99	11.55	9.56	7.93	6.60	5.50	43
44	37.11	30.36	24.92	20.51	16.92	14.01	11.62	9.67	8.06	6.74	5.65	44
45	36.18	29.76	24.56	20.32	16.85	14.02	11.69	9.78	8.20	6.89	5.80	45
46	35.28	29.18	24.20	20.13	16.79	14.04	11.77	9.89	8.33	7.04	5.96	46
47	34.41	28.61	23.86	19.95	16.72	14.06	11.85	10.01	8.47	7.19	6.12	47
48	33.57	28.06	23.52	19.77	16.66	14.08	11.92	10.13	8.62	7.35	6.29	48
49	32.75	27.52	23.19	19.60	16.60	14.10	12.01	10.25	8.77	7.52	6.46	49
50	31.96	27.01	22.88	19.43	16.55	14.13	12.09	10.38	8.92	7.69	6.64	50
51	31.21	26.51	22.58	19.28	16.51	14.17	12.19	10.51	9.08	7.87	6.83	51
52	30.48	26.03	22.29	19.13	16.47	14.21	12.28	10.65	9.25	8.05	7.02	52
53	29.79	25.57	22.01	19.00	16.43	14.25	12.39	10.79	9.42	8.24	7.23	53
54	29.12	25.13	21.75	18.87	16.41	14.30	12.50	10.94	9.60	8.44	7.44	54

Table 23: Multipliers for loss of pension commencing age 70 (males) ***continued***

Age at date of trial	Multiplier calculated with allowance for projected mortality from the 2008–based population projections and rate of return of											Age at date of trial
	–2.0%	***–1.5%***	***–1.0%***	***–0.5%***	***0.0%***	***0.5%***	***1.0%***	***1.5%***	***2.0%***	***2.5%***	***3.0%***	
55	28.48	24.71	21.50	18.75	16.39	14.36	12.61	11.10	9.79	8.65	7.66	55
56	27.88	24.32	21.27	18.65	16.39	14.43	12.74	11.27	9.99	8.88	7.90	56
57	27.30	23.94	21.05	18.55	16.39	14.51	12.88	11.45	10.20	9.11	8.15	57
58	26.74	23.58	20.84	18.46	16.40	14.59	13.02	11.63	10.42	9.35	8.40	58
59	26.19	23.22	20.63	18.38	16.40	14.68	13.16	11.82	10.64	9.59	8.67	59
60	25.65	22.86	20.42	18.29	16.41	14.76	13.30	12.01	10.86	9.85	8.94	60
61	25.13	22.52	20.22	18.20	16.42	14.84	13.44	12.20	11.10	10.11	9.23	61
62	24.63	22.19	20.03	18.13	16.44	14.94	13.60	12.41	11.34	10.38	9.52	62
63	24.16	21.88	19.86	18.07	16.47	15.04	13.77	12.63	11.60	10.67	9.84	63
64	23.72	21.60	19.71	18.03	16.52	15.17	13.95	12.86	11.87	10.98	10.18	64
65	23.33	21.35	19.59	18.01	16.59	15.31	14.16	13.12	12.17	11.32	10.54	65
66	22.97	21.14	19.50	18.02	16.69	15.48	14.39	13.40	12.50	11.68	10.93	66
67	22.66	20.96	19.44	18.06	16.81	15.68	14.65	13.71	12.86	12.07	11.36	67
68	22.38	20.82	19.40	18.12	16.96	15.90	14.93	14.05	13.24	12.50	11.82	68
69	22.13	20.70	19.40	18.21	17.13	16.15	15.24	14.42	13.66	12.96	12.31	69
70	21.91	20.60	19.41	18.32	17.32	16.41	15.58	14.81	14.10	13.44	12.84	70

Table 24: Multipliers for loss of pension commencing age 70 (females)

Age at date of trial	Multiplier calculated with allowance for projected mortality from the 2008–based population projections and rate of return of											Age at date of trial
	–2.0%	***–1.5%***	***–1.0%***	***–0.5%***	***0.0%***	***0.5%***	***1.0%***	***1.5%***	***2.0%***	***2.5%***	***3.0%***	
0	134.74	86.70	56.06	36.43	23.78	15.60	10.28	6.80	4.52	3.01	2.02	0
1	131.93	85.35	55.49	36.25	23.79	15.68	10.38	6.91	4.61	3.09	2.08	1
2	128.66	83.68	54.69	35.92	23.69	15.70	10.45	6.99	4.69	3.16	2.14	2
3	125.45	82.03	53.90	35.58	23.60	15.72	10.52	7.07	4.77	3.23	2.20	3
4	122.32	80.42	53.12	35.25	23.50	15.74	10.58	7.15	4.85	3.30	2.25	4
5	119.26	78.83	52.35	34.93	23.41	15.76	10.65	7.23	4.93	3.37	2.32	5
6	116.28	77.27	51.59	34.60	23.31	15.77	10.72	7.31	5.01	3.44	2.38	6
7	113.36	75.74	50.83	34.27	23.21	15.79	10.78	7.39	5.09	3.52	2.44	7
8	110.51	74.23	50.09	33.95	23.11	15.80	10.85	7.48	5.18	3.59	2.51	8
9	107.73	72.75	49.35	33.63	23.01	15.82	10.92	7.56	5.26	3.67	2.57	9
10	105.03	71.30	48.63	33.31	22.92	15.83	10.98	7.65	5.35	3.75	2.64	10
11	102.39	69.89	47.92	33.00	22.82	15.85	11.05	7.73	5.43	3.83	2.71	11
12	99.81	68.49	47.21	32.68	22.72	15.86	11.12	7.82	5.52	3.92	2.79	12
13	97.30	67.13	46.52	32.37	22.62	15.87	11.18	7.91	5.61	4.00	2.86	13
14	94.85	65.79	45.83	32.07	22.53	15.89	11.25	8.00	5.71	4.09	2.94	14
15	92.46	64.48	45.16	31.76	22.43	15.90	11.32	8.09	5.80	4.17	3.01	15
16	90.13	63.19	44.49	31.46	22.33	15.92	11.39	8.18	5.89	4.26	3.09	16
17	87.86	61.93	43.84	31.16	22.24	15.93	11.46	8.27	5.99	4.36	3.18	17
18	85.65	60.70	43.19	30.86	22.14	15.95	11.53	8.36	6.09	4.45	3.26	18
19	83.51	59.49	42.56	30.57	22.05	15.96	11.60	8.46	6.19	4.55	3.35	19
20	81.42	58.32	41.94	30.29	21.96	15.98	11.67	8.55	6.29	4.64	3.44	20
21	79.38	57.16	41.33	30.00	21.86	15.99	11.74	8.65	6.40	4.74	3.53	21
22	77.38	56.02	40.72	29.72	21.77	16.01	11.81	8.75	6.50	4.85	3.62	22
23	75.43	54.90	40.12	29.43	21.67	16.02	11.88	8.85	6.61	4.95	3.72	23
24	73.52	53.80	39.52	29.15	21.58	16.03	11.95	8.94	6.71	5.06	3.82	24
25	71.67	52.72	38.94	28.87	21.48	16.05	12.03	9.04	6.82	5.16	3.92	25
26	69.86	51.67	38.37	28.60	21.39	16.06	12.10	9.14	6.93	5.28	4.03	26
27	68.11	50.64	37.80	28.32	21.30	16.07	12.17	9.25	7.05	5.39	4.13	27
28	66.39	49.63	37.25	28.05	21.21	16.09	12.24	9.35	7.16	5.50	4.24	28
29	64.72	48.64	36.70	27.79	21.11	16.10	12.32	9.46	7.28	5.62	4.36	29
30	63.09	47.68	36.16	27.52	21.03	16.12	12.39	9.56	7.40	5.74	4.47	30
31	61.51	46.73	35.63	27.27	20.94	16.13	12.47	9.67	7.52	5.87	4.59	31
32	59.98	45.81	35.11	27.01	20.85	16.15	12.55	9.78	7.65	6.00	4.72	32
33	58.48	44.91	34.60	26.76	20.76	16.16	12.62	9.89	7.77	6.13	4.84	33
34	57.02	44.02	34.10	26.51	20.68	16.18	12.70	10.00	7.90	6.26	4.97	34
35	55.59	43.14	33.60	26.26	20.59	16.20	12.78	10.12	8.03	6.39	5.10	35
36	54.20	42.29	33.11	26.01	20.50	16.21	12.86	10.23	8.16	6.53	5.24	36
37	52.85	41.45	32.63	25.77	20.42	16.23	12.94	10.35	8.30	6.67	5.38	37
38	51.53	40.64	32.16	25.53	20.33	16.25	13.02	10.46	8.44	6.82	5.53	38
39	50.24	39.83	31.69	25.29	20.25	16.26	13.10	10.58	8.57	6.97	5.67	39
40	48.99	39.05	31.23	25.06	20.17	16.28	13.18	10.70	8.72	7.12	5.83	40
41	47.77	38.28	30.78	24.82	20.08	16.30	13.27	10.83	8.86	7.27	5.98	41
42	46.58	37.53	30.34	24.60	20.00	16.32	13.35	10.95	9.01	7.43	6.14	42
43	45.43	36.80	29.90	24.37	19.93	16.34	13.44	11.08	9.16	7.59	6.31	43
44	44.31	36.08	29.48	24.15	19.85	16.36	13.52	11.21	9.31	7.76	6.48	44
45	43.23	35.39	29.06	23.94	19.78	16.39	13.61	11.34	9.47	7.93	6.66	45
46	42.17	34.70	28.65	23.73	19.70	16.41	13.70	11.47	9.63	8.11	6.84	46
47	41.14	34.04	28.25	23.52	19.63	16.44	13.80	11.61	9.80	8.29	7.03	47
48	40.14	33.39	27.86	23.32	19.57	16.47	13.89	11.75	9.97	8.47	7.22	48
49	39.18	32.77	27.49	23.12	19.51	16.50	13.99	11.90	10.14	8.67	7.42	49
50	38.25	32.16	27.12	22.93	19.45	16.54	14.10	12.05	10.32	8.86	7.63	50
51	37.34	31.56	26.76	22.75	19.39	16.57	14.20	12.20	10.51	9.07	7.84	51
52	36.46	30.99	26.41	22.57	19.34	16.62	14.31	12.36	10.69	9.28	8.06	52
53	35.61	30.43	26.07	22.40	19.29	16.66	14.42	12.52	10.89	9.49	8.30	53
54	34.79	29.89	25.74	22.23	19.25	16.71	14.54	12.69	11.09	9.72	8.53	54

Table 24: Multipliers for loss of pension commencing age 70 (females) *continued*

Age at date of trial	Multiplier calculated with allowance for projected mortality from the 2008–based population projections and rate of return of											Age at date of trial
	–2.0%	***–1.5%***	***–1.0%***	***–0.5%***	***0.0%***	***0.5%***	***1.0%***	***1.5%***	***2.0%***	***2.5%***	***3.0%***	
55	34.00	29.36	25.43	22.08	19.21	16.77	14.67	12.86	11.30	9.95	8.78	55
56	33.24	28.86	25.12	21.93	19.19	16.83	14.80	13.04	11.52	10.19	9.04	56
57	32.51	28.37	24.83	21.79	19.16	16.89	14.93	13.23	11.74	10.44	9.31	57
58	31.79	27.90	24.54	21.65	19.14	16.96	15.07	13.42	11.97	10.70	9.59	58
59	31.10	27.43	24.26	21.51	19.12	17.03	15.21	13.61	12.21	10.97	9.88	59
60	30.41	26.97	23.98	21.37	19.10	17.10	15.35	13.81	12.44	11.24	10.17	60
61	29.74	26.52	23.71	21.24	19.08	17.17	15.49	14.01	12.69	11.52	10.48	61
62	29.10	26.09	23.44	21.11	19.06	17.25	15.64	14.22	12.94	11.81	10.80	62
63	28.48	25.67	23.19	21.00	19.06	17.33	15.80	14.43	13.21	12.11	11.13	63
64	27.90	25.28	22.96	20.90	19.07	17.43	15.97	14.67	13.49	12.43	11.48	64
65	27.36	24.92	22.75	20.82	19.10	17.55	16.17	14.92	13.79	12.78	11.86	65
66	26.86	24.60	22.58	20.77	19.15	17.69	16.38	15.19	14.12	13.15	12.26	66
67	26.40	24.30	22.43	20.74	19.22	17.85	16.61	15.49	14.47	13.54	12.69	67
68	25.97	24.04	22.30	20.73	19.32	18.03	16.87	15.81	14.84	13.96	13.15	68
69	25.57	23.79	22.19	20.74	19.43	18.23	17.14	16.15	15.24	14.40	13.64	69
70	25.19	23.57	22.10	20.76	19.55	18.44	17.43	16.50	15.65	14.87	14.15	70

Table 25: Multipliers for loss of pension commencing age 75 (males)

Age at date of trial	Multiplier calculated with allowance for projected mortality from the 2008–based population projections and rate of return of											Age at date of trial
	−2.0%	*−1.5%*	*−1.0%*	*−0.5%*	*0.0%*	*0.5%*	*1.0%*	*1.5%*	*2.0%*	*2.5%*	*3.0%*	
0	97.81	62.36	39.93	25.68	16.58	10.74	6.99	4.57	2.99	1.97	1.30	0
1	95.69	61.34	39.49	25.52	16.56	10.79	7.06	4.63	3.05	2.02	1.34	1
2	93.15	60.03	38.85	25.24	16.47	10.79	7.09	4.68	3.10	2.06	1.37	2
3	90.66	58.74	38.22	24.97	16.37	10.78	7.12	4.73	3.15	2.10	1.41	3
4	88.23	57.47	37.59	24.69	16.28	10.77	7.16	4.77	3.19	2.14	1.44	4
5	85.86	56.23	36.98	24.41	16.18	10.76	7.19	4.82	3.24	2.19	1.48	5
6	83.55	55.01	36.37	24.14	16.08	10.75	7.22	4.86	3.29	2.23	1.52	6
7	81.31	53.82	35.77	23.86	15.98	10.74	7.25	4.91	3.33	2.27	1.55	7
8	79.12	52.65	35.18	23.59	15.88	10.73	7.28	4.95	3.38	2.32	1.59	8
9	76.97	51.50	34.59	23.32	15.79	10.72	7.31	5.00	3.43	2.36	1.63	9
10	74.89	50.37	34.02	23.06	15.69	10.71	7.34	5.05	3.48	2.41	1.67	10
11	72.85	49.27	33.45	22.79	15.59	10.70	7.37	5.09	3.53	2.46	1.71	11
12	70.88	48.19	32.89	22.53	15.49	10.69	7.40	5.14	3.58	2.50	1.76	12
13	68.96	47.14	32.34	22.27	15.39	10.67	7.43	5.19	3.63	2.55	1.80	13
14	67.09	46.10	31.80	22.02	15.29	10.66	7.46	5.23	3.68	2.60	1.84	14
15	65.27	45.10	31.27	21.76	15.20	10.65	7.49	5.28	3.74	2.65	1.89	15
16	63.50	44.11	30.75	21.51	15.10	10.64	7.52	5.33	3.79	2.71	1.94	16
17	61.78	43.15	30.24	21.27	15.01	10.63	7.55	5.38	3.85	2.76	1.98	17
18	60.12	42.21	29.74	21.03	14.92	10.62	7.58	5.43	3.90	2.81	2.03	18
19	58.50	41.29	29.25	20.79	14.82	10.61	7.61	5.48	3.96	2.87	2.08	19
20	56.93	40.40	28.77	20.55	14.74	10.60	7.65	5.53	4.02	2.92	2.13	20
21	55.40	39.52	28.29	20.32	14.65	10.59	7.68	5.59	4.08	2.98	2.19	21
22	53.90	38.66	27.82	20.09	14.55	10.58	7.71	5.64	4.13	3.04	2.24	22
23	52.44	37.81	27.36	19.86	14.46	10.57	7.74	5.69	4.19	3.10	2.30	23
24	51.02	36.99	26.90	19.63	14.37	10.55	7.77	5.74	4.25	3.16	2.35	24
25	49.64	36.18	26.46	19.41	14.28	10.54	7.81	5.80	4.31	3.22	2.41	25
26	48.31	35.40	26.02	19.19	14.20	10.53	7.84	5.85	4.38	3.29	2.47	26
27	47.02	34.64	25.60	18.98	14.11	10.52	7.87	5.91	4.44	3.35	2.53	27
28	45.74	33.88	25.17	18.76	14.02	10.51	7.90	5.96	4.51	3.42	2.60	28
29	44.50	33.14	24.75	18.54	13.93	10.50	7.94	6.01	4.57	3.48	2.66	29
30	43.30	32.41	24.34	18.33	13.85	10.49	7.97	6.07	4.64	3.55	2.73	30
31	42.14	31.71	23.94	18.13	13.76	10.48	8.00	6.13	4.70	3.62	2.79	31
32	41.02	31.04	23.56	17.93	13.69	10.48	8.04	6.19	4.77	3.69	2.86	32
33	39.94	30.38	23.18	17.74	13.61	10.47	8.08	6.25	4.85	3.77	2.94	33
34	38.89	29.74	22.81	17.54	13.53	10.47	8.12	6.31	4.92	3.84	3.01	34
35	37.86	29.10	22.44	17.35	13.45	10.46	8.15	6.37	4.99	3.92	3.09	35
36	36.86	28.49	22.08	17.16	13.38	10.46	8.19	6.43	5.07	4.00	3.16	36
37	35.88	27.88	21.73	16.98	13.30	10.45	8.23	6.50	5.14	4.08	3.24	37
38	34.93	27.29	21.38	16.79	13.23	10.44	8.27	6.56	5.22	4.16	3.33	38
39	34.00	26.71	21.03	16.61	13.15	10.44	8.31	6.62	5.30	4.24	3.41	39
40	33.10	26.14	20.69	16.43	13.07	10.43	8.34	6.69	5.38	4.33	3.49	40
41	32.22	25.58	20.36	16.25	13.00	10.43	8.38	6.75	5.46	4.42	3.58	41
42	31.38	25.04	20.04	16.07	12.93	10.42	8.42	6.82	5.54	4.51	3.67	42
43	30.55	24.51	19.72	15.90	12.86	10.42	8.46	6.89	5.62	4.60	3.77	43
44	29.75	24.00	19.41	15.73	12.79	10.42	8.50	6.96	5.71	4.69	3.86	44
45	28.98	23.50	19.10	15.57	12.72	10.41	8.55	7.03	5.79	4.79	3.96	45
46	28.22	23.01	18.80	15.41	12.65	10.41	8.59	7.10	5.88	4.88	4.06	46
47	27.49	22.53	18.51	15.25	12.59	10.41	8.63	7.17	5.97	4.99	4.17	47
48	26.78	22.07	18.23	15.09	12.52	10.41	8.68	7.25	6.07	5.09	4.28	48
49	26.10	21.62	17.95	14.94	12.46	10.42	8.73	7.33	6.16	5.20	4.39	49
50	25.44	21.18	17.68	14.80	12.41	10.43	8.78	7.41	6.26	5.31	4.50	50
51	24.80	20.77	17.43	14.66	12.36	10.44	8.83	7.49	6.37	5.42	4.62	51
52	24.20	20.37	17.18	14.53	12.31	10.45	8.89	7.58	6.48	5.54	4.75	52
53	23.61	19.98	16.95	14.41	12.27	10.47	8.96	7.67	6.59	5.67	4.88	53
54	23.05	19.61	16.72	14.29	12.23	10.50	9.02	7.77	6.70	5.80	5.02	54

Table 25: Multipliers for loss of pension commencing age 75 (males) *continued*

Age at date of trial	Multiplier calculated with allowance for projected mortality from the 2008–based population projections and rate of return of											Age at date of trial
	–2.0%	***–1.5%***	***–1.0%***	***–0.5%***	***0.0%***	***0.5%***	***1.0%***	***1.5%***	***2.0%***	***2.5%***	***3.0%***	
55	22.52	19.26	16.51	14.18	12.20	10.53	9.09	7.87	6.83	5.93	5.16	55
56	22.01	18.93	16.31	14.08	12.18	10.56	9.17	7.98	6.96	6.08	5.31	56
57	21.53	18.61	16.12	13.99	12.17	10.60	9.26	8.10	7.09	6.23	5.47	57
58	21.06	18.30	15.94	13.91	12.16	10.65	9.34	8.21	7.23	6.38	5.64	58
59	20.60	18.00	15.76	13.82	12.15	10.69	9.43	8.33	7.38	6.54	5.81	59
60	20.15	17.70	15.58	13.73	12.13	10.74	9.52	8.45	7.52	6.70	5.98	60
61	19.71	17.41	15.40	13.65	12.12	10.78	9.61	8.58	7.67	6.87	6.16	61
62	19.29	17.13	15.23	13.57	12.12	10.84	9.71	8.71	7.83	7.04	6.35	62
63	18.89	16.86	15.08	13.51	12.12	10.89	9.81	8.85	7.99	7.23	6.55	63
64	18.52	16.62	14.94	13.45	12.13	10.96	9.92	8.99	8.16	7.42	6.76	64
65	18.18	16.40	14.82	13.41	12.16	11.05	10.05	9.16	8.35	7.63	6.99	65
66	17.87	16.21	14.73	13.40	12.21	11.15	10.20	9.34	8.56	7.86	7.23	66
67	17.60	16.04	14.65	13.40	12.28	11.27	10.36	9.53	8.79	8.11	7.50	67
68	17.35	15.90	14.60	13.42	12.37	11.41	10.54	9.75	9.03	8.38	7.78	68
69	17.12	15.78	14.56	13.46	12.47	11.56	10.73	9.98	9.30	8.67	8.09	69
70	16.92	15.67	14.54	13.51	12.58	11.72	10.94	10.23	9.58	8.97	8.42	70
71	16.72	15.57	14.53	13.57	12.70	11.90	11.17	10.49	9.87	9.30	8.77	71
72	16.53	15.48	14.52	13.64	12.83	12.08	11.40	10.77	10.18	9.64	9.14	72
73	16.36	15.40	14.52	13.71	12.97	12.28	11.64	11.05	10.51	10.00	9.53	73
74	16.19	15.33	14.53	13.80	13.12	12.49	11.90	11.36	10.86	10.39	9.95	74
75	16.04	15.27	14.56	13.90	13.29	12.72	12.19	11.70	11.24	10.81	10.40	75

Table 26: Multipliers for loss of pension commencing age 75 (females)

Age at date of trial	Multiplier calculated with allowance for projected mortality from the 2008–based population projections and rate of return of											Age at date of trial
	–2.0%	*–1.5%*	*–1.0%*	*–0.5%*	*0.0%*	*0.5%*	*1.0%*	*1.5%*	*2.0%*	*2.5%*	*3.0%*	
0	114.99	73.05	46.61	29.87	19.22	12.42	8.06	5.25	3.43	2.25	1.48	0
1	112.51	71.86	46.09	29.69	19.21	12.48	8.13	5.33	3.50	2.31	1.53	1
2	109.64	70.40	45.40	29.40	19.12	12.48	8.18	5.38	3.56	2.36	1.57	2
3	106.83	68.96	44.71	29.10	19.02	12.49	8.23	5.44	3.61	2.41	1.61	3
4	104.08	67.55	44.02	28.81	18.93	12.49	8.27	5.50	3.67	2.46	1.65	4
5	101.41	66.16	43.35	28.52	18.84	12.49	8.32	5.56	3.73	2.51	1.69	5
6	98.79	64.80	42.69	28.23	18.75	12.50	8.36	5.62	3.79	2.56	1.74	6
7	96.24	63.47	42.03	27.94	18.65	12.50	8.41	5.67	3.84	2.61	1.78	7
8	93.75	62.16	41.38	27.66	18.56	12.50	8.45	5.73	3.90	2.67	1.83	8
9	91.32	60.87	40.74	27.37	18.46	12.50	8.50	5.79	3.97	2.72	1.88	9
10	88.95	59.61	40.11	27.09	18.37	12.50	8.54	5.85	4.03	2.78	1.92	10
11	86.65	58.38	39.49	26.82	18.28	12.50	8.59	5.92	4.09	2.84	1.97	11
12	84.41	57.17	38.88	26.54	18.18	12.51	8.63	5.98	4.15	2.90	2.03	12
13	82.21	55.99	38.27	26.26	18.09	12.51	8.68	6.04	4.22	2.96	2.08	13
14	80.08	54.83	37.68	25.99	18.00	12.51	8.72	6.10	4.28	3.02	2.13	14
15	78.00	53.69	37.09	25.73	17.91	12.51	8.77	6.16	4.35	3.08	2.19	15
16	75.98	52.58	36.52	25.46	17.81	12.51	8.81	6.23	4.42	3.14	2.24	16
17	74.00	51.48	35.95	25.20	17.72	12.51	8.86	6.29	4.49	3.21	2.30	17
18	72.08	50.42	35.39	24.94	17.63	12.51	8.90	6.36	4.55	3.27	2.36	18
19	70.22	49.37	34.84	24.68	17.54	12.51	8.95	6.42	4.63	3.34	2.42	19
20	68.41	48.36	34.31	24.43	17.45	12.51	9.00	6.49	4.70	3.41	2.48	20
21	66.64	47.36	33.78	24.18	17.36	12.51	9.05	6.56	4.77	3.48	2.55	21
22	64.91	46.38	33.26	23.93	17.27	12.51	9.09	6.63	4.85	3.55	2.61	22
23	63.22	45.41	32.73	23.68	17.18	12.51	9.14	6.69	4.92	3.63	2.68	23
24	61.56	44.46	32.22	23.43	17.09	12.51	9.18	6.76	4.99	3.70	2.75	24
25	59.96	43.53	31.71	23.18	17.00	12.51	9.23	6.83	5.07	3.78	2.82	25
26	58.40	42.63	31.22	22.94	16.91	12.51	9.28	6.90	5.15	3.85	2.89	26
27	56.88	41.74	30.73	22.70	16.82	12.51	9.32	6.97	5.23	3.93	2.97	27
28	55.40	40.87	30.25	22.47	16.74	12.50	9.37	7.04	5.31	4.01	3.04	28
29	53.96	40.02	29.78	22.23	16.65	12.50	9.42	7.12	5.39	4.10	3.12	29
30	52.56	39.19	29.32	22.00	16.56	12.50	9.47	7.19	5.47	4.18	3.20	30
31	51.20	38.38	28.86	21.78	16.48	12.50	9.52	7.26	5.56	4.27	3.28	31
32	49.88	37.59	28.42	21.55	16.39	12.51	9.57	7.34	5.65	4.35	3.37	32
33	48.59	36.82	27.98	21.33	16.31	12.51	9.62	7.42	5.73	4.44	3.45	33
34	47.33	36.05	27.55	21.11	16.23	12.51	9.67	7.49	5.82	4.54	3.54	34
35	46.10	35.30	27.12	20.89	16.14	12.51	9.72	7.57	5.91	4.63	3.63	35
36	44.91	34.57	26.70	20.68	16.06	12.51	9.77	7.65	6.00	4.73	3.73	36
37	43.75	33.86	26.29	20.47	15.98	12.51	9.82	7.73	6.10	4.82	3.82	37
38	42.62	33.16	25.88	20.26	15.90	12.51	9.87	7.81	6.19	4.92	3.92	38
39	41.52	32.48	25.48	20.05	15.82	12.51	9.92	7.89	6.29	5.02	4.02	39
40	40.44	31.81	25.09	19.84	15.73	12.51	9.97	7.97	6.39	5.13	4.13	40
41	39.40	31.15	24.70	19.64	15.66	12.51	10.03	8.05	6.49	5.23	4.23	41
42	38.38	30.51	24.32	19.44	15.58	12.52	10.08	8.14	6.59	5.34	4.34	42
43	37.40	29.89	23.95	19.24	15.50	12.52	10.13	8.22	6.69	5.45	4.46	43
44	36.44	29.28	23.59	19.05	15.43	12.52	10.19	8.31	6.80	5.57	4.57	44
45	35.52	28.69	23.23	18.86	15.35	12.53	10.25	8.40	6.90	5.69	4.69	45
46	34.61	28.10	22.88	18.68	15.28	12.53	10.31	8.49	7.01	5.81	4.82	46
47	33.73	27.54	22.54	18.49	15.21	12.54	10.36	8.58	7.13	5.93	4.94	47
48	32.89	26.99	22.21	18.32	15.14	12.55	10.43	8.68	7.24	6.06	5.07	48
49	32.07	26.46	21.88	18.15	15.08	12.56	10.49	8.78	7.36	6.19	5.21	49
50	31.27	25.94	21.57	17.98	15.02	12.58	10.56	8.88	7.48	6.32	5.35	50
51	30.50	25.43	21.26	17.81	14.96	12.59	10.62	8.98	7.61	6.46	5.49	51
52	29.75	24.94	20.96	17.65	14.90	12.61	10.69	9.09	7.74	6.60	5.64	52
53	29.03	24.47	20.67	17.50	14.85	12.63	10.77	9.20	7.87	6.75	5.80	53
54	28.33	24.01	20.39	17.35	14.80	12.66	10.84	9.31	8.01	6.90	5.96	54

Table 26: Multipliers for loss of pension commencing age 75 (females) *continued*

Age at date of trial	Multiplier calculated with allowance for projected mortality from the 2008–based population projections and rate of return of										Age at date of trial
	–2.0%	***–1.5%***	***–1.0%***	***–0.5%***	***0.0%***	***0.5%***	***1.0%***	***1.5%***	***2.0%***	***2.5%***	***3.0%***	
55	27.66	23.56	20.12	17.21	14.76	12.69	10.92	9.43	8.15	7.06	6.12	55
56	27.02	23.14	19.86	17.08	14.72	12.72	11.01	9.55	8.30	7.22	6.30	56
57	26.39	22.72	19.60	16.95	14.69	12.75	11.10	9.67	8.45	7.39	6.48	57
58	25.78	22.32	19.36	16.83	14.66	12.79	11.19	9.80	8.60	7.56	6.66	58
59	25.19	21.92	19.11	16.70	14.62	12.83	11.28	9.93	8.76	7.74	6.85	59
60	24.61	21.53	18.87	16.57	14.59	12.86	11.37	10.06	8.92	7.92	7.05	60
61	24.04	21.14	18.63	16.45	14.55	12.90	11.46	10.19	9.08	8.11	7.25	61
62	23.49	20.77	18.40	16.33	14.52	12.94	11.55	10.33	9.25	8.30	7.46	62
63	22.96	20.41	18.17	16.22	14.50	12.99	11.65	10.47	9.43	8.50	7.68	63
64	22.46	20.07	17.97	16.12	14.48	13.04	11.76	10.63	9.62	8.71	7.91	64
65	22.00	19.76	17.78	16.04	14.49	13.11	11.89	10.79	9.82	8.94	8.16	65
66	21.56	19.48	17.62	15.97	14.51	13.20	12.03	10.98	10.03	9.19	8.42	66
67	21.16	19.22	17.48	15.93	14.54	13.30	12.18	11.17	10.27	9.45	8.71	67
68	20.79	18.98	17.36	15.90	14.59	13.41	12.35	11.39	10.51	9.72	9.01	68
69	20.44	18.76	17.25	15.88	14.65	13.54	12.53	11.61	10.78	10.02	9.33	69
70	20.11	18.55	17.15	15.87	14.72	13.67	12.72	11.85	11.05	10.33	9.66	70
71	19.78	18.35	17.05	15.87	14.79	13.81	12.91	12.09	11.34	10.65	10.01	71
72	19.46	18.14	16.95	15.86	14.86	13.95	13.11	12.34	11.63	10.98	10.38	72
73	19.13	17.93	16.84	15.84	14.93	14.08	13.31	12.59	11.93	11.32	10.75	73
74	18.80	17.72	16.74	15.83	15.00	14.23	13.51	12.86	12.24	11.68	11.15	74
75	18.48	17.53	16.64	15.83	15.08	14.38	13.74	13.14	12.58	12.06	11.58	75

Table 27: Discounting factors for term certain

Term	Factor to discount value of multiplier for a period of deferment											Term
	−2.0%	*−1.5%*	*−1.0%*	*−0.5%*	*0.0%*	*0.5%*	*1.0%*	*1.5%*	*2.0%*	*2.5%*	*3.0%*	
1	1.0204	1.0152	1.0101	1.0050	1.0000	0.9950	0.9901	0.9852	0.9804	0.9756	0.9709	1
2	1.0412	1.0307	1.0203	1.0101	1.0000	0.9901	0.9803	0.9707	0.9612	0.9518	0.9426	2
3	1.0625	1.0464	1.0306	1.0152	1.0000	0.9851	0.9706	0.9563	0.9423	0.9286	0.9151	3
4	1.0842	1.0623	1.0410	1.0203	1.0000	0.9802	0.9610	0.9422	0.9238	0.9060	0.8885	4
5	1.1063	1.0785	1.0515	1.0254	1.0000	0.9754	0.9515	0.9283	0.9057	0.8839	0.8626	5
6	1.1289	1.0949	1.0622	1.0305	1.0000	0.9705	0.9420	0.9145	0.8880	0.8623	0.8375	6
7	1.1519	1.1116	1.0729	1.0357	1.0000	0.9657	0.9327	0.9010	0.8706	0.8413	0.8131	7
8	1.1754	1.1285	1.0837	1.0409	1.0000	0.9609	0.9235	0.8877	0.8535	0.8207	0.7894	8
9	1.1994	1.1457	1.0947	1.0461	1.0000	0.9561	0.9143	0.8746	0.8368	0.8007	0.7664	9
10	1.2239	1.1632	1.1057	1.0514	1.0000	0.9513	0.9053	0.8617	0.8203	0.7812	0.7441	10
11	1.2489	1.1809	1.1169	1.0567	1.0000	0.9466	0.8963	0.8489	0.8043	0.7621	0.7224	11
12	1.2743	1.1989	1.1282	1.0620	1.0000	0.9419	0.8874	0.8364	0.7885	0.7436	0.7014	12
13	1.3004	1.2171	1.1396	1.0673	1.0000	0.9372	0.8787	0.8240	0.7730	0.7254	0.6810	13
14	1.3269	1.2356	1.1511	1.0727	1.0000	0.9326	0.8700	0.8118	0.7579	0.7077	0.6611	14
15	1.3540	1.2545	1.1627	1.0781	1.0000	0.9279	0.8613	0.7999	0.7430	0.6905	0.6419	15
16	1.3816	1.2736	1.1745	1.0835	1.0000	0.9233	0.8528	0.7880	0.7284	0.6736	0.6232	16
17	1.4098	1.2930	1.1863	1.0889	1.0000	0.9187	0.8444	0.7764	0.7142	0.6572	0.6050	17
18	1.4386	1.3126	1.1983	1.0944	1.0000	0.9141	0.8360	0.7649	0.7002	0.6412	0.5874	18
19	1.4679	1.3326	1.2104	1.0999	1.0000	0.9096	0.8277	0.7536	0.6864	0.6255	0.5703	19
20	1.4979	1.3529	1.2226	1.1054	1.0000	0.9051	0.8195	0.7425	0.6730	0.6103	0.5537	20
21	1.5285	1.3735	1.2350	1.1110	1.0000	0.9006	0.8114	0.7315	0.6598	0.5954	0.5375	21
22	1.5596	1.3944	1.2475	1.1166	1.0000	0.8961	0.8034	0.7207	0.6468	0.5809	0.5219	22
23	1.5915	1.4157	1.2601	1.1222	1.0000	0.8916	0.7954	0.7100	0.6342	0.5667	0.5067	23
24	1.6240	1.4372	1.2728	1.1278	1.0000	0.8872	0.7876	0.6995	0.6217	0.5529	0.4919	24
25	1.6571	1.4591	1.2856	1.1335	1.0000	0.8828	0.7798	0.6892	0.6095	0.5394	0.4776	25
26	1.6909	1.4814	1.2986	1.1392	1.0000	0.8784	0.7720	0.6790	0.5976	0.5262	0.4637	26
27	1.7254	1.5039	1.3117	1.1449	1.0000	0.8740	0.7644	0.6690	0.5859	0.5134	0.4502	27
28	1.7606	1.5268	1.3250	1.1507	1.0000	0.8697	0.7568	0.6591	0.5744	0.5009	0.4371	28
29	1.7966	1.5501	1.3384	1.1565	1.0000	0.8653	0.7493	0.6494	0.5631	0.4887	0.4243	29
30	1.8332	1.5737	1.3519	1.1623	1.0000	0.8610	0.7419	0.6398	0.5521	0.4767	0.4120	30
31	1.8706	1.5976	1.3656	1.1681	1.0000	0.8567	0.7346	0.6303	0.5412	0.4651	0.4000	31
32	1.9088	1.6220	1.3793	1.1740	1.0000	0.8525	0.7273	0.6210	0.5306	0.4538	0.3883	32
33	1.9478	1.6467	1.3933	1.1799	1.0000	0.8482	0.7201	0.6118	0.5202	0.4427	0.3770	33
34	1.9875	1.6717	1.4074	1.1858	1.0000	0.8440	0.7130	0.6028	0.5100	0.4319	0.3660	34
35	2.0281	1.6972	1.4216	1.1918	1.0000	0.8398	0.7059	0.5939	0.5000	0.4214	0.3554	35
36	2.0695	1.7230	1.4359	1.1978	1.0000	0.8356	0.6989	0.5851	0.4902	0.4111	0.3450	36
37	2.1117	1.7493	1.4504	1.2038	1.0000	0.8315	0.6920	0.5764	0.4806	0.4011	0.3350	37
38	2.1548	1.7759	1.4651	1.2098	1.0000	0.8274	0.6852	0.5679	0.4712	0.3913	0.3252	38
39	2.1988	1.8030	1.4799	1.2159	1.0000	0.8232	0.6784	0.5595	0.4619	0.3817	0.3158	39
40	2.2437	1.8304	1.4948	1.2220	1.0000	0.8191	0.6717	0.5513	0.4529	0.3724	0.3066	40
41	2.2894	1.8583	1.5099	1.2282	1.0000	0.8151	0.6650	0.5431	0.4440	0.3633	0.2976	41
42	2.3362	1.8866	1.5252	1.2343	1.0000	0.8110	0.6584	0.5351	0.4353	0.3545	0.2890	42
43	2.3838	1.9153	1.5406	1.2405	1.0000	0.8070	0.6519	0.5272	0.4268	0.3458	0.2805	43
44	2.4325	1.9445	1.5561	1.2468	1.0000	0.8030	0.6454	0.5194	0.4184	0.3374	0.2724	44
45	2.4821	1.9741	1.5719	1.2530	1.0000	0.7990	0.6391	0.5117	0.4102	0.3292	0.2644	45
46	2.5328	2.0042	1.5877	1.2593	1.0000	0.7950	0.6327	0.5042	0.4022	0.3211	0.2567	46
47	2.5845	2.0347	1.6038	1.2657	1.0000	0.7910	0.6265	0.4967	0.3943	0.3133	0.2493	47
48	2.6372	2.0657	1.6200	1.2720	1.0000	0.7871	0.6203	0.4894	0.3865	0.3057	0.2420	48
49	2.6911	2.0971	1.6363	1.2784	1.0000	0.7832	0.6141	0.4821	0.3790	0.2982	0.2350	49
50	2.7460	2.1291	1.6529	1.2848	1.0000	0.7793	0.6080	0.4750	0.3715	0.2909	0.2281	50
51	2.8020	2.1615	1.6696	1.2913	1.0000	0.7754	0.6020	0.4680	0.3642	0.2838	0.2215	51
52	2.8592	2.1944	1.6864	1.2978	1.0000	0.7716	0.5961	0.4611	0.3571	0.2769	0.2150	52
53	2.9175	2.2278	1.7035	1.3043	1.0000	0.7677	0.5902	0.4543	0.3501	0.2702	0.2088	53
54	2.9771	2.2617	1.7207	1.3109	1.0000	0.7639	0.5843	0.4475	0.3432	0.2636	0.2027	54
55	3.0378	2.2962	1.7381	1.3174	1.0000	0.7601	0.5785	0.4409	0.3365	0.2572	0.1968	55

Table 27: Discounting factors for term certain *continued*

Term	Factor to discount value of multiplier for a period of deferment											Term
	−2.0%	***−1.5%***	***−1.0%***	***−0.5%***	***0.0%***	***0.5%***	***1.0%***	***1.5%***	***2.0%***	***2.5%***	***3.0%***	
56	3.0998	2.3312	1.7556	1.3241	1.0000	0.7563	0.5728	0.4344	0.3299	0.2509	0.1910	56
57	3.1631	2.3667	1.7733	1.3307	1.0000	0.7525	0.5671	0.4280	0.3234	0.2448	0.1855	57
58	3.2277	2.4027	1.7913	1.3374	1.0000	0.7488	0.5615	0.4217	0.3171	0.2388	0.1801	58
59	3.2935	2.4393	1.8094	1.3441	1.0000	0.7451	0.5560	0.4154	0.3109	0.2330	0.1748	59
60	3.3607	2.4764	1.8276	1.3509	1.0000	0.7414	0.5504	0.4093	0.3048	0.2273	0.1697	60
61	3.4293	2.5141	1.8461	1.3577	1.0000	0.7377	0.5450	0.4032	0.2988	0.2217	0.1648	61
62	3.4993	2.5524	1.8647	1.3645	1.0000	0.7340	0.5396	0.3973	0.2929	0.2163	0.1600	62
63	3.5707	2.5913	1.8836	1.3713	1.0000	0.7304	0.5343	0.3914	0.2872	0.2111	0.1553	63
64	3.6436	2.6308	1.9026	1.3782	1.0000	0.7267	0.5290	0.3856	0.2816	0.2059	0.1508	64
65	3.7180	2.6708	1.9218	1.3852	1.0000	0.7231	0.5237	0.3799	0.2761	0.2009	0.1464	65
66	3.7938	2.7115	1.9412	1.3921	1.0000	0.7195	0.5185	0.3743	0.2706	0.1960	0.1421	66
67	3.8713	2.7528	1.9608	1.3991	1.0000	0.7159	0.5134	0.3688	0.2653	0.1912	0.1380	67
68	3.9503	2.7947	1.9806	1.4061	1.0000	0.7124	0.5083	0.3633	0.2601	0.1865	0.1340	68
69	4.0309	2.8373	2.0007	1.4132	1.0000	0.7088	0.5033	0.3580	0.2550	0.1820	0.1301	69
70	4.1132	2.8805	2.0209	1.4203	1.0000	0.7053	0.4983	0.3527	0.2500	0.1776	0.1263	70
71	4.1971	2.9243	2.0413	1.4275	1.0000	0.7018	0.4934	0.3475	0.2451	0.1732	0.1226	71
72	4.2827	2.9689	2.0619	1.4346	1.0000	0.6983	0.4885	0.3423	0.2403	0.1690	0.1190	72
73	4.3702	3.0141	2.0827	1.4418	1.0000	0.6948	0.4837	0.3373	0.2356	0.1649	0.1156	73
74	4.4593	3.0600	2.1038	1.4491	1.0000	0.6914	0.4789	0.3323	0.2310	0.1609	0.1122	74
75	4.5503	3.1066	2.1250	1.4564	1.0000	0.6879	0.4741	0.3274	0.2265	0.1569	0.1089	75
76	4.6432	3.1539	2.1465	1.4637	1.0000	0.6845	0.4694	0.3225	0.2220	0.1531	0.1058	76
77	4.7380	3.2019	2.1682	1.4710	1.0000	0.6811	0.4648	0.3178	0.2177	0.1494	0.1027	77
78	4.8347	3.2507	2.1901	1.4784	1.0000	0.6777	0.4602	0.3131	0.2134	0.1457	0.0997	78
79	4.9333	3.3002	2.2122	1.4859	1.0000	0.6743	0.4556	0.3084	0.2092	0.1422	0.0968	79
80	5.0340	3.3504	2.2345	1.4933	1.0000	0.6710	0.4511	0.3039	0.2051	0.1387	0.0940	80

Table 28: Multipliers for pecuniary loss for term certain

Term	Multiplier for regular frequent payments for a term certain at rate of return of											Term
	-2.0%	*-1.5%*	*-1.0%*	*-0.5%*	*0.0%*	*0.5%*	*1.0%*	*1.5%*	*2.0%*	*2.5%*	*3.0%*	
1	1.01	1.01	1.01	1.00	1.00	1.00	1.00	0.99	0.99	0.99	0.99	1
2	2.04	2.03	2.02	2.01	2.00	1.99	1.98	1.97	1.96	1.95	1.94	2
3	3.09	3.07	3.05	3.02	3.00	2.98	2.96	2.93	2.91	2.89	2.87	3
4	4.17	4.12	4.08	4.04	4.00	3.96	3.92	3.88	3.85	3.81	3.77	4
5	5.26	5.19	5.13	5.06	5.00	4.94	4.88	4.82	4.76	4.70	4.65	5
6	6.38	6.28	6.18	6.09	6.00	5.91	5.82	5.74	5.66	5.58	5.50	6
7	7.52	7.38	7.25	7.12	7.00	6.88	6.76	6.65	6.54	6.43	6.32	7
8	8.68	8.50	8.33	8.16	8.00	7.84	7.69	7.54	7.40	7.26	7.12	8
9	9.87	9.64	9.42	9.21	9.00	8.80	8.61	8.42	8.24	8.07	7.90	9
10	11.08	10.80	10.52	10.25	10.00	9.75	9.52	9.29	9.07	8.86	8.66	10
11	12.32	11.97	11.63	11.31	11.00	10.70	10.42	10.15	9.88	9.63	9.39	11
12	13.58	13.16	12.75	12.37	12.00	11.65	11.31	10.99	10.68	10.39	10.10	12
13	14.87	14.37	13.89	13.43	13.00	12.59	12.19	11.82	11.46	11.12	10.79	13
14	16.18	15.59	15.03	14.50	14.00	13.52	13.07	12.64	12.23	11.84	11.46	14
15	17.52	16.84	16.19	15.58	15.00	14.45	13.93	13.44	12.98	12.54	12.12	15
16	18.89	18.10	17.36	16.66	16.00	15.38	14.79	14.24	13.71	13.22	12.75	16
17	20.28	19.38	18.54	17.75	17.00	16.30	15.64	15.02	14.43	13.88	13.36	17
18	21.71	20.69	19.73	18.84	18.00	17.22	16.48	15.79	15.14	14.53	13.96	18
19	23.16	22.01	20.94	19.93	19.00	18.13	17.31	16.55	15.83	15.17	14.54	19
20	24.64	23.35	22.15	21.04	20.00	19.03	18.14	17.30	16.51	15.78	15.10	20
21	26.16	24.71	23.38	22.15	21.00	19.94	18.95	18.03	17.18	16.39	15.65	21
22	27.70	26.10	24.62	23.26	22.00	20.84	19.76	18.76	17.83	16.97	16.17	22
23	29.28	27.50	25.88	24.38	23.00	21.73	20.56	19.48	18.47	17.55	16.69	23
24	30.88	28.93	27.14	25.50	24.00	22.62	21.35	20.18	19.10	18.11	17.19	24
25	32.53	30.38	28.42	26.63	25.00	23.50	22.13	20.87	19.72	18.65	17.67	25
26	34.20	31.85	29.71	27.77	26.00	24.38	22.91	21.56	20.32	19.19	18.14	26
27	35.91	33.34	31.02	28.91	27.00	25.26	23.68	22.23	20.91	19.71	18.60	27
28	37.65	34.86	32.34	30.06	28.00	26.13	24.44	22.90	21.49	20.21	19.04	28
29	39.43	36.40	33.67	31.21	29.00	27.00	25.19	23.55	22.06	20.71	19.47	29
30	41.24	37.96	35.01	32.37	30.00	27.86	25.94	24.20	22.62	21.19	19.89	30
31	43.10	39.54	36.37	33.54	31.00	28.72	26.67	24.83	23.17	21.66	20.30	31
32	44.99	41.15	37.74	34.71	32.00	29.58	27.41	25.46	23.70	22.12	20.69	32
33	46.91	42.79	39.13	35.89	33.00	30.43	28.13	26.07	24.23	22.57	21.08	33
34	48.88	44.45	40.53	37.07	34.00	31.27	28.85	26.68	24.74	23.01	21.45	34
35	50.89	46.13	41.95	38.26	35.00	32.12	29.56	27.28	25.25	23.43	21.81	35
36	52.94	47.84	43.37	39.45	36.00	32.95	30.26	27.87	25.74	23.85	22.16	36
37	55.03	49.58	44.82	40.65	37.00	33.79	30.95	28.45	26.23	24.26	22.50	37
38	57.16	51.34	46.28	41.86	38.00	34.62	31.64	29.02	26.70	24.65	22.83	38
39	59.34	53.13	47.75	43.07	39.00	35.44	32.32	29.58	27.17	25.04	23.15	39
40	61.56	54.95	49.24	44.29	40.00	36.26	33.00	30.14	27.63	25.42	23.46	40
41	63.83	56.79	50.74	45.52	41.00	37.08	33.67	30.69	28.08	25.78	23.76	41
42	66.14	58.66	52.26	46.75	42.00	37.89	34.33	31.23	28.52	26.14	24.06	42
43	68.50	60.56	53.79	47.99	43.00	38.70	34.98	31.76	28.95	26.49	24.34	43
44	70.91	62.49	55.34	49.23	44.00	39.51	35.63	32.28	29.37	26.83	24.62	44
45	73.36	64.45	56.90	50.48	45.00	40.31	36.27	32.80	29.78	27.17	24.88	45
46	75.87	66.44	58.48	51.74	46.00	41.10	36.91	33.30	30.19	27.49	25.15	46
47	78.43	68.46	60.08	53.00	47.00	41.90	37.54	33.80	30.59	27.81	25.40	47
48	81.04	70.51	61.69	54.27	48.00	42.69	38.16	34.30	30.98	28.12	25.64	48
49	83.70	72.59	63.32	55.54	49.00	43.47	38.78	34.78	31.36	28.42	25.88	49
50	86.42	74.70	64.96	56.82	50.00	44.25	39.39	35.26	31.74	28.72	26.11	50
51	89.20	76.85	66.62	58.11	51.00	45.03	40.00	35.73	32.10	29.00	26.34	51
52	92.03	79.03	68.30	59.41	52.00	45.80	40.60	36.20	32.47	29.28	26.56	52
53	94.92	81.24	69.99	60.71	53.00	46.57	41.19	36.66	32.82	29.56	26.77	53
54	97.86	83.48	71.71	62.01	54.00	47.34	41.78	37.11	33.17	29.82	26.97	54
55	100.87	85.76	73.44	63.33	55.00	48.10	42.36	37.55	33.51	30.08	27.17	55

Table 28: Multipliers for pecuniary loss for term certain *continued*

Term	-2.0%	-1.5%	-1.0%	-0.5%	0.0%	0.5%	1.0%	1.5%	2.0%	2.5%	3.0%	Term
	Multiplier for regular frequent payments for a term certain at rate of return of											
56	103.94	88.08	75.18	64.65	56.00	48.86	42.93	37.99	33.84	30.34	27.37	56
57	107.07	90.43	76.95	65.98	57.00	49.61	43.50	38.42	34.17	30.59	27.56	57
58	110.27	92.81	78.73	67.31	58.00	50.36	44.07	38.84	34.49	30.83	27.74	58
59	113.53	95.23	80.53	68.65	59.00	51.11	44.63	39.26	34.80	31.06	27.92	59
60	116.85	97.69	82.35	70.00	60.00	51.85	45.18	39.67	35.11	31.29	28.09	60
61	120.25	100.18	84.19	71.35	61.00	52.59	45.73	40.08	35.41	31.52	28.26	61
62	123.71	102.72	86.04	72.71	62.00	53.33	46.27	40.48	35.70	31.74	28.42	62
63	127.25	105.29	87.91	74.08	63.00	54.06	46.81	40.88	36.00	31.95	28.58	63
64	130.85	107.90	89.81	75.46	64.00	54.79	47.34	41.26	36.28	32.16	28.73	64
65	134.53	110.55	91.72	76.84	65.00	55.52	47.86	41.65	36.56	32.36	28.88	65
66	138.29	113.24	93.65	78.23	66.00	56.24	48.39	42.02	36.83	32.56	29.02	66
67	142.12	115.97	95.60	79.62	67.00	56.95	48.90	42.40	37.10	32.75	29.16	67
68	146.03	118.75	97.57	81.03	68.00	57.67	49.41	42.76	37.36	32.94	29.30	68
69	150.02	121.56	99.56	82.44	69.00	58.38	49.92	43.12	37.62	33.13	29.43	69
70	154.10	124.42	101.57	83.85	70.00	59.09	50.42	43.48	37.87	33.31	29.56	70
71	158.25	127.32	103.61	85.28	71.00	59.79	50.91	43.83	38.12	33.48	29.68	71
72	162.49	130.27	105.66	86.71	72.00	60.49	51.41	44.17	38.36	33.65	29.80	72
73	166.82	133.26	107.73	88.15	73.00	61.19	51.89	44.51	38.60	33.82	29.92	73
74	171.23	136.30	109.82	89.59	74.00	61.88	52.37	44.85	38.83	33.98	30.03	74
75	175.74	139.38	111.94	91.04	75.00	62.57	52.85	45.18	39.06	34.14	30.15	75
76	180.33	142.51	114.07	92.50	76.00	63.26	53.32	45.50	39.29	34.30	30.25	76
77	185.02	145.69	116.23	93.97	77.00	63.94	53.79	45.82	39.51	34.45	30.36	77
78	189.81	148.92	118.41	95.45	78.00	64.62	54.25	46.14	39.72	34.60	30.46	78
79	194.69	152.19	120.61	96.93	79.00	65.29	54.71	46.45	39.93	34.74	30.56	79
80	199.68	155.52	122.83	98.42	80.00	65.97	55.16	46.75	40.14	34.88	30.65	80

ACTUARIAL FORMULAE AND BASIS

The functions tabulated are:

Tables 1 and 2	$\bar{a}_x$
Tables 3 and 4	$\bar{a}_{x:\overline{50-x}\vert}$
Tables 5 and 6	$\bar{a}_{x:\overline{55-x}\vert}$
Tables 7 and 8	$\bar{a}_{x:\overline{60-x}\vert}$
Tables 9 and 10	$\bar{a}_{x:\overline{65-x}\vert}$
Tables 11 and 12	$\bar{a}_{x:\overline{70-x}\vert}$
Tables 13 and 14	$\bar{a}_{x:\overline{75-x}\vert}$
Tables 15 and 16	$(50 - x)\vert\bar{a}_x$
Tables 17 and 18	$(55 - x)\vert\bar{a}_x$
Tables 19 and 20	$(60 - x)\vert\bar{a}_x$
Tables 21 and 22	$(65 - x)\vert\bar{a}_x$
Tables 23 and 24	$(70 - x)\vert\bar{a}_x$
Tables 25 and 26	$(75 - x)\vert\bar{a}_x$
Table 27	$1 / (1 + i)^n$
Table 28	$a_{\overline{n}\vert}$

- Mortality assumptions for 2008-based official population projections for the United Kingdom.
- Loadings: None.
- Rate of return: As stated in the tables.

A9: The Lord Chancellor's statement, July 27, 2001

THE LORD CHANCELLOR'S DEPARTMENT
Discount Rate
Setting the Discount Rate
Lord Chancellor's Reasons
July 27, 2001

Introduction

On June 25, 2001 I made the Damages (Personal Injury) Order 2001 ("the 2001 Order") pursuant to s.1 of the Damages Act 1996. In setting a rate of 2.5% in the 2001 Order I had regard to what I believed to be the accurate figure for the average gross redemption yield on Index-Linked Government Stock for the three years leading up to June 8, 2001. Following my announcement of the discount rate, questions were raised as to the correctness of the three-year average yield figure upon which I had relied.

These questions led me to have the information about the three-year average yield figure checked thoroughly. Those checks revealed certain limited inaccuracies in the information underlying the average yield figure on which I had based my reasoning in making the 2001 Order. In the light of the correction of that average yield figure, I think it right that I should consider completely afresh, on the basis of the accurate average yield figure, what rate I should have set when I made the 2001 Order on June 25, 2001, in order to determine whether the 2001 Order should be withdrawn.

Decision

Having considered all the material available to me, including the accurate, corrected average yield figure, I have come to the conclusion that a discount rate of 2.5% was the appropriate rate to set. Therefore, I do not consider that the 2001 Order should be withdrawn. This statement sets out my reasons for coming to that conclusion.

Reasons

In determining the discount rate, I have applied the appropriate legal principle laid down authoritatively by the courts, and in particular by the House of Lords in *Wells v Wells*.[1]

I also consider that it is highly desirable to exercise my powers under the Act so as to produce a situation in which claimants and defendants may have a reasonably clear idea about the impact of the discount rate upon their cases, so as to facilitate negotiation of settlements and the presentation of cases in court. In order to promote this objective, I have concluded that I should:

a set a single rate to cover all cases. This accords with the solution adopted by the House of Lords in *Wells v Wells*. It will eliminate scope for uncertainty and argument about the applicable rate. Similarly, I consider it is preferable to have a fixed rate, which promotes certainty and which avoids the complexity and extra costs that a formula would entail;

b set a rate which is easy for all parties and their lawyers to apply in practice and which reflects the fact that the rate is bound to be applied in a range of different circumstances over a period of time.

[1] [1999] 1 A.C. 345.

For this reason, I consider it appropriate to set the discount rate to the nearest half per cent, so as to ensure that the figure will be suitable for use in conjunction with the Ogden Tables, which are a ready means for parties to take into account actuarial factors in computing the quantum of damages;

c set a rate which should obtain for the foreseeable future. I consider it would be very detrimental to the reasonable certainty which is necessary to promote the just and efficient resolution of disputes (by settlement as well as by hearing in court) to make frequent changes to the discount rate. Therefore, whilst I will remain ready to review the discount rate whenever I find there is a significant and established change in the relevant real rates of return to be expected, I do not propose to tinker with the rate frequently to take account of every transient shift in market conditions.

(I consider that the reasoning and conclusions in the above paragraph, which appeared in my original reasons for setting the discount rate in the 2001 Order, continue to apply.)

The principle which I must strive to apply is clear: " . . . the object of the award of damages for future expenditure is to place the injured party as nearly as possible in the same financial position he or she would have been in but for the accident. The aim is to award such a sum of money as will amount to no more, and at the same time no less, than the net loss." (*Wells v Wells* at 390A–B per Lord Hope of Craighead). I acknowledge that claimants who have suffered severe injuries are not in the position of ordinary investors. Such claimants have a pressing need for a dependable source of income to meet the costs of their future care. It is accordingly unrealistic to require severely injured claimants to take even moderate risks when they invest their damages awards.

Setting a single rate to cover all cases, whilst highly desirable for the reasons given above, has the effect that the discount rate has to cover a wide variety of different cases, and claimants with widely differing personal and financial characteristics. Moreover, as has become clear from the consultation exercise (including responses by expert financial analysts to questions which I posed them), the real rate of return on investments of any character (including investments in Index-Linked Government Securities) involves making assumptions for the future about a wide variety of factors affecting the economy as a whole, including for example the likely rate of inflation. In these circumstances, it is inevitable that any approach to setting the discount rate must be fairly broad-brush. Put shortly, there can be no single "right" answer as to what rate should be set. Since it is in the context of larger awards, intended to cover longer periods, that there is the greatest risk of serious discrepancies between the level of compensation and the actual losses incurred if the discount rate set is not appropriate, I have had this type of award particularly in mind when considering the level at which the discount rate should be set. (The above paragraphs also formed a part of my original reasons for setting the discount rate, and I consider that they continue to apply.)

The House of Lords in *Wells v Wells* determined the real rate of return obtainable by claimants through low-risk investment by reference to the gross redemption yields on Index-Linked Government Stock. Their Lordships assumed that a claimant would use his damages award to purchase the right portfolio of Index-Linked Government Stock to ensure that in future years the sums which he received from his portfolio by way of coupon payments and payments on redemption would be sufficient to meet his financial needs. The risk that an early sale of Index-Linked Government Stock might cause capital losses was removed by assuming that such a claimant would hold all his Index-Linked Government Stock until redemption.

The House of Lords thought it appropriate to set the discount rate by reference to the average yields on Index-Linked Government Stock. There is no single correct method by which this average yield may be calculated. Among other factors, the calculation will depend upon the length of the period under consideration, the stocks which are to be included within the average, the inflation assumption made and the form of average taken.

The majority of their Lordships considered it appropriate to set a discount rate by taking a three-year average of Index-Linked Government Stock yields. I agree that, having regard to the benefits to be obtained in setting the discount rate for the foreseeable future, three years is an appropriate period over which to take an average. I note that Lord Lloyd of Berwick preferred a one-year period; this confirms the need for judgements to be made in determining the appropriate average yield.

It appears from the speech of Lord Hope at 393E–F that his Lordship had regard to an average of gross redemption yields on Index-Linked Government Stock with lives of over five years. He did not give reasons for adopting that particular approach. I am aware that this approach has also been favoured by the Ogden Working Party. However, having regard to the basic reasoning of the House of Lords in *Wells v Wells*, I do not consider that I am obliged to follow it. As noted above, the House of Lords in *Wells v Wells* assumed that a claimant would generally hold all his Index-Linked Government Stock until redemption. Further, as was stated by Lord Clyde at 395H–396A, it was to be assumed that in each year of loss a proportion of the capital would have to be used. If these two assumptions are to be rendered consistent then it will be necessary for the claimant to purchase Index-Linked Government Stock which will mature in the short term, for otherwise the claimant would have to sell a proportion of his Index-Linked Government Stock prior to redemption in order to realise, in the short term, some of the capital value of his investments. Some claimants, whose losses extend over periods of about five years or so or less, would have to purchase all or most of their Index-Linked Government Stock (if that is what they chose to do with the damages paid to them) in this category of stock. I have therefore decided that it is proper to take an average over all Index-Linked Government Stock rather than to exclude Index-Linked Government Stock with less than five years to maturity.

Nevertheless, I consider that it would be inappropriate to include the gross redemption yields of such stock which is very near maturity ("near maturity ILGS"—which is stock for which the nominal value of the final coupon and redemption payments have become known with certainty). The gross redemption yield on such near maturity ILGS is a nominal yield rather than a real yield. Accordingly, I asked for a calculation of the size of the real yield element in the gross redemption yields of the near maturity ILGS and have included those real yields within my calculation of the average yield.

The average yield figure upon which Lord Hope relied at 393E–F in *Wells v Wells* was based on an inflation assumption of 5%. I consider that, given both the current rate of inflation and the Government's policy aim of maintaining that rate within an upper limit of 2.5%, an assumption of 3% is to be preferred for present purposes.

The House of Lords in *Wells v Wells* did not discuss what form of average should be taken of Index-Linked Government Stock yields. One method is to take an average which is weighted in accordance with the market value of each stock. To my mind, such a weighted average is not relevant to the present circumstances, as the choice of Index-Linked Government Stock portfolio which is necessary to ensure that the future financial needs of a claimant are adequately and promptly met does not depend upon the prevailing market values of Index-Linked Government Stock. I have therefore decided that it is appropriate to take a simple average of Index-Linked Government Stock yields.

A calculation of the simple average of the gross redemption yields of an Index-Linked Government Stock (with an appropriate adjustment for the yields of near maturity ILGS) at an assumed rate of inflation of 3% produces an average yield figure of 2.46%. Accordingly, I conclude that the net average yield on Index-Linked Government Stock, as adjusted to take account of tax, lies in the range between 2% and 2.5%. In my opinion, following *Wells v Wells*, the discount rate should be set within this range. Further, given that the rate is to be set to the nearest 0.5%, it is clear that the discount rate should either be 2% or 2.5%. I do not consider that the choice whether a rate of 2% or one of 2.5% is appropriate is a simple arithmetical matter, nor that *Wells v Wells* requires me to set one rate or the other. I must have regard to the basic principle to which I have referred above, and I have taken account of matters which I consider are relevant to the setting of a discount rate which is just as between claimants as a group and defendants as a group.

In the light of all the information now available to me, and considering the matter completely afresh, I have decided that on June 25, 2001 I should have set the discount rate at 2.5%.

In doing so, I have noted that the real rate of return to be expected from Index-Linked Government Securities tends to be higher the lower the rate of inflation is assumed to be (figures at assumed rates of inflation of 3% and 5% are readily available for comparison). The average gross redemption yield figure of 2.46% assumes an inflation figure of 3% extending into the future. But over recent years inflation has been kept close to or below the 2.5% target set by the Government, and Government policy and the function of the Bank of England remains firmly to maintain inflation according to that target. Although economists differ as to what inflation rates may be expected for the future, I note that the market's general expectation as to the rate of inflation for the future (as implied by market valuations of gilts) is well below 3%. I consider that it is reasonable to assume an inflation rate for the foreseeable future somewhere below 3%, and this in turn provides comfort that a discount rate set at 2.5% is reasonable. (The above paragraph and the larger part of the following four paragraphs were contained in my original reasons for setting the discount rate. They set out considerations which I consider continue to apply).

I am further supported in my conclusion that a discount rate of 2.5% is reasonable by indications that the rate of return in respect of Index-Linked Government Securities does not represent a pure and undistorted measure of the real rate of return which markets would afford in relation to investments with minimal risk which have emerged from the information which was provided in the responses to the consultation paper and the responses from expert financial analysts which I obtained, and by consideration of rates of return on other investments which are available at low risk to claimants. I have treated the following points as significant.

First, some responses to the consultation maintained that the market in Index-Linked Government Securities is at present distorted so that the prevailing yields are artificially low, and do not necessarily give a reliable indication of the real rate of return which markets would afford in relation to investments with minimal risk. The expert financial analysts whom I consulted concurred that the market is distorted at present. This appears to be a result of the minimum funding requirement introduced by the Pensions Act 1995 (which has, in effect, created additional demand for such securities on the part of pension funds) combined with a reduced supply of government securities generally, as the Government has reduced the national debt. The market in Index-Linked Government Securities has changed significantly since *Wells v Wells* was argued and decided. It is widely held that the continuing high demand for Index-Linked Government Stock and the scarcity of supply has led to yields being artificially low as compared with both past record and the yields presently available on similar investment instruments issued by other, comparable, national governments. I consider that the fact that yields in Index-Linked Government Stock appear to be artificially low at present militates against the suggestion that these yields over recent years should be taken as the sole indication of the rates of return that can be achieved through low risk investment in the market. Also, I consider that there is some reasonable prospect of a return to higher rates of return in respect of Index-Linked Government Stock when the Government's already announced plans to abolish the minimum funding requirement are carried into effect. Any distorting effect of the minimum funding requirement would be expected to be particularly pronounced in relation to the longer maturity stocks, whose yields have recently been lower than shorter maturity stocks.

Second, I have noted that the Court of Protection, even in the wake of *Wells v Wells*, has continued to invest, on the behalf of claimants, in multi-asset portfolios, including an equity element. Investment in this manner could be expected to produce real rates of return well in excess of 2.5%. The Court of Protection has specific responsibility to ensure that the financial needs of those for whose benefit it acts will be met, ie its investment objectives are closely similar to those of the prudent claimant which the House of Lords identified in *Wells v Wells*. The Court of Protection takes competent financial advice as to the investment strategy which will best secure those objectives. Despite the decision of the House of Lords in *Wells v Wells* to set the discount rate by reference to yields on Index-Linked Government Securities, the Court of Protection has continued its former policy, with the agreement of the families concerned, of investing in portfolios comprising of a mixture of equities, gilts and cash. Master Lush of the Court of Protection has stated that none of the families of the Court's patients have chosen to invest in Index-Linked Government Stock since *Wells v Wells*, despite having been offered that option. Thus it appears that there are sensible, low risk investment strategies available to claimants which would enable them comfortably to achieve a real rate of return at 2.5% or above, without their being unduly exposed to risk in the equity markets. Although the House of Lords in *Wells v Wells* chose not to be guided by the practice of the Court of Protection, this was principally on the grounds that what the Court of Protection might do in the future was uncertain, and not on the grounds that its practice was irrelevant. I consider it is appropriate to take account of what has happened in the period since that decision.

Third, I consider that it is likely that real claimants with a large award of compensation, who sought investment advice and instructed their advisers as to the particular investment objectives which they needed to fulfil (as they could reasonably be expected to do) would not be advised to invest solely or even primarily in Index-Linked Government Securities, but rather in a mixed portfolio, in which any investment risk would be managed so as to be very low. This view is supported by the experience of the Court of Protection as to the independent financial advice they receive. It is also supported by the responses of the expert financial analysts whom I have consulted. No one responding to the consultation identified a single case in which the claimant had invested solely in Index-Linked Government Securities and doubts were expressed as to whether there was any such case. This suggests that setting the discount rate at 2.5% would not place an intolerable burden on claimants to take on excessive, i.e. moderate or above, risk in the equity markets, and would be a rate more likely to accord with real expectations of returns, particularly at the higher end of awards.

Finally, in deciding that a single rate of 2.5% should have been set by me on June 25, 2001, I have borne in mind that it will, of course, remain open for the Courts under s.1(2) of the Damages Act 1996 to adopt a different rate in any particular case if there are exceptional circumstances which justify it in doing so.

Irvine of Lairg
Lord Chancellor
July 27, 2001

Group B
Damages

B

B1: General damages table following *Heil v Rankin* and *Simmons v Castle*

General introduction

On the following pages are tables for use in updating awards of general damages in the light of the Court of Appeal's judgments in *Heil v Rankin*[1] and in *Simmons v Castle*.[2] At Table E1 will be found a Retail Prices Index table and at Table E2 an inflation table.

1. Annexed to the Court of Appeal's judgment in *Heil* was a rather smudged graph provided to show "very approximately" the scale of the increase. The line is a shallow curve. In discussion after judgment was given, their Lordships said that they had not intended to lay down a mathematical formula. We must therefore assume that the top line was intended to fit around what had actually been done in *Heil* (i.e. nothing) and the other seven cases.

2. Despite this, and with a little diffidence (though some confidence) we suggest the following formula. It is calculated on the following assumptions—

   a. the highest award of general damages at March 23, 2000 was around £150,000: awards of this amount or higher were increased by $33\frac{1}{3}$ per cent;

   b. there is no increase in awards that were worth up to £10,000 before that date; and

   c. the uplift is 0% at £10,000 and rises *in a straight line* to $33\frac{1}{3}$ per cent.

3. To find the value of an *old* award in *new* terms, that award must first be updated to March 23, 2000 using the Retail Prices Index (reproduced below), in the usual way. Let us call this updated figure A. The formula is:

   $$\pounds A + [{}^{\pounds A - 10{,}000}/_{420{,}000} \times \pounds A]$$

   The part in square brackets is the *Heil* uplift.

4. In *Simmons v Castle* the Court of Appeal decided that general damages for personal injury (and certain other losses) will increase by 10 per cent (as proposed in the Final Report on Civil Litigation Costs by Sir Rupert Jackson), unless the claimant falls within s.44(6) of the Legal Aid, Sentencing and Punishment of Offenders Act 2012. The effect of this is that in a case where the claimant entered into a Conditional Fee Agreement before April 1, 2013, he recovers the success fee as part of his costs (as before) but does not get the 10 per cent increase in general damages: in any other case the claimant gets the 10 per cent increase in damages but does not get the success fee.

5. For example:

   a. On January 26, 1988, McNeill J. awarded the claimant in *Chan v Chan* general damages of £75,000.

   b. Updating £75,000 to March 23, 2000 in line with the Retail Prices Index gives £122,250.

   c. Subtract £10,000 from £122,250, and divide it by £420,000. This gives ${}^{112{,}250}/_{420{,}000}$ = 0.27. This is the percentage uplift.

   d. Applying this uplift to the original award gives [0.27 × £122,250] = £33,008.

   e. The award in *Chan v Chan* was therefore worth [£122,250 + £33,008] = **£155,258** on March 23, 2000.

[1] [2000] 2 W.L.R. 1173.
[2] [2012] EWCA Civ 1039 and [2012] EWCA Civ 1288.

f. The £155,258 should then be updated from March 23, 2000 to the present and, unless s.44(6) applies, it should also be increased by 10 per cent. Multiply by [present RPI] × 1.10 / [RPI March 2000].

6. Because the degree of uplift varies with the size of the old award, it is inaccurate to apply the *Heil v Rankin* uplift to a figure already adjusted for inflation to a date later than March 23, 2000. The *Simmons v Castle* uplift of 10 per cent does not depend on the size of the award. In June 2015 the RPI was 258.9.

TO UPDATE A PRE-*HEIL v RANKIN* AWARD

The table on this page shows the factor to allow for inflation from an earlier judgment date to March 23, 2000. The table overleaf shows the appropriate new figure, following *Heil v Rankin* in relation to the conventional level of damages at £1,000 intervals up to £150,000.

Note that the uplift should be applied to the damages adjusted for inflation to March 23, 2000, thus:

(1) Damages awarded, say, January 1990 × Inflation increase January 1, 1990–March 23, 2000 (from first table) = old award as at March 23, 2000.

(2) Award uplifted under *Heil v Rankin* (from second table).

(3) Then multiply by an inflation uplift from March 23, 2000 onwards to the date of trial; plus the additional 10 per cent (unless s.44(6) applies).

TABLE TO UPDATE FOR INFLATION TO MARCH 2000

	J	F	M	A	M	J	J	A	S	O	N	D	
1980	2.708	2.670	2.634	2.547	2.524	2.500	2.480	2.474	2.459	2.443	2.424	2.411	1980
1981	2.396	2.374	2.339	2.274	2.259	2.246	2.236	2.220	2.207	2.187	2.165	2.151	1981
1982	2.139	2.138	2.120	2.078	2.063	2.057	2.057	2.056	2.057	2.047	2.037	2.041	1982
1983	2.038	2.030	2.026	1.998	1.990	1.985	1.974	1.965	1.957	1.950	1.943	1.938	1983
1984	1.939	1.931	1.925	1.900	1.893	1.888	1.890	1.872	1.869	1.857	1.852	1.853	1984
1985	1.846	1.832	1.815	1.777	1.769	1.765	1.768	1.764	1.765	1.762	1.756	1.753	1985
1986	1.750	1.743	1.741	1.724	1.721	1.722	1.727	1.722	1.713	1.710	1.696	1.690	1986
1987	1.684	1.677	1.674	1.654	1.653	1.653	1.654	1.649	1.645	1.637	1.629	1.630	1987
1988	1.630	1.624	1.618	1.592	1.586	1.580	1.578	1.561	1.554	1.538	1.531	1.527	1988
1989	1.517	1.506	1.500	1.473	1.464	1.459	1.458	1.454	1.444	1.433	1.421	1.418	1989
1990	1.409	1.401	1.387	1.346	1.334	1.329	1.328	1.315	1.302	1.292	1.295	1.296	1990
1991	1.293	1.286	1.282	1.265	1.261	1.256	1.259	1.256	1.251	1.246	1.242	1.241	1991
1992	1.242	1.236	1.232	1.213	1.209	1.209	1.213	1.212	1.208	1.204	1.205	1.210	1992
1993	1.221	1.213	1.209	1.198	1.193	1.194	1.197	1.192	1.187	1.188	1.189	1.187	1993
1994	1.192	1.185	1.182	1.168	1.164	1.164	1.169	1.164	1.161	1.160	1.159	1.153	1994
1995	1.153	1.146	1.142	1.130	1.126	1.124	1.129	1.123	1.118	1.124	1.124	1.117	1995
1996	1.121	1.116	1.112	1.104	1.101	1.101	1.105	1.100	1.095	1.095	1.094	1.091	1996
1997	1.091	1.086	1.084	1.077	1.073	1.069	1.069	1.062	1.057	1.056	1.055	1.053	1997
1998	1.056	1.051	1.047	1.036	1.030	1.031	1.033	1.029	1.024	1.024	1.024	1.024	1998
1999	1.031	1.029	1.026	1.019	1.017	1.017	1.020	1.018	1.013	1.011	1.010	1.007	1999
2000	1.011	1.005											2000
	J	F	M	A	M	J	J	A	S	O	N	D	

UPLIFT FOR INFLATION, AND *SIMMONS v CASTLE*, FROM MARCH 2000 TO THE DATE OF TRIAL

The Retail Prices Index on March 23, 2000 was 168.4. 168.4 ÷ 110% = 153.1. In June 2015 the RPI was 258.9.
The uplift for inflation from March 2000 is calculated as follows:
£award × (RPI at date of trial) / 153.1. (Note that using the figure of 153.1 already takes account of the Jackson 10% uplift.)
For an award that was worth £5,000 in March 2000, this would give at June 2015:
£5,000 × 258.9 / 153.1 = £8,455.

	2015						2016						
Month	Jul	Aug	Sep	Oct	Nov	Dec	Jan	Feb	Mar	Apr	May	Jun	Jul
Current RPI													
Uplift (current RPI ÷ 153.1)													

TABLE OF UPLIFTS FOLLOWING *HEIL v RANKIN*

Old	New	Old	New	Old	New
0–10,000	No change	57,000	63,378	104,000	127,276
11,000	11,026	58,000	64,628	105,000	128,745
12,000	12,057	59,000	65,883	106,000	130,229
13,000	13,092	60,000	67,142	107,000	131,712
14,000	14,133	61,000	68,407	108,000	133,200
15,000	15,178	62,000	69,676	109,000	134,693
16,000	16,228	63,000	70,949	110,000	136,190
17,000	17,283	64,000	72,228	111,000	137,693
18,000	18,342	65,000	73,511	112,000	139,200
19,000	19,407	66,000	74,799	113,000	140,712
20,000	20,476	67,000	76,092	114,000	142,229
21,000	21,549	68,000	77,390	115,000	143,750
22,000	22,628	69,000	78,692	116,000	142,276
23,000	23,711	70,000	79,999	117,000	146,807
24,000	24,799	71,000	81,311	118,000	148,343
25,000	25,892	72,000	82,628	119,000	149,883
26,000	26,990	73,000	83,950	120,000	151,428
27,000	28,092	74,000	85,276	121,000	152,979
28,000	29,199	75,000	86,607	122,000	154,533
29,000	30,311	76,000	87,942	123,000	156,093
30,000	31,428	77,000	89,283	124,000	157,657
31,000	32,550	78,000	90,629	125,000	159,226
32,000	33,676	79,000	91,979	126,000	160,800
33,000	34,807	80,000	93,333	127,000	162,379
34,000	35,942	81,000	94,693	128,000	163,962
35,000	37,083	82,000	96,057	129,000	165,549
36,000	38,228	83,000	97,426	130,000	167,143
37,000	39,378	84,000	98,800	131,000	168,740
38,000	40,533	85,000	100,179	132,000	170,343
39,000	41,692	86,000	101,562	133,000	171,950
40,000	42,857	87,000	102,945	134,000	173,562

TABLE OF UPLIFTS FOLLOWING *HEIL v RANKIN continued*

Old	New	Old	New	Old	New
41,000	44,026	88,000	104,343	135,000	175,179
42,000	45,199	89,000	105,740	136,000	176,800
43,000	46,378	90,000	107,142	137,000	178,426
44,000	47,561	91,000	108,549	138,000	180,057
45,000	48,750	92,000	109,961	139,000	181,692
46,000	49,942	93,000	111,378	140,000	183,333
47,000	51,140	94,000	112,800	141,000	184,978
48,000	52,342	95,000	114,226	142,000	186,628
49,000	53,549	96,000	115,657	143,000	188,283
50,000	54,761	97,000	117,092	144,000	189,942
51,000	55,978	98,000	118,533	145,000	191,607
52,000	57,200	99,000	119,978	146,000	193,276
53,000	58,426	100,000	121,428	147,000	194,949
54,000	59,657	101,000	122,883	148,000	196,628
55,000	60,892	102,000	124,342	149,000	198,311
56,000	62,133	103,000	125,807	150,000	200,000

TO UPDATE A POST-*HEIL v RANKIN,* BUT PRE-*SIMMONS v CASTLE,* AWARD

Awards since *Heil v Rankin* but before the *Simmons v Castle* uplift (generally awards between March 23, 2000 and April 1, 2013), should be updated in this way:

£award × 1.1 × (RPI at date of trial)/(RPI at date of award)

For an award that was worth £5,000 in June 2008, this would give at June 2015 (unless s.44(6) applies):

£5,000 × 1.1 × 258.9 / 216.8 = £6,568

TO UPDATE A POST-*SIMMONS v CASTLE* AWARD

Awards which already include the *Simmons v Castle* uplift (generally awards since April 1, 2013 unless s.44(6) applied to them), should be updated in this way:

£award x (RPI at date of trial)/(RPI at date of award)

For an award that was worth £5,000 in June 2013, this would give at June 2015:

£5,000 × 258.9 / 249.7 = £5,184

B2: Bereavement damages

1. Damages for bereavement are awarded under s.1A of the Fatal Accidents Act 1976. This is a fixed sum, set by statute as amended (see below).
2. The claim for bereavement damages can only be brought by:
   (i) a bereaved spouse, or

   (ii) where the deceased was a minor who never married, by:
      (a) either of his parents if the deceased was legitimate; or
      (b) the mother if the deceased was illegitimate.

3. Where there is a claim for damages for bereavement for the benefit of the parents of the deceased, s.1A(4) of the Fatal Accidents Act 1976 provides that:

   "The sum awarded shall be divided equally between them (subject to any deduction falling to be made in respect of costs not recovered from the defendant)."

   Where the parents are divorced or separated and only one parent makes the claim, that parent will hold half of the bereavement damages on trust for the other parent.

4. The Administration of Justice Act 1982 contains a provision (at s.1A(5)) for the Lord Chancellor to vary the statutory sum. The original statute fixed the sum at £3,500, and that was raised by four subsequent statutory instruments (SI 1990/2575, SI 2002/644, SI 2007/3488 and SI 2013/510). Hence the relevant dates and statutory sums are as follows:

– if the death was before January 1, 1983, the award is	**nil**
– if the death was between January 1, 1983 and March 31, 1991, the award is	**£3,500**
– if the death was between April 1, 1991 and March 31, 2002, the award is	**£7,500**
– if the death was between April 1, 2002 and December 31, 2007, the award is	**£10,000**
– if the death was between January 1, 2008 and March 31, 2013, the award is	**£11,800**
– if the death was on or after April 1, 2013, the award is	**£12,980**

5. The claimant is entitled to interest on bereavement damages from the date of death to the date of trial or settlement of the action—see *Prior v Hastie*.[1]

[1] [1987] C.L.Y. 1219.

B3: *Auty v National Coal Board* (pension claims)

In *Wells v Wells*, the House of Lords made only passing reference to the calculation of future pension losses. The implication is that the multipliers for such losses are to be taken from the Ogden Tables, as are those for pecuniary losses for life and for loss of earnings. There is no justification for adopting a different approach. Since the mid-1980s, pension claims have often been based on the principles set out in *Auty v National Coal Board*.[1] This analysis is a guide to those principles, but is included with the caution that the method of selecting multipliers and discount factors has been superseded by *Wells v Wells*.

It is important to remember that the trial judge in *Auty* was not working from the Ogden Tables, but from a table of life expectation. Here is the calculation carried out in *Auty*:

1. The net annual pension loss after tax: £443.
2. The claimant and his wife were both aged 34 at the date of trial.
3. The life tables showed that the claimant's life expectation beyond the age of 65 was 6.68 years, and his wife's life expectation beyond the age of 65 was 12.26 years. She was therefore expected to survive him by 5.58 years. She was entitled to a two-thirds widow's pension, so the judge added two-thirds of 5.58 years (i.e. 3.72 years) to the claimant's life expectancy beyond 65 of 6.68 to give a total period of loss of 10.4 years.
4. ***First step***: the judge considered an appropriate multiplier (at a 5 per cent discount rate) for 10.4 years to be seven. This is the equivalent of the discounting calculation that would now be performed (at 2.5 per cent) by using the Ogden Tables.
5. The basic pension loss at 65 was therefore [7 × £443] = £3,101.
6. Loss of lump sum gratuity: £1,899.
7. Total capital value of loss at retirement age [£3,101 + £1,899] = £5,000.
8. ***Second step***: Mr Auty was 34 years old. He was therefore being compensated for his pension loss 31 years prematurely. The judge discounted the sum of £5,000 at 5 per cent over 31 years, leaving £1,100. This discount would now be performed by Ogden Table 27 at 2.5 per cent.
9. ***Third step***: The judge discounted the pension claim by a further 27 per cent for contingencies. This brought the sum of £1,100 down to £800. Of this step the Court of Appeal said[2]:

   "The discount for imponderables which the judge made in Auty's case was 27 per cent. The judge said that the imponderables included voluntary wastage, redundancy, dismissal, supervening ill-health, disablement or death before 65, and said that death was the major discount."
10. Add value of loss of death in service benefit (£200).
11. Total value of award: **£1,000**.

Note: The three steps bring the annual pension element alone (ignoring the lump sum and the death in service benefit) down to below £500. If one simply applied the Ogden Tables and a 2.5 per cent discount rate to the above annual pension loss the claimant would receive [7.98 × £443] = £3,535, before contingencies. It should also be noted that, when using the Ogden Tables, no further discount should be made in the contingencies deduction for mortality, as this is incorporated into the Ogden Tables, so applying a further contingency discount would amount to a 'double discount'.

Employment tribunals have developed a different approach to the calculation of pension loss. Those interested are referred to the guidelines in Sneath, Sara, Daykin and Gallop, *Industrial Tribunals: Compensation for loss of pension rights* (2003, 3rd edn) HMSO, approved by the Employment Appeal Tribunal in *Benson v Dairy Crest*.[3]

[1] [1985] 1 All E.R. 930.
[2] Waller L.J. in *Auty*, at 937.
[3] (EAT/192/89).

B4: *Roberts v Johnstone* (accommodation claims)

1. Seriously injured claimants will often require special accommodation which may have to be adapted for their particular needs. This will often mean that they have to move to a more expensive house. The applicable principles of law were set out by the Court of Appeal in *Roberts v Johnstone*.[1]

2. **Example**: A paraplegic claimant lives in an unsuitable house with a market value of £150,000. She wishes to buy a more suitable house for £230,000 and alter it (because of her disabilities) at a cost of £20,000. The alterations will not (in themselves) make any difference to the value of the adapted house. The claimant will continue to live in the adapted house for the rest of her life and the agreed life multiplier is 10. Following *Roberts v Johnstone*, the claim for accommodation costs is calculated as follows:

   (i) Costs of adaption: **£20,000**
   Recovered in full because wholly attributable to injuries and will not add value to the house.

   (ii) Costs of moving house: **£10,000**
   Recovered in full if the claimant would not have moved house but for the accident.

   (iii) Loss of Use of Capital:
   As a result of the move, the claimant is obliged to invest in the house, thereby foregoing the use of a part of her capital. The discount rate of 2.5% is taken as the annual loss caused by this. Hence the claim is:

   £80,000 (extra cost of the house) × 2.5% (discount rate) × 10 (agreed life multiplier) = **£20,000**

   Note that the claimant does not recover the full additional capital cost of the house; if she did, the estate would derive a windfall benefit.

   (iv) Extra Annual Costs of Accommodation:
   If the costs of living in the more expensive house are higher, the claimant can claim them. Items might include council tax, decorating costs and water charges. If these costs were £500 p.a., the claim would be:

   £500 (extra annual costs) × 10 (agreed life multiplier) = **£5,000**

3. The total claim for accommodation in the example is therefore **£55,000**.

4. If the discount rate is varied from the present figure of 2.5 per cent, *Roberts v Johnstone* claims will also change. For instance, if the rate were to be reduced to 1 per cent, the calculation of loss of capital in para.2 (iii), above, would be £80,000 × 1% × 10 = £8,000.

[1] [1989] Q.B. 878.

B5: Periodical payments

The circumstances in which a periodical payment should be made

The Damages Act 1996 as amended now empowers the Court to order Periodical Payments for future losses. Provisions dealing with the making of a periodical payments order are contained in CPR rr.41.4 to 41.10 and the attendant Practice Directions. Rule 41.7 provides that:

> "When considering–
>
> (a) its indication as to whether periodical payments or a lump sum is likely to be the more appropriate form for all or part of an award of damages under rule 41.6; or
>
> (b) whether to make an order under section 2(1)(a) of the 1996 Act,
>
> the court shall have regard to all the circumstances of the case and in particular the form of award which best meets the claimant's needs, having regard to the factors set out in the practice direction."

The factors involved are derived from the Practice Direction supplementing Part 41 which provides that:

> "The factors which the court shall have regard to under rule 41.7 include–
>
> (1) the scale of the annual payments taking into account any deduction for contributory negligence;
>
> (2) the form of award preferred by the claimant including–
>
> (a) the reasons for the claimant's preference; and
>
> (b) the nature of any financial advice received by the claimant when considering the form of award; and
>
> (3) the form of award preferred by the defendant including the reasons for the defendant's preference."

Practitioners representing claimants may wish to obtain financial advice in order to decide whether or not to ask the Court to make an award for Periodical Payments. Such advice will be particularly useful in difficult cases such as those involving incomplete recovery (contributory negligence or agreed reduction of damages for litigation risk in a clinical negligence claim).

Circumstances in which periodical payments are not available

Section 2(3) of the 1996 Act provides that:

> "(3) A court may not make an order for periodical payments unless satisfied that the continuity of payment under the order is reasonably secure."

Continuity of payment will only be secure in three situations, each dignified by its own sub-clause in subsection 2(4):

> "(4) For the purposes of subsection (3) the continuity of payment under an order is reasonably secure if–

(a) it is protected by a guarantee given under section 6 of or the Schedule to this Act,

(b) it is protected by a scheme under section 213 of the Financial Services and Markets Act 2000 (compensation) (whether or not as modified by section 4 of this Act), or

(c) the source of payment is a government or health service body."

The effect of this is that Periodical Payments will not be available unless the defendant is either a government body (such as the NHSLA) or a UK insurer within one of the two statutory schemes. Hence practitioners must ascertain whether or not the defendant is within those schemes well before the matter comes to trial or settlement meeting.

The indexation of periodical payments

Section 2(8) of the Damages Act 1996 (as amended) provides that orders for periodical payments are to be treated as providing for the amount of the payment ordered to vary with the Retail Prices Index ("RPI"). However, section 2(9) of the Damages Act 1996 then stipulates that an order for periodical payments may include provision disapplying section 2(8) or modifying its effect.

In *Thompstone v Tameside and Glossop NHS Trust* [2008] AER 72, the Court of Appeal held that the appropriate means of indexation of future costs of care and case management would be by reference to ASHE 6115 (see next section of *Facts & Figures*) which was the most reliable way of "tracking" changes to these costs.

Consequently, the ASHE 6115 indexation will apply to periodical payments in respect of future care and case management. The Retail Prices Index will be used for future losses which are goods-based (such as future equipment and assistive technology). In *Sarwar v Ali and Motor Insurers Bureau* [2007] LS Law Med 375, Lloyd Jones J awarded a periodical payment for future losses of earnings and index-linked the loss by reference to the ASHE aggregated earnings data for male full-time employees. Theoretically, it would be possible for a party to contend for another means of indexation, although to our knowledge this has not been successfully attempted in a reported case.

"Model Order" for periodical payments

The leading case is now *RH v University Hospitals Bristol NHS Foundation Trust* [2013] EWHC 229. Swift J. held that since there had been a change in statistical methodology used to generate the ASHE 6115 indexation, there was a need to adapt the previous model order made by Sir Christopher Holland on December 2, 2008, which is reported at [2009] P.I.Q.R. P153. The model order approved in *RH* may be used for periodical payments and it deals with the complex issues of indexation and changes to payments caused by that indexation. The NHSLA continues to uprate indexed payments on December 15 each year although other defendants and insurers may have different preferences. Clearly, the starting date must be set at sufficient distance to allow its satisfactory introduction; this is likely to be more protracted if the Claimant has a Deputy.

Is the Claimant still alive?

In *Long v Norwich Union* [2009] EWHC 715 QB, Mackay J held that a claimant was not entitled to recover the costs of proving that he was still alive at the date of periodical payment. The court held that this cost would be covered by the award for the costs of deputyship; alternatively, it might be said that the modest costs of this type borne by the claimant would be covered by the interest generated on the advance payments to be made under the order.

B6: Step-by-step guide to finding the annual estimates for hourly pay in ASHE SOC 2000 6115

The data collection point for the Annual Survey of Hours and Earnings (ASHE) is April each year. The data are collected over the summer and the first release of estimates takes place in November/December of that year. These are provisional estimates which are revised and published as final estimates the following November/December. The following estimates were published for ASHE SOC 2000 on November 22, 2012, December 12, 2013 and November 19, 2014. Estimates for 2014 are provisional and will be replaced by final estimates in November/December 2015.

ASHE SOC 2000 6115 Centile estimates for hourly earnings £ for UK employees

Centile	10	20	25	30	40	50	60	70	75	80	90
ASHE 6115 2011 Final release	6.05	6.44	6.65	6.87	7.28	7.83	8.45	9.17	9.67	10.22	11.92
ASHE 6115 2012 Final release	6.21	6.57	6.80	7.00	7.44	7.92	8.51	9.21	9.69	10.25	11.97
ASHE 6115 2013 Final release	6.30	6.61	6.80	7.00	7.40	7.91	8.50	9.22	9.73	10.29	12.02
ASHE 6115 2014 First release	6.41	6.74	6.94	7.12	7.53	8.00	8.55	9.23	9.72	10.21	11.94

Source: ONS ASHE published November 22, 2012, December 12, 2013 and November 19, 2014.

ASHE estimates are only available online. They can be found on the website of the UK Statistics Authority. This requires some navigation from the home page. Step-by-step instructions follow. You need not follow all these instructions each time you consult the tables as you can either download the tables as an Excel file or you can save the web link to the tables in Bookmarks.

Estimates for 2011 are based on the Standard Occupational Classification (SOC) 2010 weights. Reclassification of occupational categories occurs every ten years and occurred in ASHE (SOC 2010) 2011 released in March 2012. The reclassification of occupations introduces a time discontinuity into the statistical series which creates two problems for calculating an annual escalation in a PPO. First, the occupational weights upon which all the ASHE estimates are based change between 2010 and 2011 from SOC 2000 to SOC 2010. Estimates are available for 2011 using both sets of weights. When calculating a growth rate, care must be taken that estimates in different years are made on the basis of the same occupational weights. When comparing earnings in any year from 2011 onwards with 2011, use the 2011 final release. When comparing earnings in any year before 2011, use the 2011 first release.

Secondly, the classification for carers changed in SOC 2010 to include two separate categories, ASHE 6145 care workers and home carers and ASHE 6146 senior care workers. Aside from the potential escalation difficulty, this new classification introduces problems associated the definition of the "senior" care workers who would populate the additional group and the small sample size of the group. For the purposes of the indexation of future care, the new classification for care can be ignored. From 2011 until at least 2022, the ASHE team at ONS has agreed to continue to publish statistics relating to the SOC 2000 classification of carers, that is occupational group 6115. The occupational earnings tables for 6115 can be found at Table 26. The title for this Table is 'Care workers (SOC 6145 and 6146)' and the description is 'Care workers, home carers and senior care workers'.

1. Find the home page of the Office for National Statistics (ONS) at www.ons.gov.uk.
2. Type in ASHE 2014 in the search box at the top of this page and click Search.

3. All the ASHE spreadsheets (1–26) are listed in the search results together with many other documents. To restrict your search to the statistical tables, check the box marked Reference tables under Filter Results on the right hand side of the screen. Click on 'Apply selected filters'.

4. Scroll down the list to find the Reference table that you require. For carers, you need Table 26 which provides earnings estimates disaggregated to the four-digit SOC 2000 classification for 6115. The title for this Table is 'Care workers (SOC 6145 and 6146)'.

5. Double-clicking on the table title will take you to a zip file. Opening the zip file will produce a contents list of Excel files, each of which contain an occupational breakdown of a different set of earnings estimates for carers.

6 Hourly pay for carers is in Table 26.5a 'Hourly Pay – Gross'. Double-clicking on the table title will take you to a worksheet in an Excel file. If you are sure that you have located the file that you want, save it using File-->Save in Excel.

7. Once in the Excel file, check the bottom tab. 'All' refers to all employees (male and female, part- and full-time).

8. Read across the centile estimates. Shading indicates the reliability of the estimate. Where the estimate of the error is less than 5 per cent (reliable), there is no shading. ASHE 6115 estimates are normally reliable due to a large sample size. The key to the shading can be found at the bottom and at the right hand side of the table.

9. If you have not already saved this file at step 7 above, this table can be saved now, either in part or in full. If the file is saved before the final release in November/December 2015, make a note that the 2014 estimates are provisional. They will be replaced in the final release under the same title.

10. Details of any changes to the estimates and/or to the step-by-step guide which occur after publication of *Facts & Figures 2015/16* and links to sources of further information on reclassification can be found on www.victoriawass-laboureconomics.co.uk under Indexation.

This guide has been prepared by Dr Victoria Wass, Cardiff Business School, May 2015.

Group C

Interest Rates

C

C1: Interest base rates

Introductory notes

1. The data for this table are obtained from retail banks Barclays, Lloyds TSB, HSBC and National Westminster.
2. Where these banks' base rates did not change on the same day, an average rate is shown (and asterisked in the table).
3. Since August 3, 2006, these retail banks' base rates have been identical to the Bank of England's Official Bank Rate.

Date	New rate (%)
1982	
August 2	11.50
August 18	11.00
August 31	10.50
October 7	10.00
October 14	9.50
November 4	9.00
November 26	10.125*
1983	
January 12	11.00
March 15	10.50
April 15	10.00
June 15	9.50
October 4	9.00
1984	
March 7	8.875*
March 15	8.625*
May 10	9.125*
June 27	9.25
July 9	10.00
July 11	11.00*
July 12	12.00
August 9	11.50
August 10	11.00
August 20	10.50
November 7	10.00
November 20	9.875*
November 23	9.625*
1985	
January 11	10.50
January 14	12.00
January 28	14.00
March 20	13.75*
March 21	13.50
March 29	13.25*
April 2	13.125*
April 12	12.875*
April 19	12.675*
June 12	12.50
July 7	12.25*
July 16	12.00
July 29	11.75*
July 30	11.50
1986	
January 9	12.50
March 19	11.50
April 8	11.25*
April 9	11.00
April 24	10.50
May 27	10.00
October 14	11.00
1987	
March 10	10.50
March 19	10.00
April 29	9.50
May 11	9.00
August 7	10.00
October 26	9.50
November 5	9.00
December	8.50
1988	
February 2	9.00
March 17	8.50
April 11	8.00
May 18	7.50
June 3	8.00
June 6	8.25*
June 7	8.50
June 22	9.00
June 29	9.50
July 5	10.00
July 19	10.50
August 8	10.75*
August 9	11.00
August 25	11.50
August 26	12.00
November 25	13.00
1989	
May 24	14.00
October 5	15.00
1990	
October 8	14.00
1991	
February 13	13.50
February 27	13.00
March 25	12.50
April 12	12.00
May 24	11.50
July 12	11.00
September 4	10.50
1992	
May 5	10.00
September 16	12.00
September 17	10.00
September 22	9.00
October 16	8.00
November 13	7.00
1993	
January 26	6.00
November 23	5.50
1994	
February 8	5.25
September 12	5.75
December 7	6.25
1995	
February 2	6.75
December 13	6.50
1996	
January 18	6.25
March 8	6.00
June 6	5.75
October 30	6.00
1997	
May 7	6.25
June 9	6.50
July 11	6.75
August 8	7.00
November 7	7.25
1998	
June 5	7.50
October 9	7.25
November 6	6.75
December 1	6.25

C1: Interest base rates

Date	New rate (%)
1999	
January 8	6.00
February 5	5.50
April 8	5.25
June 10	5.00
September 8	5.25
November 4	5.50
2000	
January 13	5.75
February 10	6.00
2001	
February 8	5.75
April 5	5.50
May 10	5.25
August 2	5.00
September 18	4.75
October 4	4.50
November 8	4.00
2003	
February 7	3.75
July 10	3.50
November 6	3.75
2004	
February 5	4.00
May 6	4.25
June 10	4.50
August 5	4.75
2005	
August 4	4.50
2006	
August 3	4.75
November 9	5.00
2007	
January 11	5.25
May 10	5.50
July 5	5.75
December 6	5.50
2008	
February 7	5.25
April 10	5.00
October 8	4.50
November 6	3.00
December 4	2.00
2009	
January 8	1.50
February 5	1.00
March 5	0.50

C2: Real and nominal interest rates and price inflation

Introductory notes

1. Price inflation is calculated as the rate of change of the Retail Prices Index.
2. The nominal interest rate is based on the rate on 20-year British Government Securities.
3. No account has been taken of tax in these figures.

	Price Inflation %	**Nominal Interest Rate** %	**Real Interest Rate** %
1980	18.03	13.78	(4.25)
1981	11.88	14.74	2.86
1982	8.70	12.88	4.18
1983	4.44	10.80	6.36
1984	5.01	10.69	5.68
1985	6.04	10.62	4.58
1986	3.40	9.87	6.47
1987	4.16	9.47	5.31
1988	4.92	9.36	4.44
1989	7.79	9.58	1.79
1990	9.44	11.08	1.64
1991	5.91	9.92	4.01
1992	3.73	9.12	5.39
1993	1.57	7.87	6.30
1994	2.48	8.05	5.57
1995	3.41	8.26	4.85
1996	2.44	8.10	5.66
1997	3.12	7.09	3.97
1998	3.42	5.45	2.03
1999	1.56	4.70	3.14
2000	2.93	4.70	1.77
2001	1.84	4.78	2.94
2002	1.62	4.83	3.21
2003	2.91	4.64	1.73
2004	2.96	4.78	1.82
2005	2.84	4.39	1.55
2006	3.20	4.29	1.09
2007	4.26	4.73	0.47
2008	4.00	4.68	0.68
2009	(0.53)	4.25	4.78
2010	4.61	4.25	(0.36)
2011	5.21	3.83	(1.38)
2012	3.22	2.87	(0.35)
2013	3.05	3.27	0.22
2014	2.38	3.17	0.79
Averages:			
1980–89	7.44	11.18	3.74
1990–99	3.71	7.96	4.25
2000–09	2.60	4.61	2.01
2010–14	3.69	3.48	(0.21)

Real Interest Rates 1970–2014

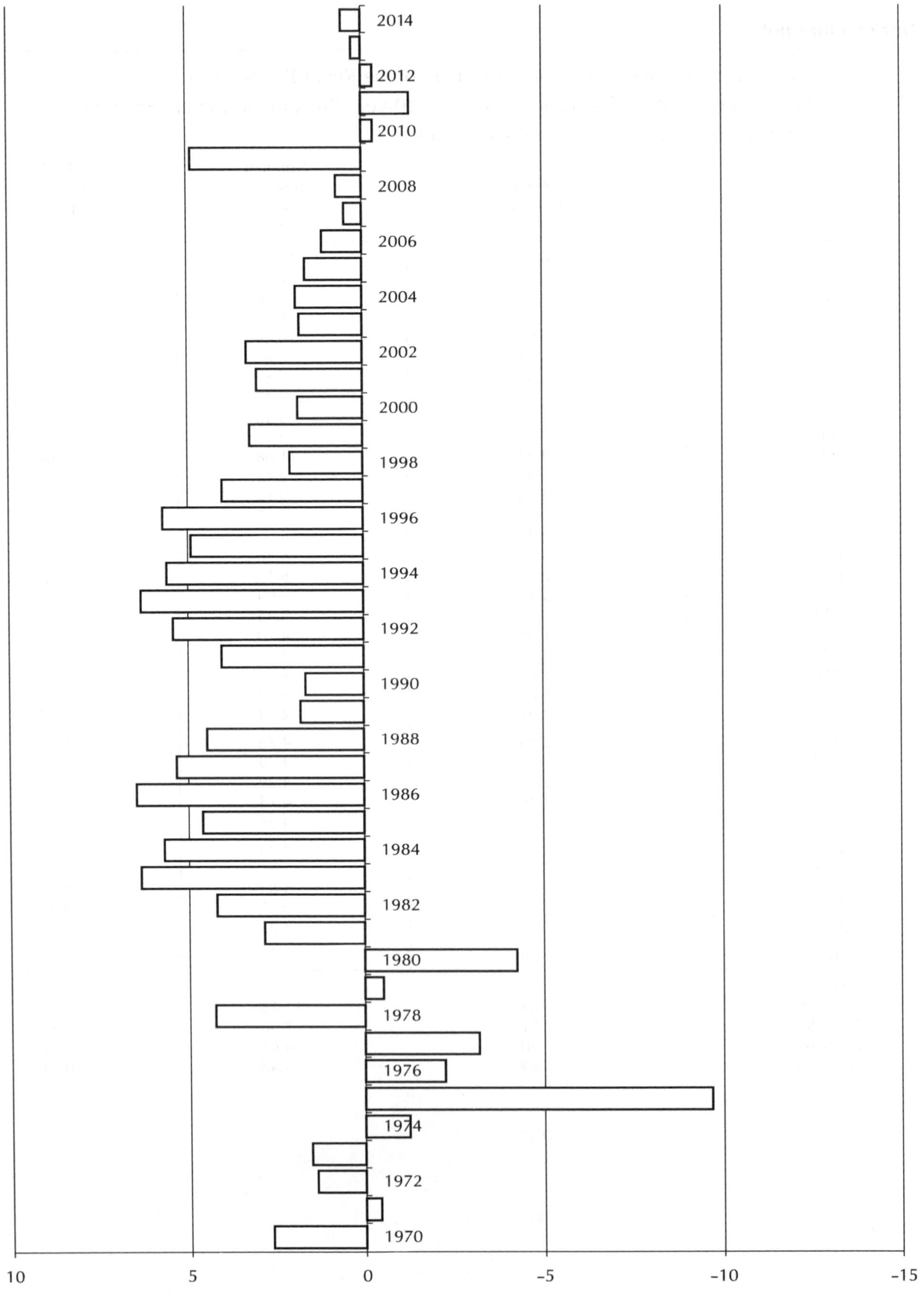

C3: Special investment account rates

Introductory notes

This is a composite table including both the Short-term Investment Account rate and the succeeding High Court Special Investment Account rate.

The manner of crediting interest is set out in Court Fund Rules 1987 r.27. Interest accruing to a special investment account is credited without the deduction of income tax.

From:		%
October 1	1965	5.0
September 1	1966	5.5
March 1	1968	6.0
March 1	1969	6.5
March 1	1970	7.0
March 1	1971	7.5
March 1	1973	8.0
March 1	1974	9.0
February 1	1977	10.0
March 1	1979	12.5
January 1	1980	15.0
January 1	1981	12.5
December 1	1981	15.0
March 1	1982	14.0
July 1	1982	13.0
April 1	1983	12.5
April 1	1984	12.0
August 1	1986	11.5
January 1	1987	12.25
April 1	1987	11.75
November 1	1987	11.25
December 1	1987	11.0
May 1	1988	9.5
August 1	1988	11.0
November 1	1988	12.25
January 1	1989	13.0
November 1	1989	14.25
April 1	1991	12.0
October 1	1991	10.25
February 1	1993	8.0
August 1	1999	7.0
February 1	2002	6.0
February 1	2009	3.0
June 1	2009	1.5
July 1	2009	0.5

C4: Special and general damages interest

Introductory notes

Special damages

The appropriate rate of interest for special damages is the rate, over the period for which the interest is awarded, which is payable on the court special account. This rate was reduced to 0.5 per cent on July 1, 2009. Interest since June 1987 has been paid daily on a 1/365th basis, even in a leap year such as 2012.

In cases of continuing special damages, half the appropriate rate from the date of injury to the date of trial is awarded. In cases where the special damages have ceased and are thus limited to a finite period, there are conflicting Court of Appeal decisions as to whether the award should be half the appropriate rate from injury to trial (*Dexter v Courtaulds*[1]) or the full special account rate from a date within the period to which the special damages are limited (*Prokop v DHSS*[2]).

The relevant rates since 1965 are set out in Table C3.

The table on the next page records the total of these rates from January 1981. In the left-hand column is shown the month from the first day of which interest is assumed to run. The right-hand column shows the percentage interest accumulated from the first day of each month to June 30, 2015.

Continued use may be made of this table by adding to the figures in it 1/365th of the special account rate for each day from July 1, 2015 onwards, using Table C6, which records the number of days between two dates in a two-year period.

Suppose that interest runs from January 1, 2001 to October 13, 2015. The total to June 30, 2015 is 53.74 per cent (see Table C4). From Table C6, July 1 to October 13 is 286–182 days = 104 days, but add 1 day as both days are to be included = 105 days. If the rate remains at 0.5 per cent p.a., the appropriate addition will be 0.5 per cent × 105/365 = 0.14 per cent. Thus the grand total from January 1, 2001 to October 13, 2015 will be 53.74 + 0.14 = 53.88 per cent.

General damages

In personal injury cases, the normal rate of interest on general damages for pain, suffering and loss of amenity was by convention 2 per cent per annum. In *Lawrence v Chief Constable of Staffordshire*[3] the Court of Appeal held that in spite of *Wells v Wells*,[4] the rate should remain at 2 per cent. Interest runs from the date of service of proceedings.

[1] [1984] 1 All E.R. 70.
[2] [1985] C.L.Y. 1037.
[3] CA, transcript June 29, 2000.
[4] [1999] A.C. 345.

Table of cumulative interest at the special account rate from the first day of each month to June 30, 2015.

	1981	1982	1983	1984	1985	1986	1987	1988	1989	1990
January	263.94	251.23	237.57	224.95	212.82	200.82	189.03	177.26	166.40	153.19
February	262.88	249.95	236.46	223.88	211.80	199.80	187.99	176.33	165.30	151.98
March	261.92	248.80	235.47	222.92	210.88	198.88	187.05	175.45	164.30	150.89
April	260.86	247.61	234.36	221.86	209.86	197.86	186.01	174.52	163.20	149.68
May	259.83	246.46	233.34	220.88	208.88	196.88	185.05	173.62	162.13	148.51
June	258.77	245.27	232.27	219.86	207.86	195.86	184.05	172.81	161.02	147.30
July	257.74	244.12	231.25	218.87	206.87	194.87	183.08	172.03	159.96	146.13
August	256.68	243.02	230.18	217.85	205.85	193.85	182.08	171.22	158.85	144.92
September	255.62	241.91	229.12	216.83	204.83	192.88	181.09	170.29	157.75	143.71
October	254.59	240.85	228.10	215.85	203.85	191.93	180.12	169.38	156.68	142.53
November	253.53	239.74	227.03	214.83	202.83	190.95	179.12	168.45	155.57	141.32
December	252.50	238.67	226.01	213.84	201.84	190.01	178.20	167.44	154.40	140.15
	1991	**1992**	**1993**	**1994**	**1995**	**1996**	**1997**	**1998**	**1999**	**2000**
January	138.94	126.83	116.55	108.36	100.36	92.36	84.34	76.34	68.34	60.76
February	137.73	125.96	115.68	107.68	99.68	91.68	83.66	75.66	67.66	60.16
March	136.64	125.14	115.07	107.07	99.07	91.05	83.05	75.05	67.05	59.61
April	135.43	124.27	114.39	106.39	98.39	90.37	82.37	74.37	66.37	59.01
May	134.44	123.43	113.73	105.73	97.73	89.71	81.71	73.71	65.71	58.44
June	133.42	122.56	113.05	105.05	97.05	89.03	81.03	73.03	65.03	57.84
July	132.44	121.72	112.39	104.39	96.39	88.37	80.37	72.37	64.37	57.27
August	131.42	120.85	111.71	103.71	95.71	87.69	79.69	71.69	63.69	56.67
September	130.40	119.98	111.03	103.03	95.03	87.01	79.01	71.01	63.10	56.08
October	129.41	119.13	110.38	102.38	94.38	86.35	78.35	70.35	62.52	55.50
November	128.54	118.26	109.70	101.70	93.70	85.68	77.68	69.68	61.93	54.91
December	127.70	117.42	109.04	101.04	93.04	85.02	77.02	69.02	61.35	54.33
	2001	**2002**	**2003**	**2004**	**2005**	**2006**	**2007**	**2008**	**2009**	**2010**
January	53.74	46.74	40.65	34.65	28.64	22.64	16.64	10.64	4.62	2.75
February	53.14	46.14	40.14	34.14	28.13	22.13	16.13	10.13	4.11	2.71
March	52.61	45.68	39.68	33.67	27.67	21.67	15.67	9.65	3.88	2.67
April	52.01	45.17	39.17	33.16	27.16	21.16	15.16	9.14	3.63	2.63
May	51.44	44.68	38.68	32.66	26.66	20.66	14.66	8.65	3.38	2.58
June	50.84	44.17	38.17	32.15	26.15	20.15	14.15	8.14	3.12	2.54
July	50.27	43.68	37.68	31.66	25.66	19.66	13.66	7.65	3.00	2.50
August	49.67	43.17	37.17	31.15	25.15	19.15	13.15	7.14	2.96	2.46
September	49.08	42.66	36.66	30.64	24.64	18.64	12.64	6.63	2.92	2.42
October	48.50	42.17	36.17	30.15	24.15	18.15	12.15	6.13	2.88	2.38
November	47.91	41.66	35.66	29.64	23.64	17.64	11.64	5.62	2.83	2.33
December	47.33	41.16	35.16	29.15	23.15	17.15	11.15	5.13	2.79	2.29
	2011	**2012**	**2013**	**2014**	**2015**					
January	2.25	1.75	1.25	0.75	0.25					
February	2.21	1.71	1.21	0.71	0.21					
March	2.17	1.67	1.17	0.67	0.17					
April	2.13	1.62	1.12	0.62	0.12					
May	2.08	1.58	1.08	0.58	0.08					
June	2.04	1.54	1.04	0.54	0.04					
July	2.00	1.50	1.00	0.50						
August	1.96	1.46	0.96	0.46						
September	1.92	1.42	0.92	0.42						
October	1.88	1.37	0.87	0.37						
November	1.83	1.33	0.83	0.33						
December	1.79	1.29	0.79	0.29						

If the rate remains at 0.5%, interest to the last day of successive later months can be found to a date after June 30, 2015 by adding the figure from the following table:

	2015	2016
January		0.29
February		0.33
March		0.38
April		0.42
May		0.46
June		0.50
July	0.04	
August	0.08	
September	0.13	
October	0.17	
November	0.21	
December	0.25	

C5: Base rate + 10%

Introductory notes

1. Under the Civil Procedure Rules 1998 r.36.21, where the judgment against a defendant is more advantageous to the claimant than the proposals in a claimant's Part 36 offer, the court may order interest on the sum awarded and on the costs, for some or all of the period starting with the latest date on which the defendant could have accepted the Part 36 offer without needing the permission of the court, at a rate not exceeding 10% above base rate. In *All-in-One Design & Build Ltd v Motcomb Estates Ltd*,[1] it was held that r.36.21 is not ultra vires.

2. Rule 36.21(4) provides that where the rule applies, the court will make those orders unless it considers it unjust to do so; sub-rule (5) sets out the factors to be considered in deciding whether it would be unjust.

3. Since 1998 base rates plus 10% have been as follows:

		Rate + 10%			Rate + 10%			Rate + 10%
1997	November 7	17.25%	**2001**	April 5	15.50%	**2006**	August 3	14.75%
1998	June 4	17.50%		May 10	15.25%		November 9	15.00%
	October 8	17.25%		August 2	15.00%	**2007**	January 11	15.25%
	November 5	16.75%		September 18	14.75%		May 10	15.50%
	December 10	16.25%		October 4	14.50%		July 5	15.75%
1999	January 7	16.00%		November 8	14.00%		December 6	15.50%
	February 4	15.50%	**2003**	February 6	13.75%	**2008**	February 7	15.25%
	April 8	15.25%		July 10	13.50%		April 10	15.00%
	June 10	15.00%		November 6	13.75%		October 8	14.50%
	September 8	15.25%	**2004**	February 5	14.00%		November 6	13.00%
	November 4	15.50%		May 6	14.25%		December 4	12.00%
2000	January 13	15.75%		June 10	14.50%	**2009**	January 8	11.50%
	February 10	16.00%		August 5	14.75%		February 5	11.00%
2001	February 8	15.75%	**2005**	August 4	14.50%		March 5	10.50%

The following table shows cumulative interest at 10% above base rate from the first day of each month until June 30, 2015. Interest for parts of a month can be found by following the method in the notes to Table C4.

	2004	2005	2006	2007	2008	2009	2010	2011	2012	2013	2014	2015
January	142.20	127.82	113.18	98.54	83.03	68.35	57.71	47.21	36.71	26.21	15.71	5.21
February	141.04	126.57	111.94	97.25	81.71	67.37	56.82	46.32	35.82	25.32	14.82	4.32
March	139.93	125.44	110.83	96.08	80.50	66.52	56.01	45.51	35.01	24.51	14.01	3.51
April	138.75	124.19	109.60	94.78	79.21	65.62	55.12	44.62	34.12	23.62	13.12	2.62
May	137.60	122.97	108.41	93.53	77.97	64.76	54.26	43.75	33.25	22.75	12.25	1.75
June	136.40	121.72	107.18	92.22	76.70	63.87	53.37	42.86	32.36	21.86	11.36	0.86
July	135.21	120.51	105.98	90.94	75.47	63.00	52.50	42.00	31.50	21.00	10.50	
August	133.99	119.26	104.75	89.61	74.20	62.11	51.61	41.11	30.61	20.11	9.61	
September	132.74	118.02	103.50	88.27	72.93	61.22	50.72	40.22	29.72	19.22	8.72	
October	131.53	116.83	102.29	86.98	71.70	60.36	49.86	39.35	28.85	18.35	7.85	
November	130.28	115.60	101.04	85.64	70.46	59.46	48.96	38.46	27.96	17.46	6.96	
December	129.07	114.41	99.81	84.35	69.38	58.60	48.10	37.60	27.10	16.60	6.10	

[1] *The Times*, April 4, 2000.

If there are no further changes of rate after that on March 5, 2009, interest to the last day of successive later months can be found to a date after June 30, 2015 by adding the figure from the following table:

	2015	2016
January		6.18
February		7.00
March		7.89
April		8.75
May		9.64
June		10.50
July	0.89	
August	1.78	
September	2.65	
October	3.54	
November	4.40	
December	5.29	

C6: Number of days between two dates

Introductory notes

Deduct the number of the opening date from the number of the closing date (where necessary adding a day for February 29).
Example: October 14th–March 19th is 443 – 287 = 156 days.
Note that the calculation produces the *interval* between the two dates; so that January 1st to February 1st is 31 days, not 32.

Day of month	Day numbers																							Day of month
	Jan	Feb	Mar	Apr	May	Jun	Jul	Aug	Sep	Oct	Nov	Dec	Jan	Feb	Mar	Apr	May	Jun	Jul	Aug	Sep	Oct	Nov	Dec	
1	1	32	60	91	121	152	182	213	244	274	305	335	366	397	425	456	486	517	547	578	609	639	670	700	**1**
2	2	33	61	92	122	153	183	214	245	275	306	336	367	398	426	457	487	518	548	579	610	640	671	701	**2**
3	3	34	62	93	123	154	184	215	246	276	307	337	368	399	427	458	488	519	549	580	611	641	672	702	**3**
4	4	35	63	94	124	155	185	216	247	277	308	338	369	400	428	459	489	520	550	581	612	642	673	703	**4**
5	5	36	64	95	125	156	186	217	248	278	309	339	370	401	429	460	490	521	551	582	613	643	674	704	**5**
6	6	37	65	96	126	157	187	218	249	279	310	340	371	402	430	461	491	522	552	583	614	644	675	705	**6**
7	7	38	66	97	127	158	188	219	250	280	311	341	372	403	431	462	492	523	553	584	615	645	676	706	**7**
8	8	39	67	98	128	159	189	220	251	281	312	342	373	404	432	463	493	524	554	585	616	646	677	707	**8**
9	9	40	68	99	129	160	190	221	252	282	313	343	374	405	433	464	494	525	555	586	617	647	678	708	**9**
10	10	41	69	100	130	161	191	222	253	283	314	344	375	406	434	465	495	526	556	587	618	648	679	709	**10**
11	11	42	70	101	131	162	192	223	254	284	315	345	376	407	435	466	496	527	557	588	619	649	680	710	**11**
12	12	43	71	102	132	163	193	224	255	285	316	346	377	408	436	467	497	528	558	589	620	650	681	711	**12**
13	13	44	72	103	133	164	194	225	256	286	317	347	378	409	437	468	498	529	559	590	621	651	682	712	**13**
14	14	45	73	104	134	165	195	226	257	287	318	348	379	410	438	469	499	530	560	591	622	652	683	713	**14**
15	15	46	74	105	135	166	196	227	258	288	319	349	380	411	439	470	500	531	561	592	623	653	684	714	**15**
16	16	47	75	106	136	167	197	228	259	289	320	350	381	412	440	471	501	532	562	593	624	654	685	715	**16**
17	17	48	76	107	137	168	198	229	260	290	321	351	382	413	441	472	502	533	563	594	625	655	686	716	**17**
18	18	49	77	108	138	169	199	230	261	291	322	352	383	414	442	473	503	534	564	595	626	656	687	717	**18**
19	19	50	78	109	139	170	200	231	262	292	323	353	384	415	443	474	504	535	565	596	627	657	688	718	**19**
20	20	51	79	110	140	171	201	232	263	293	324	354	385	416	444	475	505	536	566	597	628	658	689	719	**20**
21	21	52	80	111	141	172	202	233	264	294	325	355	386	417	445	476	506	537	567	598	629	659	690	720	**21**
22	22	53	81	112	142	173	203	234	265	295	326	356	387	418	446	477	507	538	568	599	630	660	691	721	**22**
23	23	54	82	113	143	174	204	235	266	296	327	357	388	419	447	478	508	539	569	600	631	661	692	722	**23**
24	24	55	83	114	144	175	205	236	267	297	328	358	389	420	448	479	509	540	570	601	632	662	693	723	**24**
25	25	56	84	115	145	176	206	237	268	298	329	359	390	421	449	480	510	541	571	602	633	663	694	724	**25**
26	26	57	85	116	146	177	207	238	269	299	330	360	391	422	450	481	511	542	572	603	634	664	695	725	**26**
27	27	58	86	117	147	178	208	239	270	300	331	361	392	423	451	482	512	543	573	604	635	665	696	726	**27**
28	28	59	87	118	148	179	209	240	271	301	332	362	393	424	452	483	513	544	574	605	636	666	697	727	**28**
29	29		88	119	149	180	210	241	272	302	333	363	394		453	484	514	545	575	606	637	667	698	728	**29**
30	30		89	120	150	181	211	242	273	303	334	364	395		454	485	515	546	576	607	638	668	699	729	**30**
31	31		90		151		212	243		304		365	396		455		516		577	608		669		730	**31**

C7: Decimal years

An alternative way of calculating interest is with a table expressing intervals as decimals of a year. It is in some respects simpler than using Table C6 (Number of Days) as it avoids the need to divide by 365.

The first table below gives days, weeks and months as decimals of a year.

The second table gives the period between corresponding days of two months, with the earlier month down the left-hand side and the later month across the top. Thus from the two figures in bold one sees that from April 1–June 1 is 0.167 years; from June 1 to the next April 1 is 0.833 years. The calculation again produces the *interval* between the dates: January 1st to February 1st is 31 days (not 32).

Days, weeks and months expressed as decimals of a year

Days

1	0.003	2	0.005	3	0.008	4	0.011	5	0.014	6	0.016	7	0.019	8	0.022	9	0.025	10	0.027
11	0.030	12	0.033	13	0.036	14	0.038	15	0.041	16	0.044	17	0.047	18	0.049	19	0.052	20	0.055
21	0.058	22	0.060	23	0.063	24	0.066	25	0.068	26	0.071	27	0.074	28	0.077	29	0.079	30	0.082

Weeks

1	0.019	2	0.038	3	0.058	4	0.077	5	0.096	6	0.115	7	0.134	8	0.153	9	0.173	10	0.192

Months

28 days	0.077	29 days	0.079	30 days	0.082	31 days	0.085

Intervals between corresponding days of months as decimals of a year

Later month

Earlier month	Jan	Feb	Mar	Apr	May	Jun
Jan	1.000	0.085	0.162	0.247	0.329	0.414
Feb	0.915	1.000	0.077	0.162	0.244	0.329
Mar	0.838	0.923	1.000	0.085	0.167	0.252
Apr	0.753	0.838	0.915	1.000	0.082	**0.167**
May	0.671	0.756	0.833	0.918	1.000	0.085
Jun	0.586	0.671	0.748	**0.833**	0.915	1.000
Jul	0.504	0.589	0.666	0.751	0.833	0.918
Aug	0.419	0.504	0.581	0.666	0.748	0.833
Sept	0.334	0.419	0.496	0.581	0.663	0.748
Oct	0.252	0.337	0.414	0.499	0.581	0.666
Nov	0.167	0.252	0.329	0.414	0.496	0.581
Dec	0.085	0.170	0.247	0.332	0.414	0.499

Earlier month	Jul	Aug	Sept	Oct	Nov	Dec
Jan	0.496	0.581	0.666	0.748	0.833	0.915
Feb	0.411	0.496	0.581	0.663	0.748	0.830
Mar	0.334	0.419	0.504	0.586	0.671	0.753
Apr	0.249	0.334	0.419	0.501	0.586	0.668
May	0.167	0.252	0.337	0.419	0.504	0.586
Jun	0.082	0.167	0.252	0.334	0.419	0.501
Jul	1.000	0.085	0.170	0.252	0.337	0.419
Aug	0.915	1.000	0.085	0.167	0.252	0.334
Sept	0.830	0.915	1.000	0.082	0.167	0.249
Oct	0.748	0.833	0.918	1.000	0.085	0.167
Nov	0.663	0.748	0.833	0.915	1.000	0.082
Dec	0.581	0.666	0.751	0.833	0.918	1.000

Example: to calculate interest at 8 per cent from June 3, 2014 to April 15, 2015

June 3 to June 15	= 12 days	=	0.033 years		
June 15 to April 15 the following year		=	0.833		
Total 3.6.14 to 15.4.15		=	0.866 years		
Interest at 8% from 3.6.14 to 15.4.15		=	0.866 × 8	=	6.928%

C8: Judgment debt interest rates (England and Wales)

Introductory notes

Interest rates under the Judgments Act 1838 s.17.

This table sets out the interest rates as determined by the Judgment Debts (Rate of Interest) Orders. Such orders are made under the Administration of Justice Act 1970 s.44.

By virtue of The County Courts (Interest on Judgment Debts) Order 1991, the general rule is that every judgment debt of not less than £5,000 carries interest from the date on which it was given, at the same rate as that payable on High Court judgments.

From	At %	Order
April 20, 1971	7.5	SI 1971/491
March 1, 1977	10	SI 1977/141
December 3, 1979	12.5	SI 1979/1382
June 9, 1980	15	SI 1980/672
June 8, 1982	14	SI 1982/696
November 10, 1982	12	SI 1982/1427
April 16, 1985	15	SI 1985/437
April 1, 1993 to date	8	SI 1993/564

C9: Judicial rates of interest (Scotland)

From	At %	Act of Sederunt
May 4, 1965 – January 5, 1970	5	SI 1965/321
January 6, 1970 – January 6, 1975	7	SI 1969/1819
January 7, 1975 – April 4, 1983	11	SI 1974/2090
April 5, 1983 – August 15, 1985	12	SI 1983/398
August 16, 1985 – March 31, 1993	15	SI 1985/1178
April 1, 1993 to date	8	SI 1993/770 and SI 1994/1443

Group D
Investment

D

D1: Share price index (FTSE 100)

FTSE® 100 (on last day of month)

	1987	1988	1989	1990	1991	1992	1993	1994
January	1808.30	1790.80	2051.80	2337.30	2170.30	2571.20	2807.20	3491.80
February	1979.20	1768.80	2002.40	2255.40	2380.90	2562.10	2868.00	3328.10
March	1997.60	1742.50	2075.00	2247.90	2456.50	2440.10	2878.70	3086.40
April	2050.50	1802.20	2118.00	2103.40	2486.20	2654.10	2813.10	3125.30
May	2203.00	1784.50	2114.40	2345.10	2499.50	2707.60	2840.70	2970.50
June	2284.10	1857.60	2151.00	2374.60	2414.80	2521.20	2900.00	2919.20
July	2360.90	1853.60	2297.00	2326.20	2588.80	2399.60	2926.50	3082.60
August	2249.70	1753.60	2387.90	2162.80	2645.70	2312.60	3100.00	3251.30
September	2366.00	1826.50	2299.40	1990.20	2621.70	2553.00	3037.50	3026.30
October	1749.80	1852.40	2142.60	2050.30	2566.00	2658.30	3171.00	3097.40
November	1579.90	1792.40	2276.80	2149.40	2420.20	2778.80	3166.90	3081.40
December	1713.90	1793.10	2422.70	2143.50	2493.10	2846.50	3418.40	3065.50
	1995	**1996**	**1997**	**1998**	**1999**	**2000**	**2001**	**2002**
January	2991.60	3759.30	4275.80	5458.50	5896.00	6268.50	6297.50	5164.80
February	3009.30	3727.60	4308.30	5767.30	6175.10	6232.60	5917.90	5101.00
March	3137.90	3699.70	4312.90	5932.20	6295.30	6540.20	5633.70	5271.80
April	3216.70	3817.90	4436.00	5928.40	6552.20	6327.40	5967.00	5165.60
May	3319.40	3747.80	4621.30	5870.70	6226.20	6359.40	5796.20	5085.10
June	3314.60	3711.00	4604.60	5832.60	6318.50	6312.70	5642.50	4656.40
July	3463.30	3703.20	4907.50	5837.10	6231.90	6365.30	5529.10	4246.20
August	3477.80	3867.60	4817.50	5249.40	6246.40	6672.70	5345.00	4227.30
September	3508.20	3953.70	5244.20	5064.40	6029.80	6294.20	4903.40	3721.80
October	3529.10	3979.10	4842.30	5438.40	6255.70	6438.40	5039.70	4039.70
November	3664.30	4058.00	4831.80	5743.90	6597.20	6142.20	5203.60	4169.40
December	3689.30	4118.50	5135.50	5882.60	6930.20	6222.50	5217.40	3940.40
	2003	**2004**	**2005**	**2006**	**2007**	**2008**	**2009**	**2010**
January	3567.40	4390.70	4852.30	5760.30	6203.10	5879.80	4149.60	5188.50
February	3655.60	4492.20	4968.50	5791.50	6171.50	5884.30	3830.10	5354.50
March	3613.30	4385.70	4894.40	5964.60	6308.00	5702.10	3926.10	5679.60
April	3926.00	4489.70	4801.70	6023.10	6449.20	6087.30	4243.70	5553.50
May	4048.10	4430.70	4964.00	5723.80	6621.50	6053.50	4417.90	5188.40
June	4031.20	4464.10	5113.20	5833.40	6607.90	5625.90	4249.20	4916.90
July	4157.00	4413.10	5282.30	5928.30	6360.10	5411.90	4608.40	5258.00
August	4161.10	4459.30	5296.90	5906.10	6303.30	5636.60	4908.90	5225.20
September	4091.30	4570.80	5477.70	5960.80	6466.80	4902.50	5133.90	5548.60
October	4287.60	4624.20	5317.30	6129.20	6721.60	4377.30	5044.60	5675.20
November	4342.60	4703.20	5423.20	6048.80	6432.50	4288.00	5190.70	5528.30
December	4476.90	4814.30	5618.80	6220.80	6456.90	4434.20	5412.90	5899.90
	2011	**2012**	**2013**	**2014**	**2015**			
January	5862.90	5681.60	6276.90	6510.40	6749.40			
February	5994.00	5871.50	6360.80	6809.70	6946.70			
March	5908.80	5768.50	6411.70	6598.40	6773.00			
April	6069.90	5737.80	6430.10	6780.00	6960.60			
May	5990.00	5320.90	6583.10	6844.50	6984.40			
June	5945.70	5571.20	6215.50	6743.90				
July	5815.20	5635.30	6621.10	6730.10				
August	5394.50	5711.50	6412.90	6819.80				
September	5128.50	5742.10	6462.20	6622.70				
October	5544.20	5782.70	6731.40	6546.50				
November	5505.40	5866.80	6650.60	6722.60				
December	5572.30	5897.80	6749.10	6566.10				

D2: Graph of share price index

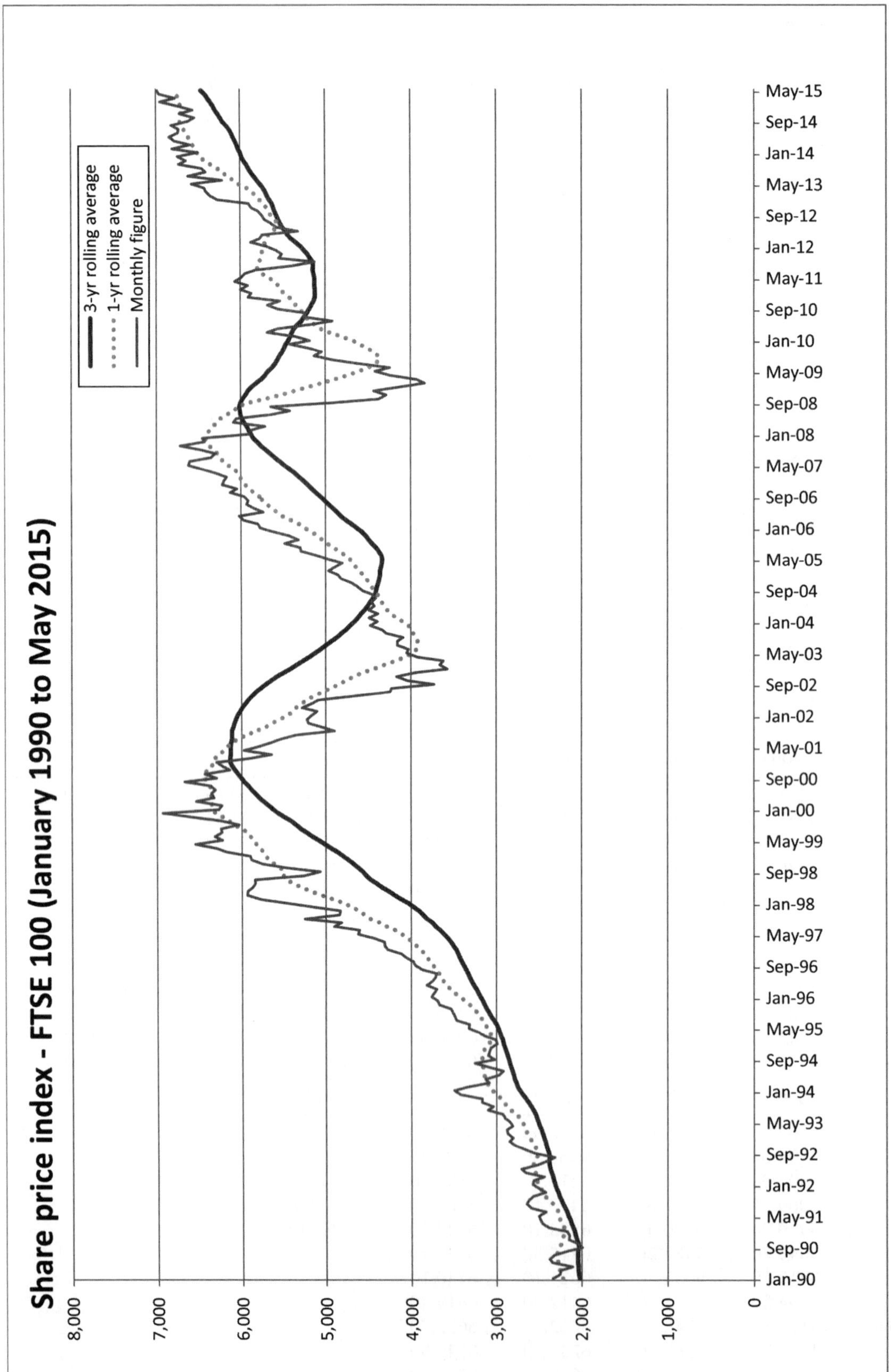

D3: Index-linked stock

Return on index-linked government securities

	2001		2002		2003		2004		2005	
	Gross %	Net %	Gross %	Net %	Gross %	Net %	Gross %	Net %	Gross %	Net %
January	1.99%	1.69%	2.36%	2.01%	1.99%	1.69%	1.97%	1.68%	1.69%	1.44%
February	2.02%	1.72%	2.35%	2.00%	1.87%	1.59%	1.84%	1.56%	1.68%	1.43%
March	2.33%	1.98%	2.36%	2.01%	1.94%	1.65%	1.75%	1.49%	1.69%	1.44%
April	2.60%	2.21%	2.38%	2.03%	2.00%	1.70%	1.91%	1.62%	1.64%	1.39%
May	2.56%	2.18%	2.34%	1.99%	1.82%	1.55%	1.99%	1.69%	1.62%	1.37%
June	2.50%	2.13%	2.23%	1.89%	1.85%	1.57%	1.96%	1.67%	1.46%	1.21%
July	2.40%	2.04%	2.41%	2.05%	2.06%	1.75%	2.00%	1.70%	1.57%	1.32%
August	2.20%	1.87%	2.12%	1.80%	2.02%	1.72%	1.84%	1.56%	1.38%	1.13%
September	2.46%	2.09%	2.10%	1.78%	1.93%	1.64%	1.79%	1.53%	1.40%	1.15%
October	2.20%	1.87%	2.22%	1.89%	2.19%	1.86%	1.77%	1.51%	1.37%	1.12%
November	2.26%	1.92%	2.35%	2.00%	2.19%	1.86%	1.70%	1.44%	1.30%	1.05%
December	2.38%	2.03%	2.11%	1.79%	1.92%	1.63%	1.62%	1.37%	1.14%	0.89%

	2006		2007		2008		2009		2010	
	Gross %	Net %	Gross %	Net %	Gross %	Net %	Gross %	Net %	Gross %	Net %
January	1.04%	0.79%	1.50%	1.25%	0.98%	0.73%	1.03%	0.88%	0.76%	0.61%
February	1.05%	0.80%	1.27%	1.02%	0.95%	0.70%	1.26%	1.11%	0.81%	0.66%
March	1.25%	1.00%	1.45%	1.20%	0.87%	0.62%	1.05%	0.90%	0.68%	0.53%
April	1.44%	1.19%	1.70%	1.45%	0.99%	0.74%	1.09%	0.94%	0.72%	0.57%
May	1.42%	1.17%	1.75%	1.50%	1.06%	0.81%	0.99%	0.84%	0.76%	0.61%
June	1.50%	1.25%	1.74%	1.49%	0.92%	0.67%	0.88%	0.73%	0.71%	0.56%
July	1.31%	1.06%	1.54%	1.29%	1.01%	0.76%	0.96%	0.81%	0.84%	0.69%
August	1.18%	0.93%	1.37%	1.12%	0.64%	0.39%	0.74%	0.59%	0.51%	0.36%
September	1.22%	0.97%	1.39%	1.14%	1.01%	0.76%	0.73%	0.58%	0.51%	0.36%
October	1.10%	0.85%	1.36%	1.11%	1.61%	1.36%	0.60%	0.45%	0.63%	0.48%
November	1.11%	0.86%	1.17%	0.92%	1.73%	1.48%	0.52%	0.37%	0.65%	0.50%
December	1.29%	1.04%	1.06%	0.81%	1.02%	0.77%	0.72%	0.57%	0.52%	0.37%

	2011		2012		2013		2014		2015	
	Gross %	Net %	Gross %	Net %	Gross %	Net %	Gross %	Net %	Gross %	Net %
January	0.72%	0.57%	–0.23%	–0.38%	–0.24%	–0.39%	–0.01%	–0.16%	–0.95%	–1.10%
February	0.64%	0.49%	–0.15%	–0.30%	–0.23%	–0.38%	–0.02%	–0.17%	–0.73%	–0.88%
March	0.66%	0.51%	–0.09%	–0.24%	–0.41%	–0.56%	–0.08%	–0.23%	–0.92%	–1.07%
April	0.57%	0.42%	–0.06%	–0.21%	–0.45%	–0.60%	–0.11%	–0.26%	–0.87%	–1.02%
May	0.53%	0.38%	–0.18%	–0.33%	–0.27%	–0.42%	–0.15%	–0.30%	–0.86%	–1.01%
June	0.51%	0.36%	–0.08%	–0.23%	–0.01%	–0.16%	–0.10%	–0.25%		
July	0.35%	0.20%	–0.09%	–0.24%	–0.03%	–0.18%	–0.14%	–0.29%		
August	0.38%	0.23%	–0.10%	–0.25%	–0.02%	–0.17%	–0.41%	–0.56%		
September	0.18%	0.03%	0.11%	–0.04%	–0.02%	–0.17%	–0.35%	–0.50%		
October	0.24%	0.09%	0.11%	–0.04%	–0.08%	–0.23%	–0.42%	–0.57%		
November	–0.11%	–0.26%	–0.01%	–0.16%	–0.05%	–0.20%	–0.66%	–0.81%		
December	–0.23%	–0.38%	–0.05%	–0.20%	0.05%	–0.10%	–0.73%	–0.88%		

Notes:

1. Up to and including December 2014 the above table shows the month end gross redemption yields of British Government index-linked stocks with over five years to maturity assuming 3 per cent inflation (the standard assumption in recent years), by interpolation of the 0 per cent and 5 per cent published figures for inflation (Source: *Financial Times* or FT website).

2. From January 2015 the figures in the above table allow for 3 per cent inflation in eight-month lagged Gilts (those issued prior to April 1, 2005) and no adjustment for inflation in three-month lagged Gilts (those issued from April 1, 2005), in accordance with the UK Debt Management Office's calculations.

3. The net percentage yield shown above up to and including 2004 is stated after deducting tax at 15 per cent (this was the assumption used in *Wells v Wells* and by the Lord Chancellor when he set the discount rate in 2001).
4. From 2005 to 2008 (inclusive) a fixed deduction of 0.25 per cent has been allowed for tax instead of a percentage. This is because, in spite of reducing yields in this period, taxable interest remained high in this period so that applying a percentage to the combined gross yield would understate the deduction for tax. The actual average tax rate will vary depending on the size of the award.
5. From 2009 a fixed deduction of 0.15 per cent has been allowed for tax. The average Income Tax deduction on taxable interest has been calculated by expert accountants as ranging from 0 per cent to 0.30 per cent depending on the size of the award, so 0.15 per cent is adopted as the midpoint of the range.

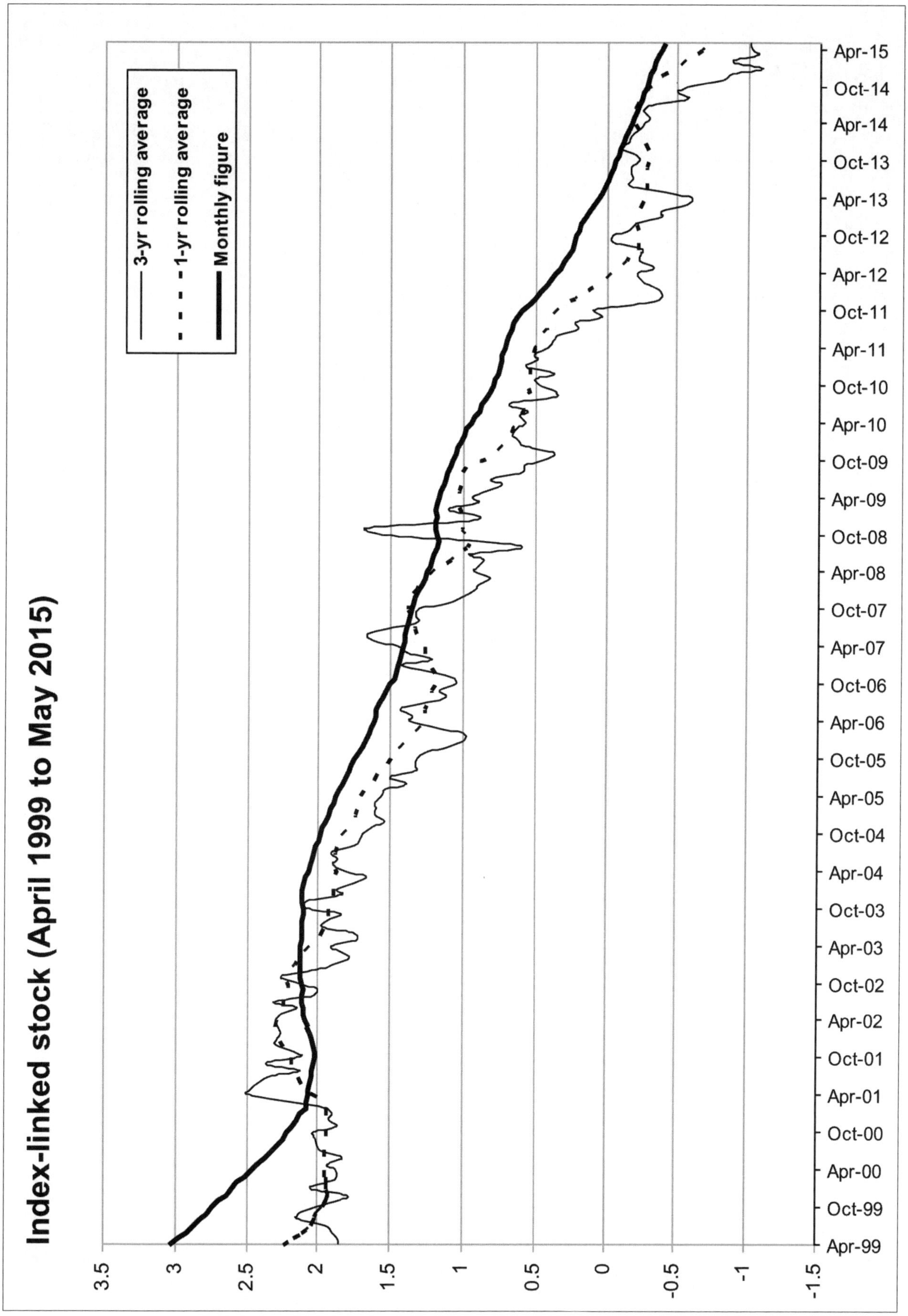
Index-linked stock (April 1999 to May 2015)
3-yr rolling average
1-yr rolling average
Monthly figure
3.5
3
2.5
2
1.5
1
0.5
0
-0.5
-1
-1.5
Apr-99
Oct-99
Apr-00
Oct-00
Apr-01
Oct-01
Apr-02
Oct-02
Apr-03
Oct-03
Apr-04
Oct-04
Apr-05
Oct-05
Apr-06
Oct-06
Apr-07
Oct-07
Apr-08
Oct-08
Apr-09
Oct-09
Apr-10
Oct-10
Apr-11
Oct-11
Apr-12
Oct-12
Apr-13
Oct-13
Apr-14
Oct-14
Apr-15

Group E
Prices

E1: Retail Prices Index

	Jan	Feb	Mar	Apr	May	June	July	Aug	Sept	Oct	Nov	Dec	
2015	255.4	256.7	257.1	258.0	258.5	258.9							**2015**
2014	252.6	254.2	254.8	255.7	255.9	256.3	256.0	257.0	257.6	257.7	257.1	257.5	**2014**
2013	245.8	247.6	248.7	249.5	250.0	249.7	249.7	251.0	251.9	251.9	252.1	253.4	**2013**
2012	238.0	239.9	240.8	242.5	242.4	241.8	242.1	243.0	244.2	245.6	245.6	246.8	**2012**
2011	229.0	231.3	232.5	234.4	235.2	235.2	234.7	236.1	237.9	238.0	238.5	239.4	**2011**
2010	217.9	219.2	220.7	222.8	223.6	224.1	223.6	224.5	225.3	225.8	226.8	228.4	**2010**
2009	210.1	211.4	211.3	211.5	212.8	213.4	213.4	214.4	215.3	216.0	216.6	218.0	**2009**
2008	209.8	211.4	212.1	214.0	215.1	216.8	216.5	217.2	218.4	217.7	216.0	212.9	**2008**
2007	201.6	203.1	204.4	205.4	206.2	207.3	206.1	207.3	208.0	208.9	209.7	210.9	**2007**
2006	193.4	194.2	195.0	196.5	197.7	198.5	198.5	199.2	200.1	200.4	201.1	202.7	**2006**
2005	188.9	189.6	190.5	191.6	192.0	192.2	192.2	192.6	193.1	193.3	193.6	194.1	**2005**
2004	183.1	183.8	184.6	185.7	186.5	186.8	186.8	187.4	188.1	188.6	189.0	189.9	**2004**
2003	178.4	179.3	179.9	181.2	181.5	181.3	181.3	181.6	182.5	182.6	182.7	183.5	**2003**
2002	173.3	173.8	174.5	175.7	176.2	176.2	175.9	176.4	177.6	177.9	178.2	178.5	**2002**
2001	171.1	172.0	172.2	173.1	174.2	174.4	173.3	174.0	174.6	174.3	173.6	173.4	**2001**
2000	166.6	167.5	168.4	170.1	170.7	171.1	170.5	170.5	171.7	171.6	172.1	172.2	**2000**
1999	163.4	163.7	164.1	165.2	165.6	165.6	165.1	165.5	166.2	166.5	166.7	167.3	**1999**
1998	159.5	160.3	160.8	162.6	163.5	163.4	163.0	163.7	164.4	164.5	164.4	164.4	**1998**
1997	154.4	155.0	155.4	156.3	156.9	157.5	157.5	158.5	159.3	159.5	159.6	160.0	**1997**
1996	150.2	150.9	151.5	152.6	152.9	153.0	152.4	153.1	153.8	153.8	153.9	154.4	**1996**
1995	146.0	146.9	147.5	149.0	149.6	149.8	149.1	149.9	150.6	149.8	149.8	150.7	**1995**
1994	141.3	142.1	142.5	144.2	144.7	144.7	144.0	144.7	145.0	145.2	145.3	146.0	**1994**
1993	137.9	138.8	139.3	140.6	141.1	141.0	140.7	141.3	141.9	141.8	141.6	141.9	**1993**
1992	135.6	136.3	136.7	138.8	139.3	139.3	138.8	138.9	139.4	139.9	139.7	139.2	**1992**
1991	130.2	130.9	131.4	133.1	133.5	134.1	133.8	134.1	134.6	135.1	135.6	135.7	**1991**
1990	119.5	120.2	121.4	125.1	126.2	126.7	126.8	128.1	129.3	130.3	130.0	129.9	**1990**
1989	111.0	111.8	112.3	114.3	115.0	115.4	115.5	115.8	116.6	117.5	118.5	118.8	**1989**
1988	103.3	103.7	104.1	105.8	106.2	106.6	106.7	107.9	108.4	109.5	110.0	110.3	**1988**
1987	100.0	100.4	100.6	101.8	101.9	101.9	101.8	102.1	102.4	102.9	103.4	103.3	**1987**
1986	96.25	96.60	96.73	97.67	97.85	97.79	97.52	97.82	98.30	98.45	99.29	99.62	**1986**
1985	91.20	91.94	92.80	94.78	95.21	95.41	95.23	95.49	95.44	95.59	95.92	96.05	**1985**
1984	86.84	87.20	87.48	88.64	88.97	89.20	89.10	89.94	90.11	90.67	90.95	90.87	**1984**
1983	82.61	82.97	83.12	84.28	84.64	84.84	85.30	85.68	86.06	86.36	86.67	86.89	**1983**
1982	78.73	78.76	79.44	81.04	81.62	81.85	81.88	81.90	81.85	82.26	82.66	82.51	**1982**
1981	70.29	70.93	71.99	74.07	74.55	74.98	75.31	75.87	76.30	76.98	77.79	78.28	**1981**
1980	62.18	63.07	63.93	66.11	66.72	67.35	67.91	68.06	68.49	68.92	69.48	69.86	**1980**
1979	52.52	52.95	53.38	54.30	54.73	55.67	58.07	58.53	59.11	59.72	60.25	60.68	**1979**
1978	48.04	48.31	48.62	49.33	49.61	49.99	50.22	50.54	50.75	50.98	51.33	51.76	**1978**
1977	43.70	44.13	44.56	45.70	46.06	46.54	46.59	46.82	47.07	47.28	47.50	47.76	**1977**
1976	37.49	37.97	38.17	38.91	39.34	39.54	39.62	40.18	40.71	41.44	42.03	42.59	**1976**
	Jan	Feb	Mar	Apr	May	June	July	Aug	Sept	Oct	Nov	Dec	

	Jan	Feb	Mar	Apr	May	June	July	Aug	Sept	Oct	Nov	Dec	
1975	30.39	30.90	31.51	32.72	34.09	34.75	35.11	35.31	35.61	36.12	36.55	37.01	**1975**
1974	25.35	25.78	26.01	26.89	27.28	27.55	27.81	27.83	28.14	28.69	29.20	29.63	**1974**
1973	22.64	22.78	22.92	23.35	23.52	23.64	23.75	23.82	24.03	24.50	24.69	24.87	**1973**
1972	21.01	21.12	21.19	21.38	21.49	21.63	21.70	21.87	21.99	22.30	22.37	22.49	**1972**
1971	19.43	19.53	19.69	20.11	20.25	20.39	20.51	20.52	20.55	20.67	20.79	20.89	**1971**
1970	17.91	18.00	18.11	18.38	18.44	18.49	18.62	18.61	18.70	18.90	19.03	19.16	**1970**
1969	17.06	17.15	17.22	17.41	17.38	17.46	17.46	17.42	17.47	17.60	17.64	17.76	**1969**
1968	16.07	16.15	16.20	16.49	16.51	16.57	16.59	16.61	16.63	16.71	16.74	16.97	**1968**
1967	15.66	15.67	15.67	15.79	15.78	15.85	15.75	15.71	15.70	15.82	15.91	16.02	**1967**
1966	15.11	15.12	15.15	15.33	15.44	15.48	15.41	15.50	15.48	15.52	15.61	15.63	**1966**
1965	14.47	14.47	14.52	14.80	14.85	14.89	14.89	14.92	14.93	14.95	15.01	15.08	**1965**
1964	13.84	13.85	13.90	14.02	14.14	14.19	14.19	14.25	14.25	14.26	14.38	14.43	**1964**
1963	13.57	13.69	13.71	13.74	13.73	13.73	13.65	13.61	13.65	13.71	13.74	13.77	**1963**
1962	13.22	13.23	13.28	13.47	13.51	13.60	13.55	13.43	13.41	13.40	13.45	13.52	**1962**
1961	12.63	12.63	12.68	12.74	12.78	12.89	12.89	13.01	12.99	13.01	13.15	13.17	**1961**
1960	12.36	12.36	12.34	12.41	12.41	12.47	12.50	12.42	12.43	12.53	12.59	12.62	**1960**
1959	12.42	12.41	12.41	12.32	12.27	12.29	12.26	12.29	12.23	12.28	12.37	12.40	**1959**
1958	12.16	12.10	12.19	12.33	12.28	12.40	12.20	12.18	12.19	12.31	12.35	12.40	**1958**
1957	11.74	11.73	11.71	11.75	11.77	11.89	11.99	11.97	11.93	12.05	12.11	12.17	**1957**
1956	11.25	11.25	11.39	11.55	11.53	11.52	11.47	11.51	11.48	11.55	11.60	11.63	**1956**
1955	10.70	10.70	10.70	10.76	10.74	10.97	11.00	10.93	11.00	11.11	11.29	11.29	**1955**
1954	10.28	10.26	10.35	10.39	10.36	10.42	10.60	10.53	10.51	10.56	10.61	10.66	**1954**
1953	10.14	10.17	10.24	10.33	10.30	10.35	10.35	10.29	10.27	10.27	10.30	10.26	**1953**
1952	9.71	9.72	9.77	9.93	9.93	10.09	10.08	10.02	10.00	10.09	10.08	10.15	**1952**
1951	8.60	8.68	8.74	8.88	9.10	9.13	9.27	9.31	9.38	9.44	9.48	9.54	**1951**
1950	8.28	8.30	8.32	8.35	8.37	8.33	8.33	8.30	8.35	8.44	8.47	8.52	**1950**
1949	7.99	8.01	7.98	7.96	8.11	8.14	8.15	8.16	8.19	8.23	8.23	8.25	**1949**
1948	7.64	7.78	7.80	7.91	7.90	8.04	7.92	7.92	7.93	7.95	7.97	7.98	**1948**
1947	–	–	–	–	–	7.33	7.38	7.34	7.37	7.43	7.58	7.60	**1947**
	Jan	**Feb**	**Mar**	**Apr**	**May**	**June**	**July**	**Aug**	**Sept**	**Oct**	**Nov**	**Dec**	

Source: Office for National Statistics licensed under the Open Government Licence V.I.O.

Note:

To calculate the equivalent value of a lump sum, divide by the RPI at the time and multiply the result by the current RPI. Thus £460 in June 1981 would be calculated as:

$$\left(\frac{460}{74.98}\right) \times \text{current RPI}$$

to show the relative value of that amount in "today's money".

E2: Inflation table

Introductory notes

The table shows the value each January in earlier years equivalent to £1 in January 2015, after taking account of inflation over time.

Price inflation is measured by reference to the Retail Prices Index.

Year	Multiplier	Year	Multiplier
1948	33.44	1982	3.24
1949	31.96	1983	3.09
1950	30.86	1984	2.94
1951	29.70	1985	2.80
		1986	2.65
1952	26.29		
1953	25.19	1987	2.55
1954	24.85	1988	2.47
1955	23.86	1989	2.30
1956	22.71	1990	2.14
		1991	1.96
1957	21.75		
1958	21.01	1992	1.88
1959	20.57	1993	1.85
1960	20.66	1994	1.81
1961	20.22	1995	1.75
		1996	1.70
1962	19.32		
1963	18.82	1997	1.65
1964	18.46	1998	1.60
1965	17.65	1999	1.56
1966	16.91	2000	1.53
		2001	1.49
1967	16.31		
1968	15.89	2002	1.47
1969	14.97	2003	1.43
1970	14.26	2004	1.39
1971	13.15	2005	1.35
		2006	1.32
1972	12.15		
1973	11.28	2007	1.27
1974	10.08	2008	1.22
1975	8.40	2009	1.22
1976	6.81	2010	1.17
		2011	1.12
1977	5.84		
1978	5.32	2012	1.07
1979	4.86	2013	1.04
1980	4.11	2014	1.01
1981	3.63	2015	1.00

E3: House price indices

Introductory notes

1. There are several price indices available in April 2014. These include the Halifax, Nationwide, the Financial Times, the Royal Institute of Chartered Surveyors, Hometrack, Rightmove, the Government Index and the Land Registry index.

2. The editors of *Facts & Figures* have used the Halifax table in previous editions and continue to do so. The Index Year for the Halifax table is 1983. In certain circumstances, the data offered by other indices may be useful. For example the Land Registry figures are broken down regionally and contain information about the numbers of first-time buyers. However, they exclude cash purchases which account for about a quarter of all transactions. Each table has strengths and weaknesses of this sort.

3. None of the indices should be treated as definitive. They can only be used as guides to the movement of prices over longer periods of time. Readers should be cautious about over-interpreting the analysis of short-term price changes.

All Houses

	U.K.		
Year	**Index**	**%**	**Average Price £**
92	208.1	–5.6	64,309
93	202.1	–2.9	62,455
94	203.1	0.5	62,750
95	199.6	–1.7	61,666
96	208.6	4.5	64,441
97	221.7	6.3	68,504
98	233.7	5.4	72,196
99	250.5	7.2	77,405
00	275.1	9.8	85,005
01	298.6	8.5	92,256
02	350.6	17.4	108,342
03	429.1	22.4	132,589
04	507.6	18.3	156,831
05	536.6	5.7	165,807
06	581.3	8.3	179,601
07	635.9	9.4	196,478
08	585.9	–7.9	181,032
09	524.6	–10.5	162,085
10	539.6	2.9	166,739
11	525.4	–2.6	162,322
12	522.1	–0.6	161,308
13	547.0	4.77	169,003
14	593.5	8.51	183,391

Year	North		Yorks/Humb		N. West		E. Midlands	
	Index	%	Index	%	Index	%	Index	%
92	210.1	−1.6	231.9	−3.6	226.1	−4.3	214.4	−5.9
93	206.3	−1.8	228.3	−1.6	219.3	−3.0	208.3	−2.8
94	203.6	−1.3	226.3	−0.9	215.8	−1.6	209.1	0.4
95	195.9	−3.8	219.2	−3.1	207.8	−3.7	203.9	−2.5
96	201.9	3.1	224.5	2.4	210.7	1.4	209.4	2.7
97	206.5	2.3	228.5	1.8	216.7	2.9	221.5	5.8
98	211.2	2.3	229.8	0.5	220.4	1.7	229.9	3.8
99	220.1	4.2	236.5	2.9	231.0	4.8	244.8	6.5
00	221.9	0.8	243.9	3.2	242.6	5.0	265.0	8.2
01	234.0	5.5	257.5	5.6	255.7	5.4	287.3	8.4
02	271.4	16.0	297.7	15.6	292.8	14.5	361.7	25.9
03	370.6	36.5	395.6	32.9	366.3	25.1	457.5	26.5
04	490.3	32.3	495.0	25.1	472.8	29.1	541.4	18.3
05	533.3	8.8	549.3	11.0	523.7	10.8	564.9	4.3
06	567.3	6.4	602.4	9.7	565.1	7.9	599.4	6.1
07	601.8	6.1	640.5	6.3	596.8	5.6	632.4	5.5
08	547.2	−9.1	580.0	−9.5	558.3	−6.5	582.0	−8.0
09	500.2	−8.6	526.3	−9.3	492.8	−11.7	518.2	−11.0
10	511.5	2.3	538.2	2.3	486.7	−1.3	541.7	4.5
11	483.1	−5.6	513.2	−4.6	485.0	−0.4	517.9	−4.4
12	478.1	−1.0	509.1	−0.8	468.6	−3.4	523.1	1.0
13	496.8	3.9	527.3	3.6	501.9	7.1	539.2	3.1
14	507.7	2.2	562.1	6.6	540.4	7.7	584.3	8.4

Year	W. Midlands		E. Anglia		S. West		S. East	
	Index	%	Index	%	Index	%	Index	%
92	229.4	−4.6	198.5	−7.4	193.9	−7.8	192.8	−8.5
93	219.1	−4.5	193.2	−2.7	185.9	−4.1	186.4	−3.3
94	218.3	−0.4	195.8	1.3	186.6	1.5	189.8	1.8
95	215.6	−1.2	193.5	−1.1	186.1	−1.3	190.3	0.3
96	224.6	4.2	197.7	2.1	195.1	4.8	199.9	5.0
97	237.3	5.6	211.0	6.7	209.7	7.5	221.2	10.7
98	250.0	5.4	224.4	6.4	226.4	8.0	244.2	10.4
99	254.7	1.9	241.1	7.5	248.8	9.9	271.2	11.0
00	282.2	10.8	279.7	16.0	291.0	17.0	318.3	17.4
01	301.5	6.8	322.6	15.4	327.8	12.6	354.7	11.4
02	363.7	20.7	386.0	19.6	403.4	23.0	413.7	16.6
03	460.7	26.7	465.0	20.5	477.7	18.4	483.8	17.0
04	540.5	17.3	522.3	12.3	545.4	14.2	528.8	9.3
05	565.4	4.6	536.0	2.6	552.6	1.3	537.0	1.5
06	602.8	6.6	581.1	8.4	587.5	6.3	571.2	6.4
07	640.4	6.2	637.3	9.7	641.9	9.3	636.9	11.5
08	591.9	−7.6	600.8	−5.7	583.2	−9.1	588.6	−7.6
09	534.1	−9.8	520.2	−13.4	540.0	−7.4	532.1	−9.6
10	549.5	2.9	540.9	4.0	568.5	5.3	561.4	5.5
11	530.9	−3.4	544.1	0.6	547.3	−3.7	553.1	−1.5
12	528.8	−0.4	540.7	−0.6	553.1	1.1	558.8	1.0
13	540.7	2.3	551.1	1.9	565.8	2.3	591	5.8
14	574.3	6.2	601.2	9.1	610.5	7.9	654.6	10.8

Year	Gr. London		Wales		Scotland		N. Ireland	
	Index	%	Index	%	Index	%	Index	%
92	202.0	−9.4	207.7	−4.3	193.2	0.2	145.5	−1.0
93	192.0	−4.9	204.5	−1.6	196.4	1.6	151.7	4.3
94	195.5	1.8	201.9	−1.2	199.4	1.6	162.1	6.9
95	194.9	−0.4	194.2	−3.8	199.4	0.0	172.8	6.6
96	212.4	9.0	205.5	5.9	204.9	2.8	204.5	18.3
97	246.3	16.0	212.0	3.1	204.7	0.1	210.6	3.0
98	272.3	10.5	220.2	3.8	209.8	2.5	235.6	11.9
99	317.9	16.8	232.3	5.5	212.8	1.4	248.8	5.6
00	373.6	17.5	245.0	5.5	214.2	0.7	264.4	6.3
01	428.3	14.7	263.8	7.7	220.0	2.7	296.8	12.2
02	499.4	16.6	299.8	13.6	238.5	8.4	307.4	3.6
03	563.3	12.8	397.2	32.5	274.5	15.1	340.3	10.7
04	608.5	8.0	516.3	30.0	330.6	20.4	397.9	16.9
05	621.4	2.1	553.7	7.3	375.7	13.6	486.0	22.1
06	680.9	9.6	589.7	6.5	421.7	12.2	581.3	32.6
07	777.6	14.2	640.7	8.7	488.2	15.8	844.5	31.1
08	705.3	−9.3	579.4	−9.6	478.2	−2.1	679.2	−19.6
09	622.0	−11.8	512.0	−11.6	426.6	−10.8	563.7	−17.0
10	659.9	6.1	530.3	3.6	421.4	−1.2	506.2	−10.2
11	659.6	0.0	521.5	−1.7	406.8	−3.5	444.1	−12.3
12	674.4	2.2	505.6	−3.0	384.3	−5.5	405.4	−8.7
13	737.2	9.3	557.3	10.2	400.5	4.2	368.9	−9.0
14	855.2	16.0	572.8	2.8	430.2	7.4	430.8	16.8

E4: Average semi-detached house prices by region

Prices are as of first quarter of 2015.

Region	£
North	131,136
North West	157,954
West Midlands	165,276
South East	290,413
Greater London	461,250
Yorkshire & Humberside	139,906
East Midlands	142,681
East Anglia	197,088
South West	206,985

E5: How prices have changed over 12 years

PRICE COMPARISON 2003–2015

Item	Price in 2003	Price in 2015	% change	Source
Milk (pint)	37p	49p	32.4%	ONS
Loaf of white sliced bread (800g)	58p	75p	29.3%	ONS
Sugar (kg)	69p	80p	15.9%	ONS
Draught lager (pint)	£2.26	£3.55	57.1%	ONS
Cigarettes (20)	£4.25	£8.23	93.6%	ONS
Unleaded petrol per litre	81p	124.9p	54.2%	AA
House prices	£132,589	£183,391	38.3%	Halifax
Weekly State Pension	£77.45	£115.95	49.7%	The Pensions Advisory Service AXA
Price of oil (per barrel)	$31.85	$44.35	39.2%	EIA
Price of gold (per ounce)	$363.38	$1312	261.1%	NMA
McDonald's Big Mac	£1.99	£2.69	35.2%	McDonald's

Read more: *http://www.thisismoney.co.uk/historic-inflation-calculator#ixzz1Bm4ygOL6*

Group F
Earnings

F

F1: Earnings losses in personal injury and fatal accident cases

1. **Purpose of note**

The purpose of this note is to provide some basic guidance on what information to request from a claimant in order to make an initial assessment as to whether an earnings loss is likely to arise.

2. **Nature of occupation**

Identify at an early stage into which category of occupation the claimant falls:

Employment
— Employee without ownership rights.
— Director/shareholder (of private company).

Self-employment
— Sole trader.
— Partner.

3. **Relevant dates**

For the purposes of proposing the periods for which information should be requested, relevant dates will be identified as follows:

For an individual in employment
(References here are to tax years ending on April 5, although the tax for many salaried employees will often effectively run from April 1 to March 31.)

D1 April 6 three years before D2
D2 April 5 immediately preceding D3
D3 Incident date
D4 April 5 immediately preceding D5
D5 Present time

For business accounts
D6 Date of beginning of accounting period three years before D7
D7 Date of end of accounting period immediately preceding D3
D8 Date of end of accounting period immediately preceding D5

A full three years' pre-accident financial information should often be sufficient (having regard to the need for proportionality), although documentation for a longer period may be appropriate if it emerges that business results have been volatile.

For an individual in employment

D1		D2	[D3 Incident]		D4	D5
April 6 April 5	April 6 April 5	April 6 April 5	April 6 April 5	April 6 April 5	April 6 April 5	April 6 Present time
Tax year –3	Tax year –2	Tax year –1	Tax year 0	Tax year +1	Current tax year –1	Current tax year

For business accounts

D6		D7	D3 [Incident]		D8	D5
Beginning End	Beginning End	Beginning End	Beginning End	Beginning End	Beginning End	Beginning Present time
Accounts year −3	Accounts year −2	Accounts year −1	Accounts year 0	Accounts year +1	Current accounts year −1	Current accounts year

4. **Employment: Employee without ownership rights**

This is the likely category for most employees—but excluding in particular those who are directors and/or shareholders with a degree of control over private companies.

In the absence of detailed representations from the employer, or from an employment expert, the earnings history may be the only useful guide to potential earnings but for the incident giving rise to the claim.

The most useful documentation will usually be a comprehensive set of pay advices (monthly, sometimes four-weekly, or weekly) because these may be expected to show:

- basic pay level (and dates/amounts of periodic increases),
- overtime (if paid) and any other regular or periodic enhancements,
- bonuses (and dates/amounts paid),
- sick pay (and dates), and
- employee pension contributions.

Request:

- **Pay advices (whether from employment or subsequent pension) from D1 to D5.**
- **Details of benefits other than pay for each tax year between D1 and D2 and for each tax year since D2.**

5. **Employment: Director/shareholders**

This category relates mainly to those individuals who have a degree of ownership or control, probably in a private company, and whose remuneration as such may not be a fair reflection of the personal reward available from the business.

For instance:

- profits may have been drawn by way of dividend for reasons of tax efficiency; or
- profits (which the claimant could have drawn) have been re-invested in the business.

It may well be appropriate to assess loss along the lines that would be adopted in relation to a sole trader or partner, that is:

- first to identify whether a business loss has occurred that is attributable to the claim incident, and
- if so, go on to identify the share of the business loss suffered personally by the claimant.

In such a case, it will often be appropriate to review not only the remuneration history of the individual but also the dividend history. Benefits history may also be important.

Request:

Regarding the Business

- **full accounts (including detailed profit and loss accounts) from D6 to D8,**
  and consider requesting

- **figures for monthly (preferably) or quarterly sales from D6 to D5.**
  (Important if the claimant's role is likely to have influenced sales levels; the figures should show up trends and seasonality, etc.)

Regarding the claimant

- **pay advices (whether from employment or pension) from D1 to D5, and**
- **tax returns from D1 to D4.**
  (Mainly to check remuneration and dividends received in each tax year, but also benefits and any personal pension contributions, etc.)

6. **Self-employment: Sole trader**

Request:

- **full accounts from D6 to D8,**
- **figures for monthly or quarterly sales from D6 to D5, and**
- **tax returns from D1 to D4.**
  (Mainly to check private usage deductions from business expenses, capital allowances, personal pension contributions, etc.)

7. **Self-employment: Partner**

Approach will be:

- first to identify whether a business loss has occurred that is attributable to the claim incident, and
- if so, go on to identify the share of the business loss suffered personally by the claimant.

Request:

Regarding the Business

- **full partnership accounts from D6 to D8, and**
- **figures for monthly (preferably) or quarterly sales from D6 to D5.**

Regarding the claimant

- **personal tax returns from D1 to D4.**
  (Mainly to check personal pension contributions, etc.)

8. **Benefits other than pay (employees)**

In the first instance, it is probably sufficient simply to ask, in relation to any employee (including a company director), for:

- **details of any non-pecuniary benefits in employment, and any pension benefits.**

9. **Other points**

- **Company searches**

Searches of small UK limited companies seldom yield helpful results as regards accounts because the contents of the accounts to be filed are invariably in abbreviated form, sometimes only a balance sheet.

In cases where there are doubts about full disclosure, a search may be useful in identifying whether a claimant has more directorships than advised, or possibly a history of connections with insolvent companies.

- **Permanent Health Insurance income**

Where a claimant receives insurance money through his employer, this will usually be evident from review of the pay advices.

As to whether credit needs to be given by the claimant for such insurance money for claim purposes will probably depend on the nature of the underlying policy. See *Gaca v Pirelli General plc.*[1]

- **Ill-health pension**

Where a claimant receives an ill-health pension following an incident, this should again be evident from review of the pay advices.

Generally, no credit is to be given for actual pension in a loss of earnings claim: *Parry v Cleaver.*[2]

- **Partnerships**

There may be cases where the profit-sharing arrangements do not reflect the realistic commercial input of the respective partners. This issue may arise particularly where spouses are business partners. The court may be prepared to put aside the historic arrangements in assessing loss: *Ward v Newalls Insulation Co Ltd.*[3]

[1] [2004] 1 W.L.R. 2683.
[2] [1970] A.C. 1.
[3] [1998] 1 W.L.R. 1722.

F2: Payroll documents

SPECIMEN PAY ADVICE

Employee name	Employer name
MR D CAMERON	FirstLord Limited

Pay date	Tax period	Taxcode
31 MARCH 2015	12	1,000L

Pay and allowances (* non-taxable)	£	Deductions/ (Refunds)	£	Totals to date	£
Salary	2,500.00			Taxable gross	33,800.00
Car allowance *	275.00			Car allowance *	1,650.00
		Income tax	313.33	Income tax	4,760.00
		National insurance	194.72	National insurance	2,523.80
		Pension	100.00	Pension	1,200.00
Total	2,775.00	Total	608.05	Net pay	2,166.95

Points to note

1 As good a starting point as any is usually a pay advice for the **last full tax year**, but try also to obtain all subsequent pay advices whether to date of trial in a personal injury case or to date of death if a fatal accident.

2 It is worth bearing in mind that some employers pay every four weeks, and on rare occasions every two weeks, rather than necessarily monthly or weekly. The tax period should help to identify payment frequency.

3 The tax code, **1000L**, represents the basic tax allowance of £10,000. This indicates that the tax inspector has no reason to make any adjustment to the standard code to collect additional tax due in the year.

This in turn implies that the employee has no taxable benefits from the employer.

The most common taxable benefits are probably health insurance cover and those related to private use of motor vehicles.

By way of example, were the employee enjoying taxable benefits to a value of £1,000 pa, the code could be expected to be 900L. Application of this code would result in the tax due on the benefit being collected under PAYE over the course of the tax year.

4 In the illustration shown above, the **gross taxable income** figure requires some reconciliation to other figures.

The year-end figures suggest that salary has probably been running consistently at £2,500 per month (i.e. £30,000 per annum), with a £100 per month pension contribution. That would produce a taxable total of £28,800 in the year, suggesting that there has been additional pay of £5,000 in arriving at the taxable gross figure of £33,800.

The figure for the year's total **National Insurance** for the year is consistent with a salary of £2,500 per month, with a single addition of £5,000.

So the gross taxable appears likely to comprise £30,000 salary, a one-off addition of £5,000 less £1,200 pension contributions.

5 The combination of a **pension deduction,** which appears to represent exactly 4 per cent of salary, together with the fact that it can readily be established that the National Insurance contributions are at contracted out rates, suggests that the employee is a member of a final salary pension scheme, which may give rise to a pension loss claim.

(In the case of a money purchase pension scheme, the deductions are made less basic rate tax, 20 per cent in 2014/15, so it is unlikely that the amount of £100.00 is a monthly contribution to such a scheme.)

6 A **car allowance** is shown, but it is marked as non-taxable.

Note also that the totals to date suggest that the allowance has been in payment for only six months in the year.

Generally, if an allowance is non-taxable, it is unlikely to represent a valuable benefit. Perhaps the car allowance in this case is a fixed level reimbursement of business costs on a prescribed formula, which will be adjusted after the year-end in accordance with actual business mileage or the like.

Nevertheless it would be worth establishing why the car allowance was not in payment throughout the year.

F3: National minimum wage

Introductory notes

1. The National Minimum Wage became law on April 1, 1999.

2. The National Minimum Wage is the minimum amount of pay to which workers over a specified age are entitled. Up to September 30, 2004, the minimum age was 18. Since October 1, 2004 a new rate has been available to workers under 18 who are no longer of compulsory school age.

3. Most adult workers who are resident in the UK, who have a written, oral or implied contract and who are not genuinely self-employed, are entitled to the National Minimum Wage.

4. The National Minimum Wage is enforced by HM Revenue and Customs.

5. There are currently four levels of National Minimum Wage: a development rate for those aged between 18 and 20; a main rate for workers aged 21 or over; from October 1, 2004, a rate for workers under 18 who are no longer of compulsory school age; and, from October 1, 2010, an apprentice minimum wage (see note 8, below).

6. The main rate was extended to workers aged 21 or over from October 2010. Prior to that the qualifying age for the main rate was 22. Correspondingly the development rate has been available to those aged between 18 and 20 from October 2010. Prior to that it was available to those aged between 18 and 21.

7. A development rate available, subject to various conditions, to workers aged 22 or over who started a new job with a new employer and did accredited training, being a course approved by the UK government to obtain a vocational qualification, was abolished for pay reference periods starting on or after October 1, 2006. When applicable, the accredited training rate could only be paid for the first six months of the new job, after which the National Minimum Wage main rate applied.

8. A new apprentice minimum wage was introduced with effect from October 1, 2010, available to apprentices aged under 19, or apprentices aged 19 or over but in the first year of their apprenticeship.

	Pay reference periods starting on or after October 1						
	2009 £/hr	2010 £/hr	2011 £/hr	2012 £/hr	2013 £/hr	2014 £/hr	Proposed 2015 £/hr
Workers under 18 who are no longer of compulsory school age (notes 2 and 5)	3.57	3.64	3.68	3.68	3.72	3.79	3.87
Development rate for workers aged 18 to 21 years (from October 2010) (notes 5 and 6)	4.83	4.92	4.98	4.98	5.03	5.13	5.30
Rate for apprentices aged under 19, or 19 or over but in the first year of their apprenticeship (note 8)	N/A	2.50	2.60	2.65	2.68	2.73	3.30
Main rate for workers aged 21 or over (from October 2010) (notes 5 and 6)	5.80	5.93	6.08	6.19	6.31	6.50	6.70

F4: Regional unemployment statistics

In previous years, tables showing the average duration of claims for Jobseeker's Allowance have been drawn from the Office of National Statistics Economic and Labour Market Review. This is no longer being produced.

The tables below have been based on data available on the Nomis website for March 2015.

North East
Median duration (weeks)

Age	Female	Male	All
Under 17	5.0	2.0	5.0
17	5.0	8.0	5.7
18	10.9	9.4	10.1
19	12.9	12.3	12.6
20–24	15.3	15.2	15.3
25–29	19.9	18.6	18.9
30–34	22.5	20.0	20.7
35–39	26.8	23.4	24.4
40–44	26.4	28.3	27.7
45–49	25.0	31.8	28.9
50–54	24.0	33.5	29.4
55–59	25.3	37.0	32.8
60 and over	25.3	29.5	27.5
All ages	20.8	21.2	21.1

North West
Median duration (weeks)

Age	Female	Male	All
Under 17	3.0	1.0	3.0
17	5.0	6.5	6.0
18	11.9	11.5	11.6
19	18.0	19.7	19.0
20–24	21.9	21.6	21.7
25–29	21.3	21.6	21.5
30–34	22.7	22.6	22.6
35–39	24.2	23.7	23.9
40–44	27.7	27.9	27.9
45–49	25.4	31.9	29.3
50–54	23.6	33.0	28.7
55–59	23.6	38.6	32.1
60 and over	24.7	30.7	28.2
All ages	23.1	24.8	24.2

Yorkshire and the Humber
Median duration (weeks)

Age	Female	Male	All
Under 17	3.3	1.0	2.4
17	5.0	4.7	4.8
18	7.8	7.7	7.7
19	12.6	11.7	12.1
20–24	16.1	13.2	14.1
25–29	20.4	17.7	18.5
30–34	21.9	20.4	20.9
35–39	25.1	22.4	23.3
40–44	27.0	25.4	25.8
45–49	25.1	26.6	25.8
50–54	22.6	31.8	26.8
55–59	23.8	32.6	28.2
60 and over	25.7	28.5	27.4
All ages	20.8	20.2	20.4

East Midlands
Median duration (weeks)

Age	Female	Male	All
Under 17	5.0	6.0	5.3
17	4.7	4.5	4.6
18	8.2	8.0	8.1
19	12.1	11.4	11.6
20–24	13.5	12.5	12.8
25–29	18.4	14.6	15.9
30–34	19.6	16.8	17.8
35–39	21.1	19.3	20.0
40–44	24.6	20.9	22.2
45–49	24.1	23.6	23.8
50–54	22.5	24.9	24.0
55–59	22.6	27.1	25.1
60 and over	23.8	26.0	25.2
All ages	18.8	17.6	18.0

West Midlands
Median duration (weeks)

Age	Female	Male	All
Under 17	0.5	4.0	2.0
17	6.5	6.0	6.3
18	8.1	8.2	8.2
19	12.4	10.4	11.1
20–24	13.5	12.1	12.5
25–29	20.9	18.2	19.2
30–34	26.2	22.2	23.6
35–39	28.8	24.8	25.8
40–44	37.1	31.6	34.0
45–49	33.5	37.0	35.6
50–54	33.6	46.0	40.7
55–59	35.4	50.7	44.6
60 and over	47.7	48.8	48.3
All ages	23.2	21.8	22.3

East
Median duration (weeks)

Age	Female	Male	All
Under 17	13.0	8.0	10.5
17	5.3	3.0	4.3
18	7.8	7.7	7.8
19	11.7	10.9	11.1
20–24	11.9	11.2	11.4
25–29	13.5	12.6	12.9
30–34	16.7	14.2	15.2
35–39	18.8	15.2	16.5
40–44	20.8	18.8	19.6
45–49	20.2	20.0	20.1
50–54	19.0	21.7	20.7
55–59	20.2	23.9	22.4
60 and over	23.1	23.9	23.6
All ages	16.2	15.4	15.7

London
Median duration (weeks)

Age	Female	Male	All
Under 17	4.0	6.0	6.0
17	4.8	5.0	4.9
18	7.9	7.4	7.6
19	10.9	10.5	10.6
20–24	12.1	11.6	11.8
25–29	15.1	14.3	14.6
30–34	19.1	16.9	17.8
35–39	21.9	20.2	20.9
40–44	26.2	23.5	24.6
45–49	28.3	28.4	28.3
50–54	30.0	33.5	32.0
55–59	33.8	41.6	37.9
60 and over	36.0	42.7	39.9
All ages	20.7	20.0	20.3

South East
Median duration (weeks)

Age	Female	Male	All
Under 17	8.0	4.8	5.4
17	4.6	5.5	5.1
18	7.2	6.9	7.1
19	10.2	9.9	10.0
20–24	11.0	11.2	11.2
25–29	14.3	11.8	12.5
30–34	16.1	13.5	14.5
35–39	16.6	15.8	16.1
40–44	18.9	17.7	18.2
45–49	19.8	20.3	20.1
50–54	19.0	21.4	20.6
55–59	17.6	22.8	20.9
60 and over	20.2	22.5	21.9
All ages	15.2	15.2	15.2

South West
Median duration (weeks)

Age	Female	Male	All
Under 17	3.3	4.0	3.4
17	5.6	5.5	5.6
18	7.7	7.6	7.6
19	11.2	11.0	11.1
20–24	11.5	11.1	11.2
25–29	13.2	12.2	12.5
30–34	12.6	13.0	12.9
35–39	14.6	15.6	15.3
40–44	17.6	17.1	17.3
45–49	17.0	18.9	18.2
50–54	15.7	19.8	18.3
55–59	15.3	22.1	19.6
60 and over	18.4	20.3	19.7
All ages	13.3	14.3	14.0

England
Median duration (weeks)

Age	Female	Male	All
Under 17	4.6	4.4	4.6
17	5.2	5.4	5.3
18	8.2	7.9	8.0
19	12.2	11.5	11.8
20–24	13.6	12.7	12.9
25–29	17.6	16.0	16.5
30–34	20.2	18.3	19.0
35–39	22.2	20.5	21.1
40–44	25.1	23.4	24.0
45–49	24.6	25.5	25.1
50–54	23.5	28.5	25.8
55–59	24.0	32.7	28.6
60 and over	25.9	29.8	28.4
All ages	19.7	19.4	19.5

Wales
Median duration (weeks)

Age	Female	Male	All
Under 17	2.0	1.0	1.7
17	6.0	7.0	6.4
18	9.3	8.8	9.0
19	13.5	12.8	13.0
20–24	15.2	14.9	15.0
25–29	18.9	18.0	18.3
30–34	23.4	20.7	21.6
35–39	24.2	24.0	24.0
40–44	25.2	25.0	25.1
45–49	26.0	27.5	26.9
50–54	23.0	28.5	25.5
55–59	25.5	32.4	29.7
60 and over	24.9	26.4	25.8
All ages	20.3	20.3	20.3

Scotland
Median duration (weeks)

Age	Female	Male	All
Under 17	6.7	7.0	6.9
17	5.6	6.1	5.8
18	8.7	7.8	8.0
19	11.0	11.0	11.0
20–24	11.8	12.4	12.2
25–29	15.1	15.4	15.3
30–34	17.0	17.3	17.2
35–39	20.0	19.9	19.9
40–44	21.0	21.9	21.6
45–49	21.7	23.7	23.0
50–54	20.1	24.6	23.2
55–59	21.6	26.7	24.8
60 and over	22.7	25.8	24.8
All ages	16.8	18.0	17.6

Northern Ireland
Median duration (weeks)

Age	Female	Male	All
Under 17	0.0	0.0	0.0
17	16.2	16.2	16.2
18	10.7	13.7	12.4
19	19.8	21.5	20.9
20–24	22.0	23.3	22.9
25–29	25.0	34.2	32.0
30–34	31.1	37.1	35.7
35–39	37.7	39.4	38.9
40–44	44.0	45.1	44.7
45–49	45.1	50.2	48.6
50–54	45.3	51.6	49.3
55–59	45.3	53.1	50.5
60 and over	54.8	67.4	63.4
All ages	32.0	35.0	34.1

United Kingdom
Median duration (weeks)

Age	Female	Male	All
Under 17	5.1	4.8	5.0
17	5.4	5.8	5.6
18	8.5	8.1	8.3
19	12.4	12.0	12.1
20–24	13.9	13.3	13.5
25–29	17.7	17.0	17.2
30–34	20.4	19.2	19.6
35–39	22.6	21.4	21.8
40–44	25.3	24.1	24.6
45–49	25.0	26.5	25.8
50–54	23.9	29.4	26.5
55–59	24.6	33.3	29.6
60 and over	26.4	30.9	29.5
All ages	19.9	20.1	20.0

Thousands, seasonally adjusted

Labour Force Survey (November–January 2015)

	Total aged 16–64	Economically active						Employment						Unemployment					
	Total	Total		Men		Women		Total		Men		Women		Total		Men		Women	
	Level	Level	Rate (%)*	Level	Rate(%)*	Level	Rate (%)*	Level	Rate (%)*	Level	Rate (%)*	Level	Rate (%)**	Level	Rate (%)**	Level	Rate (%)**	Level	Rate (%)**
	1	2	3	4	5	6	7	8	9	10	11	12	13	14	15	16	17	18	19
North East	1652	1259	76.2	651	79.7	608	72.8	1,161	70.2	598	73.2	563	67.3	1,161	7.8	598	8.1	563	7.5
North West	4496	3,415	76	1,813	81.1	1,602	70.9	3,200	71.2	1,699	76	1,500	66.4	216	6.3	114	6.3	102	6.3
Yorkshire & the Humber	3,374	2,603	77.2	1,377	81.8	1,226	72.5	2,443	72.4	1,289	76.6	1,154	68.2	160	6.2	88	6.4	72	5.9
East Midlands	2,892	2,260	78.1	1,200	843.4	1,060	72.9	2,142	74.1	1,134	78.9	1,008	69.3	117	5.2	65	5.4	52	4.9
West Midlands	3,536	2,699	76.3	1,459	82.6	1,240	70	2,516	71.2	1,353	76.7	1,163	65.7	182	6.8	106	7.2	77	6.2
East	3,697	2,958	80.7	1,601	87.3	1,384	74.3	2,832	76.6	1,513	82.4	1,319	70.8	154	5.2	88	5.5	65	4.7
London	5,778	4,452	77.1	2,412	83.8	2,040	70.4	4,175	72.3	2,272	78.9	1,903	65.6	277	6.2	141	5.8	137	6.7
South East	5,474	4,397	80.3	2,329	85.7	2,068	75	4,190	76.5	2,226	81.9	1,964	71.2	207	4.7	103	4.4	104	5
South West	3,281	2,623	79.9	1,378	84.7	1,245	75.3	2,502	76.3	1,309	80.4	1,193	72.1	121	4.6	69	5	52	4.2
England	34,181	26,694	78.1	14,221	83.7	12,474	72.6	25,161	73.6	13,394	78.8	11,767	68.5	1,533	5.7	827	5.8	706	5.7
Wales	1,913	1,423	74.4	749	78.7	674	70.2	1,333	69.7	698	73.3	635	66.1	90	6.3	51	6.8	39	5.8
Scotland	3,414	2,688	78.8	1,366	89.1	1,322	75.7	2,528	74	1,268	76	1,260	72.2	160	6	99	7.2	61	4.6
N Ireland	1,165	841	72.2	451	78.3	390	66.2	789	67.7	419	72.7	370	62.6	52	6.2	32	7.1	20	5.1
United Kingdom[1]																			

Relationship between columns: 2 = 4+6 = 8+14; 8 = 10+12; 14 = 16+18

Data source: Labour Force Survey
Labour market statistics enquiries: labour.market@ons.gov.uk

[1] Due to slight methodological differences between the way the national and regional LFS estimates have been interim adjusted for the 2001 Census, there may be small differences between the UK totals and the sum of the regional components.

* Denominator = all persons of working age

** Denominator = Total economically active

Labour Force Survey

The table reports headline labour market indicators for the UK and its constituent regions and nations. These are reported for the working age population (16–64 years) and include the number economically active in the working age population, the number in employment or self-employment (or Government employment scheme) and the number unemployed. The statistics are derived from the Labour Force Survey (LFS) for November to January 2015. Updated statistics are available on NOMIS (*www.nomisweb.co.uk*). The UK statistics are reported in Table A02 and the regional statistics are reported in Tables HI01 to HI11.

Unemployment is defined using the ILO definition and includes those who were without work during the reference week but who are currently available for work and who were either actively seeking work in the past four weeks or who had already found a job to start within the next three months. This definition of unemployment is independent of whether or not the individual is eligible to claim benefit.

Those who are either employed or unemployed (and looking for work) are defined as economically active. The economically inactive are calculated by the difference between the estimate in column 1, the working age population and the estimate in column 2, the economically active working age population. Many people who are disabled will be inactive rather than unemployed.

Non-employment includes unemployment and inactivity. It is the difference between column 1 and column 8.

Claimant Count v ILO Unemployment

Along with a large number of other countries, the United Kingdom publishes two defined measures of unemployment that complement each other.

One comes from a monthly count of those claiming unemployment-related benefits. This administrative measure is known as the "Claimant Count".

The other comes from a quarterly survey of households, the Labour Force Survey (LFS). This survey measure is accepted as an international standard because it is based on methods recommended by the International Labour Organisation (ILO). It is known as the *p* and is used by the European Union (EU) and the Organisation for Economic Co-operation and Development (OECD).

Both measures have their advantages and disadvantages.

The advantage of the Claimant Count is that it is available quickly and monthly and because it is a 100% count, it also provides precise information on very small areas.

The ILO measure on the other hand as well as being internationally standard, springs from a data source (the Labour Force Survey) which allows unemployment to be analysed in the context of other labour market information and a variety of demographic characteristics.

A disadvantage of the Claimant Count is that it can be affected if there are changes to the benefit system from which it is derived.

Although changes in the benefit system may also affect the labour market behaviour of respondents to the LFS, the ILO definition itself is entirely independent of the benefit system. Comparatively the LFS results, based on the ILO measure, are not reliable for areas smaller than counties or the larger local authority districts, because of sample size restrictions. Estimates of less than 10,000 persons unemployed (after grossing up) are not shown in published tables because they are subject to unacceptably high sampling error and are, therefore, unreliable.

This said, government statistics apply recognised statistical procedures in order to minimise these disadvantages and maintain the relevance of both measures as accurate labour market indicators.

Claimant Count Rates

Area	2006	2007	2008	2009	2010	2011	2012	2013	2014	2015
North East	4.1	4.1	4.5	6.9	6.7	4.7	5.4	5.4	4.2	4.0
North West	3.4	3.2	3.4	5.4	5.2	4.0	4.4	4.2	3.2	2.2
Yorkshire and the Humber	3.4	3.1	3.4	5.7	5.6	4.2	4.7	4.7	3.8	3.2
East Midlands	2.9	2.6	2.8	4.9	4.6	3.4	3.7	3.6	2.7	2.2
West Midlands	3.9	3.8	3.9	6.3	5.9	4.6	4.7	4.5	3.6	3.0
East	2.3	2.1	2.2	4.0	3.8	2.9	3.0	3.0	2.2	1.6
London	3.5	3.0	2.8	4.3	4.5	4.0	4.1	3.9	2.9	2.1
South East	1.9	1.6	1.7	3.3	3.1	2.5	2.5	2.4	1.8	1.3
South West	1.8	1.6	1.7	3.4	3.1	2.5	2.6	2.5	1.9	1.3
England	2.9	2.7	2.8	4.7	4.5	3.7	3.9	3.7	2.9	2.1
Wales	3.1	2.9	3.3	5.5	5.2	3.8	4.0	4.0	3.4	3.2
Scotland	3.2	2.8	2.9	4.6	4.9	4.0	4.2	4.0	3.2	2.9
Northern Ireland	3.2	2.8	3.1	5.5	6.4	6.1	5.3	5.5	4.9	5.1
United Kingdom	**3.0**	**2.7**	**2.8**	**4.7**	**4.6**	**3.7**	**3.9**	**3.7**	**2.9**	**2.3**

Percentages, seasonally adjusted annual averages

ILO Unemployment Rates

Area	2006	2007	2008	2009	2010	2011	2012	2013	2014	2015
North East	6.6	5.8	8.6	9.5	10.2	9.8	10.8	10.0	9.7	7.7
North West	5.2	5.9	7.7	8.5	7.7	8.5	9.5	8.2	8.3	6.2
Yorkshire and the Humber	5.7	5.5	7.1	9.6	9.3	8.7	9.7	9.3	8.8	6.0
East Midlands	5.2	5.7	6.4	7.8	8.0	7.9	8.3	8.0	7.2	5.0
West Midlands	5.8	6.3	7.9	9.5	9.9	8.7	8.5	9.5	8.4	6.5
East	4.8	5.0	5.5	6.6	6.2	6.7	6.6	6.9	5.9	5.1
London	7.8	6.4	7.5	8.9	9.4	9.4	8.9	8.7	8.2	6.2
South East	4.5	4.6	4.8	6.4	6.3	5.7	6.3	6.8	5.3	4.5
South West	3.7	3.9	5.1	6.4	6.3	5.7	5.9	6.4	6.0	4.5
England	5.5	5.4	6.6	8.0	7.9	7.8	8.1	8.0	7.3	5.6
Wales	3.7	5.1	7.6	6.4	8.7	7.9	9.0	8.3	6.9	6.2
Scotland	5.2	4.6	5.1	7.8	8.1	7.7	7.9	7.5	7.1	5.9
Northern Ireland	4.4	4.0	5.7	6.4	8.0	7.1	6.9	8.3	7.7	6.0
United Kingdom	**5.6**	**5.3**	**6.5**	**8.0**	**8.0**	**7.8**	**8.1**	**8.0**	**7.3**	**5.6**

Percentages, Spring each year, seasonally adjusted

F5: Average weekly earnings index

Average weekly earnings index

Whole economy, excluding bonuses and arrears of pay, and seasonally adjusted.

	2000	2001	2002	2003	2004	2005
January	99.0	102.5	107.1	110.8	114.6	119.3
February	98.9	102.5	107.9	111.1	114.7	119.5
March	98.7	103.2	108.1	111.3	115.1	120.2
April	98.7	104.0	108.4	111.7	115.6	120.6
May	99.3	104.1	108.4	112.0	116.0	120.8
June	99.4	104.3	109.1	112.2	116.3	121.2
July	99.7	105.0	109.3	112.5	116.7	121.9
August	100.1	105.7	109.0	112.9	117.2	122.4
September	100.9	105.8	109.3	113.3	117.4	122.8
October	101.3	106.2	109.5	113.6	118.0	123.0
November	101.7	106.6	109.8	114.0	118.3	123.3
December	102.2	106.7	109.8	114.5	119.1	123.6
Yearly Average	100.0	104.7	108.8	112.5	116.6	121.6

	2006	2007	2008	2009	2010	2011
January	124.2	128.9	134.1	137.9	140.5	143.7
February	124.6	129.4	134.8	138.3	140.4	143.5
March	124.8	130.0	135.3	138.3	141.1	143.6
April	125.0	130.1	136.2	138.7	140.7	143.7
May	125.7	131.0	135.9	138.9	140.6	144.0
June	126.3	131.6	136.3	139.0	141.0	144.0
July	126.3	132.1	136.7	138.6	141.7	144.1
August	126.5	132.7	137.0	138.8	142.0	144.2
September	127.1	132.9	137.3	139.1	142.2	144.8
October	127.9	132.9	137.8	139.2	142.4	145.1
November	128.2	133.6	137.9	139.3	142.6	145.3
December	128.7	133.8	138.0	139.8	142.6	145.4
Yearly Average	126.3	131.6	136.4	138.9	141.5	144.3

	2012	2013	2014	2015
January	145.2	146.7	149.4	151.8
February	146.0	147.1	148.9	152.4
March	146.4	147.3	148.7	153.0
April	146.3	148.3	148.9	153.2(p)
May	146.5	148.1	149.1	
June	146.8	148.2	149.4	
July	146.9	148.4	149.6	
August	147.3	148.3	150.0	
September	147.1	148.2	150.8	
October	147.0	148.5	151.3	
November	147.4	148.5	151.0	
December	147.2	149.1	151.4	

(p) = provisional figure.

Index base: 2000 = 100.0

ONS index reference: K54L

F5: Average weekly earnings index

Notes

This table has previously shown the Average Weekly Earnings Index for the whole economy, including bonuses and not seasonally adjusted.

The Average Earnings Index has been withdrawn and replaced as the lead measure of short-term changes in average earnings in Great Britain by the Average Weekly Earnings ["AWE"] statistic.

The index figures which now feature in this table are for the whole economy, excluding bonuses and arrears of pay, and seasonally adjusted.

F6: Average weekly earnings

These figures are the average (mean) gross weekly earnings of full-time employees on adult rates whose pay was not affected by absence.

	Men	Women
	£	£
1985	192.40	126.40
1986	207.50	137.20
1987	224.00	148.10
1988	245.80	164.20
1989	269.50	182.30
1990	295.60	201.50
1991	318.90	222.40
1992	340.10	241.10
1993	353.50	252.60
1994	362.10	261.50
1995	374.60	269.80
1996	391.60	283.00
1997	408.70	297.20
1998	427.10	309.60
1999	442.40	326.50
2000	453.30	337.60
2001	490.50	366.80
2002	513.80	383.20
2003	525.00	396.00
2004	556.80	420.20
2005	568.00	435.60
2006	589.80	450.00
2007	606.10	462.80
2008	631.10	485.50
2009	643.00	501.20
2010	653.30	513.10
2011	658.10	515.40
2012	660.10	524.40
2013	676.70	532.90
2014	673.00	539.20

Until 2004 these figures were taken from the New Earnings Survey.
In 2004 the Annual Survey of Hours and Earnings (ASHE) was developed to replace the New Earnings Survey.
Both the New Earnings Survey and ASHE are published by HMSO.

F7: Average earnings statistics

Introductory notes

1. It will usually be possible to obtain agreement, or a direction, that the earnings shown in the Annual Survey of Hours and Earnings (ASHE) may be adduced in evidence without formal proof but occasionally it is necessary to adduce formal proof. This is done by calling a witness from the Office for National Statistics (ONS).

2. ASHE provides information about the levels, distribution and make-up of earnings and hours for paid employees. The data are collected and published by the ONS. ASHE replaced the New Earnings Survey (NES) in 2004.

3. ASHE is based upon a one per cent sample of employees taken from HM Revenue and Customs PAYE records. ASHE does not cover the self-employed nor employees not covered in the reference period.

4. ASHE is collected in April of each year and is published as a first release the following November. A second release is published a year later which includes any revisions to the estimates which may be required. The revisions are usually small.

5. The Tables reproduced here relate to a sample restricted to full-time employees on adult rates of pay whose pay was not affected by absence. The estimates are disaggregated by sex and by a four digit occupational classification. They are first release estimates.

6. The earnings information relates to weekly and annual gross pay before tax, national insurance or other deductions and excludes payments in kind. Earnings are reported for full-time employees who are defined as those who work more than 30 paid hours per week.

7. Two measures of typical earnings are reported, the mean and median. The median is ONS's preferred measure of average earnings as it is less affected by the relatively small number of very high earners which skews the distribution of earnings. The median provides a better indication of typical earnings than does the mean.

8. It is helpful to understand the Standard Occupational Classification (SOC) as an ordered taxonomy of jobs in which narrowly defined jobs at the four digit level (unit groups) are included within a wider definition at the three digit level which in turn are included within a wider category at the two digit level and a still wider category at the one digit level. The hierarchy is based upon the concepts of the type of job and on the level of skill. There are 369 four digit occupational unit groups in SOC 2010 which cluster to form 90 minor groups, 25 sub major groups and 9 major groups. As an example, Rail Travel Assistants, 6215, are included within the three digit group Leisure and Travel Services (621) and at the two digit level, within Leisure, Travel and Related Personal Service Occupations (62), and, at the one digit level, within Caring, Leisure and other Personal Service Occupations (6). n.e.c. stands for 'not elsewhere classified'.

9. Reclassification of occupational categories occurs every ten years and occurred in ASHE 2011 released in March 2012. For 2011 there is a dual set of tables, one using the SOC 2000 and the second using SOC 2010.

10. Statistics derived from samples are called 'estimates' because they estimate the population parameters that we are interested in. All sample estimates are subject to a degree of unreliability due to sampling variation. This is measured by ONS in the form of the coefficient of variation (CV) and is

published in the series of Tables b which accompany the sample estimates in the series of Tables a. The CV is the ratio of the standard error of the estimate to the estimate itself. The smaller is the CV, the higher the precision (or quality) of the estimate. The ONS define four standards of reliability in relation to the size of the CV: less than 5 per cent, 5–10 per cent, 10 to 20 per cent and greater than 20 per cent. An estimate with a CV of less than 5 per cent is the most reliable. Estimates with CVs of greater than 20 per cent are considered insufficiently reliable and are not published. Those in-between are shaded in the ONS publication, though not in the reproduction here.

11. Tables of ASHE estimates are published online where alternative breakdowns can be found, for example by region, age group, industrial sector etc. After November/December 2015, the estimates published online for 2014 will be the revised final release ones. A further advantage of the online source is the shading according to the levels of reliability referred to in 10 above. The tables can be found on the website of the Office for National Statistics (ONS). This requires some navigation from the home page. Step-by-step instructions to find the estimates produced here are provided below. You need not follow all these step-by-step instructions each time you consult the tables as you can either download the tables as an Excel file or you can save the web link to bookmarks/favourites.

12. Find the home page of the ONS at: *www.ONS.gov.uk*

13. Type in ASHE 2014 in the search box at the top right hand side of this page and click Search.

14. All the ASHE spreadsheets (1–26) are listed in the search results together with many other documents. To restrict your search to the statistical tables, check the box marked Reference tables under Filter Results on the right hand side of the screen. Click 'Apply selected filters'.

15. Scroll down the list to find the Reference table that you require. Table 14 provides earnings estimates disaggregated by Occupation at the level of the four-digit Standard Occupation Classification (SOC). If you are interested in carers' earnings you should consult the advice at B6.

16. Click on the table title and this will take you to a .zip file which contains a contents list of Excel files containing an occupational breakdown of a different set of earnings estimates.

17. For example, double-click on Table 14.1a for Weekly Pay–Gross or Table 14.7a Annual Pay–Gross. This will take you to a worksheet in an Excel file. If you are sure that you have located the file that you want, save it using File → Save in Excel.

18. Note that all files marked with a file extension 'b' report the coefficient of variation on the estimate (see 10 above).

19. Once in the Excel file, check the bottom tabs. Choose 'Male Full-time' or 'Female Full-time' to view the tables reproduced here. The median is reported in column 3 and the mean in column 5.

20. The shading indicates the reliability of the estimate. Where the estimate of the error is less than 5 per cent, there is no shading. The key to the shading can be found at the bottom and at the right hand side of the table. The shading is not reproduced here.

21. If you have not already saved this file at step 17 above, this table can be saved now either in part or in full. If the file is saved prior to the final release, make a note that the 2014 estimates are provisional. They will be replaced in the final release in November/December 2015 under the same title.

This guide has been prepared by Dr Victoria Wass, Cardiff Business School, May 2015.

Full-time males on adult rates (where pay was not affected by absence)

n.e.c. = not elsewhere classified X = unreliable	Gross Weekly Pay (in April) 2014		Gross Annual Pay (in April) 2014	
Occupation SOC 2010	**Median £**	**Mean £**	**Median £**	**Mean £**
All employees	557.8	673.0	29,441	37,028
Managers, directors and senior officials	827.5	1,043.1	43,901	62,176
Corporate managers and directors	877.1	1,092.0	46,462	65,255
Chief executives and senior officials	1,629.0	1,853.0	89,811	124,294
Chief executives and senior officials	1,652.6	1,906.9	93,426	128,036
Elected officers and representatives	X	455.9	X	25,095
Production managers and directors	846.1	988.3	44,413	55,756
Production managers and directors in manufacturing	862.6	1,005.7	45,374	56,466
Production managers and directors in construction	789.0	891.7	40,000	52,418
Production managers and directors in mining and energy	874.4	X	X	X
Functional managers and directors	1,179.5	1,383.2	63,411	86,748
Financial managers and directors	1,255.4	1,483.4	69,575	97,464
Marketing and sales directors	1,331.0	1,547.1	74,030	92,858
Purchasing managers and directors	893.5	998.2	48,161	55,341
Advertising and public relations directors	X	1,399.7	X	76,946
Human resource managers and directors	955.4	1,110.5	51,702	73,286
Information technology and telecommunications directors	1,226.0	1,322.4	64,576	X
Functional managers and directors n.e.c.	1,013.4	1,156.9	51,453	66,402
Financial institution managers and directors	1,222.8	1,561.8	64,558	100,537
Financial institution managers and directors	1,222.8	1,561.8	64,558	100,537
Managers and directors in transport and logistics	600.3	674.5	32,085	36,164
Managers and directors in transport and distribution	709.0	793.9	37,416	42,840
Managers and directors in storage and warehousing	548.2	595.1	29,562	31,733
Senior officers in protective services	1,057.0	1,123.4	54,915	57,141
Officers in armed forces				
Senior police officers	1,106.4	1,197.5	57,701	58,781
Senior officers in fire, ambulance, prison and related services	876.5	994.1	47,623	53,960
Health and social services managers and directors	898.5	1,007.8	45,558	53,145
Health services and public health managers and directors	943.5	1,028.1	47,239	53,894
Social services managers and directors	771.6	943.3	X	50,366
Managers and directors in retail and wholesale	551.9	644.5	29,166	36,504
Managers and directors in retail and wholesale	551.9	644.5	29,166	36,504
Other managers and proprietors	597.6	729.2	31,722	41,899
Managers and proprietors in agriculture related services	540.7	622.0	X	32,400
Managers and proprietors in agriculture and horticulture	572.8	639.9	29,598	33,475
Managers and proprietors in forestry, fishing and related services	485.0	572.8	X	X
Managers and proprietors in hospitality and leisure services	516.3	598.6	25,616	32,062
Hotel and accommodation managers and proprietors	552.3	681.3	27,496	36,526
Restaurant and catering establishment managers and proprietors	449.9	518.1	22,798	27,212
Publicans and managers of licensed premises	453.6	498.0	23,077	24,890
Leisure and sports managers	546.6	643.9	27,787	34,150
Travel agency managers and proprietors	X	X	X	X
Managers and proprietors in health and care services	693.0	732.0	35,291	37,850
Health care practice managers	756.3	767.5	39,465	41,678
Residential, day and domiciliary care managers and proprietors	667.2	725.2	34,012	37,044
Managers and proprietors in other services	656.0	814.2	36,119	48,703
Property, housing and estate managers	724.2	876.9	39,721	56,347

Full-time males on adult rates (where pay was not affected by absence)

n.e.c. = not elsewhere classified X = unreliable	**Gross Weekly Pay (in April) 2014**		**Gross Annual Pay (in April) 2014**	
Occupation SOC 2010	**Median £**	**Mean £**	**Median £**	**Mean £**
Garage managers and proprietors	599.1	786.6	32,316	41,022
Hairdressing and beauty salon managers and proprietors	X	457.7	X	25,557
Shopkeepers and proprietors – wholesale and retail	X	964.4	X	X
Waste disposal and environmental services managers	716.6	817.8	37,669	43,601
Managers and proprietors in other services n.e.c.	613.3	733.7	32,022	40,541
Professional occupations	766.6	858.1	39,886	45,835
Science, research, engineering and technology professionals	766.6	824.9	40,348	44,406
Natural and social science professionals	709.3	783.4	37,023	43,486
Chemical scientists	618.2	649.2	32,884	37,385
Biological scientists and biochemists	775.1	811.0	40,502	45,089
Physical scientists	779.0	1,010.9	X	57,073
Social and humanities scientists	581.0	621.9	28,075	31,177
Natural and social science professionals n.e.c.	700.8	734.9	36,556	39,683
Engineering professionals	757.5	807.9	39,324	42,718
Civil engineers	775.5	815.7	39,256	41,373
Mechanical engineers	784.2	843.3	40,764	44,436
Electrical engineers	808.3	857.1	43,915	47,934
Electronics engineers	745.3	840.9	X	44,075
Design and development engineers	733.1	783.4	38,698	42,074
Production and process engineers	717.6	765.9	37,166	39,285
Engineering professionals n.e.c.	762.2	811.9	39,365	43,147
Information technology and telecommunications professionals	785.7	841.3	41,645	45,463
IT specialist managers	878.4	950.6	46,076	51,841
IT project and programme managers	928.3	948.6	51,940	52,219
IT business analysts, architects and systems designers	814.0	867.6	42,849	46,827
Programmers and software development professionals	766.6	806.3	40,558	42,224
Web design and development professionals	548.2	585.1	29,739	31,252
Information technology and telecommunications professionals n.e.c.	744.3	802.1	40,387	43,317
Conservation and environmental professionals	612.4	652.5	31,898	33,301
Conservation professionals	625.1	646.5	32,964	31,826
Environment professionals	611.8	654.0	30,193	33,687
Research and development managers	923.0	1,040.2	X	60,591
Research and development managers	923.0	1,040.2	X	60,591
Health professionals	823.8	1,064.3	40,823	56,013
Health professionals	1,098.2	1,330.7	64,001	74,530
Medical practitioners	1,353.2	1,517.4	85,517	89,183
Psychologists	722.6	824.3	X	42,141
Pharmacists	866.0	855.0	45,904	46,764
Ophthalmic opticians	835.2	843.5	X	48,530
Dental practitioners	X	1,015.0	X	57,095
Veterinarians	841.3	829.3	43,297	45,856
Medical radiographers	673.0	748.0	35,354	38,393
Podiatrists	633.0	619.1	33,127	32,525
Health professionals n.e.c.	669.3	721.9	35,205	37,035
Therapy professionals	611.1	711.4	30,455	36,739
Physiotherapists	610.3	739.9	31,246	38,410
Occupational therapists	555.0	573.3	28,574	29,051
Speech and language therapists				
Therapy professionals n.e.c.	661.6	733.6	32,893	36,640
Nursing and midwifery professionals	641.7	679.3	33,375	33,576
Nurses	641.7	678.9	33,341	33,550
Midwives				

Full-time males on adult rates (where pay was not affected by absence)

n.e.c. = not elsewhere classified
X = unreliable

Occupation SOC 2010	Gross Weekly Pay (in April) 2014 Median £	Gross Weekly Pay (in April) 2014 Mean £	Gross Annual Pay (in April) 2014 Median £	Gross Annual Pay (in April) 2014 Mean £
Teaching and educational professionals	768.0	816.5	39,538	41,902
Teaching and educational professionals	768.2	816.9	39,541	41,924
Higher education teaching professionals	927.9	1,012.8	48,073	51,933
Further education teaching professionals	682.2	713.9	35,259	36,095
Secondary education teaching professionals	753.3	756.4	38,814	38,320
Primary and nursery education teaching professionals	686.1	706.9	36,544	37,047
Special needs education teaching professionals	732.0	667.7	36,991	34,495
Senior professionals of educational establishments	1,075.3	1,120.3	55,914	58,319
Education advisers and school inspectors	629.5	667.3	32,218	34,537
Teaching and other educational professionals n.e.c.	583.8	621.6	30,538	31,238
Business, media and public service professionals	745.7	845.8	38,699	46,384
Legal professionals	903.3	1,157.8	X	67,374
Barristers and judges	X	1,157.8	X	63,575
Solicitors	805.2	987.2	43,363	55,528
Legal professionals n.e.c.	1,398.7	1,503.8	X	X
Business, research and administrative professionals	781.9	882.2	41,522	49,081
Chartered and certified accountants	782.0	840.1	41,651	47,130
Management consultants and business analysts	785.8	877.8	41,661	49,377
Business and financial project management professionals	877.0	977.0	46,880	54,602
Actuaries, economists and statisticians	862.5	1,094.8	44,133	66,963
Business and related research professionals	637.8	672.4	33,055	35,571
Business, research and administrative professionals n.e.c.	679.5	771.8	35,494	39,984
Architects, town planners and surveyors	700.2	781.7	36,849	42,161
Architects	731.7	893.2	X	49,379
Town planning officers	637.9	621.8	33,101	32,253
Quantity surveyors	766.6	801.3	39,769	42,822
Chartered surveyors	682.8	732.6	35,900	39,117
Chartered architectural technologists	520.8	601.9	29,601	33,651
Construction project managers and related professionals	672.3	797.6	35,517	42,977
Welfare professionals	568.6	571.8	29,309	30,048
Social workers	648.6	648.0	32,979	33,192
Probation officers	634.4	634.6	31,777	32,205
Clergy	435.9	476.1	23,966	25,961
Welfare professionals n.e.c.	590.8	653.8	X	35,693
Librarians and related professionals	589.7	595.7	28,752	30,615
Librarians	611.8	615.1	X	32,028
Archivists and curators	515.2	563.7	24,944	28,297
Quality and regulatory professionals	747.6	834.6	37,479	44,564
Quality control and planning engineers	708.0	731.7	35,656	37,318
Quality assurance and regulatory professionals	791.4	922.3	39,475	50,535
Environmental health professionals	685.9	691.8	33,387	33,733
Media professionals	655.0	742.8	33,245	38,712
Journalists, newspaper and periodical editors	625.3	701.0	32,804	37,105
Public relations professionals	586.3	665.3	29,534	34,265
Advertising accounts managers and creative directors	862.4	933.2	42,338	47,107
Associate professional and technical occupations	624.9	721.5	33,611	40,812
Science, engineering and technology associate professionals	555.4	599.1	29,301	31,497
Science, engineering and production technicians	562.8	599.9	29,613	31,248
Laboratory technicians	455.0	514.4	24,995	27,100
Electrical and electronics technicians	588.9	588.0	31,011	30,449
Engineering technicians	666.4	694.9	34,006	35,517
Building and civil engineering technicians	556.3	624.9	X	33,415

Full-time males on adult rates (where pay was not affected by absence)

n.e.c. = not elsewhere classified
X = unreliable

Occupation SOC 2010	Gross Weekly Pay (in April) 2014 Median £	Gross Weekly Pay (in April) 2014 Mean £	Gross Annual Pay (in April) 2014 Median £	Gross Annual Pay (in April) 2014 Mean £
Quality assurance technicians	530.5	573.9	28,324	29,813
Planning, process and production technicians	584.9	648.0	31,030	33,756
Science, engineering and production technicians n.e.c.	515.2	548.4	26,990	28,855
Draughtspersons and related architectural technicians	536.6	582.7	28,128	30,812
Architectural and town planning technicians	537.9	581.9	28,154	29,781
Draughtspersons	532.1	583.0	28,120	31,129
Information technology technicians	539.3	601.4	28,922	32,064
IT operations technicians	543.9	613.5	28,299	32,804
IT user support technicians	537.4	592.6	29,006	31,519
Health and social care associate professionals	524.1	565.8	27,724	29,404
Health associate professionals	649.4	665.3	33,925	34,043
Paramedics	736.9	766.8	37,969	38,892
Dispensing opticians	X	621.5	X	X
Pharmaceutical technicians	498.1	524.3	25,958	26,897
Medical and dental technicians	574.0	613.6	30,002	31,704
Health associate professionals n.e.c.	512.8	507.3	26,578	26,723
Welfare and housing associate professionals	493.6	510.5	25,519	26,547
Youth and community workers	497.6	529.7	26,309	27,665
Child and early years officers	486.5	489.2	24,240	24,587
Housing officers	514.9	517.2	26,104	26,685
Counsellors	X	489.8	X	31,491
Welfare and housing associate professionals n.e.c.	480.4	497.6	25,071	25,714
Protective service occupations	706.8	721.1	36,806	37,124
Protective service occupations	706.8	721.1	36,806	37,124
NCOs and other ranks				
Police officers (sergeant and below)	762.3	781.4	40,276	40,381
Fire service officers (watch manager and below)	626.7	657.0	32,027	33,067
Prison service officers (below principal officer)	557.8	566.9	29,144	28,895
Police community support officers	509.1	517.1	26,383	26,962
Protective service associate professionals n.e.c.	652.1	695.5	34,042	36,487
Culture, media and sports occupations	529.3	698.8	28,461	34,548
Artistic, literary and media occupations	632.4	706.4	33,024	38,240
Artists	541.1	527.2	25,339	27,092
Authors, writers and translators	516.4	632.6	27,467	34,994
Actors, entertainers and presenters	X	X	X	X
Dancers and choreographers				
Musicians	708.7	689.2	36,785	36,674
Arts officers, producers and directors	749.2	797.8	38,121	41,399
Photographers, audio-visual and broadcasting equipment operators	500.9	580.2	27,438	31,184
Design occupations	524.1	553.3	27,500	29,745
Graphic designers	505.0	536.3	25,966	28,621
Product, clothing and related designers	574.6	587.1	31,111	31,798
Sports and fitness occupations	407.8	X	21,458	35,596
Sports players	X	X	X	X
Sports coaches, instructors and officials	441.4	536.0	23,451	30,604
Fitness instructors	307.0	342.8	16,616	18,040
Business and public service associate professionals	665.3	792.6	36,557	48,118
Transport associate professionals	1,385.0	1,481.4	78,005	77,742
Air traffic controllers	1,673.7	1,653.4	83,193	82,645
Aircraft pilots and flight engineers	1,746.6	1,849.7	90,420	94,179
Ship and hovercraft officers	590.7	718.7	40,206	40,544
Legal associate professionals	590.4	750.6	34,036	47,154
Legal associate professionals	590.4	750.6	34,036	47,154
Business, finance and related associate professionals	689.7	866.6	37,000	54,566

Full-time males on adult rates (where pay was not affected by absence)

n.e.c. = not elsewhere classified X = unreliable	**Gross Weekly Pay (in April) 2014**		**Gross Annual Pay (in April) 2014**	
Occupation SOC 2010	**Median £**	**Mean £**	**Median £**	**Mean £**
Estimators, valuers and assessors	573.5	667.0	30,135	37,463
Brokers	X	1,834.1	X	X
Insurance underwriters	673.8	866.9	35,113	50,777
Finance and investment analysts and advisers	697.2	856.2	37,512	53,992
Taxation experts	844.9	922.7	44,208	50,697
Importers and exporters	611.0	625.7	28,346	31,141
Financial and accounting technicians	889.0	1,171.0	47,243	58,401
Financial accounts managers	766.6	898.1	42,803	54,241
Business and related associate professionals n.e.c.	574.9	697.0	31,162	40,842
Sales, marketing and related associate professionals	695.6	793.1	38,794	48,835
Buyers and procurement officers	609.1	680.2	33,009	36,751
Business sales executives	546.2	647.9	32,431	37,669
Marketing associate professionals	574.9	679.6	30,701	39,578
Estate agents and auctioneers	474.6	593.1	26,652	31,594
Sales accounts and business development managers	826.1	911.4	45,684	58,167
Conference and exhibition managers and organisers	494.1	508.3	X	X
Conservation and environmental associate professionals	447.6	490.8	23,794	26,153
Conservation and environmental associate professionals	447.6	490.8	23,794	26,153
Public services and other associate professionals	568.6	626.7	30,054	33,895
Public service associate professionals	582.5	638.9	30,816	34,857
Human resources and industrial relations officers	519.5	624.5	31,189	36,689
Vocational and industrial trainers and instructors	539.9	596.9	28,297	31,510
Careers advisers and vocational guidance specialists	500.0	526.7	25,888	26,620
Inspectors of standards and regulations	589.7	616.2	30,311	31,938
Health and safety officers	705.1	718.0	34,981	36,269
Administrative and secretarial occupations	438.9	497.3	23,312	26,448
Administrative occupations	441.6	500.0	23,500	26,527
Administrative occupations: Government and related organisations	455.7	491.5	23,730	25,368
National government administrative occupations	428.1	472.9	22,495	24,260
Local government administrative occupations	506.2	527.1	26,301	27,371
Officers of non-governmental organisations	521.8	593.9	X	31,140
Administrative occupations: Finance	453.6	517.1	23,867	27,605
Credit controllers	440.9	483.5	23,848	25,340
Book-keepers, payroll managers and wages clerks	517.5	565.8	27,431	29,608
Bank and post office clerks	408.2	478.8	22,335	26,715
Finance officers	477.6	561.0	24,257	29,087
Financial administrative occupations n.e.c.	402.7	462.6	X	24,729
Administrative occupations: Records	437.5	480.5	22,749	25,216
Records clerks and assistants	450.1	490.4	23,637	26,071
Pensions and insurance clerks and assistants	412.2	460.2	21,585	25,618
Stock control clerks and assistants	420.7	458.2	21,583	23,680
Transport and distribution clerks and assistants	479.1	526.9	24,952	27,127
Library clerks and assistants	359.7	376.4	17,748	18,306
Human resources administrative occupations	382.5	411.8	X	21,309
Other administrative occupations	387.7	446.1	20,898	23,599
Sales administrators	383.3	423.9	22,429	23,710
Other administrative occupations n.e.c.	388.2	448.8	20,775	23,585
Administrative occupations: Office managers and supervisors	615.3	673.2	32,000	36,046
Office managers	641.9	699.3	34,303	37,937
Office supervisors	534.3	569.0	27,254	29,198
Secretarial and related occupations	369.3	451.7	19,749	25,011
Secretarial and related occupations	369.3	451.7	19,749	25,011
Medical secretaries	X	495.1	X	X

Full-time males on adult rates (where pay was not affected by absence)

n.e.c. = not elsewhere classified X = unreliable	Gross Weekly Pay (in April) 2014		Gross Annual Pay (in April) 2014	
Occupation SOC 2010	**Median £**	**Mean £**	**Median £**	**Mean £**
Legal secretaries				
School secretaries	X	484.2	X	27,550
Company secretaries	X	737.5	X	40,138
Personal assistants and other secretaries	473.7	607.7	25,491	X
Receptionists	311.1	331.3	16,376	17,130
Typists and related keyboard occupations	375.8	436.9	18,734	22,488
Skilled trades occupations	490.1	533.7	25,812	27,486
Skilled agricultural and related trades	357.6	386.6	18,947	20,006
Agricultural and related trades	357.6	386.6	18,947	20,006
Farmers	457.9	515.6	X	25,987
Horticultural trades	368.9	423.9	18,560	19,470
Gardeners and landscape gardeners	357.6	380.4	18,791	19,731
Groundsmen and gamekeepers	347.1	372.0	18,484	19,470
Agricultural and fishing trades n.e.c.	407.6	420.7	20,734	22,045
Skilled metal, electrical and electronic trades	545.8	586.4	28,586	30,093
Metal forming, welding and related trades	499.5	557.0	25,699	28,049
Smiths and forge workers	X	515.0	X	X
Moulders, core makers and die casters	409.9	451.7	21,952	22,887
Sheet metal workers	504.5	592.0	27,540	28,137
Metal plate workers, and riveters	574.8	616.1	30,543	30,254
Welding trades	469.1	524.1	24,703	26,989
Pipe fitters	648.6	756.0	36,873	37,798
Metal machining, fitting and instrument making trades	555.8	596.7	28,523	30,108
Metal machining setters and setter-operators	505.0	563.0	26,061	27,721
Tool makers, tool fitters and markers-out	510.9	565.8	25,591	27,604
Metal working production and maintenance fitters	561.7	604.0	28,888	30,649
Precision instrument makers and repairers	559.4	579.5	30,202	30,611
Air conditioning and refrigeration engineers	617.0	640.9	31,672	31,262
Vehicle trades	485.4	519.1	25,618	27,111
Vehicle technicians, mechanics and electricians	469.0	494.2	24,797	25,793
Vehicle body builders and repairers	461.7	485.5	24,853	25,303
Vehicle paint technicians	463.5	506.5	24,652	25,051
Aircraft maintenance and related trades	646.4	662.9	36,204	35,259
Boat and ship builders and repairers	505.7	569.8	30,335	31,087
Rail and rolling stock builders and repairers	831.3	846.1	40,901	44,020
Electrical and electronic trades	563.2	600.2	30,005	31,333
Electricians and electrical fitters	570.0	607.9	30,195	31,221
Telecommunications engineers	566.2	610.1	31,565	32,741
TV, video and audio engineers	474.3	500.9	27,397	28,045
IT engineers	481.2	507.8	24,365	26,711
Electrical and electronic trades n.e.c.	572.6	607.0	29,796	31,767
Skilled metal, electrical and electronic trades supervisors	640.0	699.3	33,567	36,248
Skilled metal, electrical and electronic trades supervisors	640.0	699.3	33,567	36,248
Skilled construction and building trades	491.6	531.3	25,670	26,682
Construction and building trades	483.3	512.4	25,300	25,792
Steel erectors	527.6	530.9	26,512	26,220
Bricklayers and masons	467.2	498.1	24,806	25,381
Roofers, roof tilers and slaters	428.1	444.2	22,346	23,053
Plumbers and heating ventilating engineers	530.1	556.6	28,309	28,317
Carpenters and joiners	484.2	500.0	25,236	25,189
Glaziers, window fabricators and fitters	423.7	431.0	20,780	21,307
Construction and building trades n.e.c.	500.0	555.3	25,945	27,648
Building finishing trades	455.4	474.9	22,580	23,449
Plasterers	460.0	438.6	22,495	22,361

Full-time males on adult rates (where pay was not affected by absence)

n.e.c. = not elsewhere classified
X = unreliable

Occupation SOC 2010	Gross weekly pay (in April) 2014 Median £	Gross weekly pay (in April) 2014 Mean £	Gross annual earnings (in April) 2014 Median £	Gross annual earnings (in April) 2014 Mean £
Floorers and wall tilers	449.9	460.7	24,011	24,409
Painters and decorators	444.7	491.0	22,036	23,478
Construction and building trades supervisors	635.7	693.8	32,970	34,999
Construction and building trades supervisors	635.7	693.8	32,970	34,999
Textiles, printing and other skilled trades	383.3	409.3	19,912	21,297
Textiles and garments trades	433.9	481.4	22,708	22,984
Weavers and knitters	404.0	414.3	20,871	21,600
Upholsterers	455.6	515.3	22,111	22,324
Footwear and leather working trades	423.5	448.7	23,177	24,011
Tailors and dressmakers	354.4	398.7	21,536	21,281
Textiles, garments and related trades n.e.c.	X	612.6	25,652	26,737
Printing trades	460.3	513.5	23,731	25,990
Pre-press technicians	430.8	506.6	22,407	26,536
Printers	525.1	546.0	26,031	27,634
Print finishing and binding workers	419.1	460.4	20,990	22,826
Food preparation and hospitality trades	359.2	382.3	18,605	19,867
Butchers	352.5	368.6	18,725	19,236
Bakers and flour confectioners	348.0	369.0	18,157	18,944
Fishmongers and poultry dressers	323.5	359.1	16,295	18,883
Chefs	361.3	379.0	18,572	19,724
Cooks	328.9	366.7	17,350	18,809
Catering and bar managers	392.1	429.1	20,073	22,476
Other skilled trades	403.7	438.9	20,936	22,698
Glass and ceramics makers, decorators and finishers	397.0	444.6	20,457	22,593
Furniture makers and other craft woodworkers	400.5	408.0	20,461	20,720
Florists				
Other skilled trades n.e.c.	410.2	465.6	22,046	24,672
Caring, leisure and other service occupations	375.5	405.3	19,575	20,921
Caring personal service occupations	369.3	387.6	18,927	19,581
Childcare and related personal services	313.8	346.7	16,505	18,002
Nursery nurses and assistants	342.8	363.1	13,902	16,227
Childminders and related occupations				
Playworkers	276.6	317.2	X	X
Teaching assistants	297.8	340.2	14,925	17,821
Educational support assistants	326.5	357.2	18,393	19,340
Animal care and control services	393.1	407.3	20,108	20,774
Veterinary nurses	300.5	328.5		
Pest control officers	407.7	437.4	20,104	20,258
Animal care services occupations n.e.c.	358.7	396.2	21,170	21,693
Caring personal services	374.7	393.7	19,244	19,767
Nursing auxiliaries and assistants	381.5	406.4	19,970	20,673
Ambulance staff (excluding paramedics)	461.6	474.9	23,645	24,920
Dental nurses	325.0	357.4	17,372	18,994
Houseparents and residential wardens	416.8	471.7	23,371	24,237
Care workers and home carers	344.7	368.3	17,396	18,026
Senior care workers	385.8	402.2	20,603	20,674
Care escorts	335.4	336.2	X	16,354
Undertakers, mortuary and crematorium assistants	451.7	434.1	22,160	21,083
Leisure, travel and related personal service occupations	384.7	436.0	20,885	23,070
Leisure and travel services	441.0	489.7	25,050	26,382
Sports and leisure assistants	308.6	327.9	16,588	17,182
Travel agents	377.8	403.1	22,806	24,081
Air travel assistants	527.5	561.2	X	X
Rail travel assistants	633.6	651.5	32,228	32,871
Leisure and travel service occupations n.e.c.	X	487.4	X	25,038
Hairdressers and related services	309.1	325.0	16,739	17,701

Full-time males on adult rates (where pay was not affected by absence)

n.e.c. = not elsewhere classified
X = unreliable

Occupation SOC 2010	Gross Weekly Pay (in April) 2014 Median £	Gross Weekly Pay (in April) 2014 Mean £	Gross Annual Pay (in April) 2014 Median £	Gross Annual Pay (in April) 2014 Mean £
Hairdressers and barbers	294.7	308.7	14,701	17,041
Beauticians and related occupations	386.0	380.7	20,164	20,199
Housekeeping and related services	370.2	383.6	19,319	19,788
Housekeepers and related occupations	288.9	339.8	X	X
Caretakers	372.2	386.7	19,409	19,952
Cleaning and housekeeping managers and supervisors	382.6	435.0	21,011	22,376
Cleaning and housekeeping managers and supervisors	382.6	435.0	21,011	22,376
Sales and customer service occupations	345.0	388.9	18,279	20,458
Sales occupations	327.2	367.0	17,450	19,222
Sales assistants and retail cashiers	311.8	351.9	16,376	18,331
Sales and retail assistants	309.3	348.8	16,158	18,195
Retail cashiers and check-out operators	289.1	303.8	14,856	15,458
Telephone salespersons	346.7	374.1	20,019	20,688
Pharmacy and other dispensing assistants	292.1	338.4	15,303	17,910
Vehicle and parts salespersons and advisers	396.5	447.7	20,742	22,803
Sales related occupations	366.4	415.1	20,198	22,578
Collector salespersons and credit agents	X	X	X	X
Debt, rent and other cash collectors	325.7	356.1	18,750	19,493
Roundspersons and van salespersons	419.8	420.9	22,992	22,525
Market and street traders and assistants	X	X	X	X
Merchandisers and window dressers	368.5	435.0	19,474	23,314
Sales related occupations n.e.c.	383.3	468.5	21,861	26,484
Sales supervisors	380.5	408.3	19,531	21,264
Sales supervisors	380.5	408.3	19,531	21,264
Customer service occupations	376.4	434.1	20,574	23,040
Customer service occupations	356.5	394.9	18,995	20,486
Call and contact centre occupations	328.9	355.5	15,997	17,265
Telephonists	317.1	325.9	17,320	17,355
Communication operators	581.0	623.4	30,533	32,340
Market research interviewers	348.5	383.6	X	X
Customer service occupations n.e.c.	357.3	390.6	19,241	20,500
Customer service managers and supervisors	569.7	619.8	30,387	33,917
Customer service managers and supervisors	569.7	619.8	30,387	33,917
Process, plant and machine operatives	457.0	495.6	23,648	25,202
Process, plant and machine operatives	442.9	484.2	23,153	24,818
Process operatives	394.9	442.8	20,821	23,069
Food, drink and tobacco process operatives	360.0	395.1	18,968	20,487
Glass and ceramics process operatives	396.9	448.7	19,193	21,611
Textile process operatives	422.2	459.6	21,968	23,881
Chemical and related process operatives	518.7	557.1	26,230	28,965
Rubber process operatives	564.9	565.4	30,397	29,365
Plastics process operatives	389.4	454.6	21,083	24,142
Metal making and treating process operatives	453.3	494.5	23,888	25,411
Electroplaters	397.2	446.3	22,003	23,093
Process operatives n.e.c.	506.5	490.2	25,858	26,242
Plant and machine operatives	454.1	491.4	23,607	25,190
Paper and wood machine operatives	384.1	418.8	20,293	21,914
Coal mine operatives	531.1	722.8	29,178	33,102
Quarry workers and related operatives	668.1	697.8	X	34,833
Energy plant operatives	556.5	600.8	29,176	30,654
Metal working machine operatives	428.3	448.4	21,437	22,931
Water and sewerage plant operatives	536.4	574.3	29,684	30,392
Printing machine assistants	427.1	450.5	23,713	23,380
Plant and machine operatives n.e.c.	464.8	508.6	24,132	25,870

Full-time males on adult rates (where pay was not affected by absence)

n.e.c. = not elsewhere classified
X = unreliable

Occupation SOC 2010	Gross Weekly Pay (in April) 2014 Median £	Gross Weekly Pay (in April) 2014 Mean £	Gross Annual Pay (in April) 2014 Median £	Gross Annual Pay (in April) 2014 Mean £
Assemblers and routine operatives	448.7	491.2	23,639	25,211
Assemblers (electrical and electronic products)	429.0	434.5	22,046	22,406
Assemblers (vehicles and metal goods)	602.8	618.4	29,580	30,775
Routine inspectors and testers	484.5	511.8	25,124	26,542
Weighers, graders and sorters	368.3	389.0	20,127	20,836
Tyre, exhaust and windscreen fitters	361.0	384.9	20,442	21,519
Sewing machinists	367.7	379.1	18,228	18,061
Assemblers and routine operatives n.e.c.	376.2	426.1	20,063	21,723
Construction operatives	483.0	524.1	25,071	26,371
Scaffolders, stagers and riggers	601.4	626.4	28,885	30,007
Road construction operatives	503.0	531.7	25,726	26,956
Rail construction and maintenance operatives	670.1	722.0	35,359	36,222
Construction operatives n.e.c.	431.3	463.6	22,883	23,611
Transport and mobile machine drivers and operatives	471.9	505.8	24,091	25,558
Road transport drivers	453.2	476.7	23,171	23,819
Large goods vehicle drivers	522.0	536.1	26,365	26,619
Van drivers	393.9	424.7	20,243	21,321
Bus and coach drivers	446.9	478.7	23,085	24,046
Taxi and cab drivers and chauffeurs	370.1	430.3	19,358	20,859
Driving instructors	X	609.5	X	31,813
Mobile machine drivers and operatives	493.0	527.5	24,931	26,177
Crane drivers	634.3	675.9	33,555	34,996
Fork-lift truck drivers	399.9	445.0	20,631	22,171
Agricultural machinery drivers	582.0	578.0	29,019	25,437
Mobile machine drivers and operatives n.e.c.	504.0	538.9	25,404	26,556
Other drivers and transport operatives	776.4	758.0	42,036	39,647
Train and tram drivers	922.7	918.2	47,953	47,298
Marine and waterways transport operatives	624.1	707.9	37,840	37,564
Air transport operatives	505.3	557.0	25,933	28,864
Rail transport operatives	750.6	746.6	X	40,146
Other drivers and transport operatives n.e.c.	458.7	485.3	24,702	25,605
Elementary occupations	360.8	388.2	19,172	20,055
Elementary trades and related occupations	372.8	404.8	19,609	20,963
Elementary agricultural occupations	371.6	398.5	19,311	20,342
Farm workers	390.3	418.6	20,336	21,132
Forestry workers	375.7	406.2	20,049	20,929
Fishing and other elementary agriculture occupations n.e.c.	339.1	355.6	17,721	18,322
Elementary construction occupations	400.0	434.9	20,937	22,171
Elementary construction occupations	400.0	434.9	20,937	22,171
Elementary process plant occupations	362.2	396.2	19,237	20,725
Industrial cleaning process occupations	333.9	373.4	18,060	19,379
Packers, bottlers, canners and fillers	342.9	373.7	18,254	19,753
Elementary process plant occupations n.e.c.	378.5	413.6	20,033	21,507
Elementary administration and service occupations	356.8	383.7	19,017	19,826
Elementary administration occupations	437.7	464.7	23,922	24,516
Postal workers, mail sorters, messengers and couriers	446.8	479.2	24,257	25,035
Elementary administration occupations n.e.c.	313.4	340.2	16,711	18,343
Elementary cleaning occupations	318.2	338.9	16,500	17,114
Window cleaners	361.0	340.5	18,153	19,130
Street cleaners	347.0	360.2	17,962	18,586
Cleaners and domestics	302.8	326.2	15,600	16,026
Launderers, dry cleaners and pressers	267.8	291.5	X	X
Refuse and salvage occupations	367.5	394.2	19,385	20,469
Vehicle valeters and cleaners	290.2	302.9	14,877	15,533
Elementary cleaning occupations n.e.c.	334.0	380.6	19,555	18,973
Elementary security occupations	409.6	427.2	21,034	21,907

Full-time males on adult rates (where pay was not affected by absence)

n.e.c. = not elsewhere classified X = unreliable	**Gross Weekly Pay (in April) 2014**		**Gross Annual Pay (in April) 2014**	
Occupation SOC 2010	**Median £**	**Mean £**	**Median £**	**Mean £**
Security guards and related occupations	414.7	431.5	21,329	22,097
Parking and civil enforcement occupations	375.5	386.3	18,753	20,018
School midday and crossing patrol occupations	291.4	388.5	16,762	20,144
Elementary security occupations n.e.c.	416.5	443.5	X	23,076
Elementary sales occupations	312.4	329.8	15,710	16,695
Shelf fillers	317.7	331.1	15,917	16,759
Elementary sales occupations n.e.c.	287.1	289.8	14,507	14,767
Elementary storage occupations	364.8	396.9	19,413	20,222
Elementary storage occupations	364.8	396.9	19,413	20,222
Other elementary services occupations	271.7	287.3	13,932	14,155
Hospital porters	362.9	370.2	18,720	18,974
Kitchen and catering assistants	270.8	283.8	13,671	13,653
Waiters and waitresses	265.9	283.0	X	13,710
Bar staff	259.5	275.7	13,680	13,966
Leisure and theme park attendants	255.7	305.8	X	X
Other elementary services occupations n.e.c.	289.6	317.3	15,928	16,837
Not Classified				

Source: *Annual Survey of Hours and Earnings, Office for National Statistics,* Tables 14.1a and 14.7a.

Full-time Females on adult rates (where pay was not affected by absence)

n.e.c. = not elsewhere classified X = unreliable	Gross Weekly Pay (in April) 2014		Gross Annual Pay (in April) 2014	
Occupation SOC 2010	**Median £**	**Mean £**	**Median £**	**Mean £**
All employees	461.9	539.2	23,889	27,991
Managers, directors and senior officials	670.8	809.8	34,473	43,690
Corporate managers and directors	731.6	871.3	37,084	47,204
Chief executives and senior officials	1,169.9	1,336.3	60,528	72,913
Chief executives and senior officials	1,191.1	1,377.9	61,714	75,328
Elected officers and representatives	X	X	X	X
Production managers and directors	759.8	891.9	39,319	47,291
Production managers and directors in manufacturing	776.5	893.2	39,373	47,000
Production managers and directors in construction	699.2	890.4	X	X
Production managers and directors in mining and energy				
Functional managers and directors	937.5	1,062.8	47,971	58,566
Financial managers and directors	937.7	1,070.5	48,104	58,889
Marketing and sales directors	1,209.7	1,351.1	64,134	76,936
Purchasing managers and directors	794.8	924.6	42,586	49,414
Advertising and public relations directors	1,324.7	1,426.4	X	X
Human resource managers and directors	862.4	932.2	42,524	50,735
Information technology and telecommunications directors	1,198.1	1,229.3	X	64,329
Functional managers and directors n.e.c.	856.9	919.7	42,911	49,725
Financial institution managers and directors	740.4	983.8	38,632	55,210
Financial institution managers and directors	740.4	983.8	38,632	55,210
Managers and directors in transport and logistics	488.3	576.3	25,622	30,826
Managers and directors in transport and distribution	669.4	764.8	X	X
Managers and directors in storage and warehousing	460.4	521.9	23,984	27,392
Senior officers in protective services	954.5	965.3	52,673	53,694
Officers in armed forces				
Senior police officers	1,065.9	989.9	59,871	57,143
Senior officers in fire, ambulance, prison and related services	834.1	932.8	X	48,605
Health and social services managers and directors	777.3	893.9	40,494	46,385
Health services and public health managers and directors	811.3	963.2	41,531	50,330
Social services managers and directors	702.8	724.7	X	37,057
Managers and directors in retail and wholesale	406.0	469.5	20,731	24,323
Managers and directors in retail and wholesale	406.0	469.5	20,731	24,323
Other managers and proprietors	536.6	591.3	27,944	31,043
Managers and proprietors in agriculture related services	464.1	490.2	24,851	24,068
Managers and proprietors in agriculture and horticulture	517.2	553.6	26,000	26,960
Managers and proprietors in forestry, fishing and related services	253.5	273.6	13,088	14,188
Managers and proprietors in hospitality and leisure services	446.2	501.7	22,887	26,524
Hotel and accommodation managers and proprietors	483.1	493.3	20,778	24,798
Restaurant and catering establishment managers and proprietors	413.5	453.5	19,756	24,050
Publicans and managers of licensed premises	X	501.4	X	25,562
Leisure and sports managers	513.7	553.2	26,538	29,237
Travel agency managers and proprietors	418.7	490.5	X	30,218
Managers and proprietors in health and care services	595.1	613.5	30,000	30,951
Health care practice managers	587.0	618.4	30,540	32,337
Residential, day and domiciliary care managers and proprietors	602.8	612.2	29,553	30,551
Managers and proprietors in other services	560.7	636.4	29,230	33,954

Full-time Females on adult rates (where pay was not affected by absence)

n.e.c. = not elsewhere classified
X = unreliable

Occupation SOC 2010	Gross Weekly Pay (in April) 2014 Median £	Gross Weekly Pay (in April) 2014 Mean £	Gross Annual Pay (in April) 2014 Median £	Gross Annual Pay (in April) 2014 Mean £
Property, housing and estate managers	579.7	646.0	X	34,578
Garage managers and proprietors				
Hairdressing and beauty salon managers and proprietors	436.0	467.8	25,634	23,900
Shopkeepers and proprietors – wholesale and retail	X	752.0	X	34,446
Waste disposal and environmental services managers	651.6	648.7	32,581	31,799
Managers and proprietors in other services n.e.c.	528.9	640.6	27,194	34,678
Professional occupations	661.7	708.8	33,827	36,039
Science, research, engineering and technology professionals	661.3	720.8	34,530	38,031
Natural and social science professionals	668.3	709.3	34,546	37,111
Chemical scientists	500.4	594.4	24,432	28,827
Biological scientists and biochemists	687.6	733.6	35,901	38,165
Physical scientists	697.7	684.1	36,417	35,960
Social and humanities scientists	X	550.2		
Natural and social science professionals n.e.c.	661.5	705.2	33,459	37,653
Engineering professionals	644.4	678.0	32,980	35,226
Civil engineers	557.2	645.9	30,729	33,394
Mechanical engineers	718.7	757.0	X	X
Electrical engineers	827.7	915.3	42,174	44,390
Electronics engineers				
Design and development engineers	648.5	695.1	32,177	34,929
Production and process engineers	615.9	608.9	31,904	31,556
Engineering professionals n.e.c.	623.9	667.0	33,840	35,698
Information technology and telecommunications professionals	696.9	756.2	35,948	40,420
IT specialist managers	720.0	793.4	36,034	41,684
IT project and programme managers	775.1	828.3	38,829	39,579
IT business analysts, architects and systems designers	695.1	829.9	37,945	48,539
Programmers and software development professionals	694.1	737.7	35,879	38,436
Web design and development professionals	513.5	547.8	28,287	28,060
Information technology and telecommunications professionals n.e.c.	670.8	717.7	34,961	37,965
Conservation and environment professionals	585.9	589.4	28,133	29,581
Conservation professionals	616.7	583.1	X	26,711
Environment professionals	571.1	591.8	28,310	30,671
Research and development managers	723.0	796.9	39,080	42,596
Research and development managers	723.0	796.9	39,080	42,596
Health professionals	641.7	703.4	32,455	34,969
Health professionals	805.2	933.9	40,409	48,765
Medical practitioners	956.7	1,156.5	54,147	63,258
Psychologists	746.5	747.7	39,173	39,931
Pharmacists	738.6	721.7	39,023	38,818
Ophthalmic opticians	691.5	654.7	37,047	36,302
Dental practitioners	692.7	845.4	X	42,025
Veterinarians	698.6	766.3	38,063	40,722
Medical radiographers	648.4	671.0	33,355	34,465
Podiatrists	572.3	604.9	29,363	31,046
Health professionals n.e.c.	605.7	608.5	30,914	30,885
Therapy professionals	619.8	640.0	31,319	32,162
Physiotherapists	618.8	633.3	31,264	32,228
Occupational therapists	608.8	618.9	30,888	30,691
Speech and language therapists	590.3	630.3	X	32,260
Therapy professionals n.e.c.	777.3	769.3	X	X
Nursing and midwifery professionals	617.5	634.8	31,582	31,426
Nurses	613.3	630.9	31,211	31,140

Full-time Females on adult rates (where pay was not affected by absence)

n.e.c. = not elsewhere classified
X = unreliable

Occupation SOC 2010	Gross Weekly Pay (in April) 2014 Median £	Gross Weekly Pay (in April) 2014 Mean £	Gross Annual Pay (in April) 2014 Median £	Gross Annual Pay (in April) 2014 Mean £
Midwives	684.9	703.2	35,678	36,227
Teaching and educational professionals	686.1	699.7	34,954	35,461
Teaching and educational professionals	686.1	699.6	34,946	35,458
Higher education teaching professionals	862.8	873.2	42,690	44,044
Further education teaching professionals	645.6	660.1	33,135	33,573
Secondary education teaching professionals	707.7	692.9	35,966	34,692
Primary and nursery education teaching professionals	661.6	659.8	34,200	33,482
Special needs education teaching professionals	723.9	697.0	X	35,130
Senior professionals of educational establishments	893.8	897.4	46,009	46,183
Education advisers and school inspectors	574.8	700.1	32,292	36,270
Teaching and other educational professionals n.e.c.	475.1	502.9	24,862	26,274
Business, media and public service professionals	652.5	723.7	33,661	37,650
Legal professionals	804.9	927.9	41,999	50,325
Barristers and judges	637.5	700.3	X	35,844
Solicitors	747.4	826.1	39,000	44,097
Legal professionals n.e.c.	1,116.6	1,221.4	60,779	68,696
Business, research and administrative professionals	665.0	744.0	34,015	38,357
Chartered and certified accountants	661.4	702.5	32,844	36,008
Management consultants and business analysts	728.3	799.7	38,028	43,280
Business and financial project management professionals	716.1	814.2	36,002	40,394
Actuaries, economists and statisticians	795.7	827.8	42,541	X
Business and related research professionals	588.9	590.5	29,998	30,055
Business, research and administrative professionals n.e.c.	660.3	711.8	33,064	35,407
Architects, town planners and surveyors	586.7	619.3	31,169	32,534
Architects	623.1	653.7	32,318	33,553
Town planning officers	X	620.4	30,687	33,015
Quantity surveyors	576.6	648.2	32,071	33,388
Chartered surveyors	580.6	609.7	31,101	32,605
Chartered architectural technologists				
Construction project managers and related professionals	497.6	498.7	22,201	25,491
Welfare professionals	611.4	605.1	31,421	30,967
Social workers	615.8	616.5	32,006	31,489
Probation officers	607.7	622.8	31,425	32,181
Clergy	425.7	440.8	X	23,447
Welfare professionals n.e.c.	575.3	583.0	29,364	29,739
Librarians and related professionals n.e.c.	492.1	539.0	24,445	27,027
Librarians	460.2	523.2	23,824	26,611
Archivists and curators	543.7	589.8	27,370	28,391
Quality and regulatory professionals	697.6	760.0	36,372	39,406
Quality control and planning engineers	669.7	699.7	37,602	37,002
Quality assurance and regulatory professionals	699.5	783.2	36,180	40,707
Environmental health professionals	701.3	696.0	33,979	34,268
Media professionals	574.6	626.4	30,484	33,524
Journalists, newspaper and periodical editors	568.4	640.9	29,319	34,344
Public relations professionals	536.8	582.2	28,741	31,372
Advertising accounts managers and creative directors	669.8	671.4	34,676	35,187
Associate professional and technical occupations	527.8	586.1	27,686	31,091
Science, engineering and technology associate professionals	469.9	503.1	24,230	26,086
Science, engineering and production technicians	440.8	467.3	22,321	24,508
Laboratory technicians	363.2	410.5	19,336	21,494
Electrical and electronics technicians				
Engineering technicians	575.8	632.6	29,209	32,536

Full-time Females on adult rates (where pay was not affected by absence)

n.e.c. = not elsewhere classified X = unreliable	Gross Weekly Pay (in April) 2014		Gross Annual Pay (in April) 2014	
Occupation SOC 2010	**Median £**	**Mean £**	**Median £**	**Mean £**
Building and civil engineering technicians	391.3	466.8		
Quality assurance technicians	479.1	503.5	24,048	25,885
Planning, process and production technicians	465.6	472.3	24,274	26,987
Science, engineering and production technicians n.e.c.	416.4	434.6	20,917	22,355
Draughtspersons and related architectural technicians	521.5	521.3	X	X
Architectural and town planning technicians	514.0	522.7	29,183	30,053
Draughtspersons	521.4	519.4	X	X
Information technology technicians	506.6	544.7	25,884	27,816
IT operations technicians	507.3	545.2	26,186	28,591
IT user support technicians	500.8	544.3	25,769	27,050
Health and social care associate professionals	464.4	486.6	24,018	25,106
Health associate professionals	459.0	513.9	25,375	27,123
Paramedics	671.8	694.9	36,341	36,815
Dispensing opticians	410.1	430.8	21,097	22,378
Pharmaceutical technicians	390.1	427.3	20,066	22,420
Medical and dental technicians	459.9	522.5	23,665	26,378
Health associate professionals n.e.c.	519.4	538.3	26,255	27,992
Welfare and housing associate professionals	464.6	479.2	23,945	24,583
Youth and community workers	477.1	483.3	24,316	24,596
Child and early years officers	458.9	482.0	23,395	24,750
Housing officers	481.2	489.7	24,984	24,976
Counsellors	458.3	506.0	24,276	25,798
Welfare and housing associate professionals n.e.c.	453.8	465.3	22,991	24,156
Protective service occupations	642.6	652.3	33,389	33,629
NCOs and other ranks				
Police officers (sergeant and below)	706.8	701.3	35,990	36,112
Fire service officers (watch manager and below)	575.9	641.6	30,573	31,361
Prison service officers (below principal officer)	458.0	482.3	24,319	25,689
Police community support officers	497.3	501.4	25,500	25,675
Protective service associate professionals n.e.c.	660.3	703.0	33,407	35,087
Culture, media and sports occupations	498.3	540.5	25,104	27,076
Artistic, literary and media occupations	563.8	604.6	28,120	31,065
Artists	X	607.8	X	31,450
Authors, writers and translators	517.4	610.0	26,056	31,241
Actors, entertainers and presenters	X	590.7	X	X
Dancers and choreographers	X	736.4	X	X
Musicians				
Arts officers, producers and directors	694.4	702.7	34,247	37,307
Photographers, audio-visual and broadcasting equipment operators	425.8	416.7	22,202	21,130
Design occupations	496.2	517.9	25,579	26,531
Graphic designers	474.0	482.5	24,187	24,286
Product, clothing and related designers	520.7	551.2	25,901	28,432
Sports and fitness occupations	423.7	452.0	X	20,943
Sports players				
Sports coaches, instructors and officials	432.6	459.5	X	X
Fitness instructors	388.2	429.8	18,336	21,685
Business and public service associate professionals	544.7	614.9	28,727	33,123
Transport associate professionals	X	1,242.5	X	61,286
Air traffic controllers	X	1,242.5	X	61,286
Aircraft pilots and flight engineers				
Ship and hovercraft officers				
Legal associate professionals	480.7	554.3	25,735	29,224
Legal associate professionals	480.7	554.3	25,735	29,224
Business, finance and related associate professionals	565.4	637.3	29,136	34,970

Full-time Females on adult rates (where pay was not affected by absence)

n.e.c. = not elsewhere classified X = unreliable	Gross Weekly Pay (in April) 2014		Gross Annual Pay (in April) 2014	
Occupation SOC 2010	**Median £**	**Mean £**	**Median £**	**Mean £**
Estimators, valuers and assessors	479.1	525.1	25,902	28,376
Brokers	X	991.4	X	X
Insurance underwriters	618.4	689.4	29,664	37,195
Finance and investment analysts and advisers	589.5	711.9	30,198	39,150
Taxation experts	862.1	923.5	43,869	46,755
Importers and exporters	417.9	473.9	X	X
Financial and accounting technicians	589.1	706.7	30,273	40,523
Financial accounts managers	613.8	658.0	32,025	34,994
Business and related associate professionals n.e.c.	498.3	524.2	25,782	27,673
Sales, marketing and related associate professionals	570.2	647.5	30,000	35,004
Buyers and procurement officers	535.7	576.6	27,704	30,188
Business sales executives	466.9	532.3	25,482	29,583
Marketing associate professionals	489.5	510.7	25,378	26,435
Estate agents and auctioneers	383.3	472.1	21,304	28,045
Sales accounts and business development managers	702.7	790.1	36,860	42,872
Conference and exhibition managers and organisers	473.8	504.8	24,425	27,223
Conservation and environmental associate professionals	420.3	431.7	22,106	23,455
Conservation and environmental associate professionals	420.3	431.7	22,106	23,455
Public services and other associate professionals	516.1	544.7	27,214	28,668
Public service associate professionals	524.0	551.2	27,644	28,922
Human resources and industrial relations officers	513.6	546.8	27,480	28,983
Vocational and industrial trainers and instructors	507.3	518.9	25,969	27,106
Careers advisers and vocational guidance specialists	498.0	519.5	27,750	27,214
Inspectors of standards and regulations	506.1	570.4	26,172	26,495
Health and safety officers	575.9	654.3	30,250	35,526
Administrative and secretarial occupations	394.4	430.9	20,502	22,333
Administrative occupations	394.3	431.7	20,524	22,345
Administrative occupations: Government and related organisations	416.5	440.8	21,350	22,950
National government administrative occupations	409.8	436.3	21,056	22,290
Legal government administrative occupations	427.5	440.8	22,206	22,744
Officers of non-governmental organisations	479.7	537.8	X	X
Administrative occupations: Finance	403.8	440.0	21,112	22,851
Credit controllers	395.5	418.5	20,985	22,144
Book-keepers, payroll managers and wages clerks	421.6	464.6	21,794	23,910
Bank and post office clerks	375.2	403.8	19,992	21,394
Finance officers	458.9	489.7	23,495	26,056
Financial administrative occupations n.e.c.	390.7	416.0	20,057	21,483
Administrative occupations: Records	383.3	413.4	19,798	21,495
Records clerks and assistants	375.2	410.1	19,328	21,396
Pensions and insurance clerks and assistants	372.5	413.7	19,586	21,396
Stock control clerks and assistants	381.5	410.4	19,711	21,566
Transport and distribution clerks and assistants	424.5	454.9	21,515	22,951
Library clerks and assistants	379.8	398.7	19,162	20,375
Human resources administrative occupations	388.8	401.3	20,806	20,936
Other administrative occupations	364.7	398.6	18,749	20,245
Sales administrators	376.2	397.5	19,561	20,972
Other administrative occupations n.e.c.	363.6	398.7	18,687	20,166
Administrative occupations: Office managers and supervisors	523.5	549.8	26,752	28,616
Office managers	532.5	558.6	27,433	29,113
Office supervisors	465.9	486.6	23,431	25,387
Secretarial and related occupations	394.7	428.2	20,462	22,289
Secretarial and related occupations	394.7	428.2	20,462	22,289
Medical secretaries	415.4	403.4	21,386	20,633

Full-time Females on adult rates (where pay was not affected by absence)

n.e.c. = not elsewhere classified X = unreliable	Gross Weekly Pay (in April) 2014		Gross Annual Pay (in April) 2014	
Occupation SOC 2010	**Median £**	**Mean £**	**Median £**	**Mean £**
Legal secretaries	384.3	425.6	20,000	22,398
School secretaries	381.2	407.0	19,932	20,973
Company secretaries	452.7	551.8	22,327	28,798
Personal assistants and other secretaries	477.6	503.4	24,488	26,235
Receptionists	311.6	334.0	16,174	17,095
Typists and related keyboard occupations	355.0	378.3	18,609	19,806
Skilled trades occupations	348.9	391.7	17,833	20,170
Skilled agricultural and related trades	335.6	395.3	17,894	20,453
Agricultural and related trades	335.6	395.3	17,894	20,453
Farmers	X	X	X	X
Horticultural trades	291.0	329.4	15,743	18,158
Gardeners and landscape gardeners	343.1	382.8	17,872	19,256
Groundsmen and gamekeepers	333.7	382.3	16,182	18,387
Agricultural and fishing trades n.e.c.				
Skilled metal, electrical and electronic trades	498.3	518.3	25,384	26,420
Metal forming, welding and related trades	X	X	14,073	15,092
Smiths and forge workers				
Moulders, core makers and die casters				
Sheet metal workers				
Metal plate workers, and riveters				
Welding trades				
Pipe fitters				
Metal machining, fitting and instrument making trades	411.2	488.6	22,702	25,283
Metal machining setters and setter-operators	X	421.7	X	20,349
Tool makers, tool fitters and markers-out				
Metal working production and maintenance fitters	464.4	508.4	X	26,731
Precision instrument makers and repairers	X	479.7	X	25,958
Air conditioning and refrigeration engineers				
Vehicle trades	431.5	456.6	24,029	24,829
Vehicle technicians, mechanics and electricians	429.1	410.3	X	20,288
Vehicle body builders and repairers				
Vehicle paint technicians				
Aircraft maintenance and related trades	483.6	491.7	25,705	27,127
Boat and ship builders and repairers				
Rail and rolling stock builders and repairers				
Electrical and electronic trades	520.5	559.2	X	X
Electricians and electrical fitters	472.0	534.6	23,345	26,246
Telecommunications engineers	482.9	493.4	X	24,321
TV, video and audio engineers				
IT engineers	X	612.1	X	X
Electrical and electronic trades n.e.c.	535.0	561.4	X	X
Skilled metal, electrical and electronic trades supervisors	601.1	615.9	29,643	30,404
Skilled metal, electrical and electronic trades supervisors	601.1	615.9	29,643	30,404
Skilled construction and building trades	406.4	468.0	X	25,881
Construction and building trades	414.6	486.3	X	27,159
Steel erectors				
Bricklayers and masons				
Roofers, roof tilers and slaters				
Plumbers and heating and ventilating engineers	403.6	444.5	X	25,987
Carpenters and joiners				
Glaziers, window fabricators and fitters				
Construction and building trades n.e.c.	X	557.0	X	X
Building finishing trades	352.5	367.1		
Plasterers				

Full-time Females on adult rates (where pay was not affected by absence)

n.e.c. = not elsewhere classified
X = unreliable

Occupation SOC 2010	Gross Weekly Pay (in April) 2014 Median £	Gross Weekly Pay (in April) 2014 Mean £	Gross Annual Pay (in April) 2014 Median £	Gross Annual Pay (in April) 2014 Mean £
Floorers and wall tilers				
Painters and decorators	352.5	367.1		
Construction and building trades supervisors	417.1	460.7	20,222	22,021
Construction and building trades supervisors	417.1	460.7	20,222	22,021
Textiles, printing and other skilled trades	327.3	354.6	17,073	18,081
Textiles and garments trades	312.2	348.6	14,470	16,652
Weavers and knitters				
Upholsterers	X	336.3	14,604	16,513
Footwear and leather working trades	312.2	362.3	14,322	16,523
Tailors and dressmakers	363.7	422.5		
Textiles, garments and related trades n.e.c.				
Printing trades	328.0	346.3	17,265	17,202
Pre-press technicians				
Printers	X	359.0		
Print finishing and binding workers	316.5	342.9	17,262	17,183
Food preparation and hospitality trades	328.2	353.6	17,122	18,114
Butchers	322.1	352.0	X	17,695
Bakers and flour confectioners	308.4	324.1	16,554	17,344
Fishmongers and poultry dressers	291.6	305.7	12,956	14,056
Chefs	339.1	359.2	18,709	19,018
Cooks	290.6	295.4	14,967	15,255
Catering and bar managers	374.8	398.9	18,500	19,635
Other skilled trades	344.0	379.0	17,035	19,529
Glass and ceramics makers, decorators and finishers	301.9	320.3	15,273	16,366
Furniture makers and other craft woodworkers	395.5	416.5	20,475	21,579
Florists	307.9	332.7	14,722	17,124
Other skilled trades n.e.c.	X	454.6	X	X
Caring, leisure and other service occupations	324.7	346.6	16,450	17,253
Caring personal service occupations	325.5	344.6	16,413	16,998
Childcare and related personal services	298.9	318.3	15,139	16,004
Nursery nurses and assistants	284.8	306.4	14,311	15,339
Childminders and related occupations	356.0	362.1	18,377	X
Playworkers	334.9	341.0	15,501	15,260
Teaching assistants	307.7	321.8	15,704	16,216
Educational support assistants	303.9	320.8	15,268	15,876
Animal care and control services	336.3	350.1	17,520	18,092
Veterinary nurses	363.2	371.1	17,747	18,302
Pest control officers				
Animal care services occupations n.e.c.	300.0	329.5	17,017	17,829
Caring personal services	338.2	356.9	17,090	17,459
Nursing auxiliaries and assistants	364.4	378.5	18,729	18,848
Ambulance staff (excluding paramedics)	409.2	455.2	21,498	23,457
Dental nurses	346.9	367.8	17,505	18,318
Houseparents and residential wardens	392.4	406.6	20,284	20,948
Care workers and home carers	313.7	337.1	15,426	16,080
Senior care workers	353.6	373.4	18,025	18,382
Care escorts	301.5	349.7	13,618	13,651
Undertakers, mortuary and crematorium assistants	466.4	484.0	X	25,211
Leisure, travel and related personal service occupations	317.2	360.3	16,599	18,942
Leisure and travel services	356.5	411.3	20,303	22,351
Sports and leisure assistants	289.3	326.0	16,253	17,100
Travel agents	336.2	362.3	17,873	19,763
Air travel assistants	438.9	477.0	23,984	25,778
Rail travel assistants	604.1	602.0	29,131	30,222
Leisure and travel service occupations n.e.c.	X	428.6	X	22,427
Hairdressers and related services	280.4	294.8	14,143	14,873

Full-time Females on adult rates (where pay was not affected by absence)

n.e.c. = not elsewhere classified X = unreliable	**Gross Weekly Pay (in April) 2014**		**Gross Annual Pay (in April) 2014**	
Occupation SOC 2010	**Median £**	**Mean £**	**Median £**	**Mean £**
Hairdressers and barbers	260.0	281.4	13,133	14,412
Beauticians and related occupations	297.0	312.6	X	15,668
Housekeeping and related services	314.6	339.5	16,216	17,637
Housekeepers and related occupations	297.4	318.3	15,426	16,593
Caretakers	359.0	390.9	18,646	19,950
Cleaning and housekeeping managers and supervisors	333.6	358.8	16,914	18,288
Cleaning and housekeeping managers and supervisors	333.6	358.8	16,914	18,288
Sales and customer service occupations	322.6	354.7	16,396	17,983
Sales occupations	295.1	322.3	14,814	16,087
Sales assistants and retail cashiers	282.9	309.9	14,048	15,258
Sales and retail assistants	280.0	310.1	13,765	15,102
Retail cashiers and check-out operators	268.3	279.6	13,362	13,887
Telephone salespersons	344.8	366.1	19,165	20,115
Pharmacy and other dispensing assistants	297.7	302.6	15,220	15,672
Vehicle and parts salespersons and advisers	343.1	353.6	18,019	18,915
Sales related occupations	358.3	392.6	19,016	20,902
Collector salespersons and credit agents	295.7	310.5		
Debt, rent and other cash collectors	308.3	328.2	16,196	17,537
Roundspersons and van salespersons				
Market and street traders and assistants				
Merchandisers and window dressers	421.6	440.2	21,586	23,462
Sales related occupations n.e.c.	362.3	396.1	19,735	21,000
Sales supervisors	333.7	351.7	17,178	18,060
Sales supervisors	333.7	351.7	17,178	18,060
Customer service occupations	370.1	404.6	19,533	21,100
Customer service occupations	355.3	377.0	18,661	19,537
Call and contact centre occupations	322.2	339.5	16,903	17,570
Telephonists	348.1	358.3	18,997	18,925
Communication operators	527.7	538.5	28,412	28,387
Market research interviewers	X	422.6		
Customer service occupations n.e.c.	357.4	376.6	18,631	19,476
Customer service managers and supervisors	488.0	538.3	25,549	27,951
Customer service managers and supervisors	488.0	538.3	25,549	27,951
Process, plant and machine operatives	334.3	368.8	16,843	18,552
Process, plant and machine operatives	330.5	356.8	16,628	17,741
Process operatives	320.3	340.4	15,858	16,788
Food, drink and tobacco process operatives	317.9	333.5	15,554	16,486
Glass and ceramics process operatives				
Textile process operatives	334.9	326.2	17,982	16,699
Chemical and related process operatives	348.3	381.9	18,261	18,869
Rubber process operatives				
Plastics process operatives	381.4	379.9	X	18,189
Metal making and treating process operatives				
Electroplaters				
Process operatives n.e.c.	303.7	355.9	X	15,008
Plant and machine operatives	326.7	377.4	16,829	18,654
Paper and wood machine operatives	X	375.5	X	17,802
Coal mine operatives				
Quarry workers and related operatives				
Energy plant operatives	X	X	X	X
Metal working machine operatives	326.0	349.0	16,298	17,478
Water and sewerage plant operatives	X	602.4	X	29,949
Printing machine assistants	322.2	363.9	16,833	18,661
Plant and machine operatives n.e.c.	332.3	404.5	X	17,903

Full-time Females on adult rates (where pay was not affected by absence)

n.e.c. = not elsewhere classified X = unreliable	Gross Weekly Pay (in April) 2014		Gross Annual Pay (in April) 2014	
Occupation SOC 2010	**Median £**	**Mean £**	**Median £**	**Mean £**
Assemblers and routine operatives	330.4	356.9	16,803	18,012
Assemblers (electrical and electronic products)	343.8	351.6	17,779	17,945
Assemblers (vehicles and metal goods)	374.2	456.5	20,506	23,027
Routine inspectors and testers	356.6	388.6	18,860	20,377
Weighers, graders and sorters	270.6	313.9	14,131	15,935
Tyre, exhaust and windscreen fitters				
Sewing machinists	294.0	326.7	14,596	15,514
Assemblers and routine operatives n.e.c.	327.4	344.5	16,464	17,535
Construction operatives	406.2	446.6	19,868	21,300
Scaffolders, stagers and riggers				
Road construction operatives				
Rail construction and maintenance operatives	560.4	654.3		
Construction operatives n.e.c.	400.7	429.6	19,345	20,270
Transport and mobile machine drivers and operatives	366.4	429.6	18,998	22,839
Road transport drivers	349.3	381.1	18,179	19,435
Large goods vehicle drivers	385.6	407.3	20,791	21,876
Van drivers	294.7	337.5	14,801	16,880
Bus and coach drivers	397.8	440.6	20,607	22,129
Taxi and cab drivers and chauffeurs	301.4	352.8	X	19,640
Driving instructors				
Mobile machine drivers and operatives	318.0	375.4	15,597	18,276
Crane drivers				
Fork-lift truck drivers	X	450.7	X	20,011
Agricultural machinery drivers				
Mobile machine drivers and operatives n.e.c.	278.3	299.7	14,553	15,518
Other drivers and transport operatives	756.0	719.2	42,582	40,233
Train and tram drivers	922.7	877.2	48,573	50,979
Marine and waterways transport operatives				
Air transport operatives				
Rail transport operatives	714.3	727.2	39,162	38,960
Other drivers and transport operatives n.e.c.	X	483.2	X	23,194
Elementary occupations	285.9	308.8	14,477	15,306
Elementary trades and related occupations	298.6	320.6	15,679	16,322
Elementary agricultural occupations	301.9	335.2	15,311	15,830
Farm workers	301.8	343.5	16,007	17,406
Forestry workers				
Fishing and other elementary agriculture occupations n.e.c.	297.4	326.1	X	14,337
Elementary construction occupations	341.4	361.3	18,696	20,334
Elementary process plant occupations	341.4	361.3	18,696	20,334
Elementary process plant occupations	296.4	318.1	15,537	16,304
Industrial cleaning process occupations	327.8	328.6	17,735	17,012
Packers, bottlers, canners and fillers	294.0	314.8	15,489	16,296
Elementary process plant occupations n.e.c.	293.5	323.7	15,057	16,188
Elementary administration and service occupations	283.2	306.8	14,264	15,125
Elementary administration occupations	340.5	366.1	18,313	19,205
Postal workers, mail sorters, messengers and couriers	417.7	414.7	21,916	21,791
Elementary administration occupations n.e.c.	275.3	289.8	13,960	14,396
Elementary cleaning occupations	268.3	286.6	13,410	13,719
Window cleaners				
Street cleaners				
Cleaners and domestics	268.5	286.3	13,320	13,596
Launderers, dry cleaners and pressers	255.7	279.8	13,395	14,201
Refuse and salvage occupations	367.7	362.8	18,877	18,525
Vehicle valeters and cleaners	288.7	284.3	15,262	14,705
Elementary cleaning occupations n.e.c.	288.4	316.8	X	18,355
Elementary security occupations	401.9	430.7	21,382	22,698

Full-time Females on adult rates (where pay was not affected by absence)

n.e.c. = not elsewhere classified
X = unreliable

Occupation SOC 2010	Gross Weekly Pay (in April) 2014 Median £	Gross Weekly Pay (in April) 2014 Mean £	Gross Annual Pay (in April) 2014 Median £	Gross Annual Pay (in April) 2014 Mean £
Security guards and related occupations	413.5	450.2	22,526	23,722
Parking and civil enforcement occupations	397.4	421.0	20,464	21,558
School midday and crossing patrol occupations	305.2	343.9	15,726	17,424
Elementary security occupations n.e.c.	374.9	400.7	19,566	21,118
Elementary sales occupations	301.9	318.4	15,479	15,796
Shelf fillers	301.1	317.0	15,323	15,658
Elementary sales occupations n.e.c.	341.9	349.5	17,256	19,015
Elementary storage occupations	312.7	343.5	16,355	16,744
Elementary storage occupations	312.7	343.5	16,355	16,744
Other elementary services occupations	261.4	273.6	12,811	13,084
Hospital porters	332.2	402.8	16,747	19,342
Kitchen and catering assistants	267.2	278.8	13,154	13,398
Waiters and waitresses	254.3	266.2	12,092	12,024
Bar staff	249.4	259.7	12,499	12,423
Leisure and theme park attendants	275.9	276.4	14,797	14,053
Other elementary services occupations n.e.c.	245.1	261.7	12,646	12,943
Not Classified				

Source: Annual Survey of Hours and Earnings, Office for National Statistics, Tables 14.1a and 14.7a.

F8: Public sector comparable earnings

In the table below we show gross salary ranges and compare with equivalent gross salaries in the public sector

Gross salary range From (£)	To (£)	Comparable gross salaries
10,000	14,999	National minimum wage (adults, 39 hours per week) £13,182; Army (new entrants) £14,637
15,000	19,999	Porter or Cook (NHS, B) £15,100; Porter or Cook (NHS, T) £17,800; Army Private (B) £18,125
20,000	24,999	Nurse (newly qualified, B) £21,692; Teacher (newly qualified, B) £22,023; Trainee Hospital Doctor (B) £22,636
25,000	29,999	Trainee Hospital Doctor (T) £25,461; Nurse Team Leader (B) £26,041; Army Private (T) £27,324; Army Corporal (B) £27,324; NHS Registrar (B) £28,076; Nurse (non-specialist, T) £28,180
30,000	34,999	Army Sergeant (B) £31,058; Teacher (main pay scale, T) £32,187; Dean £33,780; Bishop (B) £33,780; Army Corporal (T) £34,338; Army Staff Sergeant (B) £34,380; Teacher (upper scale, B) £34,869; Nurse Team Leader (T) £34,876
35,000	39,999	Warrant Officer 2 (B) £37,304; Teacher (upper scale, T) £37,496; Army Sergeant (T) £38,215; Army Captain (B) £39,236; Warrant Officer 1 (B) £39,944
40,000	44,999	Bishop (T) £41,410; Head Teacher (B) £43,232; Army Staff Sergeant (T) £43,508; Warrant Officer 2 (T) £44,758
45,000	49,999	Army Captain (T) £46,660; NHS Registrar (T) £47,175; Warrant Officer 1 (T) £48,381; Major (B) £49,424
50,000	59,999	Teacher (advanced skills, T) £58,096; Major (T) £59,191; Bishop of London £59,920
60,000	69,999	Archbishop of York £65,370; MP £67,060; Lieutenant Colonel (B) £69,366
70,000	79,999	NHS Consultant (B) £75,249; Archbishop of Canterbury £76,280
80,000	99,999	Lieutenant Colonel (T) £80,320; Colonel (B) £84,037; Colonel (T) £92,381; Minister of State £98,740
100,000	119,999	Brigadier (T) £100,146; NHS Consultant (excluding clinical excellence awards, T) £101,451; GP (Primary Medical Services contact, A) £102,000; Brigadier (T) £104,198; District Judge £106,040; Head Teacher (T) £107,210; Major General (B) £111,567
120,000	139,999	Major General (T) £122,914; Lieutenant General (B) £129,811; Circuit Judge and Senior District Judge £132,184; Cabinet Minister £134,565
140,000	159,999	Permanent Secretary (B) £142,000; Prime Minister £142,500; Senior Circuit Judge £142,745; Lieutenant General (T) £157,355; Chief Executive, Health & Safety Executive (M) £157,500
160,000	179,999	General (B) £170,292; NHS Consultant (including maximum clinical excellence awards, T) £177,247; High Court Judge £177,988
180,000	199,999	General (T) £190,795; Government Actuary (M) £197,500; Director of Public Prosecutions (M) £197,500
200,000	219,999	Permanent Secretary (T) £200,000; Lord Justice of Appeal £202,668; Supreme Court Justice & Family Division President £213,125
220,000	and over	Master of the Rolls £220,655; Lord Chief Justice £247,112; Chief of Defence Staff (M) £247,500; Chief Executive, Nuclear Decommissioning Authority (M) £277,500; Chief Executive, Civil Aviation Authority (M) £302,500; Chief Executive, Green Investment Bank (M) £327,500

Notes: All categories are subject to varying terms and conditions. (A), (B) and (T) indicate average, bottom and top of range or seniority for post or rank. (M) indicates midpoint of published £5,000 pay band, including taxable benefits and allowances

F9: Public sector earnings websites

Websites and other sources that provide helpful information about pay and retirement benefits in the public sector include:

Sector/ annual review date	Sources of information
Armed forces (April 1)	*http://www.army.mod.uk* *http://www.royalnavy.mod.uk* *http://www.raf.mod.uk*
Health service (April 1)	*http://www.nhscareers.nhs.co.uk* *http://www.nhsemployers.org*
Police (September 1)	*http://www.police-information.co.uk*
Teachers (September 1)	*http://www.teachers.org.uk* *http://www.atl.org.uk*
Local government (April 1)	*http://www.navca.org.uk* [National Association for Voluntary and Community Action] *http://www.lgps.org.uk* [Local Government Pension Scheme]
Civil service (April 1)	*http://www.civilservice.gov.uk*

Group G

Tax and National Insurance

G

G1: Net equivalents to a range of gross annual income figures

	2004/05 Net equivalent income		2005/06 Net equivalent income		2006/07 Net equivalent income	
	Employed	Self-employed	Employed	Self-employed	Employed	Self-employed
Gross income £pa	£pa	£pa	£pa	£pa	£pa	£pa
1,000	1,000	1,000	1,000	1,000	1,000	1,000
2,000	2,000	2,000	2,000	2,000	2,000	2,000
3,000	3,000	3,000	3,000	3,000	3,000	3,000
4,000	4,000	4,000	4,000	4,000	4,000	4,000
5,000	4,946	4,847	4,977	4,872	5,000	4,891
6,000	5,736	5,667	5,767	5,692	5,797	5,717
7,000	6,498	6,459	6,556	6,511	6,587	6,537
8,000	7,168	7,159	7,226	7,211	7,280	7,260
9,000	7,838	7,859	7,896	7,911	7,950	7,960
10,000	8,508	8,559	8,566	8,611	8,620	8,660
11,000	9,178	9,259	9,236	9,311	9,290	9,360
12,000	9,848	9,959	9,906	10,011	9,960	10,060
13,000	10,518	10,659	10,576	10,711	10,630	10,760
14,000	11,188	11,359	11,246	11,411	11,300	11,460
15,000	11,858	12,059	11,916	12,111	11,970	12,160
16,000	12,528	12,759	12,586	12,811	12,640	12,860
17,000	13,198	13,459	13,256	13,511	13,310	13,560
18,000	13,868	14,159	13,926	14,211	13,980	14,260
19,000	14,538	14,859	14,596	14,911	14,650	14,960
20,000	15,208	15,559	15,266	15,611	15,320	15,660
21,000	15,878	16,259	15,936	16,311	15,990	16,360
22,000	16,548	16,959	16,606	17,011	16,660	17,060
23,000	17,218	17,659	17,276	17,711	17,330	17,760
24,000	17,888	18,359	17,946	18,411	18,000	18,460
25,000	18,558	19,059	18,616	19,111	18,670	19,160
26,000	19,228	19,759	19,286	19,811	19,340	19,860
27,000	19,898	20,459	19,956	20,511	20,010	20,560
28,000	20,568	21,159	20,626	21,211	20,680	21,260
29,000	21,238	21,859	21,296	21,911	21,350	21,960
30,000	21,908	22,559	21,966	22,611	22,020	22,660
31,000	22,578	23,259	22,636	23,311	22,690	23,360
32,000	23,276	23,979	23,306	24,011	23,360	24,060
33,000	24,046	24,749	23,976	24,728	24,030	24,760
34,000	24,816	25,519	24,646	25,498	24,746	25,492
35,000	25,586	26,288	25,541	26,268	25,516	26,262
40,000	28,742	29,444	28,904	29,631	29,066	29,812
45,000	31,692	32,394	31,854	32,581	32,016	32,762
50,000	34,642	35,344	34,804	35,531	34,966	35,712
55,000	37,592	38,294	37,754	38,481	37,916	38,662
60,000	40,542	41,244	40,704	41,431	40,866	41,612
65,000	43,492	44,194	43,654	44,381	43,816	44,562
70,000	46,442	47,144	46,604	47,331	46,766	47,512
75,000	49,392	50,094	49,554	50,281	49,716	50,462
80,000	52,342	53,044	52,504	53,231	52,666	53,412
85,000	55,292	55,994	55,454	56,181	55,616	56,362
90,000	58,242	58,944	58,404	59,131	58,566	59,312
95,000	61,192	61,894	61,354	62,081	61,516	62,262
100,000	64,142	64,844	64,304	65,031	64,466	65,212
150,000	93,642	94,344	93,804	94,531	93,966	94,712
200,000	123,142	123,844	123,304	124,031	123,466	124,212
250,000	152,642	153,344	152,804	153,531	152,966	153,712
300,000	182,142	182,844	182,304	183,031	182,466	183,212

G1: Net equivalents to a range of gross annual income figures

Gross income £pa	2007/08 Employed Net equivalent income £pa	Net per £100 extra £pa	Reason
1,000	1,000	100	
2,000	2,000	100	
3,000	3,000	100	
4,000	4,000	100	
5,000	5,000	100	
5,225	*5,225*	*79*	← *10% tax payable and 11% NIC Class 1 payable*
6,000	5,837	79	
7,000	6,627	79	
7,455	*6,986*	*67*	← *22% tax payable*
8,000	7,352	67	
9,000	8,022	67	
10,000	8,692	67	
11,000	9,362	67	
12,000	10,032	67	
13,000	10,702	67	
14,000	11,372	67	
15,000	12,042	67	
16,000	12,712	67	
17,000	13,382	67	
18,000	14,052	67	
19,000	14,722	67	
20,000	15,392	67	
21,000	16,062	67	
22,000	16,732	67	
23,000	17,402	67	
24,000	18,072	67	
25,000	18,742	67	
26,000	19,412	67	
27,000	20,082	67	
28,000	20,752	67	
29,000	21,422	67	
30,000	22,092	67	
31,000	22,762	67	
32,000	23,432	67	
33,000	24,102	67	
34,000	24,772	67	
34,840	*25,335*	*77*	← *NIC Class 1 reduced to 1%*
35,000	25,458	77	
37,500	27,382	77	
39,825	*29,172*	*59*	← *40% tax payable*
40,000	29,276	59	
45,000	32,226	59	
50,000	35,176	59	
55,000	38,126	59	
60,000	41,076	59	
65,000	44,026	59	
70,000	46,976	59	
75,000	49,926	59	
80,000	52,876	59	
85,000	55,826	59	
90,000	58,776	59	
95,000	61,726	59	
100,000	64,676	59	
150,000	94,176	59	
200,000	123,676	59	
250,000	153,176	59	
300,000	182,676	59	

Gross income £pa	2007/08 Self–employed Net equivalent income £pa	Net per £100 extra £pa	Reason
1,000	1,000	100	
2,000	2,000	100	
4,000	4,000	100	
4,635	*4,635*	*	← *£114 NIC Class 2 payable*
5,000	4,886	*	
5,225	*5,111*	*82*	← *10% tax payable and 8% NIC Class 4 payable*
6,000	5,747	82	
7,000	6,567	82	
7,455	*6,940*	*70*	← *22% tax payable*
8,000	7,321	70	
9,000	8,021	70	
10,000	8,721	70	
11,000	9,421	70	
12,000	10,121	70	
13,000	10,821	70	
14,000	11,521	70	
15,000	12,221	70	
16,000	12,921	70	
17,000	13,621	70	
18,000	14,321	70	
19,000	15,021	70	
20,000	15,721	70	
21,000	16,421	70	
22,000	17,121	70	
23,000	17,821	70	
24,000	18,521	70	
25,000	19,221	70	
26,000	19,921	70	
27,000	20,621	70	
28,000	21,321	70	
29,000	22,021	70	
30,000	22,721	70	
31,000	23,421	70	
32,000	24,121	70	
33,000	24,821	70	
34,000	25,521	70	
34,840	*26,109*	*77*	← *NIC Class 4 reduced to 1%*
35,000	26,233	77	
37,500	28,157	77	
39,825	*29,947*	*59*	← *40% tax payable*
40,000	30,051	59	
45,000	33,001	59	
50,000	35,951	59	
55,000	38,901	59	
60,000	41,851	59	
65,000	44,801	59	
70,000	47,751	59	
75,000	50,701	59	
80,000	53,651	59	
85,000	56,601	59	
90,000	59,551	59	
95,000	62,501	59	
100,000	65,451	59	
150,000	94,951	59	
200,000	124,451	59	
250,000	153,951	59	
300,000	183,451	59	

**£2.20 x 52 weeks =£114 pa fixed for any level of income in excess of £4,635 pa. So net equivalent of £4,650 gross is £4,536.*

2008/09 — Employed

Gross income £pa	Net equivalent income £pa	Net per £100 extra £pa	Reason
1,000	1,000	100	
2,000	2,000	100	
3,000	3,000	100	
4,000	4,000	100	
5,000	5,000	100	
5,435	*5,435*	*89*	*← 11% NIC Class 1 payable*
6,000	5,938	89	
6,035	*5,969*	*69*	*← 20% tax payable*
7,000	6,635	69	
8,000	7,325	69	
9,000	8,015	69	
10,000	8,705	69	
11,000	9,395	69	
12,000	10,085	69	
13,000	10,775	69	
14,000	11,465	69	
15,000	12,155	69	
16,000	12,845	69	
17,000	13,535	69	
18,000	14,225	69	
19,000	14,915	69	
20,000	15,605	69	
21,000	16,295	69	
22,000	16,985	69	
23,000	17,675	69	
24,000	18,365	69	
25,000	19,055	69	
26,000	19,745	69	
27,000	20,435	69	
28,000	21,125	69	
29,000	21,815	69	
30,000	22,505	69	
31,000	23,195	69	
32,000	23,885	69	
33,000	24,575	69	
34,000	25,265	69	
35,000	25,955	69	
37,500	27,680	69	
40,000	29,405	69	
40,040	*29,432*	*79*	*← NIC Class 1 reduced to 1%*
40,835	*30,060*	*59*	*← 40% tax payable*
45,000	32,518	59	
50,000	35,468	59	
55,000	38,418	59	
60,000	41,368	59	
65,000	44,138	59	
70,000	47,268	59	
75,000	50,218	59	
80,000	53,168	59	
85,000	56,118	59	
90,000	59,068	59	
95,000	62,018	59	
100,000	64,968	59	
150,000	94,468	59	
200,000	123,968	59	
250,000	153,468	59	
300,000	182,968	59	

2008/09 — Self-employed

Gross income £pa	Net equivalent income £pa	Net per £100 extra £pa	Reason
1,000	1,000	100	
2,000	2,000	100	
4,000	4,000	100	
4,825	*4,825*	*	*← £120 NIC Class 2 payable*
5,000	4,880	100	
5,435	*5,315*	*92*	*←8% NIC Class 4 payable*
6,000	5,835	92	
6,035	*5,867*	*72*	*← 20% tax payable*
7,000	6,562	72	
8,000	7,282	72	
9,000	8,002	72	
10,000	8,722	72	
11,000	9,442	72	**£2.30 x 52 weeks =£120 pa fixed for any level of income in excess of £4,825 pa. So net equivalent of £4,850 gross is £4,730.*
12,000	10,162	72	
13,000	10,882	72	
14,000	11,602	72	
15,000	12,322	72	
16,000	13,042	72	
17,000	13,762	72	
18,000	14,482	72	
19,000	15,202	72	
20,000	15,922	72	
21,000	16,642	72	
22,000	17,362	72	
23,000	18,082	72	
24,000	18,802	72	
25,000	19,522	72	
26,000	20,242	72	
27,000	20,962	72	
28,000	21,682	72	
29,000	22,402	72	
30,000	23,122	72	
31,000	23,842	72	
32,000	24,562	72	
33,000	25,282	72	
34,000	26,002	72	
35,000	26,722	72	
37,500	28,522	72	
40,000	30,322	72	
40,040	*30,351*	*79*	*← NIC Class 4 reduced to 1%*
40,835	*30,979*	*59*	*← 40% tax payable*
45,000	33,436	59	
50,000	36,386	59	
55,000	39,336	59	
60,000	42,286	59	
65,000	45,236	59	
70,000	48,186	59	
75,000	51,136	59	
80,000	54,086	59	
85,000	57,036	59	
90,000	59,986	59	
95,000	62,936	59	
100,000	65,886	59	
150,000	95,386	59	
200,000	124,886	59	
250,000	154,386	59	
300,000	183,886	59	

G1: Net equivalents to a range of gross annual income figures

	2009/10 Employed		
	Net equivalent income	Net per £100 extra	Reason
Gross income £pa	£pa	£pa	
1,000	1,000	100	
2,000	2,000	100	
3,000	3,000	100	
4,000	4,000	100	
5,000	5,000	100	
5,715	*5,715*	*89*	*← 11% NIC Class 1 payable*
6,000	5,969	89	
6,475	*6,391*	*69*	*← 20% tax payable*
7,000	6,754	69	
8,000	7,444	69	
9,000	8,134	69	
10,000	8,824	69	
11,000	9,514	69	
12,000	10,204	69	
13,000	10,894	69	
14,000	11,584	69	
15,000	12,274	69	
16,000	12,964	69	
17,000	13,654	69	
18,000	14,344	69	
19,000	15,034	69	
20,000	15,724	69	
21,000	16,414	69	
22,000	17,104	69	
23,000	17,794	69	
24,000	18,484	69	
25,000	19,174	69	
26,000	19,864	69	
27,000	20,554	69	
28,000	21,244	69	
29,000	21,934	69	
30,000	22,624	69	
31,000	23,314	69	
32,000	24,004	69	
33,000	24,694	69	
34,000	25,384	69	
35,000	26,074	69	
37,500	27,799	69	
40,000	29,524	69	
43,875	*32,197*	*59*	*← NIC Class 1 reduced to 1% and 40% tax payable*
45,000	32,861	59	
50,000	35,811	59	
55,000	38,761	59	
60,000	41,711	59	
65,000	44,661	59	
70,000	47,611	59	
75,000	50,561	59	
80,000	53,511	59	
85,000	56,461	59	
90,000	59,411	59	
95,000	62,361	59	
100,000	65,311	59	
150,000	94,811	59	
200,000	124,311	59	
250,000	153,811	59	
300,000	183,311	59	

	2009/10 Self-employed		
	Net equivalent income	Net per £100 extra	Reason
Gross income £pa	£pa	£pa	
1,000	1,000	100	
2,000	2,000	100	
3,000	3,000	100	
4,000	4,000	100	
5,075	*5,075*	*	*← £125 NIC Class 2 payable*
5,715	*5,590*	*92*	*← 8% NIC Class 4 payable*
6,000	5,852	92	
6,475	*6,289*	*72*	*← 20% tax payable*
7,000	6,667	72	
8,000	7,387	72	
9,000	8,107	72	**£2.40 x 52 weeks =£125 pa fixed for any level of income in excess of £5,075 pa. So net equivalent of £5,100 gross is £4,975.*
10,000	8,827	72	
11,000	9,547	72	
12,000	10,267	72	
13,000	10,987	72	
14,000	11,707	72	
15,000	12,427	72	
16,000	13,147	72	
17,000	13,867	72	
18,000	14,587	72	
19,000	15,307	72	
20,000	16,027	72	
21,000	16,747	72	
22,000	17,467	72	
23,000	18,187	72	
24,000	18,907	72	
25,000	19,627	72	
26,000	20,347	72	
27,000	21,067	72	
28,000	21,787	72	
29,000	22,507	72	
30,000	23,227	72	
31,000	23,947	72	
32,000	24,667	72	
33,000	25,387	72	
34,000	26,107	72	
35,000	26,827	72	
37,500	28,627	72	
40,000	30,427	72	
43,875	*33,217*	*59*	*← NIC Class 4 reduced to 1% and 40% tax payable*
45,000	33,881	59	
50,000	36,831	59	
55,000	39,781	59	
60,000	42,731	59	
65,000	45,681	59	
70,000	48,631	59	
75,000	51,581	59	
80,000	54,531	59	
85,000	57,481	59	
90,000	60,431	59	
95,000	63,381	59	
100,000	66,331	59	
150,000	95,831	59	
200,000	125,331	59	
250,000	154,831	59	
300,000	184,331	59	

	2010/11 Employed		
	Net equivalent income	Net per £100 extra	Reason
Gross income £pa	£pa	£pa	
1,000	1,000	100	
2,000	2,000	100	
3,000	3,000	100	
4,000	4,000	100	
5,000	5,000	100	
5,715	*5,715*	*89*	*← 11% NIC Class 1 payable*
6,000	5,969	89	
6,475	*6,391*	*69*	*← 20% tax payable*
7,000	6,754	69	
8,000	7,444	69	
9,000	8,134	69	
10,000	8,824	69	
11,000	9,514	69	
12,000	10,204	69	
13,000	10,894	69	
14,000	11,584	69	
15,000	12,274	69	
16,000	12,964	69	
17,000	13,654	69	
18,000	14,344	69	
19,000	15,034	69	
20,000	15,724	69	
21,000	16,414	69	
22,000	17,104	69	
23,000	17,794	69	
24,000	18,484	69	
25,000	19,174	69	
26,000	19,864	69	
27,000	20,554	69	
28,000	21,244	69	
29,000	21,934	69	
30,000	22,624	69	
31,000	23,314	69	
32,000	24,004	69	
33,000	24,694	69	
34,000	25,384	69	
35,000	26,074	69	
37,500	27,799	69	
40,000	29,524	69	
43,875	*32,197*	*59*	*← NIC Class 1 reduced to 1% and 40% tax payable*
45,000	32,861	59	
50,000	35,811	59	
55,000	38,761	59	
60,000	41,711	59	
65,000	44,661	59	
70,000	47,611	59	
75,000	50,561	59	
80,000	53,511	59	
85,000	56,461	59	
90,000	59,411	59	
95,000	62,361	59	
100,000	*65,311*	*39*	*← PA reduces here*
112,950	*70,362*	*59*	*← PA reduced to zero*
150,000	*92,221*	*49*	*← 50% tax payable*
200,000	116,721	49	
250,000	141,221	49	
300,000	165,721	49	

	2010/11 Self-employed		
	Net equivalent income	Net per £100 extra	Reason
Gross income £pa	£pa	£pa	
1,000	1,000	100	
2,000	2,000	100	
3,000	3,000	100	
4,000	4,000	100	
5,075	*5,075*	*	*← £125 NIC Class 2 payable*
5,715	*5,590*	*92*	*← 8% NIC Class 4 payable*
6,000	5,852	92	
6,475	*6,289*	*72*	*← 20% tax payable*
7,000	6,667	72	
8,000	7,387	72	
9,000	8,107	72	** £2.40 x 52 weeks = £125 pa fixed for any level of income in excess of £5,075 pa. So net equivalent of £5,100 gross is £4,975.*
10,000	8,827	72	
11,000	9,547	72	
12,000	10,267	72	
13,000	10,987	72	
14,000	11,707	72	
15,000	12,427	72	
16,000	13,147	72	
17,000	13,867	72	
18,000	14,587	72	
19,000	15,307	72	
20,000	16,027	72	
21,000	16,747	72	
22,000	17,467	72	
23,000	18,187	72	
24,000	18,907	72	
25,000	19,627	72	
26,000	20,347	72	
27,000	21,067	72	
28,000	21,787	72	
29,000	22,507	72	
30,000	23,227	72	
31,000	23,947	72	
32,000	24,667	72	
33,000	25,387	72	
34,000	26,107	72	
35,000	26,827	72	
37,500	28,627	72	
40,000	30,427	72	
43,875	*33,217*	*59*	*← NIC Class 4 reduced to 1% and 40% tax payable*
45,000	33,881	59	
50,000	36,831	59	
55,000	39,781	59	
60,000	42,731	59	
65,000	45,681	59	
70,000	48,631	59	
75,000	51,581	59	
80,000	54,531	59	
85,000	57,481	59	
90,000	60,431	59	
95,000	63,381	59	
100,000	*66,331*	*39*	*← PA reduces here*
112,950	*71,381*	*59*	*← PA reduced to zero*
150,000	*93,241*	*49*	*← 50% tax payable*
200,000	117,741	49	
250,000	142,241	49	
300,000	166,741	49	

G1: Net equivalents to a range of gross annual income figures

	2011/12		
	Employed		
	Net equivalent income	Net per £100 extra	Reason
Gross income £pa	£pa	£pa	
1,000	1,000	100	
2,000	2,000	100	
3,000	3,000	100	
4,000	4,000	100	
5,000	5,000	100	
6,000	6,000	100	
7,000	7,000	100	
7,225	*7,225*	*88*	*← 12% NIC Class 1 payable*
7,475	*7,445*	*68*	*← 20% tax payable*
8,000	7,802	68	
9,000	8,482	68	
10,000	9,162	68	
11,000	9,842	68	
12,000	10,522	68	
13,000	11,202	68	
14,000	11,882	68	
15,000	12,562	68	
16,000	13,242	68	
17,000	13,922	68	
18,000	14,602	68	
19,000	15,282	68	
20,000	15,962	68	
21,000	16,642	68	
22,000	17,322	68	
23,000	18,002	68	
24,000	18,682	68	
25,000	19,362	68	
26,000	20,042	68	
27,000	20,722	68	
28,000	21,402	68	
29,000	22,082	68	
30,000	22,762	68	
31,000	23,442	68	
32,000	24,122	68	
33,000	24,802	68	
34,000	25,482	68	
35,000	26,162	68	
37,500	27,862	68	
40,000	29,562	68	
42,475	*31,245*	*58*	*← NIC Class 1 reduced to 2% and 40% tax payable*
45,000	32,709	58	
50,000	35,609	58	
55,000	38,509	58	
60,000	41,409	58	
65,000	44,309	58	
70,000	47,209	58	
75,000	50,109	58	
80,000	53,009	58	
85,000	55,909	58	
90,000	58,809	58	
95,000	61,709	58	
100,000	*64,609*	*38*	*← PA reduces here*
114,950	*70,290*	*58*	*← PA reduced to zero*
150,000	*90,619*	*48*	*← 50% tax payable*
200,000	114,619	48	
250,000	138,619	48	
300,000	162,619	48	

	2011/12		
	Self-employed		
	Net equivalent income	Net per £100 extra	Reason
Gross income £pa	£pa	£pa	
1,000	1,000	100	
2,000	2,000	100	
3,000	3,000	100	
4,000	4,000	100	
5,315	*5,315*	*	*← £130 NIC Class 2 payable*
6,000	5,870	*	
7,000	6,870	*	
7,225	*7,095*	*91*	*← 9% NIC Class 4 payable*
7,475	*7,322*	*71*	*← 20% tax payable*
8,000	7,695	71	
9,000	8,405	71	** £2.50 x 52 weeks = £130 pa fixed for any level of income in excess of £5,315 pa. So net equivalent of £5,400 gross is £5,270.*
10,000	9,115	71	
11,000	9,825	71	
12,000	10,535	71	
13,000	11,245	71	
14,000	11,955	71	
15,000	12,665	71	
16,000	13,375	71	
17,000	14,085	71	
18,000	14,795	71	
19,000	15,505	71	
20,000	16,215	71	
21,000	16,925	71	
22,000	17,635	71	
23,000	18,345	71	
24,000	19,055	71	
25,000	19,765	71	
26,000	20,475	71	
27,000	21,185	71	
28,000	21,895	71	
29,000	22,605	71	
30,000	23,315	71	
31,000	24,025	71	
32,000	24,735	71	
33,000	25,445	71	
34,000	26,155	71	
35,000	26,865	71	
37,500	28,640	71	
40,000	30,415	71	
42,475	*32,172*	*58*	*← NIC Class 4 reduced to 2% and 40% tax payable*
45,000	33,636	58	
50,000	36,536	58	
55,000	39,436	58	
60,000	42,336	58	
65,000	45,236	58	
70,000	48,136	58	
75,000	51,036	58	
80,000	53,936	58	
85,000	56,836	58	
90,000	59,736	58	
95,000	62,636	58	
100,000	*65,536*	*38*	*← PA reduces here*
114,950	*71,217*	*58*	*← PA reduced to zero*
150,000	*91,546*	*48*	*← 50% tax payable*
200,000	115,546	48	
250,000	139,546	48	
300,000	163,546	48	

	2012/13		
	Employed		
Gross income	Net equivalent income	Net per £100 extra	Reason
£pa	£pa	£pa	
1,000	1,000	100	
2,000	2,000	100	
3,000	3,000	100	
4,000	4,000	100	
5,000	5,000	100	
6,000	6,000	100	
7,000	7,000	100	
7,605	*7,605*	*88*	← 12% NIC Class 1 payable
8,000	7,953	88	
8,105	*8,045*	*68*	← 20% tax payable
9,000	8,654	68	
10,000	9,334	68	
11,000	10,014	68	
12,000	10,694	68	
13,000	11,374	68	
14,000	12,054	68	
15,000	12,734	68	
16,000	13,414	68	
17,000	14,094	68	
18,000	14,774	68	
19,000	15,454	68	
20,000	16,134	68	
21,000	16,814	68	
22,000	17,494	68	
23,000	18,174	68	
24,000	18,854	68	
25,000	19,534	68	
26,000	20,214	68	
27,000	20,894	68	
28,000	21,574	68	
29,000	22,254	68	
30,000	22,934	68	
31,000	23,614	68	
32,000	24,294	68	
33,000	24,974	68	
34,000	25,654	68	
35,000	26,334	68	
37,500	28,034	68	
40,000	29,734	68	
42,475	*31,417*	*58*	← NIC Class 1 reduced to 2% and 40% tax payable
45,000	32,881	58	
50,000	35,781	58	
55,000	38,681	58	
60,000	41,581	58	
65,000	44,481	58	
70,000	47,381	58	
75,000	50,281	58	
80,000	53,181	58	
85,000	56,081	58	
90,000	58,981	58	
95,000	61,881	58	
100,000	*64,781*	*38*	← PA reduces here
116,210	*70,941*	*58*	← PA reduced to zero
150,000	*90,539*	*48*	← 50% tax payable
200,000	114,539	48	
250,000	138,539	48	
300,000	162,539	48	

	2012/13		
	Self-employed		
Gross income	Net equivalent income	Net per £100 extra	Reason
£pa	£pa	£pa	
1,000	1,000		
2,000	2,000		
3,000	3,000		
4,000	4,000		
5,595	*5,595*	*	← £130 NIC Class 2 payable
6,000	5,862	*	
7,000	6,862	*	
7,605	*7,467*	*91*	← 9% NIC Class 4 payable
8,000	7,826	91	
8,105	*7,922*	*71*	← 20% tax payable
9,000	8,557	71	* £2.65 x 52 weeks = £138 pa fixed for any level of income in excess of £5,595 pa. So net equivalent of £5,600 gross is £5,462.
10,000	9,267	71	
11,000	9,977	71	
12,000	10,687	71	
13,000	11,397	71	
14,000	12,107	71	
15,000	12,817	71	
16,000	13,527	71	
17,000	14,237	71	
18,000	14,947	71	
19,000	15,657	71	
20,000	16,367	71	
21,000	17,077	71	
22,000	17,787	71	
23,000	18,497	71	
24,000	19,207	71	
25,000	19,917	71	
26,000	20,627	71	
27,000	21,337	71	
28,000	22,047	71	
29,000	22,757	71	
30,000	23,467	71	
31,000	24,177	71	
32,000	24,887	71	
33,000	25,597	71	
34,000	26,307	71	
35,000	27,017	71	
37,500	28,792	71	
40,000	30,567	71	
42,475	*32,325*	*58*	← NIC Class 4 reduced to 2% and 40% tax payable
45,000	33,789	58	
50,000	36,689	58	
55,000	39,589	58	
60,000	42,489	58	
65,000	45,389	58	
70,000	48,289	58	
75,000	51,189	58	
80,000	54,089	58	
85,000	56,989	58	
90,000	59,889	58	
95,000	62,789	58	
100,000	*65,689*	*38*	← PA reduces here
116,210	*71,849*	*58*	← PA reduced to zero
150,000	*91,447*	*48*	← 50% tax payable
200,000	115,447	48	
250,000	139,447	48	
300,000	163,447	48	

G1: Net equivalents to a range of gross annual income figures

Gross income £pa	2013/14 Employed — Net equivalent income £pa	Net per £100 extra £pa	Reason
1,000	1,000	100	
2,000	2,000	100	
3,000	3,000	100	
4,000	4,000	100	
5,000	5,000	100	
6,000	6,000	100	
7,000	7,000	100	
7,755	*7,755*	*88*	*← 12% NIC Class 1 payable*
8,000	7,971	88	
9,000	8,851	*88*	
9,440	*9,238*	*68*	*← 20% tax payable*
10,000	9,619	68	
11,000	10,299	68	
12,000	10,979	68	
13,000	11,659	68	
14,000	12,339	68	
15,000	13,019	68	
16,000	13,699	68	
17,000	14,379	68	
18,000	15,059	68	
19,000	15,739	68	
20,000	16,419	68	
21,000	17,099	68	
22,000	17,779	68	
23,000	18,459	68	
24,000	19,139	68	
25,000	19,819	68	
26,000	20,499	68	
27,000	21,179	68	
28,000	21,859	68	
29,000	22,539	68	
30,000	23,219	68	
31,000	23,899	68	
32,000	24,579	68	
33,000	25,259	68	
34,000	25,939	68	
35,000	26,619	68	
37,500	28,319	68	
40,000	30,019	68	
41,450	*31,005*	*58*	*← NIC Class 1 reduced to 2% and 40% tax payable*
45,000	33,064	58	
50,000	35,964	58	
55,000	38,864	58	
60,000	41,764	58	
65,000	44,664	58	
70,000	47,564	58	
75,000	50,464	58	
80,000	53,364	58	
85,000	56,264	58	
90,000	59,164	58	
95,000	62,064	58	
100,000	64,964	*38*	*← PA reduces here*
118,880	*72,138*	*58*	*← PA reduced to zero*
150,000	*90,188*	*53*	*← 45% tax payable*
200,000	116,688	53	
250,000	143,188	53	
300,000	169,688	53	

Gross income £pa	2013/14 Self-employed — Net equivalent income £pa	Net per £100 extra £pa	Reason
1,000	1,000		
2,000	2,000		
3,000	3,000		
4,000	4,000		
5,725	*5,725*	*	*← £140 NIC Class 2 payable*
6,000	5,860	*	
7,000	6,860	*	
7,755	*7,615*	*91*	*← 9% NIC Class 4 payable*
8,000	7,838	91	
9,000	8,748	91	
9,440	*9,148*	*71*	*← 20% tax payable*
10,000	9,546	71	** £2.70 x 52 weeks = £140 pa fixed for any level of income in excess of £5,725 pa. So net equivalent of £6,100 gross is £5,960.*
11,000	10,256	71	
12,000	10,966	71	
13,000	11,676	71	
14,000	12,386	71	
15,000	13,096	71	
16,000	13,806	71	
17,000	14,516	71	
18,000	15,226	71	
19,000	15,936	71	
20,000	16,646	71	
21,000	17,356	71	
22,000	18,066	71	
23,000	18,776	71	
24,000	19,486	71	
25,000	20,196	71	
26,000	20,906	71	
27,000	21,616	71	
28,000	22,326	71	
29,000	23,036	71	
30,000	23,746	71	
31,000	24,456	71	
32,000	25,166	71	
33,000	25,876	71	
34,000	26,586	71	
35,000	27,296	71	
37,500	29,071	71	
40,000	30,846	71	
41,450	*31,875*	*58*	*← NIC Class 4 reduced to 2% and 40% tax payable*
45,000	33,934	58	
50,000	36,834	58	
55,000	39,734	58	
60,000	42,634	58	
65,000	45,534	58	
70,000	48,434	58	
75,000	51,334	58	
80,000	54,234	58	
85,000	57,134	58	
90,000	60,034	58	
95,000	62,934	58	
100,000	65,834	38	*← PA reduces here*
118,880	*73,008*	*58*	*← PA reduced to zero*
150,000	*91,058*	*53*	*← 45% tax payable*
200,000	117,558	53	
250,000	144,058	53	
300,000	170,558	53	

	2014/15		
	Employed		
	Net equivalent income	Net per £100 extra	Reason
Gross income £pa	£pa	£pa	
1,000	1,000	100	
2,000	2,000	100	
3,000	3,000	100	
4,000	4,000	100	
5,000	5,000	100	
6,000	6,000	100	
7,000	7,000	100	
7,956	*7,956*	*88*	← *12% NIC Class 1 payable*
8,000	7,995	88	
9,000	8,875	*88*	
10,000	9,755	68	← *20% tax payable*
11,000	10,435	68	
12,000	11,115	68	
13,000	11,795	68	
14,000	12,475	68	
15,000	13,155	68	
16,000	13,835	68	
17,000	14,515	68	
18,000	15,195	68	
19,000	15,875	68	
20,000	16,555	68	
21,000	17,235	68	
22,000	17,915	68	
23,000	18,595	68	
24,000	19,275	68	
25,000	19,955	68	
26,000	20,635	68	
27,000	21,315	68	
28,000	21,995	68	
29,000	22,675	68	
30,000	23,355	68	
31,000	24,035	68	
32,000	24,715	68	
33,000	25,395	68	
34,000	26,075	68	
35,000	26,755	68	
37,500	28,455	68	
40,000	30,155	68	
41,865	*31,423*	*58*	← *NIC Class 1 reduced to 2% and 40% tax payable*
45,000	33,241	58	
50,000	36,141	58	
55,000	39,041	58	
60,000	41,941	58	
65,000	44,841	58	
70,000	47,741	58	
75,000	50,641	58	
80,000	53,541	58	
85,000	56,441	58	
90,000	59,341	58	
95,000	62,241	58	
100,000	65,141	*38*	← *PA reduces here*
120,000	*72,741*	*58*	← *PA reduced to zero*
150,000	*90,141*	*53*	← *45% tax payable*
200,000	116,641	53	
250,000	143,141	53	
300,000	169,641	53	

	2014/15		
	Self-employed		
	Net equivalent income	Net per £100 extra	Reason
Gross income £pa	£pa	£pa	
1,000	1,000	100	
2,000	2,000	100	
3,000	3,000	100	
4,000	4,000	100	
5,885	*5,885*	*	← *£140 NIC Class 2 payable*
6,000	5,857	*	
7,000	6,857	*	
7,956	*7,813*	*91*	← *9% NIC Class 4 payable*
8,000	7,853	91	
9,000	8,763	91	
10,000	9,673	71	← *20% tax payable*
11,000	10,383	71	
12,000	11,093	71	** £2.75 x 52 weeks*
13,000	11,803	71	*= £143 pa fixed for any*
14,000	12,513	71	*level of income in excess of*
15,000	13,223	71	*£5,725 pa. So net*
16,000	13,933	71	*equivalent of £6,100*
17,000	14,643	71	*gross is £5,957.*
18,000	15,353	71	
19,000	16,063	71	
20,000	16,773	71	
21,000	17,483	71	
22,000	18,193	71	
23,000	18,903	71	
24,000	19,613	71	
25,000	20,323	71	
26,000	21,033	71	
27,000	21,743	71	
28,000	22,453	71	
29,000	23,163	71	
30,000	23,873	71	
31,000	24,583	71	
32,000	25,293	71	
33,000	26,003	71	
34,000	26,713	71	
35,000	27,423	71	
37,500	29,198	71	
40,000	30,973	71	
41,865	*32,297*	*58*	← *NIC Class 4 reduced to 2% and 40% tax payable*
45,000	34,115	58	
50,000	37,015	58	
55,000	39,915	58	
60,000	42,815	58	
65,000	45,715	58	
70,000	48,615	58	
75,000	51,515	58	
80,000	54,415	58	
85,000	57,315	58	
90,000	60,215	58	
95,000	63,115	58	
100,000	66,015	38	← *PA reduces here*
120,000	*73,615*	*58*	← *PA reduced to zero*
150,000	*91,015*	*53*	← *45% tax payable*
200,000	117,515	53	
250,000	144,015	53	
300,000	170,515	53	

G1: Net equivalents to a range of gross annual income figures

	2015/16 Employed		
	Net equivalent income	Net per £100 extra	Reason
Gross income £pa	£pa	£pa	
1,000	1,000	100	
2,000	2,000	100	
3,000	3,000	100	
4,000	4,000	100	
5,000	5,000	100	
6,000	6,000	100	
7,000	7,000	100	
8,000	8,000	100	
8,060	*8,060*	*88*	← *12% NIC Class 1 payable*
9,000	8,887	*88*	
10,000	9,767	68	
10,600	10,295	68	← *20% tax payable*
11,000	10,567	68	
12,000	11,247	68	
13,000	11,927	68	
14,000	12,607	68	
15,000	13,287	68	
16,000	13,967	68	
17,000	14,647	68	
18,000	15,327	68	
19,000	16,007	68	
20,000	16,687	68	
21,000	17,367	68	
22,000	18,047	68	
23,000	18,727	68	
24,000	19,407	68	
25,000	20,087	68	
26,000	20,767	68	
27,000	21,447	68	
28,000	22,127	68	
29,000	22,807	68	
30,000	23,487	68	
31,000	24,167	68	
32,000	24,847	68	
33,000	25,527	68	
34,000	26,207	68	
35,000	26,887	68	
37,500	28,587	68	
40,000	30,287	68	
42,385	*31,909*	*58*	← *NIC Class 1 reduced to 2% and 40% tax payable*
45,000	33,426	58	
50,000	36,326	58	
55,000	39,226	58	
60,000	42,126	58	
65,000	45,026	58	
70,000	47,926	58	
75,000	50,826	58	
80,000	53,726	58	
85,000	56,626	58	
90,000	59,526	58	
95,000	62,426	58	
100,000	65,326	*38*	← *PA reduces here*
121,200	*73,382*	*53*	← *PA reduced to zero*
150,000	90,086	53	← *45% tax payable*
200,000	116,586	53	
250,000	143,086	53	
300,000	169,586	53	

	2015/16 Self-employed		
	Net equivalent income	Net per £100 extra	Reason
Gross income £pa	£pa	£pa	
1,000	1,000	100	
2,000	2,000	100	
3,000	3,000	100	
4,000	4,000	100	
5,965	*5,965*	*	← *£146 NIC Class 2 payable*
6,000	5,854	*	
7,000	6,854	*	
8,000	7,854	*	
8,060	*7,914*	*91*	← *9% NIC Class 4 payable*
9,000	8,769	91	
10,000	9,679	91	
10,600	10,225	71	← *20% tax payable*
11,000	10,509	71	
12,000	11,219	71	**£2.80 x 52 weeks = £146 pa fixed for any level of income in excess of £5,965 pa. So net equivalent of £6,100 gross is £5,954.*
13,000	11,929	71	
14,000	12,639	71	
15,000	13,349	71	
16,000	14,059	71	
17,000	14,769	71	
18,000	15,479	71	
19,000	16,189	71	
20,000	16,899	71	
21,000	17,609	71	
22,000	18,319	71	
23,000	19,029	71	
24,000	19,739	71	
25,000	20,449	71	
26,000	21,159	71	
27,000	21,869	71	
28,000	22,579	71	
29,000	23,289	71	
30,000	23,999	71	
31,000	24,709	71	
32,000	25,419	71	
33,000	26,129	71	
34,000	26,839	71	
35,000	27,549	71	
37,500	29,324	71	
40,000	31,099	71	
42,385	*32,793*	*58*	← *NIC Class 4 reduced to 2% and 40% tax payable*
45,000	34,310	58	
50,000	37,210	58	
55,000	40,110	58	
60,000	43,010	58	
65,000	45,910	58	
70,000	48,810	58	
75,000	51,710	58	
80,000	54,610	58	
85,000	57,510	58	
90,000	60,410	58	
95,000	63,310	58	
100,000	66,210	38	← *PA reduces here*
121,200	*74,266*	*58*	← *PA reduced to zero*
150,000	90,970	53	← *45% tax payable*
200,000	117,470	53	
250,000	143,970	53	
300,000	170,470	53	

G2: Illustrative net earnings calculations

Man under 65 at 2015/16 tax rates

		Employed person					Self-employed person				
		£pa	**£pa**	**£pa**	**£pa**	**£pa**	**£pa**	**£pa**	**£pa**	**£pa**	**£pa**
Gross income	[a]	15,000	35,000	50,000	110,000	160,000	15,000	35,000	50,000	110,000	160,000
Income tax											
Gross		15,000	35,000	50,000	110,000	160,000	15,000	35,000	50,000	110,000	160,000
Personal allowance (note 1)		(10,600)	(10,600)	(10,600)	(5,600)	–	(10,600)	(10,600)	(10,600)	(5,600)	–
Taxable		4,400	24,400	39,400	104,400	160,000	4,400	24,400	39,400	104,400	160,000
Tax payable											
– At 20%		880	4,880	6,357	6,357	6,357	880	4,880	6,357	6,357	6,357
– At 40%				3,046	29,046	47,286			3,046	29,046	47,286
– At 45%						4,500					4,500
	[b]	880	4,880	9,403	35,403	58,143	880	4,880	9,403	35,403	58,143
National insurance											
Class 1											
– At 12%		833	3,233	4,119	4,119	4,119					
– At 2%				152	1,352	2,352					
Class 2							146	146	146	146	146
Class 4											
– At 9%							625	2,425	3,089	3,089	3,089
– At 2%									152	1,352	2,352
	[c]	833	3,233	4,271	5,471	6,471	771	2,571	3,387	4,587	5,587
Net income	[a–b–c]	13,287	26,887	36,326	69,126	95,386	13,349	27,549	37,210	70,010	96,270
Net % of gross		88.6%	76.8%	72.7%	62.8%	59.6%	89.0%	78.7%	74.4%	63.6%	60.2%
Note 1: personal allowance											
Personal allowance		10,600	10,600	10,600	10,600	10,600	10,600	10,600	10,600	10,600	10,600
Restriction for excess of income over limit*		–	–	–	(5,000)	(10,600)	–	–	–	(5,000)	(10,600)
Net allowance		10,600	10,600	10,600	5,600	–	10,600	10,600	10,600	5,600	–

*If gross pay does not exceed £100,000, no restriction.
If gross pay does exceed £100,000, restriction is the lower of:
(a) (gross pay–£100,000)/2; and
(b) £10,600

G3: Income tax reliefs and rates

Introductory notes

Personal allowance

Every taxpayer resident in the UK (as well as certain non-UK residents) is entitled to a personal allowance.

From 2010/11, the personal allowance has been subject to an income limit of £100,000. Where total income exceeds this limit, the personal allowance is reduced by 50 per cent of the excess. Accordingly, no personal allowance is available on incomes in excess of £121,200 in 2015/16.

Age-related personal allowance

Higher personal allowances are available to taxpayers who were born before April 6, 1938, subject to an income limit—£27,700 for 2015/16.

Where total income exceeds the prescribed income limit, the higher personal allowance is reduced by 50 per cent of the excess, although for years up to and including 2009/10 the allowance cannot be reduced below the ordinary personal allowance. However, from 2010/11, the personal allowance for people born before April 6, 1938 can be reduced below the ordinary personal allowance where the income exceeds £100,000.

For 2015/16, the higher personal allowances available are:

Those born before April 6, 1938	£10,660

The age-related personal allowance has been frozen from 2012/13 onwards.

Age-related married couple's allowance

Where a couple married before December 5, 2005, live together and at least one spouse was born before April 6, 1935, the husband can claim married couple's allowance.

Where a couple married or entered into a civil partnership on or after December 5, 2005, live together and at least one spouse or partner was born before April 6, 1935, the person with the higher income can claim married couple's allowance.

For 2015/16, the allowance is £8,355 and the rate of tax relief is 10 per cent.

The same income limit applies as in the case of the age-related personal allowance (£27,700 for 2015/16).

Where the claimant's income exceeds the income limit, the married couple's allowance is reduced by 50 per cent of the excess less any reduction of the personal allowance (as above), until the allowance is equal to the following amounts:

Tax year 2006/07	Minimum allowance £2,350	Tax relief £235
Tax year 2007/08	Minimum allowance £2,440	Tax relief £244
Tax year 2008/09	Minimum allowance £2,540	Tax relief £254
Tax year 2009/10	Minimum allowance £2,670	Tax relief £267
Tax year 2010/11	Minimum allowance £2,670	Tax relief £267
Tax year 2011/12	Minimum allowance £2,800	Tax relief £280
Tax year 2012/13	Minimum allowance £2,960	Tax relief £296
Tax year 2013/14	Minimum allowance £3,040	Tax relief £304
Tax year 2014/15	Minimum allowance £3,140	Tax relief £314
Tax year 2015/16	Minimum allowance £3,220	Tax relief £322

Child Tax Credit

Child Tax Credit is a means-tested benefit paid directly into the bank account of the main carer of the child(ren), on a weekly or four-weekly basis.

Child Tax Credit neither is affected by, nor affects, Child Benefit (see below).

Child Tax Credit is based initially on the income of the previous tax year.

The claim is corrected to actual income basis in due course.

Before April 2012 Child Tax Credit was usually available if income did not exceed a limit of £41,300. From April 6, 2012 this limit is lower for most people and depends on the claimant's individual circumstances. As a rough guide, no Child Tax Credit will be available from April 6, 2012 where the claimant has:

—one child and annual income of more than about £26,000; or

—two children and annual income of more than about £32,200.

Child Benefit

From January 2013, if an individual's income is more than £50,000 and they, or their partner, choose to carry on getting Child Benefit payments, they will need to declare these payments by registering for Self Assessment and filling in a tax return as they may be liable for a High Income Benefit charge, being 1% of the Child Benefit for each £100 of income between £50,000 and £60,000.

Taxation of savings income

Savings income is subdivided into dividends and other savings income, with dividends treated as the top slice of savings income.

Tax is payable on dividend income at the dividend ordinary rate of 10 per cent up to the basic rate limit, and at the dividend upper rate of 32.5 per cent thereafter up to the higher rate limit.

From 2010/11, in addition to these rates tax is payable on dividend income falling into the additional rate band at the dividend additional rate, as follows:

Tax year 2010/11	42.5 per cent
Tax year 2011/12	42.5 per cent
Tax year 2012/13	42.5 per cent
Tax year 2013/14	37.5 per cent
Tax year 2014/15	37.5 per cent
Tax year 2015/16	37.5 per cent

Tax is payable on other savings income at 10 per cent on income in the starting rate band, at 20 per cent on income in the basic rate band, and at 40 per cent thereafter up to the higher rate limit.

From 2010/11, in addition to these rates, tax is payable on other savings income falling into the additional rate band at the following rates:

Tax year 2010/11	50 per cent
Tax year 2011/12	50 per cent
Tax year 2012/13	50 per cent
Tax year 2013/14	45 per cent
Tax year 2014/15	45 per cent
Tax year 2015/16	45 per cent

Between 2008/09 and 2014/15 there was a 10 per cent starting rate for savings income only. For 2015/16 there is a 0 per cent starting rate for savings only, so the following rates and limits apply:

	Rate	Limit
Tax year 2008/09	10%	£2,320
Tax year 2009/10	10%	£2,440
Tax year 2010/11	10%	£2,440
Tax year 2011/12	10%	£2,560
Tax year 2012/13	10%	£2,710
Tax year 2013/14	10%	£2,790
Tax year 2014/15	10%	£2,880
Tax year 2015/16	0%	£5,000

If the taxpayer's non-savings income exceeds these limits, the savings rate does not apply.

2007/08 to 2015/16

Fiscal year:	2007/08 £	2008/09 £	2009/10 £	2010/11 £	2011/12 £	2012/13 £	2013/14 £	2014/15 £	2015/16 £
Income tax reliefs									
Personal allowance	5,225	6,035	6,475	6,475*	7,475*	8,105*	9,440*	10,000*	10,600*
Income tax rates									
Starting rate band									
– Payable at 10%	2,230	–	–	–	–	–	–	–	–
Basic rate band									
– Payable at 20%	–	34,800	37,400	37,400	35,000	34,370	32,010	31,865	31,785
Basic rate band									
– Payable at 22%	32,370	–	–	–	–	–	–	–	–
Higher rate band									
– Payable at 40%	Balance	Balance	Balance	112,600	115,000	115,630	117,990	118,135	118,215
Additional rate band									
– Payable at 45%	–	–	–	–	–	–	Balance	Balance	Balance
– Payable at 50%	–	–	–	Balance	Balance	Balance	–	–	–

* Please refer to the preceding note on personal allowance for possible restriction.

G4: National Insurance contributions

Introductory notes

1. Married women and widows have been able to elect to pay a reduced contribution as follows:

   - 4.85% on earnings between primary threshold and upper earnings limit, and 1 per cent on earnings above upper earnings limit from 2003/04 to 2010/11.

   - 5.85% on earnings between primary threshold and upper earnings limit, and 2 per cent on earnings above upper earnings limit in 2011/12 to 2015/16.

2. Class 1 employee contributions and Class 2 contributions cease to be payable when a man has reached 65 and a woman 60.

3. Class 4 contributions are not payable in respect of any fiscal year that starts after pensionable age has been reached.

4. Class 3 contributions are voluntary at a flat weekly rate (£14.10pw in 2015/16).

5. From April 6, 2009 an Upper Accrual Point (UAP) was introduced at a frozen rate of £770.00 per week for the calculation of the State Second Pension (S2P) and Class 1 National Insurance rebates under contracted-out schemes. From the same date the Upper Earnings Limit (UEL) previously used for these purposes was aligned with the higher rate threshold for income tax.

2007/08 to 2010/11

Fiscal year:	2007/08 £	2008/09 £	2009/10 £	2010/11 £
Class 1 contributions (Employees)				
Lower earnings limit (LEL) (pa)	4,524	4,680	4,940	5,044
Primary threshold (PT) (pa)	5,225	5,435	5,715	5,715
Upper Accrual Point			40,040	40,040
Upper earnings limit (UEL) (pa)	34,840	40,040	43,875	43,875
Standard rate				
If earnings below LEL:	Nil	Nil	Nil	Nil
If earnings at or above LEL: – Contribution rate on earnings up to PT	Nil	Nil	Nil	Nil
– Contribution rate on earnings between PT and UEL	11%	11%	11%	11%
– Contribution rate on earnings above UEL	1%	1%	1%	1%
Maximum contribution (pa)	3,258 +1% of excess over UEL	3,807 +1% of excess over UEL	4,198 +1% of excess over UEL	4,198 +1% of excess over UEL
Contracted out rate				
As standard rate except – Contribution rate on earnings between PT and UEL	9.4%	9.4%		
– Contribution rate on earnings between PT and UAP			9.4%	9.4%
– Contribution rate on earnings between UAP and UEL			11.0%	11.0%
Maximum contribution (pa)	2,784 +1% of excess over UEL	3,253 +1% of excess over UEL	3,648 +1% of excess over UEL	3,648 +1% of excess over UEL
Class 2 contributions (Self-employed)				
Small earnings exception limit	4,635	4,825	5,075	5,075
Fixed weekly contributions (pw)	2.20	2.30	2.40	2.40
Class 4 contributions (Self-employed)				
Lower profits limit (LPL) (pa)	5,225	5,435	5,715	5,715
Upper profits limit (UPL) (pa)	34,840	40,040	43,875	43,875
Contribution rate on profits between LPL and UPL	8.0%	8.0%	8.0%	8.0%
Contribution rate on profits above UPL	1.0%	1.0%	1.0%	1.0%
Maximum contribution (pa)	2,369 +1% of excess over UPL	2,768 +1% of excess over UPL	3,053 +1% of excess over UPL	3,053 +1% of excess over UPL

2011/12 to 2014/15

Fiscal year:	2011/12 £	2012/13 £	2013/14 £	2014/15 £
Class 1 contributions (Employees)				
Lower earnings limit (LEL) (pa)	5,304	5,564	5,668	5,772
Primary threshold (PT) (pa)	7,225	7,605	7,755	7,956
Upper Accrual Point	40,040	40,040	40,040	40,040
Upper earnings limit (UEL) (pa)	42,475	42,475	41,450	41,865
Standard rate				
If earnings below LEL:	Nil	Nil	Nil	Nil
If earnings at or above LEL: – Contribution rate on earnings up to PT	Nil	Nil	Nil	Nil
– Contribution rate on earnings between PT and UEL	12%	12%	12%	12%
– Contribution rate on earnings above UEL	2%	2%	2%	2%
Maximum contribution (pa)	4,230 +2% of excess over UEL	4,184 +2% of excess over UEL	4,043 +2% of excess over UEL	4,069 +2% of excess over UEL
Contracted out rate				
As standard rate except – Contribution rate on earnings between PT and UEL				
– Contribution rate on earnings between PT and UAP	10.4%	10.6%	10.6%	10.6%
– Contribution rate on earnings between UAP and UEL	12.0%	12.0%	12.0%	12.0%
Maximum contribution (pa)	3,705 +2% of excess over UEL	3,730 +2% of excess over UEL	3,591 +2% of excess over UEL	3,620 +2% of excess over UEL
Class 2 contributions (Self-employed)				
Small earnings exception limit	5,315	5,595	5,725	5,885
Fixed weekly contributions (pw)	2.50	2.65	2.70	2.75
Class 4 contributions (Self-employed)				
Lower profits limit (LPL) (pa)	7,225	7,605	7,755	7,956
Upper profits limit (UPL) (pa)	42,475	42,475	41,450	41,865
Contribution rate on profits between LPL and UPL	9.0%	9.0%	9.0%	9.0%
Contribution rate on profits above UPL	2.0%	2.0%	2.0%	2.0%
Maximum contribution (pa)	3,173 +2% of excess over UPL	3,138 +2% of excess over UPL	3,033 +2% of excess over UPL	3,052 +2% of excess over UPL

2015/16

Fiscal year:	2015/16 £
Class 1 contributions (Employees)	
Lower earnings limit (LEL) (pa)	5,824
Primary threshold (PT) (pa)	8,060
Upper Accrual Point	40,040
Upper earnings limit (UEL) (pa)	42,385
Standard rate	
If earnings below LEL:	Nil
If earnings at or above LEL: – Contribution rate on earnings up to PT	Nil
– Contribution rate on earnings between PT and UEL	12%
– Contribution rate on earnings above UEL	2%
Maximum contribution (pa)	4,119 +2% of excess over UEL
Contracted out rate	
As standard rate except – Contribution rate on earnings between PT and UEL	
– Contribution rate on earnings between PT and UAP	10.6%
– Contribution rate on earnings between UAP and UEL	12.0%
Maximum contribution (pa)	3,671 +2% of excess over UEL
Class 2 contributions (Self-employed)	
Small earnings exception limit	5,965
Fixed weekly contributions (pw)	2.80
Class 4 contributions (Self-employed)	
Lower profits limit (LPL) (pa)	8,060
Upper profits limit (UPL) (pa)	42,385
Contribution rate on profits between LPL and UPL	9.0%
Contribution rate on profits above UPL	2.0%
Maximum contribution (pa)	3,089 +2% of excess over UPL

G5: VAT registration thresholds and rates

Registration is required when a person's turnover (taxable supplies from all the person's businesses) exceeds prescribed limits.

Past and future turnover limits apply (looking one year back and one year forward).

Registration is also required if a turnover limit is to be exceeded in a period of 30 days.

The registration levels are:

	Past turnover		Future turnover
	1 year	Unless turnover for next year will not exceed	30 days
	£	£	£
April 1, 2004 to March 31, 2005	58,000	56,000	58,000
April 1, 2005 to March 31, 2006	60,000	58,000	60,000
April 1, 2006 to March 31, 2007	61,000	59,000	61,000
April 1, 2007 to March 31, 2008	64,000	62,000	64,000
April 1, 2008 to April 30, 2009	67,000	65,000	67,000
May 1, 2009 to March 31, 2010	68,000	66,000	68,000
April 1, 2010 to March 31, 2011	70,000	68,000	70,000
April 1, 2011 to March 31, 2012	73,000	71,000	73,000
April 1, 2012 to March 31, 2013	77,000	75,000	77,000
From April 1, 2013 to March 31, 2014	79,000	77,000	79,000
From April 1, 2014 to March 31, 2015	81,000	79,000	81,000
From April 1, 2015	82,000	80,000	82,000

De-registration depends on satisfying HM Revenue & Customs that the future annual limit (being the same as the "unless turnover for next year will not exceed"in the table above, e.g. £80,000 from April 1, 2015) will not be exceeded.

Note:

These registration and de-registration limits can be of particular relevance in considering likely turnover levels for businesses such as taxis and driving schools, where VAT registration may render charges uncompetitive (because most such businesses operate below the registration limits).

VAT Rates

Date	VAT Rate
From January 4, 2011	20.0%
January 1, 2010 to January 3, 2011	17.5%
December 1, 2008 to December 31, 2009	15.0%
April 1, 1991 to November 30, 2008	17.5%

Group H

Pension

H

H1: Net equivalents to a range of gross annual pension figures

Introductory notes

1. The following table sets out the net equivalents to a range of annual pension figures in 2015/16, distinguishing between:

   - a single person born after April 5, 1938 (i.e. under age 77 at the start of the tax year);
   - a single person born before April 6, 1938 (i.e. age 77 or over at the start of the tax year);
   - a married person born after April 5, 1938 (i.e. under age 77 at the start of the tax year);
   - a married person born before April 6, 1938 (i.e. age 77 or over at the start of the tax year);.

2. The table is followed by illustrative net pension calculations for each marital status and age category, at income levels of £15,000, £20,000, £30,000, £50,000, £110,000 and £160,000 per annum.

3. The age ranges selected reflect the availability of age-related personal and married couple's allowances, as detailed in G3.

4. Since pensions are not subject to National Insurance contributions, the net equivalent figures represent the gross pension less income tax. Given that liability to primary Class 1 National Insurance contributions falls away when the earner has reached pensionable age [note 2 of G4], it follows that the net equivalent figures for those that have reached State pension age apply equally to earnings from employment and pensions.

   Similarly, given that Class 4 contributions are not payable in respect of any fiscal year that starts after pensionable age has been reached [note 3 of G4], it follows that the net equivalent figures for those that have reached State pension age apply also to earnings from self-employment where State pensionable age has been reached in a prior fiscal year.

	2015/16 Net equivalent pension							
	Single, or married where neither spouse was born before 6.4.35				Married, where either spouse was born before 6.4.35			
Gross pension £pa	**Aged under 77* £pa**	**Net per £100 extra**	**Aged 77* or over £pa**	**Net per £100 extra**	**Aged under 77* £pa**	**Net per £100 extra**	**Aged 77* or over £pa**	**Net per £100 extra**
1,000	1,000	100	1,000	100	1,000	100	1,000	100
2,000	2,000	100	2,000	100	2,000	100	2,000	100
3,000	3,000	100	3,000	100	3,000	100	3,000	100
4,000	4,000	100	4,000	100	4,000	100	4,000	100
5,000	5,000	100	5,000	100	5,000	100	5,000	100
6,000	6,000	100	6,000	100	6,000	100	6,000	100
7,000	7,000	100	7,000	100	7,000	100	7,000	100
8,000	8,000	100	8,000	100	8,000	100	8,000	100
9,000	9,000	100	9,000	100	9,000	100	9,000	100
10,000	10,000	100	10,000	100	10,000	100	10,000	100
10,600	10,600	80			10,600	100		
10,660			10,660	80			10,660	100
11,000	10,920	80	10,932	80	11,000	100	11,000	100
12,000	11,720	80	11,732	80	12,000	100	12,000	100
13,000	12,520	80	12,532	80	13,000	100	13,000	100
14,000	13,320	80	13,332	80	14,000	100	14,000	100
14,780					14,780	80		
14,840							14,840	80
15,000	14,120	80	14,132	80	14,956	80	14,968	80
16,000	14,920	80	14,932	80	15,756	80	15,768	80
17,000	15,720	80	15,732	80	16,556	80	16,568	80
18,000	16,520	80	16,532	80	17,356	80	17,368	80
19,000	17,320	80	17,332	80	18,156	80	18,168	80
20,000	18,120	80	18,132	80	18,956	80	18,968	80
21,000	18,920	80	18,932	80	19,756	80	19,768	80
22,000	19,720	80	19,732	80	20,556	80	20,568	80
23,000	20,520	80	20,532	80	21,356	80	21,368	80
24,000	21,320	80	21,332	80	22,156	80	22,168	80
25,000	22,120	80	22,132	80	22,956	80	22,968	80
26,000	22,920	80	22,932	80	23,756	80	23,768	80
27,000	23,720	80	23,732	80	24,556	80	24,568	80
27,700			24,292	70	25,116	75	25,128	70
27,820			24,376	80	25,206	75	25,212	75
28,000	24,520	80	24,520	80	25,341	75	25,347	75
29,000	25,320	80	25,320	80	26,091	75	26,097	75
30,000	26,120	80	26,120	80	26,841	75	26,847	75
31,000	26,920	80	26,920	80	27,591	75	27,597	75
32,000	27,720	80	27,720	80	28,341	75	28,347	75
33,000	28,520	80	28,520	80	29,091	75	29,097	75
34,000	29,320	80	29,320	80	29,841	75	29,847	75
35,000	30,120	80	30,120	80	30,591	75	30,597	75
37,970					32,818	80		
38,090							32,914	80
40,000	34,120	80	34,120	80	34,442	80	34,442	80
41,785	35,548	60	35,548	60				
42,465					36,414	60	36,414	60
45,000	37,597	60	37,597	60	37,935	60	37,935	60
50,000	40,597	60	40,597	60	40,935	60	40,935	60
55,000	43,597	60	43,597	60	43,935	60	43,935	60
60,000	46,597	60	46,597	60	46,935	60	46,935	60
65,000	49,597	60	49,597	60	49,935	60	49,935	60
70,000	52,597	60	52,597	60	52,935	60	52,935	60
75,000	55,597	60	55,597	60	55,935	60	55,935	60
80,000	58,597	60	58,597	60	58,935	60	58,935	60
85,000	61,597	60	61,597	60	61,935	60	61,935	60
90,000	64,597	60	64,597	60	64,935	60	64,935	60
95,000	67,597	60	67,597	60	67,935	60	67,935	60
100,000	70,597	40	70,597	40	70,935	40	70,935	40
121,200	79,077	60	79,077	60	75,175	60	79,415	60
150,000	96,357	55	96,357	55	91,925	55	96,695	55
200,000	123,857	55	123,857	55	119,425	55	124,195	55
250,000	151,357	55	151,357	55	146,925	55	151,695	55
300,000	178,857	55	178,857	55	174,425	55	179,195	55

* = Age at start of tax year (i.e. April 6, 2015)
Under 77 years of age are those born after April 5, 1938
Over 77 years of age are those born before April 6, 1938

H2: Illustrative net pension calculations

Single person* aged under 77 at 2015/16 rates

		£pa	£pa	£pa	£pa	£pa	£pa
Gross pension	[a]	15,000	20,000	30,000	50,000	110,000	160,000
Income tax							
Gross		15,000	20,000	30,000	50,000	110,000	160,000
Personal allowance (see note 1 below)		(10,600)	(10,600)	(10,600)	(10,600)	(5,600)	–
Taxable		4,400	9,400	19,400	39,400	104,400	160,000
Tax payable							
– At 20%		880	1,880	3,880	6,357	6,357	6,357
– At 40%					3,046	29,046	47,286
– At 45%							4,500
	[b]	800	1,880	3,880	9,403	35,403	58,143
Net income	[a–b]	14,120	18,120	26,120	40,597	74,597	101,857
Net % of gross		94.1%	90.6%	87.1%	81.2%	67.8%	63.7%
Note 1: personal allowance							
Personal allowance		10,600	10,600	10,600	10,600	10,600	10,600
Restriction for excess of income over limit#		–	–	–	–	(5,000)	(10,600)
Net allowance		10,600	10,600	10,600	10,600	5,600	–

#If gross pay does not exceed £100,000, no restriction.
If gross pay does exceed £100,000, restriction is the lower of:
(a) (gross pay–£100,000)/2; and
(b) £10,600.
* = and married persons that do not meet the criteria shown in the married persons' calculations below

Single person* aged 77 or over at 2015/16 rates

		£pa	£pa	£pa	£pa	£pa	£pa
Gross pension	[a]	15,000	20,000	30,000	50,000	110,000	160,000
Income tax							
Gross		15,000	20,000	30,000	50,000	110,000	160,000
Personal allowance (see note 1 below)		(10,660)	(10,660)	(10,600)	(10,600)	(5,000)	–
Taxable		4,340	9,340	19,400	39,400	105,000	160,000
Tax payable							
– At 20%		868	1,868	3,880	6,373	6,373	6,373
– At 40%					3,014	29,254	47,254
– At 45%							4,500
	[b]	868	1,868	3,880	9,387	35,627	58,127
Net income	[a–b]	14,132	18,132	26,120	40,613	74,373	101,873
Net % of gross		94.2%	90.7%	87.1%	81.2%	67.6%	63.7%
Note 1: personal allowance							
Allowance for age 75 and over		10,660	10,660	10,660	10,660	10,660	10,660
Restriction for excess of income over limits#		–	–	(60)	(60)	(5,660)	(10,660)
Net allowance		10,660	10,660	10,600	10,600	5,000	–

#If gross pension does not exceed £27,700, no restriction.
If gross pension does exceed £27,700, but does not exceed £100,000, restriction is the lower of:
(a) (gross pension–£27,700)/2; and
(b) £10,660 – £10,600 = £60
If gross pay does exceed £100,000, restriction is the lower of:
(a) (gross pay–£100,000)/2; and
(b) £10,660
* = and married persons that do not meet the criteria shown in the married persons' calculations below

Married person aged under 77 at 2015/16 rates

(But only applies if at least one spouse born before April 6, 1935 and full married couple's allowance allocated to pensioner in this calculation)*

		£pa	£pa	£pa	£pa	£pa	£pa
Gross pension	[a]	15,000	20,000	30,000	50,000	110,000	160,000
Income tax							
Gross		15,000	20,000	30,000	50,000	110,000	160,000
Personal allowance (see note 1 below)		(10,600)	(10,600)	(10,600)	(10,600)	(5,600)	–
Taxable		4,400	9,400	19,400	39,400	104,400	160,000
Tax payable							
– At 20%		880	1,880	3,880	6,357	6,357	6,357
– At 40%					3,046	29,046	47,286
– At 45%							4,500
		880	1,880	3,880	9,403	35,403	58,143
Relief for married couple's allowance (note 2)		(836)	(836)	(721)	(322)	(322)	(322)
	[b]	44	1,044	3,159	9,081	35,081	57,821
Net income	[a–b]	14,956	18,956	26,841	40,919	74,919	102,179
Net % of gross		99.7%	94.8%	89.5%	81.8%	68.1%	63.9%

Note 1: personal allowance

Personal allowance	10,600	10,600	10,600	10,600	10,600	10,600
Restriction for excess of income over limits#	–	–	–	–	(5,000)	(10,600)
Net allowance	10,600	10,600	10,600	10,600	5,600	–

#If gross pension does not exceed £100,000, no restriction.
If gross pension does exceed £100,000, restriction is the lower of:
(a) (gross pension–£100,000)/2; and
(b) £10,600

Note 2: married couple's allowance

Married couple's allowance for age 77 and over	8,355	8,355	8,355	8,355	8,355	8,355
Restriction for excess of income over limit^	–	–	(1,150)	(5,135)	(5,135)	(5,135)
Net allowance	8,355	8,355	7,205	3,220	3,220	3,220
Relief at 10%	836	836	721	322	322	322

^ If gross pension does not exceed £27,700, no restriction.
If gross pension does exceed £27,700, restriction is the lower of:
(a) [(gross pension–£27,700)/2] **less** restriction of personal allowance; and
(b) £8,355 – £3,220 = £5,135

* If these criteria are not met, use Single Person calculator shown above

Married person aged 77 or over at 2015/16 rates

(But only applies if at least one spouse born before April 6, 1935 and full married couple's allowance allocated to pensioner in this calculation)*

		£pa	£pa	£pa	£pa	£pa	£pa
Gross pension	[a]	15,000	20,000	30,000	50,000	110,000	160,000
Income tax							
Gross		15,000	20,000	30,000	50,000	110,000	160,000
Personal allowance (see note 1 below)		(10,660)	(10,660)	(10,600)	(10,600)	(5,600)	–
Taxable		4,340	9,340	19,400	39,400	104,400	160,000
Tax payable							
– At 20%		868	1,868	3,880	6,373	6,373	6,373
– At 40%					3,014	29,014	47,254
– At 45%							4,500
Relief for married couple's		868	1,868	3,880	9,387	35,387	58,127
allowance (note 2)		(836)	(836)	(727)	(322)	(322)	(322)
	[b]	32	1,032	3,153	9,065	35,065	57,805
Net income	[a–b]	14,968	18,968	26,847	40,935	74,935	102,195
Net % of gross		99.8%	94.8%	89.5%	81.9%	68.1%	63.9%

Note 1: personal allowance

Personal allowance for age 76 and over	10,660	10,660	10,660	10,660	10,660	10,660
Restriction for excess of income over limits#	–	–	(60)	(60)	(5,060)	(10,660)
Net allowance	10,660	10,660	10,600	10,600	5,600	–

If gross pension does not exceed £27,700, no restriction.
If gross pension does exceed £27,700, but does not exceed £100,000, restriction is the lower of:
(a) (gross pension–£27,700)/2; and
(b) £10,660 – £10,600 = £60
If gross pension does exceed £100,000, restriction is the lower of:
(a) (gross pension–£100,000)/2; and
(b) £10,660

Note 2: married couple's allowance

Married couple's allowance for age 77 and over	8,355	8,355	8,355	8,355	8,355	8,355
Restriction for excess of income over limit^	–	–	(1,090)	(5,135)	(5,135)	(5,135)
Net allowance	8,355	8,355	7,265	3,220	3,220	3,220
Relief at 10%	836	836	727	322	322	322

^ If gross pension does not exceed £27,700, no restriction.
If gross pension does exceed £27,700, restriction is the lower of:
(a) [(gross pension–£27,700)/2] **less** restriction of personal allowance; and
(b) £8,355 – £3,220 = £5,135

* If these criteria are not met, use Single Person calculator shown above

H3: Note on pension losses

1. Purpose of note

The purpose of this note is to provide some basic guidance to practitioners who need to consider whether a pension loss is likely to arise in any specific case.

2. "Final Salary" or "Money Purchase" scheme?

Ascertain which type of scheme was being contributed to.

There are two types of Defined Benefit schemes:

1) Final Salary schemes

- benefits are defined in advance, usually in terms of:
  - final salary,
  - number of years of service,
  - a factor (often 1/60th or 1/80th for each year of service), and
- the financial risk of ensuring that benefits are paid lies with the employer.

2) Career Average Revalued Earnings schemes (also known as CARE schemes)

- benefits depend on a combination of:
  - each year's pensionable earnings;
  - annual increases;
  - the scheme's accrual rate, and
- the financial risk of ensuring that benefits are paid lies with the employer.

There are also **Money Purchase schemes** (also known as Personal Pensions and/or Defined Contribution schemes)

- benefits depend on a combination of:
  - the amounts paid in by the member, (if any);
  - the amounts paid in by the employer (if any and if there is one),
  - the investment returns (net of charges) achieved up to retirement,
  - the annuity rates available on retirement, and
- the financial risk lies with the member.

By definition, a self-employed person will have no employer contributions.

3. Is there likely to be a loss?

Start by assuming that there will be a loss to be evaluated, if:

- the claimant (and/or the employer) was contributing to a pension scheme;

- there is a claim for loss of earnings; and
- in respect of Money Purchase schemes, annual contributions were greater than £3,600.

4. Final salary scheme member

Potential pension:

- Obtain a copy of the members' guide (which will often be in simple terms).
- Obtain a copy of the most recent statement of the individual member's scheme benefits (an estimate of pension at normal retirement age based on current salary).
- With these documents, and the projection of final salary being used for evaluating loss of earnings, it should be possible to calculate the expected pension at retirement date (at its present day value).

Actual pension:

- Establish the actual (reduced) pension that will be payable at normal retirement date (at its present day value).

Proceed by:

- Applying *Wells v Wells*[1] principles, follow the step-by-step guide at Table B3.
- Calculating loss of annual pension (after tax). Table H1 will assist.
- Applying an appropriate multiplier drawn from the Ogden tables. Tables A1 and A8 refer.

Calculations incorporating a loss of lump sum benefit can be complex and will only be possible if the effect that taking the lump sum has on the annual pension can be ascertained with reasonable certainty. (Public pension schemes usually provide separately for lump sum and annual pension benefits, so the figures are generally straightforward to ascertain.)

5. Career Average Revalued Earnings scheme member

Potential pension:

- Obtain a copy of the members' guide (which will often be in simple terms).
- Obtain a copy of the most recent statement of the individual member's scheme benefit (an estimate of pension at normal retirement age based on current salary) – note: this may include estimated future inflation to normal retirement age, which must be ignored.
- With these documents, and the projection of annual salary being used for evaluating loss of earnings, it should be possible to calculate pension at retirement date (at its present day value), by following the step-by-step guide at Table B3.

[1] [1999] 1 A.C. 345.

Actual pension:

- Establish the actual (reduced) pension that will be payable at normal retirement date (at its present day value).
  Proceed by:

- Applying *Wells v Wells*[2] principles, follow the step-by-step guide at Table B3.

- Calculating loss of annual pension (after tax). Table H1 will assist.

- Applying an appropriate multiplier drawn from the Ogden Tables. Tables A1 and A8 refer.

Calculations incorporating a loss of lump sum benefit can be complex and will only be possible if the effect that taking the lump sum has on the annual pension can be ascertained with reasonable certainty. (Public pension schemes usually provide separately for lump sum and annual pension benefits, so the figures are generally straightforward to ascertain).

6. Money purchase scheme member

A forensic accountant will often approach evaluation of loss along the following lines:

Potential pension:

- Ascertain current value of pension fund.

- Calculate contributions foregone (payable by member and by employer if applicable).

- Calculate value of potential pension fund at retirement, based on contributions foregone and an assumed rate of investment return within the fund.

- Calculate in turn:

  - the lump sum benefit available on retirement (discounted to present day value), and
  - the gross annual pension (based on annuity tables or the drawdown method).

Actual pension:

- Calculate value of actual pension fund at retirement, based on any future contributions to the scheme and the assumed rate of investment return within the fund.

- Calculate in turn:

  - the lump sum benefit available (discounted to present day value), and
  - the gross annual pension.

Proceed by:

- Calculating the loss of lump sum (at present day value).

- Calculating the loss of annual pension (after tax). Table H1 will assist.

[2] = [1999] 1 A.C. 345.

- Applying an appropriate multiplier drawn from the Ogden tables.
- Consider whether any further adjustments should be applied for contingencies.

7. Important cases

Have regard to:

- *Parry v Cleaver*[1]:

  Briefly: pension loss only runs from anticipated retirement age.

  So that: no credit need be given against earnings losses for an early/ill health pension

- *Longden v British Coal Corporation*[2]:

  Briefly: explains how to apportion an actual tax-free lump sum received ahead of expected retirement age between pre- and post-retirement periods.

  So that: treatment of the actual lump sum is brought into line with *Parry v Cleaver* principles.

- *Aboul-Hosn v Trustees of the Italian Hospital*[3]:

  Briefly: allows for a simple calculation in which pension loss is based on the tax relief foregone on the claimant's potential personal pension contributions.

8. Further points

- Do not rely on quotations from pension providers; they invariably incorporate inflation and are not therefore compatible with conventional multipliers.
- Keep in mind the reality of life expectancy. If life expectancy is impaired, pension loss will be reduced.
- That said, do not overlook the possibility of a "lost years" claim in respect of pension losses between the end of the post-accident life expectancy and the end of the pre-accident life expectancy.
- Do not assume that individuals necessarily retire at State retirement age.
- Bear in mind that, between April 2010 and April 2018, the State pension age for women will gradually increase from 60 to 65. The State pension age is then set to increase from 65 to 68 between 2020 and mid 2030s. There is a State pension age calculator at *http://www.thepensionservice.gov.uk*.
- Claims for loss of State pension may also need to be considered, following the above principles.
- Smaller pension losses may sometimes not be worth pursuing, given the safety net of the State Pension Credit. See Table I2.

[1] [1970] A.C. 1.
[2] [1998] A.C. 653.
[3] (1987) (unreported).

Group I

Benefits, Allowances, Charges

I

I1: Social security benefits (non-means-tested)

How they work

Generally, all of these benefits may be claimed independently of each other. However, there are overlapping benefit rules which prevent more than one income replacement benefit being payable. If the claimant is entitled to more than one income replacement benefit, then the amount of the highest will be payable.

Many benefits are contributory, entitlement being dependent on satisfying conditions as to amount of national insurance contributions paid.

Until April 2003, increases were payable for many benefits for dependent children, subject to an earnings limit. The increases have now been replaced by child tax credit (see section I2) but people in receipt of the increases on April 5, 2003 have transitional protection.

Entitlement to non-means-tested benefits is frequently affected if claimants are in hospital or in full-time care.

Claims for all benefits must be made in writing. Claims can be backdated only to a limited extent (varying according to the type of benefit).

A. Income replacement

1. Retirement

Retirement Pension	**2015–2016**
Claimant (Category A)	£115.95
(Category B)	£69.50
Adult dependant	£69.50

Either spouse/civil partner may qualify in their own right (Category A) or as a spouse or civil partner (Category B). Special rules apply for parents, carers, divorced people, widows and widowers. Women's State Pension age is gradually increasing to 65 by November 2018.

Highly variable rates according to contribution history.

Contributory and taxable.

For information for Form E submit Form BR20 (for valuation of additional state pension); or Form BR19 (for benefit forecast): downloadable at *http://www.direct.gov.uk*

2. Ill Health

i. Statutory Sick Pay	**2015–2016**
Standard rate	£88.45

Paid by the employer for up to 168 days (28 six-day weeks), to employees earning not less than £107 gross p.w. Taxable.

ii. Employment and Support Allowance (ESA)	**2015–2016**
Single person under 25:	£57.90
Single person 25 or over:	£73.10
Lone parent under 18	£57.90
Lone parent 18 or over:	£73.10
Couple, both under 18:	£57.90
Couple, both under 18, with a child:	£87.50
Couple, both over 18:	£114.85
Single people with work-related activity component:	£49.05
Single people with the support group component:	£41.90
Single people with no component:	£78.10
Couples in which the claimant gets the work-related activity component:	£86.95
Couples in which the claimant gets the support group component:	£79.80
Couples with no component:	£116.00
Premiums	
Severe disability-single:	£61.85
Severe disability-couple:	£123.70
Enhanced disability-single:	£15.75
Enhanced disability-couple:	£22.60
Carer premium:	£34.60

Includes both contributory and "income-related" (means-tested) benefit, based on either limited capability for work (placed in "work-related activity group", helped to prepare for suitable work) or limited capability for work-related activity (not expected to work, placed in support group).

Benefit paid at basic rate during 13-week assessment phase. Lower rates for under 25s during assessment period; youth ESA abolished for new claimants from April 2012; existing claimants able to go on claiming, but only for one year from entitlement, disregarding time in support group. Contributory ESA: time-limited to one year for those in work-related activity group; also no age or spouse's additions, and no housing costs allowances. Income related ESA (IRESA): assessment, housing costs and capital rules modelled on IS (Table 29). Child maintenance and up to £20 earnings p.w. disregarded (or 16 hours p.w. earning up to £97.50 p.w. for 52 weeks). Passport to other benefits including full HB and CTB (HB & CTB: Table 29). Contributory ESA taxable: IRESA not.

iii. Carer's Allowance	**2015–2016**
Claimant	£62.10

Paid to people over 16 who spend at least 35 hours p.w. caring for recipient of higher or middle rates of

Entitlement to contributory benefits depends on payment of National Insurance Contributions. Amounts are per week.

Care Component of Disability Living Allowance, Attendance Allowance, or Constant Attendance Allowance at or above the normal rate with a related pension. Claimant can earn no more than £100 p.w. net and must not be in full-time education; however, entitled to offset against earnings up to half any sums paid to someone else (not close relative) to care for either recipient of allowances or carer's children under 16.

Claimant's benefit and adult dependency increases are taxable; child dependency increases are not.

3. Unemployment—Jobseeker's Allowance (JSA)

i. Contribution-based JSA		**2015–2016**
Claimant	18–24	£57.90
	25 and over	£73.10

ii. Income-based JSA (IBJSA)		**2015–2016**
Claimant	16–24	£57.90
	25 and over	£73.10
Couple Both over 18		£114.85
Dependent children —(existing claimants only— others see Child Tax Credit) till day before 20th birthday		£66.90

Premiums: as for IS (Table 29)

Contributory JSA is age-related flat-rate payment; without dependant allowances: paid for up to 26 weeks. IBJSA is paid with, or from expiry of, contributory JSA, with IS-style rules for income, capital, premiums and mortgage interest.
Personal allowance payments and premiums for children being phased out (replaced by child tax credit). Child maintenance is disregarded. Claimants must be under State Pension age, available for and actively seeking work, and have a current Jobseeker's Agreement: IBJSA is a passport to other benefits including full HB & CTB. Men are eligible for Pension Credit (PC) although those who are not yet 65 may claim PC instead.
Main rates only given. Not usually available for those under 18 or those working 16+ hours p.w. Only main rates shown.
Personal allowance taxable.

4. Maternity/paternity/adoption

i. Statutory Maternity Pay (SMP)	**2015–2016**
Payable to employees earning on average at least £112 a week.	
Higher rate (first 6 weeks)	90 per cent of average weekly wage
Lower rate (for up to next 33 weeks)	£139.58[2]

Paid by employer for a maximum of 39 weeks. Taxable.

ii. Statutory Paternity Pay (SPP)	**2015–2016**
Rate	£139.58[2]

Payable for up to two weeks. Additional SPP at same rate if upon mother's return to work, baby 20 weeks old and she would otherwise still be entitled to SMP, SAP or MA. Not payable beyond mother's 39-week maternity period. Taxable.

iii. Maternity Allowance	**2015–2016**
Average earnings threshold	£27.00
Standard rate	£139.58[2]

Paid to claimants not entitled to SMP but employed or self-employed for at least 26 weeks in 66 weeks before due date, and average pay over earnings threshold. Maximum 39 weeks (during which may work up to 10 days). Adult dependency increases no longer paid. Non-taxable.

iv. Statutory Adoption Pay[1]	**2015–2016**
Standard rate	£139.58

Paid by employer for a maximum of 39 weeks. Taxable.

v. Surestart Maternity Grant	**2015–2016**
Standard one-off payment	£500.00

Subject to complex conditions. Available only for first child.

5. Bereavement

i. Bereavement Benefit	**2015–2016**
Lump sum	£2,000.00

ii. Bereavement allowance (age-related)	£33.77 to £104.67

Available to bereaved spouses/civil partners over 45 but under State Pension age who do not remarry or cohabit and who are not bringing up children. Standard rate £112.55 for those 55 and over.
Payable for up to 52 weeks from date of bereavement.

iii. Widowed Parent's Allowance	£112.55

Available to bereaved spouses/civil partners under State Pension age and in receipt of child benefit who do not remarry or cohabit.
Widowed Parent's Allowance and Bereavement Allowance cannot be claimed together.
All benefits are contributory and (save lump sum) taxable.

[1] *Qualifying conditions based on length of service and average earnings*
[2] *Or (if less) 90% of the parent's weekly average earnings*

Entitlement to contributory benefits depends on payment of National Insurance Contributions. Amounts are per week.

B. Special needs

1. Personal Independence Payment (PIP)

		2015–2016
Care Component	Enhanced	£82.30
	Standard	£55.10
Mobility Component	Enhanced	£57.45
	Standard	£21.80

The claimant must qualify before reaching 65. Available to under-16s too.

2. Attendance Allowance

	2015–2016
Higher rate	£82.30
Lower rate	£55.10

Paid for care needs of those over 65.
Both allowances are based on need, but there are no restrictions on how they are used. Both allowances are non-contributory, non-means-tested, non-taxable and are ignored as income for means-tested benefits

C. Children

1. Child Benefit (CB)

	2015
Only/elder/eldest child	£20.70
Each subsequent child	£13.70

A child must be under 16, or under 20 and in full-time secondary education, or under 18 and registered for work or work-based training. Will no longer be available to all high rate tax payers from 2013 onwards. Non-contributory and non-taxable.
Administered by HMRC.

2. Guardian's allowance

	2015–2016
Guardian's allowance	£16.55

Payable with child benefit to those raising the children of deceased (or, sometimes, unavailable) parents. Non-contributory, non-taxable. Administered by HMRC.

Entitlement to contributory benefits depends on payment of National Insurance Contributions.
Amounts are per week except for the Surestart Maternity Grant payment and Bereavement benefit lump sum.

I2: Social security benefits and tax credits (means-tested)

Income Support (IS) 2015–2016

For reduced cohort of those under pension age on low income, working less than 16 hrs p.w. (e.g. lone parents of young children, carers, some sick workers and some students). Not for the unemployed (see JSA: Table 28) or new claimants who are sick/disabled (see ESA: ibid.) or most childless people under 18. Children remain dependent while CB (ibid.) is payable, but replacement of allowances by CTC continues.

With some exceptions for existing claimants, new conditions restrict entitlement for lone parents as youngest child reaches threshold age: *5+*.

Main rates only are shown.

IS brings automatic entitlement on income grounds to other benefits including maximum HB and CTC.

A need level is established from the allowances and Premiums right, plus mortgage interest at Bank of England's published monthly average mortgage rate (currently 3.63 per cent) on loans of up to £200,000 (with restrictions on increases during a claim and a reduction for resident non-dependants; current maximum interest payment is £139 p.w.). IS is then paid to supplement other income to the need level. There are detailed rules on the application of premiums and disregarded income. Payments from a former partner may disqualify, including a lump sum payment of any amount (treated as income) but all child maintenance disregarded. No disregard for childcare costs.

Capital up to £6,000 is disregarded (£10,000 for those in residential/nursing homes; £3,000 for child). Capital between £6,000 and £16,000 is deemed to produce tariff income of £1 for each £250 (or part) over £6,000. There is no entitlement to IS if capital exceeds £16,000, disregarding value of home. Notional capital rules penalise deliberate deprivation of capital to obtain IS.

Non-contributory. Rarely taxable.

Personal allowances

		p.w.	p.a.
Single person	16–24	57.90	3,010.80
	25 or over	73.10	3,801.20
Lone parent	Under 18	57.90	3,010.80
	Over 18	73.10	3,801.20
Couple	Both over 18	114.85	5,972.20
Main Premiums			
Carer		34.60	1,799.20
Enhanced disability			
Single		15.75	819.00
Couple		22.60	1,175.20
Severe disability			
Single (or one of couple)		61.85	3,216.20
Couple (both qualifying)		123.70	6,432.40
Existing claimants only (others see CTC):			
Family/lone parent family		17.45	907.40
Disabled child		60.06	3,123.12
Enhanced disability (child)		24.43	1,270.36

Pension Credit (PC) 2015–2016

PC comprises two elements: Guarantee Credit (GC) for those of qualifying age whose income is below the "standard minimum guarantee"; and Savings Credit for those 65 and over with modest savings or income. Either or both are claimable.

Age at which GC available is rising gradually in line with increases in State Pension age; this is key date for other benefits and retirement age-related provisions: for current law see Pensions Act 1995 Sch.4.

Means-tested, some income disregarded. No upper capital limit. £10,000 disregarded; thereafter tariff income is £1 for every £500 (or part).

Not a tax credit. State pension is not affected. Administered by the Pension Service. Child maintenance disregarded; other maintenance disregarded only for savings credit. No provision for childcare costs. Housing costs as for IS. Guarantee Credit is a passport to maximum HB and CTB.

Non-contributory. Not taxable.

Standard Minimum Guarantee		**p.w.**
Single		151.20
Couple		230.85
Additional amount for severe disability		
Single		61.85
Couple (both qualify)		123.70
Additional amount for carers		34.60
Savings Credit		
Threshold	Single	126.50
	Couple	201.80
Maximum	Single	14.82
	Couple	17.43

Working Tax Credit (WTC) 2015–2016

	p.a.
First Income threshold	6,420.00
Withdrawal rate (41%)	
Basic element	1,960.00
Additional couple's/lone parent element	2,010.00
30 hours element	810.00
Disabled worker element	2,970.00
Severe disability element	1,275.00

Childcare element	**p.w.**
Percentage of eligible costs covered (70%)	
Maximum eligible cost (maximum payable £210 p.w.)	300.00
Maximum eligible cost for one child (maximum payable £122.50 p.w.)	175.00

Based on gross annual income: in-work support for families with child/children where lone parent over 16 works at least 16 hours p.w., or couple's combined work hours total 24 hours p.w., with one parent working at least 16 hours p.w. Extra payment for working at least 30 hours p.w. Also in-work support for some households without child, including those 25+ working at least 30 hours p.w., and those 60+ or with disability working at least 16 hours p.w. Up to first threshold, claimants receive the maximum. Credit then tapers by 41p per £1 of income as income rises. Above first threshold, claimant loses main element of WTC first, then childcare element, then child element of any CTC.

Elements are cumulative. Complex assessment rules. Maintenance ignored. Assessment on annual income, joint incomes for couples (disregarding £300 of certain types of unearned income).

Awards provisional until end of year notice identifies under/overpayments. Disregard of £2,500 before in-year falls in income affect entitlement; disregard of £10,000 before in-year rises in income affect entitlement. Administered by HMRC.

Child Tax Credit (CTC) 2015–2016

	p.a.
First Income threshold for those entitled to CTC only	16,105.00
Withdrawal rate (41%)	

Family elements

Family element	545.00

Child elements

Child element (per child)	2,780.00
Disabled child additional element	3,140.00
Severely disabled child additional element	1,275.00

Based on gross annual income, support for families with child/children. First the per child element then the family element taper by 41p per £1 of income once income above £16,105.00 (WTC abated first).

One family element per family. The child elements are cumulative, including any disabled child or severely disabled child additional elements. Paid to nominated main carer.

Replaces most benefit additions for children.

Administered by HMRC.

13: Personal injury trusts

Introduction

Following a serious personal injury a client may receive substantial sums of money, be they from a claim for damages, personal accident insurance payouts, charitable gifts, or other sources.

Such clients often have to live for many years, if not the rest of their lives, with the personal, social and financial repercussions that arise because of their injury. They may be left unable to work, their family members may give up jobs to provide care, and they may have expensive ongoing costs to pay for, such as the costs of private care, case management, specialist aids and equipment. They will also continue to have their regular living costs to meet, including the maintenance of any children or dependant relatives.

Therefore, it is important to ensure that each client is provided with proper and complete advice, and practical support where required, to ensure that:

- they get the best possible award from their personal injury claim;
- they are able to claim all of the state benefits they are entitled to and statutory care and support they need, both now and in years to come; and
- they have a suitable structure in place to properly manage and invest their award in the future.

It is, of course, important for any legal advisor to ensure that they have given each and every client the proper advice with regard to each of these matters. To fail to do so has in the past led to a number of personal injury lawyers being found to have been negligent because they have not provided their clients with proper advice about the possible use of personal injury trusts.

What is a personal injury trust?

A personal injury trust is a formal structure in which to hold and manage any funds which the client has received as a consequence of their personal injury.

A formal trust deed should be put in place, which sets out the rules for the management of the funds. It is important that it is the right kind of trust, that best suits the client's requirements in their particular circumstances.

The trust deed should specify the trustees—two or more people, or a trust corporation, who are then in charge of the trust. The trustees should together make decisions about the management of the trust funds, including any payments made out of those funds, and are under an obligation to exercise their powers for the benefit of those named as beneficiaries. In most cases there will only be one beneficiary, the injured person.

The benefits of a personal injury trust

There are several benefits of having a personal injury trust in place, which include the following (albeit not an exhaustive list):

- If held in a personal injury trust, capital derived from a payment made in consequence of any personal injury to the claimant or the claimant's partner is disregarded for the purpose of many means-tested state benefits and services.
  Therefore, a client (and their partner if they claim benefits together) can continue to receive these benefits, despite having funds within the trust which, if held by them personally, would have left them with too much capital to remain entitled.
  These means-tested state benefits include Income Support, Income Related Employment Support Allowance, Income Based Job Seekers Allowance, Universal Credit, Housing Benefit and Council Tax Support. A personal injury trust exempts capital from means testing for a disabled facilities grant. A trust also protects entitlement to Local Authority funding for care.
- The trust structure can help to protect the interests of young, older, disabled or otherwise vulnerable clients.
  Because of the requirement to have trustees in place who must each authorise all transactions within the trust, a client can be protected if their trustees are vigilant to any inappropriate proposals for the use of the funds.
  A steadfast trustee, be they a solicitor, interested family friend or parent, can exercise their effective veto against the use of trust funds to ensure that the funds are only applied in the client's best interests. The balance of power will depend on the type of trust chosen, and clients who fear that they may need extra safeguards should be advised carefully about this.
- A client can benefit from the knowledge, experience and wisdom of their trustees.
  Having appropriate trustees appointed can provide a client with important advice and support when making big decisions. Particularly when dealing with a large lump sum, this can be invaluable to ensure that decisions are appropriate to protect and ensure the long-term interests of the client.
  Some clients prefer to have an appropriately experienced solicitor appointed as one of their trustees, so that they can give advice on matters such as investment decisions, budgeting, and large items of capital expenditure.
- The personal injury trust helps to define and "ring fence" the funds that arise as a consequence of the client's personal injury, keeping them separate from other assets that may belong to the client.
  This can be of help if the client's circumstances change in the future and they suddenly find that they may be eligible for means-tested benefits or care funding; for example, if they have to go in to a care home, or if they separate from a working partner.
  The personal injury trust "wrapper" can also help to define what funds were awarded for their future needs. This can help to differentiate the funds if the client goes through a divorce or any other process where their personal finances are taken into consideration.

The basic rules for entitlement to means-tested benefits

As you may imagine, the rules for assessing a client's entitlement to means-tested benefits are detailed and complex.

However, when considering how personal injury funds may affect a client's entitlement to means-tested benefits, the key principles for Income Support, Income Related Employment Support Allowance, Income Based Job Seeker's Allowance, Universal Credit, Housing Benefit and Council Tax Support are, broadly speaking, as follows:

- When considering a client's capital, it is important to consider both the personal injury funds that they are due to receive, as well as any savings or investments that they already hold.
- The first payment of any money derived from a personal injury will be ignored for 52 weeks from the date of receipt. An interim payment, or indeed any other payment received as a consequence

of the injury, will qualify as the first payment. The intention of this disregard is that the claimant will have an appropriate period to seek advice and set up the trust.
- If a client has capital below £6,000, then their capital will not affect their entitlement. This lower threshold is £10,000 for those living in a care home or independent hospital.
- If a client has capital between £6,000 and £16,000, then their entitlement will be reduced. For capital between those two thresholds they will be treated as having income of £1 for every £250 or part thereof above £6,000.
- If a client has capital over £16,000 they will be excluded from entitlement altogether.
- A client and their partner (with whom they live) will share a capital allowance, so it is important to look at their capital together. They should ideally have less than £6,000 between them both, if they are to maintain full entitlement.
- Certain assets, such as the value of the home a client lives in and their personal possessions, are disregarded when calculating capital.
- Any income received by the client, including that received by their partner, is deducted from the amount of benefits payable, albeit subject to some personal disregards and allowances.

The basic rules for entitlement to means-tested benefits for elderly clients

For Pension Credit (currently available for new claimants after age 62, which age will increase gradually to 65 by 2018), the lower capital threshold is £10,000, and above that amount tariff income from a client's capital is assumed at a rate of £1 for every £500, or part thereof. There is no upper capital threshold. Income derived from a personal injury settlement is ignored, whether paid from a trust or otherwise. Actual capital is ignored, except to the extent that it creates assumed tariff income.

For Housing Benefit and Council Tax Support, if a client is in receipt of Pension Guarantee Credit, all capital, including partner's capital, is ignored. The effect is that personal injury funds are also ignored. If a client is over 60 and not receiving a qualifying benefit (such as Income Support, Income Related Employment Support Allowance, Income Based Job Seekers Allowance), the lower capital threshold is £6,000 and the capital threshold is £16,000. However, personal injury monies are ignored completely, whether in a trust or not, both in respect of capital and income. Due to the vagaries of the rules, there is a concern that growth on capital assets may not be disregarded. In addition, in order to access the disregard for residential care funding a trust will be required and so it is best to advise clients to consider a trust even if it appears their damages will be disregarded at the moment.

Welfare reform

Since the implementation of the Welfare Reform Act 2012 in March 2013, Council Tax Benefit was abolished from March 31, 2013 and replaced by a discretionary scheme designed by local authorities. Each local authority has its own scheme although there is a national precedent scheme which local authorities can adopt. Ten per cent less money is available to reduce people's Council Tax than was previously available under the Council Tax Benefit scheme. Local authorities have to protect the position of pensioners. The net result is that in many local authority areas, people of working age are having to pay a proportion of their Council Tax even if they would previously have been entitled to full Council Tax Benefit. A number of people have been caught out by this in the belief that they are entitled to full Council Tax Support and so have not paid a great deal of attention to the Council Tax statement which comes once a year until they receive a summons for non-payment.

The primary income related benefits are being replaced by Universal Credit for new claims. That started with October 2013. There can be no new claims for Income Support, Income Related Employment Support Allowance and Income Based Job Seeker's Allowance, after October 2013 and no new claims for Housing Benefit after April 2014. Current claimants for these benefits will be migrated to Universal Credit by 2017.

Readers will be aware that benefits have been a very hot topic recently and it is fair to say that we have not yet seen the full effects of the reforms. It also remains to be seen how far this will have a knock-on effect on social care funding, the calculation of which is closely tied to the existing income-related benefits regulations.

Care funding

The Care Act 2014

The Care Act was implemented on April 1, 2015. It applies in England only. Part 1 of the Act introduces significant changes to the law on care provision and charging for that provision. However under transitional provisions, Part 1 does not apply to cases where immediately before April 1, 2015, support or services were being provided, or payments towards the cost of support or services are being made by the local authority.

The transitional provisions order requires local authorities to complete a reassessment in such cases before April 1, 2016. That reassessment will be carried out under Part 1 Care Act. If no assessment is carried out before April 1, 2016, Part 1 Care Act will apply after that date in any event.

Pre Care Act cases in England and cases in Wales

Residential care

For existing cases in England, and all cases in Wales, the old law will continue to apply as follows:

When a client moves into a residential or nursing care home, they are assessed to see if they should contribute towards some or all of the care home costs. The means-testing regulations are the National Assistance (Assessment of Resources) Regulations 1992 (the "assessment regulations") and there is statutory guidance entitled the "Charging for Residential Accommodation Guidance".

The assessment regulations also apply in Wales but Wales has its own version of CRAG. The principal difference between the English and Welsh versions of CRAG is that there is no tariff income scheme in Wales and hence only one capital limit.

The key principles are as follows:

- The means test applies to the resident only. Any capital or income belonging to their partner beneficially is ignored.
- The value of any assets of the client will be included in the capital calculation, unless they are disregarded under the regulations.
- Changes to the personal injury claimant's residence are common so it is useful to set out the disregards applying to domestic real property.
  The resident's main residence before moving into residential care is subject to a number of potential disregards which include the following:
  - Occupation by the client's partner, former partner or civil partner (except where they are estranged).
  - A lone parent who is the client's estranged or divorced partner.
  - A member of the client's family who is either:

    - aged 60 or over;
    - a child under 16 whom the client is responsible to maintain; or
    - incapacitated.
- Where the stay in the accommodation is temporary, i.e. less than 52 weeks and the resident either intends to return to their home or sell it and buy other accommodation to move into within 52 weeks.
- During the first 12 weeks of a permanent stay.
- A house purchased for the resident within the last 26 weeks or such longer period as is reasonable to allow and which they are taking steps to occupy.
- The proceeds of sale of the former residence if sold within the last 26 weeks or such longer period as is reasonable to allow, where the resident intends to use the proceeds to buy another property for their occupation.

- When considering a resident's capital, the following thresholds are applicable in England in 2015–16:

    - lower threshold £14,250 (England)
    - upper threshold £23,750 (England)

If a resident's capital is above the upper threshold then they pay the costs in full, until or unless their capital is reduced to that amount.

In England, if a resident's capital falls between those two thresholds then they are treated as having income of £1 for every £250 of capital over the lower threshold.

For residents living in Wales, there is only one capital threshold of £24,000, above which clients pay the costs of their care in full, until or unless their capital is reduced to that amount. As noted above, there is no tariff income on capital in Wales.

a) Income received by the client is taken into account subject to the definitions of income contained in the assessment regulations and the disregards contained in Sch.3 to the regulations. A personal allowance of £24.40 per week in England or £25.50 per week in Wales is also disregarded. Income on capital invested under the personal injury trust is disregarded.

b) The first capital payment made to the resident which is derived from a personal injury to them is disregarded for 52 weeks whether or not it is within a personal injury trust, but any sum which a court has specifically identified as being for care is excluded from the disregard (see below for further information).

c) Income paid to the resident from their personal injury trust is disregarded unless it was intended for use and actually used for the payment of elements of the fees that were not taken into account when the local authority standard rate was fixed for the accommodation. The standard rate is the cost of accommodation provided by the local authority. This provision is likely to be intended to apply also to the "usual rate" the local authority charges when placing a resident in independent residential accommodation but the regulation does not make this clear.

Domiciliary care funding

England

Local authorities have discretionary powers under s.17 of the Health and Social Services and Social Security Adjudications Act 1983 to make reasonable charges for adult service users where care is provided at home. The Department of Health has issued mandatory guidance on the operation of such charging schemes entitled "Fairer Charging".

In the case of *Crofton v NHSLA*,[1] the Court of Appeal held that the Fairer Charging guidance incorporates CRAG, but only in so far as CRAG deals with capital. This means that the income provisions of CRAG do not apply to assessments of income and so are at the discretion of the relevant local authority.

Periodical payments would normally be treated as income and therefore fall to be treated at the local authority's discretion. Where the local authority takes account of income, they will usually not be disregarded. It may be possible to avoid this result and specialist advice should be taken if this is likely to impact on the client's ability to afford their care, for example in a reduced liability case.

A new award of a periodical payment will cause reassessment which should bring the matter under the Care Act charging provisions—see below.

The capital within personal injury trusts should be disregarded in the trust because it is a capital asset. However, some local authorities have sought to argue that where a lump sum contains money for care, this is a good reason to depart from the Fairer Charging guidance and they may take such capital into account. In the author's view this is unlawful but the advent of the Care Act will make the issue increasingly obsolete over the 12 months to April 1, 2016—see below.

In England, the assessment of investment income to the trust appears to be a matter for the local authority's discretion. Specialist advice should be sought in relation to setting up a personal trust for those who may need to claim local authority funding for domiciliary care in cases where there is only partial recovery of loss.

Wales

Charges for domiciliary care are subject to the Social Care Charges (Wales) Measure 2010 and associated regulations.[2] Section 1 of the measure provides a power to charge for chargeable care services which are defined in s.13, broadly speaking, as domiciliary care services. At present the maximum weekly charge for domiciliary care is £60.

The Fairer Charging guidance no longer applies in Wales, having been replaced in April 2011 by new statutory guidance. The case of *Crofton* is thus not authority on the question of the applicability of CRAG to a person living in Wales.

The provisions of Pt 3 of the "assessment regulations" relating to capital are incorporated in the means test by regulation[3] save that the main residence is disregarded in any event and the requirements of the assessment regulations are without prejudice to any policy of the local authority to adopt more generous provision. Regulations also provide for the manner in which income is to be assessed. Earnings are disregarded[4]. Investment income to a trust is probably potentially assessable but is subject to the £60 limit.

[1] [2007] EWCA Civ 71.
[2] Social Care Charges (Means Assessment and Determination of Charges) (Wales) Regulations 2011.
[3] Social Care Charges (Means Assessment and Determination of Charges) (Wales) Regulations 2011, reg.14(2)(a).
[4] Social Care Charges (Means Assessment and Determination of Charges) (Wales) Regulations 2011, reg.14(4).

Care Act 2014

The Care and Support (Charging and Assessment of Resources) Regulations 2014 (CSCAR) will apply to all cases that were not receiving a care and support service on March 31, 2015, upon reassessment after April 1, 2015 or from April 1, 2016, whichever is earlier.

The single most significant difference with the previous charging arrangements is that they apply to both domiciliary and residential care. The differences between the new provisions as they apply to each are minor.

Capital placed in a personal injury trust is disregarded for means assessment purposes, both for home and residential care. The arguments previously raised by local authorities that they had discretion to take account of the care element of such assets in domiciliary care cases have no arguable basis under the CSCAR.

Investment income received by trustees upon trust assets is disregarded.

Periodical payments placed in a personal injury trust are also disregarded as income but an issue may arise if this was done to avoid care fees.

Payments made out of a trust to the claimant by the trustees are disregarded unless they are to pay for care. If they are to pay for care, they are only disregarded if the payment was intended to pay for care which the council in its own assessment recognises as a need but which they have not found to be eligible for support by them and the payments are actually used for that purpose. The aim is to allow such payments to be used for topping up care.

Payments made by trustees directly to a domiciliary care provider are disregarded. Regular payments made by trustees to a residential care provider may be treated as the income of the resident.

Care capping proposals

Section 15 of the Care Act provides that the cost to an adult of their care and support other than for daily living costs may be capped.

A consultation on the detail of the measures to be implemented under this section closed on March 30, 2015.

The proposals were to the effect that:

- Care capping would commence on April 1, 2016.
- The care cap would be nil for adults whose care and support needs began before the commencement of the provision and who were aged under 25 at the commencement of the provision.
- For any other adult, the care cap at commencement would be £72,000.
- The cap relates to costs which the local authority assess as eligible for support under the statutory eligibility criteria and are the amount of the personal budget which the authority allows to meet those needs.

At the time of writing the Department of Health has not produced final proposals further to the consultation.

The Social Services & Well-being (Wales) Act 2014

This Act represents the complete separation of legislation relating to social care between England and Wales. It is proposed that the Act will be implemented on April 1, 2016.

The Act allows the current capping of contributions to continue but does not contain proposals for a total payment care cap of the type contained in s.15 of the English Care Act 2014.

At the date of writing, a consultation on the detail of the charging proposals was due but had not been published.

What funds can go into a personal injury trust?

The benefits regulations for most benefits take a wide definition, allowing any sums of capital to be disregarded if they are "derived from a payment made in consequence of any personal injury to the claimant or the claimant's partner". However, the Universal Credit regulations refer to "compensation". The effect of that may be to narrow the types of funds which can be protected in a personal injury trust for injured people who are claiming Universal Credit. Some clients may find that they are in a dual system where certain funds within a trust might be disregarded for care purposes for example but not for Universal Credit. For most benefits however the wider definition means that

The use of personal injury trusts are not just limited to awards of damages, and can include:

- A personal injury award, including interim payments received during the course of a claim.
- A Criminal Injuries Compensation Authority award.
- A Motor Insurers' Bureau award.
- Payments from the Armed Forces Compensation Scheme, and similar schemes.
- Payments from various "no fault" schemes, sometimes set up by government bodies both here and abroad, such as payments from the Irish Residential Institutions Redress Board.
- Funds received from a Periodical Payment or Structured Settlement.
- Charitable or public donations following an accident.
- Funds received from accident or travel insurance.
- Funds received from a professional negligence claim paid to compensate for an undervalued or negligently pursued personal injury claim.

It is vitally important to remember that, although the capital disregard is quite wide, the income disregard is rather more restricted. Where a person receives income from, for example, a personal accident policy or an occupational ill health pension, it is unlikely that those funds would be able to be disregarded or enter a personal injury trust. The author is aware of at least one case working its way through the court process at the moment on this very point.

When to set up a personal injury trust

It is important that, if at all possible, a personal injury trust is set up before a client receives their funds.

Lawyers should be aware that any client funds held on their Client Account may be treated as the client's money by the benefits agency and local authority. Therefore, any funds held on Client Account can jeopardise a client's benefit entitlement and consideration should be given to the suitability of a personal injury trust straight away.

Lawyers also run the risk that if funds remain on their client account, and they are aware that the client has not notified the benefits agency, they could find their firm obliged to report the client's non-disclosure as defrauding the benefits agency. Furthermore, they run the risk that they may be construed as aiding and abetting the client in a possible benefits fraud.

While it is usually best advice that a personal injury trust should be set up sooner rather than later, it is possible to set up a trust after the funds have been received and held personally by the client for some time. There is no restriction upon when personal injury funds must be placed into a trust, so funds can be held for months, or years, before a client arranges to place them in a trust. This does not allow the client to claim retrospectively for any benefits that they have missed out on prior to the trust being set up.

However, a client will have to demonstrate to the satisfaction of the benefits agency, or local authority, that the funds placed into the trust are purely those arising from their personal injury. There is a risk that the funds may over time have been mixed up with, or diluted by, other income or capital belonging to the client. Therefore, clients may find that they have some difficulty persuading the authorities that all of the funds should be disregarded.

Setting up a personal injury trust

It will be necessary to appoint appropriate trustees. There should be at least two trustees, and no more than four. They must be over 18 years of age and mentally capable of acting as a trustee. It is usually best to avoid trustees whose health and age might make them incapable of fulfilling their obligations in the foreseeable future.

The choice of trustees is an important one, as they will for all intents and purposes have full control over the personal injury trust and the assets held within it. It is important to consider whether they will be able to work well together and continue to act in the best interests of the beneficiaries. For this reason, some caution should be exercised before appointing partners, spouses, or other family members as trustees, if there is a risk of the relationship breaking down in the future.

Some clients may prefer to have an appropriately experienced solicitor appointed as one of their trustees. This allows an impartial and professional person to assist in the trustees' deliberations and decision making. It can help to ensure that the trustees are making decisions together which are appropriate to the needs of the beneficiaries, as well as providing the professional expertise and experience that can be invaluable when making difficult decisions.

It is also important that a client receives the correct advice about the right kind of trust to put in place. Consideration needs to be given to the client's particular circumstances, their potential liability to tax and the provision that they may wish to make for their family in the future. This will in turn affect whether the client is named as the sole beneficiary of the trust, or whether other beneficiaries are named and, if so, whether the trustees have any discretion in how they apply funds for their benefit.

The client being advised about Personal Injury Trusts should be advised about wills at the same time.

Once the advice is given, and the necessary decisions are made, the trust deed will need to be prepared by the instructed lawyer, before being signed in the presence of witnesses, and dated. The personal injury trust will usually have a suitable title, such as the "John Smith Personal Injury Trust."

Once a personal injury trust is set up

Once a personal injury trust is set up, the trustees' first act will usually be to open a bank or building society account to hold the trust funds. The account should be suitably named, such as the "Josephine

Anne Bloggs Personal Injury Trust". The account should usually require that each and every one of the trustees is required to sign to authorise all transactions on account, including all cheques.

Once the trustees have set up the trust bank account, the personal injury lawyer can confidently arrange for a cheque to be issued for the personal injury funds, ensuring that the cheque is made payable to the trust, i.e. payable to the "Josephine Anne Bloggs Personal Injury Trust", and not to the client personally.

The trustees will need to keep to certain rules in order to be able to use funds from the trust without affecting the client's benefit entitlement, namely:

- Any income arising from the funds in the trust, such as interest or dividends, should be paid into a trust account, and not paid to the client personally.
- The trustees can transfer funds into the client's own personal account, but should take care to ensure that the client's capital (including the capital held by their partner if they are claiming benefits as a couple) stays below £6,000 at all times, which is the lower capital threshold for most means-tested benefits.
- Possibly the simplest way to use funds from the trust is to make direct payments from the trust to third parties. This way the funds go directly from the trust account, to the third party and do not go through the client's hands in any way.
- Any further assets set up to be held by the trustees, be they bank accounts, investments or property, should be set up with the same restrictions as the original trust bank account, namely:
  - in the name of the trust, or trustees; and
  - with the restriction that each and every one of the trustees is required to sign all transactions with regard to that asset.

Is a client likely to benefit from a personal injury trust in the future?

For many clients it is easy to determine that they are entitled to means-tested benefits, or care funding, at the time that they receive their funds, and so it makes sense to protect their entitlement straight away by setting up a personal injury trust.

However, some clients may at the time have no entitlement to means-tested benefits, and so a personal injury trust may not seem immediately relevant. In such cases careful consideration should be given to the client's potential to claim means-tested benefits in the future.

A client may become entitled to means-tested benefits in the future if their relevant circumstance change, which may include:

- If they need to move to live in a care home.
- If they move out of the family home to live on their own.
- If they leave full- or part-time education.
- If they are discharged from hospital or residential care.
- If they and their spouse divorce or separate.
- When they reach a significant age for benefits purposes, such as 16, 18 or 60 years of age or within state pension age, currently 62.
- If they or their partner lose their job, retire or are medically unable to continue to work.
- If they, or their partner, lose their entitlement to another benefit or source of income.
- If they, or their partner, find their health deteriorates and they become entitled to higher rates of disability benefits, which in turn have a knock-on effect for some means-tested benefits.
- If they, or their partner, find that they have used up their pre-existing savings (those which have not arisen from the personal injury claim and which have previously prevented them claiming means-

tested benefits) and so find that they would become entitled to means-tested benefits if their personal injury funds were disregarded as capital.

In such cases clients should be advised to use up their pre-existing savings with some caution. The benefits agency or local authority can ask to look at a person's history of expenditure, and any gifts made, to see if the client has in the opinion of the authority, deliberately depleted their estate in order to gain entitlement to means-tested benefits or services. If the authority feels that a client has deliberately depleted their estate in such a manner, they can decide to treat the spent funds as "notional capital", essentially treating the client as if they still have the funds and leaving them with no entitlement to the means-tested benefit or service which they have applied for. Therefore, it is important that clients keep a careful record of their expenditure to demonstrate that their use of funds has been reasonable and not a deliberate attempt to deplete their estate.

The 52-week rule

Payments received as a consequence of a personal injury are disregarded for the purpose of assessing entitlement to means tested benefits for the first 52 weeks after they are received.

However, that disregard applies only to the first payment received as a consequence of that personal injury, which may often be the client's first interim payment. It is also important to check to see a client has received other earlier payments, which may count as their "first payment", such as payments from an accident insurance policy or even a capital payment from a charity.

Any later payments, including further interim payments, are not protected by this disregard after the expiry of the original 52-week period.

Under the Universal Credit regulations there is a disregard of 52 weeks for every payment. That may be helpful for some clients who receive smaller awards but if they decide not to set up a trust they will need to be extremely careful in monitoring the various 52 week disregard periods. Establishing which funds form part of which interim and when the disregard therefore runs out could be quite tricky and the client would be caught out.

Therefore, when receiving a first payment as a consequence of a personal injury, a client may choose not to set up a trust if they anticipate spending enough of that sum to bring their capital below the relevant threshold by the end of the 52-week period. However, they should be advised to hold that payment in a bank account separate from any other funds. That way, if towards the end of period they find that they unexpectedly have funds remaining, they can still arrange to place them into a personal injury trust safe in the knowledge that the funds have not become mixed up with other capital in any way.

However, in many cases it will be appropriate to set up a personal injury trust as soon as any funds are received, regardless of the 52-week rule. Where the amount of funds due to the client overall are almost certainly going to last longer than that period, there is little if no benefit in delaying the setting up of a personal injury trust which is likely to remain in place to manage the client's funds for many years to come.

Personal injury trusts for children and protected parties

In most cases the decision as to whether or not to set up a personal injury trust is one for the client to make for themselves, albeit with the benefit of good advice from a lawyer. The matter does not require court approval in any way.

However, if a client is unable to make their own decision it will be necessary to obtain approval from the appropriate court with authority to make a decision on behalf of the client (CPR r.21.11 and supplementary Practice Direction), namely:

- The High Court will need to approve the establishment of a personal injury trust to manage an infant's funds until the infant reaches 18 years of age.
- In cases involving mentally incapable people, the Court of Protection will need to approve the establishment of a personal injury trust, in preference to the appointment of a Deputy for Property and Affairs. Following the case of *Re HM*,[5] the court is likely to approve the establishment of trusts in limited circumstances only.

It is important to note that the disregards which apply for benefits for funds derived from a personal injury are also available for injury derived funds held under the auspices of the Court of Protection.

As regards disregards for care and support under the Care Act 2014, the disregards for deputies and personal injury trusts are very similar.

[5] (2011) C.O.P. 11875043 April 11, 2011.

14: Claims for loss of earnings and maintenance at public expense

The Administration of Justice Act 1982 s.5 provides that where an injured claimant seeks to recover damages for loss of earnings, the defendant can set off against that claim any saving attributable to maintenance (either wholly or partly) at public expense in a hospital, nursing home or other institution.

This deduction is comparable to (but not the same as) the common law principle that where a claimant is in a private hospital or home (in respect of which damages are claimed from the defendant), credit must be giving for the domestic expenses thereby saved. This is the "domestic element" which was discussed in *Fairhurst v St Helens and Knowsley Health Authority.*[1]

15: Foster care allowances

Introductory notes:

Every April the Fostering Network publishes the cost of bringing up a child in its own home for the next 12 months. Contact Fostering Network Publications, 87 Blackfriars Road, London SE1 8HA (tel: 020 7620 6400; *http://www.fostering.net*).

The Fostering Network publishes Foster Care Finance, with recommended minimum weekly allowances for fostering in the UK and a full survey of allowances paid by each local authority. The Fostering Network's recommended minimum allowance depends on the age of the child and whether or not the placement is in London. The allowances do not include any form of reward for carers themselves. The Fostering Network recommends four extra weeks' payment, to cover the cost of birthdays, holidays and a religious festival. It encourages local authorities to pay allowances to all carers at least in line with its recommended rates. Despite such encouragement the majority of local authorities give foster carers less than the Fostering Network's recommended minimum allowances for spending on the care of fostered children. From a survey published by the Fostering Network in September 2003, 53 per cent of local authorities in England and 87 per cent of local authorities in Wales paid below the Fostering Network's recommended minimum allowance.

Fostering Network recommended costs of bringing up a child in its own home for the year beginning April 6, 2015

Age of child (years)	London (£ per week)	South East (£ per week)	Rest of the UK (£ per week)
0–4	145.00	140.00	126.00
5–10	163.00	156.00	139.00
11–15	184.00	177.00	159.00
16+	216.00	208.00	185.00

In *Spittle v Bunney*[2] it was said that the cost of fostering services is not an appropriate measure for the value of the loss of a (deceased) mother's services, but the case is not uncontroversial.

[1] [1995] P.I.Q.R. Q1, at Q8 and Q9.
[2] [1988] 1 W.L.R. 847.

Group J
Court of Protection

J

J1: Note on the Court of Protection

The Mental Capacity Act 2005 and the Court of Protection

It is important to understand some of the background to, and the purpose of, the legislation. The original bill was known as the Mental Incapacity Bill. This became the Mental Capacity Act (the Act). That change is critical in that the removal of those two letters make all the difference to the tone of the Act. The Act is very much intended to empower incapacitated adults. All of us practitioners in this field need to acknowledge that fact and continually keep the principles as set out in s.1 of the Act in the forefront of our minds at all times:

1. A person must be assumed to have capacity unless it is established that he lacks capacity.
2. A person is not to be treated as unable to make a decision unless all practicable steps to help him to do so have been taken without success.
3. A person is not to be treated as unable to make a decision merely because he makes an unwise decision.
4. An act done, or decision made, under this Act for or on behalf of a person who lacks capacity must be done, or made, in his best interests.
5. Before the act is done, or the decision is made, regard must be had to whether the purpose for which it is needed can be as effectively achieved in a way that is less restrictive of the person's rights and freedom of action.

It is easy to assume that, because the Court of Protection has not changed its name and the Public Guardianship Office has only changed slightly to the Office of the Public Guardian, nothing much occurred on October 1, 2007 when the Act came fully into force. In fact fundamental changes took place.

It is also important to note that there is a complete separation now between the Office of the Public Guardian (OPG) and the Court of Protection.

The old Court of Protection was merely an Office of the Supreme Court, whereas the new court is a superior Court of Record with equal authority to that of the High Court. Indeed certain functions of the High Court concerning termination of life cases have been transferred to the new Court of Protection. However, it is important to remember that an application to the court is the last remedy to consider. The Code of Practice established under the Act sets out clearly that matters should, wherever possible, be reached by negotiation rather than an application to the court.

The PGO was the administrative office of the old court, whereas the new Office of the Public Guardian has no connection with the court. Its role is purely to act on behalf of the Public Guardian and its role so far as this note is concerned is to supervise the conduct of Deputies. It has no part in the administration of cases.

The new court has no administrative arm and has no continuing record of clients, or case workers dealing with their affairs. Its role is purely to make decisions by the issuing of declarations or orders which might or might not involve the appointment of a Deputy.

The new court has wider powers than the old court and can make orders about welfare issues as well as financial matters.

The aim of the court is always to resolve matters in the manner least intrusive into a person's affairs. As a result the process of appointing a Financial Deputy is only to be pursued when it is quite clear, based on medical evidence, that a client lacks capacity to manage his financial affairs. The Mental Capacity Act is an evolving piece of legislation. Since coming fully into force on October 1, 2007 the Act has had significant amendments to it. The Mental Health Act 2008 amended the Act in respect of

Deprivation of Liberty issues and brought in a second Code of Practice on Deprivation of Liberty safeguards. Furthermore, from the outset the OPG announced an intention to review the implementation of the Act 12 months after coming into force in order to review its aims and ambitions, of both empowering and protecting those who lacked capacity, were being met.

This has resulted in a series of consultation papers which have amended from time to time the numerous statutory instruments supporting the principle legislation. The first related to "Forms, supervision and fees". This resulted in two new statutory instruments coming into force on May 1, 2010. One related to Enduring Powers of Attorney. The other made minor amendments to the fees exemption region and the bonding process.

This was followed by a consultation on rule changes. Recommendations were made as a result of that consultation but as yet no changes have been implemented.

A third consultation ended in May 2011 in relation to OPG fees and a new structure of fees came in to effect from October 1, 2011.

1. The scope and authority of the Court of Protection

As mentioned above it is important to remember that the court is a solution of last resort in most respects. However, as far as the Personal Injury/Clinical Negligence lawyer is concerned it is the first resort to obtain the appointment of a Deputy to deal with an incapacitated client's financial affairs.

To make an application it has to be established that a person lacks capacity in accordance with the definition as set out in s.2 of the Act:

"A person lacks capacity in relation to a matter if at the material time he is unable to make a decision for himself in relation to the matter because of an impairment of, or a disturbance, in the functioning of the mind or brain".

It is important to remember that there is no general level below which a client lacks capacity and above which he does not. The statement that a person "lacks capacity" in itself is meaningless. When and in connection with what issues does a person lack capacity? Clearly some clients will lack capacity concerning all their financial affairs but most clients retain some capacity and it is for the Deputy to establish the areas and the extent to which the client has capacity and ensure that he does not trespass there. All Deputyship Orders make it absolutely clear that the Deputy has no authority to decide any matters on which the client retains capacity.

The second part of the test is equally important. One must establish that the lack of capacity is as a result of "an impairment of, or a disturbance in the functioning of the mind or brain". A COP3 Assessment of Capacity form establishing both heads is required in support of the application.

Section 3 of the Act sets out that for the purposes of establishing the lack of capacity it is necessary to show that the client is unable:

"(a) to understand the information relevant to the decision;
(b) to retain that information;
(c) to use or weigh that information as part of the process of making the decision; or;
(d) to communicate his decision (whether by talking, using sign language or any other means)."

In essence failing to meet any one of the first three tests will establish the lack of capacity on a specific decision. However, someone who passes all three tests yet is unable to communicate his decision also is deemed to lack capacity in this context, even though medically he may have full capacity.

Putting all this in the context of Personal Injury or Clinical Negligence litigation one of the first occasions where capacity may be an issue, apart from the actual commencement of proceedings, is when the first interim payment is to be made. Can the client manage this? It is quite possible that a head-injured client may have capacity to manage modest funds of say a few thousand pounds. However, when a significant interim payment is made, he may not. A Deputy is not needed until you reach the point where the client cannot manage the funds available. However, if a Deputy is appointed knowing a significant settlement is due eventually, then the role of the Deputy in respect of minor interims may be just to stand aside and let the client deal with them.

2. The appointment of a property and affairs Deputy

Practitioners need to understand that the role of a Deputy is different to that of the pre-MCA Receiver. The appointment of a receiver was based on the concept of a one-off assessment of capacity. If it was found that the client "lacked capacity" then the power of the Receiver meant that the Receiver could take over all financial decision-making from the client and there was no need to re-consider the matter again. All Deputyship orders make it quite clear that whilst the Deputy may have wide powers to manage all of a client's financial affairs, under no circumstances can a Deputy make a decision on a matter where the client has the capacity to make his own decision. Furthermore, if the Deputy did do so then that decision would be invalid. A Deputy's authority only extends to matters where it is "established" that the client lacks capacity himself. As a result a lot more time and effort needs to be taken on a decision-by-decision basis for many clients to establish a lack of capacity.

Often there can be conflicting medical evidence as to the question of capacity. If that is the case then all such evidence must be put before the court when making an application. This can be a problem for litigators because there may be contrary evidence in existence which they do not wish to disclose in the litigation. It has to be disclosed in the Court of Protection application.

3. The timing of an application

It is important not to apply sooner than necessary. For instance, a client may have capacity to manage small interim payments but not to manage a larger sum.

Applications will usually be dealt with within the terms of the court's service levels of 21 weeks. However, Orders can be issued more quickly in some cases. As from September 1, 2010 Orders are only issued once the surety bond is in place. Previously the Order was issued but did not come into force until one calendar month after issue to allow for the bond to be put in place. This change in procedure means a slight delay in the issuing of Orders but it means the Order is fully effective from the date of its issue.

4. Professional or lay Deputy

In cases involving recovery of large amounts of say £500,000 or more (excluding Deputyship costs) it is reasonable to apply for the appointment of a professional Deputy and recover the costs of the Professional Deputyship as a specific head of future loss. There is no prescribed figure for the application for the appointment of a professional Deputy. A lot will depend on the circumstances of the individual claimant. However, in larger damages cases it is suggested that a professional is preferred as it can often remove family tensions that get in the way when a family member is appointed. Also if no professional costs are claimed at the outset then, if in later life a professional is needed, his costs are a real drain on the funds of the claimant.

5. Decision making by Deputies

When a Deputy makes a decision on behalf of a person he needs to make that decision in the person's best interests. There is no definition of "best interests" under the Act; merely guidelines of what to consider in deciding what is in a person's best interests. These guidelines are set out in s.4 of the Act. The overriding rule is that the decision maker must consider all relevant circumstances. In that respect the client has a role to play in the decision making process. The Deputy *must* consider whether it is likely that the client will have capacity at some time in relation to the decision and if so, when. Also the Deputy "so far as reasonably practicable" *must* permit and encourage the client to be involved as far as possible in the decision making process. He must also "if it is practicable" *and appropriate* consult certain others such as family, and carers, etc. The need to consult these others is often referred to whereas the need to consult and involve the client, which is a stronger obligation, is often forgotten. It may be uncomfortable but it is required.

6. The role of the financial Deputy

It is often assumed that the role of the financial Deputy is akin to that of a bank manager or book keeper. This is not so. Whilst there is a high element of routine involved, in high value cases there is a lot of highly technical and complex work to be carried out in connection with such things as house adaptations, carer employment, and investments. It is important to allocate the lowest appropriate grade or fee earner to each piece of work. As a result the Deputy will probably only be able to charge at grade A or B for small amounts of work.

In summary, the routine work of a professional Deputyship includes the following, amongst other things:

(a) liaison with an application to the Court of Protection and the Office of the Public Guardian where necessary;
(b) preparation of annual accounts/reports to the Office of the Public Guardian;
(c) completion of tax returns and payment to the Inland Revenue as necessary;
(d) dealing with requests for capital expenditure;
(e) setting appropriate budgets and regular payments as appropriate;
(f) considering and approving investment proposals;
(g) overseeing and arranging the employment and retention of care workers and other employed staff, and liaison as appropriate with the case manager;
(h) overseeing and arranging payment of national insurance contributions and PAYE tax in respect of any employees' wages;
(i) liaising with the person whose affairs are being dealt with and, wherever possible, taking all practical steps to enable them to make their own decisions;
(j) liaising with the person's family, associates, care managers and other parties as appropriate (in accordance with the "best interests" criteria);
(k) ensuring that the person receives the correct state benefits, council tax benefits and exemptions, housing benefit and local authority/public funding for care; and
(l) payment of bills, fees and regular expenses.

Most of these items should be carried out at grade C or D where possible. If there is not such a grade fee earner available then higher grade fee earners will only recover the lower grade hourly rates. The Supreme Court Costs Office are becoming very focused on the proportionality of charges.

7. Welfare Deputies

When the Act came into being there was much talk about appointing welfare Deputies in some numbers. However, in reality very few welfare Deputies have been appointed. This is because if you follow through the principles of the Act and in particular the concept of dealing with decisions in a way which is least restrictive of the person's rights and freedoms then the idea of having a welfare Deputy is, in fact, the most restrictive way of dealing with welfare matters. Accordingly, welfare Deputyships are only really for the most severely disabled who require constant welfare decisions made for them. The concept of a professional welfare Deputy is also extremely rare and the payment structure under the court's rules extremely limited as a consequence.

8. Approval of damages awards by the Court of Protection

Prior to October 2007 the Master of the Court of Protection would often provide email approval of a personal injury settlement, but this procedure has now ceased as from October 1, 2007. The Civil Procedure (Amendment) Rules 2007 set out amendments to CPR Pt 21 which provides that only a Master, designated Civil Judge or his nominee should normally hear applications for the approval of a settlement or compromise involving a "protected beneficiary" (a person who lacks capacity to manage or control any money recovered by him or on his behalf in the proceedings). Therefore, the approval of the Court of Protection is no longer required.

9. Charges for the appointment of Deputies and management by professional Deputies.

The costs of a professional Deputy is a significant item of any large personal injury or clinical negligence claim (including CICA and MIB) involving a head-injured client.

It is important to put together the claim for Deputyship costs extremely carefully as they will be a significant item of any claim. Even if you have the in-house experience to prepare your own costs statement there is a line of argument that an independent expert's statement is to be preferred merely to establish objectivity.

Whilst many elements of a claim will be standard, e.g. court fees and OPG fees, the annual costs of acting as a professional Deputy will vary from case to case. It may well be that a "difficult" client's costs will be significantly higher than those of a very passive head-injured client. Costs will vary between the early and late years of a case. It is impossible to be prescriptive about the costs of a professional Deputy. The role is not like that of a carer or even a case manager where exact numbers of hours are claimed each month. It is therefore prudent in the case of a Deputy to include some contingency for unexpected events. It is very difficult to weigh up accurately how many head-injured clients will behave on a long-term basis. A lot comes down to experience.

The requirements of the MCA and the Code of Practice means in ensuring that a Deputy does not make decisions which the client can make for himself mean a lot more time can be spent on assessing capacity now. When it is established that there is a lack of capacity in respect of a specific decision, it is necessary for the Deputy to assess what will be in the client's best interests. All this takes time.

It is a requirement for the Deputy, or at least someone on his behalf, to visit the client at least once a year at home, but it may be that such visits are necessary more frequently for some clients. It would be usual for more visits to be required in the early stages, particularly after settlement, owing to the number of decisions which will be required at that time.

Regarding the terms of the Deputyship Order, it should also be borne in mind that a Deputy may need to make further applications from time to time to the court. Orders can be limited as to time and the amount of funds that can be spent in a year. Time-limited Orders are typically given at the outset before a compensation claim has been settled. Financially limited Orders may be given to reduce the surety bond costs or for many other reasons. All Orders are not the same.

10. Fixed costs in the Court of Protection

A new Practice Direction lays down categories of fixed costs effective from February 1, 2011. They provide an alternative in low cost cases to having your bills assessed. Court Orders will state whether fixed costs are to apply. Normally Deputyship Orders will give the option to take fixed costs or have detailed assessment.

The Practice Direction deals with the following:

(a) Payments on account—where detailed assessment applies, a professional Deputy may take payments on account for the first three quarters of the year which are proportionate to the work undertaken but which must not exceed 20 per cent of the estimated annual charges. The balance is then recovered following the detailed assessment. The only bill submitted for assessment is at the end of the Deputyship year.

(b) Solicitors costs in court proceedings:

(i) Work up to and including the making of the Order appointing a Deputy for Property and Affairs—an amount not exceeding £850 plus VAT.
(ii) Annual management fees for the first year of Deputyship—an amount not exceeding £1,500 plus VAT: for the second and subsequent years £1,185 plus VAT.
(iii) Preparation and lodgement of accounts—an amount up to £235 plus VAT.
(iv) Preparation of HMRC Income Tax return—an amount up to £235 plus VAT.

(c) Conveyancing costs—for the first time for many years there are fixed fees for conveyancing. On sales or purchases a value element of 0.15 per cent of the consideration may be charged subject to a minimum of £350 and a maximum of £1,500 plus VAT and disbursements. This is a reduction from previous fixed rates. There are other fixed fees in the Practice Direction—see the details on the HMCS website.

11. Court fees in relation to Deputyship

As mentioned previously the OPG's fees are undergoing review in a consultation that ends on May 21, 2011. The new fees are intended to apply from July 1, 2011. The editors do not know what they will be but the proposals are outlined below.

The current fees are:

OPG fees

1. Deputy Assessment fee £100

A one-off fee for carrying out a risk assessment to decide the level of supervision to apply.

2. Supervision fees:

• Type I supervision (highest)	£320 per annum
• Type IIA (intermediate)	£320 per annum
• Type II supervision (lower)	£320 per annum
• Type III supervision (minimal)	£35 per annum

Supervision will vary. Typically on larger cases with a professional Deputy there will be Type 1 Supervision until the case settles and then it will move to II or IIA. Type III applies to small value cases for which the capital threshold is currently £18,000 increasing to £19,500 in April 2013 and then £21,000 in April 2014.

Court of Protection fees

• Application fee for the appointment of a Deputy	£400
• Application fee for any other application, e.g. statutory will	£400
• Appeal fee for filing a notice appealing a court decision	£400
• Hearing fee—in addition to the application fee	£500

Fee remissions and exemptions

There are fee exemptions and remissions available for both the OPG and Court of Protection fees.

For both OPG and Court of Protection fees a full exemption is available if a person is in receipt of any of the following means-tested benefits:

- Income Support /ESA.
- Income-based Jobseeker's Allowance.
- State Pension Guarantee Credit.
- A combination of Working Tax Credit and either Child Tax Credit, Disability Element or Severe Disability Element.
- Housing Benefit.
- Council Tax Benefit.

AND the person has not been awarded damages of more than £16,000 which were disregarded in calculating chargeability for any of the above benefits.

For Court of Protection fees a person is eligible for the relevant fee remission if their gross annual income falls within the following bands

Up to £12,000	Full remission
£12,001–£13,500	75% remission
£13,501–£15,000	50% remission
£15,501–£16,500	25% remission
£16,501 and above	No remission

For OPG fees a person is eligible for a 50 per cent reduction if their gross annual income is less than £12,000.

12. Surety Bonds for Deputies

Initially, there was a great deal of uncertainty about Surety Bonds. Judicial independence meant that there was no set scale and there was clear evidence that different judges had different attitudes to bonding and the amount of surety required. As a result of the case of *Re H*[1] (COP) this has now been resolved. Judge Hazel Marshall laid down clear guidelines to be followed in calculating a suitable level of surety.

Typically, bond premiums for solicitors acting as professional Deputies in high value Personal Injury/Clinical Negligence claims are no more than £250–£350 per annum, even where settlement levels are several million pounds. (This takes account of the existence of the solicitors' professional indemnity policy.) Where a large portion of a settlement is met by periodic payments then that will serve to reduce the level of bonding.

13. Wills and statutory wills

No one under the age of 18 may make a will. This principle cannot be avoided even by the use of trusts for minors who, it may be thought, will not survive beyond 18.

If a person of 18 or over has testamentary capacity he can make a will for himself and give his own instructions. If not, then it is possible for a statutory will to be made.

In order to give instructions for a will a person must be able to understand the following:

(a) The nature of the document to be executed.
(b) The extent of his property and estate.
(c) The nature of the claims of those he proposes to benefit or exclude from participation in the will.

These are the criteria set down in the case of *Banks v Goodfellow.*[2]

[1] [2009] EWHC B31.
[2] (1870) L.R. 5 Q.B.

Many clients whose financial affairs are dealt with by a Deputy have such testamentary capacity. If the Deputy obtains a certificate of testamentary capacity the client can give instructions and execute his will in the usual way. However, if it is established that the client lacks testamentary capacity then an application to the Court of Protection for a statutory will to be executed on his behalf should be made.

Practice Direction F supplemental to Pt 9 of the Court of Protection Rules 2007 sets out the detailed procedure.

The cost of such an application can be significant as the procedure requires the involvement of the Official Solicitor on behalf of the client and the notification of anyone adversely affected by the applications, e.g. those who might lose their entitlement under an intestacy by the terms of the proposed will.

A Medical Certificate will be required. The court fee of £400 will apply to the application and if it goes to a hearing a further £500 court fee will apply. Many applications are dealt with on the papers and no attendance is required. Hearings will normally only be required if there are serious disputes over the proposed will. Costs can amount in the simplest of cases to a few thousand pounds and in the most difficult of cases tens of thousands of pounds. The usual rule about costs is that all parties' costs are paid out of the testator's estate. However, the court has discretion to order costs against any party if it believes he has acted unreasonably. It is important to claim this item properly in the compensation claim.

14. Keeping up to date

As from April 2011 the OPG website has closed. Information about the OPG is now found in the DIRECTGOV site and that for the Court of Protection on the HMCS website. Neither is as easy to navigate as the OPG site but hopefully that will change.

SOME IMPORTANT INFORMATION ABOUT BENEFITS RELEVANT TO DEPUTIES

Income Support (Amended) Regulations 1987 as amended.

52-week disregard

Under para.12A of Sch.10 to the Regulations (which since April 7, 2008 extend to means testing for Local Authority funded care or Direct Payments) practitioners have to be careful when receiving interim payments.

In essence there is a period of 52 weeks running from the day of receipt of the first payment (no matter how small) in consequence of a personal injury claim, during which the capital received will be disregarded. However, you do not receive a separate 52-week period on future payments.

e.g. £10,000 interim received six months ago.
£100,000 final compensation received today.

The 52-week period starts on the date of the first payment, so that the disregard for the £100,000 will actually expire in 26 weeks' time.

In most cases interims are received over a much longer period such that the disregard will run out well before the interim is exhausted. As a result the funds received do have to be disclosed. However, if the funds are held by the Deputy under the Deputyship order then they are disregarded regardless of the 52-week period. There is no need to put funds in a personal injury trust if they are held by a Deputy under a Court of Protection Order.

Payments other than the interim may also trigger the 52-week disregard period if they are paid "in consequence of" a personal injury, e.g. personal accident insurance or a statutory "no fault" scheme.

Funds held in or out of court

Under the Regulations funds received as a consequence of a personal injury are disregarded entirely if they are either held in trust or are under the control of the Court of Protection.

Most practitioners are aware of the trust exception but may not fully understand the Court of Protection exemption. Originally, in order to qualify for the exemption the funds of a Deputy had to be held in court, i.e. actually be invested through Court Funds Office. However, since April 7, 2008 as a result of SI 593/2008 that restriction no longer applies. Now funds held "to the Order of the Court" are disregarded. As a result funds invested more freely, including in property, remain disregarded as long as they are in the Deputy's name. Accordingly there is no need to contemplate personal injury trusts where there is a Deputyship.

J2: The incidence of Deputyship costs over a claimant's life

1. The appointment of a Deputy is likely to arise for a personal injury/clinical negligence claimant when he lacks capacity to manage his financial and property affairs, i.e. he is a protected person for the purpose of the Mental Capacity Act 2005 prior to the index injury or insult or as a consequence thereof. In either case Deputyship costs are a recoverable head of loss:
   - where the incapacity preceded the index injury or insult, but it is only in consequence of that injury or insult that the claimant has financial affairs and property of sufficient size and complexity to warrant the appointment of a Deputy, and
   - where the incapacity is a direct consequence of the injury/insult.
2. Minority is not of itself an incapacity for these purposes but it is the Court of Protection's practice to appoint a Deputy for infants where the damages are significant and the probability is that the infant will not acquire legal capacity on attaining his majority.
3. At the latest admission of liability and/or judgement an application should be made without delay. This is in order that a decision maker, i.e. the Deputy, can be put in place as soon as possible to enable interim funds to be applied for the claimant's benefit. An application may be made earlier if the circumstances in which an eventual award is a probability.
4. The process of application for a Deputy will involve the solicitor concerned in undertaking a fact-find with the claimant and his family for preparation and completion of the application; service in person upon the claimant and close members of family of notice of intention to apply; and of the application itself once issued. Fees will arise for the Court of Protection on application; and on appointment with the office of the public guardian. Work may typically be undertaken by the Deputy and/or solicitors acting on his behalf on an interim basis in relation to the management of the claimant's property and affairs either in anticipation of, or with the benefit of, interim authorities provided on application by the court.
5. The order appointing a Deputy is also authority for assessment of costs involved in the application. Cost Draftsman and SCCO assessment fees will arise accordingly to the claimant's account.
6. The court will in addition require the Deputy to enter into a security bond. The extent of the bond appropriate is in the discretion of the judge. Considerations are detailed in the case of *Re H*. They include whether the Deputy is a professional and has the benefit of PII and in a Solicitor's case of the compensation fund; the extent of the annual income; and the size of assets generally which are readily accessible by the Deputy without further reference to the court. The figure provided in the accompanying cost breakdown is an estimate in a typical cerebral palsy and/or catastrophic brain injury case.
7. It is important to check the terms in which the first general order is made to ensure that it provides the Deputy with the authorities sought on the application and/or likely to be required, for example to purchase a property and/or to invest. Failing this, short of the court's accepting an error which requires correction, a separate application for amendment will be required and will attract a fee and costs associated with its preparation and conduct. Applications will generally be dealt with on paper without a hearing but nonetheless can take three months to be processed even on that basis. The initial application can be anticipated to take at least six months as will an application for appointment of a new Deputy.
8. The management of the claimant's property and affairs then proceeds in annual stages—Deputyship years. The anniversary of the initial order appointing the Deputy is authority for the Deputy's assessment of his/her costs of the preceding year. The Deputy can take payments on account during the year at quarterly intervals: currently the amount is 20 per cent of the total anticipated annual costs per quarter, for the first three quarters of the Deputyship year, which will be set-off against the eventual bill once approved by the SCCO.

9. The security bond will be renewed on an annual basis and in addition an OPG annual supervision fee will be payable. This is charged according to a scale and depends upon the level of supervision deemed appropriate by the OPG. It will generally be higher in the case of a lay, as opposed to a professional, Deputy. Initially a claim is ongoing and in the immediate post-settlement years the level of supervision may also be set at a higher level (probably type 2A intermediate), being reduced once a routine is in place (down to type 2 light touch). All levels of supervision, apart from level three supervision where a client has minimal assets, now carry a fixed fee of £320 per annum.

10. In the initial years of a Deputyship, costs can be anticipated to be higher than they will be in subsequent years. Costs are given in the accompanying breakdown for the "first two Deputyship years" within which it is contemplated that significant structural issues will be addressed including;

    - acquisition and adaptation of accommodation,
    - the major/initial investment decisions, and
    - the establishment, through Case Managers or otherwise, of care and other support regimes.

11. The impact of the litigation should be factored in while this is being undertaken. Litigation will inevitably increase costs because:

    - long-term budgeting even on an annual basis will not generally be possible while the Deputyship is in its infancy and the claimant is dependent upon interim payments,
    - liaison with the litigation team will be required including as to the claimant's requirements for interim funding; the adequacy of offers made in these connections; the provision of evidence in support of applications; the provision of copy financial and other records and their appropriate collation; and the consideration of the eventual form of order and of financial advice in relation thereto, and
    - Stresses will occur to the claimant and his family. These can be anticipated to extend beyond settlement of the action/final judgment. It is a commonplace that the first year or two post-litigation are likely to be unsettled.

12. Thus "the first two Deputyship years" may extend over a greater period of time. When the conclusion of the assessment of damages approaches, there are likely to be a number of years that are already "history". When concluding assessment of damages approaches, these are likely to be a number of years for which the bills for Deputyship costs have been assessed and paid. Heightened costs associated with the litigation itself and the major structural adjustments in prospect will extend beyond the end of the litigation. At least one year should be allowed for the major investment decisions and for the claimant and family to settle down (even if relocation to suitable alternative accommodation has already taken place).

13. The general management costs identified for "the first two Deputyship years" are for a case of medium level complexity. Depending on all the circumstances and needs of the claimant including importantly the interplay and relationship with his/her family, the costs could be greater or less. All is contingent upon the level of activity required of the Deputy and their team. The range might be between £12/13,000 and £30,000 or more for general management costs.

14. Matters usually settle down to a general routine after that period. A range of £8,000–12,000 for general management costs might be anticipated in a typical cerebral palsy/acquired brain injury claim. Decisions may have to be taken about the claimant and his best interest and those of the family. Previous decisions should be revised.

15. It must be borne in mind that the MCA requires the deputy to consult on decisions to be made. A claimant will often require face-to-face meetings so that the Deputy is able to provide him with appropriate explanations for decisions. The time and cost of dealing with this appropriately should not be underestimated.

16. "Some claimants will have behavioural problems, these include excessive contact, abusive behaviour, and the claimant working against the Deputy. The claimant may feel the Deputy is intruding into his life and taking his money. The claimant may also be exhibiting these behaviours to other professionals and the care/support team around him. Where these behaviours occur it is often difficult to overcome these and the resultant costs from the Deputy having to deal with these behaviours, or indeed the aftermath in terms of the breakdown of a care team or support regime, are often significant. Careful consideration should be given to the nature of the clients behaviours and additional costs should be included to allow for these where they occur. It is not unusual for such cases to see annual costs well in excess of £30,000.00 plus VAT per annum and these costs should not be underestimated."

17. "As with everyone, issues arise in the clients life periodically which are impossible to foresee. These can be changes in family circumstances for example the death of a close family member. A contingency sum has been allowed in the accompanying schedule, however this should be amended to reflect the clients life expectancy as a longer life expectancy will mean that inevitably as higher contingency sum should be allowed and of course the reverse for clients with a shorter life expectancy."

18. On attaining majority the claimant requires a will. If he has testamentary capacity (as opposed to capacity to manage financial and property affairs), the will can be prepared on his instructions and subject to the court's approval, signed on his behalf by the Deputy. If not, a statutory will must be made by the court on application. The Official Solicitor will be appointed to act on behalf of the claimant. In either case the application will need to be supported by evidence as to those who might be required as having a claim upon the claimant's natural love and affection, and as to the claimant's best interest (*Re P*). In either case a medical report will be required concerning capacity. The costs given in the accompanying breakdown are estimated on the assumption that an attended hearing will be required. Depending upon the degree of contention, the costs may be greater or smaller. All parties that may be affected by any new will must be notified. If the claimant would have been intestate this will include a natural parent even if the parent has re-married and estranged children from former relationships, etc. If the proposed will is contested the cost will increase significantly.

19. The will requires periodic review in the light of changed circumstances and provision is accordingly made for the preparation of a further will every 10 years.

20. The application for a new Deputy amounts to a fresh application, but as much of the information will already be available, the costs incurred are likely to be lower. A medical certificate will be required concerning capacity and the application might be expected to take up to six months, again. The appointment of a new Deputy will give rise to an authority for assessment of the existing/retiring Deputy's costs.

21. The Deputyship will come to an end either on: (a) application by the claimant for discharge on the footing that he or she now has sufficient capacity to manage his or her own finances and affairs; or (b) death. In either case there will be winding-up costs associated with accounting to the protected person or to the representatives of their estate. An application for discharge on the ground of regained capacity of the protected person will generally require to be supported by a Medical Certificate.

22. No provision has been made in the accompanying breakdown for incidental applications for additional or special authority but each will cost £400 in application fee.

23. A professional Deputy will be required to submit an annual bill of costs to the Senior Court Costs Office (SCCO) on the anniversary of each deputyship year. The bill will need to be prepared by a Costs Draftsman and the costs of the bill being prepared will be around 5.5 per cent of the profit costs claimed. Additionally there is an assessment fee of £225 which is payable to the SCCO on application for the assessment.

J3: Deputyship costs

One-off cost of application for a Deputy to be appointed

1	Solicitors' costs	£4,000	Total setup costs: £6,563
2	*Plus VAT*	£800	
3	Disbursements (medical cert/travel)	£400	
4	*Plus VAT*	£80	
5	Court of Protection Application fee	£400	
6	Office of the Public Deputy Assessment Fee	£100	
7	Security Bond Premium	£337.50	
8	Cost Draftsman's fees	£220	
9	SCCO Assessment Fee	£225	

Estimated annual costs for each of the first two Deputyship years

10	General management costs	£18,000	Total annual cost for each of the first two years: £23,653 pa
11	*Plus VAT*	£3,600	
12	Plus Disbursements	£150	
13	*Plus VAT*	£30	
14	Costs Draftsman's fee	£990	
15	SCCO Annual Assessment fee	£225	
16	Security Bond Premium	£337.50	
17	OPG Annual Supervision fee	£320	

Estimated annual costs for following years

18	General management costs	£10,000	Total annual cost: £13,613
19	*Plus VAT*	£2,000	
20	Plus Disbursements	£150	
21	*Plus VAT*	£30	
22	Costs Draftsman's fee	£550	
23	SCCO Annual Assessment fee	£225	
24	Security Bond Premium	£337.50	
25	OPG Annual Supervision fee	£320	

Other future costs

26	Solicitors' costs in dealing with a statutory will application (assuming a hearing is required)	£5,500	Each of these items to be incurred every 10 years = total of £12,720 every 10 years
27	*Plus VAT*	£1,100	
28	Official Solicitor's costs in dealing with statutory will (assuming a hearing is required)	£2,500	
29	*Plus VAT*	£500	
30	Court of Protection fee for statutory will	£400	
31	Disbursements involved in statutory will	£400	
32	*Plus VAT*	£80	
33	Solicitors' Costs for appointment of new Deputy/Obtaining new order	£1,200	
34	*Plus VAT*	£240	
35	Disbursements (Medical Cert)	£250	
36	*Plus VAT*	£50	
37	CP Application Fee for appointment of a new Deputy	£400	
38	OPG Deputy Assessment Fee	£100	
39	Winding-up costs	£1,500	One off
40	*Plus VAT*	£300	One off
41	Contingency sum	£30,000	One off
42	*Plus VAT*	£6,000	One off

Notes

There has been little change in costs from the previous years, the main reason being that the guideline hourly rates have been retained at the 2010 levels. This remains the case this year.

There is a reduction in the Security Bond premiums as, where there is a Professional Deputy, the Courts have been setting lower bonds, and the premiums have also reduced in the past couple of years as competition has come into the market.

The Senior Court Costs Office assessment fee has risen by £5 to £225 per annum.

The costs of Capacity assessments are rising and it is getting increasingly difficult to get GPs to complete the COP3 forms. In injury cases it is usually the expert who completes the form and they are usually charging higher fees for this now.

A big issue affecting Deputies, who employ care staff on behalf of clients, is the pension auto-enrolment requirements. These requirements are time consuming and will add to the costs. There will be ongoing additional costs to the Deputy of administering the monthly payments and returns for the carers' pensions to comply with the regulations.

Group K

Carer Rates and Rehabilitation

K1: Care and attendance

Introduction

1. A series of cases since 2005 involving injuries of the utmost severity has led to highly developed claims for care and attendance including case management.[1] This section aims to be a source of practical assistance to practitioners and courts setting about the task of assessing damages for care and attendance.

Past non-commercial care

2. Damages awarded in respect of non-commercial care, usually by family members, are governed by the following rules/practical advice.
3. The aim is to award the reasonable value of/proper recompense for gratuitous services rendered—*Hunt v Severs* [1994] 2 A.C. 350.[2]
4. Accordingly, a claimant holds the damages on trust for those who provided the care.[3]
5. If a tortfeasor has himself provided the care, there can be no recovery of damages on that score.[4]
6. If a claimant has fallen out with the care provider so that the recovery on trust will not be honoured, again there will be no award in damages.[5]
7. There is no threshold requirement to be satisfied before an award can be made.[6] Extra domestic services are sufficient.[7]
8. While there is no threshold to satisfy, there must be actual care. So, when a claimant is still in hospital, damages are not to be awarded for mere visiting—only for any periods of care given during the course of the visit.[8]

[1] Readers interested in the finer detail of big cases can find it set out in the paper by James Rowley QC, "Serious PI litigation—a Quantum Update" with the accompanying tables at: *http://www.byromstreet.com.*

[2] At 363Aff. These are special damages. While not referred to expressly in the speeches, the rationale in *Daly v General Steam Navigation Co Ltd* 1981] 1 W.L.R. 120 CA—awarding general damages in respect of past non-commercial domestic services—was overruled by the House of Lords through the result in *Hunt v Severs.*

[3] *Hunt v Severs* supra also expressly overruled the line of authority derived from *Donnelly v Joyce* [1974] QB 454 in favour of that derived from Lord Denning's judgment in *Cunningham v Harrison* [1973] QB 942. No longer is an award for services considered as a claimant's damages (based on his need for the care) for him then to make a present to the carer. Rather it is recompense to the carer and only held by a claimant on trust.

[4] Ibid at 363D. This is a common occurrence when passengers are suing a member of the family who was the negligent driver. Where liability is split, there is no known authority but also there is no reason in principle why a tortfeasor carer cannot recover to the extent of another tortfeasor's share of the blame.

[5] See *ATH v MS* [2003] PIQR Q1 at [30] as to the principle; but in this case of fatal accident, the court was already ordering damages to be paid into court for investment on behalf of dependent children and felt able to enforce the trust through the investment control of the court. It would be otherwise if the monies were simply to be paid over to a claimant and the court really felt that the trust would not be honoured.

[6] The Court of Appeal in *Giambrone v Sunworld Holidays Ltd* [2004] PIQR Q4, Q36 decided that dicta in *Mills v British Rail Engineering Ltd* [1992] PIQR Q130 to the effect that there was a threshold of devoted care or care well beyond the ordinary call of duty (and similar phrases) were obiter and not to be followed.

[7] The Court of Appeal in *Mills* had overlooked a passage from Lord Denning in *Cunningham v Harrison*—quoted with apparent approval by Lord Bridge in *Hunt v Severs*, above at 360E—"Even though she had not been doing paid work but only domestic duties in the house, nevertheless all extra attendance on him certainly calls for compensation." [1973] QB 942, 952B–C.

[8] *Havenhand v Jeffrey* (unreported, February 24, 1997 CA); *Tagg v Countess of Chester Hospital Foundation NHS Trust* [2007] EWHC 509 (QB), [85]; *Huntley v Simmons* [2009] EWHC 405 (QB), [65].

9. Compensable care must relate to the person—the claimant himself or, under the rule in *Lowe v Guise*,[9] another disabled member of the same household, usually cared for by the claimant but who, because of the claimant's injury, is cared for by another. So, where the provision spreads out into non-commercial cover for the claimant in his business, different considerations apply; there is no compensable claim here for the hours provided by analogy with real care.[10]
10. Claims are rarely put on the following footing but where a carer has lost earnings in the provision of services, the value can be assessed as the lost net earnings up to a ceiling of the commercial value of the care provided.[11]
11. In the majority of cases the exercise is to examine the care and make a fair assessment of the number of hours in fact provided. (In doing this, one will in passing register if care has been given at anti-social hours or has been particularly demanding.) The assessment is easy in respect of discrete blocks of care; but calls for more subtle evidence/judgment when care is given in multiple short bursts over the course of day and night or constitutes more general supervision/support in the home while daily life continues.
12. Hourly rates are then applied to the determined number of hours.
13. Many different scales have been used in the past; but now there is uniformity in taking rates derived from Local Authority Spinal Point 8.
14. The suggested starting points are the basic (daytime weekday) rate or the enhanced aggregate rate (which takes into account care in the evenings, at night and at weekends). Both are set out in the table below.
15. The aggregate rate balances all the hours of the week by their relative number and appropriate rate. It is logically entirely apt only when care is spread out evenly through the whole week and the hours of the day and night. The odd hour here and there in the evening will not justify an aggregate rate; but intensive care given only at night and not by day, seven days a week (for example, when commercial daytime care has been purchased but a relative left to care at night), would logically justify more than the aggregate rate. Where a spouse has gotten up early to provide care before going to work and then carried on in the evenings on returning home, no care has been given when the daytime weekday rate is applicable.
16. There is no reason in principle why different rates cannot be used in different periods—the aggregate rate during more intensive care in early convalescence and the basic rate afterwards; or a rate over the whole period averaged somewhere between the two. No doubt the exercise would have to be relatively broad brush but it may be none the worse for that.[12] The overarching aim is to attach a reasonable value to the actual care and award proper recompense.
17. Notwithstanding the logical attraction, however, of choosing a rate close to the circumstances of the actual provision, following *Fairhurst v St Helens & Knowsley Health Authority* [1995] PIQR the

[9] [2002] QB 1369, [38]. What the ratio of this case is (and how widely or narrowly the rule established should be construed) is a fertile area for argument. Is it really confined to care of a disabled member or will care of a baby or child suffice? Is the element of provision being within the same household essential to the legal rule? Is it an important difference if a disabled mother has come to rely on her daughter's care while living in the next street; or in a self-contained granny-flat within the curtilage of the daughter's house; or in the spare room of her house?

[10] *Hardwick v Hudson* [1999] 1 W.L.R. 1770.

[11] *Housecroft v Burnett* [1986] 1 All E.R. 332 O'Connor LJ at 343e albeit his view of the *Cunningham v Harrison* and *Donnelly v Joyce* debate was overruled in *Hunt v Severs*. The ceiling of the commercial rate has sometimes been criticised on the basis that it would have been enough simply to apply a wider test of reasonableness to the evaluation of the mother's claim for care of her daughter. However, that evaluation was at the very heart of the appeal and it would be difficult to contend that the invocation of the commercial ceiling was not part of the ratio.

[12] Averaging things with a broad brush appealed to Stuart-Smith J in *Ali v Caton & MIB* [2013] EWHC 1730 (QB) at [323b–d] and he effectively reached a rate between the aggregate and basic ones. He took the starting point of the claimant's expert's figures and discounted them by 25% on account of arguments over both rates and the number of hours. ". . . *Adoption of a basic rate throughout would lead to under-compensation while adoption of the enhanced rate would have the opposite effect.*" See below for more about this case.

basic rate was used for over a decade in reported cases, even those of maximum severity when the care was of an onerous nature and much of it provided at nights and at weekends.[13]

18. Notwithstanding *Wells v Wells*[14] and modernisation of the assessment of damages for personal injuries, it took until *Massey v Tameside* [2007] EWHC 317 (QB) for there to be a reported case at the aggregate rate. Since then there has been a move away from using the basic rate as the universal starting point in very serious cases at least.[15]
19. It is unclear whether, in more routine cases where a significant proportion of the care has been carried out at anti-social times, a rate other than the basic rate is being awarded in unreported decisions[16]; or if the basic rate still rules.
20. It is increasingly common for experts in very valuable cases to break the past down into a large number of periods with minor fluctuations in hours and annual increases in rates. It may be fine in that type of case, albeit use of properly considered averages would surely simplify things considerably at no significant cost in overall accuracy. In cases without experts, practical experience suggests focussing on fewer distinct periods of care and taking into account minor fluctuations through the reasoned choice of an average number of hours or average rate[17] rather than embarking on over-elaborate calculation. Where cases involve gradually diminishing care from a point on hospital discharge to recovery or a plateau of continuing need, looking to the level of care midway through that period has much to commend it as a starting point in picking an overall average.
21. Since personal injury damages are awarded net of tax and NI, there is now invariably an appropriate reduction in respect of past non-commercial care.[18] It is now almost always

[13] Many settlements were negotiated with an enhancement for a higher rate, but there was no reported case until *Massey v Tameside* [2007] EWHC 317 (QB).

[14] [1999] 1 A.C. 345.

[15] After *Massey* supra came *Noble v Owens* [2008] EWHC 359 (QB)—a serious case but not quite of the utmost severity—in which the Court retreated to *Fairhurst* and the basic rate. Since then, in *Crofts* (2008) QBD Lawtel, *Smith* [2008] EWHC 2234 (QB) and *Whiten* [2011] EWHC 2066 (QB)—all cases of the utmost severity—the Court has awarded the aggregate rate or (*Crofts*) a broad-brush average rate close to it. Recently, in a case of more moderate value (arthritis and pain syndrome-—general damages £93,000), Sir David Eady awarded the basic rate at [44]; he had been shown *Noble v Owens* but no other authorities are mentioned.

[16] In the asbestosis case of *Nicholas v MoD* [2013] EWHC 2351 (QB), HHJ Burrell QC (sitting as a High Court Judge) awarded the aggregate rate at [23]. In *Knauer v MOJ* [2014] EWHC 2553 (QB) Bean J (as he then was) awarded the aggregate rate in respect of general household tasks [13]. In neither case does it appear there was any spirited resistance.

[17] See also *Ali v Caton & MIB*, supra.

[18] At a time when the basic rate was being used as the universal starting point, a few very serious cases emerged where it was felt that a deduction from such a low rate would leave a carer with inadequate recompense; and some courts refused to make a deduction. Now that the quality and difficulty of care is beginning to be reflected through higher rates, this method of achieving a fair result is no longer required. Choose the appropriate rate for the quality/intensity of care; but then make the principled deduction for tax and NI. As with any rule, however, there is the odd reasoned departure to be found: in *AC v Farooq & MIB* [2012] EWHC 1484 QB) King J did not make deduction from the £7.11 rate used by one of the nursing experts since it already represented a compromise over what was the appropriate commercial rate—see [131]. Recently in *Totham v King's College Hospital NHS Foundation Trust* [2015] EWHC 97 (QB), the Parties agreed the rate and the hours. Late in the day, the claimant tried to get round that agreement by arguing that Mrs Totham had given up highly paid work and consequently there should be no discount at all for the non-commercial element. The attempt was rejected by Laing J at [25]–[28]: the argument in respect of Mrs Totham's work did not go to the correct non-commercial reduction (principally to do with tax and NI), rather it went to the correct rate to be allowed for the hours (which had already been compromised). The moral of the tale is to take the advice in the earlier part of this footnote to heart.

25 per cent[19] but the bracket appears historically to have been between 20 per cent and 33 per cent.[20]

22. A sum equivalent to any Carer's Allowance received is to be deducted from an award for non-commercial care.[21] The value of direct payments also stands to be deducted.[22] There is no loss to the extent that there is NHS continuing care.

Example schedule[23]

Care while an in-patient—2 weeks Average of 2 hours actual care at the bedside each evening (including Saturday and Sunday): 2 hours x 14 days @ the aggregate rate (£8.98)	251	
Care during 4 weeks intensive convalescence at home: 6 hours provided daily, including weekends and evenings: 6 hours x 28 days @ the aggregate rate (£8.98)	1,509	
Further 6 months of care gradually diminishing from 6 hours a day to nil, more during the evenings and weekends at the beginning than at the end: Average of 3 hours a day care x 365/2 x the average of the basic and aggregate rates (£7.91)	4,331	
	6,091	
Non-commercial discount	×0.75	
		4,568
No continuing personal care but assistance still required in respect of heavier DIY, gardening, etc. chores		

[19] This was the considered reduction in *Whiten* supra from the already chosen aggregate rate—see [144]. It was described by Stuart-Smith J in *Ali v Caton & MIB* supra footnote 12 as the *conventional 25% discount* and he refused to make more adjustment [323c]. 25% has been the reduction in *Loughlin v Singh* [2013] EWHC 1641 (QB); *Farrugia* [2014] EWHC 1036 (QB); *Tate v Ryder Holdings* [2014] EWHC 4256 (QB); *Ellison v University Hospitals of Morecambe Bay NHS Foundation* Trust [2015] EWHC 366 (QB); *Totham* supra; *Robshaw v United Lincolnshire Hospitals NHS Trust* [2015] EWHC 923 (QB) and other cases too numerous to specify.

[20] *Evans v Pontypridd Roofing Limited* [2002] PIQR Q5 is the leading general authority on the non-commercial reduction. In *Zambarda v Shipbreaking (Queenborough) Ltd* [2013] EWHC 2263 (QB), John Leighton Williams QC (sitting as a Deputy High Court Judge) made only a 20% discount [64] because the sum was so small that income tax would not be paid. It is a very long time since an argued and reported decision at 33%: *Nash v Southmead Health Authority* [1993] P.I.Q.R. Q.156, decided in late 1992, is the case usually cited.

[21] Teare J in *Massey* supra at [52]:

> "To the extent that the carer has received benefits in respect of his or her voluntary care the claimant does not need a sum of money to give proper recompense for that care. It therefore seems to me that the Defendant's contention is right in principle."

[22] *Crofton v NHS Litigation Authority* [2007] 1 W.L.R. 923.

[23] The example will pick up the threads of the "logical" approach as outlined in the text. No doubt a counter schedule, as well as attempting to reduce the number of hours, would take a point that the basic rate only should be allowed in a case beneath that of maximum severity. Readers should report decided cases on the issue of hourly rate applied and kindly inform the writer when a case reference is available via james.rowley@byromstreet.com.

Making allowance from £1,500 pa[24] for the chores still possible: £750 pa × 10 (discounted lifetime multiplier to say 70):	7,500
Total	£12,068

Past commercial care

23. Where there has been actual expenditure in the past on commercial care, it should be capable of easy proof (or reasonably accurate estimation if records have not been kept).
24. It will usually be awarded in full unless the defendant raises issues of unreasonable provision (or elements of separate causation leading to unrelated provision).[25]

[24] Mackay J in *Fleet v Fleet* [2009] EWHC 3166 (QB):

"25. This is claimed based on a multiplicand of £1500 p.a. I do not understand the multiplier to be controversial. The defendant contends for between £750 and £1000 per annum as a "more conventional sum" than the £1500 sought by the Claimant. The evidence on this issue is that Mr Fleet did all the DIY in the house and had in the past installed a new bathroom according to his wife. He was a skilled man albeit he was busy and worked long days and sometimes long weeks. He also said that he had plans to redecorate the house, and Mrs Fleet said that the living room now needs redecoration; though she could do some of the preparatory work, and did do so when her husband did the work, she could not in my judgement be reasonably expected to fill the gap left by him.

26. Equally, there is considerable garden at the house which Mrs Fleet tends but she cannot manage the trimming of the trees a screen of which separates the house from its neighbours and which has to be kept in order, or cut the grass.

27. I believe I am justified in saying that I can take into account the general level of awards under this head of damage from past experience. It would be dismal if experts had to be called to say how much it costs to mow a lawn or paint a room; after all judges do have some experience of that kind of activity and what it cost to buy it in the market place.

28. I see nothing wrong with the figure of £1,500 per annum claimed by the plaintiff and I think that is the right sum."

John Leighton Williams QC (sitting as a High Court Judge) allowed £1,250 pa to age 77 in *Zambarda v Shipbreaking (Queenborough) Ltd* supra at [88]. Contrast Stuart-Smith J in *Ali v Caton & MIB* supra and infra at [337] where he awarded £250 pa to a young man with no track record for DIY, decorating and gardening. In *McGinty v Pipe* [2012] EWHC 506 (QB) HHJ Foster QC (sitting as a Judge of the High Court) awarded a woman of 51 £750pa for gardening and DIY with a multiplier of 16 (to just beyond 70). Kenneth Parker J in *Tate v Ryder Holdings* supra discounted the claim for a 24-year-old man heavily to a lump sum award of £15,000 because of the considerable uncertainty whether he would have carried out such activities. HHJ McKenna (sitting as a Deputy High Court Judge) awarded [96] £900pa between the ages of 25 and 70 in *FM v Ipswich Hospital NHS Trust* [2015] EWHC 775 (QB). Foskett J [421] awarded £1,500pa in *Robshaw* supra from age 25 when life expectancy was reduced to 63.

[25] In *O'Brien v Harris* (transcript of February 22, 2001) the BIRT rehabilitation costs (£21,860) significantly exceeded those originally estimated (£13,700) [191]. There was no evidence from BIRT explaining the difference or resiling from the estimate [192]. The case manager was not called to justify the additional case management costs (£10,834 v £6,461) [193]. Some increased costs were allowed based on inferences from the invoices to the effect that a higher quality of support worker had been provided than in the estimate [195]. There had, however, been inadequate management of cost (see [194]) (but by whom?—see below) and Pitchford J made an overall award of £18,500 [196].

In the case of *Loughlin v Singh* [2013] EWHC 1641 (QB), Parker J was invited [62] to disallow the costs of past care and case management on the basis that *the standard of such care and management fell significantly below that which could reasonably be expected to meet the exigencies of the claimant's condition and circumstances.* The full submission was rejected as *wholly disproportionate and unjust*; but the claim was reduced by 20 per cent with a broad brush on account of the case manager's failure to address the claimant's need for a specific and effective sleep hygiene regime in timely fashion. Parker J made a finding that *the efforts made on this fundamental aspect of the rehabilitation were simply not adequate* [61]. . . . *Principle requires that I should take due account of the fact, that I have found, that the standard of the care and case management services did, in an important respect, fall significantly below the standard that could reasonably have been expected. In other words, the objective value of what the claimant received was less than the amount of the charges made for the relevant services* [62].

There was no finding in *Loughlin* that the claimant through his Financial Deputy had knowingly appointed an incompetent case manager. Parker J made no finding of failure to mitigate against the claimant/Financial Deputy in the handling/funding of the case manager (although this may have been an undercurrent in the case). As long as Parker J's findings amounted to *gross* negligence on the part of the case manager, his observations can be squared with wider principles of novus actus under *Rahman v Arearose Ltd* [2001] QB 351: insofar as the increased costs of failing to implement a sleep hygiene regime were

25. The primary measure of damage against which to judge the claimed level of provision is one of reasonable care to meet a claimant's needs.[26]

26. If, at first blush, the claim in the past appears to exceed the primary measure of damage, principles of mitigation of loss may yet come to a claimant's aid if some evidence is adduced to explain the apparent over-spend. Once a claimant raises such arguments, the burden of proof lies on a defendant to prove a failure in mitigation; and the standard against which to judge a claimant's actions is not a harsh one.[27]

Future non-commercial care

27. If non-commercial care is to be carried on long into the future, the potential break down of the package is a contingency to be assessed. Where there is detailed expert evidence, there will often be an alternative package laid out drawing on greater commercial care. It will then be a matter for the judge to reach a fair balanced assumption in monetary terms between two or more packages, weighting the award according to the available evidence.[28]

28. Where the evidence is not so detailed and there is no provision elsewhere in the calculations for a break down in the non-commercial care package, it may well be appropriate to reflect adverse contingencies by refusing to apply the usual non-commercial discount. In this way some allowance is made with a broad brush for the possibility of more expensive commercial care on separation/ill health/death in the family member who is to supply the care.[29]

caused by the gross negligence of a third party, they were separately caused. It is difficult to see, however, why a finding of mere negligence as against gross negligence in the past on the part of a case manager should break the chain of causation and lead to the disallowance of part of the claim.

In the more recent case of *Ali v Caton & MIB*, supra and infra, Stuart-Smith J awarded the full claim for past support workers, the regime having been set up in accordance with apparently competent third party advice. *The position of a significantly brain-damaged claimant who acts on the basis of apparently reasonable advice is strong, though not always impregnable, when seeking to recover the costs of doing so from a tortfeasor. On this item, the balance of the argument strongly favours the claimant* [323f–h]. This approach is in keeping with the writer's understanding of the real legal issue set out in the previous paragraph.

[26] The principle was put succinctly by Lord Lloyd in *Wells v Wells* [1999] 1 A.C. 345, 377F in just 17 words: "Plaintiffs are entitled to a reasonable standard of care to meet their requirements, but that is all."

Stephenson LJ traced in *Rialis v Mitchell* (Court of Appeal transcript July 6, 1984) how the 100 per cent principle was finessed through a series of Victorian cases involving fatal accidents on the railways to reflect the recovery of reasonable rather than perfect compensation. Reasonable compensation is now 100 per cent compensation since it is the primary measure of damage. Professor Andrews Burrows, writing Chapter 28 of the leading practitioner's textbook *Clerk & Lindsell*, 21st edn, clearly espouses what this chapter has considered the orthodox line: see §28–23. For an alternative view, see Dr Harvey McGregor in *McGregor on Damages*, 19th edn, at 38-056 (but his line ignores *Rialis* and Lord Lloyd in *Wells* supra, as well as practice over decades and the other decisions mentioned in footnote 206 within his own section).

Recently, claimants and defendants are jousting, the one using the language of *full compensation* and the other *proportionality*. It is far from clear what these ideas add if the primary measure of damage is *reasonable compensation*: this test is infinitely flexible and requires no gloss; all the decisions are ultimately explicable applying a simple test of *reasonableness* to the very specific facts. Readers interested in seeing the development of this trend can look to *Whiten* supra at [4]–[5]; *Totham* supra at [12]; *Ellison* supra at [9]; *Robshaw* supra at [161]–[167].

[27] The topic is beyond the scope of this chapter; an obvious source of assistance lies in *McGregor on Damages*, 18th edn (London: Sweet & Maxwell, 2012), para.7–070 and in the surrounding paragraphs.

[28] In *C v Dixon* [2009] EWHC 708 (QB) King J assessed damages where the relationship between the claimant and his partner was far from assured in the long run. He took an assumed period of 10 years before break up as a fair reflection of the chances and proceeded to do the arithmetic from that starting point.

[29] See *Willbye v Gibbons* [2004] PIQR P15 at [12] and [16] in which, on a quality of evidence which was insufficient to warrant fine alternative contingency calculations in the event of breakdown in the non-commercial package, Kennedy LJ varied the sum awarded by removing the non-commercial discount allowed by the Recorder.

Future commercial care

Care—hourly rates

29. There is no "conventional" hourly rate for future commercial care, whether recruited through direct employment or an agency. All depends on the nature/difficulty of the required care; the level of need for continuity in carers; and the prevailing rates local to a claimant's home. Evidence on all three scores is highly desirable.[30] The most recent cases have not involved argument over the hourly rate. Examples in the biggest cases (direct employment not agency rates) are as follows:

Case[31]	Weekday - £	Weekend - £	Location
Farrugia[32] (determined –Mar. '14)	11.50	14	Hants.
Streeter[33] (determined – Sept. '13)	9	10	Aylesbury
Whiten (agreed – mid-2011)	13	15	"Good" London rates
Sklair (agreed – late 2009)	11	13	Beckenham, Kent
C v Dixon (determined – evidence as at mid 2008)	10	11	Barnsley
Huntley (determined – aggregate rate for late 2008)	9.50	9.50	Portsmouth Cosham/Hillsea
XXX (agreed – late 2008)	12	14	Guildford
Smith (determined – mid 2008)	10	12	Herts.
Crofts (agreed composite rate – summer 2008)	12	12	Herts.

Case management—hourly rate

30. As with support worker rates there is no "conventional" hourly rate for case management; but the rate for this (as against the number of hours required) is usually uncontroversial. The rate has crept

[30] Jack J. bewailed the lack of evidence of decent quality in *XXX* [2008] EWHC 2727 (QB) at [16].

[31] Full case references can be found in wider text of this chapter and footnotes.

[32] [2014] EWHC 1036 (QB) Jay J at [102].

[33] [2013] EWHC 2841 (QB): the judgment at [209] did not articulate the figures beyond the annual multiplicands but the accepted rates were as set out in Mrs Gough's evidence in the Joint Statement. This was a tetraplegia case and Mrs Gough adduced evidence of actual research into local rates.

up gradually and £90 an hour+ travel time (£45 an hour plus mileage) was agreed in *Whiten.* £95 an hour was awarded in *Ali v Canton* [332], Streeter [217] (noting the agreement of Mrs Gough's costing) and Farrugia at [107], all supra. The required number of hours varies greatly and will be lower where there is agency care as against direct employment.

Provision for holidays, sick pay, etc.

31. Where future care is to be provided through direct employment rather than agency provision, it is now customary to take into account: (i) paid holidays, (ii) higher hourly rates paid on Bank holidays, (iii) sick leave, and (iv) down time in the package for training days by adopting calculations based on a notional 60 weeks in the year.[34] While a few experts continue to use it, the alternative method of taking 52 weeks in the year and a percentage uplift to cover the required extras (which started at around 27 per cent and rose steadily) has fallen out of favour in reported cases. Jay J in Farrugia supra described [100] taking a 60-week year as *standard practice.*

ERNIC

32. Calculation of ERNIC on carer's wages is often misunderstood. It is currently (tax year 2015/16) payable at 13.8 per cent on wages above the secondary threshold[35] (£156 a week × 52 weeks = £8,112 pa). So, to reach the annual sum of ERNIC, calculate the annual wage's bill and deduct from it (£8,112 × the likely number of carers in the package) to give the sum on which 13.8 per cent is likely to be paid.

NEST pension contributions

33. The following information comes from the NEST website on 23 May 2014 and may be subject to change.
34. If enrolled within the scheme, employers pay a percentage of *qualifying earnings*: for tax year 2015/16 this is between £5,824 and £42,385 pa.
35. Enrolment is compulsory for all workers aged at least 22 but under State Retirement age who earn at least £10,000 pa from that employer, who work (or normally work) in the UK and who are not already an active member of a qualifying scheme with that employer.
36. Enrolment is at a worker's own option if aged at least 16 and under 75, with the employer having to contribute if they have *qualifying earnings* i.e. earn over £5,824 pa.
37. There will be a staged introduction of the duties depending on the size of the employer; but all care packages have fewer than 30 employees so will stand to be introduced into the scheme late on—between January 2016 and April 2017.

[34] See: *XXX* supra at [24] and *Whiten v St George's Healthcare NHS Trust* [2011] EWHC 2066 (QB) at [167]–[168]. For the evolution of the 60-week calculation, see the paper at footnote 1. *Streeter* supra is an exception, where the experts both adopted 59.6 weeks but made an additional allowance on Bank Holidays—ruled on by Baker J in line with Mrs Gough at £1 an hour uplift. It is clear that down time for training days, additional pay for bank holidays, etc. are included in the 60-week calculation. Those care experts who take 60 weeks and routinely bill for training time and so on in addition might be said to be trying too hard. The taking of 60 weeks, however, might be distinguished up or down for the specific training, etc. requirements of any case since it has evolved out of the bigger cases—it might be easier to distinguish down rather than up (or the attempt not worth the effort). In *HS v Lancashire Teaching Hospitals NHS Trust* [2015] EWHC 1376 (QB), the claimant's care expert asked for a 5% contingency uplift (5% x 60 weeks = 3 more weeks) *in order to cover holidays, sickness and other unexpected and sudden absences on the part of employed carers.* William Davis J rejected the argument at [31] on the basis that the 60-week calculation included holidays and sickness. He continued: *Any maternity leave will be funded from the public purse given the number of employees. Any other absences will almost certainly be accommodated with the carers' shift patterns.*

[35] There is an upper ceiling; but no carer is ever paid enough to bring it into play.

38. Once the duties have bitten on an employer, the full impact of the contributions is also to be phased in: the plan at time of writing is:

	Minimum percentage of qualifying earnings that must be paid in total	Minimum percentage of qualifying earnings that ***employers*** must pay
To end September 2017	2%	**1%**
Oct 2017 to end Sept 2018	5%	**2%**
Oct 2018 onwards	8%	**3%**

Child care as a possibility

39. The possible costs of caring for children have been claimed recently in *Totham* and *Robshaw* both supra. Both were cases of cerebral palsy and the claims were resisted on the basis that neither claimant would realistically have children. The defences succeeded with slightly different formulations in the rationale. In *Totham*, Laing J found [71] that she was *not satisfied that there is a more than fanciful chance that Eva will have children.* In *Robshaw*, Foskett J [191] would not go so far as to say the chance was *merely speculative or fanciful* but nevertheless said that the discount for contingencies would have to be so significant that *it would reduce the figure to something that would bear no real relationship to that actual cost if the event itself materialised. An award of such a sum would, in my view, be wholly artificial.* And he made no award at all [192].

Parental contribution to the future care package

40. The court's attitude to any fair offset from future commercial care of very severely damaged children on account of parental involvement has evolved since 2006. The seeds sown by Sir Rodger Bell in *Iqbal*[36]—to the effect that parents are not to be presumed to take part in the care of grievously injured children requiring onerous care—have grown on strongly via Teare J in *Massey* [64], Lloyd Jones J in *A v Powys* [57] and HHJ Collender QC (sitting as a High Court judge) in *Crofts* [120]. By the time of *Whiten* (2011) the NHSLA was no longer apparently arguing for any real offset: the only point at which the parents' potential contribution was considered relevant was in allowing for a single night sleeper in the commercial package on the basis that they would be available in an emergency [205]. In *Farrugia* supra [96] care was awarded for 14 hours a day × 2 commercial carers except when a family member would take the place of one commercial carer in outings spread over 10 hours each week. This modest adjustment to the rates for family provision covered only 48 weeks in the year up to the claimant's age of 49. While not arguing for any offset in *Robshaw* supra (claimant 12 years old), the NHSLA renewed its fight in *HS v Lancs.* [2015] EWHC 1376 (QB) (claimant only 8) but were again unsuccessful.

Offset for care required anyway?

41. In *Sklair v Haycock*,[37] the claimant (aged 49 and looked after informally by his "bohemian" father) had suffered with Asperger's Syndrome and Obsessive Compulsive Disorder before the accident. The defence focussed on and valued what were described as merely the few extra hours of care required as a result of the accident.

[36] [2006] EWHC 3111 (QB), [20].
[37] [2009] EWHC 3328 (QB).

42. The narrow approach of the defence was rejected. Edwards-Stuart J found that the claimant's elderly father would have continued to look after him for 5–10 years longer, when his wider family would have looked after him at a financial cost to them of £150–£200 per week for 5–10 years, after which a residential placement in local authority care would have been likely.
43. The accident had turned (as a matter of fact) the claimant's need for this lower level of care into a reasonable need for 24–hour commercial care [80]. There was no question in the judge's mind [78] after *Peters v East Midlands SHA*[38] of the claimant now having to mitigate into local authority care: he could pursue the tortfeasor as of right. The only real issue, therefore, was how, if at all, to credit the mixture of family non-commercial care and family-funded commercial care he would have received anyway against the full cost of 24-hour commercial care.
44. As to family non-commercial care, Edwards-Stuart J rejected any offset at all [89].
45. As to family expenditure on commercial care, Edwards-Stuart J gave credit for its net value, reasoning at [91] that if the family had lent the claimant money to pay for care (and he had paid for it himself) he would have had to give credit for the value of that care. It should make no difference whether the family channel the money through the claimant or pay for the care directly.
46. The approach in *Sklair* was endorsed by Foskett J in *Reaney v University Hospital of North Staffordshire NHS Trust and another* [2014] EWHC 3016 (QB) at [72].

Resident carers

47. The old arguments for residential agency care have completely fallen away in the most serious cases. There may still be a place for such a provision, however, in cases requiring a lighter touch, as with care of the partial tetraplegic claimant in *Davies*[39] (between the ages of 70 and 75, after which extensive top up for double up hours was added). The last gasp of the argument for residential care in the most serious cases came when the NHSLA in *Whiten* supra tried to run a *Davies*-post-75-style argument in the case of a grievously injured child with mixed spastic-dystonic, severe, quadriplegic cerebral palsy. It suggested the bedrock of a care package through a residential agency carer with extensive hourly top up. Swift J rejected that potential solution without hesitation [204].

Risk/benefit applied to care regimes

48. *Davies* and *C v Dixon*, both supra, have also been interesting in the detailed way in which Wilkie J and King J balanced risk and benefit to the claimant in reaching the appropriate care package. In each case the defendant argued that the package suggested by the claimant's experts amounted to substantial over-provision and would be stifling of the claimant. In *Davies* some risk of falling was found to be acceptable without a resident carer always on hand before the age of 70: a resident carer package before that age did not take into account the contribution which a degree of self-reliance has to a person's sense of worth and well-being. In *C v Dixon* the claimant was not to be wrapped in cotton wool with unnecessary commercial and double up provision—he could have the required 24-hour care in a looser sense, including some down time in the package as long he had someone to contact in an emergency. Since his partner was assumed to be with him for the next 10 years, there was no need for commercial overnight care during that period.
49. In the moderate (general damages £147,500—July 2013) brain injury case of *Ali v Caton & MIB* supra Stuart-Smith J described scope of the care package there allowing 15 hours a week of support as follows [331ii)]:

[38] [2009] 3 W.L.R. 737.
[39] [2008] EWHC 740 (QB), Wilkie J.

"The purpose of the future care regime should be to provide sufficient support to enable [the Claimant] to pursue a structured and constructive existence so far as possible, reinforcing constructive routines and being available to assist when he is confronted by the new, the unfamiliar or the complex."

Two carers throughout the day

50. Whether two carers are required throughout the day has not been litigated to a formal decision recently—it was common ground in the 2014 case of *Farrugia* supra (severe brain injury) that it was necessary and in *Streeter* supra in 2013 (C5/6 motor tetraplegia) that it was not. In *A v B*[40] two carers were required throughout waking hours (essentially in respect of transfers for toileting which could not be forecast as to timing) in a case of severe compromise in dystonic athetoid tetraplegic cerebral palsy. A similar result ensued in *XXX*. In both cases the claimants had little or no appreciation of their predicament but swift availability of changing was necessary for their health and comfort. The result was the same in *Massey* for a different reason: here the claimant had substantially retained intellect in a grossly malfunctioning body: for him the availability of two carers was essential for transfers and transport so that he could exercise autonomy and make decisions to act on impulse rather than live in the straight-jacket of double-up provision which was less than continuous and at fixed hours of the day.

51. In *Farrugia* supra, while awarding care based on two carers in attendance during waking hours, Jay J said this when considering whether two *commercial* carers had to be present throughout:

> "I do not accept . . . that Jack should, in effect, be free to do whatever he wishes at the spur of the moment. I do not consider that Jack's personal autonomy is overridden, or the dictates of spontaneity are unreasonably quelled, by providing for a regime which presupposes a modest degree of pre-planning and organisation. This, after all, reflects the realities of ordinary life."

52. The case for two carers in respect of a sentient adult who can give basic co-operation with hoisted transfers (in the sense of not lashing out or being subject to spasm) has not yet been clearly made out for transfers within the home. While the NHS commonly uses two nurses for such transfers even with a hoist on hospital wards, that appears to be at least partly because two nurses are available in such a setting and the use of two speeds things up.

Day centre provision

53. The argument for offset from a commercial care package for down time while a claimant attends a local authority day centre was never strong. With its lack of forensic success and further funding cuts and closure of day centres, the argument is not currently being aired.

Team leaders

54. Although the payment of a higher rate to a member of the support worker team did not find favour over five years ago in *Crofton* or *Iqbal*, the allowance of a team leader (reducing the amount and cost of case management intervention) has become pretty standard more recently in really serious cases. £2 an hour extra was conceded in *XXX*. In *Whiten* the principle was disputed; and as a fall back it was suggested by the defendant that any provision could be by reference to a small

[40] [2006] EWHC 1178 (QB).

proportion of the hours worked by the team leader, i.e. only those hours when in fact engaged on team leader duties. Swift J at [164] rejected that line and allowed 30 hours a week at a weekday rate enhanced by £3 an hour (London). The whole point was to attract someone to the post with experience and ability: the defendant's suggestion would not achieve the aim. Contrast *Farrugia,* in which Jay J awarded an increase of £5 an hour (Hants.) [104] but over only 22 hours a week [103], commenting that he simply could not accept that a full week's work was required for the combination of tasks required of the team leader. In *Streeter,* Baker J allowed an increment of £2 an hour over 15 hours a week (see footnote 32). Much appears to depend on the nature of the precise nature of the case (and perhaps the experts and judge).

Hand over meetings

55. Claiming hand over periods of up to half an hour at the conclusion of each shift has never appeared an attractive argument and is not generally being run at the moment unless in unusual circumstances.

Liaison/team meetings

56. Recently, these were not contended for in *Whiten* or *Farrugia*; allowed as to merely one hour a month in *C v Dixon*, and substantially conceded in *XXX*. There may have been oversight when these allowances have been made or conceded: as the "60 weeks in the year" evolved, it was probably supposed to take into account a routine allowance for training and team meetings—see the discussion of the evidence in the judgment of Penry-Davy J in *Smith*.[41]
57. The result was more complicated in *Robshaw* supra, where Foskett J allowed for the costs of therapists attending multi-disciplinary meetings but decided—in line with the above discussion —that the attendance of the case manager, team leader and support workers should be funded out of the normal working time already awarded within the 60-week year. He allowed five meetings in the first year; four per annum then until age 18; three per annum then to age 25; the claim was limited to one per annum then for life but he would have awarded two per annum. All meetings were said to require two hours allocated to them and should not be rushed. See [474]–[479].

The status of family choice on behalf of a claimant

58. The issue of the status of a future family choice on behalf of a claimant raised its head in the very recent case of *Harman v East Kent Hospitals NHS Foundation Trust* [2015] EWHC 1662 (QB). The claimant, aged 13 and suffering severe autism with significant cognitive impairment, was being cared for in a specialist placement funded by the LEA but spending eight weeks a year at home. The issue was where the Claimant would live when his education came to an end in 12 years at age 25: the parents wanted him then to come home. Turner J found in favour of that course, following expert evidence that a care package which met with the aspirations of the parents would be more likely to succeed than one which did not [38]. As to the underlying point of law, however, the parents' choice did not trump the view of the court of the primary measure of damage in the future:

> "[36] Care must be taken in cases such as this not to equiparate the preferences of relatives with the regime of care and support the cost of which should be the basis of reasonable compensation. Each case must be looked at on its own facts. There may well be circumstances

[41] [2008] EWHC 2234 (QC)—the transcript lacks numbered paragraphs.

in which, however strong and genuine the desire of the parents or a spouse or partner may be to have the claimant home, there are good reasons for taking a contrary course. The purpose of damages in a personal injury claim is to compensate the victim and not to accommodate the wishes of his family whatever the extent of the inevitable personal sympathy one might have for those who are left to pick up the pieces and suffer the inevitable and sustained emotional impact of serious injury to someone dear to them."

Chance contingencies and PPOs for care

59. Huntley[42] illustrates that the essential chance assessment of damages for future loss has survived the new PPO regime, which purports to trace everything back to a claimant's needs. There the claimant, who had suffered a frontal lobe injury and whose rehabilitation had not gone well up to trial, contended for 24 hours of care per day as the long-term solution: the defendant submitted for 21 hours per week. Underhill J approached matters by evaluating first of all the hard-core minimum level that he thought was reasonable, which he assessed at six hours a day [109]. This hard-core cost he would have put within a PPO [114] but not the full chance reasonable amount that he went on to evaluate as follows. He uplifted the package by 50 per cent from six hours to nine hours a day with a broad brush for all the possibilities of needing greater care. He then discounted that back by one hour to eight hours a day for the chance that the claimant would not in fact engage all the care that he might reasonably require. There was a real chance that he would reject care (as he would if he entered a stable relationship) and small chances of imprisonment and detention under the Mental Health Act. The resulting additional two hours a day beyond the core six hours Underhill J would have provided within an additional lump sum award; but the whole PPO submission was withdrawn when the claimant did not recover for 24-hour care.

60. For a further example taking contingencies into account, see the decision of Kenneth Parker J in *Tate v Ryder Holdings* supra [38]–[42] where he averaged the cost of caring for the claimant in his own and residential accommodation, catering for different times in his life, and adjusted further for the chances of non-compliance by 20 per cent for reasons similar to those set out by Underhill J in *Huntley*. As in *Huntley*, the adjustments led to a lump sum award rather than PPO.

[42] [2009] EWHC 405 (QB).

National Joint Council Payscales – Spinal Column Point 8

Year	Time of day	Hourly rate £	Hours pw	Cost pw £	Divided by hours pw	Aggregate rate
Jul 1992 to Jun 1993	Basic Evening Weekend	£4.04 £5.05 £6.06	55 65 48	£222.20 + £328.25 + £290.88 = £841.33	168	£5.01
Jul 1993 to Aug 1994	Basic Evening Weekend	£4.21 £5.26 £6.32	55 65 48	£231.55 + £341.90 + £303.36 = £876.81	168	£5.22
Sep 1994 to May 1995	Basic Evening Saturday Sunday	£4.44 £5.55 £6.66 £8.88	55 65 24 24	£244.20 + £360.75 + £159.84 + £213.12 = £977.91	168	£5.82
Jun 1995 to Mar 1996	Basic Evening Saturday Sunday	£4.56 £5.70 £6.84 £9.12	55 65 24 24	£250.80 + £370.50 + £164.16 + £218.88 = £1,004.34	168	£5.98
Apr 1996 to Mar 1997	Basic Evening Saturday Sunday	£4.69 £5.86 £7.03 £9.38	55 65 24 24	£257.95 + £380.90 + £168.72 + £225.12 = £1,032.69	168	£6.15
Apr 1997 to Mar 1998	Basic Evening Saturday Sunday	£4.84 £6.05 £7.26 £9.68	55 65 24 24	£266.20 + £393.25 + £174.24 + £232.32 = £1,066.01	168	£6.35
Apr 1998 to Mar 1999	Basic Evening Saturday Sunday	£4.98 £6.22 £7.47 £9.96	55 65 24 24	£273.90 + £404.30 + £179.28 + £239.04 = £1,096.52	168	£6.53
Apr 1999 to Mar 2000	Basic Evening Saturday Sunday	£5.13 £6.41 £7.69 £10.26	55 65 24 24	£282.15 + £416.65 + £184.56 + £246.24 = £1,129.60	168	£6.72
Apr 2000 to Mar 2001	Basic Evening Saturday Sunday	£5.29 £6.61 £7.93 £10.58	55 65 24 24	£290.95 + £429.65 + £190.32 + £253.92 = £1,164.84	168	£6.93
Apr 2001 to Mar 2002	Basic Evening Saturday Sunday	£5.49 £6.86 £8.23 £10.97	55 65 24 24	£301.95 + £455.90 + £197.52 + £263.28 = £1,208.61	168	£7.19
Apr 2002 to Sep 2002	Basic Evening Saturday Sunday	£5.65 £7.06 £8.47 £11.30	55 65 24 24	£310.75 + £458.90 + £203.28 + £271.20 = £1,244.13	168	£7.41
Oct 2002 to Mar 2003	Basic Evening Saturday Sunday	£5.71 £7.14 £8.56 £11.42	55 65 24 24	£314.05 + £464.10 + £205.44 + £274.08 = £1,257.67	168	£7.49

Year	Time of day	Hourly rate £	Hours pw	Cost pw £	Divided by hours pw	Aggregate rate
Apr 2003 to Mar 2004	Basic Evening Saturday Sunday	£5.90 £7.37 £8.85 £11.80	55 65 24 24	£324.50 + £479.05 + £212.40 + £283.20 = £1,299.15	168	£7.73
Apr 2004 to Mar 2005	Basic Evening Saturday Sunday	£6.06 £7.57 £9.09 £12.12	55 65 24 24	£333.30 + £492.05 + £218.16 + £290.88 = £1,334.39	168	£7.94
Apr 2005 to Mar 2006	Basic Evening Saturday Sunday	£6.24 £7.80 £9.36 £12.48	55 65 24 24	£343.20 + £507.00 + £224.64 + £299.52 = £1,374.36	168	£8.18
Apr 2006 to Mar 2007	Basic Evening Saturday Sunday	£6.43 £8.04 £9.65 £12.86	55 65 24 24	£353.65 + £522.60 + £231.60 + £308.64 = £1,416.49	168	£8.43
Apr 2007 to Mar 2008	Basic Evening Saturday Sunday	£6.59 £8.24 £9.88 £13.18	55 65 24 24	£362.45 + £535.60 + £237.12 + £316.32 = £1,451.49	168	£8.64
Apr 2008 to Mar 2009	Basic Evening Saturday Sunday	£6.75 £8.44 £10.13 £13.50	55 65 24 24	£371.25 + £548.60 + £243.12 + £324.00 = £1,486.97	168	£8.85
Apr 2009 to Mar 2013	Basic Evening Saturday Sunday	£6.85 £8.56 £10.28 £13.70	55 65 24 24	£376.75 £556.40 £246.72 £328.80 = £1,508.67	168	£8.98
April 2013 to Dec 2014	Basic Evening Saturday Sunday	£6.90 £9.21 £10.36 £13.81	70 50 24 24	£483.32 £460.31 £248.57 £331.42 = £1,523.62	168	£9.07
Jan 2015 to 31 Mar 2016	Basic Evening Saturday Sunday	£7.19 £9.59 £10.78 £14.38	70 50 24 24	£503.28 £479.31 £258.83 £345.11 = £1,586.53	168	£9.44

Notes for 2015–16

Agreement between the LGA and UNISON was reached in November 2014 with uplifted rates being implemented on January 1, 2015. Employees on Spinal Point 8 received a 4.13 per cent increase plus a non-consolidated payment in December 2014.

Employees on Spinal Point 8 also received a non-consolidated payment of £150 in January 2015. This is not incorporated into the above figures.

Bank holiday pay is not incorporated into the above as the LGA provision is for staff to be paid at the normal rate for the period in question and to take either a half or full day time off in lieu, according to time worked. Specific calculation is therefore difficult and is likely to make minimal difference at 0.03 per cent overall.

Source for above rates: National Joint Council for Local Government Services Green Book

K2: Nannies, cleaners and school fees

The death or incapacity of a spouse frequently involves incurring the costs of a nanny or a housekeeper or of sending a child to boarding school so that the surviving parent can continue working. Also, with some employments, typically when they involve overseas postings or frequent moves, school fees are part of the remuneration and will be lost if the employee dies or is disabled from that particular employment.

Nannies

	Live-out		Live-in	
	Weekly net	**Annual gross**	**Weekly net**	**Annual gross**
Central London	£476	£32,020	£351	£22,507
Outer London/Home Counties	£458	£30,687	£359	£23,135
Other areas	£405	£26,626	£302	£18,707

The figures are derived from the 2014 survey by *Nannytax.* The total cost to the client will be more than the gross wage as it is necessary to pay for holidays, sickness, employer's national insurance contribution, agency fees and so on. (See the discussion in the notes to Table K1: Care and attendance.)

Cleaners

The services of cleaners in London are currently (April 2015) advertised at the following rates. These are commonly for three or more hours a week: one-off visits usually cost more.

Homeclean	£8.73 per hour	(three hours a week)
	£9.10 per hour	(two hours a week: the cleaner is paid separately avoiding VAT; and there is an annual agency fee)
MK Londyn	£12.00 per hour	(£10.00 plus VAT)
Amy Cleaning	£10.50 per hour	(Varies. The cleaner is paid separately, avoiding VAT; there is also an agency fee).

School fees

Annual school fees for a three-term year are as follows.

Public school	
Boarders (Upper school)	£33,792
Day pupils (Upper school)	£23,400
Day pupils (Under school or preparatory school)	£16,380

Independent Schools Council (average)	
Boarder	£29,685
Day pupil (boarding school)	£17,598
Day pupil (day school)	£13,143

Notes:

1. Fees for pupils entering in the sixth form may be higher.

2. Fees for weekly as opposed to full-time boarders may be lower.

The information has been obtained from the websites of Nannytax, Homeclean, MK Londyn, Amy Cleaning, Westminster School, and the Independent Schools Council.

K3: DIY, gardening and housekeeping

1. Claimants are entitled to damages for the loss of the ability to do these tasks. Anyone who is responsible for the running of a house knows that there is a real cost in bringing in an electrician, tiler, carpenter, joiner, plumber or other skilled tradesmen to carry out tasks that they themselves cannot do. "The loss of ability to do work in the home is a recoverable head of damages and includes 'services' such as general housekeeping, gardening and maintenance".[1]

2. The same principle applies to loss of housekeeping skills. Claimants can be compensated for their inability to carry out the tasks which occur in most households—e.g. cleaning, shopping, laundry, ironing, cooking, and washing up. Even sewing on buttons, cleaning the windows, and performing the mundane routines of daily existence, such as putting out the bins and dealing with the milkman, all have to be carried out by someone, though it is too easy to forget them.

3. The loss can be valued commercially. In *Phipps v Brooks Dry Cleaning Services*[2] Stuart-Smith L.J. says that such skills have "a real money value", and Brandon J. in *Daly v General Steam Navigation Co Ltd*[3] says:

   "The loss occurred and the cost of employing someone else is no more than a way of measuring it".

4. The difficulty is always in finding an appropriate rate and working out a number of hours every week which such housekeeping tasks take to perform. Whether as a "jury award" or by using a multiplier/multiplicand approach, a judge is perfectly able to assess the evidence and make an award which reflects the reality of the loss to the claimant or the dependants. The courts have made a wide range of awards, which are analysed in *Kemp & Kemp*, Vol.1, Ch.17. In *Lawrence v Osborn*,[4] the defendant insurers accepted an annual rate of £750 per annum as the standard figure for inability to perform DIY functions. In *Wells v Wells*,[5] the Court of Appeal accepted an award under this head of £1,000 per annum. In *Dixon v Wene*,[6] Gross J. awarded £15,000 (a global sum), for loss of services: gardening and DIY.

5. Evidence is needed to support such a claim, photographs being an excellent addition to witness statement evidence. A report from a local surveyor and/or an independent agency can also strengthen this claim.

6. It should be borne in mind that often, as people get older, their appetite and energy for such tasks diminishes. This is not true for all, however; some 70- and 80-year-olds seem to have an undiminished enthusiasm for these activities.

7. A claimant need not prove an actual intention to employ replacement services (paid or unpaid). It is worth remembering the words of Bridge L.J. in *Daly v General Steam Navigation Co*[7]:

"It has been energetically argued by Mr Bennett, for the defendants, that before future loss of capacity to undertake housekeeping duties can properly be assessed at the estimated cost of

[1] Damages for Personal Injury: Medical, Nursing and Other Expenses; Law Commission, Law Com. No.262 (1999), para.2.34.
[2] [1996] P.I.Q.R. Q 100.
[3] [1979] 1 Lloyd's Rep. 257.
[4] Unreported November 7, 1997, Anthony May J., QBD.
[5] [1997] 1 W.L.R. 652.
[6] [2004] EWHC 2273 (QB).
[7] [1981] W.L.R. 120, 127.

employing some third person to come in and do that which the plaintiff is unable to do for herself, the plaintiff has to satisfy the court that she has a firm intention in any event that such a person shall be employed. For my part, I am quite unable to see why that should be so. Once the judge had concluded, as this judge did, that, to put the plaintiff, so far as money could do so, in the position in which she would have been if she had never been injured, she was going to need, in the future, domestic assistance for eight hours a week, it seems to me that it was entirely reasonable and entirely in accordance with principle in assessing damages, to say that the estimated cost of employing labour for that time, for an appropriate number of years having regard to the plaintiff's expectation of life, was the proper measure of her damages under this heading. It is really quite immaterial, in my judgment, whether having received those damages, the plaintiff chooses to alleviate her own housekeeping burden, which is an excessively heavy one, having regard to her considerable disability to undertake housekeeping tasks, by employing the labour which has been taken as the basis of the estimate on which damages have been awarded, or whether she chooses to continue to struggle with the housekeeping on her own and to spend the damages which have been awarded to her on other luxuries which she would otherwise be unable to afford".

		Hourly range	Daily range
Handymen	London	£25–£50	£180–£240
	Outside London	£15–£35	£100–£180
Gardeners	London	£25–£30	n/a
	Outside London	£15–£20	n/a

Charges will vary depending on the complexity of the work undertaken.
Charges often increase for the first hour of work undertaken and/or at weekends.
Companies that cater exclusively to seniors or those on low income and consequently charge a much reduced rate have not been included in these ranges.
Handyman charges are exclusive of plumbing or electrical charges which are invariably set at a higher rate.

K4: Hospital self-pay (uninsured) charges

The following figures are inclusive of hospital charges and surgeons' and anaesthetists' fees. The charges are approximate, as certain factors affecting cost, such as length of stay or prosthesis used, vary from patient to patient.

Treatment	Cost
breast lump removal	£1,190
cardiac catheterisation	£3,130
carpal tunnel release	£2,150
cataract removal	£2,490
circumcision	£1,518
colonoscopy	£1,895
colposcopy	£850
coronary angioplasty	£3,755
coronary artery bypass	£17,860
cruciate ligament repair	£5,632
cystoscopy	£1,456
epidural injection	£1,235
gall bladder removal	£5,110
facet joint injection under x-ray and anaesthetic	£1,240
ganglion removal	£1,830
gastric banding	£5,100
gastric balloon insertion	£2,145
gastric bypass	£9,300
gastroscopy	£1,335
grommets insertion	£1,910
haemorrhoids removal	£2,598
hernia repair (inguinal)	£2,305
hip replacement	£11,515
hysterectomy	£6,635
hysteroscopy	£2,270
knee arthroscopy	£3,295
knee replacement	£12,745
laparoscopy	£2,471
prostate removal	£5,230
sigmoidoscopy	£985
sterilisation (female)	£2,395
termination of pregnancy	£1,580
tonsillectomy	£2,380
vaginal repair	£3,455
varicose vein surgery (both legs)	£3,560
varicose vein surgery (one leg)	£2,585
varicose vein laser treatment—EVLT (both legs)	£3,250
varicose vein laser treatment—EVLT (one leg)	£2,760
vasectomy	£1,030
vasectomy reversal	£2,775
wisdom teeth extraction replacement	£1,895

These figures are drawn from around the country. Charges vary from hospital to hospital and between different areas of the country. They are generally higher in London than elsewhere.

K5: NHS charges

NHS prescriptions (from April 1, 2015)

Charge per prescribed item		£8.20
Prescription prepayment certificate:	three months	£29.10
	12 months	£104.00

For items dispensed in combination (duo) packs, there is a charge for each different drug in the pack.

NHS dental treatment (from April 1, 2015)

If a patient is not exempt from charges, he should pay one of the following rates for each course of treatment he receives:

Course of treatment	Cost	Scope
Band 1	£18.80	This covers an examination, diagnosis (e.g. x-rays), advice on how to prevent future problems, and a scale and polish if needed.
Band 2	£51.30	This covers everything listed in Band 1, plus any further treatment such as fillings, root canal work or extractions.
Band 3	£222.50	This covers everything listed in Bands 1 and 2 above, plus crowns, dentures or bridges.

Notes

1. These are the only charges for NHS dental treatment.
2. A patient only has to pay one charge for each course of treatment, even if it takes more than one visit to the dentist to finish it.
3. If the patient needs more treatment within the same or lower charge band (e.g. an additional filling), within two months of completing a course of treatment, there is no extra charge.
4. There is no charge for repairing dentures or for having stitches removed.
5. Children under 18, and many adults, do not have to pay NHS charges. (See form HC11, "Help with Health Costs", which can be found on the Department of Health website: *http://www.dh.gov.uk*.)

NHS wigs and fabric supports (from April 1, 2014)

Stock modacrylic wig	£67.75
Partial wig—human hair	£179.45
Full bespoke wig—human hair	£262.45
Abdominal support	£41.50
Spinal support	£41.50
Surgical brassière	£27.45

K6: The 2007 Rehabilitation Code

(Code of Best Practice on Rehabilitation, Early Intervention and Medical Treatment in Personal Injury Claims)

The aim of this code is to promote the use of rehabilitation and early intervention in the compensation process so that the injured person makes the best and quickest possible medical, social and psychological recovery. This objective applies whatever the severity of the injuries sustained by the claimant. The Code is designed to ensure that the claimant's need for rehabilitation is assessed and addressed as a priority, and that the process of so doing is pursued on a collaborative basis by the claimant's lawyer and the compensator.

Therefore, in every case, where rehabilitation is likely to be of benefit, the earliest possible notification to the compensator of the claim and of the need for rehabilitation will be expected.

1. INTRODUCTION

1.1 The purpose of the personal injury claims process is to put the individual back into the same position as he or she would have been in had the accident not occurred, insofar as money can achieve that objective. The purpose of the rehabilitation code is to provide a framework within which the claimant's health, quality of life and ability to work are restored as far as possible before, or simultaneously with, the process of assessing compensation.

1.2 Although the Code is recognised by the Personal Injury Pre-Action Protocol, its provisions are not mandatory. It is recognised that the aims of the Code can be achieved without strict adherence to the terms of the Code, and therefore it is open to the parties to agree an alternative framework to achieve the early rehabilitation of the claimant.

1.3 However, the Code provides a useful framework within which claimant's lawyers and the compensator can work together to ensure that the needs of injured claimants are assessed at an early stage.

1.4 In any case where agreement on liability is not reached it is open to the parties to agree that the Code will in any event operate, and the question of delay pending resolution of liability should be balanced with the interests of the injured party. However, unless so agreed, the Code does not apply in the absence of liability or prior to agreement on liability being reached.

1.5 In this code the expression "the compensator" shall include any loss adjuster, solicitor or other person acting on behalf of the compensator.

2. THE CLAIMANT'S SOLICITOR

2.1 It should be the duty of every claimant's solicitor to consider, from the earliest practicable stage, and in consultation with the claimant, the claimant's family, and where appropriate the claimant's treating physician(s), whether it is likely or possible that early intervention, rehabilitation or medical treatment would improve their present and/or long-term physical and mental well being. This duty is ongoing throughout the life of the case but is of most importance in the early stages.

2.2 The claimant's solicitors will in any event be aware of their responsibilities under section 4 of the Pre-Action Protocol for Personal Injury Claims.

2.3 It shall be the duty of a claimant's solicitor to consider, with the claimant and/or the claimant's family, whether there is an immediate need for aids, adaptations, adjustments to employment to enable the claimant to keep his/her existing job, obtain suitable alternative employment with the same employer or retrain for new employment, or other matters that would seek to alleviate problems caused by disability, and then to communicate with the compensators as soon as practicable about any such rehabilitation needs, with a view to putting this Code into effect.

2.4 It shall not be the responsibility of the solicitor to decide on the need for treatment or rehabilitation or to arrange such matters without appropriate medical or professional advice.

2.5 It is the intention of this Code that the claimant's solicitor will work with the compensator to address these rehabilitation needs and that the assessment and delivery of rehabilitation needs shall be a collaborative process.

2.6 It must be recognised that the compensator will need to receive from the claimant's solicitors sufficient information for the compensator to make a proper decision about the need for intervention, rehabilitation or treatment. To this extent the claimant's solicitor must comply with the requirements of the Pre-Action Protocol to provide the compensator with full and adequate details of the injuries sustained by the claimant, the nature and extent of any or any likely continuing disability and any suggestions that may have already have been made concerning the rehabilitation and/or early intervention.

2.7 There is no requirement under the Pre-Action Protocol, or under this code, for the claimant's solicitor to have obtained a full medical report. It is recognised that many cases will be identified for consideration under this code before medical evidence has actually been commissioned or obtained.

3. THE COMPENSATOR

3.1 It shall be the duty of the compensator, from the earliest practicable stage in any appropriate case, to consider whether it is likely that the claimant will benefit in the immediate, medium or longer-term from further medical treatment, rehabilitation or early intervention. This duty is ongoing throughout the life of the case but is most important in the early stages.

3.2 If the compensator considers that a particular claim might be suitable for intervention, rehabilitation or treatment, the compensator will communicate this to the claimant's solicitor as soon as practicable.

3.3 On receipt of such communication, the claimant's solicitor will immediately discuss these issues with the claimant and/or the claimant's family pursuant to his duty set out above.

3.4 Where a request to consider rehabilitation has been communicated by the claimant's solicitor to the compensator, it will usually be expected that the compensator will respond to such request within 21 days.

3.5 Nothing in this or any other code of practice shall in any way modify the obligations of the compensator under the Protocol to investigate claims rapidly and in any event within three months (except where time is extended by the claimant's solicitor) from the date of the formal claim letter. It is recognised that, although the rehabilitation assessment can be done even where liability investigations are outstanding, it is essential that such investigations proceed with the appropriate speed.

4. ASSESSMENT

4.1 Unless the need for intervention, rehabilitation or treatment has already been identified by medical reports obtained and disclosed by either side, the need for and extent of such intervention, rehabilitation or treatment will be considered by means of an assessment by an appropriately qualified person.

4.2 An assessment of rehabilitation needs may be carried out by any person or organisation suitably qualified, experienced and skilled to carry out the task. The claimant's solicitor and the compensator should endeavour to agree on the person or organisation to be chosen.

4.3 No solicitor or compensator may insist on the assessment being carried out by a particular person or organisation if (on reasonable grounds) the other party objects, such objection to be raised within 21 days from the date of notification of the suggested assessor.

4.4 The assessment may be carried out by a person or organisation which has a direct business connection with the solicitor or compensator, only if the other party agrees. The solicitor or compensator will be expected to reveal to the other party the existence of and nature of such a business connection.

5. THE ASSESSMENT PROCESS

5.1 Where possible, the agency to be instructed to provide the assessment should be agreed between the claimant's solicitor and the compensator. The method of providing instructions to that agency will be agreed between the solicitor and the compensator.

5.2 The assessment agency will be asked to carry out the assessment in a way that is appropriate to the needs of the case and, in a simple case, may include, by prior appointment, a telephone interview but in more serious cases will probably involve a face-to-face discussion with the claimant. The report will normally cover the following headings:

1. The injuries sustained by the claimant.
2. The current disability/incapacity arising from those injuries. Where relevant to the overall picture of the claimant's needs, any other medical conditions not arising from the accident should also be separately annotated.
3. The claimant's domestic circumstances (including mobility accommodation and employment) where relevant.
4. The injuries/disability in respect of which early intervention or early rehabilitation is suggested.
5. The type of intervention or treatment envisaged.
6. The likely cost.
7. The likely outcome of such intervention or treatment.

5.3 The report should not deal with issues relating to legal liability and should therefore not contain a detailed account of the accident's circumstances.

5.4 In most cases it will be expected that the assessment will take place within 14 days from the date of the letter of referral to the assessment agency.

5.5 It must be remembered that the compensator will usually only consider such rehabilitation to deal with the effects of the injuries that have been caused in the relevant accident and will normally not be expected to fund treatment for conditions which do not directly relate to the accident unless the effect of such conditions has been exacerbated by the injuries sustained in the accident.

6. THE ASSESSMENT REPORT

6.1 The report agency will, on completion of the report, send copies on to both the claimant's solicitor and compensator simultaneously. Both parties will have the right to raise questions on the report, disclosing such correspondence to the other party.

6.2 It is recognised that for this assessment report to be of benefit to the parties, it should be prepared and used wholly outside the litigation process. Neither side can therefore, unless they agree in writing, rely on its contents in any subsequent litigation.

6.3 The report, any correspondence related to it and any notes created by the assessing agency to prepare it, will be covered by legal privilege and will not be disclosed in any legal proceedings unless the parties agree. Any notes or documents created in connection with the assessment process will not be disclosed in any litigation, and any person involved in the preparation of the report or involved in the assessment process, shall not be a compellable witness at court. This principle is also set out in para.4.4, above, of the Pre-Action Protocol.

6.4 The provision in para.6.3, above as to treating the report, etc. as outside the litigation process is limited to the assessment report and any notes relating to it. Any notes and reports created during the subsequent case management process will be covered by the usual principle in relation to disclosure of documents and medical records relating to the claimant.

6.5 The compensator will pay for the report within 28 days of receipt.

6.6 This code intends that the parties will continue to work together to ensure that the rehabilitation which has been recommended proceeds smoothly and that any further rehabilitation needs are also assessed.

7. RECOMMENDATIONS

7.1 When the assessment report is disclosed to the compensator, the compensator will be under a duty to consider the recommendations made and the extent to which funds will be made available to implement all or some of the recommendations. The compensator will not be required to pay for intervention treatment that is unreasonable in nature, content or cost or where adequate and timely provision is otherwise available. The claimant will be under no obligation to undergo intervention, medical or investigation treatment that is unreasonable in all the circumstances of the case.

7.2 The compensator will normally be expected to respond to the claimant's solicitor within 21 days from the date upon which the assessment report is disclosed as to the extent to which the recommendations have been accepted and rehabilitation treatment would be funded and will be expected to justify, within that same timescale, any refusal to meet the cost of recommended rehabilitation.

7.3 If funds are provided by the compensator to the claimant to enable specific intervention, rehabilitation or treatment to occur, the compensator warrants that they will not, in any legal proceedings connected with the claim, dispute the reasonableness of that treatment, nor the agreed costs, provided of course that the claimant has had the recommended treatment. The compensator will not, should the claim fail or be later discontinued, or any element of contributory negligence be assessed or agreed, seek to recover from the claimant any funds that they have made available pursuant to this Code.

K7: Rehabilitation: a practitioner's guide

Compiled by the Bodily Injury Claims Management Association

Norman W. Cottington, The Injury Care Clinics (President)
David Blofeld, past Claims Manager, Hart Re
Christopher Crook, Solicitor, Edwards Duthie
Tony Goff, Solicitor, George Ide Phillips
Graham Plumb, Claims Manager, AXA Insurance
Keith O. Popperwell, Solicitor Silverbeck Rymer
Bernard Rowe, Solicitor, Lyons Davidson (Treasurer)
Martin Saunders, Allianz Cornhill Insurance
Martin Staples, Solicitor, Vizards
Janet Tilley, Solicitor, Colemans CTTS (Secretary)
Ian Walker, Solicitor, Russell Jones and Walker (Vice President)

CONTENTS

1. CASE MANAGEMENT

One of the first decisions to make is who will manage the rehabilitative process. The various specialist disciplines are outlined below. The task of organising so many disciplines may seem daunting, but help can be found.

One way is to use a case manager to act as case co-ordinator.

The appointment of a case manager at an early stage in the claim will need to be discussed and preferably agreed with the claimant and the insurer. A case manager must have close contact with the claimant and his/her family.

A case manager must have the time available to deal with the claimant and preferably be based close to the claimant.

Case managers can come from a variety of disciplines, but look for someone trained and committed to the standards laid down by the Case Management Society of the UK (CMSUK).

There are a number of specialist case management organisations in the UK, although the number of claimants is likely to outweigh the availability of specialists for some time to come.

A case manager will co-ordinate all of the available services and should be required as appropriate to:

- assess the personal circumstances and needs of the claimant and his/her family;
- monitor medical rehabilitation and, if necessary, provide for multi-disciplinary assessment;
- liaise with the DSS and claim appropriate benefits;
- liaise with the local authority for interim support prior to a statutory assessment (currently Community Care Act 1990); review such assessment and negotiate the provision of services and financial assistance from the local authority;
- arrange for therapies;
- monitor the needs of the claimant's family and arrange for respite care, if necessary;
- assist the claimant in obtaining training and monitoring carers;
- facilitate employment rehabilitation;
- arrange appropriate accommodation;
- review personal transport arrangements;
- consider mobility issues; and
- consider funding arrangements for rehabilitation.

Cost
Following an initial assessment, case management will normally be charged on an hourly basis (expect to pay between £65 and £85 per hour). Input by a case manager should reduce once rehabilitation needs have been addressed.

2. IMMEDIATE NEEDS ASSESSMENT

Why?
Rehabilitation in the long-term will be difficult, if not impossible, if short-term needs are overlooked. "First Aid" support is essential to overcome the immediate aftermath of an injury and to provide a platform on which to build long-term rehabilitation.

At what level?
As a rule of thumb, an immediate needs assessment is applicable to claimants who have sustained injuries likely to cause incapacity for several months or longer.

When?
The assessment should be done as soon as possible, even before discharge from hospital, with a view to ensuring the home environment to which the claimant will be discharged is suitable at least for the basic needs of the claimant and his/her family. However, an assessment undertaken years after the event of the injury can still help.

What to expect
The report should provide preliminary background information about the claimant's circumstances, including the following:

a. the nature and extent of the injury;
b. any relevant medical background;
c. family circumstances;
d. immediate home adaptation needs;

e. steps to improve the claimant's quality of life and support for family carers; and
f. how, and at what cost, recommendations can be implemented.

Relatively simple and inexpensive measures can make a big difference, for example, stair handrails, ramps for wheelchair access, raised toilet seats, widened doorways, and lowered light switches or doorknobs.

Recommendations should be capable of being put into immediate effect and at proportionate, reasonable cost.

Do not confuse an immediate needs assessment with long-term care needs and costs, which will be addressed by appropriate experts in the claim.

By whom?
A case manager trained and committed to the standards laid down by the Case Management Society of the UK (CMSUK) is the most obvious choice.

An occupational therapist or anyone with a social care background, for example, a community care nurse, a social worker or a general practitioner, may similarly be able to conduct the assessment.

Cost
The Code requires that the insurer be responsible for the cost.

The charge will depend upon the complexity of the report and travel expenses, but expect to pay between £750 and £1,750.

The defendant's insurer should usually fund reasonable recommendations by way of an interim payment (see section 7 of the Code).

Liability
Only a complete denial of liability should prevent a defendant's insurer from considering an immediate needs assessment (but also consider an assessment via Social Services).

If the dispute is confined to contributory negligence, the comparatively low cost of an assessment will be justified.

3. EMOTIONAL AND PSYCHOLOGICAL CARE

Why?
Anyone who has suffered a serious injury has experienced a major life event. The injured person, his/her family and close friends will be totally unprepared for either the injury or what follows.

Those who have suffered a serious injury will need to come to terms with what has happened to them. There may also be psychological disorders triggered by the accident, which must be recognised and dealt with. Failure to do so may prevent other treatments from being effective and may hinder a return to work.

Emotional, and in many cases psychological support needs to be given to help the claimant and those upon whom he/she depends.

When?

Support should be offered as soon as possible. Often this will be determined by the willingness of the injured claimant and/or his/her family to accept outside help. Many people are frightened by their feelings or by the idea of sharing them with someone. Proper counselling can also be of great assistance to relatives acting as carers.

An early assessment can in itself help identify problems or potential problems in time to prevent prolonged post-traumatic stress disorder.

An assessment and, where needed, counselling or psychological treatment are best considered soon after the injury and/or return home from hospital (i.e. within the first three months of injury). The need for emotional and psychological support may last much longer than the medical treatment.

By whom?

Clinical psychologists should normally carry out an initial assessment. If there is any suggestion of brain injury, then a neuropsychologist should be used.

It is useful to check first whether the claimant's hospital team has already involved a psychologist to help with rehabilitation or whether there is a facility within the GP's practice.

Arrangements should be made with a clinical psychologist close to the claimant's home. Where necessary, appointments can be arranged at the claimant's home, which is important if the claimant is distressed by travel.

There are a number of agencies that have panels of psychologists available or you can contact the British Psychological Society at St. Andrew's House, 48 Princess Road East, Leicester LE1 7DR or by telephone on 0116 254 9568.

What to expect

Most assessments involve some psychological testing. This is necessary to determine what help is needed. Better insight and understanding by the claimant and/or his/her family of what to expect of themselves and their feelings will help to achieve maximum recovery.

Cost

A clinical psychologist's assessment and recommendations will cost between £200 and £500.

A neuropsychologist's assessment will cost between £750 and £1,750.

Psychological therapy costs between £75 and £150 per session.

4. PHYSIOTHERAPY, OSTEOPATHY AND CHIROPRACTIC

Why?

Early mobilisation following injury is now widely recognised as an important part of treatment and needs to be encouraged, provided that it is consistent with medical advice. Damaged tissue needs careful handling. Injury victims need to be shown how to regain movement and function as soon as possible. Whilst treatment methods vary amongst the different professions, these all work towards maximising useful function and can help prevent an injury from becoming a permanent disability.

When?
In the case of serious injuries, this type of treatment is normally determined by the hospital medical team. After discharge from hospital, it is all too easy to overlook the benefit to be gained from continuing physiotherapy and other treatments. Treatment is not just about relieving pain, but equally about achieving the best possible recovery of movement, strength and function. In the case of soft tissue injuries, treatment should be assessed as soon as possible, i.e. within a few weeks, not months, of the injury. In more serious cases, initial treatment should be considered as part of the overall medical management of the patient. After discharge, treatment should be considered as part of the overall nursing plan or by direct referral to a practitioner.

By whom?
This type of treatment is provided by chartered physiotherapists, osteopaths or chiropractors. Increasingly, it is possible to find that two or more of these disciplines are offered at the same clinic. There are a number of specialist agencies that will provide and co-ordinate treatment. Details of local practitioners can also be found in the Yellow Pages. Alternatively, information is available from:

- Chartered Society of Physiotherapists: 0207 306 6666
- General Council of Osteopaths: 0207 357 6655
- British Chiropractic Association: 0118 950 5950

What to expect
Make sure the practitioner is a member of a relevant professional body and that there are well-equipped treatment rooms. All practitioners will want to assess the patient before offering treatment. The assessment may involve x-rays as well as a physical examination.

If treatment is offered, a treatment plan should be prepared that identifies the number of treatments and when they are to be given. Often a patient will be taught exercises to help speed up the recovery process.

Cost
The cost will vary from clinic to clinic. Average costs for an assessment will be in the order of £40–£60. Treatment is likely to cost in the order of £30–£45 per session depending upon locality.

5. ACCOMMODATION

Why?
A secure, comfortable and accessible home is likely to be a pre-requisite for any home-based rehabilitation plan. Accommodation that was suitable for a claimant before an injury may be unsuitable after injury.

When?
Assessment of accommodation needs should be undertaken as soon as possible. For many patients, the only obstacle to being discharged from hospital is their inability to access their own home.

The need for substantial adaptations to accommodation or even a purpose-built property is normally a long-term consideration. Permanent arrangements are best dealt with when it is reasonably clear what the long-term requirements will be.

Physical needs will be identified in medical, occupational therapist and nursing reports.

Short-term needs are as important a consideration as long-term needs. Short-term may, in fact, mean several months or even longer. Immediate needs may have been dealt with under an immediate needs report, but this will need to be updated.

By whom?
A case manager or occupational therapist may be able to advise upon minor alterations that are needed until permanent needs become clear. Once these needs have been identified, a good local builder will be able to carry out minor works such as installing rails, ramps and widening doorways.

If major alterations are needed, a report will be required from an accommodation expert, usually a surveyor or architect, and preferably one with experience of designing accommodation for use by people with disabilities. Whoever carries out the assessment should be familiar with and liaise with the local authority, from which grants may be available. This is particularly relevant in cases where damages may be reduced as a result of an apportionment of liability.

What to expect
A visit to the claimant's home or proposed home, after consideration of the medical and other reports. This will lead to a report detailing the physical requirements of the property that are necessary in order for the claimant to maximise his/her potential for independent living. In addition, it will take into account the possibility that a carer might need accommodation.

The report should detail the work needed, together with costs, including likely maintenance and/or replacement costs.

Cost
The cost of this report will vary from case to case. Hourly charge-out rates will be in the order of £100–£150 per hour. A detailed report is likely to cost £1,000 or more.

6. NURSING, CARE AND EQUIPMENT

Why?
The objective will be to establish the most beneficial regime, aimed at ensuring the health and welfare of the injured person, and optimising independence and self-esteem by the most cost-effective means.

When?
It is important to establish in advance what arrangements will be beneficial at each stage of the recovery process, and not address each stage as it occurs. At each stage, it is vital that the case manager, or those reporting, are fully aware of the current medical prognosis, including any anticipated changes.

By whom?
The appointed case manager is likely to be the best choice, as they often possess all of the relevant experience. The person chosen must have an understanding of the medical and physical needs of the claimant, and how to provide for them. Not all nursing/care experts may deal with aids and equipment. Separate advice may be needed from an occupational therapist.

What to expect

The expert will need to see all existing reports and it may be beneficial for the different disciplines to confer.

The expert will need to speak to the claimant and his/her family and carers as well as those responsible for medical treatment. The report should address:

- the injured person's capacity for coping with the challenges of his/her injury and impairment;
- existing care, by whom and in what environment;
- external features impacting on the situation, e.g. accommodation, social contact, locality and family dynamics;
- the level of nursing care required;
- vulnerabilities—health and safety issues for the claimant and his/her carers at present and in the future;
- the need for an enabler;
- the need for domestic assistance;
- details of equipment needed;
- detailed cost of recommendations and suggested providers; and
- objectives and their timescales.

Cost

This will depend upon the circumstances and the complexity of each case. Reports will cost from £1,000. Hourly charging rates are likely to range from £65–£90 per hour, but could possibly be higher.

7. SOCIAL SERVICES

Social services are provided pursuant to the National Health Service Community Care Act 1990 by local authorities' Social Services departments, which are entitled to call upon:

- Health Authorities.
- Housing Departments.

The trigger for support is an assessment by the local authority pursuant to s.47 of the NHS and Community Care Act 1990. The right to an assessment is absolute.

Once an assessment has been carried out, a written copy must be provided to the Social Services department. A complaints and review procedure is available if the assessment is considered unsatisfactory.

Following assessment, the local authority will make a decision about whether to provide services and the type of services to be provided.

Social services available include:

- home helps or carers;
- respite breaks for carers;
- laundry service;
- therapies;
- odd job scheme;
- rehabilitation;

- carer support;
- residential care;
- transport;
- housing adaptation; and
- provision of accommodation suitable to the claimant's needs.

The provision of services may be dependent upon the resources of the local authority. Each local authority publishes eligibility criteria. Certain services must be provided under a legal duty. Other services may be provided on a discretionary basis, but there is no duty to do so.

Section 2 of the Chronically Sick and Disabled Persons Act sets out services that must be supplied as a legal duty:

- home help;
- provision of radio, television, library or residential services;
- home adaptations for greater safety, comfort or convenience;
- holidays;
- meals; and
- telephone.

The local authority will formulate a case plan, which will be administered by a case manager. This will specify all needs, including those that cannot be met due to budget restraints.

Local authorities are empowered to make direct cash payments to disabled persons so that they can purchase care services for themselves (Community Care (Direct Payments) Act 1996). In addition, cash payments are available from Independent Living Funds and from the DWP.

If the claimant needs suitable accommodation, the local authority has a duty to provide this pursuant to s.21 of the National Assistance Act.

Residential care can be arranged by both local authorities and health authorities. Provision of residential care by a health authority is free, but DWP benefits are treated as if the claimant were in hospital. Local authority residential care is subject to means testing. Residential care includes the provision of basic accommodation.

A claimant can choose his/her preferred accommodation and can ask a third party (e.g. an insurer or tortfeasor) to meet any shortfall if the cost is more than the local authority would normally pay.

If a local authority provides services free of charge, a claimant cannot make a claim against the insurer in respect of such services.

A local authority has discretion to charge for services other than residential care.

The right to charge for services is subject to a two-stage test:

1. whether it is reasonable in all the circumstances; and
2. whether the claimant has sufficient means to pay for the services.

Where residential accommodation is provided by a local authority, there is a duty to charge, subject to means testing.

However, such charges can be avoided by the creation of a trust or if the damages are administered by the court (see Preservation of Benefits, below).

8. SOCIAL SECURITY BENEFITS

Aim

To maximise benefits and to preserve the right to means-tested benefits.

Non-means-tested benefits

There are four main groups of non-means-tested benefits that are payable as a consequence of disability:

1. Incapacity for Work
   Incapacity Benefit
   Severe Disablement Allowance

2. Care and Supervision
   Disability Living Allowance
   Care Component
   Constant Attendance Allowance

3. Mobility
   DLA Mobility Component

4. Degree of Disablement
   Severe Disablement Allowance
   Industrial Disablement Benefit

Income Support

This is paid to the claimant if he/she is incapable of working, and to a carer if regularly and substantially engaged in caring for another person.

If the claimant has capital in excess of £8,000 (or £16,000 if in residential care), he/she does not qualify for income support.

Disability Working Allowance

This is intended to encourage people with disabilities to return to work. It is paid to people who work 16 hours or more per week. If a claimant (or his/her partner) has capital of more than £16,000, the claimant does not qualify for this allowance.

Disability Living Allowance

The DLA is not means-tested.

This allowance comprises a care component and a mobility component. The care component is for personal care needs and is paid at three different rates. The mobility component is paid at two different rates.

Tests are administered by an Adjudication Officer.

Receipt of the DLA acts as a gateway to the following benefits:

- Disability Premium.

- Severe Disability Premium.
- Independent Living Funds.
- Motability Scheme.

Industrial Injuries Benefit
This benefit is paid to those who are disabled by a loss of physical and mental capacity caused by an industrial accident or disease.

It is paid in addition to any other non means-tested benefit.

Incapacity Benefit
This is paid to those who are unable to work due to disability. It is non-means-tested, but it is only payable if sufficient national insurance contributions (NIC) have been made.

Severe Disablement Allowance
This allowance is paid for 28 weeks to those who are incapable of working but have made insufficient NIC to qualify for the incapacity benefit.

How to claim
Benefit is generally paid from the date that a claim is received by a DWP Office.

There is discretion to accept anything in writing "as sufficient" in the circumstances of a particular case.

The DLA is paid from the date a claim form is requested, so long as the claim form is returned within six weeks.

Income support is paid from the date of notifying the DWP, so long as the claim form is returned within one month. There is discretion to extend time limits in some cases.

Claims should be made to a local DWP Office or by telephoning the Benefit Enquiry Line on 0800 882200.

Appeals are made to the local DWP Office. An appeal can be made within three months of any decision. There is some discretion to extend the time limit up to six years, but it is difficult to make a late appeal.

The effect of receipt of damages on income-related benefits
Lump sum payments of compensation are treated as capital and are added to any other capital that the claimant may have. The effect is that:

- a claimant or partner may have up to £8,000 (£16,000 if in residential care) in capital and benefit will not be affected;
- deductions are made on a sliding scale in Income Support, DLA, Housing Benefit and Council Tax Benefit, depending on the amount of capital;
- income support is not payable where there is capital in excess of £8,000 (or £16,000 if in residential care); and
- no Housing Benefit, Council Tax Benefit or DLA is payable if capital exceeds £16,000.

Preservation of benefits
Benefits paid to a claimant can be managed by creating a trust or ensuring the damages fund is administered by the court.

Trusts
The trust may be set up by the claimant or someone acting on behalf of the claimant. If a trust is created:

- the capital value of the trust fund is wholly disregarded;
- payments from the trust fund to the claimant or on his/her behalf will be treated as income or capital, depending on frequency of payment and the terms of the trust; and
- regular discretionary payments will be disregarded, provided they are used for needs other than those intended to be covered by benefits.[1]

Funds administered by the court
A decision of the Social Security Commissioner[2] makes it clear that money in the Court of Protection should not be taken into account for entitlement to Income Support under the terms of para.12 to Sch.120 to the Income Support (General) Regulations (as amended).

9. MOBILITY

Why?
Restricted mobility emphasises impairment and threatens independence. Mobility contributes toward independence.

When?
Immediate thought should be given to mobility within the home, which is often effectively achieved by simple steps such as providing ramps and widening doorways for wheelchair users.

Longer-term projects, such as specialised wheelchairs or appropriate motor vehicles, may have to await medical recovery.

What to expect?
A driving assessment can identify and address any barriers to independent driving ability, and can identify aids, adaptations or controls required to overcome those barriers.

The Disability Living centres identify and cost aids and equipment for mobility and dexterity.

By whom?
Personal mobility can be assessed by an occupational therapist.

Disability Living centres exhibit and assist in identifying appropriate aids, including wheelchairs, vehicles and prosthetic appliances.

[1] This is no longer so. It was changed by the 2006 Regulations. See H4.
[2] (1996) 3 J.S.S.L.D. 136.

Driving Assessment centres can assist in determining the right choice of vehicle and wheelchair.

The claimant or his/her family can apply to the DWP for a Mobility Allowance and/or payment under the Motability Scheme to defray the cost of a vehicle.

Disabled living experts, usually architects, can advise on property alterations to ensure ease of access.

Cost
A driving assessment is unlikely to cost £50–£100 or more, at a mobility centre.

The Disability Living centres provide their services at no cost, although the equipment they recommend can cost anything from a few pounds for a wide-handled toothbrush to more than £1,000 for a suitable wheelchair.

10. VOCATIONAL

Why?
A return to work is more likely to raise a claimant's self-esteem than anything else. It provides independence and self-respect.

When?
A claimant should be helped to return to work, if appropriate, as soon as possible.

It is vital to:

- take early steps to consider, with the involvement of the employer, the preservation of the claimant's pre-accident job, by adapting the workplace or duties in accordance with the Equality Act 2010; and
- if remaining with the pre-accident employer is not possible, then consider all alternative avenues.

Insurers may be willing to fund the necessary steps to achieve these goals.

By whom?
A vocational or employment rehabilitation expert should assess the claimant's suitability to return to work and his/her requirements.

A vocational report should not be confused with the reports commonly commissioned from employment consultants. The latter are generally designed to assist in the quantification of loss, whereas the former is intended to identify the injured person's potential and motivation for employment, and to recommend how to achieve a return to suitable work. The expert should know the local area and sympathetic employers, whilst having a good working relationship with the Disability Employment Advisor.

What to expect
A detailed interview should be undertaken to identify the claimant's former work experience abilities and qualifications, his/her aspirations, and a general assessment of his/her current physical and mental ability.

The next stage should, ideally, be a meeting between the vocational assessor and the previous employer with a view to identifying whether re-employment is possible, either in full or reduced capacity; whether other placements may be available; and/or whether adaptations to the work place may be necessary to facilitate such employment.

If employment with the pre-accident employer is not possible for whatever reason, then consideration will be given to other suitable local job opportunities.

If no such opportunities exist, a more detailed vocational assessment, carried out over a period of one week, may be recommended.

There are numerous facilities nationwide where such assessments can take place either on a day or residential basis. Assessments take place in a working environment and measure dexterity, co-ordination, ability, communication skills, confidence, and motivation. Speed, ability and quality of work is recorded, assessed and reported upon.

Following assessment, recommendations may include finding a work placement properly suited to the claimant's skills and abilities or sending the claimant on a training scheme to learn new skills. Another possibility is for the claimant to be supported by a trainer or friend, who would work alongside him/her in a work placement until confidence is gained in employment skills.

A return to some form of remunerative employment is the most effective way an injured person can regain his/her self-esteem and achieve an improved quality of life.

Cost

This will vary depending upon the type of assessment and the time it takes. Expect charges of £750–£1,500 for a vocational interview and report. More detailed assessments will cost more. A residential five-day assessment is likely to cost £2,000 or more.

Case management—the early days

As health care options, delivery methods and financing mechanisms became more complex, with inconsistent incentives and accountability, the need for assistance in obtaining timely and appropriate care to achieve recovery and optimal functioning has become increasingly evident.

The first Case Management Society was established in America in 1990 (CMSA) after recognition of the need for a supportive body for this rapidly expanding profession. In 1996, the Case Management Society International was established to provide an umbrella for global affiliation. Canada, Australia, South Africa and a number of European countries already have their own case management societies.

In response to this growth in case management, an informal group of care professionals involved in case management practice started meeting during 2000 to explore the possibility of a national, non-profit, professional membership association for case managers.

About CMSUK

The overall goals and ambitions are to:

- advise on the development of a professional case management qualification;
- develop and encourage consistent professional standards of best practice, competence, service and conduct of case managers;

- provide comprehensive continuing education programmes;
- provide support for its members;
- instil confidence for purchasers when employing the services of a CMSUK member;
- development of case managers within existing public/private health and social environment; and
- one of our main aims is to be affiliated with and accredited by the main professional bodies that currently register practising case managers.

With evolving care structures, CMSUK will play an integral part in setting and upholding standards to ensure that cost-effective and timely outcomes are achieved.

If you would like to know more about CMSUK, please write to: CMSUK, 100 Fetter Lane, London, EC4A 1BN. Email: cmsukltd@yahoo.co.uk

L

Group L

Motoring and Allied Material

L1: Motoring costs

AA motoring costs

Petrol cars

	Cost New (£)				
	Up to £13,000	£13,000 to £18,000	£18,000 to £25,000	£25,000 to £32,000	Over £32,000
Standing charges per annum (£s)					
Vehicle Excise Duty (Road tax)	110.00	145.00	180.00	283.00	609.00
Insurance	360.00	409.00	481.00	571.00	762.00
Cost of capital	203.00	251.00	355.00	494.00	877.00
Depreciation	1190.00	2156.00	2611.00	3672.00	6974.00
Breakdown cover	50.00	50.00	50.00	50.00	50.00
Total, standing charges only (£s)	1913.00	3011.00	3678.00	5070.00	9271.00
Standing charges per mile (pence)					
at 5,000 miles per year	37.78	59.36	72.51	99.93	182.64
10,000	19.13	30.11	36.78	50.70	92.71
15,000	13.07	20.65	25.21	34.78	63.67
20,000	10.16	16.13	19.69	27.18	49.84
25,000	8.22	13.08	15.96	22.04	40.43
30,000	6.89	10.97	13.39	18.49	33.93
Running costs per mile (pence)					
Petrol*	10.84	13.12	14.55	16.22	18.04
Tyres	1.37	1.57	1.94	2.32	3.35
Service labour costs	2.10	2.07	2.09	2.04	2.34
Replacement parts	2.24	2.39	2.25	2.73	3.34
Parking and tolls	2.00	2.00	2.00	2.00	2.00
Total, running costs only (pence)	18.56	21.14	22.83	25.31	29.06
* Petrol @ 129.0 p/litre. For every penny more or less, add or subtract	0.08	0.10	0.11	0.13	0.14

Total of standing charges and running costs (in pence) based on annual mileage:

at 5,000 miles per year	56.34	80.51	95.34	125.24	211.70
10,000 miles	37.68	51.26	59.60	76.01	121.78
15,000 miles	31.63	41.79	48.04	60.09	92.73
20,000 miles	28.72	37.28	42.52	52.49	78.91
25,000 miles	26.78	34.22	38.79	47.35	69.50
30,000 miles	25.45	32.12	36.22	43.80	62.99

Please see the associated notes for more detail. These figures are typical but do not represent all types of vehicle and conditions of use. The figures change from time to time.

Diesel cars

	Cost New (£)				
	Up to £16,000	£16,000 to £22,000	£22,000 to £26,000	£26,000 to £36,000	Over £36,000
Standing charges per annum (£s)					
Vehicle Excise Duty (Road tax)	30.00	110.00	180.00	180.00	361.00
Insurance	424.00	499.00	511.00	601.00	771.00
Cost of capital	245.00	325.00	429.00	541.00	823.00
Depreciation (at 10,000 miles/annum)	1705.00	2426.00	2618.00	3373.00	5197.00
Breakdown cover	50.00	50.00	50.00	50.00	50.00
Total, standing charges only (£s)	2454.00	3411.00	3788.00	4745.00	7203.00
Standing charges per mile (pence)					
at 5,000 miles per year	48.40	67.24	74.71	93.55	141.98
10,000	24.54	34.11	37.88	47.45	72.03
15,000	16.81	23.38	25.95	32.53	49.40
20,000	13.12	18.27	20.25	25.41	38.61
25,000	10.63	14.81	16.41	20.60	31.31
30,000	8.92	12.42	13.76	17.28	26.26
Running costs per mile (pence)					
Diesel fuel*	9.28	10.20	12.65	12.88	16.79
Tyres	1.15	1.49	2.06	2.02	2.87
Service labour costs	2.10	2.14	2.29	2.24	2.76
Replacement parts	2.73	2.43	2.53	2.99	3.44
Parking and tolls	2.00	2.00	2.00	2.00	2.00
Total, running costs only (pence)	17.26	18.25	21.54	22.14	27.85
* Diesel fuel @ 137.0 p/litre. For every penny more or less, add or subtract	0.07	0.07	0.09	0.09	0.12

Total of standing charges and running costs (in pence) based on annual mileage:					
at 5,000 miles per year	65.66	85.49	96.25	115.69	169.83
10,000 miles	41.80	52.35	59.41	69.59	99.88
15,000 miles	34.08	41.64	47.49	54.67	77.26
20,000 miles	30.39	36.52	41.79	47.55	66.47
25,000 miles	27.90	33.06	37.94	42.74	59.16
30,000 miles	26.18	30.67	35.30	39.42	54.11

Notes to the AA tables

The AA tables are published annually as a guide to the likely cost to the average private user to run a car. (In previous years tables were also produced for motorcycles and scooters.) The figures given can only be a guide, as individual vehicles will vary: for instance fuel consumption will depend on traffic conditions and the type of journey, and repairs can be very unpredictable. The aim is to show a representative cost that reflects all the important items, so that the motorist can see how it all adds up. This should help make the most suitable choice of economical and environmentally less damaging transport.

Standing Charges The basic costs which you have to pay whether you use the car or not. They include the Road Tax (annual VED), insurance, the cost of the capital used for the vehicle, the loss of value of the vehicle or depreciation, and AA breakdown cover. Depreciation is affected by mileage.

Running Costs The actual costs of using the car include petrol, oil, tyres, routine servicing, repairs and parking.

Vehicle Groups Cars are put into groups depending on the new car price, as this is a better guide to what they cost to run than for instance the engine size. Take the new car list price when it was first registered (including the main options such as automatic gearbox, air conditioning etc supplied with the car), not the current list price. If in doubt, used-car price guides will give the original list prices.

Claiming Mileage How much an employer pays for mileage is a matter for negotiation between them and the employees, as circumstances will vary. The Inland Revenue operates the Approved Mileage Allowance Payment (AMAP) system (in our Table L2)—further details from your local tax office or:

http://www.hmrc.gov.uk/mileage/index.htm, and
http://www.hmrc.gov.uk/cars/fuel_company_cars.htm.

The figures given in our tables are VAT inclusive.

The AA Website The Motoring Costs tables are also on the AA website at *http://www.theaa.com* Here some of the data will be updated throughout the year, and there is an interactive version that can tailor the costs to an individual car model and, for instance, the actual insurance premium paid.

Road Tax For cars registered after 1st March 2001 the rate of Vehicle Tax depends on their fuel type and their emissions of carbon dioxide in the legislated Type Approval tests. In the tables, averages for the price groups are used for the rate. For older (pre-March 2001) cars, if the engine capacity is 1,549 cc or less the duty is £145, and if it is over 1,549 cc the duty is £230.

Insurance The UK average cost for a comprehensive policy with a 60 per cent no-claims discount.

Cost of capital This represents the loss of income from the owner's having money tied up in a vehicle, which could otherwise be earning interest in a deposit account, calculated at 2.2 per cent (the AA's online saving rate) of the average value for the car cost group. If the money is borrowed, the cost of capital will instead consist of the charges for loans or hire-purchase finance.

Depreciation Cars lose value at different rates, depending on make, age, mileage, condition and even colour. Older cars will in general depreciate at a slower rate. The tables assume that depreciation costs are averaged over four years from purchase, and include typical adjustments for the different annual mileage in that period. Different rates are used for mileages differing from 10,000 miles per annum.

AA breakdown cover For AA "Roadside" annual vehicle based cover.

Fuel cost Based on the average UK price, but can be adjusted for price changes using the factors given. The fuel consumption figures taken are typical for each of the car bands listed.

Tyres Based on using six tyres in a four-year period. Actual tyre life will vary with individual driving style. The prices in each car category are based on prices from high street retailers for a well-known brand: they include valve, balance, and the disposal charge for the old tyre. The prices at main dealers will be higher.

Service and labour costs Average cost for each car cost group for normal servicing and parts replacement at a dealer, taking average UK labour rates. Actual labour rates vary between different parts of the country and different brands.

Replacement parts The replacement parts included cover those likely to be needed under normal driving conditions, such as brake materials, oils, filters, bulbs, wipers, and hoses, plus the cost of one MOT.

Parking and tolls The allowance for parking and road tolls is based on a national average for an urban driver. You may pay more or less depending on patterns of use.

Editors' note:

1. The AA notes have been re-arranged by us, with the AA's permission, in the interests of space.
2. Figures for the taxation of car and fuel benefits are at Table L2.
3. The current Vehicle Tax bands are as follows:

Bands	**CO_2 Emission**	**Petrol or Diesel Car**	
		Standard rate	**First year rate**
	(g/km)	**£**	**£**
Band A	Up to 100	0	0
Band B	101–110	20.00	0
Band C	111–120	30.00	0
Band D	121–130	110.00	0
Band E	131–140	130.00	130.00
Band F	141–150	145.00	145.00
Band G	151–165	180.00	180.00
Band H	166–175	205.00	295.00
Band I	176–185	225.00	350.00
Band J	186–200	265.00	490.00
Band K	201–225	290.00	640.00
Band L	226–255	490.00	870.00
Band M	Over 255	505.00	1100.00

Band K includes cars with a CO2 figure over 225 g/km which were registered before 23 March 2006.

An alternative fuel car has a discount of £10 for all Bands.

The first year rate applies to new car purchases only. The duty reverts to the standard rate in subsequent years.

The CO_2 emission of a particular vehicle can be found at a website provided by the Vehicle Certification Agency (VCA): *www.carfueldata.direct.gov.* It is also on the V5 registration document.

Illustrative motorcycle running costs

RAC Motoring Services, in conjunction with Emmerson Hill Associates (Vehicle Management Consultants), have compiled the following illustrative motorcycle running costs. The figures represent a guide to the cost of running a privately-owned motorcycle for a period of three years with an annual mileage of 6,000 miles.

Engine size (cc)	**100cc**	**125cc**	**250**	**up to 400cc**	**600cc**	**750cc**	**1000cc**	**over 1000cc**
Assumed fuel consumption	80	68	56	48	45	43	37	33
Average cost new	1,950	2,150	2,950	4,250	4,500	4,950	5,950	7,500
Average value @ 3 years	950	1,250	1,850	2,150	2,650	3,100	3,500	4,450
Projected depreciation	1,000	900	1,100	2,100	1,850	1,850	2,450	3,050
Financing charges @ 6% APR	195	215	295	425	450	495	595	750
Fuel cost @ **£1.35/litre**	1,384	1,628	1,977	2,306	2,460	2,574	2,992	3,355
Insurance & repairs	650	825	975	1,050	1,325	1,325	1,550	1,550
Servicing & maintenance	250	295	525	550	600	725	795	825
Tyres & replacement parts	330	420	630	650	725	800	800	900
Excise licences 3 years	51	51	111	111	171	234	234	234
RAC Membership	150	150	150	150	150	150	150	150
Protective clothing/helmet	425	425	525	525	525	525	525	525
Total cost	4,435	4,909	6,288	7,867	8,256	8,678	10,091	11,339
Annual cost	1,478	1,636	2,096	2,622	2,752	2,893	3,364	3,780
Cost per mile in pence	**24.6**	**27.3**	**34.9**	**43.7**	**45.9**	**48.2**	**56.1**	**63.0**
Standing costs per mile	**13.7**	**14.3**	**17.5**	**24.2**	**24.9**	**25.4**	**30.6**	**34.8**
Running costs per mile	**10.9**	**13.0**	**17.4**	**19.5**	**21.0**	**22.8**	**25.5**	**28.2**
Adjustment for change in fuel price of 1p +/-	**0.06**	**0.07**	**0.08**	**0.09**	**0.10**	**0.10**	**0.12**	**0.14**

Note to the RAC motorcycle figures above:

The standing and running costs per mile and the adjustment for changes in fuel price have been calculated by the editors from the RAC figures.

Standing costs include Vehicle Tax, insurance and repairs, finance charges, depreciation, protective clothing and RAC membership.

Running costs include fuel, tyres and replacement parts, service and maintenance.

L2: Taxation of car and fuel benefits

Car benefit 2006/07 to 2014/15

CO_2 emissions (g/km)										Percentage of car's price taxed if car does not run solely on diesel (%)	Percentage of car's price taxed if car does run solely on diesel (%)
2006/07	2007/08	2008/09	2009/10	2010/11	2011/12	2012/13	2013/14	2014/15	2015/16		
N/A	N/A	N/A	N/A	1-75	1-75	1-75	1-75	1-75	0-50	5	8
N/A	N/A	N/A	N/A	N/A	N/A	N/A	N/A	N/A	51-75	9	12
N/A	N/A	0-120	0-120	76-120	76-120	76-99	76-94	N/A	N/A	10	13
N/A	N/A	N/A	N/A	N/A	N/A	100	95	76-94	N/A	11	14
N/A	N/A	N/A	N/A	N/A	N/A	105	100	95	N/A	12	15
N/A	N/A	N/A	N/A	N/A	N/A	110	105	100	76-94	13	16
N/A	N/A	N/A	N/A	N/A	N/A	115	110	105	95	14	17
0-144	0-144	121-139	121-139	121-134	121-129	120	115	110	100	15	18
145	145	140	140	135	130	125	120	115	105	16	19
150	150	145	145	140	135	130	125	120	110	17	20
155	155	150	150	145	140	135	130	125	115	18	21
160	160	155	155	150	145	140	135	130	120	19	22
165	165	160	160	155	150	145	140	135	125	20	23
170	170	165	165	160	155	150	145	140	130	21	24
175	175	170	170	165	160	155	150	145	135	22	25
180	180	175	175	170	165	160	155	150	140	23	26
185	185	180	180	175	170	165	160	155	145	24	27
190	190	185	185	180	175	170	165	160	150	25	28
195	195	190	190	185	180	175	170	165	155	26	29
200	200	195	195	190	185	180	175	170	160	27	30
205	205	200	200	195	190	185	180	175	165	28	31
210	210	205	205	200	195	190	185	180	170	29	32
215	215	210	210	205	200	195	190	185	175	30	33
220	220	215	215	210	205	200	195	190	180	31	34
225	225	220	220	215	210	205	200	195	185	32	35
230	230	225	225	220	215	210	205	200	190	33	35
235	235	230	230	225	220	215	210	205	195	34	35
240	240	235	235	230	225	220	215	210	200	35	35
N/A	N/A	N/A	N/A	N/A	N/A	N/A	N/A	N/A	205	36	37
N/A	N/A	N/A	N/A	N/A	N/A	N/A	N/A	N/A	210	37	37

Notes

1. From April 6, 2002, although the benefit of a company car is still to be calculated as a percentage of the price of the car (normally list price), the percentage is graduated according to carbon dioxide (CO_2) emissions and adjustments for business mileage and older cars no longer apply.
2. There are discounts for certain cleaner alternatively-propelled cars, which may reduce the minimum charge to that shown in the table.
3. The diesel supplement and the discounts for cleaner alternatives apply only to cars first registered on January 1, 1998 or later.
4. Cars without an approved CO_2 emissions figure are taxed according to engine size. This includes all cars registered before 1998 but only a tiny proportion of those registered 1998 and later.
5. Except where otherwise indicated, the exact CO_2 figure is rounded down to the nearest 5 grams per kilometre when using the above table.
6. From April 6, 2008 there was a new lower rate of 10 per cent (13 per cent for diesel) for cars with CO_2 emissions of 120 grams per kilometre or less.
7. From April 6, 2010 cars and vans with zero CO_2 emissions were exempt from company car tax for five tax years.
8. From April 6, 2010 an ultra low carbon cars band was introduced for five years.

Car fuel benefit — petrol and diesel — cash equivalent 2003/04 to 2015/16

Notes

1. From April 6, 2003, the car fuel benefit is, like the car benefit, linked directly to the CO_2 emissions of the company car.
2. There are the same diesel supplement and discounts for cleaner alternatively-propelled cars as there are in calculating the car benefit.
3. To calculate the car fuel benefit the percentage in the table used for calculating car benefit is multiplied against a set figure for the year:

2003/04 to 2007/08	£14,400
2008/09 to 2009/10	£16,900
2010/11	£18,000
2011/12	£18,800
2012/13	£20,200
2013/14	£21,100
2014/15	£21,700
2015/16	£22,100

   Thus, if the car benefit percentage for 2015/16 is 23%, the fuel benefit would be £22,100 × 23% = £5,083.
4. For cars registered before January 1, 1998 and cars with no approved CO_2 emissions figure, the percentage to be applied is the same as that used to calculate the car benefit.

Authorised Mileage Allowance Payments — tax-free rates in pence per mile 2002/03 to 2015/16

	Annual mileage	*Pence per mile*
Cars and vans	Up to 10,000	45p*
	10,001 +	25p
Motorcycles		24p
Bicycles		20p
Business Passengers		5p

* For 2002/03 to 2010/11 (inclusive) this rate was 40 pence per mile

L3: The Motability Scheme

Disabled people who need a motor vehicle may obtain one by utilising most if not all of the Higher Rate component of the Disability Living Allowance, the War Pensioner's Mobility Supplement or the Armed Forces Independence Payment. Motability is only available to those in receipt of any of these benefits who assign all or some of them to the scheme for the duration of the contract. Because of the very wide range of physical and mental disabilities of those in receipt of them the scheme does not require the person seeking to use it to be a driver: anyone in receipt of one of these allowances who is over three is entitled to use it. Under the Scheme there are three available options:

1. A new car can be obtained on a three-year hire lease contract.
2. A wheelchair accessible vehicle (WAV) can be obtained on a five-year lease hire contract.
3. A powered wheelchair or scooter may be taken on a three-year contract hire.

A national network of some 4,500 dealers provides a wide range of suitably adapted new and used cars. In the case of any option, the scheme requires a capital sum and a monthly payment which is provided for by the assignment of the relevant state benefit to the scheme. As well as the adapted vehicle, all maintenance is provided to include the cost of tyres, as is insurance for two named drivers who are over 25, annual road fund disc and roadside recovery. Fuel, oil and other incidentals are the responsibility of the driver. There is a 60,000-mile limit on use over the three years of the contract for Option 1 or 100,000 miles for a WAV, with an annual limit of 20,000 miles in the case of Option 2. Any mileage over that limit attracts a penalty of 5p per mile. At the end of the contract period the car reverts to the scheme. Hire purchase is no longer available under the scheme.

When costing, care must be taken to distinguish between the three elements of any claim:

(i) the capital cost of both purchase and adaptation which recur every three years;
(ii) the monthly running costs covered by the Motability Scheme; and
(iii) the running costs not covered by the scheme such as oil, petrol and car washes.

Not all cars are available and advice must be obtained as to whether what is available adequately meets the needs of the disabled person. When experts have recommended that a car be obtained under the scheme practitioners should ensure that they are clear which option is being recommended and ensure that they compare like for like.

The condition precedent for using the Motability Scheme is that the beneficiary is in receipt of a state benefit which falls within the Second Schedule of the Social Security (Recovery of Benefits) Act 1997. It is now clear, following *Eagle v Chambers (No.2)*[1], that s.17 of the Act precludes a court from insisting that the mobility component of the Disabled Living Allowance should be used by any recipient to mitigate her loss. Henceforth no defendant can insist that a claimant use the mobility allowance to participate in the Motability Scheme.

DLA, hitherto the gateway into Motability, is over the next 4 years being replaced by the Personal Independence Payment (PIP). When this is fully implemented only those receiving the enhanced rate of the mobility component of PIP will be eligible to use the Motability Scheme. During the transitional period those with the higher rate of the mobility component of DLA continue to be eligible. PIP is assessed in a less generous way than DLA and it is likely that as the shift occurs to PIP some will cease to be eligible for Motability.

Further reading and assistance in specific cases can be obtained at:
http://www.motabilitycarscheme.co.uk and Customer Services (0300) 456 4566.

[1] [2004] EWCA Civ 1033.

L4: The costs of buying and replacing cars

There are a number of commonly encountered calculations involving the cost of cars. This section contains tables and examples of calculations dealing with the following and should be read along with the table of Motoring costs in section L1:

1. New car prices.
2. Cost of future replacements.
3. Cost of more frequent replacement.
4. Cost of automatic cars.
5. Cost of additional mileage.
6. Cost of professional servicing.
7. Cost of Assessment.

We have classified cars as follows:

Mini:	Most cars of 1.1 litre or under, such as Toyota Aygo 1.0, Vauxhall Corsa 1.0
Super mini:	Similar cars between 1.1 and 1.4, Ford Fiesta 1.25, Suzuki Swift 1.2
Small:	Cars of the smaller Ford Focus, VW Golf type, mostly 1.3–1.6 litre
Medium:	The Ford Mondeo, VW Passat type, mostly cars from 1.6–1.9 litre
Executive:	The larger Passat, Volvo S60 type, mostly 2.0–2.8 litre
Prestige:	The BMW 330d, Jaguar 3.0, mostly up to 3.5 litre
Luxury:	The Jaguar XJ, Audi A8 4.2, mostly over 3.5 litre and expensive
Estate etc:	Self-explanatory

Notes:

1. The first table is intended to convey in broad terms the purchase costs of cars across a range of models. The material is taken from *Parker's Car Price Guide* and *What Car?* with the kind permission of the publishers.

   The *New Price* is the recommended retail price (including VAT) according to the latest manufacturer's price list: all prices stated are "on the road" and include delivery charges, 12 months' road fund licence, number plates and £25 registration tax. *Tax band* is the vehicle tax band.

2. Depreciation: Different cars, even produced by the same manufacturer, depreciate at different rates. As a model of car may change after a few years even if the same name is retained, losses over a long period cannot be calculated for individual models but only by reference to the general position.

3. Automatics: The comparison of manual and automatic cars is similarly a generalisation. The calculation for depreciation assumes that the new price of the automatic is higher than for the manual model. There is considerable variation, even among cars of similar type with similar new prices, in the rate at which the premium for the automatic version is eroded. With some cars the gap disappears very quickly: with some the premium for the automatic version is actually greater for used cars than for new ones.

4. Where the current new price of the manual and automatic versions is the same, which is often the case with expensive cars, the used automatic tends to retain its value *better* than the manual model. It may nevertheless have higher fuel consumption but whether it will be more expensive overall may depend on the mileage.

1. New Car Prices

	New Price (£)	Tax band
Mini Citroën C1 1.0i VT 68 Touch 3d	8,345	A
Toyota Aygo 1.0 3d	8,695	A
Vauxhall Corsa 1.0 Design S 3d	12,910	B
Super Mini Citroën DS3 1.2 82 Dsign 3d	12,865	B
Ford Fiesta 1.25 82 Style 3d	12,345	C
Suzuki Swift 1.2 SZ2 3d	8,999	B
Vauxhall Corsa 1.2 SE 3d	12,420	D
Volkswagen Polo 1.2 90SE 3d	13,730	B
Small Citroën C4 1.6v 90 VTR 5d	16,355	B
Ford Focus 1.6 Zetec 5d	19,545	F
Honda Civic 1.4 i VTEC 5d	15,975	D
Renault Megane 1.6 110 Expr 5d	16,750	G
Toyota Auris 1.6 Icon 5d	17,995	E
Vauxhall Astra 1.6i SRi 5d	19,580	F
Volkswagen Golf 1.6 105 S 5d	20,455	A
Medium BMW 316i ES 4d	24,255	E
Ford Mondeo 2.0 Style 5d	21,845	B
Toyota Avensis 1.8 Active 4d	17,700	G
Vauxhall Insignia 1.8SRi 5d	18,629	G
Volkswagen Passat TDI 2.0 S 4d	23,340	B
Volvo V40 2.0 D3 SE 5d	23,770	C
Executive BMW 320i SE 4d	27,270	F
Honda Accord 2.0i VTEC EX 4d	26,580	G
Toyota Avensis 2.2 D-4D Icon 4d	23,450	F
Volkswagen Passat 2.0 TDi 150 GT 4d	26,430	B
Volvo S60 2.0 D SE S/S 4d	28,645	A

	New Price (£)	Tax band
Prestige Audi Quattro A4 3.0 245 SE 4d	35,360	F
BMW 330d SE 5d	36,105	E
Jaguar XF 3.0 V6 Luxury 4d	46,615	G
Mercedes-Benz E250 SE 4d	36,820	D
Volvo S80 2.4 D5 SE Lux 4d	36,835	C
Luxury Audi Quattro A8 4.2 SE Exec 4d	72,790	J
BMW 550i Lux 5d	59,515	K
Jaguar XJ 3.0 V6 Prem Lux 4d	60,670	G
Mercedes-Benz S350 Bluetec SE 4d	66,910	F
Estate Citroën C5 1.6 HDi 115 VTR 5d	22,770	D
Ford Mondeo Estate 2.0 Zetec 5d	22,745	C
Honda Accord 2.0i VTEC ES 5d	24,680	G
Mercedes-Benz E250 CDI SE 5d	38,755	F
Volkswagen Passat 2.0 TDi 150 S 5d	24,870	B
4 x 4 Honda CR-V 2.0 i-VTEC S 5d	22,340	H
Nissan Pathfinder 2.5 dCi Tekna 5d	36,280	K
Toyota Landcruiser 3.0 D-4D LC3 5d	37,015	K
Volkswagen Touareg 3.0 SE TDi 5d	43,415	H
Volvo XC90 2.0 D5 Momentum 5d	45,750	F
People carriers Citroën C4 Grand Picasso HDi 150 Excl 5d	24,710	B
Ford Galaxy 2.0 Zetec 5d	26,645	E
Renault Grand Scenic 1.6 dCi 130 Dyn 5d	23,715	C
Toyota Verso 1.6 D-4D Icon 5d	21,995	C
Vauxhall Zafira 1.8 VVT 140 Design 5d	23,370	H

2. Cost of future replacements

Table 1 below has representative trade-in values of used *manual* cars expressed as a proportion of the *current* new price (calculated from material in *Parker's Car Price Guide*). Automatic cars may depreciate faster. Where the new price of an automatic car is *higher* than that of the corresponding manual car, there is a tendency for the automatic to depreciate by about 1 per cent more (altogether, not per year).

Table 1 Trade-in values of used manual cars

Age of car	Residual value	Loss of value	Equivalent annual depreciation
1	0.64	0.36	0.360
2	0.50	0.50	0.256
3	0.41	0.59	0.204
4	0.36	0.64	0.168
5	0.33	0.67	0.143
Adjustment for automatics	–0.01	+0.01	

The table can be used to calculate the future net costs of replacements where the replacements will be second hand as well as where they will be new.

Example 1: The claimant is 54 and needs a people carrier such as a Chrysler Grand Voyager 3.3 LE Auto 5d, automatic version. He will need to replace it every four years, the final replacement being when he is 70. He would not otherwise have had a car (or the car is additional to whatever vehicle would have been bought in any event).

Initial price of people carrier, say		£32,995.00
Proportion of price lost at each replacement (Table 1 above, + 0.01)	0.65	
Cost of each replacement	0.65 × 32,995 = 21,446.75	
Multiplier for 16 years (Table A5, 2.5%, four-yearly)	3.14	
Cost of future replacements	3.14 × 21,446.75 =	£67,342.80
Total		£100,337.80

Example 2: The same claimant currently runs a manual Volvo S80 2.4 SE and will replace it with the Chrysler people carrier. The additional cost is the future cost of the Chryslers *minus* the corresponding figure saved on Volvos. (If either both cars are manual or both automatic the calculation is simpler.)

Initial price of Volvo saved, say		£28,245.00
Proportion of price saved at each replacement (Table 1 above, manual)	0.64	
Cost of each replacement	0.64 × 28,245.00 = 18,076.80	
Multiplier for 16 years (Table A5, 2.5%, four-yearly)	3.14	
Cost of future replacements saved	3.14 × 18,076.80 =	£56,761.15
Total saved		£85,006.15
Net future cost of Chryslers instead of Volvos (100,337.80 – 85,006.15)	=	£15,331.65

3. Cost of more frequent replacement

Claimants are sometimes advised that because of their condition they need a more reliable car and should therefore replace it more often than they needed to do before the injury. Table 2, which is derived from Table 1, shows the additional annual cost, expressed as a proportion of the new price. Find the row corresponding to the new interval in years and the column corresponding to the old interval.

Note that the table expresses the multiplier as an *annual* cost, not the cost *on each exchange*. Thus in row 2, column 4, the figure 0.088 means that the additional expense of replacing a car every two years, instead of every four years, is 8.8 per cent of the price of the car per year for however long the claimant continues to drive.

Table 2 Multipliers for additional annual cost of replacing car more frequently

		Old interval in years				
		1	**2**	**3**	**4**	**5**
	1	0	0.104	0.156	0.192	0.217
New	**2**		0	0.052	0.088	0.113
interval	**3**			0	0.036	0.061
in	**4**				0	0.025
years	**5**					0

Example: The claimant is 40 and drives a car currently costing £11,995 new. She has just bought one. She can continue to drive a similar car, with modifications. She has been advised that because of her disability she should now change it every three years rather than every five as she has until now. She should stop driving at about 73, so the last change will be at about age 70.

Multiplier for additional annual cost from table above		
– new frequency three years, old frequency five years	0.061	
Multiplier for woman of 40 until age 70 (Table A1)	20.65	
Multiplier for additional cost of more frequent replacement	0.61 × 20.65	= 1.26
Current cost of car		£11,995.00
Additional cost of replacing car more frequently until age 70		£15,113.70

4. Cost of automatic cars

Claimants' injuries sometimes make it necessary for them to have an automatic car which they would not otherwise have needed. Generally this involves additional costs in three respects: the automatic car is more expensive to buy, is more expensive to run and tends to depreciate faster than the corresponding manual model (but see the notes in the introduction).

Table 3 Added cost of automatic cars

		Mini and Super Mini	Small	Medium and Executive	Prestige and Luxury	Estate, 4×4 and MPV
Added cost of new car in £		850	1,075	1,145	1,275	1,245
Petrol at 129.0p per litre	Added cost in pence per mile	3.42	1.73	1.42	0.41	–
	For every penny more/less, add/subtract	0.030	0.015	0.012	0.004	–

Greater depreciation

Where the new price of an automatic model of a car is *higher* than that of the corresponding manual car, there is a tendency for the automatic to depreciate by about 1 per cent more (altogether, not per year)—see Table 1 above. Thus:

New manual model	£11,000	three-year-old manual	11,000 × 0.41 = £4,510
New automatic	£12,000	three-year-old automatic	12,000 × 0.40 = £4,800

Example: The claimant is 48. He drives a manual car of medium type whose price new is about £16,000. He drives about 10,000 miles a year and changes his car every three years. Because of his injury he now needs an automatic. He is likely to stop driving in about 30 years.

Extra cost of automatic car:			
On first purchase (from Table 3, column 3 above):			£1,145.00
Cost at each replacement of automatic (Table 1, row 3):	17,145 × 0.60 =	10,287.00	
less cost at each replacement of manual	16,000 × 0.59 =	9,440.00	
Additional cost at each replacement		£ 847.00	
Crude multiplier for replacements (Table A5, 27 years, three-yearly)	6.33		
Multiplier for 27 years certain (Table A5, cont's loss)	19.71		
Multiplier for man of 48 until age 75 (Table A1)	18.42		
Multiplier discounted for mortality	(6.33 × 18.42/19.71) =	5.92	£5,014.24
Extra cost per mile, petrol at 135.7 p/litre = 1.42 + (6.7 × 0.012) = 1.50 pence			
Extra running cost 10,000 miles pa		£150.00	
Crude multiplier (table A5, 30 years, cont's loss)	21.19		
Multiplier discounted for mortality (21.19 × 18.42/19.71) =		19.80	£2,970.00
Total extra cost:			£9,129.24

5. Cost of additional mileage

The AA figures for *running* costs at Table L1 do not include depreciation. Mileage reduces the value of a car by a factor which varies with the type of car and its age on resale. Age on resale is not necessarily the length of time the claimant had the car. The categories A, B, C, etc. are derived from *Parker's Price Guide*.

The table may not be appropriate for mileages below 1,000 miles a year or above 30,000 miles a year.

Table 4 Adjustment for depreciation for extra mileage

Age on resale	Depreciation in pence per mile							
	A	B	C	D	E	F	G	H
1	3.00	4.00	5.00	6.00	7.00	8.50	10.50	13.50
2	2.50	3.50	4.50	5.50	6.50	7.50	9.00	11.00
3	2.00	3.00	3.50	4.50	5.00	6.00	7.50	10.00
4	1.20	2.00	2.50	3.50	4.00	5.00	6.00	8.00
5	1.00	1.50	2.00	2.50	3.00	4.00	5.00	7.00
6	0.70	1.20	1.50	2.00	2.50	3.00	4.00	6.00
7	0.50	0.90	1.00	1.50	2.00	2.50	3.50	5.00
8	0.40	0.60	0.90	1.00	1.50	2.00	2.50	4.00

Example: The claimant would have had a car anyway. His mileage is increased by 4,000 miles a year because of his injury. He buys a one-year-old car and changes it after four years costing about £14,500 in category C in the mileage adjustment table. Petrol costs 135.7 pence per litre.

Running cost per mile from AA figures (Table L1)	21.14 pence
Adjustment for petrol price (from Table L1) (6.7p × 0.10)	0.67
Adjustment for mileage (category C, Four years old)	2.50
Total per mile	24.31 pence
Total annual cost (4,000 × 24.31)	£ 972.40

6. Cost of professional servicing

Some claimants will have carried out the routine servicing of their cars themselves, but their injury may make that impracticable and they will in future need to have the car serviced professionally.

The resulting increased cost consists essentially in the labour element in the cost of servicing. Costs such as the cost of the Ministry of Transport test itself will remain the same and will not form an element of the loss. There will be *some* increase in the cost of materials such as replacement parts and oil, as these may be less expensive online or at a supermarket rather than at a garage. On the other hand, particularly with newer models, the more complex servicing tasks may not be feasible without specialised equipment, and so even mechanically minded car owners may be unable to do these jobs themselves. This section therefore takes the loss as equivalent to the cost of labour and treats these other factors as neutral overall.

Labour costs vary between main dealers and independent garages, and between different parts of the country. They are generally cheaper in the north and away from London, but do not conform to any clear pattern. In a 2011 survey Gwynedd was one of the most expensive areas, but Clwyd, not far away, was one of the cheapest. Also, as will be seen from the figures in Table L1: Motoring Costs, the most expensive cars involve higher labour costs but the cheapest cars to buy are not the cheapest to service. For those reasons it is not straightforward to try to produce figures independently on the basis of time estimates and hourly labour charges, and the editors recommend using the following figures derived from Table L1.

Table 5 Additional cost of professional servicing

	Additional cost in pence per mile				
Cost of car new	**Up to £13,000**	**£13–18,000**	**£18–25,000**	**£25–32,000**	**over £32,000**
Petrol cars	2.10	2.07	2.09	2.04	2.34
Cost of car new	**Up to £16,000**	**£16–22,000**	**£22–26,000**	**£26–36,000**	**over £36,000**
Diesel cars	2.10	2.14	2.29	2.24	2.76

Example: The same claimant as in section 5 used to do his own servicing and because of his injury is now unable to do so. His car cost £14,500 new. Before the accident he drove 12,000 miles a year, but because of the accident he must now drive a further 4,000 miles, making 16,000 miles in all. He incurs the additional cost of professional servicing, as well as the additional cost of extra mileage.

Extra cost of professional servicing per mile		2.07 pence
Annual cost (for *12,000* miles)	12,000 × 2.07 pence	£ 241.40
Cost of additional 4,000 mileage (from section 5 example)		£ 972.40
Total annual cost		£1,213.80

Note that the figure for running costs used to calculate the cost of additional mileage already includes service labour costs. The extra cost of servicing must therefore be based on the pre-accident 12,000 miles: there will be double counting if it is calculated on the basis of the post-accident 16,000 miles.

7. Cost of assessment

At the Banstead Mobility Centre in Surrey, the Queen Elizabeth Foundation for Disabled People conducts a variety of driving assessments, such as car adaptation assessments, for people with disabilities, and will provide a report. (See section M7 for address etc.) The centre also provides advice and training but does not provide costings or carry out adaptations itself.

The cost of an assessment for litigation purposes is £1,200 (including VAT).

There is a lower, subsidised, rate for individuals not requiring the report for litigation, but the Centre will then deal only with the client personally, and not with others such as solicitors or case managers.

Sections 2–5 are based on figures in *Parker's Car Price Guide* and from the websites of the *Vehicle Certification Agency* and the *United States Department of Transportation.*

L5: Time, speed and distance

Table of speeds and distances

Speeds				Distances in yards																			
mph	**km/h**	**yd/sec**	**m/sec**	**5**	**10**	**15**	**20**	**25**	**30**	**40**	**50**	**60**	**75**	**100**	**125**	**150**	**175**	**200**	**225**	**250**	**300**	**400**	**500**
5	8.0	2.44	2.24	2.0	4.1	6.1	8.2	10.2	12.3	16.4	20.5	24.5	30.7	40.9	51.1	61.4	71.6	81.8	92.0	102.3	122.7	163.6	204.5
10	16.1	4.89	4.47	1.0	2.0	3.1	4.1	5.1	6.1	8.2	10.2	12.3	15.3	20.5	25.6	30.7	35.8	40.9	46.0	51.1	61.4	81.8	102.3
15	24.1	7.33	6.71	0.7	1.4	2.0	2.7	3.4	4.1	5.5	6.8	8.2	10.2	13.6	17.0	20.5	23.9	27.3	30.7	34.1	40.9	54.5	68.2
20	32.2	9.78	8.94	0.5	1.0	1.5	2.0	2.6	3.1	4.1	5.1	6.1	7.7	10.2	12.8	15.3	17.9	20.5	23.0	25.6	30.7	40.9	51.1
25	40.2	12.22	11.18	0.4	0.8	1.2	1.6	2.0	2.5	3.3	4.1	4.9	6.1	8.2	10.2	12.3	14.3	16.4	18.4	20.5	24.5	32.7	40.9
30	48.3	14.67	13.41	0.3	0.7	1.0	1.4	1.7	2.0	2.7	3.4	4.1	5.1	6.8	8.5	10.2	11.9	13.6	15.3	17.0	20.5	27.3	34.1
35	56.3	17.11	15.65	0.3	0.6	0.9	1.2	1.5	1.8	2.3	2.9	3.5	4.4	5.8	7.3	8.8	10.2	11.7	13.1	14.6	17.5	23.4	29.2
40	64.4	19.56	17.88	0.3	0.5	0.8	1.0	1.3	1.5	2.0	2.6	3.1	3.8	5.1	6.4	7.7	8.9	10.2	11.5	12.8	15.3	20.5	25.6
45	72.4	22.00	20.12	0.2	0.5	0.7	0.9	1.1	1.4	1.8	2.3	2.7	3.4	4.5	5.7	6.8	8.0	9.1	10.2	11.4	13.6	18.2	22.7
50	80.5	24.44	22.35	0.2	0.4	0.6	0.8	1.0	1.2	1.6	2.0	2.5	3.1	4.1	5.1	6.1	7.2	8.2	9.2	10.2	12.3	16.4	20.5
60	96.6	29.33	26.82	0.2	0.3	0.5	0.7	0.9	1.0	1.4	1.7	2.0	2.6	3.4	4.3	5.1	6.0	6.8	7.7	8.5	10.2	13.6	17.0
70	112.7	34.22	31.29	0.1	0.3	0.4	0.6	0.7	0.9	1.2	1.5	1.8	2.2	2.9	3.7	4.4	5.1	5.8	6.6	7.3	8.8	11.7	14.6
80	128.7	39.11	35.76	0.1	0.3	0.4	0.5	0.6	0.8	1.0	1.3	1.5	1.9	2.6	3.2	3.8	4.5	5.1	5.8	6.4	7.7	10.2	12.8
90	144.8	44.00	40.23	0.1	0.2	0.3	0.5	0.6	0.7	0.9	1.1	1.4	1.7	2.3	2.8	3.4	4.0	4.5	5.1	5.7	6.8	9.1	11.4
100	160.9	48.89	44.70	0.1	0.2	0.3	0.4	0.5	0.6	0.8	1.0	1.2	1.5	2.0	2.6	3.1	3.6	4.1	4.6	5.1	6.1	8.2	10.2

Seconds

Notes:

1. The table shows the time taken to cover a given distance at a given speed, to the nearest $\frac{1}{10}$ second.

2. The table can also be used to ascertain the approximate speed of a vehicle, if the time and distance are known.

3. As an example, to find how long it would take to cover 125 yards at 35 mph, follow the vertical column down from the figure 125 and follow the horizontal row across from the figure 35: they meet at the figure 7.3, which is the number of seconds taken to cover the distance.

4. A speed of z miles per hour approximately equals [0.5z] yards per second.

5. The general formula for the number of seconds to cover a given distance at a given speed is approximately:

$$\frac{\text{distance in yards} \times 2.04545}{\text{speed in miles per hour}}$$

Typical Stopping Distances (average car length = 4 metres)

Speed (mph)	**Thinking Distance** (metres)	**Braking Distance** (metres)	**Total Stopping Distance** (metres)	(car lengths)
20	6	6	12	3
30	9	14	23	6
40	12	24	36	9
50	15	38	53	13
60	18	55	73	18
70	21	75	96	24

Extracted from The Highway Code, published by the Stationery Office.

Group M

Other Information

M

M1: Senior Court Costs Office Guideline Rates for Summary Assessment

Band One	A	B	C	D
2011–present	217	192	161	118
2010	217	192	161	118
2009	213	189	158	116
2008	203	180	151	110
2007	195	173	145	106
2005	184	163	137	100

Aldershot, Farnham, Bournemouth (including Poole), Birmingham Inner, Bristol, Cambridge City, Harlow, Canterbury, Maidstone, Medway and Tunbridge Wells, Cardiff (Inner), Chelmsford South, Essex and East Suffolk, Chester, Fareham, Winchester, Hampshire, Dorset, Wiltshire, Isle of Wight, Kingston, Guildford, Reigate, Epsom, Leeds Inner (within two-kilometres radius of the City Art Gallery), Lewes, Liverpool, Birkenhead, Manchester Central, Newcastle—City Centre (within a two-mile radius of St Nicholas Cathedral), Norwich City, Nottingham City, Oxford, Thames Valley, Southampton, Portsmouth, Swindon, Basingstoke, Watford.

Band Two	A	B	C	D
2011–present	201	177	146	111
2010	201	177	146	111
2009	198	174	144	109
2008	191	168	139	105
2007	183	161	133	101
2005	173	152	126	95

Bath, Cheltenham and Gloucester, Taunton, Yeovil, Bury, Chelmsford North, Cambridge County, Peterborough, Bury St E, Norfolk, Lowestoft, Cheshire and North Wales, Coventry, Rugby, Nuneaton, Stratford and Warwick, Exeter, Plymouth, Hull (City), Leeds Outer, Wakefield and Pontefract, Leigh, Lincoln, Luton, Bedford, St Albans, Hitchin, Hertford, Manchester Outer, Oldham, Bolton, Tameside, Newcastle (other than City Centre), Nottingham and Derbyshire, Sheffield, Doncaster and South Yorkshire, Southport, St Helens, Stockport, Altrincham, Salford, Swansea, Newport, Cardiff (Outer), Wigan, Wolverhampton, Walsall, Dudley and Stourbridge, York, Harrogate.

Band Three	A	B	C	D
2011–present	201	177	146	111
2010	201	177	146	111
2009	198	174	144	109
2008	174	156	133	99
2007	167	150	128	95
2005	158	142	121	90

Birmingham Outer, Bradford (Dewsbury, Halifax, Huddersfield, Keighley and Skipton), Cumbria, Devon, Cornwall, Grimsby, Skegness, Hull Outer, Kidderminster, Northampton and Leicester, Preston, Lancaster, Blackpool, Chorley, Accrington, Burnley, Blackburn, Rawenstall and Nelson, Scarborough and Ripon, Stafford, Stoke, Tamworth, Teesside, Worcester, Hereford, Evesham and Redditch, Shrewsbury, Telford, Ludlow, Oswestry, South and West Wales.

London City [EC1–4]	A	B	C	D
2011–present	409	296	226	138
2010	409	296	226	138
2009	402	291	222	136
2008	396	285	219	134
2007	380	274	210	129
2005	359	259	198	122

London Central [W1, WC1, WC2, SW1]	A	B	C	D
2011–present	317	242	196	126
2010	317	242	196	126
2009	312	238	193	124
2008	304	231	189	121
2007	292	222	181	116
2005	276	210	171	110
London Outer [N, E, SE, W, SW, NW, Bromley, Croydon, Dartford, Gravesend and Uxbridge]	**A**	**B**	**C**	**D**
2011–present	229–267	172–229	165	121
2010	229–267	172–229	165	121
2009	263–225	225–169	162	119
2008	256–219	219–165	158	116
2007	246–210	210–158	152	111
2005	232–198	198–149	144	105

A – Solicitors with over eight years' post-qualification experience including at least eight years' litigation experience.
B – Solicitors and legal executives with over four years' post-qualification experience including at least four years' litigation experience.
C – Other solicitors and legal executives and fee earners of equivalent experience.
D – Trainee Solicitors, para legals and fee earners of equivalent experience.
Note: "Legal Executive" means a Fellow of the Institute of Legal Executives.

Entitlement to VAT on Costs

DATE	VAT RATE
April 1, 1991–November 30, 2008	**17.5%**
December 1, 2008–December 31, 2009	**15%**
January 1, 2010–January 3, 2011	**17.5%**
January 4, 2011 to date	**20%**

Costs PD 44 para.2.3 deals with entitlement to VAT on Costs. It provides:

"VAT should not be included in a claim for costs if the receiving party is able to recover the VAT as input tax. Where the receiving party is able to obtain credit from HM Revenue and Customs for a proportion of the VAT as input tax, only that proportion which is not eligible for credit should be included in the claim for costs."

Costs PD 44 para.2.7 deals with the form of a Bill of Costs where the VAT Rate changes. It provides:

"Where there is a change in the rate of VAT, suppliers of goods and services are entitled by ss.88 (1) and 88(2) of the VAT Act 1994 in most circumstances to elect whether the new or the old rate of VAT

should apply to a supply where the basic and actual tax points span a period during which there has been a change in VAT rates."

Costs PD 44 para.2.8 provides:

"It will be assumed, unless a contrary indication is given in writing, that an election to take advantage of the provisions mentioned in paragraph 2.7 and to charge VAT at the lower rate has been made. In any case in which an election to charge at the lower rate is not made, such a decision must be justified to the court assessing the costs."

Costs PD 44 para.2.9 deals with apportionment. It provides:

"Subject to 2.7 & 2.8 all bills of costs, fees and disbursements on which VAT is included must be divided into separate parts so as to show work done before, on and after the date or dates from which any change in the rate of VAT takes effect. Where, however, a lump sum charge is made for work which spans a period during which there has been a change in VAT rates, and paragraphs 2.7 and 2.8 above do not apply, reference should be made to paragraphs 30.7 or 30.8 of the VAT Guide (Notice 700) (or any revised edition of that notice) published by HMRC. If necessary, the lump sum should be apportioned. The totals of profit costs and disbursements in each part must be carried separately to the summary."

M2: Conversion formulae

	To convert	Multiply by
Area	square inches to square centimetres	6.452
	square centimetres to square inches	0.1555
	square metres to square feet	10.7638
	square feet to square metres	0.0929
	square yards to square metres	0.8361
	square metres to square yards	1.196
	square miles to square kilometres	2.590
	square kilometres to square miles	0.3861
	acres to hectares	0.4047
	hectares to acres	2.471
Length	inches to centimetres	2.540
	centimetres to inches	0.3937
	feet to metres	0.3048
	metres to feet	3.281
	yards to metres	0.9144
	metres to yards	1.094
	miles to kilometres	1.609
	kilometres to miles	0.6214
Temperature	Centigrade to Fahrenheit Fahrenheit to Centigrade	× 9 ÷ 5 + 32 –32 × 5 ÷ 9
Volume	cubic inches to cubic centimetres	16.39
	cubic centimetres to cubic inches	0.06102
	cubic feet to cubic metres	0.02832
	cubic metres to cubic feet	35.31
	cubic yards to cubic metres	0.7646
	cubic metres to cubic yards	1.308
	cubic inches to litres	0.01639
	litres to cubic inches	61.024

	To convert		Multiply by
	gallon to litres		4.545
	litres to gallons		0.22
Weight	grains to grams		0.0647
	grams to grains		15.43
	ounces to grams		28.35
	grams to ounces		0.03527
	pounds to grams		453.592
	grams to pounds		0.0022
	pounds to kilograms		0.4536
	kilograms to pounds		2.2046
	tons to kilograms		1016.05
	kilograms to tons		0.0009842
Speed	miles per hour to kilometres per hour		1.6093
	kilometres per hour to miles per hour		0.6214
Fuel cost	pence per litre to pounds per gallon		0.045
	pounds per gallon to pence per litre		22.00
USA measures	Dry	USA pint to UK pint	0.9689
		UK pint to USA pint	1.1032
		USA pint to litres	0.5506
		litres to USA pint	1.816
		USA bushel to UK bushel	0.9689
		UK bushel to USA bushel	1.032
		USA bushel to litres	35.238
		litres to USA bushel	0.0283
	Liquid	USA pint (16 fl oz) to UK pint	0.8327
		UK pint to USA pint	1.2
		USA pint to litres	0.4732
		litres to USA pint	2.113
		USA gallon to UK gallon	0.8327
		UK gallon to USA gallon	1.2
		USA gallon to litres	3.7853
		litres to USA gallons	0.2641

Clothing

Shirts

UK/USA	14	$14\frac{1}{2}$	15	$15\frac{1}{2}$	16	$16\frac{1}{2}$	17	$17\frac{1}{2}$
Europe	36	37	38	39	40	41	42	43

Ladies clothes

UK							
Size code	10	12	14	16	18	20	22
Bust/hip inches	32/34	34/36	36/38	38/40	40/42	42/44	44/46
Bust/hip cm	84/89	88/93	92/97	97/102	102/107	107/112	112/117
USA							
Size code	6	8	10	12	14	16	18
Bust/hip inches	$34\frac{1}{2}/36\frac{1}{2}$	$35\frac{1}{2}/37\frac{1}{2}$	$36\frac{1}{2}/38\frac{1}{2}$	$37\frac{1}{2}/39\frac{1}{2}$	38/40	$39\frac{1}{2}/41\frac{1}{2}$	41/43

European sizes vary from country to country

Footwear—Men

British	6	7	8	9	10	11	12
American	$6\frac{1}{2}$	$7\frac{1}{2}$	$8\frac{1}{2}$	$9\frac{1}{2}$	$10\frac{1}{2}$	$11\frac{1}{2}$	$12\frac{1}{2}$
Continental	40	41	42	43	44	45	46

Footwear—Women

British	3	4	5	6	7	8	9
American	$4\frac{1}{2}$	$5\frac{1}{2}$	$6\frac{1}{2}$	$7\frac{1}{2}$	$8\frac{1}{2}$	$9\frac{1}{2}$	$10\frac{1}{2}$
Continental	36	37	38	39	40	42	43

Children's clothes

UK												
Age	1	2	3	4	5	6	7	8	9	10	11	12
Height/inches	32	36	38	40	43	45	48	50	53	55	58	60
Height/cm	80	92	98	104	110	116	122	128	134	140	146	152
USA												
Boys' size code	1	2	3	4	5	6	8		10		12	
Girls' size code	2	3	4	5	6	6x	7	8	10		12	
Europe												
Height/cm	80	92	98	104	110	116	122	128	134	140	146	152

M3: Perpetual calendar

The number opposite each of the years in the list below indicates which of the calendars on the following pages is the one for that year. Thus the number opposite 2000 is 14, so calendar 14 can be used as a 2000 calendar.

Leap years

Years divisible by four without remainder are leap years with 366 days instead of 365 (29 days in February instead of 28). However, the first year of the century is not a leap year except when divisible by 400.

Year	Calendar	Year	Calendar	Year	Calendar	Year	Calendar	Year	Calendar	Year	Calendar
1980	10	1992	11	2004	12	2016	13	2028	14	2040	8
1981	5	1993	6	2005	7	2017	1	2029	2	2041	3
1982	6	1994	7	2006	1	2018	2	2030	3	2042	4
1983	7	1995	1	2007	2	2019	3	2031	4	2043	5
1984	8	1996	9	2008	10	2020	11	2032	12	2044	13
1985	3	1997	4	2009	5	2021	6	2033	7	2045	1
1986	4	1998	5	2010	6	2022	7	2034	1	2046	2
1987	5	1999	6	2011	7	2023	1	2035	2	2047	3
1988	13	2000	14	2012	8	2024	9	2036	10	2048	11
1989	1	2001	2	2013	3	2025	4	2037	5	2049	6
1990	2	2002	3	2014	4	2026	5	2038	6	2050	7
1991	3	2003	4	2015	5	2027	6	2039	7	2051	1

1

	January	February	March	April
M	2 9 16 23 30	6 13 20 27	6 13 20 27	3 10 17 24
T	3 10 17 24 31	7 14 21 28	7 14 21 28	4 11 18 25
W	4 11 18 25	1 8 15 22	1 8 15 22 29	5 12 19 26
T	5 12 19 26	2 9 16 23	2 9 16 23 30	6 13 20 27
F	6 13 20 27	3 10 17 24	3 10 17 24 31	7 14 21 28
S	7 14 21 28	4 11 18 25	4 11 18 25	1 8 15 22 29
S	1 8 15 22 29	5 12 19 26	5 12 19 26	2 9 16 23 30

	May	June	July	August
M	1 8 15 22 29	5 12 19 26	3 10 17 24 31	7 14 21 28
T	2 9 16 23 30	6 13 20 27	4 11 18 25	1 8 15 22 29
W	3 10 17 24 31	7 14 21 28	5 12 19 26	2 9 16 23 30
T	4 11 18 25	1 8 15 22 29	6 13 20 27	3 10 17 24 31
F	5 12 19 26	2 9 16 23 30	7 14 21 28	4 11 18 25
S	6 13 20 27	3 10 17 24	1 8 15 22 29	5 12 19 26
S	7 14 21 28	4 11 18 25	2 9 16 23 30	6 13 20 27

	September	October	November	December
M	4 11 18 25	2 9 16 23 30	6 13 20 27	4 11 18 25
T	5 12 19 26	3 10 17 24 31	7 14 21 28	5 12 19 26
W	6 13 20 27	4 11 18 25	1 8 15 22 29	6 13 20 27
T	7 14 21 28	5 12 19 26	2 9 16 23 30	7 14 21 28
F	1 8 15 22 29	6 13 20 27	3 10 17 24	1 8 15 22 29
S	2 9 16 23 30	7 14 21 28	4 11 18 25	2 9 16 23 30
S	3 10 17 24	1 8 15 22 29	5 12 19 26	3 10 17 24 31

2

	January	February	March	April
M	1 8 15 22 29	5 12 19 26	5 12 19 26	2 9 16 23 30
T	2 9 16 23 30	6 13 20 27	6 13 20 27	3 10 17 24
W	3 10 17 24 31	7 14 21 28	7 14 21 28	4 11 18 25
T	4 11 18 25	1 8 15 22	1 8 15 22 29	5 12 19 26
F	5 12 19 26	2 9 16 23	2 9 16 23 30	6 13 20 27
S	6 13 20 27	3 10 17 24	3 10 17 24 31	7 14 21 28
S	7 14 21 28	4 11 18 25	4 11 18 25	1 8 15 22 29

	May	June	July	August
M	7 14 21 28	4 11 18 25	2 9 16 23 30	6 13 20 27
T	1 8 15 22 29	5 12 19 26	3 10 17 24 31	7 14 21 28
W	2 9 16 23 30	6 13 20 27	4 11 18 25	1 8 15 22 29
T	3 10 17 24 31	7 14 21 28	5 12 19 26	2 9 16 23 30
F	4 11 18 25	1 8 15 22 29	6 13 20 27	3 10 17 24 31
S	5 12 19 26	2 9 16 23 30	7 14 21 28	4 11 18 25
S	6 13 20 27	3 10 17 24	1 8 15 22 29	5 12 19 26

	September	October	November	December
M	3 10 17 24	1 8 15 22 29	5 12 19 26	3 10 17 24 31
T	4 11 18 25	2 9 16 23 30	6 13 20 27	4 11 18 25
W	5 12 19 26	3 10 17 24 31	7 14 21 28	5 12 19 26
T	6 13 20 27	4 11 18 25	1 8 15 22 29	6 13 20 27
F	7 14 21 28	5 12 19 26	2 9 16 23 30	7 14 21 28
S	1 8 15 22 29	6 13 20 27	3 10 17 24	1 8 15 22 29
S	2 9 16 23 30	7 14 21 28	4 11 18 25	2 9 16 23 30

3

	January	February	March	April
M	7 14 21 28	4 11 18 25	4 11 18 25	1 8 15 22 29
T	1 8 15 22 29	5 12 19 26	5 12 19 26	2 9 16 23 30
W	2 9 16 23 30	6 13 20 27	6 13 20 27	3 10 17 24
T	3 10 17 24 31	7 14 21 28	7 14 21 28	4 11 18 25
F	4 11 18 25	1 8 15 22	1 8 15 22 29	5 12 19 26
S	5 12 19 26	2 9 16 23	2 9 16 23 30	6 13 20 27
S	6 13 20 27	3 10 17 24	3 10 17 24 31	7 14 21 28

	May	June	July	August
M	6 13 20 27	3 10 17 24	1 8 15 22 29	5 12 19 26
T	7 14 21 28	4 11 18 25	2 9 16 23 30	7 14 21 28
W	1 8 15 22 29	5 12 19 26	3 10 17 24 31	6 13 20 27
T	2 9 16 23 30	6 13 20 27	4 11 18 25	1 8 15 22 29
F	3 10 17 24 31	7 14 21 28	5 12 19 26	2 9 16 23 30
S	4 11 18 25	1 8 15 22 29	6 13 20 27	3 10 17 24 31
S	5 12 19 26	2 9 16 23 30	7 14 21 28	4 11 18 25

	September	October	November	December
M	2 9 16 23 30	7 14 21 28	4 11 18 25	2 9 16 23 30
T	3 10 17 24	1 8 15 22 29	5 12 19 26	3 10 17 24 31
W	4 11 18 25	2 9 16 23 30	6 13 20 27	4 11 18 25
T	5 12 19 26	3 10 17 24 31	7 14 21 28	5 12 19 26
F	6 13 20 27	4 11 18 25	1 8 15 22 29	6 13 20 27
S	7 14 21 28	5 12 19 26	2 9 16 23 30	7 14 21 28
S	1 8 15 22 29	6 13 20 27	3 10 17 24	1 8 15 22 29

4

	January	February	March	April
M	6 13 20 27	3 10 17 24	3 10 17 24 31	7 14 21 28
T	7 14 21 28	4 11 18 25	4 11 18 25	1 8 15 22 29
W	1 8 15 22 29	5 12 19 26	5 12 19 26	2 9 16 23 30
T	2 9 16 23 30	6 13 20 27	6 13 20 27	3 10 17 24
F	3 10 17 24 31	7 14 21 28	7 14 21 28	4 11 18 25
S	4 11 18 25	1 8 15 22	1 8 15 22 29	5 12 19 26
S	5 12 19 26	2 9 16 23	2 9 16 23 30	6 13 20 27

	May	June	July	August
M	5 12 19 26	2 9 16 23 30	7 14 21 28	4 11 18 25
T	6 13 20 27	3 10 17 24	1 8 15 22 29	5 12 19 26
W	7 14 21 28	4 11 18 25	2 9 16 23 30	6 13 20 27
T	1 8 15 22 29	5 12 19 26	3 10 17 24 31	7 14 21 28
F	2 9 16 23 30	6 13 20 27	4 11 18 25	1 8 15 22 29
S	3 10 17 24 31	7 14 21 28	5 12 19 26	2 9 16 23 30
S	4 11 18 25	1 8 15 22 29	6 13 20 27	3 10 17 24 31

	September	October	November	December
M	1 8 15 22 29	6 13 20 27	3 10 17 24	1 8 15 22 29
T	2 9 16 23 30	7 14 21 28	4 11 18 25	2 9 16 23 30
W	3 10 17 24	1 8 15 22 29	5 12 19 26	3 10 17 24 31
T	4 11 18 25	2 9 16 23 30	6 13 20 27	4 11 18 25
F	5 12 19 26	3 10 17 24 31	7 14 21 28	5 12 19 26
S	6 13 20 27	4 11 18 25	1 8 15 22 29	6 13 20 27
S	7 14 21 28	5 12 19 26	2 9 16 23 30	7 14 21 28

5

	January	February	March	April
M	5 12 19 26	2 9 16 23	2 9 16 23 30	6 13 20 27
T	6 13 20 27	3 10 17 24	3 10 17 24 31	7 14 21 28
W	7 14 21 28	4 11 18 25	4 11 18 25	1 8 15 22 29
T	1 8 15 22 29	5 12 19 26	5 12 19 26	2 9 16 23 30
F	2 9 16 23 30	6 13 20 27	6 13 20 27	3 10 17 24
S	3 10 17 24 31	7 14 21 28	7 14 21 28	4 11 18 25
S	4 11 18 25	1 8 15 22	1 8 15 22 29	5 12 19 26

	May	June	July	August
M	4 11 18 25	1 8 15 22 29	6 13 20 27	3 10 17 24 31
T	5 12 19 26	2 9 16 23 30	7 14 21 28	4 11 18 25
W	6 13 20 27	3 10 17 24	1 8 15 22 29	5 12 19 26
T	7 14 21 28	4 11 18 25	2 9 16 23 30	6 13 20 27
F	1 8 15 22 29	5 12 19 26	3 10 17 24 31	7 14 21 28
S	2 9 16 23 30	6 13 20 27	4 11 18 25	1 8 15 22 29
S	3 10 17 24 31	7 14 21 28	5 12 19 26	2 9 16 23 30

	September	October	November	December
M	7 14 21 28	5 12 19 26	2 9 16 23 30	7 14 21 28
T	1 8 15 22 29	6 13 20 27	3 10 17 24	1 8 15 22 29
W	2 9 16 23 30	7 14 21 28	4 11 18 25	2 9 16 23 30
T	3 10 17 24	1 8 15 22 29	5 12 19 26	3 10 17 24 31
F	4 11 18 25	2 9 16 23 30	6 13 20 27	4 11 18 25
S	5 12 19 26	3 10 17 24 31	7 14 21 28	5 12 19 26
S	6 13 20 27	4 11 18 25	1 8 15 22 29	6 13 20 27

6

	January	February	March	April
M	4 11 18 25	1 8 15 22	1 8 15 22 29	5 12 19 26
T	5 12 19 26	2 9 16 23	2 9 16 23 30	6 13 20 27
W	6 13 20 27	3 10 17 24	3 10 17 24 31	7 14 21 28
T	7 14 21 28	4 11 18 25	4 11 18 25	1 8 15 22 29
F	1 8 15 22 29	5 12 19 26	5 12 19 26	2 9 16 23 30
S	2 9 16 23 30	6 13 20 27	6 13 20 27	3 10 17 24
S	3 10 17 24 31	7 14 21 28	7 14 21 28	4 11 18 25

	May	June	July	August
M	3 10 17 24 31	7 14 21 28	5 12 19 26	2 9 16 23 30
T	4 11 18 25	1 8 15 22 29	6 13 20 27	3 10 17 24 31
W	5 12 19 26	2 9 16 23 30	7 14 21 28	4 11 18 25
T	6 13 20 27	3 10 17 24	1 8 15 22 29	5 12 19 26
F	7 14 21 28	4 11 18 25	2 9 16 23 30	6 13 20 27
S	1 8 15 22 29	5 12 19 26	3 10 17 24 31	7 14 21 28
S	2 9 16 23 30	6 13 20 27	4 11 18 25	1 8 15 22 29

	September	October	November	December
M	6 13 20 27	4 11 18 25	1 8 15 22 29	6 13 20 27
T	7 14 21 28	5 12 19 26	2 9 16 23 30	7 14 21 28
W	1 8 15 22 29	6 13 20 27	3 10 17 24	1 8 15 22 29
T	2 9 16 23 30	7 14 21 28	4 11 18 25	2 9 16 23 30
F	3 10 17 24	1 8 15 22 29	5 12 19 26	3 10 17 24 31
S	4 11 18 25	2 9 16 23 30	6 13 20 27	4 11 18 25
S	5 12 19 26	3 10 17 24 31	7 14 21 28	5 12 19 26

7

	January	February	March	April
M	3 10 17 24 31	7 14 21 28	7 14 21 28	4 11 18 25
T	4 11 18 25	1 8 15 22	1 8 15 22 29	5 12 19 26
W	5 12 19 26	2 9 16 23	2 9 16 23 30	6 13 20 27
T	6 13 20 27	3 10 17 24	3 10 17 24 31	7 14 21 28
F	7 14 21 28	4 11 18 25	4 11 18 25	1 8 15 22 29
S	1 8 15 22 29	5 12 19 26	5 12 19 26	2 9 16 23 30
S	2 9 16 23 30	6 13 20 27	6 13 20 27	3 10 17 24

	May	June	July	August
M	2 9 16 23 30	6 13 20 27	4 11 18 25	1 8 15 22 29
T	3 10 17 24 31	7 14 21 28	5 12 19 26	2 9 16 23 30
W	4 11 18 25	1 8 15 22 29	6 13 20 27	3 10 17 24 31
T	5 12 19 26	2 9 16 23 30	7 14 21 28	4 11 18 25
F	6 13 20 27	3 10 17 24	1 8 15 22 29	5 12 19 26
S	7 14 21 28	4 11 18 25	2 9 16 23 30	6 13 20 27
S	1 8 15 22 29	5 12 19 26	3 10 17 24 31	7 14 21 28

	September	October	November	December
M	5 12 19 26	3 10 17 24 31	7 14 21 28	5 12 19 26
T	6 13 20 27	4 11 18 25	1 8 15 22 29	6 13 20 27
W	7 14 21 28	5 12 19 26	2 9 16 23 30	7 14 21 28
T	1 8 15 22 29	6 13 20 27	3 10 17 24	1 8 15 22 29
F	2 9 16 23 30	7 14 21 28	4 11 18 25	2 9 16 23 30
S	3 10 17 24	1 8 15 22 29	5 12 19 26	3 10 17 24 31
S	4 11 18 25	2 9 16 23 30	6 13 20 27	4 11 18 25

8

	January	February	March	April
M	2 9 16 23 30	6 13 20 27	5 12 19 26	2 9 16 23 30
T	3 10 17 24 31	7 14 21 28	6 13 20 27	3 10 17 24
W	4 11 18 25	1 8 15 22 29	7 14 21 28	4 11 18 25
T	5 12 19 26	2 9 16 23	1 8 15 22 29	5 12 19 26
F	6 13 20 27	3 10 17 24	2 9 16 23 30	6 13 20 27
S	7 14 21 28	4 11 18 25	3 10 17 24 31	7 14 21 28
S	1 8 15 22 29	5 12 19 26	4 11 18 25	1 8 15 22 29

	May	June	July	August
M	7 14 21 28	4 11 18 25	2 9 16 23 30	6 13 20 27
T	1 8 15 22 29	5 12 19 26	3 10 17 24 31	7 14 21 28
W	2 9 16 23 30	6 13 20 27	4 11 18 25	1 8 15 22 29
T	3 10 17 24 31	7 14 21 28	5 12 19 26	2 9 16 23 30
F	4 11 18 25	1 8 15 22 29	6 13 20 27	3 10 17 24 31
S	5 12 19 26	2 9 16 23 30	7 14 21 28	4 11 18 25
S	6 13 20 27	3 10 17 24	1 8 15 22 29	5 12 19 26

	September	October	November	December
M	3 10 17 24	1 8 15 22 29	5 12 19 26	3 10 17 24 31
T	4 11 18 25	2 9 16 23 30	6 13 20 27	4 11 18 25
W	5 12 19 26	3 10 17 24 31	7 14 21 28	5 12 19 26
T	6 13 20 27	4 11 18 25	1 8 15 22 29	6 13 20 27
F	7 14 21 28	5 12 19 26	2 9 16 23 30	7 14 21 28
S	1 8 15 22 29	6 13 20 27	3 10 17 24	1 8 15 22 29
S	2 9 16 23 30	7 14 21 28	4 11 18 25	2 9 16 23 30

9

	January	February	March	April
M	1 8 15 22 29	5 12 19 26	4 11 18 25	1 8 15 22 29
T	2 9 16 23 30	6 13 20 27	5 12 19 26	2 9 16 23 30
W	3 10 17 24 31	7 14 21 28	6 13 20 27	3 10 17 24
T	4 11 18 25	1 8 15 22 29	7 14 21 28	4 11 18 25
F	5 12 19 26	2 9 16 23	1 8 15 22 29	5 12 19 26
S	6 13 20 27	3 10 17 24	2 9 16 23 30	6 13 20 27
S	7 14 21 28	4 11 18 25	3 10 17 24 31	7 14 21 28

	May	June	July	August
M	6 13 20 27	3 10 17 24	1 8 15 22 29	5 12 19 26
T	7 14 21 28	4 11 18 25	2 9 16 23 30	6 13 20 27
W	1 8 15 22 29	5 12 19 26	3 10 17 24 31	7 14 21 28
T	2 9 16 23 30	6 13 20 27	4 11 18 25	1 8 15 22 29
F	3 10 17 24 31	7 14 21 28	5 12 19 26	2 9 16 23 30
S	4 11 18 25	1 8 15 22 29	6 13 20 27	3 10 17 24 31
S	5 12 19 26	2 9 16 23 30	7 14 21 28	4 11 18 25

	September	October	November	December
M	2 9 16 23 30	7 14 21 28	4 11 18 25	2 9 16 23 30
T	3 10 17 24	1 8 15 22 29	5 12 19 26	3 10 17 24 31
W	4 11 18 25	2 9 16 23 30	6 13 20 27	4 11 18 25
T	5 12 19 26	3 10 17 24 31	7 14 21 28	5 12 19 26
F	6 13 20 27	4 11 18 25	1 8 15 22 29	6 13 20 27
S	7 14 21 28	5 12 19 26	2 9 16 23 30	7 14 21 28
S	1 8 15 22 29	6 13 20 27	3 10 17 24	1 8 15 22 29

10

	January	February	March	April
M	7 14 21 28	4 11 18 25	3 10 17 24 31	7 14 21 28
T	1 8 15 22 29	5 12 19 26	4 11 18 25	1 8 15 22 29
W	2 9 16 23 30	6 13 20 27	5 12 19 26	2 9 16 23 30
T	3 10 17 24 31	7 14 21 28	6 13 20 27	3 10 17 24
F	4 11 18 25	1 8 15 22 29	7 14 21 28	4 11 18 25
S	5 12 19 26	2 9 16 23	1 8 15 22 29	5 12 19 26
S	6 13 20 27	3 10 17 24	2 9 16 23 30	6 13 20 27

	May	June	July	August
M	5 12 19 26	2 9 16 23 30	7 14 21 28	4 11 18 25
T	6 13 20 27	3 10 17 24	1 8 15 22 29	5 12 19 26
W	7 14 21 28	4 11 18 25	2 9 16 23 30	6 13 20 27
T	1 8 15 22 29	5 12 19 26	3 10 17 24 31	7 14 21 28
F	2 9 16 23 30	6 13 20 27	4 11 18 25	1 8 15 22 29
S	3 10 17 24 31	7 14 21 28	5 12 19 26	2 9 16 23 30
S	4 11 18 25	1 8 15 22 29	6 13 20 27	3 10 17 24 31

	September	October	November	December
M	1 8 15 22 29	6 13 20 27	3 10 17 24	1 8 15 22 29
T	2 9 16 23 30	7 14 21 28	4 11 18 25	2 9 16 23 30
W	3 10 17 24	1 8 15 22 29	5 12 19 26	3 10 17 24 31
T	4 11 18 25	2 9 16 23 30	6 13 20 27	4 11 18 25
F	5 12 19 26	3 10 17 24 31	7 14 21 28	5 12 19 26
S	6 13 20 27	4 11 18 25	1 8 15 22 29	6 13 20 27
S	7 14 21 28	5 12 19 26	2 9 16 23 30	7 14 21 28

11

	January	February	March	April
M	6 13 20 27	3 10 17 24	2 9 16 23 30	6 13 20 27
T	7 14 21 28	4 11 18 25	3 10 17 24 31	7 14 21 28
W	1 8 15 22 29	5 12 19 26	4 11 18 25	1 8 15 22 29
T	2 9 16 23 30	6 13 20 27	5 12 19 26	2 9 16 23 30
F	3 10 17 24 31	7 14 21 28	6 13 20 27	3 10 17 24
S	4 11 18 25	1 8 15 22 29	7 14 21 28	4 11 18 25
S	5 12 19 26	2 9 16 23	1 8 15 22 29	5 12 19 26

	May	June	July	August
M	4 11 18 25	1 8 15 22 29	6 13 20 27	3 10 17 24 31
T	5 12 19 26	2 9 16 23 30	7 14 21 28	4 11 18 25
W	6 13 20 27	3 10 17 24	1 8 15 22 29	5 12 19 26
T	7 14 21 28	4 11 18 25	2 9 16 23 30	6 13 20 27
F	1 8 15 22 29	5 12 19 26	3 10 17 24 31	7 14 21 28
S	2 9 16 23 30	6 13 20 27	4 11 18 25	1 8 15 22 29
S	3 10 17 24 31	7 14 21 28	5 12 19 26	2 9 16 23 30

	September	October	November	December
M	7 14 21 28	5 12 19 26	2 9 16 23 30	7 14 21 28
T	1 8 15 22 29	6 13 20 27	3 10 17 24	1 8 15 22 29
W	2 9 16 23 30	7 14 21 28	4 11 18 25	2 9 16 23 30
T	3 10 17 24	1 8 15 22 29	5 12 19 26	3 10 17 24 31
F	4 11 18 25	2 9 16 23 30	6 13 20 27	4 11 18 25
S	5 12 19 26	3 10 17 24 31	7 14 21 28	5 12 19 26
S	6 13 20 27	4 11 18 25	1 8 15 22 29	6 13 20 27

12

	January	February	March	April
M	5 12 19 26	2 9 16 23	1 8 15 22 29	5 12 19 26
T	6 13 20 27	3 10 17 24	2 9 16 23 30	6 13 20 27
W	7 14 21 28	4 11 18 25	3 10 17 24 31	7 14 21 28
T	1 8 15 22 29	5 12 19 26	4 11 18 25	1 8 15 22 29
F	2 9 16 23 30	6 13 20 27	5 12 19 26	2 9 16 23 30
S	3 10 17 24 31	7 14 21 28	6 13 20 27	3 10 17 24
S	4 11 18 25	1 8 15 22 29	7 14 21 28	4 11 18 25

	May	June	July	August
M	3 10 17 24 31	7 14 21 28	5 12 19 26	2 9 16 23 30
T	4 11 18 25	1 8 15 22 29	6 13 20 27	3 10 17 24 31
W	5 12 19 26	2 9 16 23 30	7 14 21 28	4 11 18 25
T	6 13 20 27	3 10 17 24	1 8 15 22 29	5 12 19 26
F	7 14 21 28	4 11 18 25	2 9 16 23 30	6 13 20 27
S	1 8 15 22 29	5 12 19 26	3 10 17 24 31	7 14 21 28
S	2 9 16 23 30	6 13 20 27	4 11 18 25	1 8 15 22 29

	September	October	November	December
M	6 13 20 27	4 11 18 25	1 8 15 22 29	6 13 20 27
T	7 14 21 28	5 12 19 26	2 9 16 23 30	7 14 21 28
W	1 8 15 22 29	6 13 20 27	3 10 17 24	1 8 15 22 29
T	2 9 16 23 30	7 14 21 28	4 11 18 25	2 9 16 23 30
F	3 10 17 24	1 8 15 22 29	5 12 19 26	3 10 17 24 31
S	4 11 18 25	2 9 16 23 30	6 13 20 27	4 11 18 25
S	5 12 19 26	3 10 17 24 31	7 14 21 28	5 12 19 26

13

	January	February	March	April
M	4 11 18 25	1 8 15 22 29	7 14 21 28	4 11 18 25
T	5 12 19 26	2 9 16 23	1 8 15 22 29	5 12 19 26
W	6 13 20 27	3 10 17 24	2 9 16 23 30	6 13 20 27
T	7 14 21 28	4 11 18 25	3 10 17 24 31	7 14 21 28
F	1 8 15 22 29	5 12 19 26	4 11 18 25	1 8 15 22 29
S	2 9 16 23 30	6 13 20 27	5 12 19 26	2 9 16 23 30
S	3 10 17 24 31	7 14 21 28	6 13 20 27	3 10 17 24

	May	June	July	August
M	2 9 16 23 30	6 13 20 27	4 11 18 25	1 8 15 22 29
T	3 10 17 24 31	7 14 21 28	5 12 19 26	2 9 16 23 30
W	4 11 18 25	1 8 15 22 29	6 13 20 27	3 10 17 24 31
T	5 12 19 26	2 9 16 23 30	7 14 21 28	4 11 18 25
F	6 13 20 27	3 10 17 24	1 8 15 22 29	5 12 19 26
S	7 14 21 28	4 11 18 25	2 9 16 23 30	6 13 20 27
S	1 8 15 22 29	5 12 19 26	3 10 17 24 31	7 14 21 28

	September	October	November	December
M	5 12 19 26	3 10 17 24 31	7 14 21 28	5 12 19 26
T	6 13 20 27	4 11 18 25	1 8 15 22 29	6 13 20 27
W	7 14 21 28	5 12 19 26	2 9 16 23 30	7 14 21 28
T	1 8 15 22 29	6 13 20 27	3 10 17 24	1 8 15 22 29
F	2 9 16 23 30	7 14 21 28	4 11 18 25	2 9 16 23 30
S	3 10 17 24	1 8 15 22 29	5 12 19 26	3 10 17 24 31
S	4 11 18 25	2 9 16 23 30	6 13 20 27	4 11 18 25

14

	January	February	March	April
M	3 10 17 24 31	7 14 21 28	6 13 20 27	3 10 17 24
T	4 11 18 25	1 8 15 22 29	7 14 21 28	4 11 18 25
W	5 12 19 26	2 9 16 23	1 8 15 22 29	5 12 19 26
T	6 13 20 27	3 10 17 24	2 9 16 23 30	6 13 20 27
F	7 14 21 28	4 11 18 25	3 10 17 24 31	7 14 21 28
S	1 8 15 22 29	5 12 19 26	4 11 18 25	1 8 15 22 29
S	2 9 16 23 30	6 13 20 27	5 12 19 26	2 9 16 23 30

	May	June	July	August
M	1 8 15 22 29	5 12 19 26	3 10 17 24 31	7 14 21 28
T	2 9 16 23 30	6 13 20 27	4 11 18 25	1 8 15 22 29
W	3 10 17 24 31	7 14 21 28	5 12 19 26	2 9 16 23 30
T	4 11 18 25	1 8 15 22 29	6 13 20 27	3 10 17 24 31
F	5 12 19 26	2 9 16 23 30	7 14 21 28	4 11 18 25
S	6 13 20 27	3 10 17 24	1 8 15 22 29	5 12 19 26
S	7 14 21 28	4 11 18 25	2 9 16 23 30	6 13 20 27

	September	October	November	December
M	4 11 18 25	2 9 16 23 30	6 13 20 27	4 11 18 25
T	5 12 19 26	3 10 1 24 31	7 14 21 28	5 12 19 26
W	6 13 20 27	4 11 18 25	1 8 15 22 29	6 13 20 27
T	7 14 21 28	5 12 19 26	2 9 16 23 30	7 14 21 28
F	1 8 15 22 29	6 13 20 27	3 10 17 24	1 8 15 22 29
S	2 9 16 23 30	7 14 21 28	4 11 18 25	2 9 16 23 30
S	3 10 17 24	1 8 15 22 29	5 12 19 26	3 10 17 24 31

M4: Religious festivals

2014		
☬	Birthday of Guru Gobind Singh	January 5
☪	Mawlid-al-Nabi	January 13
✝	Ash Wednesday	March 5
✡	Purim	March 16
ॐ	Holi	March 17
☬	Hola Mohalla	March 17
☬	Birthday of Guru Nanak	April 14
☬	Baisakhi Day	April 14
✡	Passover	April 15
✝	Good Friday	April 18
✝	Easter Sunday	April 20
✝	Easter Monday	April 21
✝	Ascension Day	May 29
✡	Shavuot	June 4
✝	Pentecost	June 8
☪	Ramadan begins	June 28
☪	Eid al-Fitr	July 28
✡	Rosh Hashanah	September 25
✡	Yom Kippur	October 4
ॐ	Dasarah	October 4
☪	Eid al-Adha	October 4
✡	Succot	October 9
ॐ	Diwali	October 23
☪	Ashurah	November 3
☪	Hijra – New year	November 15
✡	Chanukah	December 17
✝	Christmas Day	December 25

2015		
☬	Birthday of Guru Gobind Singh	January 5
✝	Ash Wednesday	February 25
✡	Purim	March 6
ॐ	Holi	March 6
☬	Hola Mohalla	March 6
✝	Good Friday	April 3
✡	Passover	April 4
✝	Easter Sunday	April 5
✝	Easter Monday	April 6
☬	Baisakhi Day	April 14
✝	Ascension Day	May 2
✝	Pentecost	May 24
✡	Shavuot	May 24
☪	Ramadan begins	June 18
☪	Eid al-Fitr	July 18
✡	Rosh Hashanah	September 4
✡	Yom Kippur	September 23
☪	Eid al-Adha	September 23
✡	Succot	September 28
☪	Hijra – New year	October 14
ॐ	Dasarah	October 22
☪	Ashurah	October 23
ॐ	Diwali	November 11
☬	Birthday of Guru Nanak	November 25
✡	Chanukah	December 7
☪	Mawlid-al-Nabi	December 23
✝	Christmas Day	December 25

2016		
☬	Birthday of Guru Gobind Singh	January 5
✝	Ash Wednesday	February 10
ॐ	Holi	March 23
✡	Purim	March 24
☬	Hola Mohalla	March 24
✝	Good Friday	March 25
✝	Easter Sunday	March 27
✝	Easter Monday	March 28
☬	Baisakhi Day	April 14
✡	Passover	April 23
✝	Ascension Day	May 5
✝	Pentecost	May 15
☪	Ramadan begins	June 6
✡	Shavuot	June 12
☪	Eid al-Fitr	July 7
☪	Eid al-Adha	September 11
☪	Muharram – New year	October 2
✡	Rosh Hashanah	October 3
☪	Dasarah	October 11
☪	Ashurah	October 12
✡	Yom Kippur	October 12
✡	Succot	October 17
ॐ	Diwali	October 30
☬	Birthday of Guru Nanak	November 14
☪	Mawlid-al-Nabi	December 12
✡	Chanukah	December 25
✝	Christmas Day	December 25

✝ Christian
ॐ Hindu
✡ Jewish
☪ Muslim
☬ Sikh

Note: all Islamic and Jewish holidays begin at sundown on the preceding day.

M5: Medical reference intervals and scales

Haematology—reference intervals

Measurement	Reference interval
White cell count	$4.0–11.0 \times 10^9/l$
Red cell count – Male: Female:	$4.5–6.5 \times 10^{12}/l$ $3.9–5.6 \times 10^{12}/l$
Haemoglobin – Male: Female:	13.5–18.0g/dl 11.5–16.0g/dl
Platelet count	$150.0–400.0 \times 10^9/l$
Erthrocyte sedimentation rate (ESR) – Male: Female:	Up to age in years divided by two. Up to (age in years plus 10) divided by two.
Prothrombin time (factors II, VII, X)	10–14 seconds
Activated partial thromboplastic time (VIII, IX, XI, XII)	35–45 seconds

Proposed therapeutic ranges for prothrombin time (British Society for Haematology guidelines on oral anticoagulants, 1984)

British ratio (NR)	Clinical state
2.0–2.5	Prophylaxis of deep vein thrombosis including high risk surgery (e.g. for fractured femur).
2.5–3.0	Treatment of deep vein thrombosis, pulmonary embolism, transient ischaemic attacks.
3.0–4.5	Recurrent deep vein thrombosis an pulmonary embolism, arterial disease including myocardial infarction, arterial grafts, cardiac prosthetic valves and grafts.

Cerebrospinal fluid—reference intervals

Opening pressure (mmCSF)	Infants: < 80; children: < 90; adults: < 210

Substance	**Reference interval**
Glucose	3.3–4.4 mmol/l or ≥ 2/3 of plasma glucose
Chloride	122–128 mmol/l
Lactate	< 2.8 mmol/l

Biochemistry—reference intervals

Substance	Specimen	Reference Interval
Albumin	P	*35–50 g/l
a-amylase	P	0–180 Somogyi U/dl
Bicarbonate	P	*24–30 mmol/l
C reactive protein (CRP)	P	< 6 mg/l
Calcium (ionised)	P	1.0–1.25 mmol/l
Calcium (total)	P	*2.12–2.65 mmol/l
Chloride	P	98–107 mmol/l
Cholesterol	P	3.3–6.2 mmol/l
Creatinine	P	*58–110 mmol/l
Glucose (fasting)	P	3.5–5.5 mmol/l
Glycosylated haemoglobin	B	5–8%
Phosphate	P	0.8–1.45 mmol/l
Potassium	P	3.6–5.0 mmol/l
Protein (total)	P	60–80 g/l
Sodium	P	*137–145 mmol/l
Urea	P	*2.5–7.5 mmol/l

Key: P = plasma; B = whole blood

* Reference intervals for these substances differ in pregnancy. Reference intervals in pregnancy are not reproduced here.

Arterial blood gases—reference intervals

pH:	7.35–7.45
PaO_2:	>10.6 kPa
$PaCO_2$:	4.7–6.0 kPa
Base excess	±2 mmol/l
NB: 7.6 mmHg = 1 kPa (atmospheric pressure = 100 kPa)	

Apgar scoring chart

A baby's condition is assessed at one and five minutes after birth by means of the Apgar score. This system observes five signs. A score of nought, one or two is awarded for each sign.

Sign	0	1	2
Heart rate	absent	slow (below 100)	over 100
Respiratory effect	absent	weak cry, hypoventilation	good cry
Muscle tone	limp	some flexion of extremities	well flexed
Reflex irritability	no response	some motion	cry
Colour	blue, pale	body pink, extremities blue	completely pink

NB: An Apgar score of 10 represents optimal condition. A score of three or less indicates a markedly asphyxiated infant.

Glasgow coma scale

Three types of response are assessed:

	Score	
Best motor response	6	Obeys commands
	5	Localises to pain
	4	Flexion/withdrawal to pain
	3	Abnormal flexion
	2	Abnormal extension
	1	None
Best verbal response	5	Oriented
	4	Confused
	3	Inappropriate words
	2	Incomprehensible sounds
	1	None
Eye opening	4	Spontaneously
	3	To speech
	2	To pain
	1	None

The overall score is the sum of the scores in each area, e.g. no response to pain + no verbal response + no eye opening = three.

In severe injury the score is eight or under.
In moderate injury the score is nine–12.
In minor injury the score is 13–15.

PULHHEEMS rating

This is a system of physical and mental grading used by all three branches of the British Armed Forces. It is taken from the joint Services publication JSP 346 which is issued to all Service and Civilian medical practitioners required to examine applicants for entry to the Armed Forces. It is carried out on new recruits, and repeated at five-yearly intervals after the age of 30. After the age of 50, it is performed at two-yearly intervals.

PULHHEEMS is an abbreviation for the factors to be tested. These include:

P	Physique
U	Upper limbs
L	Locomotion—i.e. lower limbs and back
H	Hearing in the left ear
H	Hearing in the right ear
E	Visual acuity—left eye
E	Visual acuity—right eye
M	Mental function
S	Stability (emotional)

The maximum score is eight (excellent) and the minimum one (unfit for service). In the form this appears in a table as follows (Lord Nelson taken as an example):

P	U	L	H	H	E	E	M	S
8	4	8	8	8	8	1	8	5

FDI World Dental Federation notation

FDI Two-Digit Notation

Permanent Teeth

upper right								upper left							
18	17	16	15	14	13	12	11	21	22	23	24	25	26	27	28
48	47	46	45	44	43	43	41	31	32	33	34	35	36	37	38
lower right								lower left							

Deciduous teeth (baby teeth)

upper right					upper left				
55	54	53	52	51	61	62	63	64	65
85	84	83	82	81	71	72	73	74	75
lower right					lower left				

Codes, names and usual number of roots

Codes		Names	Usual number of roots
11	21	maxillary central incisor	1
41	31	mandibular central incisor	1
12	22	maxillary lateral incisor	1
42	32	mandibular lateral incisor	1
13	23	maxillary canine	1
43	33	mandibular canine	1
14	24	maxillary first premolar	2
44	34	mandibular first premolar	1
15	25	maxillary second premolar	1
45	35	mandibular second premolar	1
16	26	maxillary first molar	3
46	36	mandibular first molar	2
17	27	maxillary second molar	3
47	37	mandibular second molar	2
18	28	maxillary third premolar	3
48	38	mandibular third premolar	2

How the codes are constructed

Syntax: <quadrant code><tooth code>

Quadrant codes

1	upper right
2	upper left
3	lower left
4	lower right

Tooth codes

1	central incisors
2	lateral incisors
3	canines
4	1st premolars
5	2nd premolars
6	1st molars
7	2nd molars
8	3rd molars

M6: Websites

Useful web sites

Site	Address
Acts of Parliament	*http://www.legislation.gov.uk*
Australasian Legal Information Institute	*http://www.austlii.edu.au*
Bank of England	*http://www.bankofengland.co.uk*
Bar Council	*http://www.barcouncil.org.uk*
British and Irish Legal Information Institute	*http://www.bailii.org*
Child Support Agency	*https://www.gov.uk/child-maintenance/overview*
Social Security and Child Support Commissioners' Decisions	*www.osscsc.gov.uk*
Companies House	*https://www.gov.uk/government/organisations/companies-house*
Court of Justice of the European Union	*http://europa.eu/about-eu/institutions-bodies/court-justice/index_en.htm*
Her Majesty's Court and Tribunals Service	*https://www.gov.uk/government/organisations/hm-courts-and-tribunals-service*
Carers Trust	*https://www.carers.org*
Delia Venables Legal Resources	*http://www.venables.co.uk*
DCA Human Rights site	*http://www.dca.gov.uk/peoples-rights/human-rights/index.htm*
Department of Health	*https://www.gov.uk/government/organisations/department-of-health*
Electronic Share Information (iii)	*http://www.iii.co.uk*
European Court of Human Rights	*http://www.echr.coe.int*
Financial Times	*http://www.ft.com*
Government Actuary's Department	*https://www.gov.uk/government/organisations/government-actuarys-department*
Government Information Service	*https://www.gov.uk/*
Hague Conference on Private International Law	*http://www.hcch.net/index_en.php*
Hague Convention on Child Abduction	*http://www.hcch.net/index_en.php?act=text.display&tid=21*
Hansard: House of Commons Debates	*http://www.parliament.uk/business/publications/hansard/commons*
House of Lords Debates	*http://www.parliament.uk/business/publications/hansard/lords*
Land Registry	*https://www.gov.uk/government/organisations/land-registry*
Legislation.gov.uk	*http://www.legislation.gov.uk*
House of Commons	*http://www.parliament.uk/business/commons/*
House of Lords	*http://www.parliament.uk/business/lords/*
House Price Indices (Halifax)	*http://www.lloydsbankinggroup.com/media/economic-insight/halifax-house-price-index/*
Information for Lawyers	*http://www.infolaw.co.uk*
HM Revenue & Customs	*https://www.gov.uk/government/organisations/hm-revenue-customs*
Judicial Committee of the Privy Council	*http://www.jcpc.gov.uk*
Laurie West-Knights' homepage	*http://www.lawonline.cc*
Law Society	*http://www.lawsociety.org.uk*
Legal Services Commission	*https://www.gov.uk/government/organisations/legal-services-commission*
Ministry of Justice	*http://www.justice.gov.uk*
National Savings & Investments	*http://www.nsandi.com/*
Official Solicitor and Public Trustee Office	*https://www.gov.uk/government/organisations/official-solicitor-and-public-trustee*
ONS–Consumer Price Index and Retail Price Index	*http://www.ONS.gov.uk/ons/guide-method/user-guidance/prices/cpi-and-rpi/index.html*

RPI (full table)	*http://www.ons.gov.uk/ons/datasets-and-tables/data-selector.html?cdid=CHAW&dataset=mm23&table-id=2.1*
Statutory Instruments	*http://www.legislation.gov.uk/uksi*
Sweet & Maxwell	*http://www.sweetandmaxwell.co.uk*
The Stationery Office	*http://www.tso.co.uk*
The Supreme Court	*http://www.supremecourt.uk*
The Times	*http://www.thetimes.co.uk*
UK Parliament	*http://www.parliament.uk*
Zoopla	*http://www.zoopla.co.uk*

M7: Addresses of useful organisations

Part 1—Medical

British Medical Association

BMA House
Tavistock Square
London WC1H 9JP
Tel: 020 7387 4499
http://www.bma.org.uk

General Dental Council

37 Wimpole Street
London W1G 8DQ
Tel: 020 7167 6000
Email: information@gdc-uk.org
http://www.gdc-uk.org

British Association for Accident and Emergency Medicine—merged with the College of Emergency Medicine

The Royal College of Surgeons of England
35–43 Lincoln's Inn Fields
London WC2A 3PN
Tel: 020 7831 9405
Email: communications@rceng.ac.uk

The Royal College of Emergency Medicine

7-9 Bream's Buildings
Chancery Lane
London, EC4A 1DT
Tel: 020 7404 1999
http://www.rcem.ac.uk/

General Medical Council

Regent's Place
350 Euston Road
London NW1 3JN
Tel: 0161 923 6602
Email: gmc@gmc-uk.org
http://www.gmc-uk.org

General Optical Council

41 Harley Street
London W1G 8DJ
Tel: 020 7580 3898
Email: goc@optical.org
http://www.optical.org

Nursing and Midwifery Council

23 Portland Place
London W1B 1PZ
Tel: 020 7637 7181
Email: UKenquiries@nmc-uk.org
http://www.nmc.org.uk/

Accidents

Royal Society for the Prevention of Accidents (RoSPA)
RoSPA House
28 Calthorpe Road
Edgbaston
Birmingham B15 1RP
Tel: 0121 248 2000
Email: help@rospa.co.uk
http://www.rospa.com

Alcoholism

Medical Council on Alcohol
5 St. Andrew's Place
Regent's Park
London NW1 4LB
Tel: 020 7487 4445
Email: info@m-c-a.org.uk
http://www.m-c-a.org.uk

Alzheimer's disease

Alzheimer's Society
Devon House
58 St Katherine's Way
London E1W 1LB
Tel: 020 7423 3500
Email: enquiries@alzheimers.org.uk
http://www.alzheimers.org.uk/

Anaesthetics

Obstetric Anaesthetists' Association
21 Portland Place
London W1B 1PY
Tel: 020 7631 8883
Email: secretariat@oaa-anaes.ac.uk
http://www.oaa-anaes.ac.uk/home

Asthma

18 Mansell Street
London E1 8AA
Tel: 020 7786 4900
Email: info@asthma.org.uk
http://www.asthma.org.uk/

Bereavement

Child Bereavement Charity
The Saunderton Estate
Wycombe Road
Saunderton
Buckinghamshire HP14 4BF
Tel: 01494 568 900
Email: enquiries@childbereavement.org.uk
http://www.childbereavementuk.org/

The Compassionate Friends
(counselling for bereaved parents)
14 New King St
Deptford
London SE8 3HS
Tel: 0845 120 3785
Email: info@tcf.org.uk
http://www.tcf.org.uk/

Biochemistry

Biochemical Society
Charles Darwin House
12 Roger Street
London WC1N 2JU
Tel: 020 7685 2400
Email: genadmin@biochemistry.org
http://www.biochemistry.org/

Blindness

Royal National Institute of the Blind
105 Judd Street
London WC1H 9NE
Tel: 020 7388 1266
Email: helpline@rnib.org.uk
http://www.rnib.org.uk/

Brain

Brain Research Trust
Dutch House, 307–308 High Holborn
London WC1V 7LL
Tel: 020 7404 9982
Email: info@brt.org.uk
http://www.brt.org.uk/

British Association of Brain Injury Case Managers
(BABICM)
Suite 11, Ela Mill,
Cork Street, Bury
BL9 7BW
Tel:0161 764 0602
http://www.babicm.org/

Centre for Brain Injury, Rehabilitation and
Development (BIRD)
The Old Coach House
Church Road
Eccleston, Chester
Tel: 01244 678 629
http://www.birdcharity.org.uk/

Brittle bone disease

Brittle Bone Society
30 Guthrie Street
Dundee DD1 5BS
Tel: 01382 204 446
Email: bbs@brittlebone.org
http://www.brittlebone.org/

Cancer

British Association of Cancer United
Patients (BACUP)
3 Bath Place
Rivington Street
London EC2A 3RJ
Tel: 020 7696 9003
Email: info@cancerbacup.org.uk

The Association for Cancer Surgery
Royal College of Surgeons
35–43 Lincoln's Inn Fields
London WC2A 3PE
Tel: 020 7869 6817
Email: admin@baso.org.uk
http://www.baso.org.uk/

Macmillan Cancer Relief
89 Albert Embankment
London SE1 7UQ
Tel: 020 7840 7840
Email: cancerline@macmillan.org.uk
http://www.macmillan.org.uk/

Cancer Research UK
Angel Building
407 St John Street
London EC1V 4AD
Tel: 020 7242 0200
http://www.cancerresearchuk.org/

Marie Curie Cancer Care
89 Albert Embankment
London SE1 7TP
Tel: 0800 716 146
Email: supporter.services@mariecurie.org.uk
https://www.mariecurie.org.uk/

Cardiology

British Cardiovascular Society
9 Fitzroy Square
London W1T 5HW
Tel: 020 7383 3887
Email: enquiries@bcs.com
https://www.bcs.com/pages/default.asp

British Heart Foundation
Greater London House
180 Hampstead Road
London, NW1 7AW
Tel: 020 7554 0000
http://www.bhf.org.uk

Society of Cardiothoracic Surgeons in Great Britain & Ireland
The Royal College of Surgeons
35–43 Lincoln's Inn Fields
London WC2A 3PE
Tel: 020 7869 6893/6894
Email: sctsadmin@scts.org
http://www.scts.org/

Childbirth

The Association for Post-Natal Illness
145 Dawes Road, Fulham
London SW6 7EB
Tel: 020 7386 0868
Email: info@apni.org
http://apni.org/

The National Childbirth Trust
Alexandra House
Oldham Terrace
London W3 6NH
Tel: 0800 330 0700
Email: enquiries@nct.org.uk
http://www.nct.org.uk/

Royal College of Midwives
15 Mansfield Street
London W1G 9NH
Tel: 020 7312 3535
Email: info@rcm.org.uk
https://www.rcm.org.uk/

Stillbirth and Neonatal Death Society (SANDS)
28 Portland Place
London W1B 1LY
Tel: 020 7436 7940
Email: helpline@uk-sands.org
https://uk-sands.org/

Children

The National Association for Children with Lower Limb Abnormalities (STEPS)
Warrington Lane
Lymm
Cheshire WA13 OSA
Tel: 01925 750 271
Email: info@steps-charity.org.uk
http://www.steps-charity.org.uk/

Barnardo's
Tanners Lane
Barkingside
Ilford
Essex IG6 1QG
Tel: 020 8550 8822
http://www.barnardos.org.uk

Baby Life Support Systems (Bliss)
2nd Floor,
Chapter House
18-20 Crucifix Lane
London SE1 3JW
Tel: 020 7378 1122
Email: ask@bliss.org.uk
http://www.bliss.org.uk/

Child Accident Prevention Trust
Canterbury Court (1.09)
1–3 Brixton Road
London SW9 6DE
Tel: 020 7608 3828
Email: safe@capt.org.uk
http://www.capt.org.uk/

Child Poverty Action Group (CPAG)
30 Micawber Street
London
N1 7TB
Email: info@cpag.org.uk
http://www.cpag.org.uk/

(see also **Paediatric**)

Chiropody

Institute of Chiropodists & Podiatrists
150 Lord Street
Southport
Merseyside PR9 0TL
Tel: 01704 546 141
Email: secretary@iocp.org.uk
http://www.iocp.org.uk/

Society of Chiropodists & Podiatrists
1 Fellmonger's Pass
Tower Bridge Road
London SE1 3LY
Tel: 020 7234 8620
Email: reception@scpod.org
http://www.scpod.org

Colostomy

Colostomy Association
Enterprise House
95 London Street
Reading RG1 4QA
Tel: 0118 939 1537
Email: cass@colostomyassociation.org.uk
http://www.colostomyassociation.org.uk

Counselling

British Association for Counselling and Psychotherapy
BACP House
15 St John's Business Park
Lutterworth LE17 4HB
Tel: 01455 883 300
Email: bacp@bacp.co.uk
http://www.bacp.co.uk/

Cystic fibrosis

Cystic Fibrosis Trust
One Aldgate
Second floor
London
EC3N 1RE
Tel: 020 3795 1555
Email: enquiries@cysticfibrosis.org.uk
http://www.cysticfibrosis.org.uk/

Day surgery

British Association of Day Surgery
The Royal College of Surgeons
35–43 Lincoln's Inn Fields
London WC2A 3PE
Tel: 020 7973 0308
Email: bads@bads.co.uk
http://daysurgeryuk.net/en/home/

Deafness

Royal Association for Deaf People
Century House South, Riverside Office Centre
North Station Road, Colchester, Essex CO1 1RE
Tel: 0845 688 2525
Email: info@royaldeaf.org.uk
http://www.royaldeaf.org.uk/

Royal National Institute for Deaf People
19–23 Featherstone Street
London EC1Y 8SL
Tel: 020 7296 8000
Minicom: 020 7296 8001
Email: informationline@hearingloss.org.uk
http://www.actiononhearingloss.org.uk/

Dentists

British Dental Association
64 Wimpole Street
London W1G 8YS
Tel: 020 7935 0875
Email: enquiries@bda.org
https://www.bda.org/

Dermatology

British Association of Dermatologists
Willan House
4 Fitzroy Square
London W1T 5HQ
Tel: 020 7383 0266
Email: admin@bad.org.uk
http://www.bad.org.uk/

Development

British Association for Developmental Disabilities
5 Handsworth Drive
Great Barr
Birmingham B43 6ED
Tel/Fax: 0121 360 2027

Diabetes

Diabetes UK Central Office
Macleod House
10 Parkway
London NW1 7AA
Tel: 020 7424 1000
Email: info@diabetes.org.uk
https://www.diabetes.org.uk

Diagnostics

Cellmark Diagnostics
PO Box 265
Abingdon OX14 1YX
Tel: 0800 362 522
Fax: 01235 528 141
Email: info@cellmark.co.uk
http://www.cellmark.co.uk/

University Diagnostics Ltd
Queens Road
Teddington
Middx TW11 0NJ
Tel: 020 8943 8400

Dietetics

British Dietetic Association
5th Floor Charles House
148–9 Great Charles Street
Queensway
Birmingham B3 3HT
Tel: 0121 200 8080
Fax: 0121 200 8081
Email: info@bda.uk.com
https://www.bda.uk.com/

British Nutrition Foundation
Imperial House 6th Floor
15–19 Kingsway
London, WC2B 6UN
Tel: 020 7557 7930
http://www.nutrition.org.uk

Digestion

Digestive Disorders CORE Foundation
3 Saint Andrew's Place
London NW1 4LB
Tel: 020 7486 0341
Email: info@corecharity.org.uk
http://www.corecharity.org.uk/

Disability

Disabled Living Foundation
4th Floor, Jessica House
Red Lion Square
191 Wandsworth High Street
London, SW18 4LS
Tel: 020 7289 6111
Email: info@dlf.org.uk
http://www.dlf.org.uk/

Royal Association for Disability and
Rehabilitation (RADAR)
12 City Forum
250 City Road
London EC1V 8AF
Tel: 020 7250 3222
Email: radar@radar.org.uk
http://disabilityrightsuk.org/

Disfigurement

Changing Faces
(Charity for Facially Disfigured People)
The Squire Centre
33–37 University Street
London WC1E 6JN
Tel: 0845 4500 275
Email: info@changingfaces.org.uk
https://www.changingfaces.org.uk/Home

Down's Syndrome

Down's Syndrome Association (DSA)
Langdon Down Centre
2a Langdon Park
Teddington TW11 9PS
Tel: 0333 1212 300
Email: info@downs-syndrome.org.uk
http://www.downs-syndrome.org.uk/

Drugs

Committee on Safety of Medicines (for
adverse reaction reports)
151 Buckingham Palace Road
London SW1W 9SZ
Tel: 020 3080 6000
Email: info@mhra.gsi.gov.uk

Dyslexia

Dyslexia Action
10 High Street
Egham
Surrey, TW20 9EA
United Kingdom
Tel: 0300 303 8357
Email: info@dyslexiaaction.org.uk
http://www.dyslexiaaction.org.uk/

Ear, nose and throat

British Association of Otorhinolaryngologists
ENT UK at The Royal College of Surgeons
35–43 Lincoln's Inn Fields
London WC2A 3PE
Tel: 020 7404 8373
Email: entuk@entuk.org
https://entuk.org/

(see also **Deafness**)

Elderly

British Geriatrics Society
Marjory Warren House
31 St John's Square
London EC1M 4DN

Tel: 020 7608 1369
Email: general.information@bgs.org.uk
http://www.bgs.org.uk/

British Association for Service to the Elderly (BASE)
119 Hassell Street
Newcastle-under-Lyme
Staffordshire ST5 1AX
Tel: 01782 661 033
Email: basenul@intonet.co.uk

Endocrinology

Society for Endocrinology
22 Apex Court
Woodlands
Bradley Stoke
Bristol BS32 4JT
Tel: 01454 642 200
Email: info@endocrinology.org
http://www.endocrinology.org/

Epilepsy

Epilepsy Action
New Anstey House
Gate Way Drive
Yeadon
Leeds LS19 7XY
Tel: 0113 210 8800
Email: epilepsy@epilepsy.org.uk
https://www.epilepsy.org.uk/

Forensic science

British Academy of Forensic Sciences
Anaesthetic Unit
Royal London Hospital
London E1 1BB
Tel: 020 7377 9201

Gastroenterology

British Society of Gastroenterology
3 Saint Andrew's Place
Regent's Park
London NW1 4LB
Tel: 020 7935 3150
Email: j.rother@bsg.org.uk
http://www.bsg.org.uk/

Glaucoma

International Glaucoma Association
Woodcote House
15 Highpoint Business Village
Henwood
Ashford
Kent TN24 8DH
Tel: 01233 648 164
Email: info@iga.org.uk
http://www.glaucoma-association.com/

General information

Health Information (will provide a wide range of health information for both doctors and their patients)
The Mapels
Level 2
The Lister Hospital
Coreys Mill Lane
Stevenage
Hertfordshire SG1 4AB
Tel: 0800 665 544

Haematology

British Society for Haematology
100 White Lion Street
London N1 9PF
Tel: 020 7713 0990
Email: info@b-s-h.org.uk
http://www.b-s-h.org.uk/

Haemophilia

The Haemophilia Society
Willcox House
140 – 148 Borough High Street
London, SE1 1LB
Tel: 0207 939 0780
Email: info@haemophilia.org.uk
http://www.haemophilia.org.uk/

Hand surgery

British Society of Surgery of the Hand
Royal College of Surgeons of England
35–43 Lincoln's Inn Fields
London WC2A 3PE
Tel: 020 7831 5162
Email: secretariat@bssh.ac.uk
http://www.bssh.ac.uk/

Head injuries

Headway (The Brain Injuries Association)
Bradbury House
190 Bagnall Road, Old Basford
Nottingham
NG6 8SF
Tel: 0115 924 0800
Email: enquiries@headway.org.uk
https://www.headway.org.uk/home.aspx

Health visitors

Community Practitioners' and Health Visitors Association (Amicus/CPHVA)—Unite
Unite
128 Theobold's Road
Holborn
London WC1X 8TN
Tel: 020 7611 2500
http://www.unitetheunion.org

Hysterectomy

Hysterectomy Association
2 Princes Court
Puddletown
Dorchester
Dorset, DT2 8UE
http://www.hysterectomy-association.org.uk/

Injury

(See **Rehabilitation**)

Kidneys

National Kidney Federation
The Point, Coach Road,
Shireoaks, Worksop
Nottinghamshire S81 8BW
Tel: 01909 544 999
Helpline: 0845 601 0209
Email: nfk@kidney.org.uk
http://www.kidney.org.uk/

Kidney Research UK (previously The National Kidney Research Fund)
General Enquiries: Tel: 0845 070 7601
enquiries@kidneyresearchuk.org
http://www.kidneyresearchuk.org/

Kidney Research UK
Nene Hall
Lynch Wood Park
Peterborough PE2 6FZ
Tel: 0845 300 1499
Email: kidneyhealth@kidneyresearchuk.org

Lungs

(See **Thoracic**)

Lupus

Lupus UK
St James House
Eastern Road
Romford
Essex RM1 3NH
Tel: 01708 731 251
Email: headoffice@lupusuk.org.uk
http://www.lupusuk.org.uk/

Maxillofacial surgery

(See **Oral**)

M.E.

Myalgic Encephalomyelitis Association
4 Top Angel
Buckingham Industrial Park
Buckingham MK18 1TH
Tel: 0870 444 8233
Email: enquiries@meassociation.org.uk
http://www.meassociation.org.uk/

Medicine

Committee on Safety of Medicines
151 Buckingham Palace Road
Victoria
London SW1W 9SZ
Tel: 020 3080 6000
Email: info@mhra.gsi.gov.uk

Medical Society of London
Lettsom House
11 Chandos Street
London W1G 9EB
Tel: 020 7580 1043
http://medsoclondon.org/

Medicines Commission
151 Buckingham Palace Road
Victoria London SW1W 9SZ
Tel: 020 3080 6000
Email: info@mhra.gsi.gov.uk

The Royal Society of Medicine
1 Wimpole Street
London W1G 0AE
Tel: 020 7290 2900
http://www.rsm.ac.uk

Meningitis

The National Meningitis Trust
Fern House
Bath Road
Stroud
Gloucestershire GL5 3TJ
Tel: 01453 768 000
Email: info@meningitis-trust.org.uk
https://www.meningitisnow.org/

Menopause (premature)

The Menopause Amarant Trust
80 Lambeth Road
London SE1 7PW
Tel: 01293 413 000 (Advice Line)
http://www.amarantmenopausetrust.org.uk

Mental health

National Association for Mental Health (MIND)
Granta House
15/19 Broadway
London E15 4BQ
Tel: 020 8519 2122
Email: contact@mind.org.uk
http://www.mind.org.uk/

Royal Society for Mentally Handicapped Children and Adults (MENCAP)
Mencap National Centre
123 Golden Lane
London EC1Y 0RT
Tel: 020 7454 0454
Email: information@mencap.org.uk
https://www.mencap.org.uk/

Midwives

(See **Childbirth**)

Migraine

Migraine Trust
52–53 Russell Square
London WC1B 4HP
Tel: 020 7631 6970
Email: info@migrainenetrust.org
http://www.migrainetrust.org/

Mobility

Banstead Mobility Centre
Leatherhead Court
Woodlands Road
Leatherhead
Surrey KT22 0BN
Tel: 01372 841 100
http://qef.org.uk/

Motor Neurone Disease

Motor Neurone Disease Association
PO Box 246
Northampton NN1 2PR
Tel: 01604 250 505
Tel: 0845 7626 262 (helpline)
Email: enquiries@mndassociation.org
http://www.mndassociation.org/

Multiple Sclerosis

MS Society
MS National Centre
372 Edgware Road
London NW2 6ND
Tel: 020 8438 0700
Email: info@mssociety.org.uk
http://www.mssociety.org.uk/

Muscular Dystrophy

Muscular Dystrophy Campaign
61 Southwark Street
London SE1 0BU
Tel: 020 7803 4800
Email: info@muscular-dystrophy.org
http://www.musculardystrophyuk.org/

Narcolepsy

Narcolepsy UK
PO BOX 26865
Kirkcaldy KY2 9BX
Tel: 07920 650 552
Email: nicola.rule@narcolepsy.org.uk
http://www.narcolepsy.org.uk/

Neurology

Association of British Neurologists
Ormond House
27 Boswell Street
London WC1W 3JZ
Tel: 020 7405 4060
Email: info@theabn.org
http://www.theabn.org/

Neurosurgery

Society of British Neurological Surgeons
35–43 Lincoln's Inn Fields
London WC2A 3PE
Tel: 020 7869 6892
Email: admin@sbns.org.uk
http://www.sbns.org.uk/

Nursing

Royal College of Nursing of the United Kingdom
20 Cavendish Square
London W1G 0RN
Tel: 020 7409 3333
Email: membership@rcn.org.uk // web.enquiries@rcn.org.uk
http://www.rcn.org.uk

BNA Care Assessment Services
Sutton Head Office
Group House
92–96 Lind Road
Sutton, Surrey SM1 4PL
Tel: 08718 733 324
Email: info@bna.co.uk
http://www.bna.co.uk/index.php?option=com_content&view=frontpage&Itemid=184

Carers Trust
Head office
32–36 Loman Street
London SE1 0EH
Tel: 08448 004 361
Email: info@carers.org
http://www.carers.org/

Occupational medicine

Society of Occupational Medicine
Hamilton House
Mabledon Place
London WC1H 9BB
Tel: 020 7554 8628 (or 8627)
Email: admin@som.org.uk
https://www.som.org.uk/

Occupational therapy

British Association of Occupational Therapists/
College of Occupational Therapists
106–114 Borough High Street
Southwark
London SE1 1LB
Tel: 020 7357 6480
Email: reception@cot.co.uk
http://www.cot.co.uk

Oncology

(See **Cancer**)

Oral

British Association of Oral & Maxillofacial Surgeons
Royal College of Surgeons
35–43 Lincoln's Inn Fields
London WC2A 3PE
Tel: 020 7405 8074
Email: office@baoms.org.uk
http://www.baoms.org.uk/

Orthopaedic

British Orthopaedic Association
Royal College of Surgeons
35–43 Lincoln's Inn Fields
London WC2A 3PE
Tel: 020 7405 6507
Email: secretary@boa.ac.uk
http://www.boa.ac.uk/

Osteoporosis

National Osteoporosis Society
Camerton
Bath BA2 OPJ
Tel: 01761 471 771
http://www.nos.org.uk
Email: info@nos.org.uk

Pain

The British Pain Society
Third Floor
Churchill House
35 Red Lion Square
London WC1R 4SG
Tel: 020 7269 7840
Email: info@britishpainsociety.org
https://www.britishpainsociety.org/

National Back Pain Association
Backcare
16 Elmtree Road
Teddington
Middlesex TW11 8ST
Tel: 020 8977 5474
Email: info@backcare.org.uk
http://www.backcare.org.uk/

Parkinson's disease

Parkinson's UK
215 Vauxhall Bridge Road
London SW1V 1EJ
Tel: 020 7931 8080
Email: hello@parkinsons.org.uk
http://www.parkinsons.org.uk/

Pathology

Pathological Society of Great Britain & Ireland
2 Carlton House Terrace
London SW1Y 5DG
Tel: 020 7976 1260
Email: admin@pathsoc.org.uk
http://www.pathsoc.org/

Royal College of Pathologists
4th Floor,
21 Prescot Street
London E1 8BB
Tel: 020 7451 6700
Email: info@rcpath.org
http://www.rcpath.org/

Patients

Patients Association
PO Box 935
Harrow HA1 3YJ
Tel: 020 8423 9111
Email: mailbox@patients-association.com
http://www.patients-association.org.uk/

Physiotherapy

Chartered Society of Physiotherapy
14 Bedford Row
London WC1R 4ED
Tel: 020 7306 6666
Email: csp@csphysio.org.uk
http://www.csp.org.uk/

Plastic surgery

British Association of Plastic Surgeons
The Royal College of Surgeons
35–43 Lincoln's Inn Fields
London WC2A 3PE
Tel: 020 7430 1840
Email: info@baaps.org.uk
http://baaps.org.uk/

Polio

British Polio Fellowship
Ground Floor
Unit A
Eagle Office Centre
The Runway
South Ruislip
Middlesex HA4 6SE
Tel: 0800 018 0586
Email: info@britishpolio.org
http://www.britishpolio.org.uk/

Post-natal illness

(See **Childbirth**)

Psoriasis

Psoriasis Association
Dick Coles House
2 Queensbridge
Northampton NN4 7BF
Tel: 0845 676 0076
Email: mail@psoriasis-association.org.uk
https://www.psoriasis-association.org.uk/

Psychiatry

Royal College of Psychiatrists
21 Prescot Street
London E1 8BB
Tel1: 020 7235 2351
Tel2: 020 7977 6655
Email: reception@rcpsych.ac.uk
http://www.rcpsych.ac.uk/

Psychology

British Psychological Society
Saint Andrew's House
48 Princess Road East
Leicester LE1 7DR
Tel: 0116 254 9568
Fax: 0116 227 1314
Email: enquiries@bps.org.uk
http://www.bps.org.uk/

David McGlown
Clinical Psychologist Public Trust Office
Stewart House
24 Kingsway
London WC2B 6JX
Tel: 020 7269 7085

Psychotherapy

British Association of Psychotherapists
37 Mapesbury Road
London NW2 4HJ
Tel: 020 8452 9823
Email: mail@bap-psychotherapy.org
http://www.britishpsychotherapyfoundation.org.uk/

Radiography and Radiology

Society and College of Radiographers
207 Providence Square
Mill Street
London SE1 2EW
Tel: 020 7740 7200
Email: info@sor.org
https://www.sor.org/

Royal College of Radiologists
63 Lincoln's Inn Fields
London WC2A 3JW
Tel: 020 7405 1282
Email: enquiries@rcr.ac.uk
https://www.rcr.ac.uk/

Rehabilitation

British Society of Rehabilitation Medicine
c/o Royal College of Physicians
11 Saint Andrew's Place
London NW1 4LE
Tel: 01992 638 865
Email: admin@bsrm.co.uk
http://www.bsrm.co.uk/

REMEDI (Rehabilitation and Medical Research Trust for Relief of Disability)
c/o Winterflood Securities Ltd
Elysium House
126–128 New Kings Road
London SW6 4LZ
Tel: 020 7384 2929
Email: info@remedies.org.uk
http://www.remedi.org.uk/

The Injury Care Clinics Ltd
Carnac House, Carnac Court
Carns Estate, Fareham
Hampshire PO16 8UZ
Tel: 01329 245 200
http://www.ticcs.co.uk/

Research

Medical Research Society
Charles Darwin House
12 Roger Street
London WC1N 2JU
Tel: 020 7685 2620
http://www.amrc.org.uk/

Rheumatology

British Society for Rheumatology
Bride House
18–20 Bride Lane
London EC4Y 8EE
Tel: 020 7842 0900
Email: bsr@rheumatology.org.uk
http://www.rheumatology.org.uk/

Schizophrenia

Rethink
Head Office
89 Albert Embankment
London SE1 7TP
Tel: 0300 500 0927
Email: info@rethink.org
http://www.rethink.org/

SCOPE

Scope
6 Market Road
London N7 9PW
Tel: 020 7619 7100
(Helpline: 11am–9pm Mon-Fri,
2–6pm weekend)
http://www.scope.org.uk/

Speech

Royal College of Speech & Language Therapists
2 White Hart Yard
London SE1 1NX
Tel: 020 7378 3012
Email: info@rcslt.org
http://www.rcslt.org/

Association for all Speech-Impaired
Children (AFASIC)
1st Floor
20 Bowling Green Lane
London EC1R 0BD
Tel: 020 7490 9410
Email: info@afasic.org.uk
http://www.afasicengland.org.uk

Spinal injuries

Spinal Injuries Association
SIA House
2 Trueman Place
Oldbrook
Milton Keynes MK6 2HH
Tel: 0845 678 6633
Freephone Helpline: 0800 980 0501
Email: sia@spinal.co.uk
https://www.spinal.co.uk/

(See also **Back pain under Pain**)

Stroke

The Stroke Association
Stroke House
240 City Road
London EC1V 2PR
Tel: 020 7566 0300
Email: info@stroke.org.uk
https://www.stroke.org.uk/

Torture

Freedom from Torture
111 Isledon Road
London N7 7JW
Tel: 020 7697 7777
http://www.freedomfromtorture.org

Thoracic

British Thoracic Society
17 Doughty Street
London WC1N 2PL
Tel: 020 7831 8778
Email: bts@brit-thoracic.org.uk
https://www.brit-thoracic.org.uk/

British Lung Foundation
Lung Foundation House
73–75 Goswell Road
London EC1V 7ER
Tel: 020 7688 5555
Email: enquiries@blf.org.uk
http://www.blf.org.uk/home

Society of Cardiothoracic Surgeons of Great
Britain & Ireland
35–43 Lincoln's Inn Fields
London WC2A 3PE
Tel: 020 7869 6893
Email: sctsadmin@scts.org

(See also **Asthma**)

Transplants

NHS Blood and Transplant Organ Donation and Transplantation Directorate
Oak House
Reeds Crescent
Watford, Hertfordshire WD24 4QN
Tel: 0300 123 23 23
Email: enquiries@nhsbt.nhs.uk
http://www.nhsbt.nhs.uk/

Tropical Medicine

Liverpool School of Tropical Medicine
Pembroke Place
Liverpool L3 5QA
Tel: 0151 705 3100
Email: info@lstmed.ac.uk
http://www.liv.ac.uk/lstm

London School of Hygiene and Tropical Medicine
Keppel Street
London WC1E 7HT
Tel: 020 7636 8636
Email: registry@lshtm.ac.uk
http://www.lshtm.ac.uk

HPA Malaria Reference Laboratory (for advice on prophylaxis)
London School of Hygiene and Tropical Medicine
Keppel Street
London WC1E 7HT
Tel: 020 7636 7921
Email: red.team@hPa.org.uk
http://malaria.lshtm.ac.uk/facilities/malaria-reference-laboratory-mrl

Urology

British Association of Urological Surgeons
Royal College of Surgeons
35–43 Lincoln's Inn Fields
London WC2A 3PE
Tel: 020 7869 6950
Email: admin@baus.org.uk
http://www.baus.org.uk/

Part 2—Litigation

Action Against Medical Accidents (AvMA)

Freedman House
Christopher Wren Yard
117 High St
Croydon
CR0 1QG
Tel: 020 8688 9555
Lawyers service: ls@avma.org.uk
Email: advice@avma.org.uk
Website: *http://www.avma.org.uk*

Association of Personal Injury Lawyers (APIL)

3 Alder Court
Rennie Hogg Road
Nottingham N62 1RX
Tel: 0115 958 0585
Email: mail@apil.org.uk
http://www.apil.org.uk/

Association of Trial Lawyers of America

777 6th Street
NW Suite 200
Washington DC 20001
USA
Tel: 001 800 424 2725
Email: help@justice.org
https://www.justice.org

Clinical Disputes Forum

Chairman: Dr Alastair Scotland
Medical Director and Chief Officer
National Clinical Assessment Authority
9th Floor, Market Towers
London SW8 5NQ
Tel: 0115 947 4700
Email: margaret.dangoor@blueyonder.co.uk
http://www.clinical-disputes-forum.org.uk/

Compensation Recovery Unit (CRU)

Compensation Recovery Unit
Durham House
Washington
Tyne & Wear NE38 7SF
Tel: 0191 225 2005
Email: cru-info-management@dwp.gsi.gov.uk
https://www.gov.uk/government/collections/cru

Disability Law Service

The Foundry
17 Oval Way
London SE11 5RR
Tel: 020 7791 9800
Email: aqdvice@dls.org.uk
http://www.dls.org.uk/

General Council of the Bar (Bar Council)

289–293 High Holborn
London WC1V 7HZ
Tel: 020 7242 0082
Email: ContactUs@BarCouncil.org.uk
http://www.barcouncil.org.uk/

Incorporated Council of Law Reporting for England and Wales

Megarry House
119 Chancery Lane
London WC2A 1PP
Tel: 020 7242 6471
Email: enquiries@iclr.co.uk
http://www.lawreports.co.uk/

Inquest

89–93 Fonthill Road
London N4 3JH
Tel: 020 7263 1111
Email: inquest@inquest.org.uk
http://www.inquest.org.uk/

Law Society

113 Chancery Lane
London WC2A 1PL
Tel: 020 7242 1222
http://www.lawsociety.org.uk
Practice Advice Service - 020 7320 5675
Lawyerline - 020 7320 5720

Legal Services Commission

Legal Aid Agency
Unit B8
Berkley Way
Viking Business Park
Jarrow
South Tyneside NE31 1SF
Civil general enquiries: 0300 200 2020
Crime general enquiries: 01158 526 000
Email: contactcivil@legalaid.gsi.gov.uk
https://www.gov.uk/government/organisations/legal-aid-agency

Ministry of Justice
102 Petty France
London SW1H 9AJ
Tel: 020 3334 3555
Email: general.queries@justice.gsi.gov.uk
https://www.gov.uk/government/organisations/ministry-of-justice

Legal Services Commission London/South
Exchange Tower (Area No. 1)
2 Harbour Exchange Square
London E14 9GE
Tel: 020 7718 8466
Email: london@legalservices.gov.uk

Legal Services Commission (Area No. 2)
3rd and 4th Floors Invicta House
Trafalgar Place
Cheapside
Brighton BN1 4FR
Tel: 01273 878 800

Legal Services Commission (Area No. 3)
Old Shire Hall
The Forbury
Reading
Berkshire RG1 3EH
Tel: 020 7715 3991

Legal Services Commission Wales and the West Group Area Offices (Area No. 4)
33–35 Queen Square
Bristol BS1 4LU
Tel: 0117 302 3000

Legal Services Commission (Area No. 5)
2nd Floor, Churchill House
17 Churchill Way
Cardiff
South Glamorgan CF10 2HH
Tel: 0300 200 2020
Email: Cardiff@legalservices.gsi.co.uk

Legal Services Commission Midlands Group Area Offices (Area No. 6)
1st Floor, Cannon House
18 The Priory Queensway
Birmingham B4 6BS
Tel: 0121 232 5500
Email: Birmingham@legalservices.gsi.co.uk

Legal Services Commission (Area No. 7)
2nd Floor Lee House
90 Great Bridgewater Street
Manchester M1 5JW
Tel: 0300 200 2020
Email: manchester@legalservices.gsi.co.uk

Legal Services Commission (Area No. 9)
Harcourt House
Chanceller House
21 The Calls
Leeds LS2 7EH
Tel: 0113 390 7300
Email: leeds@legalservices.gsi.co.uk

Legal Services Commission (Area No. 10)
2nd Floor, Fothergill House
16 King Street
Nottingham NG1 2AS
Tel: 0115 908 4200

Legal Services Commission (Area No. 11)
62–68 Hills Road
Cambridge CB2 1LA
Tel: 0300 200 2020
Email: legal-enquiries@legalservices.gsi.co.uk

Legal Services Commission North Western
Group Area Offices (Area No. 12)
2nd Floor, Pepper House
Pepper Row
Chester CH1 1DW
Tel: 01244 404 500
Email: Chester@legalservices.gsi.gov.uk

Legal Services Commission (Area No. 15)
Cavern Walks
8 Matthew Street
Liverpool L2 6RE
Tel: 0151 242 5200
Email: liverpool@legalservices.gsi.gov.uk

Medical Defence Union

MDU Services Limited
One Canada Square
London E14 5GS
Tel: 0800 716 646
Email: advisory@themdu.com
http://www.themdu.com

The Medical Protection Society Ltd

33 Cavendish Square
London W1G OPS
Tel: 0113 243 6436
Email: info@medicalprotection.org
http://www.medicalprotection.org/uk/home

Medico-Legal Society

Blake Lapthorn,
Watchmaker Court,
33 St John's Lane,
London EC1M 4DB
Tel: 02072890188
Email: caron.heyes@bllaw.co.uk or
https://www.medico-legalsociety.org.uk/index.asp

Motor Insurers Bureau

Linford Wood House
6–12 Capital Drive
Linford Wood
Milton Keynes MK14 6XT
Tel: 01908 830 001
Fax: 01908 671 681
Email: enquiries@mib.org.uk
Website: *http://www.mib.org.uk*

National Association of Guardians ad Litem and Reporting Officers (NAGALRO)

PO Box 264
Esher
Surrey KT10 0WA
Tel: 01372 818 504
Email: nagalro@globalnet.co.uk
http://www.nagalro.com/

Official Solicitor to the Supreme Court

Victory House
30–34 Kingsway
London WC2B 6EX
Tel: 020 7911 7127
Email: enquiries@offsol.gsi.gov.uk
https://www.gov.uk/government/organisations/official-solicitor-and-public-trustee

The Patients' Association

PO Box 935
Harrow
Middlesex HA1 3YJ
Tel: 020 8423 9111
Email: mailbox@patients-association.com
http://www.patients-association.org.uk/

Personal Injury Bar Association (PIBA)

Faircroft Avenue
Walmley
Sutton Coldfield
West Midlands B76 1HQ
Tel: 0121 240 8448
Email: admin@piba.org.uk
http://piba.org.uk/

Professional Negligence Bar Association (PNBA)

Victoria Woodbridge
Crown Office Chambers
London EC4Y 7HJ
Tel: 020 7797 8100
Email: woodbridge@crownofficechambers.com
http://pnba.co.uk/

Witnesses Against Abuse by Health and Care Workers

Verulam House
110 Luton Road
Harpenden
Hertfordshire AL5 3BL

Smith Bernal Reporting Ltd

(Court of Appeal Transcribers)
2nd Floor, 101 Finsbury Pavement
London EC2A 1ER
Tel: 020 7422 6100
Email: London@merrillcorp.com
http://mls.merrillcorp.com/index.html

Part 3—Government

Commission for Local Administration in England

(Local Government Ombudsman)
PO Box 4771
Coventry CV4 0EH
Tel: 0300 061 0614
Email: training@lgo.org.uk
http://www.lgo.org.uk/

Department of Health

Richmond House
79 Whitehall
London SW1A 2NS
Tel: 020 7210 4850
https://www.gov.uk/government/organisations/department-of-health

Department of Work and Pensions

DWP Litigation Division
2nd Floor
Caxton House
Tothill Street
London SW1H 9NA
Tel: 020 7712 2171
Email: ministers@dwp.gsi.gov.uk
http://www.dwp.gov.uk

Department of Health Social Care Group

Richmond House
79 Whitehall
London SW1A 2NL
Tel: 020 7210 4850

Health & Safety Executive

2 Southwark Bridge
London SE1 9HS
Tel: 020 7556 2100
http://www.hse.gov.uk

Health and Safety Executive—Health Policy Division

Rose Court
2 Southwark Bridge
London SE1 9HS
Tel: 020 7717 6000 (Head Office)
http://www.hse.gov.uk/

Home Office

Direct communications unit
2 Marsham Street
London SW1P 4DF
Tel: 020 7035 4848
https://www.gov.uk/government/organisations/home-office

HM Inspector of Anatomy

Dept. of Health
Richmond House
79 Whitehall
London SW1A 2NS
Tel: 020 7210 4850
https://www.gov.uk/government/organisations/department-of-health

Lord Chancellor's Department

Selbourne House
54–60 Victoria Street
London SW1E 6QW
Tel: 020 7210 8614

Care Quality Commission

Finsbury Tower
103–105 Bunhill Row
London EC1Y 8TG
Tel: 0300 616161
Email: enquiries@cqc.org.uk
http://www.cqc.org.uk/

Mental Welfare Commission for Scotland

Thistle House
91 Haymarket Terrace
Edinburgh EH12 5HE
Tel: 0131 313 8777
Email: enquiries@mwcscot.org.uk
http://www.mwcscot.org.uk/

National Blood Authority

NHS Blood and Transplant
Head Office
Oak House
Reeds Crescent
Watford
Hertfordshire WD24 4QN
Tel: 01923 486 800
Email: enquiries@nhsbt.nhs.uk
http://www.nhsbt.nhs.uk

Scottish Office Home and Health Department

St Andrew's House
Regent Road
Edinburgh EH1 3DG
Tel: 0300 244 4000
Email: ceu@scotland.gsi.gov.uk
http://www.gov.scot/Home

London Office: Dover House
Whitehall
London SW1A 2AU
Tel: 020 7270 6754
Email: scottish.secretary@scotland.gsi.gov.uk
https://www.gov.uk/government/organisations/scotland-office

Scottish National Blood Transfusion Service

21 Ellen's Glen Road, Liberton
Edinburgh EH17 7QT
Tel: 0131 536 5700
https://www.scotblood.co.uk/

Part 4—Courts and Tribunals

The Supreme Court

Parliament Square
London SW1P 3BD
Switchboard: 0207 960 1500/1900
Email: Enquiries@supremecourt.gsi.gov.uk
Website: *http://www.supremecourt.gov.uk*

Court of Appeal

Room E307
Royal Courts of Justice
Strand
London WC2A 2LL
https://www.justice.gov.uk/courts/rcj-rolls-building/court-of-appeal/civil-division
Tel: 020 7947 6000 (Listings Office)

High Court of Justice

Royal Courts of Justice
Strand
London WC2A 2LL
Tel: 020 7947 6000 (General Office)
http://www.justice.gov.uk/

Court of Protection

Royal Courts of Justice
Thomas More Building
Strand
London WC2A 2LL
Tel: 0300 456 4600
Email: courtofprotectionenquiries@hmcts.gsi.gov.uk
http://www.justice.gov.uk/courts/rcj-rolls-building/court-of-protection

Criminal Injuries Compensation Authority (CICA)

Winston Solicitors LLP
112 Street Lane
Leeds LS8 2AL
Tel: 0113 320 5000
Email: enquiries@criminal-injuries.co.uk
http://www.criminal-injuries.co.uk

Part 5—Other

Child Poverty Action Group

94 White Lion Street
London N1 9PF
Tel: 020 7837 7979
Email: info@cpag.org.uk

Fostering Network

87 Blackfriars Road
London SE1 8HA
Tel: 020 7620 6400
Email: info@fostering.net
https://www.fostering.net/

Leonard Cheshire Disability

66 South Lambeth Road
London SW8 1RL
Tel: 020 3242 0200
Email: info@LCDisability.org
https://www.leonardcheshire.org/

The Bank of England

Threadneedle Street
London EC2R 8AH
Tel: 020 7601 4444
Email: enquiries@bankofengland.co.uk
http://www.bankofengland.co.uk/Pages/home.aspx